A HISTORY OF AUSTRALIAN DEFENCE AND FOREIGN POLICY 1901–23: VOLUME 2

AUSTRALIA AND WORLD CRISIS, 1914–1923

'There is much damned nonsense being talked among a rare exhibition of statesmanship during this World's Crisis ... Sometimes the fools of one age are the seers of the next.'
    Letter, Andrew Fisher to George Pearce, 5 Sep 1916, Pearce Papers, AWM, B3/3/50.

Neville Meaney

SYDNEY UNIVERSITY PRESS

Published 2009 by Sydney University Press
SYDNEY UNIVERSITY PRESS
University of Sydney Library
www.sup.usyd.edu.au
© Neville Meaney 2009
© Sydney University Press 2009

Reproduction and Communication for other purposes
Except as permitted under the Act, no part of this edition may be reproduced, stored in a retrieval system, or communicated in any form or by any means without prior written permission. All requests for reproduction or communication should be made to Sydney University Press at the address below:
Sydney University Press
Fisher Library F03
University of Sydney NSW 2006 AUSTRALIA
Email: info@sup.usyd.edu.au

National Library of Australia Cataloguing-in-Publication entry

Author:	Meaney, N. K. (Neville Kingsley)
Title:	A history of Australian defence and foreign policy 1901-23.
	Volume 2, Australia and world crisis, 1914-1923 / Neville Meaney.
ISBN:	9781920899172 (pbk.)
	9781920899448 (hbk.)
Notes:	Includes index.
	Bibliography.
Subjects:	Australia--Foreign relations.
	Australia--Military policy.
	Australia--Defenses.
Dewey Number:	327.94

For my Mother and Father

Contents

Abbreviations vi
Acknowledgements.. vii

Introduction ix
The Onset of War and the Pacific Problem
1   Australian Leaders and the Outbreak of War 3
2   The Imperial Cause and Aid for the Mother Country..21
3   The Competition for Germany's Pacific Empire 56
4   'No Parallel in our History': The Menace of Japan...77

'Our Last Man and Our Last Shilling'? Loyalty and Conscription
5   'The Survival of the Fittest': The Crusade for the British Race 115
6   The War and the Home Front: Japan and the Defence of Australia. 152
7   'The Greatest Crisis in Our History': The Conflict over Conscription............163
8   'Loyalty' and Empire: The Nation Divided..183
9   'The Enemy within the Gate': The Attack on National Community 204

'Annexation and Indemnity': Australia's War Aims
10   The Attack on Peacemongers and the Appeasement of Japan.........................243
11   Manoeuvring for the Spoils of War: American Consultations and Imperial Councils ...256
12   'The Very Threshold of the Promised Land': Joining Battle over the Armistice Terms..280

'Not a Good Peace': The Making of the Treaty of Versailles
13   Preparing for the Paris Peace Conference..313
14   'Absolutely Unbearable': The Defeat of Hughes's Vision for the Post-War World 340

The Lessons of War, the Decline of Empire and 'Détente' in the Pacific
15   A Pacific 'Foreign Office', the Japanese Threat and Defence Planning.............407
16   The Crisis of Empire and a Pacific Settlement 466
Conclusion..500

Bibliography 515
Index..528

Abbreviations

AAP	Australian Associated Press
ADB	Australian Dictionary of Biography
ADM	Admiralty
AIF	Australian Imperial Force
ALP	Australian Labor Party
AMF	Australian Military Forces
AWM	Australian War Memorial
BD	Documents on British Foreign Policy, 1919–1939
BL	British Library
CAB	Cabinet Office
CD	Command Paper
CEB	Counter Espionage Bureau
CID	Committee of Imperial Defence
CPD	Commonwealth Parliamentary Debates
CO	Colonial Office
FO	Foreign Office
FRUS	United States Foreign Relations Document Series
IRB	Irish Republican Brotherhood
IWW	Industrial Workers of the World
LAC	Library and Archives of Canada
LC	Library of Congress
ML	Mitchell Library
NAA	National Archives of Australia
NARA	National Archives and Records Administration-USA
NAS	National Archives of Scotland
NLA	National Library of Australia
NSW	New South Wales
PRO	Public Record Office
SIB	Special Intelligence Bureau
SMH	Sydney Morning Herald
TNA	The National Archives – UK
USL	Universal Service League
WPA	War Precautions Act
WRO	Wiltshire Record Office

Acknowledgements

This work has had a long history and during its evolution I have accumulated many, many debts to institutions and individuals, indeed so many that I could not possibly acknowledge them all here. Even to name a few that stand out in my imperfect recollection of the history of this history is rather invidious.

In listing those debts I should, however, begin at the beginning and that was my appointment in 1984 as a Harold White Fellow at the National Library. My task was to begin the research and writing of this volume. This fellowship was nirvana for a scholar. I look back on that time with a great sense of nostalgia. All the resources of the library were at my disposal seven days a week and twenty-four hours a day. I had freedom of the stacks and the riches it held. I had a room of my own and could keep whatever works I needed at my desk for as long as I wished. The manuscript room was at the centre of my scholarly activity. It held nearly all the major Australian collections of personal papers which were central to my project and the library staff would photocopy whatever material I wished. The library also provided me with a contract typist who produced from my handwritten scrawl the first drafts of two early chapters which were written during the period of the fellowship. The library staff, especially Graeme Powell the head of the Manuscript Division, were always supportive and welcoming when I returned for brief periods as I intermittently continued researching the topic. Without that fellowship I would not have been able to undertake this work. It was a remarkable opportunity and many of my other publications and historical endeavours flowed from it.

Numerous other libraries and archives have also been helpful in allowing me access to primary sources, both official and unofficial, which have contributed to the making of this work. They include: in Australia – the National Australian Archives, the Australian War Memorial, the University of Melbourne Archives, the Mitchell Library and the University of Sydney Library and Archives; in the United Kingdom – the National Archives Public Record Office, the Scottish Record Office, the British Library, the Oxford University Bodleian Library, the Cambridge University Churchill College Archives, the House of Lords Record Office, the Wiltshire Record Office and the Imperial War Museum; in the United States – the National Archives and Records Administration, the Library of Congress and the Sterling Library, Yale University; and in Canada – the Library and Archives of Canada.

In turning to individuals, I have to say that without the support of many friends, students and colleagues I would have found it very difficult to maintain the commitment which has resulted in this work. Among the many, some of whom have read draft chapters from time to time and offered helpful criticisms as well as encouragement, I would mention specially Hugh White, James Curran and David McLean. I have over this long period also had the help of a number of research assistants. Perhaps of them all, the two who made the greatest contributions were Colin Milner who did a sterling job of providing me with an extensive collection of material taken from newspapers and Richard Lehane who has in the last few months worked very hard and for long hours to check the vast array of footnotes and to give them and the bibliography a systematic form. I should also mention Tetsuaki Okamoto who translated the passages I identified in the Nippon Gaiko Bunsho which are used in the book.

Finally I would be remiss if I did not recognise here the two institutions which have made it possible for the manuscript to be published – Sydney University Press and the Department of Defence.

Sydney University Press, which accepted the task of bringing the work into the public arena, has done the book proud. It is fitting that they should have agreed to reprint the first volume at the same time they are bringing out the second volume. Since the first volume was published the Press has gone through some difficult times. Indeed at the high point of managerialism the University of Sydney, to its shame, closed it down. Since its revival it has slowly grown and extended its role and hopefully this book will, in a modest way, also help to bring it back to the status as one of the first rate university presses in the country – a position it held when the first volume was published. The standing of the University in the academic world requires that it should have such a press.

The Defence Department gave a generous grant to subsidise the publishing of the work. Scholars understand that they are heirs to an intellectual tradition which values independence and integrity in what they publish to the world, and I have to pay a tribute to the Defence Department in that it did not seek to influence my work in any way, awarding the grant purely on the basis of my reputation as a scholar.

I have always been conscious that my life as a scholar has been supported by the taxes of my fellow citizens and have thus tried to bear in mind in pursuing my research and writing that I am also responsible in some lasting way to serve our Commonwealth. I would like to think that at least to some extent I have also achieved that aim.

I would like to extend my sincere thanks to all those who have played such a vital part in bringing this book into being and I hope that they will think that the outcome has justified their faith in the enterprise.

Scholarly independence and integrity require, however, that I should absolve all those who have assisted in the process of making this book from any responsibility for its shortcomings of whatever kind. That responsibility rests with me and me alone.

Introduction

The decade 1914–23 was an era of crisis in world affairs, an era of unparalleled violence and change. The Great War of 1914–18 convulsed the European continent, and the reverberations from the conflict were felt around the globe. It toppled thrones, destroyed empires, provoked insurrections, redrew frontiers and redistributed power. Indeed so profound were these disturbances to the received social and political order that it took a further five years after the end of hostilities to achieve a settled peace with the vanquished, create a *modus vivendi* among the victors and damp down the threat of world revolution.

For Australia, as for the other belligerents, this decade was a time of trial and turmoil. Australia was ineluctably caught up in these great events and their consequences. Australians experienced the full range of the world crisis; they felt its impact in the Pacific as well as Europe and at home as well as abroad. They were, so to speak, engaged simultaneously in a 'hot war' against Germany and its allies in Europe and a 'cold war' against Japan in the Pacific. As an integral part of the British Empire, a self-governing member of the Pan-Britannic alliance, Australia not only identified sentimentally with the Mother Country but also recognised that its own security was bound up with Britain's effort to contain the German thrust for hegemony in Europe. At the same time, as a small Pacific nation which had for a decade been apprehensive about Japan and its regional ambitions, it feared that this Asian great power might seize the opportunity afforded by Europe's troubles to expand southward and make unwelcome demands. Australia also experienced the internal stresses and strains of war, and with the growth of authoritarian demands for sacrifice and partisan attacks on loyalty, social and political divisions appeared to test the bonds of community, and this in turn had consequences for defence and foreign policy.

As the bloody drama unfolded, Australia, like the other belligerents, had to contend with the contingencies of war. The outcome of the war was always in the balance. The military fortunes of the rival camps teetered backwards and forwards almost until the very end. Even the Treaty of Versailles did not itself provide a clear picture of the new world that would emerge when the dust settled.

The Japanese dimension

Scholars dealing with Australia and the Great War have been inclined to treat the period as if it represented a sharp break with the past. The picture that is generally painted is one in which the war broke in upon an innocent, colonially-dependent people who since the foundation of the Commonwealth had been almost completely occupied with domestic affairs. But this is not the case. From the late-nineteenth-century, Australians had been aware that the world was being transformed. The *Sydney Morning Herald* at the end of the Franco-Prussian War, summing up this great change, declared that that war had 'opened up an epoch in which the war of the races has clearly begun; and unless Divine Providence shall interfere, instead of contending dynasties, the races will have to fight for existence.'[1] And by 'race' they meant not only peoples divided by physiological appearance or 'colour' but also peoples divided by culture. The newspaper was commenting on how in Europe mass nationalism had remade ideas of loyalty and identity and was replacing the sovereignty of the monarch with the sovereignty of the people. Looking out from their island continent, the British colonists saw with apprehension the movement of European Empires into the Pacific. They were even more affected by a growing consciousness of living in an alien Asian region, and perceiving the world in racial terms, they adopted a migration policy which shut the door against nearly all 'coloured' peoples.

Volume one of this work shows how Australia's anxieties about Asia took on a palpable form after Japan's victory over Russia in 1905 and Britain's simultaneous withdrawal of its capital ships from the Pacific. Japan had emerged from that conflict as the paramount power in the region. Britain had an alliance with Japan but as it was not based on a mutual exchange of interests, the Australians did not trust it. Since Japan had embarked on an imperial course and resented the White Australia policy they considered that it might take advantage of European tensions to make demands which in their most extreme form could even lead to an invasion.

In defiance of the British authorities, Australia, alarmed by these developments in the North Pacific, had adopted an integrated defence and foreign policy aimed at protecting the continent against this worst possibility. The British Foreign Office had assured the Australians that they could depend on the Anglo-Japanese alliance; the War Office had advised that their compulsory military training scheme was wasteful and unnecessary; the Admiralty had denied that they had any need for a naval force in the Pacific; and the Committee of Imperial Defence had asserted that they lived in the safest part of the Empire. Despite the British Government's disapproval, policy-makers in Melbourne, on the basis of their own strategic assessment that Australia was the most vulnerable part of the Empire, proceeded with preparations for their own protection.[2] It was this experience of world politics that Australian policy-makers took with them into the Great War.

During that war, Australian leaders, driven by their Pacific concerns, gave as much attention to Japan as to Germany. Japan's entry into the war on Britain's side was not reassuring. Australia's security agencies devoted almost as much time to investigating Japanese activities as German ones. Naval and military authorities were engaged in gathering information about Japanese attitudes towards the Pacific, assessing their intentions towards Australia and planning post-war defences against a threat from the north. Until the last months of the war Australian leaders thought it not impossible that Japan, should it perceive the fortunes of war to be favouring the Central Powers, might desert the Allies and try to consolidate its dominant position in the Western Pacific by reaching an accommodation with Germany. In the immediate post-war years

---

[1] *Sydney Morning Herald*, 31 December 1870. (hereinafter *SMH*)
[2] For British preoccupation with Germany after 1905, see Zara S. Steiner, *Britain and the Origins of the First World War* (London: Macmillan, 1977) and P.M. Kennedy, *The Rise of the Anglo-German Antagonism* (London: Allen and Unwin, 1980); for the origin of the Anglo-Japanese alliance and its difficulties after 1905, see Ian H. Nish, *Alliance in Decline: A Study in Anglo-Japanese Relations, 1908–1923* (London: The Athlone Press, 1972); and for Australia's strategic concerns about diplomatic and strategic developments in Europe and the Pacific see Neville Meaney, *Search for Security in the Pacific, 1901–1914* (Sydney: Sydney University Press, 1976).

the government continued with this intelligence surveillance and defence planning, focusing exclusively on Japan.

The British commitment

This preoccupation with Japan did not prevent the Australians from identifying with Britain and the British cause in the European war and playing the role which their culture dictated and their interests made logical.

Indeed Australia's sense of being British and a proud part of the British Empire grew alongside Australia's anxiety about Asia and the British Governments' indifference to its need for defence against Japan. In this age of mass nationalism Australians' psychological insecurity, intensified by their structureless democracy and geocultural isolation,[3] had drawn them to embrace Britishness with an intensity which was greater than that evinced by the people of the British Isles. Thus with the coming of this war of peoples against peoples, these apostles of what was called 'Greater Britain'[4] greeted the news of Britain's entry into the conflict with an extraordinary outburst of patriotic fervour.[5] Australians, by contrast to the British, were almost unanimous in their support for Britain's entry into the war. While in Britain two Liberal ministers resigned from the Asquith Government in protest, in Australia not one Liberal or Labor leader uttered a word of criticism. Indeed the leaders of both parties vied with one another to prove their support for the war and the Mother Country.

Australia's commitment to the British Empire's cause was driven not only by national sentiment but also by strategic interest. In many of the speeches expressing Australia's solidarity with the Mother Country, appeals to British race sentiment were mixed with arguments about national security. Australians recognised that their own survival was bound up with that of Britain and the Empire. British Australia had been created under the protective cover of Pax Britannica and should the British fleet be defeated, Germany – and Japan also, if it switched sides – would be able to impose whatever peace they chose on Australia, including a commanding influence over policy and even possibly cessions of territory. It was hard to define precisely what defeat might mean but whatever that might be Australians, rightly, could only imagine dire consequences.

Very shortly after the first contingent of the AIF was despatched, the question of how many more troops Australia should raise became a matter of dispute and this question was followed quickly by the question of conscription. In these disputes about the size of Australia's military commitment to the British cause, fear of Japan was an issue. While many other questions were mixed up in the debate over conscription this question of how best to provide for Australia's own security was always present. Two different, if more or less equally plausible, arguments were

---

[3] See D.H. Lawrence's novel, *Kangaroo* (London: Martin Secker, 1923) for an evocation of this sense of egalitarian *anomie* and the concomitant appeal of mass movements, nationalist and socialist.
[4] For an excellent study of the origins of this term and the ideas of Britishness associated with it, see Duncan Bell, *The Idea of Greater Britain: Empire and the Future of World Order: 1890–1900* (Princeton: Princeton University Press, 2007).
[5] Neville Meaney, 'Britishness and Australian Identity: The Problem of Nationalism in Australian History and Historiography', *Australian Historical Studies,* 32(April 2001), 76–90.

advanced. The conscriptionists, on the one hand, maintained that by helping Britain and its Allies to the utmost to achieve a speedy and decisive victory, Australia would free the British navy to come to the Pacific and so deter Japan from taking any hostile action against Australia. The anti-conscriptionists, on the other, claimed that conscripting Australians for the European conflict would not make any substantial difference to the outcome of that war and if Australia denuded itself of its trained military forces it would become an easy prey for Japan.

There was no simple answer to this question. E. L. Piesse, the head of military intelligence in Tasmania at the beginning of the war, who was fully convinced of the Japanese danger, would not at first volunteer for the AIF. He had grave reservations about the wisdom of the Australian Government's offer in August 1914 to send a 20,000 strong force to fight in Europe. He was only able to comfort himself by assuming that the 'War Office knows all about the Japanese situation' and in accepting Australia's expeditionary force had 'thought of our interest as well as England's'. When, however, the Allies suffered serious setbacks and the Empire's very survival seemed at stake he changed his mind, offered himself for overseas service and supported conscription for the European war. Even so, after he was appointed Director of Military Intelligence in 1916, he taught himself to read Japanese and devoted much time and energy to collecting material on Japan and writing assessments of Japan's intentions towards Australia and the region.[6] During the whole period of the war Japan remained an issue in the debates over recruitment and conscription and in Australia's diplomacy dealing with the future of Germany's possessions in the Pacific.

Peace diplomacy and the post-war crisis

War is something of a gamble. It lets loose explosive forces which are difficult to contain. War often has unexpected results, as the Hapsburg, Hohenzollern and Romanoff dynasties were to learn to their cost. Even so, belligerents act as though they are in control of their fate. They treat war not as an isolated incident but as an integral part of their national policies. In war they do not lose sight of their peacetime goals, they do not put out of mind their longstanding differences with adventitious allies, and they do not overlook the consequences of wartime strategy for the peace settlement and their future relations with both their allies and their enemies. National leaders understand, in the prophetic words of Prime Minister Joseph Cook on the eve of World War I, that 'war means a new map. New relations – new history.'[7] Aware of this truism, Australian leaders tried to devise their wartime and post-war policies – military and diplomatic – to ensure that the new map would be drawn in their favour, that the new relationships between the powers would be to their advantage and that at the end they would, as part of the British Empire, emerge masters of the new geopolitical history.

The Australian policy-makers recognised that wartime strategy and diplomacy would play an important role in shaping the peace. Writing from London in 1915, Chris Watson, Australia's first Labor Prime Minister, stressed to Prime Minister Andrew Fisher the urgent need for an imperial conference; 'The point is that probably some of the terms of peace are being agreed upon now, so

---

[6] Neville Meaney, *Fears and Phobias: E.L. Piesse and the Problem of Japan 1909–39* (Canberra: National Library of Australia, 1996), pp.3–9.
[7] Cook Diary, 1 August 1914, NAA M3580.

"if 'twere well it 'twere done, 'twere well 'twere done quickly'".[8] But Fisher did not require Watson's prompting. From December 1914 when he first learnt that Japan had taken possession of the German North Pacific islands he had been pressing London to agree to a meeting of British and Dominion leaders. Though the Australians had lost the contest over the German North Pacific islands, they pursued, during the war years, a discreet diplomacy aimed at limiting, as far as possible, Japan's southward advance.

Victory over Germany did not resolve these Pacific problems. At the Paris Peace Conference Australia's then Prime Minister William Morris Hughes was relentless in carrying out a policy aimed at securing island ramparts against a southward thrust of Japan and at blocking what he conceived to be its efforts to breakdown White Australia. But this had little impact on Japan's dominance of the region. It had emerged from the war relatively unscathed. It had acquired new territory in East Asia and the North Pacific and enhanced its position as a great power. Britain was badly weakened by the great effort that it had invested in winning the war and was unable to support or even contribute to a fleet in the Pacific. The League of Nations was new and untried and Japan as a permanent member of the League Council was in a position to quash any interference from that organisation. The United States had refused to join the League and wanted to withdraw into Western Hemispheric isolation.

As a result, policy makers remained suspicious of Japan and continued in the immediate post-war years to plan on a grand scale for defence against Japan's formidable naval forces and even against the possibility of a military invasion.

It was not until the Washington conference of 1921–22 when Japan along with the United States, the British Empire and other European allies signed treaties agreeing to limit their naval forces and respect each other's Pacific possessions that Australia's world crisis was brought to an end. For the first time in almost twenty years most Australians could agree that at last Japan might be considered 'peaceful' and that they could relax their guard.

This book, while tracing out the story of Australia's world crisis, places at its centre the nation's leaders who had the responsibility for defining the crisis for their fellow citizens, analysing the problems which the crisis posed for the country and taking the decisions which shaped the nation's defence and foreign policy. To this end it seeks to show how, within the framework of the given international conditions, the ideas and experiences that the individual leaders brought to their task shaped their respective responses to the Great War and its aftermath.

---

[8] Letter, Chris Watson to Andrew Fisher, 11 May 1915, Fisher Papers, NLA MS2919/1/107.

The Onset of War and the Pacific Problem

The Great War brought to the fore what Australian leaders had long feared. That is, they had envisaged the coming of an 'Australian crisis' in which Britain, engaged in a struggle for survival in Europe, would be unable to deter Japan from prosecuting its ambitions in the Pacific. Even in the decade since Japan's rise to power, Australia had recognised that with the British fleet based in the North Sea to protect the home islands against Germany, the danger from the north was, in principle, already present. It was, however, the outbreak of the European war which gave a palpable meaning to this dread prospect.

From the first months of the conflict Australia had to face up to the implications of being involved in a 'hot war' in Europe and a 'cold war' in the Pacific. There would be no question about supporting Britain but Japan's entry into the war on the Allies' side, rather than giving comfort, caused anxiety. There was a cloud over Japan's reliability as an ally. Japan's failure to offer military forces for the Western Front, its quite limited naval assistance in the European theatre, its occupation of the German North Pacific territories, its extreme demands on China and its pressure on Australia to enter into a commercial agreement, when taken together, created considerable disquiet. These indications of Japan's ambitions caused the Australians to try to maintain their home defence program even as they handed over their navy to the Admiralty and sent a volunteer AIF to assist the Mother Country and its Allies.

Underneath the Australian desire to help the British Empire ran a continuing thread of doubt concerning how far Australia should go in divesting itself of its military defences. As Prime Minister Fisher was to admit towards the end of his term in office Australia was facing a crisis without parallel in its history.

1
Australian Leaders and the Outbreak of War

Before beginning the story proper, it is important to look briefly at two contextual matters. The first, an examination of the immediate origins of the decision for war, shows how Britain – and thus Australia – came to be embroiled in the European cataclysm. It helps to sharpen the focus on Britain's strategic priorities and its attitude towards Australia and its interests. The second is a critical account of the ideas and experiences which informed the Australian leaders' response to this primal international event and framed their policy-making throughout the whole period of this world crisis.

The coming of the war

When news of the British declaration of war on Germany reached Australia about midday on 5 August 1914, those thin attenuated cables which had carried the message from London suddenly became chains of immense power, ineluctably drawing the Pacific Commonwealth into a great European conflict. The awesome tidings brought into sharper relief the foreign policy dilemma which had dominated the thinking of nearly all political leaders in the preceding decade. It brought to the fore the issue of the 'Australian Crisis' as it had been defined in those years, that is the possibility of having to face the menace of Japan at a time when all British resources were engaged in a struggle for the mastery of Europe.

Australia took no part in the decision for war. Despite the British assurance at the 1911 Imperial Conference that the Dominions would be consulted on the Empire's foreign policy, the British Government, in going to war, neither took the Dominions into their confidence nor discussed whether they should be consulted. After the conference the British Prime Minister, H. H. Asquith, had admitted that it was 'obviously reasonable' that the Dominions 'should be entitled to be heard in the determination of the [imperial defence and foreign] policy'[1] but he had shown no interest in giving such sentiments an institutional form or a practical expression. At the time of the European crisis of July 1914 the British Government without any second thoughts assumed the right to act for the whole Empire, and so it was that Britain alone made the decision which committed Australia and all the other Dominions.

The outbreak of hostilities in Europe took the British by surprise. For two decades continental Europe had been divided between the Dual Alliance of France and Russia and the Triple Alliance of Germany, Austria-Hungary and Italy. For a decade Britain, in response to Germany's challenge to the supremacy of the Royal Navy, had associated itself with France and Russia in this diplomatic confrontation. In this period there had been many potential flashpoints, but each of these had been resolved peacefully. As a result, it was difficult for the British Government to believe that the assassination of Archduke Franz Ferdinand at Sarajevo in Bosnia

---
[1] *Search for Security*, pp.218 and 236–37.

on 28 June and the subsequent Austrian ultimatum to Serbia on 23 July would be the trigger for a general war.[2]

During the spring and early summer of 1914 the British were distracted by the prospect of civil war in Ireland over Home Rule. In so far as the British Foreign Secretary, Sir Edward Grey, did pay heed to the Austro-Serbian tensions he had consoled himself with the thought that, as in the 1906 and 1911 Moroccan incidents and during the 1912 and 1913 Balkan squabbles, the great powers would be able to negotiate a compromise. He felt hopeful that once again Germany would restrain Austria, and France would exercise a similar influence over Russia.[3] Indeed it is possible that the British Foreign Office believed that Anglo-German relations had so improved that the chance of war with Germany was exceedingly remote. On 16 July Herbert Easton of the British Immigration League of Australia, in an interview at the Foreign Office, had claimed that 'In Australia it was everywhere held that the coming Anglo-German war would spell disaster for Australia even if Great Britain were victorious.' Australians believed that Britain would be 'so weakened' that '… in such a circumstance Japan would at once attack Australia'. Commenting on Anglo-German relations the official concerned had replied that 'a very marked improvement had taken place during the last two years so that there was no longer any reason why Australia should be particularly apprehensive on that score.'[4]

After Austria's ultimatum to Serbia, Grey warned the cabinet that it could be 'the prelude to a war in which at least four of the Great Powers might be involved.'[5] During the next few days Grey worked diligently to find a diplomatic solution to the problem. But all to no avail. Following the Austrian declaration of war on Serbia on 28 July, the four continental powers, as he had feared, lurched towards a war along the lines of the script which had been written in the 1890s. By 2 August, Russia had mobilised in defence of Serbia, Germany had declared war on Russia, France had made it clear to Germany that it would stand by its ally and Britain had to face the prospect of the German fleet engaging French forces in the North Sea and attacking France through Belgium.

Britain could no longer postpone answering the question whether it too should enter the fray. There were deep divisions and some confusion within the Liberal ministry over the best course to pursue. A majority, wedded to the tradition of Gladstonian isolationism and reflecting dominant opinion in the Liberal Party, were at first strongly against entering the conflict. Only Grey, supported by Asquith, Haldane (the Lord Chancellor) and Churchill (First Lord of the Admiralty) felt bound by the commitments without commitment that had been made to France since 1905. In the end it was Germany's threat against Belgium's neutrality which convinced the government that Britain should intervene. As Asquith explained to King George, the cabinet decided on 2

---

[2] Zara S. Steiner, *Britain and the Origins of the First World War* (London: Macmillan, 1977).
[3] Letter, Sir F. Bertie to Grey, 25 July 1914, TNA: PRO FO 800/54; Zara S. Steiner, *The Foreign Office and Foreign Policy, 1898–1914* (London: Cambridge University Press, 1969), pp.156–58.
[4] Memo of Conversation between Mr Craigie of the Foreign Office and Mr Easton of the British Immigration League of Australia, 16 July 1914, enclosed in letter, F.O. to C.O., 16 July 1914, TNA: PRO CO 418/129. This optimistic assessment of Anglo-German relations might well have been intended merely to quieten Australian alarm. Craigie added that he 'could not believe any senior Japanese statesmen contemplated … the conquest of Australia.'
[5] Cabinet Letter to the King, 25 July 1914, Asquith Papers, Bodleian Library, MSS. Asquith 7.

August that 'a substantial violation of the neutrality of that country would place us in the situation contemplated by Mr Gladstone in 1870 when interference with Belgian independence was held to compel us to take action.'[6]

On the following day, after the German ultimatum to Belgium, the cabinet authorised Grey to announce its decision to parliament and to take the steps which would lead to war with Germany. Only two ministers resigned. In the House of Commons Grey, explaining the government's position, shrewdly made the core of his brief the German treatment of Belgium. He appealed to Liberal orthodoxy and hagiography, invoking Gladstone's famous words of 1870 from the last occasion when Germany had threatened France through Belgium. Britain's response at that time had to be 'found in the answer to the question whether … the country, endowed as it is with influence and power, would quietly witness the direst crime that ever stained the pages of history and thus become participator in that sin.' Even more, though, he stressed Gladstone's prediction of the strategic consequences. Britain had to act 'to prevent the whole of the West of Europe opposite us from falling under the domination of a single power.'[7] Despite the 1839 Treaty of Guarantee, Britain's decision to enter the war in defence of Belgium would be, as Asquith had earlier written to the King, 'rather one of policy than legal obligation.'[8] And thus when the day came, the British response to the European crisis was an act of strategic calculation rather than of legal or moral duty.[9] Grey's speech, sombre in tone and substantial in content, appealing as it did to ideals and interests, to Liberals and Conservatives, was a triumph, and when on 4 August Germany ignored Britain's demand that it respect Belgium's neutrality, Asquith was able to lead a more or less united government and nation into the war.

For the British Government it had been an anxious time. Britain could have been almost as deeply divided over entry into the war as it was over Irish Home Rule. Grey and the interventionists in cabinet had acted with circumspection in not pressing the issue prematurely. They had sought to keep a free hand for Britain for as long as possible, both to give credibility to their role as peacemakers and also to allow their doubting colleagues to learn from the course of events the true nature of the German threat. Beset by so many difficulties the British leaders had no desire to add to their burdens by bringing the Dominions into this complex process of decision-making. Consequently Australia was neither informed nor consulted about these momentous questions of peace and war.

Australia's leaders' response to the war

When the news of the gathering war clouds reached Australia in the last days of July, it caught the nation off-balance. On 5 June the Governor-General, Sir Ronald Munro Ferguson, had granted

---

[6] Cabinet Letter to the King, 2 August 1914, *ibid.*
[7] Great Britain, *Parliamentary Debates* (Commons), Vol.LXV, pp.1822–24, 3 August 1914.
[8] Cabinet Letter to the King, 30 July 1914, Asquith Papers, Bodleian Library, MSS. Asquith 7.
[9] Cf. K.M. Wilson, 'The British Cabinet's Decision for War, 2 August 1914', *British Journal of International Studies,* l (1975), pp.148–57 and M. Brock, 'Britain Enters the War', in R.J.W. Evans and H. Pogge von Strandmann (eds), *The Coming of the First World War* (Oxford: Clarendon Press, 1988), pp.159–61.

the Liberal Government a double dissolution and the leaders of the country were engaged in a rather lack-lustre election campaign. The rumours of war, followed by Britain's entry into the war, quickly upstaged the debate over federal powers and industrial monopolies, social reform and national development, drought and unemployment. In Australia, unlike Britain, not one major politician questioned the wisdom of the British Government's handling of the European crisis or its decision to go to war or even the lack of consultation in the weeks leading up to the outbreak of hostilities.[10] All acted instinctively in giving their support to the cause of Britain and the Empire.

The four most important political leaders at the time, Prime Minister Joseph Cook, Attorney-General Sir William Irvine, Leader of the Opposition Andrew Fisher and shadow Attorney-General William Morris Hughes, while responding loyally, did so in a way reflecting their respective world views and prefiguring some of the subsequent differences over how Australia should manage its world crisis.

The two party leaders made their first pronouncements in the heat of the election contest and they gave voice to the emotional simplicity of the initial Australian response to the war. On 30 July, Cook declared that 'all our resources are in the Empire and for the Empire, and for the preservation and security of the Empire.' The following evening Fisher put the point even more succinctly when he promised that Australians would stand by Britain 'to help and defend her to our last man and last shilling.'[11] But there was more to these men's views than was immediately apparent. Cook and Fisher, and with them Irvine and Hughes, brought to the crisis a rich political experience which had compelled them to ponder the great problems of their times, namely the problems of morality and power, principle and expediency, empire and nation. The political philosophies and personalities that these four men had fashioned for themselves during the first years of the Commonwealth determined the way in which each understood the world crisis.

None of these four leaders was Australian-born. They had grown up in the British Isles and emigrated to Australia in their early or middle twenties – Cook and Hughes from England, Fisher from Scotland and Irvine from Ireland. Cook and Fisher were miners and sons of miners, Hughes was a teacher by training and a jack of all trades in practice, and Irvine, the son of a bankrupt linen manufacturer, was a lawyer. All arrived in the country between 1879 and 1884. Yet that they all had grown up in Britain did not mean they were any more or less British in their sentiments and loyalties, or any more or less committed to Australia's interests and welfare, than the native-born. They were the democratically elected leaders of their parties and their country.

Cook, a founder of the Miners' Union at Lithgow and the first leader of the New South Wales Parliamentary Labour Party, had broken with Labour over the Caucus solidarity pledge in 1894 and gravitated towards George Reid's Free Trade Party. His political fires were stoked by

---

[10] In Britain the prospect of war divided both the Liberal government and the Liberal parliamentary party and press. The Labour parliamentary party on 30 July unanimously resolved 'to oppose ... any action which might involve Great Britain in war.' After Grey had announced in the House of Commons Britain's decision for war both the Labour leader Ramsay MacDonald and eleven Liberals attacked Britain's involvement in the European conflict. See A.J. Anthony Morris, *Radicalism Against War, 1906–1914: The Advocacy of Peace and Retrenchment* (London: Longman, 1972), pp.403–20.

[11] *Argus*, 1 August 1914.

Methodist moralism – some said wowserism. As a lay preacher, who neither drank, smoked, gambled, nor indulged in frivolous pastimes, he saw politics through an English Nonconformist lens as the preservation of a righteous liberty.

He needed to justify Britain's entry into the war in moral terms. 'Our enemy strikes the first blow in an unrighteous cause,' he wrote. '… What is more lawful than self-defence … the issues raised by War. Not Alsace-Lorraine, not heavy armaments' but, and here he named the German philosophers, Friedrich von Bernhardi and Friedrich Nietzsche, 'a morality which was putrid. An ethic of hell.' He recoiled from the thought of the death and destruction that the war would bring about but consoled himself with the vague hope of 'the good to come. Moral tone. Luxury, frivolity and class selfishness will be less.' The war would unite the nation and prepare individuals and classes to eschew vain things and sacrifice their interests for the good of the whole.

As for so many other English Protestants there was a narrow tribal quality in this moral outlook. Linking the European conflict to one of his enduring political themes, Cook rejoiced in 'the spectacle … of the Austrian Socialist fighting the Serbian Socialist, of the Russian Socialist preparing to fight the Austrian Socialist.' It confirmed him in his view that 'the feeling of nationhood is there today. It is proof against all your brother of man principles.' He asserted that the actions of the European Socialist showed 'that there is something stronger and that is the feeling of nationalism that is behind all the principles that have come down to us.'[12] But for Australians what was 'nationalism'? It is true that during his brief term as Prime Minister, he had come to realise that Australian and British strategic interests were not identical, and had shown no compunction in arguing the Australian case against British authority. He was, like all his peers, keenly aware of the looming presence of Asia, in particular the hostility of Japan to White Australia, and in the years immediately preceding the onset of the war had taken the British Government to task for failing to honour its commitment to the defence of the Empire in the Pacific. Nevertheless these differences made him uneasy and he was most comfortable when he could believe that Australia and the Empire shared one world view which would provide for the security of the whole British race.

Despite his atavistic attachment to the British Empire, Cook shared something of British liberal fastidiousness in his attitude to war. There remained with him some residual qualms about allowing the state to use illiberal means in the defence of liberty. He was one of a handful of members from his side of parliament who questioned the unrestricted powers which Attorney-General Hughes sought to give the government under the *War Precautions Act* in October 1914. He was fearful that the military might assume too much power and that ordinary citizens might become subject to martial law. But these scruples were quickly silenced by the greater imperative of securing victory for the British Empire.

Personally he lacked the ruthlessness of spirit as well as the resources of energy which war leadership required. Thus, in early 1917, after the National Party had been formed from the fusion of the pro-conscription Labor men with the Liberals, Cook agreed, even though the Liberals had the majority in the coalition, to take second place to Hughes in the National Ministry and to be content with the rather nominal navy portfolio. In 1918 and 1919 Cook accompanied

---

[12] Cook Diary, 27 July to 3 August 1914, NAA M3580: *Argus*, 6 August 1914: *Age*, 1 August 1914.

Hughes to the Imperial War Conference and the Paris Peace Conference, and in 1920 and 1921 he was Treasurer and Acting Prime Minister while Hughes attended the 1921 Imperial Conference in London. Yet in these years he always walked in Hughes's shadow, being content to serve loyally his dynamic and masterful leader.

Cook, in this era, was a failed liberal who could neither embrace wholeheartedly the Wilsonian vision of a new world and a new diplomacy nor accept fully Hughes's harsh doctrine of the submission of the individual to the state, of the salvation of the nation through armed might. He foresaw what the war would mean for the geopolitical position of Australia and the Empire – 'New relations, new history'– but showed little desire to grapple with the issues and so help to define and shape this new history.

William Irvine, the Scotch-Irish Presbyterian, had a more severe and unsentimental outlook. There was no liberal squeamishness in his approach to the war. The embattled position of the Protestant ascendancy in Catholic Ireland had taught him the value of the British connection. For him the British Empire was the ultimate guarantor of order and identity. Thus at the approach of the European conflict he adopted a literal interpretation of the British Imperial constitution: 'When England is at war we are at war. There is no half-way home ... The statesmen of England are now charged with the terrible responsibility of determining the issues of peace and war for the whole of the people, and we are not only bound to abide by their decision, but to give them every assistance that lies in our power.'[13] Irvine was not indifferent to Australia's potential difficulties with Japan but such local problems paled into insignificance when compared with the survival of the Empire. For this reason, he accepted that citizens must be prepared to sacrifice all their liberties to the state and to place all their lives and goods at the disposal of the Mother Country. Indeed, if necessary, the Imperial parliament should be free to requisition whatever was required.

In the debate over the *War Precautions Act*, Irvine, unlike Cook, gave Hughes unqualified support, agreeing that the powers sought were 'inherent in all Governments'. The future Chief Justice of Victoria, the stickler for the strict construction of the Imperial constitution, boasted that 'In time of war Governments do – the late Government [in which he had held the post of Attorney-General] did – many things not authorised by law.'[14]

From 1915 he became a fervent advocate of conscription both of men and wealth for the British cause. He showed as much sympathy to those who opposed him in this as he had to the striking railway engine drivers whom he as Victorian Premier in 1903 had sacked and replaced with non-unionists. He refused to accept the negative results of the 1916 referendum on conscription for overseas service. In early 1917 he even suggested to the Governor-General that the 'Imperial parliament' had every right to overrule the popular decision and legislate for conscription.[15] In the May 1917 election campaign, in defiance of his party and leader, he refused to give an assurance that the Australian Parliament would not legislate for conscription without

---

[13] *SMH*, 2 August 1914.
[14] *CPD*, 1914–17 session, XXV, 369–85, 28 October 1914.
[15] Letter (personal), Governor-General Sir Ronald Munro Ferguson, to King's Private Secretary Lord Stamfordham, 21 February 1917, Novar Papers, NLA MS 696/270 – '... he [Irvine] suggested to me in private that the Imperial Parliament might very properly have decreed conscription for the Empire ... ' Even the Governor-General thought such a proposal high-handed.

first referring the matter to the people. And in late 1917 his public agitation on the subject was, in part, responsible for Hughes's decision to hold a second referendum. Irvine's ultramontane stand isolated him from dominant opinion in the National Party and helped to keep him out of office in 1917 and 1918. He was probably happy in April 1918 to accept the position of Chief Justice of Victoria, where he could escape the trammels of democracy.

The Governor-General declared of Irvine that 'He has more the mind of a statesman than anyone else in Australia … there is no public man who so often hits the right nail on the head.'[16] Munro Ferguson regarded Irvine as the most discerning and high-principled of the Australian political leaders. But this judgment said more about Munro Ferguson's position and predilections than about Australian politics. As Governor-General he was the representative of the British Government as well as the British crown – the separation of the two roles did not come about until after 1926 – and as such he was impressed by those politicians who would subordinate Australian interests to British interests, who would unquestioningly serve a London-centred Empire.

Irvine's was a principled not a partisan stand. He urged the conscription of treasure as well as troops. In order to secure the safety of the Empire, total war required total commitment. Irvine suffered politically for his principles. He was, however, a voice crying in the wilderness. Australians refused to heed him not because they were deaf to statesmanship or hostile to Britain but because he was at odds with popular sentiment. He did not appreciate the complexities of Australian Britishness, the absolute respect for Dominion self-government which accompanied a passionate commitment to a British identity. He was doomed to be the failed imperialist.

Fisher, as a Scot, was never as enamoured of Empire as Irvine, Cook or Hughes. As a Scot he had not the same sense of dependence upon the English connection as did Irvine the Ulsterman. Similarly, as a Scot, he did not feel so much at home with a British Empire controlled from London as did the English-born Cook and Hughes. Fisher never lost his distinctive Scottish Britishness. Not only did he speak with a pronounced brogue but it was Scotland's own bard, the poet of the people, Robert Burns, who was the inspiration for his socialism.

Fisher was a romantic. No work of Karl Marx or of any other significant socialist thinker can be found in his library. Nor are his speeches studded with references to such authorities. But his library does contain a number of copies of Burns's works: certainly no other writer is as well represented. A fellow Scottish Australian, Robert Anderson, in presenting a copy of *The World's Memorials of Robert Burns* to Fisher in 1912, wrote on the flyleaf 'That you may long be spared in heart and strength to Labor for the Realisation of that glorious period predicted by the grand old Burns when "Man to man the world o'er shall brithers be."' He wrote as if he and Fisher had often excited one another with Burns's vision. Throughout the book the egalitarian and idealistic lines of Burns, such as 'Princes and lords are but the breath of kings; an honest man's the noblest work of God' are marked in pencil as if they were the passages upon which Fisher dwelt.[17] He espoused a humane, almost poetic, socialism, a *socialisme sans doctrine*.

---

[16] *Ibid.*

[17] (Detroit, Michigan, 1911), Fisher Papers, NLA MS 2919/13/ 2. See also Fisher at a gathering of Scots on 25 January 1915 in Dunedin, New Zealand, to honour the 156th anniversary of the birth of Burns when he

Fisher was an ardent apostle of the sentiments celebrated in 'A man's a man for a' that'. The symbols of class pretension, especially those inherited from a superstitious past, particularly offended him. In 1911 on the occasion of George V's coronation he was only persuaded to wear court dress after the Colonial Secretary, the Governor-General, his secretary and his wife had worn down his resistance. Even so, on the day he rebelled against the lace trimmings, and when his wife refused to remove them he tore them off and went laceless to the ceremony.[18]

He subscribed to Burns's principle of the common humanity and equal dignity of all peoples. He held to the Enlightenment vision of human progress and believed that the day was approaching when wars would cease and all nations would live in peace with one another. In harmony with these views Fisher, while a supporter of the White Australia policy, made little of it. Compared to the other political leaders he was little given to using the language of race in his speeches and was much less committed to the idea of race as the defining principle for human, cultural or national relationships. His concern about Japan and its possible designs on Australia was not expressed primarily in terms of a 'Yellow Peril' but rather as a prudent consideration in the light of Japan's military strength, imperialist behaviour and geopolitical opportunism.

Of the four leaders Fisher was the only one to reveal a sustained belief in the possibility of world peace. He was more emphatic than any of his colleagues in deploring the coming of the Great War. He alone saw it as a human tragedy. He was deeply affected by the assassination of the French Socialist leader Jean Jaurès who died at the hand of a fanatical nationalist while trying to avert war by negotiating with the German Socialists. Fisher had spent a day with Jaurès in Paris in 1911 and he declared that the Frenchman was 'a great patriot'. It was his considered view that 'Among all the men he had met ... none strove harder to ameliorate conditions and promote peace, international and other, than he [Jaurès] did.' Fisher had proposed to Jaurès his own peace plan, namely that 'an international conference along the lines of the Imperial Conference' should be established to settle disputes between the nations. Fisher was an early proponent of an international organisation along the lines of what became the League of Nations. He believed that just as unions and management in Australia were compelled to take their disputes to an industrial tribunal, so countries should be expected to submit their differences to arbitration before resorting to arms.[19]

The English peace propagandist Norman Angell, with whom Fisher had 'a passing acquaintance', had confirmed him in his view that war was wasteful and foolish.[20] The bloodshed and sacrifice could only be justified if at the end they led to a better world. By 1915 Fisher had become convinced that 'the great war would leave behind it a lesson to mankind which would raise them to a higher plane of intelligence than they had yet reached. And just as poets had dreamed of it, so

---

declared of his hero, 'He was a hater of tyranny of any kind and a lover of freedom of every kind. He tore the cloak of hypocrisy, and with his incomparable wit he unbound superstition ... He foresaw what mankind could and ought to be today.' *Daily Times*, Otago, 26 January 1915.

[18] NAA A1632, 'Memoirs of M.L. Shepherd'.

[19] *Age*, 3 August 1914; *Argus*, 3 and 4 August 1914.

[20] Angell's most famous book, *The Great Illusion,* had argued that because war was unprofitable for all parties, even if it broke out, it would not last long. See J.D. Miller, *Norman Angell and the Futility of War* (London: Macmillan, 1986), pp.4–10.

he believed that in the future they would see developed a mighty power (a spiritual power) for organisation and law wherein there would be an international creed for the welfare of the people of the earth.'[21]

Despite his hatred of war Fisher, like Jaurès, had to reconcile his belief in the brotherhood of man and world peace with the need to protect his own people against aggression. He thus concluded, in much the same terms as Jaurès, that his first obligation after war had broken out was the defence of the nation. Jaurès' struggle with this question, caught up as it was in the debates of the Second International, was more ideological than Fisher's but the outcome was the same.[22]

Fisher was a practical romantic. He had long since accepted that, while the world was anarchical and given to violence, peaceable nations when confronted by armed, ambitious powers had to defend themselves. From a critic of militarism and military expenditure he had, after 1907, become one of the chief exponents of the doctrine of the 'Australian Crisis' and a chief author of Australia's defence preparedness programs. 'In these matters,' he said, '… facts are stubborn things.' But for him what the facts dictated in 1914 and 1915 was not altogether clear.

On Friday 31 July after Cook had offered all Australian resources for the protection of the Empire, Fisher had promised that Australia 'would stand beside our own [the Mother Country] to help and defend her to our last man and our last shilling.' In a country stirred by the prospect of Britain becoming engaged in a European war it was the politic phrase. Hughes later claimed that he had put Fisher up to using it.[23] In the circumstances, however, Fisher probably did not need Hughes's prompting for he was merely invoking the doctrine which Australian Boer War dissidents like himself had proclaimed at the beginning of the Commonwealth era. As Henry Bournes Higgins, one of the spokesmen for the Boer War critics, had explained, their opposition was not based on indifference to Britain's security and that if indeed Britain were in danger then he and all Australians would offer 'every man and every shilling' for the imperial cause.[24]

Yet, even as Fisher professed this emotional identity with the Mother Country, even as he allowed that Australia's welfare was inextricably bound up with that of Britain and the British Empire, he was aware that Australia, in some significant respects, had distinct interests of its own. He knew better than any of the other leaders that Australia's Pacific concerns had been ignored by

---

[21] *CPD*, 1914–17 session, LXXVII, 4843, 14 July 1915; *Official Report of the Sixth Commonwealth Conference of the ALP held in Adelaide, 31 May–7 June 1915* (Sydney: Worker Trade Union Printery, 1915).

[22] See Annie Kriegel, *Le Pain et les Roses: Jalons pour une Histoire des Socialismes* (Paris: Presses universitaires de France, 1968), pp.81 and 107–24; Roland N. Stromberg, *Redemption by War: The Intellectuals and 1914* (Lawrence: Regents Press of Kansas, 1982), chapter 6; Susan Milner, *The Dilemmas of Internationalism: French Syndicalism and the International Labour Movement, 1900–1914* (New York: Berg, 1990), pp.140 and 195–209.

[23] 'Notes from Billy Hughes', ND, Hume-Cook Papers, NLA MS 601.

Hughes told Hume-Cook that in addition to writing the major speeches and the manifesto for the Labor Party in July and August 1914, he had also been responsible for 'the now famous utterance regarding "the last man and the last shilling".'

[24] *Search for Security*, p.44.

British strategic planners. Since 1908, during his two terms as Prime Minister, he had followed Alfred Deakin's lead in defining those Pacific concerns, in arguing the Australian case against the British and in creating a defence policy to meet Australian needs. At the time of the Dreadnought crisis in March and April 1909 he had established the principles of his national and imperial policies. He had resisted the appeals to offer a battle cruiser for the Royal Navy. Panicked by the froth and bubble of public emotions, Hughes had urged capitulation to imperial fervour, but Fisher had stood firm and maintained that the government's first responsibility was the defence of Australia. He held to his decision to pursue 'a steady, persistent and determined policy to provide for the adequate defence of Australia and assist the Mother Country in the time of emergency.'[25]

Fisher's assertion of an independent defence policy was not motivated by an Australian cultural nationalism. Like the other leaders he did not draw on a mythology which identified Australians as a distinct people or race to legitimise his independent stand. Fisher's oratory, as is true of nearly all the politicians of his day, did not draw on the language of a unique Australian myth. He did not look to convicts, shearers, bushrangers to provide a separate story for Australians which would set them apart from Britons. His speeches did not invoke the names of Henry Lawson or 'Banjo' Paterson or any other members of the Bush Legend school. His decision to put Australia first was the result of a settled view that Australia as a political community had a set of interests peculiar to itself, and it was those interests which the Australian Government, elected by the Australian people, had a prime responsibility to protect. And on the eve of Britain's entry into the war – perhaps as the costs of intervention loomed more clearly before him – he reasserted the orthodox doctrine of the Dreadnought episode. On 4 August at Wangaratta he clearly put Australian interests ahead of imperial sentiment. 'My idea of patriotism,' he said, 'was to first provide for our own defence and if there was anything to spare offer it as a tribute to the Mother Country. Australians now had the opportunity of patriotism of this kind.'[26] This was a far cry from the offer of 'the last man and the last shilling'.

After being elected to office in September 1914, Fisher found himself overwhelmed by the war crisis. He recognised the important issues at stake in the war but, unlike Cook, Irvine and Hughes, was unwilling to sacrifice everything for the Empire. He hoped that Britain and its Allies would gain a quick victory and so save Australia from having to make hard choices. In the meantime Labor's plans for national development and social reform should not be abandoned. In justifying this stance he proudly proclaimed that 'It is enough for us to know that we are a progressive country … that, taking all in all … perhaps socially the most progressive in the world.' And he continued, 'We anticipated the people of the Old Land while it was yet day, and we ought not to halt while the way remains open to us.'[27] Australia was to be a model for the regeneration of the Mother Country.

Similarly, while he was willing that Australia should assist Britain he did not consider that Australia should put its own security at risk. From the outset he realised that the war would give Japan a greater opportunity to advance its aims in the Pacific. After Japan took possession of the

---

[25] *Search for Security*, p.180.
[26] *Argus*, 5 August 1914.
[27] *CPD*, 1914–17 Session, LXXVI, 2369, 15 April 1915.

German North Pacific islands in November 1914, he revived his proposal for an imperial conference on Pacific security and his plan for a Pacific fleet composed of Dominion squadrons. During 1914 and 1915 Fisher remained ever alert to the danger which Japan posed to Australia. Britain was totally dependent on Japan's goodwill for the protection of its interests in East Asia. Furthermore Britain wanted Japan to make a greater contribution to the war against Germany in the Mediterranean and the Atlantic. This was a cause for continuing anxiety since it was unclear what price Japan might demand and Britain might pay in return for such assistance.

Consequently Fisher's attitude to recruiting for the AIF was one of studied restraint. Unlike Cook, Irvine and Hughes, Fisher did not endorse an active recruitment program until after the Australian losses at Gallipoli had taken their toll and the Allied failure in Europe had ended hopes of an early and easy victory. While he supported compulsory military service for home defence, he was opposed to conscription for overseas service. Apart from his strategically based reservations, his sensitivity to the labour movement's feeling on the issue also counselled against such a course. In the 1916 conscription referendum he was the only Prime Minister, of all those who had served in that office since the inauguration of the Commonwealth, who did not sign an appeal to the people to vote for compulsory overseas service. Though he hid behind his official position, claiming that as High Commissioner in London he could not take a public stand on a controversial political subject – Edmund Barton at the time a Justice of the High Court had no such scruple – his refusal was more fundamentally an expression of his political principles and common sense.

Most of Fisher's former Labor colleagues, both the proponents and opponents of conscription, knew in their hearts as they wrote to him of their divisions in late 1916 and early 1917 that he would not have led them down such a path.[28] And their instincts were right. It would appear that Fisher, in contrast to the more doctrinaire members of the party, did not regard opposition to conscription as the ultimate test of Labor loyalty. More probably he recognised, as John Curtin – the Secretary of the Victorian Anti-Conscription League in 1916 – did in 1943, that under some circumstances, conscription for overseas service might be justified. Always reluctant to adopt such a policy, he believed in 1915 and 1916 that for reasons of domestic harmony and national security it was not wise to take such a step.

The Governor-General, on summing up Fisher, wrote that while he was honest and public-spirited 'he was absorbed in his own opinions, which are unchangeable.'[29] Hughes, who succeeded Fisher as Prime Minister and who had been a close associate of Fisher in and out of government since 1901, wrote of him that 'It was always difficult to get him to squarely face and overcome a problem. His qualities though sound were of a negative kind … He was honest and honourable and fair. He would never commit the Party to an indiscretion.' Explaining his own failure to be elected leader of the party in 1907, Hughes averred that 'in the comparative peace and quiet of the

---

[28] Letter, W.H. Demaine to Andrew Fisher, 25 and 26 December 1916, Fisher Papers, NLA MS 2919/1/290. Demaine, who was the editor of the *Maryborough Alert* and an old party comrade of Fisher, wrote 'I am delighted to read that you are still opposed to compulsion. I thought you were, reading between the lines of your September letter, but I am pleased to have my thoughts definitely confirmed.'
[29] Secret letter, Munro Ferguson to A. Bonar Law, 28 December 1915, TNA: PRO CO 418/134/472.

times he [Fisher] was regarded as "safe". But he had always to be helped.'[30] And these measures of the man have passed without question into the history books.

Both assessments, however, while containing a grain of truth, were partisan and self-serving. Munro Ferguson disliked the constitutional restrictions which Fisher had placed on the Governor-General's ability to interfere in policy-making and he considered that Fisher's approach to helping Britain was too lukewarm. Hughes resented the fact that his Labor colleagues had preferred Fisher to lead them. Since Hughes was temperamentally incapable of appreciating that some problems had no simple solutions, he could not help but see Fisher's ambivalence as indecision or Fisher's rejection of an urgent plea for action as timidity.

Fisher was not the rigid reactive leader, devoid of vision and initiative, which they depicted. His oratory often lacked eloquence and coherence, and those who judged him by his performance in parliament or on the hustings might have found some warrant for their criticisms. But both as leader of the opposition and as Prime Minister he grappled with problems, learnt from experience and sponsored significant initiatives in social reform and national development as well as defence and foreign policy.[31]

Though Fisher was a man of principle, his principles were guides to more general objectives, not inflexible standards to be applied under all circumstances. He sought to attain his ends by relying on persuasion and goodwill instead of, as so often was the case with Hughes, resorting to coercion or chicanery. Perhaps he was too straightforward for his own good. Perhaps he felt too keenly the moral dilemmas of his time. Perhaps he made too few concessions to Machiavelli's view of man and politics. Even so, on matters of politics as well as principle, from the Dreadnought Crisis of 1909 to the call for a Coalition Government in August 1914 and the conscription controversy of 1915 and 1916, Fisher's judgment proved to be sounder than Hughes's.

The world crisis taxed Fisher beyond bearing. War was not his metier. In October 1915, weary in mind and body, he resigned as Prime Minister. However, if Fisher was, in the war years, the failed Labor leader, his was an honourable failure. As the letters written to him by his former colleagues in 1916 and 1917 testify, Fisher remained the conscience of the Labor Party and even, it might be said, the nation.[32] He remained the symbol of what might have been if Hughes had not succeeded him as Prime Minister and divided the party and nation over conscription. Those who saw Fisher in this light may, however, have indulged somewhat in wishful thinking, for by the end of 1915 the signs of distress and division in the Labor ranks were already apparent, and by 1916 the Universal Service League and its Liberal sympathisers were bent on demanding conscription, no matter who was Prime Minister. Fisher, however, did not fall into the putative role of the peacemaker simply because he was absent from the country when the critical moment came. Those made distraught by what Hughes had wrought had every reason to believe that Fisher would have guided them more wisely.

---

[30] 'A Note from Billy Hughes', Hume-Cook Papers, NLA MS 601.
[31] The Governor-General, complaining of Fisher that 'once an idea is rooted in his mind … it is apt to remain there,' added that his mind was 'a prolific seed-bed.' Letter, Munro Ferguson to Harcourt, 13 April 1915, TNA: PRO CO 418/132/340–42. Munro Ferguson was complaining not so much that Fisher had original ideas as that he refused to accept the Governor-General's arguments against them.
[32] Fisher Papers, NLA MS 2919/1/124–375.

Of the four leaders, Hughes had the quickest and most incisive mind and the sharpest and most vitriolic tongue. He was, of all the Australian leaders of his time, the most brilliant, the most articulate and, not least for explaining his success, the most energetic. Moreover, he was the only one to have developed a general theory of international relations as a basis for understanding Australia's position in the world.[33]

Hughes was impressed above all else with the friable nature of the world order. To him the history of international relations was the history of war and conflict. In an article on 'International Arbitration and National Defence', he wrote 'It is unhappily true that war has been the common lot of most nations.'[34] As a Labor leader he at first gave the impression that he shared with Fisher the belief in a world progressing towards a time when all peoples would live together in peace and harmony. Here he explained the causes of war in classical liberal terms as 'the ambitions of kings and rulers, the personal interests of dynasties, court intrigues and the desire for territorial aggrandisement'. The peoples of these nations 'between whom there rarely exists real cause for enmity, who fight in obedience to command, and, in general, under a belief that in some way the welfare of their country is involved in the struggle' were the victims of 'misunderstanding born of ignorance, of distance, lack of communications and facilities for intercourse'.

Thus just as the nation had evolved from the tribe, so an international community or a consciousness of a common humanity would, as means of communication improved, evolve out of and then replace national rivalries. Once the peoples of the world became enlightened and educated, their governments would no longer be able to inveigle them into wars of mutual hatred and mass slaughter. This was 'the hope of the world'. Hughes, however, allowed that in the same way that the tribe had taken a long time to develop into a nation, so it would be a long time before loyalty to the nation was replaced by a loyalty to a common humanity.

In the meantime the best that Hughes could offer for settling disputes and preventing war was international arbitration. To some extent the efficacy of the international court would depend on 'an enlightened public opinion born of a friendly understanding between the working classes of the world'. But, most importantly, the international court, like the domestic courts, would need to have an adequate force at its disposal to ensure respect for its authority. It would require a 'league of civilised powers who would compel by force every nation to submit to the decisions of the international tribunal.'[35] When subsequently proposals for international settlement of disputes arose, as at the Commonwealth Labor Conference of June 1915, or the Paris Peace Conference of 1919, Hughes was adamant that provision for an international policeman was essential for their

---

[33] Between 1908 and 1911 Hughes wrote a series of articles dealing with Labor policy on the great issues of the day. Though many of these articles were subsequently published as *The Case for Labor* (Sydney and Melbourne: The Worker Trustees, 1910) those concerned with international relations were omitted. See for example *Daily Telegraph*, 22 February 1908; 26 June 1909; 'International Arbitration and National Defence', 17 December 1910; 'The National Defence Scheme and Its Critics', 7 October 1911; 18 October 1911. These essays, however, provide the clearest picture of Hughes's view of the nature of international relations.

[34] *Daily Telegraph*, 17 December 1910.

[35] *Ibid.*, 14 December 1910.

success, and even more importantly that that role should devolve upon the 'civilised powers' led by the British Empire.

This universalist, optimistic and cooperative language sat ill, however, with other, more fundamental strands in Hughes's philosophy and psychology. His experience in life and his observation of men and nations had engendered in him a highly sceptical, if not cynical, view of human nature and human progress. Sometimes he expressed this merely in terms of time, in questioning how long it would take for the new harmonious order to arise. More frequently, though, it appeared as a critique of progressive expectations themselves. Indeed, the questions about time and tenets merged. If the day when the peoples of the world would be able to live together happily was in the distant future, then until that time arrived Australia must act upon another set of assumptions. It had to respond to different expectations and in practice this meant discarding the liberal philosophy of international relations.

Hughes had first set out this alternative view of international relations in the debates over defence and immigration in the first Commonwealth Parliament. At that time he had advocated compulsory military training to protect Australia against the unpredictability of a violent world, and he supported the White Australia policy against the brotherhood of man principle as a means of safeguarding the British character of the new nation.[36] In answer to those socialists who foresaw national morality and sentiment giving way to a wider international morality and sentiment, he subsequently declared that 'I am sorry I cannot think that either probable or desirable.' Confuting the internationalists, he proclaimed the absolute pre-eminence of national feeling.

> A man's love for his country may not be reasonable, though I think it is – it is certainly unselfish. Without it the race would speedily degenerate, mentally, morally, and even physically. For love of one's country, like the sexual and maternal instincts, is too deeply rooted to be easily destroyed. But, it may, through false doctrine be suppressed ... There comes a time in the history of rising nations when a call to arms will fire the people who running headlong to the defence of their country, save not only their native land but themselves. Patriotism has regenerated them. They are like lovers, who in their lives see for the first time the world and their place in it.[37]

For Hughes, then, love of nation was natural and instinctual in a way that love of humanity was not. Reflecting the classic nineteenth century understanding of nationalism, Hughes saw the individual citizens realising their selfhood within the fold of the nation. He perceived the citizens achieving personal fulfilment by merging themselves with the national community and, if necessary, sacrificing everything to ensure its survival.

Within a year of his brief flirtation with internationalism and international arbitration, Hughes had to all intents and purposes renounced such notions as foolish and dangerous. In a vehement attack on 'Pacifists' and 'International Revolutionary Socialists' he rejected the idea of human perfectibility. He asked rhetorically:

---

[36] *Search for Security*, pp.45–47.
[37] *Daily Telegraph*, 22 February 1908.

> And since all the talk about honesty being the best policy the Rights and Brotherhood of Man has not yet prevented the descendants of Cain from plying their bloody trade … in these days, as in those long gone by, why should we think the men of other nations are likely to be moved by such high and noble ideals?

And then he answered his own question:

> The history of the world furnishes, indeed, sad proof to the contrary. History shows that there has never been a weak nation worth attacking that has not been attacked. That there has never been a nation which neglected to adequately provide for its defence that did not live to regret it …

Contemplating the lessons to be learnt from Italy's attack on Turkey in 1911, Hughes cut down the very props upon which he had earlier appeared to build his hopes for a new and better world.

> Italy is a civilised nation. Civilisation is opposed to war. She is a Christian nation and Christianity denounces war. Socialism has made great strides there, and Socialism desires to embrace the whole world as a family. Unionism is strong and militant. Yet we hear that the war upon Turkey which is a shameful and unprovoked attack upon a neighbour in order to steal that neighbour's land is popular amongst the people of Italy … The fact is that nations, like men, are indifferently good. All nations are, like some men, born criminals. They will break the law whenever it suits them, if they can break it safely.

The people, even the working class, were as likely to engage in wars of aggression as kings and courts. All, regardless of status or station, were born in sin. The 'Babble about peace and the Brotherhood of man will not help us.' The lesson to be learnt was that of Ancient Rome.

> There is but one way … by which we here in Australia can hope to ensure the maintenance of peace. It is by being prepared for war … There is only one way to be free, and that is to hold the means of freedom in one's own strong right hand.[38]

To Hughes 'international relations' was a struggle for survival; 'While we are in the jungle, we must beware lest the wild beasts devour us.' In this dangerous world Australia faced its peculiar perils. He pointed out that 'so far from being out of harm's way and isolated, the map shows that we are in the very middle of trouble, for we are right at the back door of the East.' Australia's racial geography obsessed him. In words similar to those he would use to frighten the Australian people in 1916 on the eve of the conscription referendum, he declared, 'Within a few days sail 100s of millions of people alien in race, creeds, and ideals are crowded together, engaged in a fierce and bitter struggle for mere existence. Can it be wondered at if these people … look with covetous eyes on our country.' Australia was 'not less the natural prey of the teeming, sweating millions of the East than Turkey was the natural prey of Italy.' Hughes maintained that 'the teeming, sweating millions' had to that time been held back not by their belief in the 'Brotherhood of Man' but by fear, 'fear of the British navy'.

However, it had to be recognised that the British navy might 'someday' – and the sense that this was a 'near-day' was conveyed – be 'engaged elsewhere, fighting for its life … In that day it will go hard with us … if we have not at our disposal something to tame the land-lust and blood-

---

[38] *Ibid.*, 7 October 1911.

lust of the men of the East.'[39] Here was the authentic voice of Hughes. There was no assessment of the intent, no measuring of the means, no concern for the geopolitical circumstances – just an assertion of an abstract racial threat to Australia and its white British people.

When Europe erupted into war in August 1914, Hughes joined with Cook, Irvine and Fisher in identifying with Britain. His first response was, like that of the other leaders, one of unqualified support based on interest and sentiment. 'Whatever needs to be done to defend the interests of the Commonwealth and of the Empire must be done …' he declared on 1 August. 'If Britain is involved and war is upon us,' he continued, 'we must face it and do our part in a fashion worthy of the tradition and spirit of our race.' But he had a greater sense of the epoch-making nature of the conflict, proclaiming that Australia must do 'what has to be done with inflexible resolution and purpose and we must face it unitedly. For this indeed is the occasion when "None shall be for the party, but all be for the state" '.[40] The crisis that he had long anticipated was upon them. As was his wont, he warned of the perils which the conflict portended; 'If Britain were defeated Australia would be left merely to choose to whom it should surrender.' Half-measures were 'absolutely useless.' The country 'must act promptly and effectively. As the crisis is without precedent, so must the measures.'[41]

Hughes would not rely on the possibility of the Entente powers achieving a quick victory. He did not consider feasible or desirable a negotiated peace between the belligerents. For him the war was a struggle for national existence, according to the jungle law of world politics, in which the fittest alone would survive. Germany had thrown down a challenge to the primacy of the British race and its destiny to maintain a civilised and righteous world order. All that the British peoples stood for was at stake. As a result, Hughes was single-minded in his determination that all aspects of national life should be made subservient to the war effort. After becoming Prime Minister in October 1915 he stated that he could only give his mind to one great question at a time. Labor's domestic program had to give way before the imperative of winning the war. Everything that Australians valued, national security, economic prosperity and social progress, was dependent on the British Empire achieving victory in Europe.

From the first, Hughes was willing to send every available man to the front, and when voluntarism seemed inadequate he embraced the cause of conscription. In their uncompromising approach to the war Hughes and Irvine were as one, believing that Australian Britons should be willing to sacrifice their lives and fortunes for the good of the race. Unlike Irvine, however, Hughes had sufficient political sense to realise that conscription could not be foisted upon the people against their will.

Hughes also understood much better than Irvine that Australian and British interests were not in any simple way one and indivisible. He held that, while Australian and British interests were inextricably linked, they were also, in some important respects, distinct and opposed. From the 1901 debates over the White Australia policy to the subsequent crises over the Japanese defeat of Russia in 1905 and the British naval retreat from the Pacific, Hughes had, like Fisher and Cook,

---

[39] *Ibid.*, 18 October 1911.
[40] *SMH*, 3 August 1914.
[41] *Daily Telegraph*, 15 August 1914.

become aware that Australia and Britain did not share the same strategic priorities and that under certain circumstances Britain might leave Australia to fend for itself. Confronted by the European war Hughes's view was that Australia had only one choice. Australia had to give every assistance to the Mother Country to defeat Germany so that the global pre-eminence of the British Empire could be restored and through that, Australia might achieve permanent security in the Pacific. No other possibility could be contemplated. Without total victory, Australia and the Empire would remain exposed to powerful enemies in Europe and the Pacific.

Hughes was temperamentally a man of action. He was not able to live easily with himself or those about him. He suffered agonies from dyspepsia and drew little comfort from his private life. Perhaps his inner suffering contributed to his unrelenting efforts to dominate the external environment. Whatever the reason, he expended great energy, far in excess of any of his contemporaries, in writing and speaking, organising and scheming to master the politics of his times. So driven, he had answers to all the great questions which came before the country. His logical faculties were not allowed to content themselves with an analysis of a problem. He required a solution, indeed *the* solution, which, once decided upon, had to be imposed on the party and the people, or if appropriate, the Empire and the world. For his whole life the chasm of insecurity yawned beneath him. Only the highest wall built to meet every contingency could be trusted. Henry Boote, editor of the Sydney *Worker,* reported of Hughes's concern about his West Sydney seat that 'every election, it seems, he is in fear and trembling of losing his seat, and is afraid his committee is not doing enough, even though he has a majority of ten thousand!'[42]

This absolutism was evident in his approach to the war and demands for the peace. In this respect it was an extreme expression of a commitment to the idea of nationalism which makes the individual and the society whole. It could be seen in his support for a total war effort and demand for a crushing victory over Germany. It was present in his persecution of German residents and even those of German descent. It dominated his campaign for conscription during the war. At the Paris Peace Conference it was apparent in his contemptuous dismissal of Wilson's 'Babble of peace' and the League of Nations, his desire for vengeance against Germany, his tenacious claim for the annexation of the German Pacific islands and his hostility to a racial equality provision, no matter how innocuous, in the League of Nations Covenant. Having failed at the Paris Peace Conference to achieve any of his aims, apart from the suppression of the racial equality principle, it is little wonder that he could write of the Treaty of Versailles, 'It is not a good peace for Australia: nor indeed for Britain.'[43] It is no wonder that shortly after returning from Paris he could imagine that Japan was about to launch a surprise attack on Australia.

By 1923 his heroic days on the political stage were over. He had to reconcile himself to the limits of power. He had to learn to live with the limits of British and Australian power in the world and the limits of his own position in the National Party and in national politics. There was nothing he could do to restore the supremacy of the Royal Navy, to re-establish the predominance of British commerce and finance, to restructure the British Empire to give Australia an effective voice in the formulation of its defence and foreign policy, to guarantee Australian security in the

---

[42] M.E. Lloyd, *Sidelights on two referendums, 1916–1917* (Sydney: William Brooks & Co., 1952), p.49.
[43] Letter, Hughes to Munro Ferguson, 17 May 1919, Novar Papers, NLA MS 696/552.

Pacific or to avoid the consequences of the Russian Revolution or the Irish Rebellion. He could rail against the implacable nature of history, but, do what he might, he was powerless to change it. Nothing that Hughes could do would win him his peace.

Leaders do matter. By the outbreak of the war each of the four leaders had acquired from the interaction of their personality, culture and experience views of history and human nature, of politics and international relations which would have a great impact on Australia's response to the world crisis.

2
The Imperial Cause and Aid for the Mother Country

The coming of the war was the occasion for a perfervid outpouring of national emotion. The European conflict was the first great trial for the myths and loyalties of late-nineteenth-century mass nationalism that had fused state power with cultural identity. The Australian people who took great pride in belonging to the British race and Empire reacted accordingly. They were as one with their leaders. In the streets and at the hustings, in the press and on the public platform, they vented their feelings. It was a spontaneous movement which embraced all sections of society.

The response to the outbreak of war

Eager citizens followed European developments from press cables posted on the outside of newspapers offices in the capital cities. From the 3 to 5 of August 1914 scenes of wild enthusiasm, sometimes spilling over into mob violence, greeted every new announcement. In Melbourne it was reported that:

> It needed only a single mouth to give the opening bars of a patriotic song, and thousands of throats took it up, hats and coats were waved, and those who were lucky enough to possess even the smallest Union Jacks were the heroes of the moment, and were raised shoulder high as the crowd surged hither and thither. Rule Britannia, Soldiers of the King and Sons of the Sea were sung again and again. The National Anthem had a sobering effect from time to time, and woe betide anyone who failed to remove his hat without hesitation.[1]

It was in an atmosphere of 'mafficking' madness that Australia's capital welcomed the war.

This hysteria led to xenophobic attacks on all enemies of White British Australia, including not only Germans and Austrians but also the Chinese community. On the evening of 3 August there were incitements to march on the German Consul's Office, on the next evening the German club, the Turnverein, was broken into and damaged, and on the evening of 5 August, after the announcement of Britain's declaration of war, there was a full scale riot. At about 10 o'clock 'a gang of about 200 youths', whose patriotic ardour had been suitably inflamed with alcohol, marched behind Union Jacks down Swanston Street. They quickly attracted a following of about 3000 sympathisers, who joined in 'with shouts, yells, mingling with cheers and snatches of public airs'. The police, fearing a repetition of the previous night's disorder (they reported that the leaders were making wild threats to 'smash-up' foreigners), tried to move the demonstrators along but only succeeded in packing them together in 'a congested, howling mob'. When the police confiscated the Union Jacks that were being used to taunt them, some in the crowd tore the whips from the cabstands and lashed out at the police. Blocked from reaching the German club, about

---

[1] *Age*, 4 August 1914.

fifty of the hard core turned their hostility against the race enemy and dashing up Little Bourke Street smashed every window in the Chinese quarter.[2]

Similar outbursts of patriotic enthusiasm occurred in all other state capitals. In Brisbane university students streamed out of the campus onto the streets chanting, 'We want war.' Thousands of citizens assembled in Market Square singing 'Rule Britannia', 'Sons of the Sea' and 'God Save the King'. The Labor *Daily Standard* reported that it 'was reminiscent of a strike scene.' Brisbane, like all the other major cities, had not ever before witnessed such an expression of public feelings and as in Melbourne there were excesses. Several hundred youths detached themselves from the main body and 'made a hostile demonstration' outside the German Consulate. As they passed German shops or houses they hooted. In Perth crowds gathered on the evening of 5 August on St George's Terrace to cheer the news from Britain and Europe as it was posted on the *West Australian* bulletin boards. There was, however, 'nothing wildly demonstrative' about the response except for 'a number of excited youths' who threw bricks at the plaque displaying the Hapsburg coat of arms outside the Austrian consulate. A reporter, stirred by the occasion, prophesied that as a result of the war, 'The long-dormant primal instincts of the race are rousing [the people] from the slothful, guarded slumbers of the years.'[3]

Adelaide greeted the news of war more sedately. Members of the civil service organised a meeting in Victoria Square. The Minister for Public Works, accompanied by other dignitaries, presided over the proceedings. The assembly quickly 'swelled to many thousands.' The Governor asked the South Australian people 'to keep a stiff upper lip'. 'The Song of Australia' was sung – the only distinctively Australian song sung at any of these assemblies or public demonstrations – followed by 'Rule Britannia', and the meeting closed with 'the National Anthem' and further cheering.[4]

Representatives of all major segments of Australian society joined together to affirm their support for Britain and the Empire. At an overflow meeting in the Melbourne Town Hall on 6 August, Sir Alexander Peacock, the Liberal Premier of Victoria, addressing his audience as 'my fellow Britishers', declared that 'When the day came that the British Empire would be endangered,

---

[2] *Age* and *Argus*, 6 August 1914.

This was not the last occasion on which patriotic fervour found an outlet in attacks on Chinese property. The Australian Government in January 1915 agreed, following a request from the Chinese Consul-General, to pay £80.00 as 'compensation for broken windows and other damage caused by riot for which soldiers were chiefly responsible'. Cabinet Minutes, undated, but from internal evidence of a meeting held between 7 and 21 January 1915, Fisher Papers, NLA MS 2919 add. ms 21/8/81, box 1. See also letter, Atlee Hunt, Secretary, External Affairs Department to Minister for External Affairs, 7 January 1915, Hunt Papers, NLA MS 52/1496.

Hew Strachan in his masterly study of the onset of war in Europe has stated that 'hatred of the enemy' was not a 'primary element in the sense of fraternity and national bonding which in Europe marked the news of the coming of the war. If this is so then Australians responded rather differently from the European belligerents. For Strachan, see *The First World War* (Cambridge: Cambridge University Press, 2001), I, 'The Call to Arms', 105.

[3] *West Australian*, 6 and 7 August 1914.
[4] *Advertiser*, 6 August 1914.

its children in the far-out dependencies would be prepared with any sacrifices for Empire and peace.' He claimed that 'They were all in the same boat (sustained applause). Never mind what their position might be; never mind whether they were rich or poor: they were all together.'

George Elmslie, the Victorian Labor leader, in endorsing the Premier's remarks, seemed to vindicate this assertion. Elmslie, the head of the most radical branch of the Australian Labor Party, made the most imperialist catchcry of the Boer War years his own. He proclaimed that 'His cry was everyone's cry: "My country, right or wrong."(Loud cheers.) If they faltered or hesitated they would be less than Britishers.'[5] There might have been a few among the more militant spirits in labour ranks who demurred at this but Elmslie spoke for the great majority of the working class.[6] At the same meeting John Gavan Duffy, the son of a Young Ireland nationalist and a long-time supporter of Home Rule, spoke for the Irish Catholic community. He appealed to his fellow Irish Australians to 'forget old injustices and stand shoulder to shoulder, knee to knee, to fight the battle of the Empire ... an Empire whose flag flew over all the world, from east to west, the greatest empire the world had ever seen.'[7]

Church leaders, even though they tended to give more weight to the righteousness of the Empire's cause, were also united in their expressions of support for the Mother Country. The Protestant clergy, especially the Anglicans, were more fervent than their Roman Catholic counterparts. In his sermon in St Andrew's Cathedral in Sydney on the Sunday following Britain's entry into the war, Archbishop J. C. Wright assured the congregation that they should have confidence that God was on their side in a war which was 'a matter of life and death, with our Empire at stake'. At a service of intercession that same afternoon attended by 20,000 people in the Domain, the Dean of Sydney elaborated on these sentiments. In an impassioned address, he urged Australians 'not to waver in their patriotism'. He asserted that the Empire 'stood for all that was highest and best', that Britain had been forced into the war by 'the pride and arrogance' of the German Emperor and that the British Empire had a great destiny which 'no proud power' could defeat. Many other preachers, Anglican, Presbyterian and Methodist, used the occasion to express similar sentiments.[8]

The Irish Catholic hierarchy, joining in these professions of loyalty, set aside old grievances, even though the very mention of them signalled a difference of emphasis from their Protestant brethren. The Archbishop of Sydney, Michael Kelly, in a sermon at St Mary's Cathedral declared that regardless of whether Britain granted Ireland Home Rule or whether their schools were treated fairly Irish Catholics would do their duty. He believed that there would be 'a disposition on the part of everyone to appreciate our action in sinking all differences in order to more effectively safeguard the interests of the Empire.'[9] At a meeting of the Catholic Young Men's

---

[5] *Age*, 7 August 1914.
[6] Ian Turner, *Industrial Labor and Politics: The Labor Movement in Eastern Australia* (Canberra: Australian National University, 1965), pp.69–70; for exceptions, see resolutions passed by a meeting of the Industrial Workers of the World in Sydney and at a meeting of the Australian Miners Association at Broken Hill. *Daily Telegraph*, 3 August 1914 and *Age*, 6 August 1914.
[7] *Age*, 7 August 1914.
[8] *Daily Telegraph*, 10 August 1914.
[9] *Ibid*.

Association the Archbishop of Melbourne, T. J. Carr, took a similar stand, maintaining that 'our religious principles, our loyalty and our interests lead us to forget the past and to join heartily with our fellow citizens in defence of the Mother Country and the best balanced constitution which the world has ever known.' Carr said that Irish Home Rule, which the British Government had approved, would be earned by Irish support for Britain's war. For those who might have had scruples about helping Ireland's oppressor, he pointed out that Britain had tried to find a peaceful solution, had held out until the last moment and had only entered the fray on behalf of 'little Belgium', which was 'apart from Ireland the most Catholic country in Europe'.[10] In taking this position the Irish Catholic community was following the lead of John Redmond and the Irish Parliamentary Party which represented Catholic Ireland in the House of Commons. Redmond had urged his supporters to give all aid to the Empire and the great majority of the Irish Volunteer Force which had been formed to fight for Home Rule enlisted to fight for the Empire.

The coming of the war then seemed to presage an endless Empire Day. *The Deeds that Won the Empire*, that heroic saga so beautifully embellished by the President of Melbourne's Presbyterian Ladies' College, the Rev. W. H. Fitchett, was now to have a new chapter, and Australians were to be permitted to participate and to take their place alongside their fellow-Britons. But the unanimity of the moment hid differences over the extent of the nation's willingness to make sacrifice for the Empire. Some approved of the war only with qualifications and reservations.[11] As, over time, the war put increasing strains upon society, these doubts, misgivings and resentments surfaced and ultimately the British cause was to be almost as much a symbol of division as of unity.

The enthusiastic public response to the European war had an immediate impact in the political arena, especially on the character of the federal election. The war not only wiped the party speeches from the press headlines but also did much to transform the campaign rhetoric. The Labor and Liberal leaders vied with one another in attesting their loyalty to the Mother Country and in claiming responsibility for Australia's defence policy and defence achievements. The politicians could not ignore the popular mood. They were also creatures of the culture that elicited this nationalist response. They shared in what one reporter called 'the quiver of tense, almost unhinged excitement.'[12]

---

[10] *Age*, 10 August 1914.
Archbishop James Duhig of Brisbane declared on 2 August that 'as an Irish-Australian I would say that if the Mother Country found herself in trouble she would find her Catholic and Irish-Australian sons loyal to her cause,' *Brisbane Courier*, 3 August 1914.

[11] See *Australian Worker*, 6 August 1914, 'We must protect our country. We must keep sacred from the mailed fist this splendid heritage. But we hope no wave of jingo madness will sweep over the land, unbalancing the judgment of its leaders, and inciting its population to wild measures ... God help Australia! God help England! Gold help Germany! God help us,' and the Melbourne Catholic *Tribune*, 8 August 1914, cited in Michael McKernan *Australian Churches at War: Attitudes and Activities of the Major Churches 1914–1918* (Sydney and Canberra: Australian War Memorial, 1980), p.35, '... it is not perhaps that we love Britain with her Irish oppression more. But we in Australia would like her enemies less.'

[12] *West Australian*, 7 August 1914.

During the election the candidates followed their leaders and pursued the politics of patriotism. The Liberals gave unqualified support to the British who were 'blood of our blood, bone of our bone'[13] and Labor, likewise, urged solidarity with the Mother Country. J. K. McDougall, Labor candidate for the Victorian seat of Flinders, who was reputed to be a radical, even a pacifist, told a meeting of electors that 'If Great Britain was at war Australia should sink all political differences and stand shoulder to shoulder for the defence of the Empire.'[14] W. F. Finlayson, Labor member for Brisbane, while endorsing the hopes of Andrew Fisher, his fellow Scottish Australian, that the war would enhance the influence of socialism and therefore the hopes for a lasting peace, expressed complete confidence in the British Government's actions in the crisis and endorsed his leader's call for assistance for the Empire.[15] Labor meetings, almost as frequently as Liberal meetings, ended with the singing of 'God Save the King'.

From all sides came appeals for national unity.[16] In all the states the opposition pledged its support to the government and the government promised to avoid contentious measures. In Western Australia the Labor Government expressed this new-found sense of common purpose by inviting the leader of the opposition to attend a special cabinet meeting.[17] In strictly political terms the Labor Party considered that the European conflict had placed them at a disadvantage.[18] The memories of how the Boer War had been used against them were still fresh. The hopes of the Liberals, on the other hand, had been boosted by the prospect of war. They believed that they could drape themselves more convincingly in the robes of imperial loyalty. A former Liberal senator wrote to the Defence Minister, Senator E. D. Millen, on 31 July: 'If I might suggest the European situation affords Liberals in Australia excellent material for a good war-cry during the current campaign.'[19] Yet though both parties may have seen political advantages and disadvantages in the war crisis, there is no reason to doubt the genuineness of the language of loyalty to Britain and the Empire which dominated their campaign oratory.[20]

---

[13] Speech by Honorary Minister W.H. Kelly in Brisbane, 1 August 1914, *Brisbane Courier*, 3 August 1914.

[14] *Age*, 4 August 1914.

[15] *Daily Standard* (Brisbane), 6 August 1914.

[16] See for example *SMH*, 4 August 1914, editorial 'The Worker and His Country'; *ibid.*, 6 August 1914, editorial 'Parliament As it Should be'; *The Mercury*, 4 August 1914, editorial 'The War and the Pending Elections'; *Advertiser*, 5 August 1914, editorial 'Closing the Ranks'; *Daily Telegraph*, 7 August 1914, editorial 'Stop the Elections'.

[17] *West Australian*, 6 August 1914.

[18] Cable, Edward A. Box, Andrew Fisher's Private Secretary, to Fisher, 27 July 1914, 'Sydney Telegraph predicts Ministerial Benefit from European situation if serious think latter worth watching … ', Fisher Papers, NLA MS 2919 add. ms. 21/8/81.

[19] Letter, I.D. Chataway to Millen, 31 July 1914, NAA MP729/1 'Odds and Ends, Personal Minister'.

[20] Whatever best describes the Australian public's response to the coming of the war it was not 'curiosity', that is a detached interest or fascination, which Hervey contends, unconvincingly, was the dominant response of the German people. See Hervey, *The Spirit of 1914: Militarism, Myth and Mobilisation in Germany* (Cambridge: Cambridge University Press, 2000), pp.38–47. Enthusiasm for the cause of their fellow Britons and their Empire would seem to be the most inclusive and accurate description of the Australian public's attitude to the conflict.

When, therefore, on the eve of Britain's entry into the war, the Liberal Premier of Victoria, Sir Alexander Peacock, suggested that there should be a political truce and that the elections should be abandoned,[21] Hughes, not willing to allow the patriotic initiative to rest with the Liberals, made the proposal his own. It spoke to his deep-seated conviction that the war represented a struggle for national survival and that this was a defining moment in the history of the British Empire. And so the following morning he published an appeal for postponing the election in the Sydney morning papers. He maintained that there were two possible ways of accomplishing this objective, either by having the Governor-General revoke the proclamation and then asking the Imperial parliament to legalise this step retrospectively by a special Act or by persuading the parties not to stand candidates against sitting members. In either case parliament could be recalled immediately to deal with the war crisis.[22]

Hughes, his mind made up, was indefatigable in pressing his argument. Having obtained the endorsement of his Sydney parliamentary colleagues and the New South Wales Labor Party executive, he then sought to convince his leader to urge such a course on Cook. Fisher, who was campaigning in the southwest of the state, had no code book and could not decipher Hughes's telegraph message. Hughes consequently sent Senator Arthur Rae post-haste to deliver his request in person.[23] Simultaneously Hughes wrote an imperative, impassioned letter almost demanding Fisher's consent. His overheated imagination exaggerated the immediate threat of the European war. His political judgment was overcome by the intensity of public feeling and his belief that the hour of Armageddon had struck. His personal sense of destiny, that he had been born for this hour, required complete submission to his will.

In his letter, written just after the announcement of Britain's entry into the war, Hughes told Fisher that 'All idea about having an election at a moment when our very existence is at stake must be put aside.' It was 'the only course at this juncture'. The British declaration of war 'finished the campaign'. He made it plain that what he wanted was an extension of the life of the dissolved parliament until the end of the war. The continuation of the parliament 'must be for the purpose only of the war and dealing with the war.' Trying to present his plan as a *fait accompli* he informed Fisher that 'The feeling here is so unanimous. State: Federal Executives P.L.L. Unions Trades Hall Kavanagh. Our Candidates: supporters – that there is no room for doubt as to what ought to be done – nor of the opinion of the people.' In the postscript he concluded, 'I urge you to do this not only for the sake of the Party – although it is suicide to act otherwise – but for the sake of the Country. Cook must not be left in charge at this juncture. It may mean ruin.'[24]

Fisher was not to be bulldozed into accepting one more of Hughes's impulsive schemes. Just as in 1909 he had turned down Hughes's proposal to appease the Imperialists in the Dreadnought crisis, so in 1914 he judged Hughes's electoral truce plan to be impracticable and unprincipled. By accepting the plan Labor would have to give up all hope of securing social or political reform

---

[21] Melbourne *Herald*, 4 August 1914.
[22] *SMH*, 5 August 1914.
[23] Cable, Hughes to Rae, Pastoral Hotel, Wagga Wagga, undated but in the context 4 August 1914, Fisher Papers, NLA MS 2919/1/189.
[24] Letter, Hughes to Fisher, 5 August 1914, Fisher Papers, NLA MS 2919/1/183–88.

during the war years. Furthermore, it was difficult to see how an extension of the life of the 1913 parliament would prevent Cook from being in charge of the war government. Did Hughes believe that by recalling parliament, government would somehow be taken out of Cook's hands, even though he continued to have a majority in the House of Representatives? Did he expect that a coalition war government would be formed and that the times would find the man in himself? Whatever the answer to these questions, Fisher saw that the proposal was seriously flawed. He did not see any need to summon parliament. And so he chastised Hughes for putting forward such an ill-conceived plan and rejected the proposal. Fisher felt confident that the assurance he had given Cook on 2 August, when he had promised to cooperate with the government on all measures needed to prosecute the war, was all that the crisis required.[25] This remained his position throughout the election.

Cook and Irvine also refused to entertain Hughes's proposal. They also denied that there was any good reason for recalling parliament. Moreover, while arguing through a smoke-screen about the details of the scheme, they probably saw that a return to the *status quo* of 1913 and 1914 would do nothing to remove the impediments to government which had led to the double dissolution and that acquiescence in the plan might well rob them of the chance of obtaining good majorities in both Houses.[26]

Hughes did not accept kindly Fisher's rebuke. The man of absolutes was 'absolutely in disagreement' with Fisher's view.[27] He knew better than his leader, and he continued to wage a one-man battle for his electoral truce.[28] But increasingly he used it as a political weapon against the Liberals. Fisher's opposition had been privately expressed; Irvine and Cook had taken a public stand. Hughes had no compunction about accusing the Liberals of putting party before the country, and Fisher allowed himself to be drawn into such tactics. In the 'Labor Manifesto' which was written by Hughes but published by Fisher as leader of the opposition and David Watkins as secretary of the federal Parliamentary Party, 'the responsibility for pressing on with the elections at a time when our very existence is at stake' was laid at the door of the government 'who have deliberately refused every suggestion put forward for a political truce.' Labor's attitude to the war, under the general heading of 'We will defend the Empire', was the theme of the Manifesto, and on this question too the pure Hughesian doctrine prevailed.

> We deplore war. We believe war to be a crime against civilisation and against humanity. But to deplore and to denounce war is not to abolish it. War is one of the greatest realities of life, and it must be faced. Our interests and our very existence are bound up with those of the Empire. In time of war half measures are worse than none. If returned with a majority we shall pursue

---

[25] *SMH*, 3 August 1914.
[26] *Age*, 5 August 1914: *Age*, 7 August 1914; *SMH*, 7 August 1914; *SMH*, 8 August 1914; Secret letter, Munro Ferguson to British Colonial Secretary Sir Lewis Harcourt, 25 August 1914, TNA: PRO CO 418/123/185. Munro Ferguson believed that Hughes's 'solution was not practical' and would not be acceptable to Cook 'who is determined not to have to meet again with the dissolved Senate'.
[27] Superscription on letter, Hughes to Fisher, 5 August 1914, Fisher Papers, NLA MS 2919/3/183. It is from this superscription that we can deduce Fisher's reply to Hughes.
[28] *Age*, 8 August 1914 and 11 August 1914.

with the utmost vigour and determination every course necessary for the defence of the Commonwealth and the Empire in any and every contingency.[29]

Fisher's heart, however, was not in the crusade to create the warfare state. He was not excited by the challenge to national existence. Writing to his wife, five days later, he stated that 'the political situation is dull on account of the war.' The war prevented him from rousing the people to support the Labor program of social reform and national development. The prospect of presiding over a government whose first task was to organise for war held no attraction for him. 'Should the war prevent success [in the election],' he added 'we may not miss much.' But, as a man who would not shrink from his duty, he was 'ready for any responsibility the Country may impose on me.'[30] In the event, Hughes's tactics were successful. Labor had defused the imperial loyalty issue. It was thus able to capitalise on the discontent caused by the drought in the rural areas and by the disruptions to industry, finance and commerce. On 5 September, Labor was elected to office with a clear majority in the House of Representatives and an overwhelming majority in the Senate.[31]

The Australian Government's initial response to the war crisis

On coming to office, Labor inherited the results of the Liberal government's war policy. During the six weeks prior to the election Cook and his ministers, with Fisher's concurrence, had put the country on a formal war footing and made important decisions about aid for the Mother Country.

In the last days of July, following British warnings, the Cook Government had begun the process of putting the country in a state of preparedness. Strategic points and defence installations

---

[29] *SMH*, 24 August 1914.

[30] Letter, Fisher to Margaret Fisher, 29 August 1914, Fisher Papers, NLA MS 2919 add. ms 21/8/81, box 2.

[31] The Governor-General, a 'new chum' of only four months standing, confidently informed the Colonial Secretary that 'the war absorbs public attention and there was no excitement, only some 50% of electors going to the polls.' Secret letter, Munro Ferguson to Harcourt, 9 September 1914, TNA: PRO CO 418/123/122.

Munro Ferguson's estimate of the percentage of voters was wrong. Some 73.53% of the electors had voted for the House of Representatives candidates and some 72.64% for the Senate candidates. The turn-out for the House of Representatives election was the highest ever and that for the Senate just marginally below the highest recorded in the 1913 election. This scarcely bespeaks the lack of interest in the election that Munro Ferguson and, indeed, Hughes had predicted.

Similarly the Governor-General informed the British Government that 'the Irish Catholic vote contributed largely to the defeat of the Government.' Secret letter, Munro Ferguson to Harcourt, 17 September 1914, TNA: PRO CO 418/133/236.

But once again this says more about Munro Ferguson's prejudices – his anti-Catholic bias – than about his political judgment. He does not give reasons for his view. But since he was perturbed by the high proportion of Irish Catholics in the Australian population compared to England and Scotland, and regarded them as a potentially disloyal section of society, he deduced that they had voted for Labor as the less imperial of the two parties. Even if the proposition were accepted it seems unlikely that it would explain Labor's success since the great body of Irish Catholics, as members of the working class, normally voted for the Labor Party on economic and social grounds.

had to be protected against the possibility of surprise attack from Germany's Pacific squadron. Commerce and communications with the outside world had to be controlled in order to prevent potential enemies from using them for hostile purposes. Plans for such an emergency had long been in the making. As part of Britain's overhaul of its defence organisation after the Boer War, the Committee of Imperial Defence by July 1914 had compiled a War Book that prescribed the actions which the major departments of state were to take as precautionary measures in the period of 'strained relations' and when war was declared.[32] The Australian Defence Scheme, which was modelled on the British War Book,[33] became the basis for the Commonwealth ministers' decisions.

On 29 July the British Government reluctantly agreed to set in motion the 'Precautionary Stage' procedures provided for in the War Book, and telegrams were sent to all British Dominions and colonies and to all British forces scattered around the globe.[34] Simultaneously the Governor-General received a message from the Admiralty asking the Minister of Defence to arrange for the ships of the Australian navy to take up their 'preliminary station' in accordance with their war orders.[35]

Munro Ferguson was not prepared for the crisis. He knew nothing of the British War Book or of the Australian Defence Scheme. Moreover, his ministers were dispersed around the country campaigning for the election. Only Senator E. D. Millen, the Minister for Defence, and W. H. Kelly, an Honorary Minister, were in Sydney and within reach on 30 July. When Millen was handed a copy of the British cable he seemed equally at a loss to know what it meant and what to do. The following day he sent for the Acting Chief of the General Staff, Major C. B. B. White,[36] and, after taking legal advice from Irvine, the Attorney-General, he ordered White 'to adopt precautionary measures' including the defence of all ports.[37] He also allowed the Australian fleet to assume its war station. On 3 August the *Commonwealth Gazette* authorised the necessary measures to achieve these ends.

As it was taking these steps, the government was also being called upon to consider what aid it should offer the Mother Country if war should break out. In reply to a British inquiry on 29 July, Millen had replied 'unofficially' that he understood that following a declaration of war, Australia would 'at once' hand over its fleet to the Admiralty.[38] The Governor-General, however, was disappointed by the failure of the government to give more urgent attention to the interna-

---

[32] Stephen Roskill, *Hankey, Man of Secrets*, 3 vols (London: Collins, 1970), 1, '1877–1918', pp.107–08; Julian Corbett, *History of the Great War: Naval Operations* (London: Longmans, Green, 1920), 1, 'To the Battle of the Falklands, December 1914', pp.18–21; Lord Hankey, *The Supreme Command, 1914–1918*, 2 vols (London: Allen and Unwin, 1961), Vol.I, p.154; Minutes of Committee of Imperial Defence, 14 July 1914, TNA: PRO CAB 38/24/35.
[33] See Defence Scheme for Australia, NAA CP290/15/2 24/11/05; NAA B197 1856/4/338; NAA MP826/1/3.
[34] Cabinet letter to the King, 30 July 1914, Asquith Papers, Bodleian Library, MSS. Asquith 1.
[35] NAA MP1049/1 14/02/6.
[36] Diary of C.B.B. White, 31 July 1914 entry, White Papers, NLA MS 5172.
[37] NAA MP792/2, box 8, 1877/92; White Diary, 2 August 1914, 'Issued orders for precautionary stage', White papers, NLA MS 5172.
[38] Cable, Munro Ferguson to Harcourt, 30 July 1914, TNA: PRO ADM 137/7.

tional crisis which was threatening to engulf the Empire, and he suggested to Cook that 'ministers should meet in order that the Imperial Govt. may know what support to expect from Australia.'[39] In a further letter of the same day he added force to his suggestion by mentioning a report that Canada had 'already acted' and by noting that 'such timely demonstrations of homogeneity have their effect on the European situation.'[40]

Interrupting his election campaign, the Prime Minister summoned a cabinet meeting for Monday 3 August in Melbourne.[41] Only five members – Cook, Millen, Irvine, Littleton E. Groom (Minister for Trade and Customs) and Senator J. S. Clemens (an Honorary Minister) – were able to be present. By the time they met, the press had confirmed that both Canada and New Zealand had offered military contingents to the Mother Country.[42] The Australian ministers, not wishing to be outshone in showing their loyalty to the Empire, therefore informed the British Government that, in the event of war, they would place the Australian navy at the disposal of the Admiralty and raise an expeditionary force of 20,000 men. Australia would bear the costs of its contributions to the imperial war effort.[43] In Australia there was virtually no criticism of these decisions. Fisher, after being informed of the government's action, replied to Cook, 'Appreciate your wire, and again assure your government opposition will support you on all measures taken in support of Mother Country and in protecting Australia's interests.'[44]

On 5 August, the day following the declaration of war, the British agreed to send an expeditionary force to France and gratefully accepted the Dominions' offers of military assistance.[45] The Colonial Secretary, in conveying this to the Australian Government, stated that the British authorities would be glad 'if it [the Australian contingent] could be despatched as soon as possible.'[46]

On 10 August, all sixteen vessels and 3800 men of the Australian navy were transferred to the Admiralty for the duration of war. At the 1911 Imperial Conference it had been agreed that Australia would have unfettered control over its naval force and therefore determine in time of war if and when it should be placed under the command of the Royal Navy.[47] The Commonwealth Government saw that it made sense to take this step. Nearly all the naval vessels had been built in Britain. The Commanding Officer as well as most other senior officers had been seconded from the Royal Navy. The relatively small force could only act effectively on the high seas in

---

[39] Letter, Munro Ferguson to Cook, 31 July 1914, NAA CP 78/23 14/89/1–2.
[40] Letter, Munro Ferguson to Cook, 31 July 1914, Novar Papers, NLA MS 696/483.
[41] NAA CP78/23 14/89/3.
[42] *Age*, 1 and 3 August 1914.
[43] Cable, Munro Ferguson to Harcourt, 3 August 1914, C of A, *Parliamentary Papers*, 1914–17 session, V, No.10, 'Naval and Military Assistance afforded to H.M.'s Government by H.M.'s Overseas Dominions – Correspondence Regarding the'.
[44] *Daily Telegraph*, 6 August 1914.
[45] Hankey, *Supreme Command*, Vol.I, p.172.
[46] Cable, Harcourt to Munro Ferguson, 6 August 1914, C of A, *Parliamentary Papers*, 1914-17 session, V, No.10.
[47] *Search for Security*, p.221.

conjunction with the British fleet. In a European war it was logical that the Admiralty should take charge.

The Australian Government, however, retained control over its naval bureaucracy. It insisted that the Admiralty should only communicate with the Naval Board through the established channels, the Governor-General and the Defence Minister. The Naval Board, divested of its navy, still had responsibility for pursuing the plans for naval expansion under the Henderson Scheme, for care of naval buildings and bases, for transport services, for training the naval brigade under the compulsory service provisions of the *Defence Act* and for surveillance of commerce and wireless telegraphy. In addition its intelligence officers gave considerable attention to the strategic implications of the war for Australia's future security, especially against Japan.

The offer of military assistance posed more complicated questions. In the first place an expeditionary force of 20,000 men was a very substantial commitment. It exceeded the total number of troops that Australia had despatched to the Boer War over a period of three years. Unlike Australia's naval personnel, its military forces could not be compelled to serve overseas. Under the *Defence Act* of 1903, while all adult males could be conscripted for the defence of the Commonwealth, no soldiers, whether professional or otherwise, could be sent outside Australia without their consent. Thus the expeditionary force had to be made up of volunteers.

Related to this was yet a further difficulty. The Australian Government had not during peacetime approved any plan for despatching a military force to Europe. In 1912 the Australian and New Zealand Defence Ministers had agreed that their respective chiefs of the General Staff might draw up plans for an expeditionary force of 18,000 men (12,000 Australian and 6000 New Zealand). In 1913 the Australian Acting Chief of the General Staff, Major C. B. B. White, presented such a plan to Senator Millen, the Defence Minister, but there is no record of the Australian Government ever approving the plan.[48] Thus in August 1914 Australia had to start from the beginning to create a military force composed entirely of volunteers, which would be quite separate from the existing home defence establishment.

The Defence Minister requested Brigadier-General W. T. Bridges, the Inspector-General of the Australian Army, to draw up plans for the expeditionary force, and on 15 August he appointed Bridges to the command of the overseas contingent, with White as his Chief of Staff. The command of the expeditionary force was quite independent of the home force. The control of the latter remained with the Military Board. Colonel J. G. Legge, who had returned from his secondment to the Imperial General Staff in Britain on 8 August, resumed his position as Chief of the General Staff with responsibility for supervising the military defence of Australia and recruiting troops for an expedition to the German Pacific islands.

The Military Board had, in accordance with the war requirements of the Australian Defence Scheme, urged the Defence Minister to appoint a General Officer Commanding for all Commonwealth military forces and to hand over the administrative functions of the Military Board to the Inspector-General. But Millen did not agree. The command structure in the Defence Scheme had been designed to meet the possibility of an invasion of Australia. The offer of a

---

[48] Guy Verney, 'The Army High Command and Australian Defence Policy, 1901–1918', PhD thesis (University of Sydney, 1985), pp.160–62, 167–68.

20,000 strong contingent to Britain cut across the smooth lines of this arrangement. There were also personnel obstacles. As Millen minuted, 'In view of the appointment of General Bridges to organise and command the Expeditionary Forces, it would not appear necessary to consider the appointment of General Officer Commanding at this juncture. Bridges fully occupied organising Expeditionary Force and cannot be expected to handle other matters. If another officer appointed – he would be junior to Bridges but would hold authority over Bridges in relation to expeditionary forces.'[49]

Bridges and White set about their task with a will. For the two professional officers here at last was an opportunity to realise the vision of their patron and mentor, Lieutenant-General E. T. H. Hutton, the first General Officer Commanding Australian Military Forces, who had attempted to establish, as part of the Commonwealth organisation, a mobile force of 20,000 men which would be 'at the disposal of the Imperial Government for general service in the case of war between Great Britain and one or more European powers.' These disciples of Hutton saw Australian defence as an integral and subsidiary part of imperial defence. He was to their mind 'the founder of the military spirit of Australia and its patron saint.'[50] Indeed, Bridges had recommended that Hutton be given command of the expeditionary force, but the Commonwealth ministers still remembered the difficulties they had had with Hutton when he was commander of the Australian army and were determined that an Australian officer should lead Australian soldiers.

Bridges, however, was able to give symbolic expression to the Hutton ideal in the naming of the Australian contingent. In contrast to the other Dominions who gave their contributions the simple designations of the 'Canadian Expeditionary Force' and the 'New Zealand Expeditionary Force', Bridges named his contingent the 'Australian Imperial Force' (AIF), a slight variation on the name which the War Office had proposed in 1902 for Hutton's mobile reserve, namely the 'Imperial Australian Force'.[51] Bridges and White did nevertheless support the Commonwealth Government's view that the Australian Imperial Force should have its own identity and not be scattered throughout the British Army.[52] One of the advantages of offering 20,000 troops was that this number allowed the Australians to be organised as a self-sufficient division, even if still under the command of the British Army.

Bridges had no trouble in raising the prescribed force. The imperial fervour which had greeted the outbreak of war marched into the recruiting offices. Notwithstanding the very rigorous physical standards that were required, the army had by 24 August, that is within a fortnight of the call for volunteers, enlisted the full complement. Despite the Governor-General's doubts as to whether the troops would be able to sail within four to six weeks as the government

---

[49] Millen, undated minute on letter, Col. W.C.N. Sellheim, Adjutant General to S.A. Pethebridge, Secretary of the Defence Department, 7 August 1914, NAA MP729/5 W7/1/2.

[50] Letter, White to Hutton, 4 March 1913, Hutton Papers, BL Add 50089, Vol.XII, p.1114.

[51] *Search for Security*, pp.60–63; letter, White to Hutton, 4 July 1915, Hutton Papers, BL, Add. 50089, Vol.XI, p.123; see also C.E.W. Bean, 'The Story of Anzac: The First Phase', *Official History of Australia in the War, 1914–1918*, 12 vols (Sydney: Angus and Robertson, 1921), Vol.I, p.36 and Bean's *Two Men I Knew. William Bridges and Brudenell White, Founders of the AIF* (Sydney: Angus and Robertson, 1957), p.34.

[52] Ernest Scott, *Australia During the War* (Sydney: Angus & Robertson, 1936), p.204

had promised,[53] Bridges and his officers proved adequate to the task. By 21 September they were ready to embark. Since, however, the Admiralty had directed British naval forces to hunt down the German Pacific squadron, to seize the German wireless stations and to occupy its island bases, no escort was available to convoy the AIF across the Indian Ocean until the beginning of November.

In the meantime Cook was so impressed by the response to recruitment that, following the appeal launched in Britain for another 100,000 volunteers, he offered to send an additional infantry brigade and light-horse brigade – approximately 8300 men in all – whom he hoped would be able to leave for Europe by the end of November.[54] The command of this second contingent was entrusted to Colonel John Monash, a militia officer, who was in 1918 to succeed to the command of the Australian forces in France and to create for himself a reputation as one of the most able senior officers in the Allied armies.[55]

The Labor Government and recruitment for the AIF

After Labor took office on 17 September 1914, the Commonwealth Government's attitude to the war became more complex. While the Liberals regarded the war as a self-sufficient program, Fisher and Labor were determined not to allow support for the Empire to block their plans for social reform, national development and local defence. Senator David Watson, President of the Miners' Association in New South Wales, who in 1916 became an anti-conscriptionist, accepted that 'We have a duty which we owe to our race … Our duty to the British Empire must never be questioned – must never be forsaken in any degree' but, in commending Labor's reforms, he asserted that 'there is no higher function of a government than to make provision for the well-being of the people.'[56] Thus Fisher and his government while supporting the raising of the initial expeditionary force did not at first actively encourage further recruitment.

Labor, under Fisher's leadership, was insistent that, in fighting for the Empire and for Australia as part of the Empire, Australians should feel that they were fighting for a society which was worthy of the sacrifice of their blood and treasure. In the debate over the Address-in-Reply, Fisher reaffirmed his campaign promise: 'We shall pledge our last man and our last shilling to see this war brought to a successful issue', but then went on to defend his program, saying that 'We are here as representatives of the people to devise means and measures that will help to develop the country. If we do not exercise our power and authority when we are practically at peace when shall we do so?'[57] Labor's fortunes seemed to be riding the crest of a wave. Its electoral victory was the culmination of incremental gains over a long period. Though this was its second federal

---

[53] Secret letter, Munro Ferguson to Harcourt, 8 August 1914, TNA: PRO CO 418/23/149; cable, Munro Ferguson to Harcourt, 8 August 1914, *Parliamentary Papers*, 1914–17 session; Vol.V, No.10.

[54] Cable, Munro Ferguson to Harcourt, 30 August 1914, *ibid.*; *Argus*, 31 August 1914.

[55] For an evaluation of Monash's qualities as a military commander, see P.A. Pedersen, *Monash as Military Commander* (Melbourne: Melbourne University Press, 1985); also Geoffrey Serle, *John Monash: a biography* (Melbourne: Melbourne University Press, 1982).

[56] *CPD*, 1914–17 session, LXXV, 18, 8 October 1914.

[57] *Ibid.*, LXXV, 174, 14 October 1914.

success, it was much more decisive than that of 1910. Fisher and the party expected great things from their political victory.[58]

The Governor-General at the opening of parliament announced Labor's ambitious agenda. After expressing satisfaction with the Dominion's response to 'the cause of civilisation and justice and those high ideals for which the Empire stands', and asseverating that additional troops would be sent to Europe 'until peace terms satisfactory to the Allies' were secured, he outlined a list of reforms which rivalled those of 1910. The government intended to undertake a public works program to deal with unemployment; to raise tariffs to protect domestic industries; to assist the elderly by introducing old age and invalid pensions; to ask the people to give the Commonwealth greater power over corporations, monopolies, industrial relations and internal trade; and to make Australia more self-sufficient by creating a Commonwealth-owned steamer line. Finally it proposed to stimulate the settlement of the Northern Territory and establish a uniform gauge for the state railways both of which were 'essential to effective defence and development.'[59]

Fisher was resolved to let neither the war nor the Governor-General interfere with the carrying out of Labor's policies. Having suffered from the meddling of Lord Dudley in his earlier administrations, he wanted to ensure that Munro Ferguson should not be able to subvert government policy either by having direct access to ministers or challenging cabinet decisions in the Executive Council. Hence, as Munro Ferguson reported to London:

> On his [Fisher's] assumption of office he laid stress on the expediency of all communications between the Governor-General and his government passing through the Prime Minister ... He also suggested that it was not the practice to discuss business at an executive council. I agreed to this as a general rule but I have insisted on receiving the minutes of executives in sufficient time to give them due consideration.

Fisher's open and generous nature, however, made it difficult for him to hold rigorously to this procedure. He, as Munro Ferguson happily noted, 'speedily relaxed the ruling [on dealings with Ministers]' and, as a result, the Governor-General 'was quickly in the close relations with the new minister of defence to which I was accustomed.' Indeed he claimed that 'Mr Fisher in fact facilitated relations between myself and all the Ministers.'[60] Despite Fisher's best efforts, events conspired against him, the war intruded more and more on the business of government, and the Governor-General abused the Prime Minister's trust and used his position to influence recruitment policy.

The first major pieces of legislation brought down by the government were the *Crimes Act*, the *Trading with the Enemy Act* and the *War Precautions Act*.[61] Attorney-General Hughes justified

---

[58] Patrick Weller (ed.), *Caucus Minutes, 1901–1949: Minutes of the Meetings of the Federal Parliamentary Labor Party*, 3 vols, (Carlton, Vic: Melbourne University Press, 1975), Vol.I, pp.378–79.
[59] *CPD*, 1914–17 session, LXXV, 7–9, 8 October 1914.
[60] Secret letter, Munro Ferguson to Colonial Secretary, Bonar Law, 28 December 1915, TNA: PRO CO 481/134/172; see also personal letter, Munro Ferguson to Colonial Secretary, Walter H. Long, 13 September 1918, Long Papers, WRO 947/625/123, 'Mr Fisher informed me, indeed, that it was the Labour custom that a Governor-General should see no minister but the P.M.'
[61] Commonwealth of Australia, Act No.12 of 1914; Commonwealth of Australia, Act No.9 of 1914; Commonwealth of Australia, Act No.10 of 1914.

all of them on grounds of national security and pushed them through parliament with the utmost despatch.

Of the three, the most important was the *War Precautions Act*. It was based on the British *Defence of the Realm Act* and gave the executive, in effect, power to govern by decree under regulations 'for securing the public safety and the defence of the Commonwealth'. The Australian statute, however, went beyond the British model and included a provision giving the government unlimited authority over aliens, whether citizens of enemy countries or not, and over 'naturalised persons', again regardless of country of birth. Under clause 5 such people, at the discretion of the government, could be deported, restricted in their movements and business or interned.[62]

Hughes made no apologies for insisting that the government should be given these powers without any delay. In answer to complaints from Cook and others that the *War Precautions Act* would enable the government 'to proclaim something like martial law', Hughes replied that it gave nothing which was not 'inherent in all Governments'. The government had to be trusted. Hughes promised that 'the aim of the Government will be to use it as little as possible, and to as limited an extent as possible', and he added that 'Nothing will be done without the approval of the Government as a whole.'

In subsequent years Hughes flagrantly violated these undertakings. More than 100 regulations were passed under this Act by 1918, including provisions for confiscation of private property; for control of commodity prices; for prohibition of telephone conversations not in the English language; for 'trespassing or loitering in the vicinity of tunnels, viaducts or culverts'; for punishment of persons 'who display hostility to the British Empire', 'who wear or display any banner, flag, badge, or symbol of an enemy country, or of a disaffected body or association', 'who interfere with shearing' or 'attempt to cause mutiny, sedition or disaffection among the forces of the civil population'; for detention of naturalised persons or natural-born British subjects one of whose parents was a subject of an enemy state in military custody; for placing the burden of proof of innocence on the accused; for establishment of a Commonwealth Police Force; for 'the holding of any race meeting for horses, or any competition or contest in boxing, football or other athletic games or sport'; for deregistration of 'industrial organisations which cease work'.[63] In drawing up and issuing these regulations, Hughes often acted alone or through his solicitor-general, R. R. Garran.[64]

Most disquiet was expressed over clause 5, especially that part allowing the government to treat naturalised citizens as aliens. Former Liberal External Affairs Minister McMahon Glynn, representing the seat of Angas, which covered the German-settled areas of the Barossa Valley, was disturbed by this provision, but he allowed that 'if the same power applies in Great Britain to naturalised persons, I shall say no more.' Hughes had himself inserted these powers into the Bill but he did nothing to disabuse Glynn of the notion that he was simply following British practice. Two Victorian Labor backbenchers, Dr William R. Maloney and Frank Brennan, raised questions about excesses by the military censors and the unreasonable harassment of naturalised Germans

---

[62] Commonwealth of Australia, Act No.10 of 1914; United Kingdom, 4 and 5 Geo.V, C.29 and 63.
[63] Commonwealth of Australia, *Official Year Book*, No.11, 1918 Melbourne 1918, pp.1033–43.
[64] Robert Randolph Garran, *Prosper the Commonwealth* (Sydney: Angus and Robertson 1958), pp.221–223.

or German aliens. Maloney was proud of his membership in the Melbourne Turnverein. He had received 'Much of the foundations of my Democracy' from such men many of whom had been forced to flee Germany after the failure of the 1848 Revolution. 'Some of these men,' he claimed, were 'our best citizens.' Brennan, for his part, was dismayed that the government would be able to treat naturalised citizens differently from native-born British subjects.

Hughes dismissed these criticisms out of hand pleading the doctrine of race survival. In replying to Brennan he turned human understanding into an argument for hate and suspicion. Hughes contended that if Australians of British origin had taken German citizenship, they would not lose their love for their native land. 'If I were in Germany for 100 years … I should still be British or Australian, and I would not think it wrong to do what I could for Great Britain or Australia. I put a German in Australia on exactly the same footing. His sympathy is for Germany in this struggle. Is it not a question of life and death with him as with us?' It had to be remembered that 'Naturalisation is nothing but a form if the substance does not accompany it – that is, if there is no change in the heart and mind.'[65] For Hughes such a change was impossible. The loyalty of citizens was determined by their 'racial' biology.

Fisher accepted the inevitability of the war measures. He accepted Hughes's assurances, and lent his prestige to the passage of the Bills. Yet his heart and mind were clearly elsewhere, and this was particularly evident in his attitude towards recruitment. Despite his repeated promises about offering 'our last man and our last shilling', he showed little enthusiasm for boosting the number of recruits.[66] The Prime Minister at first rejected special schemes to promote recruiting. He disapproved, in particular, of the New South Wales' practice of paying the police 10/- for each man they enlisted.[67] Fisher's lack of enthusiasm was in part temperamental, in part political, in part practical, and in part strategic. He disliked the jingoistic spirit often associated with recruiting meetings. He feared that too much public pressure would be construed as an attack on the voluntary principle and would make military support for the Mother Country a matter of controversy. He recognised that it was only possible to send properly trained and armed recruits, and while training facilities and arms remained in short supply it was foolish to urge more men to come forward. Moreover, appropriating additional money for the expeditionary force inevitably weakened his government's ability to carry out its domestic program, and since the Australian private was paid six shillings a day while overseas, compared to one shilling for the British 'Tommy', this was a weighty consideration. Finally, and this was not the least of his concerns, he was worried that Australia might be left defenceless to face an ambitious, aggressive Japan.

When, by November, it became clear that the Entente powers were not going to secure an early victory and that, indeed, they had emerged from the first round of the contest with loss of territory, the Liberal opposition and the press began to clamour for a more active recruiting program. Echoing Lord Kitchener's call to raise a new army in Britain, Cook demanded 'a fillip to

---

[65] *CPD*, 1914–17 session, LXXV, 369–85, 28 October 1914.
[66] *CPD*, 1914–17 session, LXXV, 906, 20 November 1914.
[67] L.L. Robson, *The First AIF: A Study of its Recruitment, 1914–1918* (Melbourne: Melbourne University Press, 1970), pp.37–38.

recruiting in Australia'.⁶⁸ On 30 November he declared that the 30,000 troops so far offered to the Mother Country were 'not half-enough' and urged the Australian Government to aim at putting '100,000 men into the fighting lines.' ⁶⁹

Fisher was not moved by these appeals. Bringing down his first budget on 3 December he reaffirmed that the Commonwealth was 'prepared to use its whole resources in men and money in order to give the greatest possible aid to the Mother Country in her hour of need.' But the budget details did little to substantiate such an assertion. Fisher in his estimates allowed for funding only 42,000 troops overseas by the end of June 1915. In addition to the 22,373 that had already been sent and the 13,000 who were due to embark by the end of December, he claimed that the Commonwealth was planning to despatch 3000 every two months.⁷⁰

The budget sought a sharp increase in total expenditure from £15,458,771 in 1913–14 to £37,583,715 for 1914–15. The defence estimates amounted to £18,254,374, and of that figure £11,742,050 was for war purposes; £1,775,800 for the naval and military forces employed in home defence and the capture of the German Pacific islands; £7,800,000 for the AIF; and £2,000,000 for the RAN in service with the Admiralty. In the exceptional war circumstances Fisher proposed running a budget deficit of £13,088,314 which would be covered by a British war loan of £18,000,000.

Fisher was, however, reluctant to abandon his domestic program. By raising the war loan he was able not only to finance public works which would alleviate unemployment but more importantly to proceed with his plans for national development and national security. Determined to carry through Australia's pre-war defence plans which he had helped to initiate, he delayed the introduction of pensions for widows and orphans. Compulsory military training for home defence was to continue and an additional £750,000 was allocated for that purpose. The government considered that there was 'a pressing need … for strategic railways and a uniform gauge linking up the various States of the Commonwealth'. Unless this was completed quickly an enemy might achieve 'an unhindered occupation' of a distant part of the country. In accordance with the 1912 Henderson Scheme, £250,000 was set aside for building a new light cruiser and, while waiting for the report of Sir Maurice Fitzmaurice on plans for the naval bases at Fremantle and Westernport, the Naval Board was authorised to push on with other works. Impressed by the value of military aviation on the Western Front, the number of pilot officers in training at Point

---

⁶⁸ *CPD*, 1914–17 session, LXXV, 467, 11 November 1914.

⁶⁹ *SMH*, 1 December 1914; Cook repeated this cry at the end of December when he called for 'nothing less than 100,000' men independent of regular reinforcements, *SMH*, 30 December 1914.

⁷⁰ Fisher's statement was confusing and misleading. On 16 December the Minister for Defence, Senator George Pearce, explained that the 42,000 mentioned in the budget was the number of troops which had enlisted up until the end of the calendar year and that the government had decided to send 3000 reinforcements each month for the subsequent six months. This suggested that in the middle of December the government had agreed to increase the AIF to 60,000 by the end of June 1915. *CPD*, 1914–17 session, LXXVI, 1970, 16 December 1914. It seems probable that Fisher's figure of 42,000 was made up of all servicemen overseas, including the 22,373 sent to Europe and the 1764 in the German Pacific islands, as well as the 16,800 or so who had enlisted and were in training in camps in Australia.

Cook was tripled from 12 to 36. The government also promised to encourage the local construction of aircraft.[71]

All these latter budget provisions were aimed at strengthening the defence of Australian territory. They were not intended to deal with a German raid or insurrection but to meet and repel a possible Japanese invasion. After the Battle of the Falkland Islands and the defeat of the German Pacific squadron, the threat of raids on ports receded; and after the failure of a 1914 Christmas Eve 'German uprising' to materialise, the fear of a German rebellion disappeared.[72] Nevertheless as the alarm bells about Germany in the Pacific were being stilled, the tocsin began to ring for Japan. Australia's apprehensions were strengthened by Japan's seizure of the German North Pacific islands in October and November 1914, by its demands on China in early 1915 and by its attempts to use the British Empire's weakness to exact immigration and commercial concessions. The rising sun of Japan cast a long shadow over the Australian political landscape.

It was nevertheless very difficult to hold the line against demands that more troops be offered to the imperial authorities. By mid-December Fisher felt obliged to make some placatory gestures and he agreed to a new target of 60,000 men. In response to Cook's criticism that this was not enough and that Australia should contribute 100,000 men to the cause, Fisher cannily declared that there was no 'limitation to the number of men that will be sent forward,' without making any further promises of reinforcements and he added that, though 60,000 was the maximum sought by the British, the Australian Government had never limited themselves to this number.[73]

---

[71] *CPD*, 1914–17 session, LXXV, 1338–48, 3 December 1914.

In his second term in office Fisher, as part of the 'Australian Crisis' defence build-up, had supported proposals for building 'strategic railways' so that troop could be moved more readily to any part of the continent that might face invasion. See E.J.G. Prince, 'Towards National Railway Planning by the Commonwealth Government: Defence Considerations and the Constitutional Referenda of 1911 and 1913', *Australian Journal of Politics and History*, XXII (April 1976), pp.62–73. After the outbreak of the war the Commonwealth Government, on the advice of Legge, the Chief of the General Staff, sought the States' cooperation to build strategic railways connecting Port Augusta in South Australia to Perth and connecting Port August to Darwin. Senator Pearce, the Minister for Defence, addressing the War Railway Council in November 1914 said that 'in view of the world-wide struggle that is going on and in view of the possibilities that may arise out of it in which we may be involved this question [strategic railways] must be faced ... to give us a ... more effective means of transporting troops to any part of the Commonwealth.' (Proceedings of the War Railway Council ... 18 and 19 November 1914', NAA MP493/3 A).

On 16 February 1915 Pearce announced plans to build military aircraft in Australia, *SMH,* 17 February 1915.

[72] Memorandum, T.H. Kelly, Victoria Barracks, Sydney, to Colonel J.G. Legge, Chief of the General Staff, 26 December 1914, NAA MP729/2 202/1/64.

The memorandum tells a remarkable story of how on the night of Christmas Eve in Sydney the authorities had gone to elaborate lengths to prepare for a German uprising. See Neville Meaney, 'Australia's Secret Service in World War I: Security, Loyalty and Abuse of Power', *Quadrant*, XXIII 9 (July 1979), 19–23.

[73] *CPD*, 1914–17 session, LXXVI, 2040 and 2046, 16 December 1914; see also Pearce on the same day, 'It has already been announced that every man who offers for service, and who is medically fit, will be accepted for training', *ibid.,* 1970.

The greatest challenge to Fisher's policy came not from the public attacks mounted by his political opponents but from the secret machinations of the Governor-General and the Attorney-General. Munro Ferguson, writing to Fisher about recruitment, seemed to accept the government's formal view that 'the numbers who can go are limited 1. by Transport, 2. Cost, & 3. Equipment'. In answering those who sought a more positive policy he explained that cost could not be 'reduced without reversing the economic policy which at present is hardly within the range of practical politics … These being the facts it is hard to see how, with any regard to Finance, it is possible to put Australians into the firing line in numerical proportion with English.'[74] Similarly he used his influence to try to prevent recruitment becoming the subject of party controversy. Following a fresh campaign against the government's attitude to recruitment at the end of the year, he urged both the Liberal and Labor leaders to exercise 'the utmost self-restraint' in discussing the matter and he succeeded in damping down the agitation.[75] Given his subsequent conduct, it might be wondered whether Munro Ferguson's seeming approval of Fisher's own arguments was meant to win his confidence and thereby make him more manageable, and whether he did not use his influence to take recruitment out of the public arena so that government policy could be more easily manipulated behind the scenes.

Throughout the war Munro Ferguson took a keen interest in recruitment for the AIF; it was, as a matter of prime concern for the British Crown and British Empire, above party politics, and so a fit subject for the Governor-General to take under his care. At the commencement of hostilities Munro Ferguson had told the Colonial Secretary that '20,000 men represent but a fraction of what the Commonwealth could contribute to the Imperial forces.'[76] In reporting the controversy over recruitment he gave Harcourt up-to-date figures on Australian manpower resources and prompted him to ask for further contingents. Munro Ferguson knew that Fisher had defended his stand on recruitment by pointing out that the British Government had not indicated a need for further assistance. Munro Ferguson thus told Harcourt that Legge, the Chief of the General Staff, 'found difficulty in advising the cabinet, not knowing whether the situation had arisen when defeat or victory depended on hurrying every available man into the field.'

Without his ministers' knowledge Munro Ferguson cabled London that 'in case of dire necessity Australia could send 30,000 more in addition to 55,000 promised by June.' And he repeated this statement in a letter to the Colonial Secretary, adding that 'To supply rifles would be

---

[74] Munro Ferguson to Fisher, 19 November 1914, Novar Papers, NLA MS 696/3847–48.
[75] Letter, Munro Ferguson to Sir William Irvine, 6 January 1915, Novar Papers, NLA MS 696/6601–02, '… to press for the instant raising of such a force [100,000 men] regardless of means available and from political platforms is not a help to the Empire. I'd hope the Government and Opposition will alike exercise the utmost self-restraint and self control.'; despatch, Munro Ferguson to Harcourt, 11 January 1915, Novar Papers, NLA MS 696/647, '… I wrote to Mr Hughes, Acting Prime Minister, urging self-restraint, and to Sir W. Irvine pointing out that this controversy … was injurious to the public interest. Both returned satisfactory replies and the subject has been dropped.'
[76] Secret letter, Munro Ferguson to Harcourt, 8 August 1914, TNA: PRO CO 418/123/152. Munro Ferguson, writing to Lord Roberts, said that 'we could provide great numbers of additional troops if the difficulty of finance in the face of drought could be overcome.' Letter, Munro Ferguson to Lord Roberts, 14 October 1914, Novar Papers, NLA MS 696/3692.

the chief difficulty.' Moreover he mentioned that he was much encouraged by the attitude of Hughes who had expressed doubts on whether 'we are sending men enough'. Hughes's words strengthened Munro Ferguson's belief 'in the opinion that the W.[War] O.[Office] could get by [European] mid-summer troops in addition to 55,000 contracted.' Then he advised Harcourt how he might persuade the Commonwealth to do Britain's bidding: 'The element of competition with Canada should be reckoned with as Australia will not like to fall far behind in the numbers sent to the front.'[77] While Fisher, the man of 'unchangeable opinions', was visiting New Zealand in late December and early January, Munro Ferguson cooperated with Hughes, the Acting Prime Minister, in promoting a more positive recruitment policy. By 11 January he was able to inform the Colonial Secretary that 'we shall send a good number more troops in addition to those already promised.'[78]

As with other war measures, recruitment was a matter neither for Caucus[79] nor for Cabinet.[80] Responsibility rested exclusively with the Prime Minister and the Defence Minister. With Hughes acting as Prime Minister, the government's policy took a different course. By 16 January Hughes and Pearce had concluded that Australia should offer a further 10,000 troops to the Mother Country and Hughes sent a cable to Fisher seeking his agreement.

> Pearce now in Sydney has sent me following message (beginning) I recommend we inform Sec. of State that we can supply additional troops as follows one Infantry brigade and three light horse brigades making ten thousand as alternative larger proportion infantry if required. Conditionally on War Office undertaking provide rifles message should make this condition absolutely clear. (ends) I want your opinion. My own is and always has been in favour sending every man we could rake up. Until Pearce's Sydney visit he did not favour going beyond what was agreed upon. Point is that this offer is absolutely contingent British authorities supplying rifles for this force. This I am of the opinion they cannot do. But unless you veto it, I will *send* message.[81]

This message was cleverly designed, almost too cleverly designed, to win Fisher's consent. Firstly, Hughes, while acknowledging that he had always supported sending every available man to the front, nevertheless attributed the initiative to Pearce, who had shared Fisher's views on recruitment. Secondly, Hughes suggested that Britain would not be able to meet the condition

---

[77] Secret letter, Munro Ferguson to Harcourt, 15 December 1914, TNA: PRO CO 418/123/486 and secret and personal telegram, Munro Ferguson to Harcourt, 28 December 1914, Harcourt Papers, Bodleian Library, MSS. Harcourt 479.

[78] Letter, Munro Ferguson to Harcourt, 11 January 1915, Novar Papers, NLA MS 696/647.

[79] There is no record of any Caucus discussion of recruitment in 1914 and 1915, Weller (ed.), *Caucus Minutes, 1901–1949*, Vol.I, pp.374–428.

[80] From the rough minutes of cabinet meetings held in the Fisher Papers it would appear that recruitment policy was discussed by cabinet on only one occasion, namely at the meeting of 7 January 1915. The minutes in Hughes's handwriting cryptically state that Pearce spoke on 'Expeditionary Force: Numbers Rifles etc. arising out of Cook & Millen's press agitation for more men. Decided that further discussion along these lines is fraught with great danger to C'Wealth & Empire, & that whatever steps are necessary to prevent its continuance be taken. Matters left to minister & Acting Prime Minister.' Fisher Papers, NLA MS 2919 add. ms 2/8/81, box 12.

[81] Cable, Hughes to Fisher, 16 January 1915, Fisher Papers, NLA MS 2919, add. ms 21/8/81, box 13.

attached to the offer and he implied therefore that the Fisher Government would be able to gain the political rewards of having made the offer without having to pay the price. Thirdly, Hughes made it appear that he was consulting Fisher and yet he stipulated that unless Fisher specifically vetoed it, he would send the cable to London. Since Fisher had rejected his wild initiatives on a number of previous occasions, perhaps Hughes was in this instance showing more guile. It would be interesting to know what had had happened in Sydney to bring about Pearce's change of mind.

The Governor-General had already prepared the ground for the request. On 6 January he had written Fisher setting out, rather obliquely, his own position.

> I incline to the view I have heard expressed that if the Army Council believes that Victory depends on putting every available man into the field at once, we could send 20,000 additional troops [for Fisher he reduced his expectation by 10,000], for in that case every Rifle in Australia should be at the front. We shall be told if the Army Council thinks that conditions have arisen which make such an immediate reinforcement imperative. As matters stand, I believe we are doing the best we can until we can secure more Rifles.[82]

On 18 January, a week after he had assured Harcourt that more troops would be sent, he made a more direct appeal but, even so, he approached Fisher circumspectly. He recounted a discussion with Hughes about 'adding to Australia's quota of men'. Since the British Government had not replied to his inquiry about the urgency of reinforcements, he claimed he could give 'no decided opinion'. However, the Army Council had agreed to provide rifles for the monthly 3000 strong reinforcements and this opened up new possibilities. He disingenuously stated that 'I gather that some talk is going on as to the immediate provision of a further force of 10,000 men.' His own judgment had been 'against recruiting great numbers of men for whom we had no equipment,' but with 'that difficulty overcome then the more we send the better, for it will need the whole strength of the Empire to secure a satisfactory and lasting Peace.'[83]

Fisher, being in New Zealand, was at a great disadvantage and succumbed to the joint pressure of Hughes and Munro Ferguson. Thus he replied that Hughes should make an unconditional offer of 10,000 troops and on 27 January the British Government formally accepted the offer.[84]

But even as they increased their contribution to the imperial cause, the responsible ministers and their advisers were still intent on completing Australia's own defences. They were loath to let the European war interfere with their plans to protect the homeland. On 5 January 1915, the Chief of the General Staff recommended to Pearce that the full structure for the local military forces should be brought into being on 30 June 1915 – one year ahead of the original timetable. Legge had been one of the few senior officers to sympathise with the Deakin and Fisher Governments' desire to introduce compulsory military training and he had been the most important officer associated with drawing up plans to give effect to the principle. He shared the

---

[82] Letter, Munro Ferguson to Fisher, 6 January 1915, Novar Papers, NLA MS 696/3855.
[83] Letter, Munro Ferguson to Fisher, 18 January 1915, Novar Papers, NLA MS 696/3861–2.
[84] Draft cable, Fisher to Hughes, 19 January 1915, Fisher papers, NLA MS 2919 add. ms 21/8/81, box 13; cable, Hughes to Fisher, 29 January 1915, containing copy of cable from Colonial Secretary to Governor-General, 27 January 1915, Fisher Papers, NLA MS 2919 add. ms 21/8/81, box 13.

political leaders' fear of Japan. While in London in 1913–14, as head of the Australian section of the Imperial General Staff, he had employed his time in working out how the Japanese might invade Australia and he had concluded, along the lines of 'the Australian Crisis', that 'there is not much doubt that they could easily send 3 divisions to Australia in less than 1 month from the day on which they commenced to mobilise. At the present time that would be more than enough for the job, and the Japs could, if they chose, do it without giving us even indirect information of more than 7 to 14 days.'[85] And Legge carried these concerns into the war years. As Munro Ferguson, in a discussion of Australia's attitude to Japan in the North Pacific islands, put it, 'Col. Legge, like some others, seems anxious that at the close of the war Australia should still be in a strong position from the point of view of defence so that should differences arise between the Allies, we may not be a totally negligible country.'[86]

Legge, in urging Pearce to hasten on the organising of the Australian Military Forces 'into a complete and mobile war machine', explained that by the middle of the year the AMF, the product of compulsory military training, would be 70,000 strong and that in time of war it could be expanded through the addition of reserves to 115,000. The AMF, while numerically an army, would unless action was taken 'remain an unwieldy mass of many independent brigades and unallotted units'. Legge, citing the Kitchener report of 1910, maintained that 'to provide adequately for local safety, it would be necessary to deal promptly with an attempted invasion.' He declared that it was 'Urgently necessary therefore that notwithstanding the present war, a higher organisation should be erected at once, in order to render such action possible', and he accordingly proposed that by 30 June 'all units in the Table of Peace Organisation should be brought into being so far as matériel and personnel will permit.'

Pearce approved the plan 'in principle' but withheld final judgment until a conference of senior officers and other members of the Military Board had an opportunity to express their views. At the conference of officers on 12 January, Legge had his way. But after the Acting Adjutant-General pointed out that the scheme would involve creating six new infantry brigades and would require the training of 1016 new officers, the Prime Minister decided at a Council of Defence meeting on 26 February that the scheme should be postponed until its cost could be ascertained. The practical and financial problems proved to be substantial, and on 7 April Pearce assented to an amended scheme which allowed the 'provisional formation' of eight divisional staffs for practical instruction with a view to the creation of the divisions themselves one year later.[87]

After offering the additional 10,000 men in January, the Australian Government became once again rather cautious about recruitment. On the one hand, the responsible ministers continued to

---

[85] *Search for Security*, p.157; letter, Legge to White, 25 July 1913, NAA MP826/3 (left with papers on Australia's Defence Scheme).

[86] Personal letter, Munro Ferguson to Harcourt, 18 February 1915, Novar Papers, NLA MS 696/657-58.

[87] Letter, Legge to Secretary, Defence Department, 5 January 1915, and Pearce's minuted decision, 6 January 1915, NAA MP133/2, 264/1/120, AIF Series 1914-17; Report of the Conference Ordered by the Minister, 12 January 1915, *ibid.*, 264/1/128; Minutes of the 12th Meeting of the Council of Defence, 26 February 1915, 'Council of Defence Meetings', 1905–15, NAA A2032; Pearce's decision on amended scheme for Divisional organisation, 7 April 1915, NAA MP133/2, 264/1/170, AIF Series 1914-17.

proclaim that they would take 'every soldier that could be trained and equipped without limit'.[88] But on the other, there was much evidence that they wished to limit the size of the AIF to the agreed figure. On 11 February the Council of Defence rejected a request from the British Government to raise a further contingent – a request prompted by Lord Kitchener's statement to the British Cabinet that he needed all available fit men,[89] explaining that 'after most careful consideration greater service would be rendered by their retention here at all events for the present.'[90] Fisher and Legge were disturbed by the way in which the growth of the expeditionary forces was affecting their ability to complete Australia's own defence program. Fisher, on 19 February, while reaffirming his government's commitment to recruitment, also repeated his Wangaratta statement of priorities, namely that it was 'the bounden duty of Australia to provide adequate home defence, and do more than had been done in the past for the Mother Country'.[91]

Though Fisher and Pearce did little to stimulate the flow of recruits, the number of men coming forward was nevertheless considerably greater than that needed to meet the targets set for the AIF. In January 10,225 men had enlisted, in February 8370, and in March 8913. In early April Pearce, more than pleased that 'men were coming forward in satisfactory numbers,' offered another infantry brigade of 4500 men to the British authorities.[92] With the troops in camp the government had little choice but to make such a gesture. Fisher, while continuing to maintain that 'every fit and free man' should offer himself, added, to curb any excessive enthusiasm, that 'there is no want yet'. He iterated that there should be 'no urging of any compulsion of any kind.'[93]

Pressures for more recruits and agitation for conscription

From May 1915, the war entered a new and more dangerous phase which undermined Fisher's hopes to keep a balance between assistance for the Mother Country and the building up of Australia's own defences. During the northern spring and summer offensives, the British and French made no headway on the Western Front and suffered very heavy casualties. In the East the Germans occupied Warsaw and advanced into Russian territory. At sea the German submarines began inflicting damage on the Allied merchant marine. These adverse developments convinced a number of leading figures in Britain and the Dominions that the war had become a war for national survival and as a result the Empire should marshal its total resources for a more wholehearted war effort. They called for the raising of an even greater number of troops, some even proposing conscription, and as a result recruitment became the central political issue.[94]

---

[88] See Pearce, *SMH*, 19 January 1915 and 2 February 1915; Hughes, *SMH*, 22 January 1915; Fisher, *SMH*, 22 March 1915 and *CPD*, 1914–17 Session, LXXVVI, 2299, 14 April 1915

[89] R.J.Q. Adams and Philip P. Poirier, *The Conscription Controversy in Great Britain 1900–18* (Basingstoke: Macmillan, 1987), p.55.

[90] Council of Defence Minutes, 11 February 1915, NAA A2032.

[91] *SMH*, 20 February 1915.

[92] *SMH*, 2 April 1915.

[93] *SMH*, 1 April 1915.

[94] Adams and Poirier, *Conscription Controversy in Great Britain 1900–18*, pp.77–89; David French, *British Strategy and War Aims, 1914–1916* (London: Allen and Unwin, 1986), pp.95–111.

The gravity of the struggle was brought home most dramatically by the AIF's participation in the Allied assault on Turkey's Gallipoli peninsula, a naval-military operation intended to wrest control of the Dardanelles from Germany's ally and so open up a warm water route to Russia. The Dardanelles offensive was ill-conceived and poorly executed and Melbourne was neither consulted nor informed about the British plans. Yet when the public learnt of the valour shown by their troops along with those of New Zealand in facing up to impossible odds, they took great pride in the stories of the Anzacs' heroism that filled the pages of the press.[95]

Even more moving for the Australian people were the casualty lists, the high cost in dead and wounded which the AIF paid for the invasion of Gallipoli. In the daily press, column on column of the fallen, illustrated by photographs of those 'killed in action', 'died of wounds' or 'missing' told a graphic story. These reports followed by the return of the wounded brought home to Australians the harsh meaning of the splendid adventure. After Gallipoli, Australians took a more serious view of the war. Its full meaning could not be ignored. After Gallipoli there was a new and greater surge of enlistments, and this time, in contrast to what has been suggested, perhaps rather flippantly, about the motives of the earlier recruits, there could not be the slightest ground for believing that these volunteers saw themselves enjoying a paid overseas holiday.

Righteous anger against the enemy was widespread, and was further inflamed by the German U-boat sinking of the British passenger liner *Lusitania* in May 1915 with the loss of 1400 lives. This act of 'frightfulness' was seen as a striking evidence of the truth of the platform phrases about German ruthlessness and militarism. The German clubs in Sydney and Brisbane were closed down for fear of riot and disturbance. New regulations were promulgated under the *War Precautions Act* placing restrictions on naturalised Australians of enemy origin, and even on natural born British subjects, one of whose parents had been a subject of an enemy country. Such Australians could be interned at the discretion of the authorities. Australian residents who were subjects of enemy countries were deprived of the right to plead in civil matters before the courts. No newspaper could be published in the German language. Some local councils refused to employ Australians who were German or Austro-Hungarian by birth or ethnic origin. Employees walked off the job in protest against being asked to work alongside naturalised Australians who had been born in enemy countries or even alongside native-born Australians who were descended from German or Austro-Hungarian migrants. A number of unions passed resolutions ordering

---

[95] The first despatch to tell the story of the Australian and New Zealand troops, that of the British correspondent, Ashmead-Bartlett, which appeared in the Australian press on 8 May, was followed by many more, all celebrating the heroic exploits of the new and better Britons from the Southern Seas. That there was some truth in the myth was vouched for by relatively independent observers. Sir Maurice Hankey, the Secretary of the British War Council and the Committee of Imperial Defence, who went to the Gallipoli peninsula at the end of the year to report on the operation, recorded in his diary that the Australian troops were 'the finest in the world' and he continued, 'I do hope that we shall have no more talk of the "indiscipline" of this extraordinary corps, for I don't believe that for military qualities of every kind their equal exists ... They do not salute as much as our men, but the relations between officers and men appeared to be of the best.' Hankey had no discernible ulterior motive in committing this judgment to his diary. Hankey, *Supreme Command*, Vol.I, pp.379 and 400.

members not to work with employees of German extraction 'whether naturalised or unnaturalised'.[96]

For others in the labour movement, Gallipoli symbolised the wanton waste of war and they could only justify the human carnage if they could see emerging from the conflict some means for achieving a lasting peace. At the Labor Party's National Conference that met in the first week of June the delegates debated a motion which called for 'The settling of international disputes by a council of civilised nations'.

Hughes, who had already worked out his position on the issue in his *Daily Telegraph* articles, believed such a proposal to be inadequate. Restating his philosophy of international relations to suit the Labor Conference, he told the delegates that wars were not the result of misunderstanding but of wrongdoing and that the efforts of civilised nations to halt aggression could only be successful through the collective force of an international policeman. 'Crimes against civilisation,' he said, 'must be dealt with in the same way as crimes against society ... The remedy for war and crimes was twofold – to remove the causes and to deal with the effects.' As he had little faith that the causes could be removed – 'They might cry "let there be peace" but there was no peace' – he addressed himself to the effects. Until a new environment was created, there was only one way of preventing war – the international policeman to deal with the international criminal just as the ordinary criminal was dealt with. Tribunals for mediation were not enough. If would-be aggressors were met with a threat to 'knock seven bells out of you', it would have a very chastening effect. Hughes did not, however, specify what he had in mind in speaking of an 'International Policeman'.

W. A. Holman, the New South Wales Labor premier, was perplexed by this notion of an 'International Policeman' and took Hughes to task for overlooking the true nature of international relations. In his view there was 'nothing more futile than the International Policeman idea. Such an authority could not be constituted.' Holman advocated rather the voluntary acceptance of arbitration. Hughes and Holman took their respective stands on different aspects of the intractable reality of international relations. Neither of their proposals offered any real hope that war would be abolished for all time.

Fisher considered both views to be too pessimistic. He had a vision of a new world in the making. In contrast to Hughes and Holman, he believed that:

> the great war would leave behind it a lesson to mankind which would raise them to a higher plane of intelligence than they had yet reached. And just as poets had dreamed of it, so he believed that in the future they would see developed a mighty power (a spiritual power) for

---

[96] *SMH*, 14, 21, 24, 25 and 31 May 1915.

Some unions, such as the United Furniture Trade Society, did try to resist this wave of intolerance, *ibid.*, 31 May 1915.

For a similar Queensland employer and union response to the sinking of the Lusitania, see Raymond Evans, *Loyalty and Disloyalty: Social conflict on the Queensland Homefront, 1914–1918* (Sydney: Allen and Unwin, 1987), pp.49–52 and also Walter Meister and John A. Moses, 'The Brisbane German Club 1883–1983', in Johannes H. Voigt, John Fletcher and John A. Moses (eds), *New Beginnings: The Germans in New South Wales and Queensland* (Stuttgart: Institute for Foreign Cultural Relations, 1983).

> organisation and law wherein there would be an international creed for the welfare of the people of the earth.

It was a cry from the heart reflecting his profound antipathy to the bloody destruction which had been let loose in Europe.

At the conclusion of the debate Hughes's argument won out and the conference agreed to support 'the prevention of war through the settlement of international disputes by a tribunal clothed with power sufficient to enforce its awards'. Nothing was said about how this tribunal would be chosen or how it would acquire the power to enforce its decisions.

But in June 1915, with no end to the war in sight, these discussions about peace-making were rather academic. The more immediate task was to ensure the success of the British Empire and its Allies on the battlefield, and the conference, in sending birthday greetings to King George V, prayed that 'during the coming years his reign will be crowned by victory for the British and Allied arms in the great war for freedom and the realisation of an enduring peace.' The loyal resolution, which had no precedent at a Labor Conference, was carried with resounding cheers and the singing of 'God Save the King'.[97]

When the Liberal Party met the following month, ordinary business was dispensed with and the occasion turned into 'a very fine recruiting meeting'. The essence of the problem, as the Liberals defined it, was whether an Australian or a German system of government should prevail in their country. Their answer to that question was to demand that Australia, in order to play its part in the world struggle, should muster and maintain a force of not less than 100,000 in the field.[98] Unlike Labor, the Liberals were not troubled about how to achieve a just and lasting peace; a British victory was the only guarantee of peace which they considered possible. But, though Labor and Liberal could differ or seem to differ about the solution for world peace, both parties, as a result of the Allies' reverses, agreed on the need to give further assistance to the Mother Country.

Moved by this new understanding of the war the Fisher Government began to adopt a more energetic recruitment policy. Fisher's earlier reservations about numbers were set aside. He allowed that Australia had 'no other policy in regard to the war than to abide by what the Imperial Government thinks necessary.'[99] On 18 June the British Government, in reply to an Australian inquiry, cabled that 'Every available man that can be recruited in Australia is wanted.'[100] Fisher was left with no alternative but to urge the recruitment of more men for the front. On 8 July he announced, following the formation of a Coalition Government in the United Kingdom, the establishment of a War Committee comprising an equal number of government and opposition members to advise on war policy.

The Committee's first act was to propose a *War Census Bill* for the purpose of compiling a register of all males from 18 to 50 and of the wealth and income of the whole population. Like the

---

[97] *Official Report of Sixth Commonwealth Conference of the A.L.P. held in Adelaide, 31 May–7 June, 1915,* Sydney 1915; *Register,* 4 June 1915.
[98] *SMH,* 8 July 1915.
[99] *CPD,* 1914–17 session, LXXVI, 3091, 13 May 1915: see also *ibid.,* LXXVII, 11 June 1915.
[100] Scott, *Australia During the War,* p.292.

British *National Registration Act* on which it was based, the Australian Bill purported to express the desire in the country for a more vigorous prosecution of the war. In effect it was a compromise intended to appease those pressing for conscription while not alienating those who held to the voluntary principle. By invoking the British example, the Labor Government was able to persuade the Liberal leaders not to raise the issue of conscription.[101] By tacking on to the Bill an asset and income census they, moreover, went some way to placating dissidents in their own ranks. The government thus hinted that if men were to be called upon for greater sacrifices, so would wealth. The government, rather disingenuously, denied that the Bill was the first step towards conscription. And it was on the basis of these assurances that the Labor Caucus approved the Bill.[102]

The debate over the Bill was an exercise in obfuscation. The leaders of both parties were committed to refuting any suggestion that the measure represented a first step to conscription. When pressed on whether the Bill was intended directly or indirectly to compel Australians to enlist for military service overseas, Fisher replied that 'It is not only not intended but it is not provided in the Bill.' He said that its purpose was to obtain information 'so that we may be able, organised and equipped to face any situation and be ready for effective action at any moment.'[103]

The Prime Minister could accept the arguments for effective organisation quite readily. It fitted well with his view of national development and national security. Experience in the war had also demonstrated the need for better management of resources. The state had been required not only to raise, equip and transport a large army overseas but also to manufacture munitions and control and coordinate many aspects of the economy, especially the primary industries on which the well-being of the Australian economy rested. Thus Fisher explained that the registration was in part necessary because Australia 'as a democracy ... [had] been proceeding on unscientific lines not only in regard to warfare, but also for civil purposes.'[104] Fisher, however, had no answers for those who said that if national efficiency were the aim then it made no sense that the Bill failed to require boys under eighteen and women, both of whom were found in the work-force, to register.

Hughes, who had the chief responsibility for steering the Bill through the House of Representatives, declared that its object was 'the organisation of the forces of the country, so that we may put forth the greatest effort of which we are capable.' Like Fisher, he denied that the Bill contemplated conscription and asserted that he did not believe conscription to be necessary. Yet, unlike Fisher, he conceded that while the immediate purpose of the Bill was to achieve 'the better waging of the conflict upon the principles of voluntary military service', he would not rule out the possibility that changed circumstances might not create new necessities, that 'the future may not hold within it possibilities which may shatter our present conception of what is necessary.'[105]

---

[101] Cable, Munro Ferguson to Andrew Bonar Law, Colonial Secretary, 10 July 1915, TNA: PRO CO 418/133/123, 'Agreement between both parties renders Federal Administration effective for war'.

[102] Weller (ed.), *Caucus Minutes,* Vol.I, pp.412–13, minutes of meeting 8 July 1915.

[103] *CPD*, 1914–17 session, LXXVII, pp.4716 and 4830–31, 14 July 1915.

[104] *Ibid.,* 4574, 2 July 1915.

[105] *Ibid.,* 4716, 8 July 1915.

Irvine, Cook and Millen, speaking for the Liberals, wholeheartedly approved the Bill, including the proposed survey of wealth. Irvine said that every person had to recognise 'he only held what he possesses, no matter what it may be, subject to the general weal and security of the community of which he is a member,' and when Hughes interjected 'That being lost, all is lost,' Irvine took over his words and repeated them.[106] Here was a meeting of minds. Irvine and Hughes were united in their acceptance of the state as the source of all civil rights, whether to life, liberty or property, and this justified the state calling upon the citizen to sacrifice everything for the defence of the nation. Irvine, as well as the other Liberal leaders, kept the agreement with the Labor Party and did not link the Bill to conscription. He did, however, advocate using the register of adult males to bring 'moral suasion' to bear upon 'shirkers', which roused the ire of some Labor backbenchers. The Liberals were content to follow the British lead and take the measure as an earnest of the government's good intentions.

The Labor rank and file gave the Bill a mixed reception. Despite the Caucus adoption of the Bill, some Labor members were very free in expressing their hopes and fears. Senator De Largie, an avowed conscriptionist, saw the Bill as a preliminary step towards compulsion for overseas service and he welcomed it as such.[107] On the other hand some anti-conscriptionists evinced their misgivings by pointing up the gap between the government's explanation of the measure and the nature of the manpower census which was being sought. Others opposed to conscription for service outside Australia were willing to accept Fisher's and Hughes's word because, as W. G. Higgs put it, 'No exception can be taken to the idea of a census because the time might come when we should have to fight locally for Australia. As history shows, nations have broken away from treaty engagements, and taken advantage of people whom they thought to be in a weak position.' For this group, which included F. W. Bamford, John Lynch, Parker Moloney, Edward Riley, and Senator David O'Keefe, fear of Japan justified such a census as it justified compulsory military training.[108] None of the Labor men pushed their doubts to a division and, as a result of careful orchestration, by 23 July the Bill had passed both Houses and six days later it became law.

The Universal Service League

Though both the British and Australian political leaders had endorsed the principle of manpower registration in order to avoid a public controversy over conscription, they were not able to quell the rising demand to marshal the total resources of the nation for victory. In Britain and then Australia an imperially-minded professional elite began to organise a movement for the purpose of persuading their respective governments to legislate for conscription.

The British campaign grew out of impatience with the Asquith Government's seeming half-hearted approach to the war. At its core was a group of intellectuals and reformers who, prior to the Great War, had developed a critique of the British liberal tradition with its suspicion of state intervention and its pride in amateurism, voluntarism and 'muddling through'. While most were

---

[106] *Ibid.*, 4845, 14 July 1915.

[107] *Ibid.*, 5083–85, 21 July 1915.

[108] *Ibid.*, 4852, 14 July 1915; *ibid.*, 5035, 16 July 1915; *ibid.*, 5045, 16 July 1915; *ibid.,* 5026, 16 July 1915; *ibid.*, 5053, 16 July 1915; *ibid.*, 5088, 21 July 1915.

to some degree attached to the Conservative Party there were also Liberal and Labour supporters in their ranks. These latter were especially critical of the inherited privileges of the aristocracy and the indifference of society to the well-being of the working-classes. They advocated restructuring British politics and society along scientific lines. They believed that Britain could only stave off the challenge to its position in Europe and the world by adopting Germany's thoroughness, professionalism and authoritarianism. They sought national efficiency and national organisation for national survival. Above all they stood for the integration of defence planning, for the introduction of national service and for the unifying of Britain with its Dominions in an imperial federation.[109] They were at once romantic nationalists and scientific idealists. Many of them were stalwarts of the National Service League, a pre-war organisation advocating compulsory military training, and the Round Table, a secret Empire-wide body committed to some form of imperial federation.

By January 1915 leading members of the British National Service League were already convinced of the need for conscription, and in May Lord Milner, the *éminence grise* behind both the League and the Round Table, issued a 'Call for Leadership', which declared that it was 'high time that the whole of our able-bodied manhood should be enrolled'.[110] L. S. Amery, a close associate of Milner's, was the first major figure to denounce publicly the *National Registration Bill* as an inadequate alternative to compulsion. Amery was one of the most ardent apostles of 'national efficiency', being a leading light in all the major ginger groups which espoused the cause, such as the 'Co-Efficients', the 'Compatriots' and the 'Round Table'.[111]

Amery, returning from military service in France, joined 'a small War Committee' made up mostly of Round Table members who since June had been meeting once a week to discuss how they could achieve their objectives.[112] In a speech to the House of Commons on 28 July, Amery gave voice to their critique of the Asquith Government. He stressed that Britain was not engaged in the war to fulfil an obligation to France or to satisfy 'some philanthropic emotion'. Britain was fighting because it was caught up 'in a struggle for its existence'. Had Britain adopted national service before the war, it would have been in a much better position to meet the present crisis: 'What they needed was guidance and leadership. At a time like this what a man wanted was an authoritative order telling him in what battalion he had to serve or in what factory he had to work.' He feared that unless the nation took drastic steps to marshal its resources, it would be defeated.[113]

---

[109] G.R. Searle, *The Quest for National Efficiency: A Study in British Politics and Political Thought, 1899–1914* (Oxford: Blackwell, 1971), especially chapter 3, 'The Ideology of National Survival' and chapter 5, 'The Liberal Revival, 1902–1908'.

[110] Adams and Poirier, *Conscription Controversy in Great Britain 1900–18,* pp.64 and 88.

[111] L.S. Amery, *My Political Life*, 2 vols, (London: Hutchinson, 1953), I, 'England before the Storm, 1896–1914', 223–26, 264–66, 346–49; John Kendle, *The Round Table Movement and Imperial Union* (Toronto: University of Toronto Press, 1975), pp.132–45.

[112] J.R.M. Butler, *Lord Lothian, Philip Kerr, 1882–1940* (London: Macmillan, 1960), p.364.

[113] *Times* (London), 29 July 1915; see also Amery, 'An Organised Nation: National Service', *Times* (London), 26 August 1915 and Amery, *My Political Life*, 2, 'War and Peace, 1914–1929', 67–70.

On 16 August, *The Times* published a Manifesto, signed by a large number of dignitaries, demanding a total national effort to win the war and specifically seeking compulsory national service whether for military or civil purposes.[114] Milner threw the support of the National Service League behind the appeal.[115] As days went by more and more prominent people added their names to the Manifesto. The Manifesto called on people throughout the length and breadth of the nation to hold meetings to demonstrate their support for national service. On 3 September, the campaign was launched in London at a public meeting of women who had relatives serving in the armed forces.[116]

In Sydney a similar movement was taking shape, and by early September it too had issued its Manifesto and established a national organisation, the Universal Service League. The founders, drawn from the Sydney branch of the Round Table, included the President of the New South Wales branch of the League, T. W. Edgeworth David, Professor of Geology and Physical Geography at the University of Sydney, one of the two secretaries and the secret national organiser, T. R. Bavin[117] and J. C. Watson, the former Labor Prime Minister who was a Vice-President of the League. Of the twenty-three members of the Sydney Round Table moot, eleven were office-bearers or members of the inaugural committee of the Universal Service League. Most of those who did not join the League held judicial or other statutory appointments and probably for that reason felt it improper to identify themselves publicly with a political cause.[118]

It may well be that the British Round Table had induced the Sydney branch to follow their lead. It was remarkable that the Sydney movement was established so soon after the publication of the Manifesto in the *Times*, and especially so since the British Manifesto was only published in the Australian press in a very summary form which avoided all reference to conscription.[119] Perhaps Watson, who had been in close touch with the Round Table during his visit to London in May, was the conduit. As in Britain it was the Round Table network that brought the Universal Service League into being and defined its purpose.

Within four days of the publication of the British Manifesto, Bavin wrote to John Latham, a prominent figure in the Melbourne Round Table, telling him of the Sydney organisation and asking him to take the lead in establishing a Victorian branch.

> This is a private and preliminary letter only. Please don't say anything – except confidentially – about the matter at present. We are starting an organisation to be called (provisionally) the Universal Service League. Its object is to induce the Govt. to introduce a measure to compel every citizen, man or woman, to render whatever kind of service, military or otherwise, in or out of Australia, he or she may be considered capable of. The primary object, I suppose will be

---

[114] *Times* (London), 16 August 1915.

[115] *Ibid.*, 19 August 1915.

[116] *Ibid.*, 4 September 1915.

[117] The headquarters of the league were situated at his address, University Chambers, Phillip Street.

[118] Compare the list of 'The N.S.W. Round Table Group', September 1916 (Round Table Papers, Bodleian Library, MSS. Eng. hist. c.797, f.128) with the list of the USL's list of office-holders and committee members, *SMH*, 11 September 1915.

[119] *SMH*, 17 August 1915. It was probably censored on the ground that it would undermine the voluntary recruitment drive.

to obtain a sufficient number of soldiers for service abroad, but we want the law to be wide enough to embrace any kind of service that may be useful to the Empire. This is only a rough outline of the objects: I will send you a more definite statement later, if you can see your way to cooperate with us, as I am going to ask.

Professor David is our President. J. C. Watson, some of the present N.S.W. ministry, leading members of the opposition and others, are identified with it; it has no party complexion whatever. We are very anxious to begin the movement in all states at once: and with David's approval I am writing to ask you what you think of starting a similar movement in Victoria, to work in cooperation, and under the same title with us – possibly under a single organisation. We are taking steps to get the thing going in other states … and want to make it a Federal movement – starting simultaneously in all the states.[120]

After three weeks of clandestine planning, the Universal Service League published their Manifesto and appealed for popular support. The organisers in Sydney had done their work well and had collected a very distinguished and representative group of community leaders to hold office in the League and endorse its principles. The list of vice-presidents and committee members included all the major church leaders – the Anglican and Roman Catholic archbishops, the Moderator of the Presbyterian Church, the President of the Methodist Conference and Rabbi F. L. Cohen; the chief state political figures – the Premier and a number of his ministers, the leader of the opposition and Liberal front-benchers and the President of the Political Labor League; the heads of employers and employee bodies – the Presidents of the Chambers of Commerce, the Chamber of Manufacturers and the Employers Federation and the General Secretaries of the Meat Industry Employees Union and the Federal Millers and Mill Employees Association; and many other dignitaries – the Vice-Chancellor of the University of Sydney and a number of professors from the University, the Lord Mayor of Sydney, the President of the National Council of Women, and the manager of the *Worker*. It was a most impressive, seemingly irresistible, expression of public opinion.

The Australian Manifesto, like the British one, put the case for national and imperial efficiency. It assumed that Australians were agreed about the meaning of imperial loyalty and had accepted that there was a complete identity of interest between the nation and the Empire. It claimed that the whole community needed to be organised so 'that every man and every woman may be able to render the best service of which he or she is capable to the Empire.' It asserted that voluntarism had failed, and that, even if it had not, it was 'often harmful' in that 'men have gone who should have stayed' and 'many more have stayed who should have gone.' The future had to be properly planned. The principle of compulsory service for the defence of Australia, embodied in the *Defence Act*, had to be logically extended to incorporate the defence of the Empire for '… today Australia is being defended in the fields of Flanders and on the hills of Gallipoli. If she is to be saved at all it must be there.'[121]

Bavin's organisation was not, however, as successful as he had hoped. In issuing their Manifesto in Sydney on 11 September, the League had declared that identical statements were

---

[120] Letter, Bavin to Latham, 20 August 1915, Latham Papers, NLA MS 1009/17/44–45.
[121] *SMH*, 11 September 1915.

being published in all the other capital cities and that branches were being formed in all states. The Manifesto was published on 11 September in newspapers across the country but, despite Bavin's and David's best efforts, the other branches came into existence very slowly and failed to attract representative backing. On 12 September the Labor premiers of Queensland and South Australia admitted that they had been approached – T. J. Ryan by the Sydney organisers, and Crawford Vaughan by David's Adelaide agent Professor Sir Douglas Mawson – but both had responded warily to these overtures.[122]

In Melbourne the Manifesto appeared over the names of Latham and Professor Orme Masson, Professor of Chemistry and Chairman of the Professorial Board at Melbourne University. Latham had great difficulty in forming a Victorian branch of the League. He had encountered resistance from political and civic leaders. The Melbourne Round Table moot contained no Labor men, let alone one of Watson's eminence and influence. In Melbourne too, the Liberal leaders took seriously their commitment to the Fisher Government not to raise the conscription issue. Thus, when on 21 September the Victorian branch was formed at a meeting in the Melbourne Town Hall, its sponsors had to be content with a committee made up almost entirely of professional and academic leaders, a very high proportion of whom were Round Table members.[123]

This campaign for national service did not result from the failure of voluntary recruiting. During the winter of 1915 the numbers enlisting had risen from 10,506 in May to 36,575 in July and in August they were still over 25,000. The response to the recruiting drive had been overwhelming. The founders of the Universal Service League, like their British counterparts, were moved not so much by a desire to enforce equity in sacrifice as by a conviction that in the great struggle for the Empire's survival the state had a responsibility to achieve efficiency in the use of national resources. Professor Masson expressed this well when, at the formation of the Victorian branch of the League, he 'likened the British Empire to a team of amateurs playing professionals'. He declared that the League wanted 'the most professional system of organisation'. Professor David, speaking at the same meeting, emphasised the inclusive character of their organisation and the need for equity in sacrifice. 'One of the chief aims of the League,' he said, 'was to convince them [the workers of Australia] that the universal service movement was not a movement to exploit workers in the interests of capitalists.' He said that 'he did not believe in conscription of men without reasonable conscription of wealth through taxation.'[124] The nation should use its men and material in a systematic way. There was no end in sight to the threat to nation and Empire – the fortunes of both being inseparable – and the total resources of the country had to be organised for victory.

---

[122] *SMH*, Brisbane *Courier*, Adelaide *Register*, *West Australian*, *Mercury*, 11 September 1915; see also 'Conscription for Australia. Views of Public Men', *Age*, 13 September 1915 and 'Conscription. The Premier's View', *Register*, 22 September 1915.
[123] *Age*, 11 and 22 September 1915.
[124] *Age*, 22 September 1915.

It is noteworthy that both Masson and David were very distinguished scientists and Presidents of the Australian Association for the Advancement of Science and that Masson helped found the Commonwealth Institute of Science and Industry and was its first vice-chairman from 1916–20.

The crusade for conscription, however, produced the very result Fisher had feared and which the *War Census Bill* had supposedly been intended to avert. It divided the nation. Two days after the Universal Service League held their inaugural meetings in Sydney and Melbourne,[125] the opponents of compulsion, mostly drawn from the trade unions, held a meeting in the Sydney Town Hall and established an Anti-Conscription League which, following the pattern of the Universal Service League, soon had branches throughout the Commonwealth. These union leaders were greatly influenced by the English Trades Union Congress which in early September, in response to the British Manifesto, had condemned the principle of compulsion.[126] The anti-conscriptionists spoke for the dependent and vulnerable in society. Equal suffrage did not produce an equal sense of belonging to the nation. Inequality of wealth and work at the whim of capital tended to qualify faith in the democratic political institutions. Increasing unemployment, rises in the cost of living, experiences of arbitrary military censorship all helped to breed discontent. Thus the Secretaries of the Boilermakers' Union and the Sydney Coal Lumpers Union asserted that 'there should be conscription of wealth before conscription.'[127] Many of those who disliked the idea of being compulsorily organised for war saw some point in the Industrial Workers of the World's poster which mocked the USL Manifesto:

To Arms!!

Capitalists, Parsons, Politicians,

Landlords, Newspaper Editors, and

Other Stay-at-home Patriots,

YOUR COUNTRY NEEDS YOU IN THE TRENCHES!!

WORKERS,

FOLLOW YOUR MASTERS.[128]

The only elite group which the poster overlooked, and that the most appropriate for inclusion, was professors.

Shortly thereafter Fisher showed his hostility to the USL's actions when he reassured a delegation of anti-conscriptionists that he was 'irrevocably opposed to conscription and he was sure he could say his colleagues were.' The government had no intention of amending the *Defence Act* to remove the territorial restrictions on compulsory military service. It was 'for every man to

---

[125] *SMH*, 22 September 1915; *Age*, 22 September 1915.
[126] *Argus*, 13 September 1915.
At a meeting of the executive of the Railway Workers and General Labourers' Association held in Sydney on 11 September it had been decided in response to the United Service League's Manifesto 'to stand by what has been done by the Trades Union Congress at Bristol' and oppose conscription.
[127] *Age*, 13 September 1915.
[128] Cited in Ian Turner, *Industrial Labor and Politics: The Labor Movement in Eastern Australia. 1900–1921* (Canberra: Australian National University Press, 1965), p.123. For a sympathetic account of the Australian IWW's ideology, see Verity Burgmann, *Revolutionary Industrial Unionism: The Industrial Workers of the World in Australia* (Melbourne: Cambridge University Press, 1995), chapter 5.

decide where he will fight'. Fisher had given public undertakings during the passage of the *War Census Bill* and he would not renege on these promises. He guaranteed that there would be no change of government policy until after the people had been consulted.[129]

Fisher's statement embarrassed the USL. In Sydney the Labor politicians doubted whether they could continue in the movement if Fisher spoke for the party. Some, citing Hughes, suggested that Fisher had not consulted his cabinet. Nevertheless, as a result of Fisher's stand, Bavin had become convinced that, as he told Latham, 'unless the Federal Government makes some pronouncement that membership with our League is not inconsistent with party loyalty, we shall be left with very few, if any, labour supporters. You will … see that the matter is vital to us.'[130] Consequently they sought Hughes's intervention – it was well-known that he sympathised with their aims – and arranged for Professor David to seek a clarification from Fisher. Following an interview with the Prime Minister on 21 October, David wrote to Fisher asking for confirmation of the results of their discussion. In his letter David, recapitulating what he had understood Fisher to say, asked whether the federal government's attitude to the League was:

> 1. The federal government does not consider that the voluntary system of Military Service has broken down.
>
> 2. The federal government at the present juncture is opposed to the adoption for the Commonwealth of Compulsory Military Service outside of Commonwealth Territories.
>
> 3. That while thus disagreeing with the views of the USL, the federal government does not wish to suppress advocacy of the principles for which the League stands, nor would it seek to debar members of any political party from belonging to the League or assisting in its work in their capacity as private citizens.

Fisher noted on the side of the letter that 'the Government has no desire to suppress views on the matter that are not in accord with its policy.'[131]

The call for conscription had a damping effect on the recruiting campaign. Since the conscriptionists believed that voluntarism had failed, many of them had little desire to prop up the bankrupt system by taking part in recruiting drives. On the other side the anti-conscriptionists became suspicious of all attempts to boost enlistments through public exhortations or moral pressure. This disenchantment with voluntary recruitment touched the Labor Party closely. William Webster, who had the task of engaging federal politicians for a new recruiting campaign scheduled to be launched in Sydney on 7 October, was discouraged by the lack of response from Commonwealth ministers and Labor members. He informed Fisher that he would not take part in 'a half-hearted campaign' and warned that 'if recruiting is really essential, my anxiety anent same is because it is the alternative of conscription.' By 1 October he was despairing of the results 'as both parties seem unconcerned at the future of any recruiting effort.'[132]

---

[129] *SMH* and *Age*, 25 and 30 September 1915.

[130] Letter, Bavin to Latham, 19 October 1915, Latham Papers, NLA MS 1009/17/53–55A.

[131] Letter, Bavin to Latham, 28 October 1915, enclosing a copy of letter from David to Fisher, 22 October 1915 with Fisher's comment, Latham Papers, NLA MS 1009/17/61–62.

[132] Letters, Webster to Fisher, 26 September and 1 October 1915, Fisher Papers, NLA MS 2919/3/296–97.

The Governor-General, who had made recruiting meetings his chief public responsibility, was also concerned by the Commonwealth ministers' apparent reluctance to assist with recruiting and urged Fisher to encourage them to spare time for the purpose. Their authority was needed to help quash the 'rowdies' who were disrupting meetings. But Fisher viewed the emotional appeals at public meetings with a certain suspicion, especially since the conscriptionists' initiative. He told Munro Ferguson that 'too much may be made of Ministers' efforts on the public platform as recruiting agents. It would not need very keen insight to discover much party politics in certain special moves. A government has higher purposes in such times as the present … Stern resolve alone will carry us through successfully to the peaceful end of victory. It is too soon in my opinion to make a dying gasp effort either in finance or otherwise. We have reserves and resources that will last for the final blow.'[133]

Fisher's approach to aiding the Empire was the very antithesis of that which informed the Universal Service League's campaign. For the League, the frittering away of reserves and resources would mean that they would never be used most effectively and that when the time came nothing would be left for a 'final blow'. For Fisher on the other hand, Australia should not move too quickly to give its last man and last shilling to the Mother Country. Conscription would not only denude Australia of resources which might be needed for its own defence, but also divide the country and tear the Labor Party apart.

Fisher was under great strain. For two years he had been in indifferent health. The conflicts in the nation and the party over war policy and recruitment had exacerbated this condition; there were even reports that a section of the party was hatching plots 'with a view to a complete reorganisation'.[134] He also had differences with Hughes, probably over both the latter's *Trading with the Enemy* and the *War Census Bills*.[135] After a 'scolding' interview with delegates from the Melbourne Trades Hall on 24 September he had confessed to journalists that 'Perhaps I am irritable, I am nervous and run down.'[136] By this time he had lost any heart for the struggle. He no longer had the wit or the will to find a way through the problems that hemmed him round. He stumbled through these last days in office, a weary and unhappy leader of his country. On 26 October he sought release from his ordeal by resigning as Prime Minister and accepting the post of Australia's High Commissioner in London.[137]

---

[133] Fisher to Munro Ferguson, 16 October 1915, Novar Papers, NLA MS 699/3975.

[134] Letter, Pearce to Fisher, 12 October 1915, Fisher Papers, NLA MS 8919/3/263.

[135] Novar Papers, Novar Diary, NLA MS 696/36, 9 June 1915.

Munro Ferguson, commenting on his talk with Fisher that day, said that while the Prime Minister 'always speaks freely, nicely and fairly of colleagues' Hughes 'gives much trouble.'

[136] *Age*, 25 September 1915.

See also Munro Ferguson's view after Fisher had resigned; 'Mr Fisher has been for some months in a state of high nervous tension aggravated by a chill, which he was unable to shake off.' Letter, Munro Ferguson to Bonar Law, 8 November 1915, Novar Papers, NLA MS 696/768.

[137] Weller (ed.), *Caucus Minutes*, Vol.I, pp.426–27.

3
The Competition for Germany's Pacific Empire

Though Australians had identified themselves with Britain's cause and rushed to offer aid to the Mother Country, they understood well the implication of the European war for their own security in the Pacific. They were worried not so much by the possibility of German raids on ports and commerce – this was seen to be a short-term and limited problem – as by the uncertainty surrounding Japanese aims and intentions. Australian leaders were aware that war was the engine of change in history. Joseph Cook, on the eve of Britain's entry into the European conflict, confided to his diary that 'The war means a new map. New relations – new history.'[1] They and their chief advisers recognised that just as the outcome of the war in Europe would shape the future structure of global politics, so Japan's actions in Asia and the Pacific would have a large influence, indeed, depending on the result of the European conflict, even a decisive influence, on the strategic balance in their region.

Japan enters the war

When Australians considered the implications of the war for their position in the Pacific, they were much troubled by the new set of circumstances with which they were confronted. The Cold War against Japan, which had dominated their defence and foreign policy for a decade, acquired a more immediate meaning. As the European great powers became absorbed in their struggle for supremacy Japan was left completely free to impose its will on the Western Pacific and East Asia. The British had no significant naval force in the Pacific and were in no position to check Japanese imperialism in the region. On the contrary Britain was obliged to appease Japan in order both to obtain its naval assistance and keep it in the camp of the Entente powers. For the Australians, then, the scenario of the 'Australian Crisis', which had haunted them since the Russo-Japanese war, seemed in danger of imminent realisation. Thus from the beginning of the war they were greatly concerned about the possibility of Japan intervening and, if it did, about the role it would play. Indeed Fisher's cautious approach to recruitment for the AIF was in part explained by his anxiety about Japan. In formulating his policy of aid to the Mother Country he always acted with one eye looking northwards over his shoulder at Japan.

During the pre-war years, out of deference to the Anglo-Japanese alliance, the Australian press and politicians often used euphemisms to express their fear of Japan. The coming of the war increased the need for discretion, and self-censorship was reinforced by official censorship which prohibited publication of any statement which might be offensive to an ally of the British Empire.[2] In parliament, Fisher had occasionally to appeal to members not to debate the Pacific question, and members themselves when they touched on Japan would even confess that they were giving

---

[1] Cook Diary, 1 August 1914, NAA M3580.
[2] See *War Precautions Act*, Clause 4 (d).

work to the censors. Nevertheless, while the unpublished records, both the government's official files and the policy-makers' private papers provide the fullest account of Australian attitudes towards Japan, the newspapers and the parliamentary debates still contain much that is revealing about Australia's apprehensions.

In the days preceding Britain's entry into the war there was considerable speculation about the possible consequences of Japan's involvement. The *Bulletin*, perhaps the most rabidly racist and anti-Japanese publication in the country, put the position most candidly. James Edmond, in his editorial for the 6 August issue – written before news of Britain's declaration of war reached Australia – warned that:

> A great European war is full of possibility for Australia. This country will be in the centre of the whirlpool, to say nothing of the fact that unlike Austria and Germany, it may be an Asiatic whirlpool of its own …

> If some adjacent Great Power – perhaps an unreasonable and combustible brown creature which objects to anybody but itself practising an exclusive policy – took the opportunity to fish in the troubled waters around our coasts new complications might arise … Australia would have to stand on its own defence, and its defence is poor. Yet the event is only the sort of thing which may be expected. Every country with a grievance or an ambition selects the handiest time to settle the question … If Japan chooses to resent Australia's absolutely necessary Colored Exclusion policy, and selects the most convenient time to do the deed, it will simply be playing the ordinary game. It will be no worse than any other power. Nothing is to be gained by appealing to treaties. All that Australia can do in such a case is to take stock of its resources.[3]

The Sydney *Daily Telegraph* hinted at the same outcome for Australia in case of war:

> Should this war begin, no-one can even faintly imagine where it will end. Australia will have her own problems to face if Great Britain is involved, and in that event there are more quarters than one from which a blow may be aimed at this Commonwealth.[4]

Senator T. J. K. Bakhap, a Liberal Senator from Tasmania of mixed Chinese and European extraction who had recently returned from a tour of East Asia told his fellow-countrymen that:

> If there was a European war involving the Greater Powers … developments in the East outside the sphere of possible European action would take place with startling rapidity, and that the undefended Commonwealth would find itself face to face with a question that would tax the ability of statesmen, the resources of nations much older than our own … A European war would be the opportunity for a strong Asiatic power to work its will in Eastern Asia and contiguous countries.

He concluded that 'he had greatly mistaken the position if such opportunity would not be availed of.'[5]

Following rumours reported in the press on 31 July and 1 August that Japan would stand by Britain, interest in the subject grew. The Sydney *Sun* looked on the prospect of Japan offering 'to

---

[3] *Bulletin*, 6 August 1914.
[4] *Daily Telegraph*, 27 July 1914.
[5] *Argus*, 1 August 1914.

protect the Commonwealth against Germany' with anything but enthusiasm. It noted cryptically that 'Australia is unlikely to view such "protection" with favour.'[6]

Many of the leading dailies, however, seemed willing to trust in Japan's good faith though their very discussion of the subject showed that there were doubts in the public's mind. Perhaps some of them hoped that, in circumstances over which Australia had little or no control, these affirmations of trust would help to win Japan's goodwill. The Adelaide *Advertiser*, arguing for all aid to the Mother Country, insisted that 'Japan is Britain's ally and we fully believe in her protestations of friendship in this hour of peril.'[7] The *Age* said that Japan's declaration of friendship towards the Empire 'removed considerable uneasiness'.[8] When Britain's entry into the war seemed inevitable, the *Daily Telegraph* also adopted a more tactful and reassuring line:

> There is a good deal of speculation as to what Japan's position is likely to be in the event of a general war ... In spite of the irresponsible talk which has been occasionally heard [and in which it itself had indulged] there is no doubt of the perfect loyalty with which Japan will observe whatever obligation she has undertaken.[9]

The *Sydney Morning Herald* took a similar stand and, like the other newspapers, seemed anxious to quieten its own fears. The Anglo-Japanese alliance was a 'live thing'. Japan was 'not likely to ignore her obligations' and, in coming to Britain's assistance, would not take the opportunity to encroach on China's territory or to gain a privileged position in China's trade. The paper frankly avowed that:

> Many Australians are discussing Japan's position with some reserve. They know that things have been said and written which have wounded the feelings of a sensitive and high-spirited people and they are wondering how far an ally may be inclined to hesitate when called upon to observe her treaty obligations.

But it ended with a forced optimism:

> There need be no debate on the matter. Japan has already shown in her international relations that she is actuated by the highest ideals of Western nations ... Whatever be the decision – and it will be taken with Great Britain's concurrence, or not at all – we may depend upon Japan's honour and honesty; and in loyalty to the Empire Australia will welcome her help.[10]

Returning to the same theme a few days later, while Japan's decision was still being awaited, the *Herald* produced an elaborate case to show why Japan must go to war with Germany, which ranged from the German 'betrayal of Japan' at the time of the Sino-Japanese war to Kaiser Wilhelm's insulting obsession with the 'Yellow Peril'.[11] Here was desperate history serving desperate times.

The Prime Minister and the Minister for External Affairs, on being questioned by reporters on the same topic, were even more circumspect. Cook, in 1913 and early 1914, when taking the

---

[6] *Sun*, 31 July 1914.
[7] *Advertiser*, 3 August 1914.
[8] *Age*, 3 August 1914.
[9] *Daily Telegraph*, 4 August 1914.
[10] *SMH*, 10 August 1914.
[11] *Ibid.*, 14 August 1914.

British to task for failing to keep their promise to help build a Pacific fleet, had maintained that the Anglo-Japanese alliance was not a credible basis for security and that indeed Japan itself posed the greatest threat to Australian interests.[12] It is not surprising therefore that in August 1914 Cook preferred not to speak on the matter and External Affairs Minister Glynn, in tune with the press, merely said what he believed would most encourage the Japanese to cooperate with the British Empire, namely that he had 'no doubt that Japan is as sensitive on points of obligation and honour as any great nation of the West.' In the light of Germany's treatment of the Belgian treaty of neutrality as a 'scrap of paper', Glynn's answer might be thought somewhat more equivocal than it appears at first sight, but this is perhaps to squeeze more out of Glynn's remarks than he had intended. He dismissed the idea that Japan might be called upon to defend Australia as 'a matter we need not consider as it is beyond the sphere of reasonable probability.'[13]

The Australian Government, like the politicians and press, were debating in the dark. Their assessments were not based on any knowledge of Japan's intentions or British actions. Britain retained as complete a control over the Empire's relations with Japan as it did with Germany. Even though on the occasion of the 1911 Imperial Conference the British Government had for the first time given the Dominion leaders an overview of the Empire's foreign policy and sought their advice on the renewal of the Anglo-Japanese alliance, it was not disposed to consult Australia about Japan's entry into the war and the role it might play in the war. It is true that the British had to act under pressure of time since events moved almost as rapidly in East Asia as in Europe. More importantly, however, the British understood that Australia had a very different perspective on the Japanese question, and they wished to avoid unnecessary friction and debate. They considered that they alone were responsible for imperial defence and foreign policy. The position of the United Kingdom was under threat and they were determined that its interests should prevail.

Britain did try to influence its Asian ally's response to the European crisis. In the cold light of war the British leaders came to recognise what the Australians had been pressing upon them for some time, namely that when Europe was rent by conflict, Japan would be the unchallenged master of East Asia. Sir Edward Grey admitted that 'the Far East and the whole of the Pacific Ocean lay open to her,'[14] and he feared that Japan might, after its entry into the war, undermine the 'Open Door' in China and thrust outward into the Pacific. The Foreign Secretary, moreover, was aware that neutral countries, notably the United States and the Netherlands, might be alienated if Japan joined the Entente powers and pursued an aggressive policy in the Pacific. Australia's concerns did not come into the British calculations.

During 1913 and early 1914, Grey had become increasingly suspicious of Japan's aims in China,[15] and he had no desire to allow Japan to take advantage of the war to realise its ambitions. As the European crisis deepened, his first impulse was to discourage the Japanese from taking

---

[12] *Search for Security*, pp.242–57.

[13] *Age*, 3 August 1914; *Advertiser*, 3 August 1914.

[14] Viscount Grey of Fallodon, *Twenty Five Years*, 1892–1916, 2 vols (London: Hodder and Stoughton, 1925), Vol.II, p.99.

[15] Peter Lowe, *Great Britain and Japan, 1911–1915: A Study of British Far Eastern Policy* (Macmillan: London, 1969), pp.175–76; Ian Nish, *Alliance in Decline: A Study in Anglo-Japanese Relations, 1908–1923* (London: The Athlone Press, 1972), pp.104–05.

part in the conflict.[16] Once Britain was in the war, however, he quickly perceived that British naval forces in East Asia were not strong enough to ensure the protection of Allied trade and territory, and on 6 August he asked the Japanese for naval assistance to deal with German armed merchantmen in the China Sea.[17] Grey deliberately tried to restrict Japan's war role to the China Sea. That is, he wanted to secure Japanese help on British terms and for British purposes.

Such ham-fisted diplomacy showed contempt for Japan as an ally and a great power, and it rebounded on Grey. When the Japanese replied that they were willing to go to war with Germany but would not limit their participation to suit 'the temporary convenience of Great Britain' and asserted they would pursue by 'all and every possible means' the destruction of German power in East Asia,[18] the Foreign Secretary was much put out. If Japan should assume such a stance, not only would the *status quo* in China be undermined but also the United States, which had made its distrust of Japan very plain, would be likely to take offence.[19]

Knowing that Japan's resolve to intervene could not be shaken, the British salvaged what they could and agreed that 'the general interests involved in the Anglo-Japanese alliance warranted and required common action, but the operation should be limited to the coasts of China and the China Seas and westward.'[20] The inclusion of 'the coasts of China' was a concession to Japan's clearly stated intention. The exclusion of the area east of the China Sea on the other hand was aimed at preventing Japan from seizing the German North Pacific islands. The call for 'common action' was designed to give the British a say in Japanese decisions. But all this elaborate scheming came to nought. Britain was helpless in face of Japan's determination.

In conveying the British Government's view to the Japanese, Grey took an even stricter view. In order to avoid being placed under any diplomatic obligation to Japan, he first denied that British interests in East Asia were 'so seriously menaced' as to justify invoking the Anglo-Japanese alliance. He then proceeded to explain that Britain was nevertheless willing to join in a call for common action to protect 'general interests' covered by the alliance. Such action would not extend beyond 'Asiatic waters' to any foreign territory 'excepting territory in German occupation on the continent of Eastern Asia'.

---

[16] Cables, Grey to British Ambassador in Tokyo, Sir Conyngham Greene, 1 August and 3 August 1914, *BD*, XI, 298 and 305; see also TNA: PRO CO 532/72/177-79.

[17] Cable, Grey to Greene, 6 August 1914, *BD*, X, Pt.II, appendix II, 823; see also Ian Nish, 'Admiral Jerram and the German Pacific Fleet', *Mariner's Mirror*, LVI, 1970, 411-421 and Bartlett, p.138.

[18] Lowe, *Great Britain and Japan,* p.185; Nish, *Alliance in Decline,* pp.119-20.

For an account of the Japanese decision-making over how to reply to the British, see Charles Schencking, 'Navalism, Naval Expansion and War; the Anglo-Japanese Alliance and the Japanese Navy', in Phillips Payson O'Brien (ed.), *The Anglo-Japanese Alliance, 1902-1922* (London: Routledge Curzon, 2004), pp.129-30.

[19] Ernest R. May, 'American Policy and Japan's Entrance into World War I', *Mississippi Valley Historical Review*, XV, 1953, 279-90; Cable, American Secretary of State, W.J. Bryan to American Ambassador to the United Kingdom, W.H. Page, 11 August 1914, US, *Foreign Relations* (hereinafter *FRUS*), 1914, 'Supplement', pp.166-67.

[20] Letter, Asquith to King George V, 11 August 1914, Asquith Papers, Bodleian Library MSS. Asquith 7.

The Japanese would not be trifled with in this way. They were pleased to be able to base their declaration of war on the Anglo-Japanese alliance but they rejected out of hand the self-denying conditions which Britain sought to impose upon them. Without further ado the Japanese, on 15 August, sent an ultimatum to Berlin demanding the withdrawal of German ships from Japanese and Chinese waters and the handing over of the German leased territory of Jiaozhou.

The critical point for the British had been reached. While waiting for Germany to reply, Grey acted. On 17 August he issued a statement through the Press Bureau in London which, while approving Japan's action under the alliance, declared that Japan had taken this step to help safeguard 'the independence and integrity of China', and that Japan would 'not extend its sphere of operations into the Pacific Ocean except to protect its shipping, nor to any territory except territory in German Occupation on the continent of Eastern Asia.' It was as though by publicly, if unilaterally, committing the Japanese to the British point of view, he expected to be able to lock them into the British terms.

The Japanese Government was unmoved by this British manoeuvre and published its own statement of its war aims. It would eliminate from Continental China 'the root of German influence which forms a constant menace to the peace of the Far East', and, more generally would only restrict its actions to those 'necessary for ... the defence of her own legitimate interests', which remained undefined. The Foreign Minister, Takaaki Kato,[21] informed Grey on 21 August that Japan did not consider itself bound by the British press release.[22] Britain, lacking any bargaining lever, had attempted to achieve its diplomatic objectives through bluff. But the Japanese had the measure of their ally. They were not willing to be browbeaten into making humiliating and unnecessary concessions. Thus Grey's Japanese policy had collapsed in ruins around him. And when, on 23 August, Japan came into the war, a new chapter opened in the history of the Pacific, a chapter that was for Australia to be peculiarly disturbing.

Planning to seize Germany's Pacific empire

Neither the British nor the Australians had made any plans for prosecuting a war against Germany in the Pacific and it was some time before they realised all its ramifications. Nevertheless the British authorities moved with commendable speed to consider what should be done. The Pacific was a peripheral part of British global planning, but it was a part of it. On 6 August, the British Cabinet agreed to ask the Commonwealth Government to mount an expedition to capture the cable and wireless telegraphy station on Yap in the German-controlled Pelew Archipelago in the North Pacific.[23] In accord with this decision the Colonial Secretary

---

[21] I have put Japanese given names first and family names second in accordance with general Western practice.
[22] Lowe, *Great Britain and Japan,* pp.188–92; Nish, *Alliance in Decline,* pp.122–25.
[23] The recommendation came from a special subcommittee of the Committee of Imperial Defence, made up of representatives of the Colonial Office, the Admiralty and the War Office, which had been created for the express purpose of considering what operations the Dominions might undertake against German-held territory in their respective geographical regions; 'Proceedings of a Joint Naval and Military Subcommittee for the consideration of Combined Operations in Foreign Territory', in CID.

cabled Melbourne inviting the Australians 'to seize German Wireless Stations at New Guinea, Yap … and Nauru.' He stressed that if they should in the process take possession of German islands, they must accept that such territory would be 'at the disposal of the Imperial Government for purpose of an ultimate settlement.'[24] In adopting this policy Britain sought both to destroy the communication system of the German Pacific squadron and its associated armed merchantmen and also to ensure that the German Pacific colonies would be available as pawns for any negotiated peace settlement in Europe.

The Australian Government readily assented to raise a force of 1500 to occupy the German bases.[25] The defence minister minuted that 'the government attached the utmost importance to the prompt accomplishment of the projected mission.'[26] It may well be that the Australian view of the mission did not altogether coincide with that of the British. The Australians undoubtedly welcomed the idea of redressing the wrong which, as they conceived it, had been done in 1883 when the British had rejected Queensland's attempt to annex east New Guinea and associated territory and thereby allowed Germany to establish a colony on their doorstep.

The entry of Japan into the war added a new dimension to Australia's interest in these islands. Britain had kept the negotiations with Japan from the Australians. Harcourt had rejected a suggestion from a junior clerk in the Colonial Office that the Pacific Dominions be kept informed of the Anglo-Japanese exchanges,[27] and Britain held to that position until Japan's ultimatum to Germany forced its hand. On 11 August, after the British Government had accepted that Japan's involvement was unavoidable, Harcourt warned the Australians of Japan's decision and, anticipating Australian disquiet, passed on the British Government's belief that Japan's belligerency would 'not extend to the Pacific Ocean beyond the China seas or to any foreign territory in German occupation on the continent of Eastern Asia.'[28]

The Japanese ultimatum gave a fresh impetus to Australian anxieties.[29] Since Japan seemed about to join the Allies, the newspapers discussed the prospect very discreetly and, while

---

113-C, October 1914, Harcourt Papers, Bodleian Library MSS. Harcourt 508; letter, Asquith to King George V, 6 August 1914, Asquith Papers, Bodleian Library MSS. Asquith 7.

[24] Cable, Harcourt to Munro Ferguson, 6 August 1914, in UK, Cd. 7975, 'Correspondence respecting Military Operations against German Possessions in the Western Pacific, November 1915'; see also cable, Harcourt to Munro Ferguson, 18 August 1914, *ibid.*, in which the colonial Secretary reaffirmed that 'no proclamation formally annexing any such territory should be made without previous communications with His Majesty's Government', and also NAA CP78/23 14/89/10.

[25] Cable, Munro Ferguson to Harcourt, 10 August 1914, UK, *Cd.* 7975.

[26] Memorandum by the Minister for Defence, Senator E.D. Millen, 10 August 1914, NAA MP1049/1 14/0307.

[27] TNA: PRO CO 532/72/175.

[28] Cable, Harcourt to Munro Ferguson, 11 August 1914 – 'copies sent to Prime Minister and Minister for Defence, 12/8/14', NAA CP 78/23 74/89/32.

[29] In the Pacific province of Canada there was an almost hysterical reaction to the news. The Premier of British Columbia, Sir Richard McBride, on reading press reports of Japanese mobilisation, urged the Canadian Prime Minister, Sir Robert Borden, to tell the British Admiralty that 'in event British loss Japan would not hesitate to cooperate with Germany. I know of treaties with Canada and England but in this time those of little or no consequence.' See copy of cable Borden to W.S. Churchill, First Lord of

elaborating at length on public apprehensions, they generally went out of their way to reassure their readers that Japan could be trusted. Following Grey's announcement that Japan's war role would be confined to East Asia and the Japanese Prime Minister's rather different statement that Japan would not go beyond the limits necessary to protect its interests, the *Sydney Morning Herald* expressed confidence that Japan would act in accordance with the British understanding. Japan's financial weakness argued against any larger policy. Japan would gain enough from the destruction of Germany's Pacific trade without seeking territorial acquisitions in the region. The editorial concluded that at all events Japan would not move out of 'Asiatic waters' without British consent.[30] At the time of Japan's formal declaration of war, the *Herald* was even more positive in its judgment of Japan. It praised Japan's civilised standards, maintained what it had denied in pre-war years, namely that Japan depended for its security on British naval cooperation, and rejected the notion that Japan's decision should be seen 'as the first part of an attack on the Pacific Islands.'[31] The press's harping on the subject was itself an acknowledgement of the extent of Australian misgivings.

Not all newspapers, however, were as diplomatic as the *Sydney Morning Herald*. The *Age* took the Japanese-declared war aims at face value. It did not believe that the British would be able to confine the sphere of Japanese naval operations. Its editorial therefore drew the obvious lesson:

> In view of the intervention of Japan in Chinese waters, the duty of the Australian Commonwealth to plant the British flag on Germany's Pacific Ocean Colonies has acquired a new and sharp significance ... That they will be wrested from Germany is certain. But under what flag will they pass? To the captors belong the prize. Australia should be first well and good, but we cannot afford to take chances in a matter so closely affecting our national interests and the future of the Commonwealth.[32]

The Commonwealth Government shared the *Age*'s alarm and sense of urgency. On 24 August, the day after the Japanese ultimatum expired, it sought confirmation from the British that the agreement 'that Japanese action will not extend to territory except on Continent Eastern Asia will be adhered to.' It stressed to the British that, in the Australian view, 'This is important.'[33] The British Government had already anticipated Australian concern about the German Pacific islands and had approached Japan for clarification of its intentions. On 16 August the British Ambassador

---

the Admiralty, 13 August 1914, Borden Papers, LAC OC 231. Churchill replied soothingly that Japan had long-standing grievances against Germany and that the alliance 'involved her very closely in the war'. He warned against any public criticism of Japan, 'as Japan enters war of her own free choice. She must be welcomed as a comrade and an ally. The naval situation is secure everywhere but entry of Japan will of course make Pacific absolutely safe very soon ... Any declaration against entry of Japan into war would do harm.' See cable, Churchill to Borden, 14 August 1914, *ibid.* and also Department of External Affairs (Canada), *Documents on Canadian External Relations* (Ottawa: Queen's Printer, 1967), I, '1909–1918', 43–44.

[30] *SMH*, 30 August 1914.
[31] *Ibid.*, 24 September 1914.
[32] *Age*, 19 August 1914.
[33] Cable, Munro Ferguson to Harcourt, 24 August 1914, NAA CP78/23 14/89/32; see also Harcourt Papers, Bodleian Library MSS. Harcourt 507.

reported that the Japanese Foreign Minister had told him, 'Japan had no such designs and he hoped that this had been made plain in … the Prime Minister's speech of last night.'[34]

Japan's pre-emptive strike

Grey hoped to nip any ambition of this kind in the bud, and so he informed the Japanese Ambassador in London that 'an expedition from New Zealand is already on its way to Samoa, and another from Australia to take Carolines, German New Guinea and other German possessions in the Pacific.'[35] Harcourt made good use of the Foreign Office material. In trying to set Australian minds at rest he cabled Melbourne that 'we have received private assurances from Japanese Government that they have no intention to seize territory outside China Seas such as German Islands in the Pacific,' and that the British had confidentially told the Japanese that the Australians were preparing an expedition to take the German islands. Harcourt, however, knew that these assurances were not all that they seemed and warned the Australian ministers not to make the message public.[36]

The British Government's uncertainty about Japan's intentions led it, at this very time, to give the Australians more specific instructions for dealing with the German Pacific islands. On 19 August Harcourt suggested to the Australian Government that it should, as soon as the naval situation allowed, occupy Rabaul and then 'at once' send out subsidiary expeditions to take the islands of Nauru, Yap and Angaur and 'as many as possible of the more valuable outlying German Islands.'[37] The Admiralty desired the seizure of Rabaul, Nauru, Yap and Angaur in order 'to break the enemy's line of intelligence' and to deny bases to the German squadron.[38] But the more general program would seem to have had a more general motive. Since the British telegraphed the Australians immediately after the Japanese Prime Minister had refused to accept Grey's restraining statement, it is not unreasonable to see the British action as a precautionary measure aimed at forestalling Japan's expansion into Micronesia.

The Australian Government was very happy for its own reasons to oblige the British. It understood the need for swift action. By 20 August it had a task force ready to depart for New Guinea. It was, however, frustrated by the inability of the Admiralty to provide an adequate naval escort for the expedition. The British naval forces in the Pacific, which included the Australian

---

[34] Cable, Greene to Grey, 10 August 1914, TNA: PRO FO 371/2017/104. A senior member of the Foreign Office thought that this should 'allay apprehension both in the Colonies and the United States.'
[35] Cable, Grey to Greene, 22 August 1914, TNA: PRO FO 371/2017/160.
[36] Cable, Harcourt to Munro Ferguson, 25 August 1914, NAA CP 78/23 14/89/32; copies in Harcourt Papers, Bodleian Library MSS. Harcourt 507.
[37] Cable, Harcourt to Munro Ferguson, 19 August 1914, NAA A981 MARS2 PART3 and 'C.O. Telegrams Circulated to the Cabinet During the War, August 1914', Harcourt Papers, Bodleian Library MSS. Harcourt 507.
[38] Cable, Admiralty to Commonwealth Naval Board Australia, 19 August 1914, TNA: PRO ADM 137/5/42. The Colonial Secretary was also interested in Angaur and Fay Islands in the Pelew (Palau) group because they were reputed to be rich in phosphates. See cable, Harcourt to Munro Ferguson, 18 August 1914, NAA A981 MARS2 PART3.

fleet, were called upon to perform many different functions. They had to search out and destroy the enemy squadron, to convoy the Australian and New Zealand contingents to the Mediterranean, to protect the troops being sent to seize the German Pacific islands, and to patrol trade routes in order to ward off attacks against British and allied commerce. Until the defeat of the German squadron at the Battle of the Falkland Islands in early December, the Admiralty never had sufficient ships at their disposal in the Pacific to accomplish more than one of these objectives at a time. The result was that the Admiralty moved its forces hither and thither as changing events and priorities dictated.[39] And the capture of the German islands was not accorded the highest priority.

Since the Australian ministers and the Naval Board considered the seizure of the German Pacific possessions a matter of great importance they pressed London to provide a convoy for the Australian island force 'as early as possible'.[40] But having committed the battle cruiser *Australia* – the only British Empire war vessel in the Pacific capable of handling the German armoured cruisers *Scharnhorst* and *Gneisenau* – to protecting the New Zealand expedition to Samoa, the Admiralty was not able to allow the *Australia* to return to help the Australians until 9 September. Four days later Colonel W. Holmes, commander of the expeditionary force, raised the British flag at Rabaul in the Bismarck Archipelago. In accordance with the Attorney-General's instruction he insisted that the German Governor should, in his capitulation, include 'the whole of the German Possessions in the Pacific Ocean lately administered from Rabaul.'[41] The German administrator in Rabaul had responsibility for all German Pacific island territories and so through the instrument of capitulation Australia acquired a legal claim to them. The Chief of the General Staff, Colonel J. G. Legge, had warned Holmes 'that Japan is desirous of immediately seizing all German possessions in the Pacific' and urged him to occupy all German territory as quickly as possible.[42]

Yet, despite the Australians' rapid mobilisation, they were not able to make their claim good. British naval weakness was their undoing. Not only did the British authorities lack a naval force that could be sent to pre-empt Japan's expansion into the North Pacific but they were also forced to seek Japan's assistance to maintain the Allies' naval supremacy in European waters. At the end of August, the Admiralty discovered that it lacked the naval strength required to establish simultaneously a clear margin of supremacy over Germany and its Allies in the North Sea, the

---

[39] On 13 August, after unsuccessfully sending the battle-cruiser *Australia* to seek out and destroy the German wireless telegraphy station at Rabaul, the Admiralty ordered Commander George Patey to divide the Australian forces, using *Australia* to escort a New Zealand expedition to Samoa and the light cruisers *Sydney* and *Melbourne* to convoy the Australian forces to New Guinea and the other German islands. The Commonwealth authorities considered that the light cruisers did not offer acceptable cover since they were no match for the German armoured cruisers *Scharnhorst* and *Gneisenau*, and so the despatch of the Australian island force was delayed until the *Australia* returned from Samoa. See cable, Admiralty to Commonwealth Naval Board Australia, 13 August 1914, TNA: PRO ADM 137/5/25.
[40] Cable, Munro Ferguson to Harcourt, 25 August 1914, CID 133, Harcourt Papers, 508; cable, Commonwealth Naval Board Australia to Admiralty, 25 August 1914, TNA: PRO ADM 137/5/72.
[41] Cable, Munro Ferguson to Harcourt, 29 October 1914, UK, Cd. 7979.
[42] Instructions to Colonel Holmes, Commanding Australian Naval and Military Expedition, n.d., Holmes and Travers Papers, ML MSS15/4.

Atlantic, the Mediterranean and the Pacific. It feared a cross-channel invasion and, at a time when Turkey seemed poised to enter the war on Germany's side, the Admiralty had to move cruisers from the Mediterranean to the North Sea.[43] As a result, on 2 September Grey, on behalf of the Admiralty, asked the Japanese Government whether they would 'send a division of the Japanese Navy to cooperate with the British and French fleets primarily in the Mediterranean, and ultimately in the decisive theatre of the naval war.'[44]

Though the Japanese would not send their naval forces so far afield, they used the invitation as a pretext to expand into the Pacific. Thus they agreed to assume larger responsibilities in the Pacific and to send a cruiser squadron into the 'South Seas' to try to locate the German warships and to destroy the German bases in the North Pacific islands. On 10 September the Australian Government was advised that it was 'very likely that Japanese ships and destroyers may cruise in Pacific around Marianne and Caroline islands in order to hunt down the German squadron.'[45]

In the following two weeks Vice-Admiral George Patey, in command of the *Australia* which was helping the Commonwealth's troops to take control of German New Guinea, endeavoured to contact the Japanese squadrons in order to plan a joint sweep through the North Pacific islands.[46] Patey realised that Australian and Japanese roles in the Pacific would have to be rationalised and he asked the Admiralty whether 'after present search northward ... I should personally quit Simpsonhafen [Rabaul] and work further southward, leaving Japan to the northward.'[47] Failing to receive any satisfactory response from the Japanese, Patey, on 1 October, set out on his own initiative to investigate the northern archipelagos.[48] But almost immediately he was halted by news that the *Scharnhorst* and *Gneisenau* had visited Tahiti and appeared to be headed for the South American coast. With this intelligence, Patey returned to New Guinea whence he was directed to Suva to combine with the Japanese first squadron for the purpose of closing the net around the German cruisers.

Meanwhile the Japanese second southern squadron was visiting the German North Pacific islands, beginning on 27 September with that most remote from Japan, Jaluit, in the southern extremity of the Marshalls. They occupied Yap, the important cable centre in the Pelews on 7 October, and within a week all the island groups – the Marshalls, the Pelews, the Carolines and

---

[43] Corbett, *History of the Great War: Naval Operations*, (London: Longmans, Green, 1920), 1, 'To the Battle of the Falklands, December 1914', p.91.

[44] Cable, Grey to Greene, 2 September 1914, Confidential Print for Cabinet, Bodleian Library MSS. Harcourt 582.
See for British discussion of Japanese assistance, including military assistance, cabinet letter, Asquith to King George V, 2 September 1914, Bodleian Library MSS. Asquith 7.

[45] Copy of cable, Harcourt to Munro Ferguson, 10 September 1914, NAA A981 MARS2 PART3 and TNA: PRO ADM 137/5/45. It may well be that it was this telegram which alerted Legge to the possibility that Japan would seize the North Pacific islands.

[46] Cable, Patey to Admiralty, 27 September 1914, TNA: PRO ADM 137/5/134.

[47] Cable, Patey to Admiralty, 29 September 1914, *ibid*.

[48] 'Most necessary that I should be informed of proceeding of Japanese First Detached Squadron. Although I have been in wireless communication, I can get no reply from Japanese Vice-Admiral. My future movements depend considerably on being informed of what he has done and what he intends to do.' Cable, Patey to Admiralty, 1 October 1914, TNA: PRO ADM 137/16/23.

the Marianas – were in their hands. The British authorities were taken by surprise. Without their quite knowing it, strands of policy had become intertwined in unexpected ways. They were caught in the web of their own weakness and found themselves left with a Japanese *fait accompli*. The British Foreign Office, Colonial Office and Admiralty along with the Australian Government were helpless before Japan's nine points of the law and had little choice in the end but to concede the formal tenth.

The Admiralty was first alerted to the territorial consequences of inviting the Japanese fleet to play a substantial part in the Pacific when Japan asked their view on a proposal to connect the Shanghai-Yap cable to Formosa. The Admiralty officials were clearly aware of what this portended. Commander W. T. Kettlewell minuted that Japan would establish itself in Yap 'at our expense'. It was 'a moral certainty' that the island would become 'a Japanese possession since Australia was not yet in occupation.' He recommended that Australian or other British forces should be sent to the island 'at once'. His immediate superior agreed and suggested that the Japanese be told Britain intended to occupy the island 'shortly'. The First Sea Lord, Prince Louis of Battenberg, approved but recognised that the business would 'require delicate handling to avoid showing any suspicion against our Allies the Japanese who are very materially helping us out of a tight corner.' Winston Churchill, the First Lord of the Admiralty, gave his assent and appropriate telegrams were drafted for the Australian Station, the Commonwealth Government and the Japanese Government.[49]

When on 10 October the Japanese informed London that their naval forces had three days earlier landed marines on Yap, the British were compelled to rethink their attitude to Japan in the North Pacific islands. The Japanese pressed for a clarification of British policy. They maintained that Yap because of its strategic importance should be permanently occupied. They wished therefore to know 'whether Australia proposed to take Yap … and station a guard there, in which case Japanese Squadron will be instructed to hand over the place.' If not, the Japanese would remain.[50] The Admiralty would have preferred not to acquiesce in the Japanese occupation. But 'the tight corner' was pinching and what was preferable had to wait upon what was practical.

Almost at the same time as the British were proposing to encourage the Australians to head off the Japanese, the Admiralty were entering into an arrangement to divide up naval responsibilities in the Pacific in such a way as to leave their Asian ally in control of the North Pacific. Under the arrangement the Japanese second squadron was to patrol north of latitude 20° South and west of 140° East longitude, the Japanese first squadron north of the equator and east of 140° east longitude, and the Australian squadron in the south-west Pacific.[51] And the Japanese promptly accepted this demarcation of duties.[52] The proposal was peculiarly ill-timed and ill-advised. Neither the Foreign Office nor the Colonial Office was consulted. The Australian

---

[49] Cable, Greene to Grey, 5 October 1914, TNA: PRO FO 371/2017/381; Kettlewell, Minute, 6 October 1914, TNA: PRO ADM 137/16/71–73 and 137/45/100.

[50] Cable, Greene to Grey, 10 October 1914, TNA: PRO FO 317/2017/436; TNA: PRO ADM 137/45/400.

[51] Copy of cable, Admiralty to Commander-in-Chief, China Station and Naval Board Melbourne, 9 October 1914, *ibid.*, 137/16/127.

[52] Cable, Admiralty to Commander-in-Chief China Station and Naval Board Melbourne, 12 October 1914, *ibid.*, 137/16/165.

Government had no inkling of what was being planned. The negotiations had been conducted through the Japanese naval attaché at the London Embassy. It illustrates well the pressures under which the Admiralty had to operate.

Faced with the Japanese occupation of Yap, the Admiralty felt obliged to set aside short-term diplomatic considerations and longer-term strategical ones in favour of immediate naval imperatives. The First Sea Lord, looking for an excuse to evade the consequences of the Admiralty's own incompetence, argued that the Japanese by their offer to withdraw had shown 'a true gentlemanly attitude and we ought to reciprocate in the same sense. As they are in occupation we ought to leave them there.' Churchill agreed. 'We must,' he said, 'treat the Japanese in the fullest confidence of Allies.' Having asked the Japanese to take part in the Pacific naval operations and bearing in mind the need to ask for further aid, they reconciled themselves to the inevitable. They scrapped the draft telegrams which they had intended for the Australian and Japanese Governments, and instead advised the Foreign Office and Colonial Office that 'in view of the occupation of the island of Yap by the Japanese, it is no longer proposed that an Australian force should proceed to Yap, and it is requested that the Japanese Government may be asked to arrange for the continued occupation of Yap by their Forces.'[53]

Grey, encouraged by Harcourt, refused to comply with the Admiralty's wishes and, acting on the basis of the earlier arrangement, the Foreign Secretary told the Japanese that it was 'still the intention of the Australians to occupy Yap as soon as possible.' He said that the British would let Tokyo know 'as soon as possible the date on which they are likely to do so.'[54] Grey and Harcourt explained to the Admiralty that it was desirable 'for political reasons that the Islands should be taken over by the Commonwealth Government from the Japanese force … at present occupying it.' They asked for a convoy to enable the Australian force to carry out its task.[55] Simultaneously Harcourt cabled Melbourne that the Japanese were ready to hand the island over to an Australian force and he stressed the urgent need for action.

> On account of strategical importance island must be occupied by some force. Your ministers will remember that it was originally intended that they should send force to occupy Yap and they will no doubt agree that it is desirable to relieve Japanese as quickly as possible of the task of holding the island.[56]

The Admiralty initially refused to cooperate. They claimed that there were no Australian cruisers available to convoy such an expedition as they were engaged in tracking down the *Scharnhorst* and the *Gneisenau*. Even when the German ships had been destroyed the naval officials had no wish to intervene in an area that had been allotted to the Japanese second southern squadron. The Chief of the Naval Staff, Admiral D. Sturdee, would 'let Australia raise the question which the

---

[53] Copy of letter, Secretary, Admiralty to Under-Secretaries of State, Foreign Office and Colonial Office, 11 October 1914, *ibid.*, 137/45/400–01.

[54] Copy of cable, Grey to Greene, 12 October 1914, TNA: PRO FO 371/2017/444–47; see also TNA: PRO ADM 137/45/404–06.

[55] Letter, Under-Secretary of State, Colonial Office to Secretary, Admiralty, 13 October 1914, *ibid.*, 137/45/430.

[56] Cable, Harcourt to Munro Ferguson, 13 October 1914, NAA CP78/23 89/68.

Admiralty are not in accord with.' Since 'the Admiralty are not in favour of the policy,' he thought they should hang fire. There was 'no real necessity … for sending an Australian force so far afield to oust the Allied forces who have been operating in their proper sphere.'[57] Churchill agreed with his officials and wrote Harcourt:

> We have no cruiser available for Yap at the present time and much inconvenience would be caused by changing existing arrangements. There appears to be no military reason which requires us to eject the Japanese at this juncture. I do not gather that the Australasian Governments are pressing us to act. On the contrary it would seem that you were pressing them. The Admiralty would strongly deprecate any action towards Japan which would appear suspicious or ungracious. We are deriving the greatest benefit from their powerful and generous aid. They have intimated that their occupation is primarily military and devoid of political significance and there I trust we may leave the matter for the present.[58]

Not for the first time nor for the last, Churchill was inventing a Pacific Dominion opinion to suit himself. The Australian Government did not need the Colonial Secretary's prodding to stir its interest in the German Pacific islands. It had been committed from the very outset to occupying all island groups north and south of the equator. In its direction to Holmes it had stipulated that the German Governor at Rabaul should surrender all German Pacific possessions to Australia. It was the Admiralty, chopping and changing naval policy in the light of the exigencies of the moment, which had prevented the Australians from accomplishing their objective.

The Labor Government, coming to office while all these crosscurrents were muddying the waters, did have some difficulty in mastering the Pacific problem. But their advisers in the Defence and External Affairs departments followed the developments very closely. When the former External Affairs Minister, Glynn, responding to newspaper reports, hoped that 'the occupation by the Japanese of Yap and Jaluit is not a surprise,' the permanent head of External Affairs, Atlee Hunt, stated he had been 'prepared by private instructions from the Defence Department that something of the kind would take place. I think we may rely on the Japanese good faith when they undertook to hand over the islands to us.'[59] Certainly Pearce seemed to expect that Australia at the end of the war would have responsibility for all the islands north and south of the Equator, telling Parliament that 'in the future … if the war turns out as we all hope it will, our sphere of influence will be widened by the fact that what were German possessions are possessions under the British flag and with consent of Allies may … remain under that flag.'[60]

On 17 October the Commonwealth Naval Board expressed enthusiasm for the Colonial Office proposal. They 'fully appreciated the importance of occupying Yap', and they announced their intention to fit out a small expedition 'to proceed to Pelew Islands, the Marshall Islands, the Caroline islands, and the Mariana Islands as soon as the situation permitted'. They reminded the

---

[57] Minute on Colonial Office letter of 13 October 1914, Sturdee to Churchill, 16 October 1914, *ibid.*, 137/45/433–35; Churchill commented 'I agree cordially.' 17 October 1914.
[58] Letter, Churchill to Harcourt, 18 October 1914, Harcourt Papers, Bodleian Library MSS. Harcourt 462.
[59] Letter, Glynn to Hunt, 10 October 1914 and Hunt to Glynn, 12 October 1914, Hunt Papers, NLA MS 52/1439 and 1438.
[60] *CPD*, 1914–17 session, LXXV, 104, 14 October 1914.

British that the Germans had already formally handed over legal control of these islands to Australia. The expedition in their view was not merely to occupy Yap but to take possession of all the island groups. 'On account of great distances to be covered,' they argued, 'arrangements should be made for such a cruise in preference to arranging for an isolated expedition to take possession of a single island.' The invitation to take Yap was to be the launching pad for completing the original grand sweep; 'These islands closely effect [sic] the whole question of the Naval Defence of Australia in the future. They are of great strategic importance.'[61]

By the end of October the Australian Government had become aware that there was something amiss in their plans for occupying the North Pacific islands and on 26 October the cabinet for the first time considered the 'Control of Pacific'.[62] The results of the meeting were not recorded but on the same day the Commonwealth replied to the Colonial Office that, 're Yap, a force consisting of 200 is being organised to garrison the principal islands. Particulars will be cabled later as to convoy dates &c.'[63]

While the Australians were raising their forces and collecting their convoy, the Pacific island trading company Burns Philp added its voice to those seeking an expansionist policy in the region. Colonel James Burns, its managing director, submitted a plan for acquisition of the great majority of the German Pacific islands and the development of Australian interests in these islands at the end of the war. It was 'the duty of Australia to maintain her increased share in the responsibilities of the British Empire by claiming the possession as an integral portion of the Commonwealth of the Groups in the Western South Seas now under British Government, and including the recently occupied German territories.' New Zealand would gain the more easterly islands, German Samoa and the Union and Phoenix groups. Britain would retain its control over Fiji and Tonga. France could keep New Caledonia though 'a great effort' should be made to persuade France to relinquish its share of the New Hebrides. Australia should gain German New Guinea, the Bismarck Archipelago, the British Solomons, the Gilbert and Ellice islands, and the Marshall and Caroline groups. Japan, it appeared, might be consoled with the Marianas, the most northerly group of islands.

All Australia's Pacific islands were to be brought under one administration with 'uniform methods of procedure and uniform laws relating to justice ... land tenure, companies, commerce etc.', and a special department of state with its headquarters in Sydney would be created to supervise this colonial empire. Australian tariff protection should be extended to the islands and their trade, which would be open only to Australian owned and registered vessels. By this means Burns foresaw that the islands 'must steadily progress to proportions of great economic value and

---

[61] Cable, Commonwealth Naval Board to Admiralty, 17 October 1914, Harcourt Papers, Bodleian Library MSS. Harcourt 508, 'Operations in British Dominions and Colonies against German Territories, August 1914' and NAA MP1049/1 1914/0455; letter, Commonwealth Naval Board to Pearce, 26 October 1914, NAA B543 W112/4/457.

[62] Cabinet Minutes '26th 1914', – from internal evidence and sequence of minutes it is evident that it should be '26th October', Fisher Papers, NLA MS 2919 add. ms. 21/8/81, box 12.

[63] Cable, Munro Ferguson to Harcourt, 26 October 1914, Harcourt Papers, Bodleian Library MSS. Harcourt 508, 'Operations in British Dominions and Colonies against German Territories, August 1914'.

importance, eventually becoming to the Commonwealth what the Dutch East Indies are to the Netherlands.'

There were also strategic arguments to be taken into account. By gaining control of 'the magnificent harbours' in these islands, Australia would deny an advantage to its enemies and have bases for its own navy. It was a comprehensive, though primarily commercial, vision of empire. The head of the External Affairs Department, to whom Burns had confided his scheme, had some reservations. He thought it unwise to publish the proposal. Burns's letter had come 'most appropriately', Hunt observed, 'because I have been thinking a great deal about this subject and have had frequent discussions with the Minister.' After talking to Hugh Mahon, the Acting Minister, he could assure Burns that 'We do not want any spurs to urge us on to take action and shall make it our aim to get control of everything we can.'[64]

'The materials for a tragic row'

The Commonwealth's interest in the Pacific and its anxiety about Japan had a long history. Neither British prodding nor commercial pressure were required to move Australia to action, and its authorities had it in mind not merely to take Yap but to gain control of all the German islands in the North Pacific. During the first two weeks of November, preparations for despatching the force were accelerated, and on 14 November the government instructed Colonel S. A. Pethebridge, the leader of the expedition, to visit the North Pacific islands 'recently held by Germany and place Australian troops in occupation.'[65]

Three days later the Colonial Office was informed that a garrison force of 200 troops and about 15 wireless telegraphists would leave Sydney on 26 November 'to relieve the Japanese troops now occupying Yap and the other islands north of Equator.'[66] The Australians had arranged their own transport and escort. The steamer *Easton* was converted to a troop carrier, and the captured merchant ship *Komet*, renamed the *Una*, became the escort. After Australian intentions had been made clear the Admiralty relented and detached the light-cruiser *Pioneer* from the Indian Ocean to join the Australian Pacific island force.[67] To tidy up the situation in the South Pacific and to

---

[64] Copies of letter, Burns to Hunt, 5 November 1914 and letter Hunt to Burns, 10 November 1914, Novar Papers, NLA MS 696/6642–54.

[65] Instructions to Col. S.A. Pethebridge, 14 November 1914, NAA MP 729/5 112/6/45.

See also for the Minute, Pearce to Secretary of the Defence Department on 'Occupation of Islands North of the Equator', 14 November 1914, setting out the government's instructions which were approved by Fisher and incorporated in Holmes's Commission, NAA A981 MARS2 PART3.

The Naval Board ordered Lieutenant Commander H.N.M. Hardy who was to accompany the expedition 'to obtain information which will be of use in considering the defence of Australasia from attack, particularly from the Northward'. See letter, Naval Secretary to Hardy, 20 November 1914, NAA MP 1049/1 1914/0455.

[66] Copy of cable, Munro Ferguson to Harcourt, 17 November 1914, TNA: PRO ADM 137/45/521; see also letter, Secretary, Prime Minister to Secretary, Governor-General, 16 November 1914 asking that the cable be sent, NAA CP 78/23 1914–16/9–10.

[67] Cable, Admiralty to Commonwealth Naval Board, 21 October 1914, Bodleian Library MSS. Harcourt 508.

prevent any further misunderstanding with Japan, Colonel Holmes at Rabaul was simultaneously directed to hoist the flag on Admiralty and Hermit islands, which were close to the Equator, and to post a garrison there.[68] On 21 November the Commonwealth gave London a more detailed outline of the expedition's itinerary; leaving Sydney on 26 November the Australian forces, after landing troops at Bougainville in the North Solomons were to proceed to Yap, Angaur, Saipan, Ponape, Jaluit, Nauru, Rabaul and then the Caroline and Marshall groups, leaving troops on islands 'where necessary'.

For some inexplicable reason, later the same day, the Australian Government cabled the British that the expedition would set out for Rabaul 'without waiting'. They now estimated that their force would reach Yap about 20 December and from there proceed to the other islands.[69] The Australians were acting on the assumption, as conveyed in the British message of 25 August, that the Japanese still had 'no intention to seize territory outside China Seas such as German lands in the Pacific'. They were proposing to make good the title granted them in the articles of the Rabaul surrender. Pearce on 18 November announced that the Japanese had agreed to hand over the North Pacific islands and that an expedition was being sent north of the Equator for that purpose.[70] By publicly setting out Australia's claim he was perhaps attempting to make it difficult for the Japanese to refuse to accede to Australia's wishes. If this were a diplomatic ploy then it was a ploy doomed to fail.

The Japanese, since their occupation of the islands, had given no indication to the British Government that they were willing to hand them over to Australian forces. They had spoken only of giving up Yap. Indeed, under pressure from Japanese public opinion and from the Japanese Navy, Foreign Minister Takaaki Kato had on 12 October hinted to the British Ambassador that a request to vacate the islands would be embarrassing.[71] Japan, by the middle of November, was much more self-confident. By 7 November the last German stronghold in China had fallen and Jiaozhou had been surrendered. On the same day the German Pacific Squadron had defeated a British naval force at Coronel off the Chilean coast and Britain had had to appeal to Japan to send the second southern squadron to join the *Australia* in hunting down the *Scharnhorst* and the *Gneisenau* in the East Pacific. The British had also asked Japan for naval assistance to help bottle up the German and Turkish fleets in the Dardanelles.[72] Aware of its enhanced value to the alliance,

---

[68] Despatch, Munro Ferguson to Harcourt, 16 February 1915, containing report of Colonel W. Holmes to Minister of Defence, 11 December 1914, UK Cd. 7979, 'Correspondence respecting Military Operations against German Possessions in the Western Pacific, November 1914.'

[69] Copy of cable, Munro Ferguson to Harcourt, 21 November 1914, TNA: PRO ADM 137/45/507.

[70] *SMH*, 19 November 1914. Pearce's public announcement caused the Japanese Consul-General to inquire of Pethebridge whether the expedition expected to take possession of the Marshall, Caroline and Ladrones islands, and Pethebridge warned Pearce that when he responded positively the Consul-General indicated that there might be a misunderstanding about Japan's willingness to surrender these territories. See minute (secret), Pethebridge to Pearce, 24 November 1914, NAA MP1049/1 1914/0455.

[71] Nish, *Alliance in Decline,* pp.143–44.

[72] Cable, Grey to Greene, 14 November 1914, TNA: PRO FO 800/67.

The Japanese agreed to the Pacific request but refused the Mediterranean which was thought to be too distant. See cables, Greene to Grey, 25 November and 1 December 1914, *ibid.*

Japan wished to see tangible rewards for its service. The Japanese reaction to a Commonwealth Naval Board inquiry about the state of wireless telegraphy equipment at Yap and Angaur brought the British up short. Greene reported to Grey that Japan had only consented to hand over Yap and that it intended 'to retain Angaur island'.[73]

The British Government was faced with a dilemma. Here, as Grey commented, were 'the materials for a tragic row'. It was so important that the cabinet had to deal with it straightaway. 'Meanwhile,' he wrote Harcourt, 'the Australians must hold their hand somehow till we have come to an understanding with the Japanese.'[74] Accordingly on 24 November the Australians were told that it was 'desirable that the expedition to occupy German islands should not proceed to any Island North of the Equator at present'.[75] The Australians were puzzled and not a little irritated by the belated British switch in plans. They replied that the Australian troops were already embarked. They reasserted the legal position that all the German Pacific islands came under the administration of German New Guinea and were ceded by the Governor to Australia. They sought 'early and definite information about what was now desired'. In the meantime the expedition would not sail.[76]

During the following days the Japanese made their intentions unmistakably clear. On 24 November they agreed to detach their squadron to join in the chase off the coast of South America, but they would not give an inch on the islands question.[77] They refuted Pearce's legal argument. In response to a report from their Consul-General in Melbourne that the Australian 'marines' – in fact the Secretary of the Defence Department, S. A. Pethebridge – had told him the German North Pacific islands had been surrendered to the Commonwealth, Kato answered that they had been given up to the Japanese navy. The British Ambassador in Tokyo gained the impression, as early as 25 November, that 'what Japan wants and will claim after the war is the German Pacific islands lying north of the Equator excepting Yap.'[78] In London the Japanese Ambassador pursued the same line. He took issue with Pearce's published statement and said that, 'it was only the island of Yap which Japan was prepared to hand over.' Japan would continue in its

---

[73] Cable, Greene to Grey, 21 November 1914, TNA: PRO FO 371/2018/218; see also ADM 137/45/521.
[74] Letter, Grey to Harcourt, 23 November 1914, TNA: PRO FO 800/91.

Beilby Alston of the Far Eastern section of the Foreign Office commented on 23 November that Japan's retention of Angaur was 'more than likely to raise apprehension in Australia' but he thought that it might be 'necessary / desirable?' to let them keep it, since 'the Japanese evidently intend to retain it.' See TNA: PRO FO 371/2018/279.

[75] Cable, Harcourt to Munro Ferguson, 24 November 1914, NAA CP78/23 1914–16/9–10 and NAA A981 MARS2 PART3.

In a telegram of the previous day Harcourt had merely asked the Australians to leave Angaur to the Japanese for 'it would be discourteous and disadvantageous to the Japanese if we turned them out of Angaur when they are helping us in every way with their Fleet throughout Pacific and in convoying Australian contingents.' See telegram, Harcourt to Munro Ferguson, 23 November 1914, NAA CP78/23 89/68.

[76] Cable, Munro Ferguson to Harcourt, 25 November 1914, Harcourt Papers, Bodleian Library MSS. Harcourt 508, 'Operations in British Dominions' and TNA: PRO ADM 137/45/560.
[77] Letter, Japanese Naval Attaché to Secretary, Admiralty, 24 November 1914, *ibid.*, 137/16/661.
[78] Copy of cable, Greene to Grey, 25 November 1914, *ibid.*, 137/45/530.

occupation of all the other islands. The Japanese Government feared that 'this misunderstanding might give rise to unpleasant consequences and wanted the attention of the Australian Government drawn to the matter.'

Grey had to admit that circumstances had changed since 19 August when it was assumed that Australia would take over the North as well as the South Pacific islands. Since then, 'the cooperation ... between Japanese and British navies has led by common agreement and desire to the occupation of various points for strategic purposes and we recognise that only strategic consideration should count.' Grey recognised that he had to embark on a strategic retreat. The best he could hope for was to lock the Japanese into the same long-term conditions that the British had imposed on the Dominions, namely that the occupation of German territory during the war was 'without prejudice to the permanent arrangement that will have to be made after the war.'[79]

On 1 December the denouement came. The Japanese, replying to a probing inquiry from Grey, affirmed that they were in control of all the island groups in the North Pacific. They expressed the wish that the Australian expedition should not visit any of the islands apart from Yap, which 'in view of a previous understanding' they would, if the British desired it, relinquish. In a 'Confidential Memorandum' and 'Note Verbale' they spelled out their attitude to the final disposition of the islands. The wording is so disingenuously final that it needs to be fully quoted:

> ... Minister for Foreign Affairs agrees that all occupation of territory belonging to Germany by Japanese and British forces will be without prejudice to final arrangement which will have to be made when the Allies come to settle terms of reference after the conclusion of the war.
>
> Minister for Foreign Affairs begs to add that, having regard to the very wide operation in which Imperial navy is and has been engaged in cooperation with the British navy, the nation would naturally insist on retaining permanently all the German islands lying north of equator, and the Imperial Government will rely on support of His Majesty's Government when the proper time arrives for fulfilment of the above object.[80]

---

[79] Cable, Grey to Greene, 26 November 1914, TNA: PRO FO 371/2018/134.

Harcourt was very unhappy with the intimation that Japan would remain in control of all North Pacific Islands save Yap. In recognising the meaning of such a concession, he wrote Grey that it was 'unthinkable as a final settlement'. Perhaps influenced by commercial interests, he was particularly irate to think that the profitable phosphate deposit on Angaur – 'the finest phosphate deposit in the world' – would go to Japan. 'It will,' he added, 'be disastrous if the Australian expedition declines to start.' See letter, Harcourt to Grey, 26 November 1914, TNA: PRO FO 371/2018/348.

[80] Greene to Grey, 1 December 1914, TNA: PRO FO 371/2018/381-2.

The Japanese were not intimidated by a US Senate resolution which opposed any Japanese attempt to take permanent possession of German leased territory in China or of the German Pacific islands. See *SMH*, 16 October 1914.

For an account of how the Japanese Navy Department and the Japanese officers in charge of closing down German telegraph stations in the North Pacific islands defied the government's wishes on the matter, occupied the islands and so presented Tokyo with a *fait accompli*, see Schencking in O'Brien, *Anglo-Japanese Alliance*, pp.131–4.

The second paragraph contradicted the first. The first was a diplomatic gesture to British feeling, the second went to the heart of the matter.

Grey complained to the Japanese that not only was their memorandum internally inconsistent but the second paragraph was also at odds with Kato's assurance of 19 August. He acknowledged that Japanese services had been more extensive and might become 'more extensive still' than had been contemplated at the outbreak of the war and that the extent of Japan's contribution to the war effort would have to be taken into account in working out peace terms. Nevertheless Britain had promised France and Russia that it would not commit itself to bilateral peace terms. Grey said that Britain had operated on the understanding that all territory taken by allied forces would be without prejudice to a final settlement and, acting on that assumption, it was requesting Australia to abandon its expedition.[81]

The accumulated events of the previous four months had taken their toll on British diplomacy. Grey had no choice but to capitulate to the Japanese. He lost no time in bringing Australia into line and thus headed off the dangers and difficulties that might have otherwise resulted from allowing the issue to remain unresolved. On the same day that he bowed to Japan's demands he explained to the Australians that as

> Pelew, Mariana, Caroline Islands and Marshall Islands are at present in military occupation by Japanese who are at our request engaged in policing waters Northern Pacific, we consider it most convenient for strategic reasons to allow them to remain in occupation for the present, leaving whole question of future to be settled at the end of the war. We should be glad therefore if the Australian expedition would confine itself to occupation of German Islands South of the Equator.

---

[81] Cable, Grey to Greene, 3 December 1914, TNA: PRO FO 371/2018/390, copy in TNA: PRO ADM 137/45/550.

The Japanese Foreign Minister denied there was a conflict between the position taken in the two paragraphs of the Memorandum. He asserted that on 19 August Japan had merely denied any desire to acquire the North Pacific islands. This had not been their motive for going to war. But as a result of the Japanese navy's extended operations, it was 'as a matter of fact not … possible for the Japanese Government to abandon and hand over islands in question to another power.' He had not sought to bind the British to support Japanese post-war claims but looked to 'rely on British good office when time for the peace settlement arrived'. Sir W. Langley noted in the British Foreign Office that Japan's aspirations would 'suit the US as little as it will suit Australia' but Britain was at that time in such a position that it could 'now only discuss [the question] with the Japanese at a disadvantage'. Grey merely reiterated his 3 December view. See cables, Greene to Grey and Grey to Greene, 16 December 1914, TNA: PRO FO 371/2018/482–84.

Two days later the Commonwealth Government indicated that they would comply with British wishes.[82] The Australians were frustrated but knew that they had no other option. The Japanese had had their way and won the day.

---

[82] Cable, Harcourt to Munro Ferguson, 3 December 1914, NAA CP78/23 89/68; Munro Ferguson to Harcourt, 5 December 1914, Harcourt Papers, Bodleian Library MSS. Harcourt 508 and TNA: PRO ADM 137/45/558–63.

The British decision to abandon Yap is something of a mystery. It might be that Grey was influenced by the second part of Kato's Memorandum of 1 December in which the Japanese had indicated they were 'retaining permanently all the German islands north of the Equator' at the peace settlement.

4
'No Parallel in our History': The Menace of Japan

The North Pacific islands episode, with its unfortunate end, focused the minds of the Australian policy makers more intensely on the Japan question. The British had not revealed Japan's ulterior aim to the Australians, but the Commonwealth Government knew that Japan would use its wartime occupation to seek annexation at the peace table. The problems and perils of the Pacific were drawing closer to Australian shores and the responsible ministers were not willing to surrender the North Pacific islands without putting up some kind of fight. Japan had shown its hand and the ministers and their advisers were determined to do what they could to prepare to meet a possible regional emergency. Pearce, in a recruiting speech at the very moment when Britain had called off Australia's expedition, declared that all who wished to defend the Empire had three options, to volunteer for overseas service, to form a rifle company and keep their eye in or to help in training militia and senior cadets, the men 'who will fight some day perhaps to guard the shores of Australia.'[1]

The Prime Minister, above all others, appreciated clearly the full import of the diplomacy that had allowed the Japanese to gain control of the North Pacific islands. He had been the key figure in each decision made by the Australian Government; only he and Pearce were privy to the full story. Fisher was exhorted from many quarters to keep his powder dry. In early October Robert Anderson, a friend and fellow Scottish Australian, had sent Fisher a warning note from London about 'the intrusion of Japan into this trouble'. Anderson wrote:

> I have reason for thinking that the British Government did all they could to dissuade them [the Japanese] from taking this step but the opportunity was too good to be lost. An incident of this kind brings out in bold relief the differences that now exist, and as time goes on, will be even more marked between the Mother Country and Australia. If you have not done so, I earnestly recommend you to most carefully peruse the style and wording of Japan's ultimatum to Germany and of her proclamation of war. Australia, after most careful deliberation, has placed its feet in the direction of White Australia at all costs, and let us never forget exactly what this means ... The Japs are very sore with Australia and especially with a section of the Press which publishes offensive cartoons about them ... These offensive cartoons are carefully kept for reference purposes in Japan, and if the time comes when she can specially employ,

---

[1] *SMH*, 13 November 1914.

In the Senate, Bakhap renewed his earlier warnings of Japan's threat to Australia: 'Whilst European civilisation is exhausting itself the power of another civilisation is becoming greater, and it does not require any large amount of prescience to foresee that there are many grave problems confronting not only the people of our Empire in general, but the people of the Commonwealth in particular.' Recognising, however, that the question was not suitable for public discussion he promised to submit his views confidentially to the Minister for Defence. *CPD*, 1914–17 session, LXXV, 116, 14 October 1914.

towards us, the insulting terms that she has used in her official despatches to Germany, that opportunity will be seized.[2]

Fisher understood this widespread concern and shared it. From his first administration in 1908 he had been aware of the storm brewing in what he had called Australia's 'Near East'. He had been the chief architect of Australia's pre-war defence policy which was single-mindedly aimed at protecting Australia from Japan. The Pacific developments in the early months of the war were further evidence of all that the Australians had feared. Summing up the meaning of this scarcely veiled confrontation with Japan Fisher concluded that Australia was faced with a crisis which had 'no parallel in our history'.[3]

Appeals for an Imperial Defence Conference and Dominion cooperation in the Pacific

Following the 1909 Imperial Defence Conference's decision to establish a Pacific fleet with contributions from the Pacific Dominions and the Mother Country, Australian leaders, including Fisher and Cook, had seen in this initiative their best hope for averting the 'Australian crisis'.[4] But Britain had reneged on its part of the arrangement and the fleet had failed to materialise. Only Australia had fulfilled its obligations and built its squadron. In the first months of the war the Empire's naval weakness in the Pacific was plain for all to see. The Admiralty's inability to deal quickly and effectively with the German Pacific squadron had delayed the despatch of the AIF and allowed the Japanese to occupy the North Pacific islands. Fisher believed that a Pacific fleet would be the only sure barrier against an expansionist Japan. Reflecting on these problems he told parliament on 11 November that 'the strength and unity of the British Empire will be increased by a wider distribution of armed forces on the sea, with greatest autonomy.' He trusted that 'the time is not far distant when the other parts of the Empire will see fit to fall into line with the Commonwealth in the matter of naval defence.'[5]

On the very day that the British Government had closed the door on Australia's North Pacific ambitions, Fisher spoke out again, linking Australia's pre-war policy with its post-war needs. In addressing the defence budget on 3 December he stated that:

> Experience during the war supports evidence gathered in time of peace that modern efficient sea defence in the South Pacific is essential for the safety and general welfare of His Majesty's Dominions ... It is the hope of the Government that the day is not far distant when the sister Dominion of New Zealand, whilst maintaining its identity unimpaired ... will be more closely

---

[2] Letter, Robert Anderson to Fisher, 27 August 1914, Fisher Papers, NLA MS 2919 add. ms 21/8/81, box 2.
[3] Copy of letter, Fisher to T.J. Ryan, Premier of Queensland, 12 June 1915, Fisher Papers, NLA MS 2919/3/282.
[4] *Search for Security*, chapters 6–9.
[5] *CPD*, 1914–17 session, LXXV, 468, 11 November 1914.

Munro Ferguson wrote Harcourt that 'There is but one opinion here, viz. that HMA Fleet and the China Squadron also have been singularly ineffective and that due to the remoteness of the Admiralty'. See secret letter, Munro Ferguson to Harcourt, 15 November 1914, TNA: PRO CO 418/123/443.

associated with the Commonwealth of Australia in the creation and maintenance of effective defence in a common sphere of action.

One effect of the war will probably be to bring us new duties and obligations in the Pacific. We can hardly hope that our problems of government will be fewer or less difficult than they have hitherto been, but it is hoped that the Governments of the Dominions will give to each other, without loss of time, opportunity for a full and frank exchange of views upon these matters of the highest national importance.[6]

Fisher had been very disturbed in 1912 when he learnt that the British Government, because of its European commitments, had no intention of carrying out its part of the Pacific fleet agreement. Both Fisher and Cook, who succeeded him as Prime Minister, had pressed for an imperial conference to revisit the question and had expected New Zealand and the other Dominions with an interest in the Indian and Pacific oceans to combine their forces to provide such a fleet.[7] In July 1914 the British Government, after much wrangling between the Colonial Office and the Admiralty, had finally agreed to hold an imperial conference to consider the issue of Pacific naval defence, but, after the outbreak of the European war, they had postponed it indefinitely. Fisher was unhappy with this decision, and he told Harcourt that, 'you will make a mistake if you decide not to hold it next year. War in my view makes the holding of a conference more urgent and valuable.'[8]

When it became clear that the Japanese were going to remain in the German North Pacific islands, Fisher urged the British Government to summon an imperial conference 'for Defence and for Pacific Administration as well as Imperial Policy'. An ordinary Imperial Conference was due in 1915 and the special Pacific conference could be combined with it. Japan's new position as Britain's co-belligerent and the dominant power in the Western Pacific was beginning to affect Australia directly. As Munro Ferguson informed Harcourt: 'Japanese Consul made courteous enquiry as to status of Japanese. This and abandonment of expedition north of the Equator excites more attention than surprise. P.M. advocates holding Imperial Conference next year preferably before close of war.'[9] The Australians were not surprised by Japan's actions – they had long anticipated something of the kind – but they were apprehensive. Japanese control of the North Pacific islands brought their frontier that much closer to Australian shores. The Commonwealth Government wanted a conference as soon as possible so that Pacific naval defence could be attended to and Pacific peace terms discussed. Fisher intended that Australia should have an effective say in the new Pacific map and the new Pacific relations that would come out of the war.

The British, understanding well Australia's objective, opposed the holding of a conference in 1915. They knew that the Admiralty was unable to allocate more naval resources to the Pacific.

---

[6] *CPD*, 1914–17 session, LXXV, 1342, 3 December 1914.
[7] *Search for Security*, pp.239–41.
[8] Letter, Fisher to Harcourt, 18 November 1914, Harcourt Papers, Bodleian Library MSS. Harcourt 463/60.
[9] Personal letter, Munro Ferguson to Harcourt, 10 December 1914, Harcourt Papers, Bodleian Library MSS. Harcourt 479 and Novar Papers, NLA MS 696/637; cable, personal and secret, Munro Ferguson to Harcourt, 11 December 1914, Harcourt Papers, Bodleian Library MSS. Harcourt 479.

They were concerned that Australian demands for the North Pacific islands might damage relations with Japan and make that country more intransigent over China and less willing to help in Europe. Harcourt explained Britain's embarrassment in a 'Private & Personal' and 'Very Secret' letter to Munro Ferguson which was 'for your eye only, and under no circumstances is to be seen by anyone else'. In the letter Harcourt explained again that London had given Australia the original assurance about the North Pacific islands when it was believed that the Japanese would limit their activities to capturing the German territory of Jiaozhou in China. The letter continued:

> But later on it was found necessary by us to ask them to extend their activities. Our fleets were so fully engaged in the North Sea, Atlantic, Mediterranean, in convoying of troops across the Indian Ocean that we could not spare enough to deal with the Pacific. We had therefore to call in Japanese aid to assist in the convoy of the Australian forces to Ceylon, and to undertake (especially after our disaster on the coast of Chile) the hunt for the Emden, Scharnhorst, Gneisenau, Dresden, etc … It has even been in contemplation (and still is) that the Japanese fleet may in the future be employed in the European theatre of war.
>
> All this has changed the character of the Japanese participation and no doubt of their eventual claim for compensation.
>
> From information which reaches me, I have very little doubt that it is the intention of the Japanese at the end of the war to claim for themselves all the German Islands north of the Equator …
>
> But it would be impossible at this moment to risk a quarrel with our ally which would be the certain or immediate result of any attempt diplomatically to oust them now from those Islands which they are occupying more or less at the invitation of the Admiralty …[10]

The British could not help Australia. Their position was fixed by the limits of their power and the priorities of their geopolitics. Consequently they were less than frank with Australia about Japan's claims for permanent possession of the occupied islands, and set about manipulating their relationship with Australia, as though it were a minor, dispensable and troublesome ally rather than an intimate and equal partner in a united empire. An imperial conference dealing with the Pacific might be damaging for British interests. At all costs the idea had to be quashed. For the sake of appearances the British Cabinet agreed to seek the opinions of the other Dominions, but Harcourt, with Asquith's approval, worded the telegrams in a way to ensure a negative reply; 'Suggestion made by Australian Government that Imperial Conference should meet next year … but it seems impossible to convene the Conference before conclusion of the war. Please let me know privately whether yr. Ministers concur in this view.' The other Dominion governments dutifully fell into line.[11]

---

[10] Letter, Harcourt to Munro Ferguson, 6 December 1914, Novar Papers, NLA MS 696/1306–09.

[11] Cables, Colonial Secretary to Governors-General and Governors of all Dominions, except Australia, 16 December 1914; cable, Canadian Governor-General to Colonial Secretary, 16 December 1914; cable New Zealand Governor to Colonial Secretary, 17 December 1914; cable, Newfoundland Governor to Colonial Secretary, 17 November 1914; cable, South African Governor-General to Colonial Secretary, 18 November 1914; Confidential Print Circulated to Cabinet, 1 January 1915, Harcourt Papers, Bodleian Library MSS. Harcourt 468.

The assertion that it was 'impossible' to hold a conference before the end of the war was neither argued nor self-evident. Subsequently the British did, in mid-1915, invite the Dominion prime ministers to London, and indeed in 1917 and 1918 held imperial conferences which dealt with all the great questions of war and peace. The Asquith Government opposed Fisher's request because they feared that the airing of the differences between Britain and Australia over the Pacific at an imperial conference might upset the delicate relationship with Japan, and they were not willing to take that risk. Thus it pleased Harcourt to inform Fisher that 'All Dominions consulted re your suggestion to hold Imperial Conference next year irrespective of war. Opinion of all concerned strongly against Conference before conclusion of war.'[12]

Ignorant of how his proposal had been treated, Fisher had no choice but to accept the decision. When the Colonial Secretary, who anticipated having to face a question in the House of Commons, sought to know, in the light of the Dominions' replies, the attitude of the Australian Government, Fisher acquiesced in the inevitable and said that the Commonwealth had 'no wish to press matter further'. As a consolatory gesture Harcourt promised Fisher that it was 'the intention of His Majesty's Government to consult him most fully and, if possible personally, when the time arises to discuss possible terms of peace.'[13]

Though Fisher had said that he would not 'press' for an imperial conference, he remained as convinced as ever that such a meeting was desirable, even essential, and he was not reluctant to make the point. He knew that if Australia were not to be consulted until the end of the hostilities, it might find itself presented with terms for the peace that were already fixed by the military and diplomatic decisions of the war years. When he shared his misgivings with the Governor-General he found little sympathy. Munro Ferguson had no appreciation of Australia's Pacific predicament. To him Fisher's tenacity was tiresome. On Fisher's advocacy of an imperial conference, he observed to Harcourt, that 'he is the kind of person who can't drop an idea once it gets into his head and his mind is well waterproofed – other people's views never reach it.'[14]

Even before receiving the British response, Fisher had decided to visit New Zealand to seek cooperation and support, believing for good reason that the neighbouring Dominion shared Australia's anxiety about Japan and naval defence in the Pacific. Since 1912 the Reform Government of W. F. Massey had identified itself with the Australian view of a Pacific threat and had taken steps to create a naval force which could act in association with the Australian navy. As a result of the two countries' experience in the Pacific in the first months of the war, Massey maintained that New Zealand should do 'a great deal more in regard to Naval defence'.[15] Fisher was heartened by these signs that New Zealand was moving closer to Australia. The Governor-

---

See also note by Lewis Harcourt, 15 December 1914, 'My tel. is the result of a Cabinet decision and the wording was approved by the P.M. and Lord Crewe,' Harcourt Papers, Bodleian Library MSS. Harcourt 503.

[12] Cable, Munro Ferguson to Fisher, 24 December 1914, Fisher Papers, NLA MS 2919/1/3.

[13] Copy of telegram, Harcourt to Munro Ferguson, 21 January 1915, and copy of cable, Fisher to Hughes and Munro Ferguson, 23 January 1915, Fisher Papers, NLA MS 919/1/3; see also TNA: PRO CAB 37/124/2.

[14] Copy of despatch, Munro Ferguson to Harcourt, 11 January 1915, Novar Papers, NLA MS 696/647.

[15] *SMH*, 11 November 1914.

General tried to discourage his Prime Minister. He thought such a meeting might be detrimental to British interests and suggested to Fisher that he had little likelihood of success.[16]

The Australian Prime Minister was not deterred by these cautioning words. Indeed Fisher approached his task with almost evangelical zeal. In response to the Prime Minister's request, Pearce armed him with a battery of arguments in favour of a joint Australian-New Zealand Pacific naval force. They derived directly from the 1912 and 1913 controversies over Pacific naval defence. Pearce first noted that the British navy, even with subsidies, could not 'unless the Naval Balance of Power is considerably altered as a result of the present war, give a guarantee against any raiding cruisers in these waters.' If Canada and New Zealand followed the Australian example and raised their own fleet units, they could train together and act together and, in time of crisis, perhaps act with the British squadron, as a Pacific fleet. The creation of a fleet in this way 'would justify, in time of war, a greater control by these Dominions of the Pacific'. Finally it was contended that 'the probable acquisition of further colonies in the Pacific as a result of the present War, hugely increased Australasian Naval responsibility, and the only way by which these colonies can be effectively held is by Naval strength.'[17] After collaborating closely over a number of years, Pearce and Fisher had formed a common mind on the 'Australian Crisis' and its meaning for Australian defence.

In his 'Progress' through New Zealand Fisher took every opportunity to appeal for naval cooperation and to put the case for an imperial conference. He was, however, inhibited by the

---

[16] Letter, Munro Ferguson to Harcourt, 24 December 1914, Novar Papers, NLA MS 696/638–40; 'The P.M. goes to New Zealand, as he told me some days ago he was likely to do. Fisher will make a "Progress" right through the Islands with the object, no doubt, of forming public opinion in favour of a common Defence System. I suggested to Mr Fisher that in the circumstances of the moment … he would not be able to effect very much, but he expects to achieve a good deal in the way of preparation.'

See also letter, Munro Ferguson to Harcourt, 28 December 1914, Novar Papers, NLA MS 696/641, 'To satisfy Mr Fisher I cabled his suggestion re holding the Imperial Conference in 1915. He urged that the Conference would be even more useful before the end of the war than afterwards and that it would emphasise the unity of the Empire. Knowing the excellence of his motives whatever the value of his judgment, and seeing he was about to visit New Zealand, I said his views would be communicated to you. I have now cabled to him the substance of your message so that he might have the information before meeting his brother P.M. in New Zealand. I have also written to him and I imagine the proposal will now be dropped … Meanwhile he cannot do harm by discussing the co-ordination of Defence in these regions. He is not a particularist in the matter, and can contemplate a wider project for the defence of the Pacific in cooperation with Canada though he is alive to the difficulties of cooperation between communities as divergent as Canada and Australia.' Frequently the tone that the Governor-General adopted in talking of the King's first minister in Australia, at least in the voice that he used for his British correspondents, was reminiscent of that employed by a Scottish laird to his crofter. He would give his man a courteous, if slightly contemptuous, hearing and when he was properly respectful and did not seek too much, might indulge him in his foolishness. But Fisher was more than a match for Munro Ferguson. He had already bested two former Governors-General. The Governor-General was never able either to silence him or to divert him from pursuing any object that he had decided was vital to Australia's interests.

[17] Copy of letter, Pearce to Fisher, 24 December 1914, Pearce Papers, AWM 3DRL 2222/7/84.

requirements of wartime diplomacy from defining in public the nature of the Pacific threat. On landing at Auckland he called for trans-Tasman cooperation in defence. He wanted the two 'sister Dominions' to 'act together amicably to protect their mutual interests, and not to be dependent upon the British taxpayer.'[18] A few days later he affirmed that an imperial conference in 1915 would be more value to the Dominions than any yet held. 'I have not,' he added, 'changed my views as to the necessity of one or more of His Majesty's Ministers in Great Britain paying an official visit to the most distant Dominions.'[19] It was the repetition of a point he had made in 1912 and 1913; the British needed to see the Empire from Melbourne and Wellington as well as from London. In Wellington he took issue with those who opposed an imperial conference:

> I still adhere to the opinion that this time, above all others, is suitable and desirable for holding a conference … All that needs to be accomplished could be gained much more easily now than later on. Things are now so red hot that the right conclusions would be arrived at very readily.[20]

Fisher had planned his campaign well. He had brought with him David Boyd, a Liberal member of the House of Representatives, who was able to demonstrate to the New Zealanders that what Fisher was advocating had bipartisan support and was truly a national policy. Fisher was also the consummate politician. In his public addresses he went out of his way to reassure the New Zealanders that Australia had no designs on their independence and no desire to weaken the imperial connection.

When Fisher returned after a month labouring in the New Zealand vineyard he had little to show for his efforts. At his first meeting with the New Zealand Prime Minister on 31 December he had presented Massey with a copy of Pearce's argument for a South Pacific navy and he subsequently put Australia's position to the Defence Minister, Colonel James Allen. As he reported it to Pearce, he had explained to the New Zealanders that Australia had a naval policy which was 'likely to be permanent as regards sea-defence', that Australia would be happy to be associated with New Zealand 'as closely as found practicable in a common defence of both Dominions on sea and land', and that the same principles could be applied to Canada and South Africa 'should they desire to come in at any time'. Massey expressed sympathy and was 'quite sincere in his desire for a very full cooperation with Australia in naval matters', but the government, faced with opposition from Sir Joseph Ward's Liberal Party, would not commit itself to anything concrete.[21] The outcome was disappointing. Massey, while believing that the war had made 'many thousands of converts' to his policy of a local navy, was unable to agree to anything more than the desirability of having annual meetings of the Australian and New Zealand leaders.[22] Back in Melbourne

---

[18] *SMH*, 29 December 1914.

[19] *Ibid.*, 2 January 1915.

[20] *Ibid.*, 13 January 1915.

[21] Letter, Fisher to Pearce, 15 January 1915, Pearce Papers, AWM 3DRL 2222/7/8; letter, Fisher to Munro Ferguson, 10 January 1915, Novar Papers, NLA MS 696/3856; and also despatch, New Zealand Governor to Harcourt, 4 January 1915, TNA: PRO CO 209/283.

[22] 'Notes on Conversation with Mr Massey, Auckland, 31 December 1914', Fisher Papers, NLA MS 2919/2/6.

Fisher announced that New Zealand naval officers would train alongside their Australian counterparts at Jervis Bay in the same way that their military officers were being trained at Duntroon.[23]

Responding to Japan's occupation of the German North Pacific islands

While Fisher was in New Zealand, the national security community in Melbourne, the military and naval authorities and the External Affairs Department, were considering how to respond to Japan's occupation of the North Pacific islands. The Army until the end of the war took a practical view of Japan's position in the former German territories. Colonel W. Holmes, commander of the Australian forces at Rabaul, in a letter to the Chief of the General Staff summed up this view quite well.

> The turn which events have now taken is no doubt to be regretted as it would seem that the Japanese who are well known to have longing eyes for some time on the Islands in the Pacific, now being in Military occupation … are hardly likely at the conclusion of the War to be dispossessed of same, as it is only reasonable to suppose that they will regard their retention as recompense for the services they have rendered.[24]

Legge and his successors as Chief of the General Staff were not inclined, at least until victory was in sight, to press Australia's legal and political claims to the North Pacific islands. They had originally been anxious to acquire the islands but accepted that Japan's occupation determined the question. Nevertheless they recognised that Japan's southward thrust to the equator had brought it into direct contact with Australia's sphere of interest. On the very day that the British had requested Australia not to send its expedition into the North Pacific, Legge showed that he was aware of what it signified. He told Holmes that 'The end of the war is not in sight yet, and the settlement may mean another war with parties re-divided – how? So we must push on Australia's preparation.'[25]

Legge's proposal of 5 January 1915 to bring the full military structure for home defence into being a year ahead of the original plan was, like Fisher's decision to increase appropriations for local military defence, a direct outcome of Japan's new position in the Pacific. Legge maintained that, 'to provide adequately for local safety, it would be necessary to deal promptly with attempt at invasion'. Continuing, he asserted that it was 'urgently necessary therefore that, notwithstanding the present war, a higher organisation should be created at once in order to render such action possible.' The Minister for Defence and the other members of the Military Board agreed in principle but were compelled because of the shortage of officers to postpone the plan for a year.

The navy, in contrast to the army, was quite unwilling to accept the Japanese *fait accompli* in the North Pacific. In Japanese hands, these islands might become naval bases from which attacks

---

[23] *SMH*, 5 February 1915.
[24] Extract from despatch, Holmes to Legge, 11 December 1914, cited in letter, Munro Ferguson to Harcourt, 24 February 1915, Novar Papers, NLA MS 696/665–66.
[25] Letter, Legge to Holmes, 25 November 1914, Holmes and Travers Papers, ML MSS 15/2.

could be launched against Australia. They wanted the Australian Government to document its claims and keep the British mindful of them. Rear-Admiral W. R. Creswell, the First Naval Member, with the approval of the other members of the Naval Board, recommended to Pearce that:

> it was important that our position in regard to the Marshall, Caroline and Mariana and Pelew groups of Islands be clearly stated, and recorded … in order to place it on record that these islands are only in temporary occupation. It is necessary that the facts should be stated so that Australia's claims in any final arrangement for their disposal may be fully taken into account.[26]

The External Affairs Department formed its view in part from disquieting intelligence from the Pacific frontier. Colonel James Burns had forwarded to External Affairs a report by F. Wallin, Manager of Burns Philp's Islands Department, who had visited the Marshall Islands during the latter part of November and early December in the normal course of trading. Since the German warships had been driven from the Pacific, Wallin could not see why it was necessary for Japan to maintain a military force on Jaluit or 'to make it into a naval base'. In a paragraph which Hunt had underscored, Wallin pointed out that the Japanese and Americans as well as the Australians and British recognised the strategic value of the islands. He was satisfied that the Japanese authorities were 'out for keeps'. Besides the strength of their naval and military occupying forces, there had 'for the last month been a staff of between 50 and 60 Japanese hydrographic officers and men, surveying the whole of the Jaluit lagoon, its islets, passages and reefs.' The Japanese had brought with them material for the erection of a powerful wireless installation, 'capable it is said of holding direct communications with Japan'. He then described how the naval authorities had placed obstacles in the way of the Burns Philp ship *Jambo* in its efforts to obtain a licence and a cargo of copra, and how they had favoured the Japanese South Ocean Trading Co. When Wallin departed, the Japanese commander refused to say whether Burns Philp steamers would be allowed to return. Hunt noted for his minister that this first news from the occupied territories confirmed their suspicions of Japan.[27]

Without waiting for Fisher's return from New Zealand, the Australian Government approached the British about Burns Philp's complaint. Cabinet instructed the Governor-General to inform London that the Japanese authorities appeared to be 'placing obstacles in the way of British traders in Marshal [sic] Island' and to inquire 'whether any arrangement has been made

---

[26] Minute, 30 December 1914, NAA MP1049/1 14/0449.
 See also Minute by Creswell, 30 December 1914, signed by all members of the Naval Board, setting out Australia's claim to the North Pacific islands NAA A981 MARS2 PART3.
[27] Letter, Burns to Hunt, 20 January 1915, enclosing letter Wallin to Burns, Ocean Island, 24 December 1914 with report of same date, NAA A1 1920/7685.

with Government of Japan respecting trading rights in islands now held by them under military occupation.'[28]

Burns Philp, not content to rely on British intervention, took steps themselves to make straight the way of trade and approached the Japanese Consul in Sydney, Seizaburo Shimizu, and at their request Shimizu asked Tokyo for clarification of Japanese policy in the islands. The reply was not very encouraging. The Japanese Navy Department, which had administrative responsibility, wished to know the numbers and names of the Burns Philp ships and asked that the company should 'defer sending any ship to the Marshall Islands until they have had definite sanction from the Japanese Government.' The company promptly furnished the information. It explained that it had been engaged in the trade with the island for ten years and reminded the Japanese that, since Burns Philp had Commonwealth Government contracts to maintain communication with the islands and to carry mails, it was 'incumbent upon us to revert to our regular sailings as soon as circumstances will permit.' Burns hoped that by invoking government authority he would help his case. On 17 February the consul told the company that it had permission to resume its shipping and trading relations with the Marshall Islands but would have to apply for permission if it replaced its old vessels or introduced new ones.[29]

The Department of External Affairs, using the pretext of the Commonwealth mail subsidy, also made representations on behalf of Burns Philp. Hunt wrote to Shimizu on 20 February asking for a copy of the rules issued by local Japanese authorities for the regulation of trade. After consulting Tokyo, the Japanese Consul reported that there were 'no published rules or regulations enforced by the Japanese Government in regard to trade, shipping or business in the South Pacific Islands occupied by the Japanese Navy.'[30] There were, however, 'a few notifications' which had to be obtained from Japanese officials on the islands, and subsequently Shimizu sent Hunt a copy of the 'notifications'. Perhaps the most significant of these was the one that stated that:

> In cases where, prior to Japanese naval occupation, interests have been held in any enterprise by individuals, and new residents should apply for permission to carry on such enterprises, such permission can be granted subject to the full recognition, by the new applicants of the right, if any, of the prior holders.

While purporting to protect established rights, it was providing a mechanism for Japanese settlers to take over existing business interests. The Japanese sought, reciprocally, to be supplied with Australian rules and regulations for trading in the German South Pacific islands. The Department

---

[28] Cable, Munro Ferguson to Harcourt, 1 February 1915, TNA: PRO CO 418/132/160; copy of letter, M.L. Shepherd, Secretary, Prime Minister's Department to G. Steward, Secretary, Governor-General, 31 January 1915, and draft cable with 'Approved by Cabinet, H[ugh]. M[ahon].', 21 January 1915, NAA CRS A1 1920/7685.

There is no record of a discussion or decision by cabinet on 21 January 1915. See Cabinet Minutes in Fisher Papers, NLA MS 2919 add. ms 21/8/81, box 12.

[29] Copy of letter, Burns to Shimizu plus enclosures in draft of cable, Shimizu to Japanese Foreign Office, Tokyo, 12 February 1915, and cable, Japanese Foreign Office to Shimizu, 17 February 1915, NAA A1 1920/7685.

[30] From the Japanese point of view the North Pacific islands were in the 'South Seas' or 'Nan'yo', which meant all islands south of Formosa, and they thus referred to them as the 'South Pacific Islands'.

of External Affairs replied pointedly that since 'these islands are only held in military occupation and have not been annexed, the laws in force in them prior to the occupation remain in force.' The only restrictions on trade applied to enemy countries.[31]

Upon arriving home from New Zealand, Fisher found the government and its advisers preoccupied with these Japanese questions, and their main concern was not trade but security. For Fisher it was a taxing time. The Council of Defence had rejected a British request for additional troops, maintaining that 'greater service would be rendered by their retention here at all events for the present.'[32] The army was recommending substantial military preparations to defend Australia. The Ministers for Defence and External Affairs were proposing that Australia should press its claim to the North Pacific islands.

From Burns Philp came further reports of Japanese interference with Australia's established trade in the North Pacific islands. Burns on 8 February had warned Hunt that, 'We have, so to speak, a swarm of Japanese coming South.' The Japanese were planning to run regular cargo and mail services to Australia and New Zealand. With their wireless stations they would 'make rings round the Southern Sea'. He feared that the British Administrator in the Gilbert and Ellice islands, 'under some misguided notion of protecting the native people' (presumably against Burns Philp's monopoly) might allow the Japanese to trade there. Burns believed that 'now is the time that some effort should be made to try and induce the Home Government to deal somewhat firmly and make some definite announcement that Australia expects that at the conclusion of the war the whole of the Island Groups adjacent to her shores will be given over to British Australian domination.' He left it to Hunt to judge 'whether or not some effort should not be made before it would be too late to have the Japanese acquainted with the expectation that they must hand over as they have promised to do the interest they have acquired.'[33]

Fisher recognised that a critical point had been reached in the shaping of the future of the Pacific. At this very time Australian suspicions were given further support when the press revealed Japan's demands on China which, if accepted, would have made China a Japanese protectorate. To the Australians it was clear that Japan would exploit to the full the opportunities afforded by the European war to expand its empire and influence in the Western Pacific.[34] Since the British had ruled out an imperial conference, the Commonwealth Government had no recourse but to take up the issue directly with London.

---

[31] Letter, Hunt to Shimizu, 20 February 1915 and letter, Shimizu to Hunt, 24 February 1915 and letter Shimizu to Hunt, 15 March 1915 and letter, Hunt to Shimizu, 13 April 1915 and letter, Shimizu to Hunt, 14 April 1915 with enclosure containing translation of 'Notifications', *ibid.*; see also Papers Prepared in the Pacific Branch in Connection with the First Assembly of the League of Nations, Geneva, November 1920, No. VII 'Australia's Interests in Islands North of the Equator and Japanese Interests in German New Guinea – A Review of Policy from September 1914 to July 1920',' NAA CAO 447/3, SC12.
[32] Council of Defence Minutes, 11th Meeting, 11 February 1915, NAA A2032.
[33] Copy of letter, Burns to Hunt, 8 February 1915, Novar Papers, NLA MS 696/6655-58. The Japanese were hoping to supply Australia with the goods no longer obtainable from Europe and were sending substantial delegations to look at the trade prospects, *SMH,* 13 and 15 January 1915.
[34] *SMH,* 15, 22 and 23 February 1915.

On 18 February the Australians asked the British whether they had made any commitment to the Japanese.

> Ministers have been considering possible bearing for future of Australia if Japan permanently retains possession of all islands formerly German now occupied by them especially Marshall and asks that they may be supplied secretly with full statement of any arrangements or understanding that may have been made upon this subject between Great Britain and Japan.[35]

The Australians believed that the Japanese were bent on annexing the islands and it seemed not improbable that Britain, in order to buy goodwill, might very well have connived with their Asian ally for this purpose. Though Burns's letter might have been the immediate occasion for the cable the request was a natural outcome of the general anxiety which had been building up ever since Japan had seized the North Pacific islands.

The Australian Government, fearing that secret deals were being made behind its back, enthusiastically took up the Naval Board's suggestion to stake its claim to the Marshall, Caroline, Marianne and Pelew islands (Palau). It was not willing to accept the inevitability of Japanese sovereignty over these territories. On 16 February Fisher ordered 'that a chronological record be made of Australia's actions in respect to the islands referred to herein [North Pacific islands] for use in negotiations on the cessation of war.'[36] On 10 February he with the support of Pearce and Mahon approved the Naval Board's proposal and a draft letter for the Colonial Secretary was prepared. The letter fleshed out the Naval Board's arguments.

SECRET

I have the honour at the instance of my Colleague the minister for external affairs to inform Your Excellency that it is desired that the position of the Commonwealth of Australia in regard to the Marshall, Caroline, Marianne and Pelew Groups of Islands should be clearly stated and recorded.

2. These Islands were surrendered to the Australian Expeditionary Force on the capture of the seat of government of the German Pacific Possessions and were definitely and distinctly included in the surrender, dated 17th September, 1914, clause 1 of which reads as follows:-

"(1) The name Deutsch Neu Guinea (German New Guinea) includes the whole of the German Possessions in the Pacific Ocean lately administered from Rabaul by the Acting Governor on behalf of the German Imperial Government, and the said possessions are hereafter referred to as 'a colony.'"

3. At the instance of the Imperial Government preparations were completed for the occupation of the above-mentioned groups of islands but it was subsequently intimated to this government that the Japanese would temporarily take under their care all the German

---

[35] Cable, Munro Ferguson to Harcourt 18 February 1915, TNA: PRO CO 418/132/218; see also letter, Hunt to Shepherd, 17 February 1915 seeking transmission of draft cable and including Mahon's minute, NAA A1 1920/7685.

[36] Minuted note by Hugh Mahon in his handwriting on 16 February 1915 on copy of draft cable about 'any arrangements or understanding' sent on 18 February 1915, NAA A1 1920/7685 and NAA A981 MARS2 PART3.

Possessions in the Pacific north of the Equator while those south of the Equator should be under the charge and control of the Commonwealth Government. The Expedition, therefore, which had been organised and was on the point of starting to occupy the Marshall, Caroline, Marianne and Pelew Groups was instructed to confine its operations to the possessions south of the Equator.

4. It is desirable that the fact should be thoroughly established that the Japanese are only in temporary occupation of the Islands to the north of the Equator so that Australian claims in any final arrangement for their disposal may be fully taken into account, and I shall be glad therefore if you will kindly bring the above facts under the notice of the Secretary of State for the Colonies.[37]

The Australians set out their legal title and the unhappy circumstances which had prevented them from making it good. The main purpose of the exercise was, however, to warn Britain that Australia had not abandoned its claims and that it expected Britain to hold Japan to its 'temporary occupation' commitment. It put the British on notice that it was going to argue for acquisition of the islands at the peace settlement.

But before the draft went to the Governor-General the government received a message from London which seemed to anticipate their inquiry and to offer some comfort. The Australian ministers were told that they could 'rest assured that we have no arrangement or understanding secret or otherwise with the Japanese Government about Islands in the Pacific except that the occupation of all territory conquered during the war by the Allies to be without prejudice final arrangement to be made at the end of the war.' The Colonial Secretary furthermore told the Australians that he was writing to them 'very fully by despatch on the subject'. The promise of a full disclosure of all the circumstances was encouraging. As a result, Fisher and Mahon decided to defer sending the draft despatch. They would be reasonable and reconsider their position after they had studied the promised information.[38]

The Australian Government faced the serious possibility of becoming involved in a major diplomatic quarrel over the Pacific islands. The prospect of such a clash helped to focus the mind. The ministers felt keenly their ignorance of Japan and Japan's intentions. They wanted a better basis for making policy. They needed to know more about Japanese attitudes towards both Australia and the islands. To this end Hunt, who had in effect been acting as the head of an Australian foreign office during the crisis, suggested that 'it would be advantageous for this Government to be informed of any expression which might indicate the public opinion of the Government and people of Japan regarding the Pacific Islands, formerly owned by Germany and now held under military occupation by the Japanese.' For this purpose he proposed that the

---

[37] *Ibid.*

[38] Minute by Pearce, 10 February 1915 on Naval Board recommendation and letter, Acting Secretary, Defence Department, H. Trumble to M. Shepherd, Secretary, Prime Minister's Department, 17 February 1915; draft letter, Secretary, Prime Minister's Department to Secretary, Governor-General, 23 February 1915; cable, Harcourt to Munro Ferguson, 23 February 1915; letter, Secretary, Prime Minister's Department to Secretary, External Affairs Department, 25 February 1915 with minute by Atlee Hunt 25 February 1915 approved by Mahon 25 February 1915; and letter, Secretary, External Affairs Department to Secretary, Prime Minister's Department, 26 February 1915, *ibid*.

British Ambassador in Tokyo should be asked to send Melbourne 'all statements in the public press or made by public men concerning these Islands'. Appreciating the difficulty of interpreting such material, he thought it would be useful if the Ambassador would also 'indicate in each case the weight which ought to be attached to such opinions'. He even allowed that the net might be widened further to include 'any political references in Japan to Australia generally'.

Not content to rely alone on British sources, Hunt also recommended that the New South Wales Government be invited to direct its Trade Commissioner in the Far East, J. B. Suttor, who was stationed at Kobe, to supply similar information. Though this might result in some duplication, 'it would probably ensure that we miss nothing of importance.' Certainly the Australians would thereby be able to check the British reports for completeness and accuracy. Mahon and Fisher adopted Hunt's proposal, and the British and New South Wales Governments, each of which was approached without the knowledge of the other, agreed to cooperate.[39] This search for more authoritative information was yet another sign of the gravity with which the Australians viewed the emerging problem of Japan in the Pacific.

The British campaign to persuade the Australians to accept the fait accompli

From the moment Japan had revealed its ultimate aim, the British knew that they would have a problem with the Australians. Sir John Anderson, the Permanent Under-Secretary at the Colonial Office, minuted on a draft of Harcourt's 6 December letter to Munro Ferguson that:

> it will be an impossible task to reconcile Australia to seeing the Japanese frontier moved halfway across the Pacific. Japan is the one power they distrust and their conscription law and Fleet would never have materialised but for the Japanese spectre.[40]

Anderson understood fully the pre-war 'Australian Crisis' and the way that the fear of Japan had shaped the Commonwealth's massive defence build-up in those years.

Alert to these sensibilities, Harcourt in his 'very secret' and 'private and personal' letter had charged the Governor-General with the task of bringing his ministers around to accepting Japan's permanent occupation of the islands. 'The moral of it,' he wrote, 'is that you ought in the most gradual & diplomatic way to begin to prepare the mind of your Ministers for the possibility at the end of the war Japan may be left in possession of the North Islands and we with everything South of the Equator.'[41] That is, the Governor-General, without ever revealing he was acting on

---

[39] Memorandum, Hunt to Mahon, 22 February 1915, approved by Mahon, 22 February 1915; copy of letter M. Shepherd, Secretary, Prime Minister's Department to G. Steward, Official Secretary, Governor-General, 24 February 1915; copy of letter, Fisher to Holman, Premier of New South Wales, 24 February 1915 and reply in letter, J.H. Cann on behalf of the Premier to Fisher, 4 March 1915, NAA A1 1920/7685; cable, Munro Ferguson to Harcourt, 26 February 1915, TNA: PRO CO 418/132/259; copy of cable, Harcourt to Munro Ferguson, 11 March 1915, *ibid.*, 418/141/86.

[40] Minute, Sir John Anderson, 7 December 1914 on draft of letter, Harcourt to Munro Ferguson, 6 December 1914, Bodleian Library MSS. Harcourt 468.

[41] Letter, Harcourt to Munro Ferguson, 6 December 1914, Novar Papers, NLA MS 696/1306.

instructions from Whitehall, was to persuade the Australians, through informal discussions, that they should resign themselves to Japan retaining possession of the North Pacific islands.

Munro Ferguson relished the role he had been given. He prided himself on his ability to manage men. He liked to think he was leading rather than being led, that he was shaping events not merely acquiescing in the decisions of his advisers. This even applied to his dealings with the Colonial Secretary. Thus, after receiving Harcourt's letter in mid-January, he felt able to boast that

> I had already done something in the direction of meeting your wishes re the post-bellum Pacific situation, and in talking over the question with ['Fisher' was crossed out] trustworthy leading men had suggested the Equator as the likely line between British and Japanese spheres in the Pacific … I … sounded those with whom I am on confidential terms in naval, military and political circles as well as Col. Burns and Sir Arthur May [former Premier of Queensland] as to their views on the matter.

According to the Governor-General, none of those to whom he had talked had expressed dissent. Seemingly his presentation of the case had been irresistible since they all had accepted his proposal as 'an inevitable consequence to the inestimable service by Japan to Australia throughout the war'.[42]

In a secret letter five days later he sounded a more cautious note. A discussion with Colonel Burns had made him less confident that Australia would fall into line. While conceding that Australians generally would recognise a Japanese sphere of influence in the Marianas and Carolinas, Burns thought that Australian Pacific traders might baulk at seeing the Marshalls remain in Japan's hands. Burns, in one of his plans for reconstructing Pacific geopolitics and geocommerce in the post-war era, had contended that, 'Now would seem to be the opportunity to fulfil what Providence evidently intended, and allow Australasia, as part of the British Empire, to control the Southern Pacific on and south of the Equator down to New Zealand and Tasmania.' Steps should be taken to prevent the Pacific from being 'Europeanised' or Balkanised.

Munro Ferguson took up Burns's ideas, hoping to use them to win over the Prime Minister. As he wrote Harcourt, if Japan could be excluded both commercially and politically from the South Pacific, and France induced to cede its interest in New Caledonia and New Hebrides – the only foreign-held territories left in the region – to the British Empire, then Australia might be reconciled to leaving the North Pacific islands to the Japanese. The Governor-General admitted that he was unable to provide 'definite information' on Australia's attitude until Fisher arrived back from New Zealand. Munro Ferguson intended to suggest to Fisher that he see Burns, and, 'This will give me an opening for attempting to lead his thoughts in the direction of some such settlement as I have indicated above.' He admitted there was a risk, and he would move 'warily lest the raising of the question could increase his desire for a Colonial Conference and lead to his pressing this point.'[43] The Governor-General was an almost too dutiful servant of Whitehall.

---

[42] Letter, secret and personal, Munro Ferguson to Harcourt, 20 January 1915, Harcourt Papers, Bodleian Library MSS. Harcourt 479; copy of letter, Novar Papers, NLA MS 696/650–51.

[43] Letter, secret, Munro Ferguson to Harcourt, despatched 25 January 1915, arrived 8 March 1915, TNA: PRO CO 418/132/93–95.

Munro Ferguson had not waited until Fisher returned to commence the process of convincing him of the wisdom and necessity of the British point of view. On 20 January he had written Fisher in the precise terms of his British instructions, urging that Japan be left undisturbed in the North Pacific in order to avoid friction in the Allied camp.[44] In Melbourne he repeated this argument, reporting to Harcourt that Fisher 'appeared convinced' that, with the additional territory Australia had acquired in the South Pacific, it would have 'enough on ... [its] hands'. He also broached the question of the acquisition of the New Hebrides and New Caledonia with the Prime Minister but Fisher was not particularly enthusiastic. 'You may therefore,' he told Harcourt, 'take it for granted that Mr. Fisher feels he would have enough new territory to handle were the Rabaul administrative area south of the line handed to Australia.'[45] A week later he reiterated this point; 'I have heard nothing to lead me to modify my opinion that my Government is likely to view with equanimity or at any rate without serious protest, a continued occupation of those Possessions by Japan should that be found expedient at the Peace Settlement.'[46]

The Governor-General, however, did not have the confidence of his ministers. He had heard what they allowed him to hear, and he had made of it what he wanted to hear. Given his assumption that he had the right to guide his inexperienced and parochial ministers on matters involving imperial policy, he took a lack of dissent to mean assent. It is apparent that he was not privy to the counsels of the Prime Minister, the Defence Minister, the External Affairs Minister or the First Member of the Naval Board all of whom were at this very time engaged in planning to make good Australia's claims to the North Pacific islands. He failed to understand what lay behind the Australian Government's cable of 18 February which sought to know whether there was any arrangements with the Japanese about the North Pacific islands. Seemingly he was ignorant also of the Naval Board's Memorandum and the steps taken by Pearce, Mahon and Fisher, culminating in the draft cable of 24 February, to reaffirm Australia's right to ultimate control of the Northern islands. He was living in a self-congratulatory world of his own making. Despite Munro Ferguson's prodding and prying, Fisher had maintained his rule of keeping the Governor-General at a respectful but safe distance from the processes of policy-making.

The Colonial Office, for their part, were in no doubt about the intent of the 18 February cable and they recognised that, if they continued to keep the Japanese demands from the Australians, they would place themselves in an untenable position. As an official noted, 'it will be only laying up trouble for the future if we don't tell the C'wealth ... what the difficulty is.' Consequently they agreed to send the Australian ministers the crucial cables that had passed between London and Tokyo, including Kato's Memorandum and Note Verbale of 1 December 1914.[47]

The British Government was not altogether pleased with Munro Ferguson's management of his ministers. They were particularly affronted by his proposal to compensate the Australians for the loss of the North Pacific territories with the acquisition, through exchange or purchase, of the

---

[44] Copy of letter, Munro Ferguson to Fisher, 24 January 1915, Novar Papers, NLA MS 696/3863–65.

[45] Letter, Munro Ferguson to Harcourt, 18 February 1915, Harcourt Papers, Bodleian Library MSS. Harcourt 479 and copy of letter, Novar Papers, NLA MS 696/656–57.

[46] Letter, Munro Ferguson to Harcourt, 24 February, Harcourt Papers, Bodleian Library MSS. Harcourt 479 and copy of letter, Novar Papers, NLA MS 696/665–66.

[47] TNA: PRO CO 418/132/216–22.

New Hebrides and New Caledonia. The permanent head of the Colonial Office declared that 'I am afraid Sir R. Munro's sense of proportion has been affected. The French would not give up New Caledonia and all their other interests for the whole of our share of the German Possessions.' Harcourt promptly cabled Munro Ferguson – the urgency of the issue precluded it being left to a leisurely despatch – warning him off such dangerous ground and urging him to try to persuade the Australians to be content with East New Guinea and the Solomon Islands.[48]

Munro Ferguson took his rebuke hardly and hastened to assure his superiors that he had made amends. On 17 March he tried to justify his meddling with the French islands by claiming that 'no general review of the situation in the Pacific could be made without referring to these Islands.' He was pleased to assure Harcourt, however, that no ill effects had followed:

> There have been so many lamentations over the loss to Australia caused by the French occupation of New Caledonia and New Hebrides – as if they were the equivalent of Heligoland, Ceylon and Ireland – that it was relief to find that no-one except an odd trader or shipper seems really now to care a jot about them.

He also assured the Colonial Office that there was 'equal indifference expressed as to the future of the Group North of the line.' From the British point of view the White Australia policy was the most difficult problem, 'for a White Australia policy appeals strongly to the spirit of Race, even if it be unsound economically and dangerous to the interests of the Empire.'[49]

Munro Ferguson's assertion about the Australian leaders' indifference to the French islands was, like his earlier assertion about their indifference to the North Pacific islands, at odds with the facts. The cabinet had on 3 March reaffirmed the established Australian position on the New Hebrides and approved a draft despatch urging the British Government to seek complete control of these islands. On reflection, however, it was agreed to wait and see how the war developed before sending this message to London. If the Governor-General had been aware of his ministers' attitude to the New Hebrides and intervened to delay them from taking action, he knowingly misled Harcourt. If, on the other hand, as seems more likely, he was ignorant of their deliberations, then it is further evidence that he was ill-informed about the policies and purposes of his government, or at least informed only to the extent that Fisher wished him to be.[50]

Having abandoned for the moment any attempt to influence Britain on the matter, the government nevertheless showed its continuing interest by setting up a royal commission to examine Australia's relationship with the islands. Just a week after offering his confident opinion on Australia's attitude, the Governor-General found himself arguing fiercely with his ministers about the terms of reference for such a royal commission. Sensitive to Whitehall's opinion he tried to scotch the whole plan. He maintained that, as such an enquiry must affect the French and their rights in the islands, it came under the jurisdiction of the British Foreign Office, and no matter

---

[48] John Anderson's Minute, 10 March 1915, TNA: PRO CO 418/132/91–106; cable, private and personal, Harcourt to Munro Ferguson, 11 March 1915, Novar Papers, NLA MS 696/1321–25.
[49] Letter, private and personal, Munro Ferguson to Harcourt, 17 March 1915, Harcourt Papers, Bodleian Library MSS. Harcourt 479 and copy, Novar Papers, NLA MS 696/669–72.
[50] Letter, Hunt to Mahon, 3 March 1915, forwarding draft despatch for Governor-General, NAA A1108, Vol.XVII.

what the 'ostensible or even real purpose' might be, the French Government might misunderstand and take offence. But Fisher was not to be put off. He denied that the proposal was a 'dangerous innovation'. He was willing that the British Government and the French, through the British, should be informed. Hinting at a larger ambition he said that 'Cabinet did not decide Commonwealth has a right to New Hebrides without consent of possessing Nations.' He did not wish to create 'foreign complications for the British'. In the end Munro Ferguson, despite serious misgivings, was obliged to permit the royal commission to proceed.

When in July the Commissioners produced the results of their labours the Governor-General's worst suspicions about 'the real purpose' of the inquiry were confirmed. In addition to a published report on improvements for trade and mail services between Australia and the New Hebrides, they also had produced a confidential report which suggested that Australia should, at the end of the war, seek to acquire the French share in the control of the islands. The confidential report made it clear that Australian interests were primarily strategic, not commercial. The additional expenditure on mail services which the Commissioners had proposed in their published report could not, they said, be justified on commercial grounds; 'The control of the New Hebrides' was 'a question of vital importance to the Commonwealth.'

The Commissioners allowed that 'Although France is our ally today, the future may develop other international relationships, in which event the possession of the New Hebrides Group by an unfriendly power would be a serious menace to the Commonwealth of Australia.' Their preferred solution, which ironically echoed the Governor-General's own earlier unauthorised thoughts on the matter, was 'an exchange of the Marshall and Caroline islands for existing French rights in the Group.' They noted that the Japanese were 'pushing South' and were making 'insidious and continuous efforts to establish themselves permanently in the Marshall Islands.' The great advantage of their plan was that 'a buffer' would be erected 'between Australian possessions and those of Asiatic powers.' Munro Ferguson considered the report to be potentially inflammatory should its content be leaked to the Japanese or the French, and so he refrained from sending a copy to London. He thought it wiser that the British should not be officially acquainted with its contents.[51]

On every side Munro Ferguson was slowly being made aware that his early assumption about the Australians' lack of serious interest in the fate of the Pacific islands was mistaken. The Liberal leaders were no less tractable on the subject than Fisher and his colleagues. When he had eventually, with Fisher's consent, consulted Irvine and Cook about the North Pacific islands, his optimism about Australian acquiescence in their Japanese destiny was given a severe jolt. He found that Irvine was 'reserved' and Cook was 'alarmed at the prospect of Japan obtaining a permanent footing so close to Australia as are those Islands North of the Line where she is now

---

[51] 'Confidential Report of the Royal Commission on Mail Services and Trade Development between Australia and the New Hebrides', 16 July 1915, NAA A1108, Vol.XV; see also cable, Hughes to Fisher, 25 March 1915 and draft of cable, Fisher to Hughes, 26 March 1915, Fisher Papers, NLA MS 2919/3/256–57, and Novar Diary, 25 and 26 March 1915, Novar Papers, NLA MS696/36.

It may well be that Munro Ferguson did not inform the Colonial Office of this major report with its international ramifications because he did not wish yet once again to admit that he could not convince his ministers to accept British policy.

established, and thinks that such alarm would be general out here.' Cook 'quite recognised the cost and difficulty of organisation for all these Islands, though he thinks the Marshalls would be a profitable possession. He is not at all inclined to quarrel with Japan, however, and frankly admits there may have to be give and take.'

The Governor-General had at last learnt something of the nature and depth of Australian concerns and he concluded that:

> The substantial objections that may be taken here to a continued occupation by the Japanese of these Islands will be two –
>
> 1) The Naval and Military danger – and
>
> 2) The Commercial advantage acquired by the Japanese in the Marshalls.
>
> With regard to the first the menace to Australia of Japanese propinquity might be serious.

After four months during which he had talked more than he had listened, the British viceroy had gained some appreciation of the Australian perspective on the Pacific. But he showed that he had no more sympathy for Australia's geopolitical world view than he had for its easy affluence and democratic mores. With an impatient flourish he added that 'This fool's paradise needs a rude awakening! and if a Japanese Naval Base near the Line should act as a solvent then it would be a blessing in disguise.'[52]

The Australians acquiesce in the inevitable

In the second week of April, Harcourt's promised despatch containing the Anglo-Japanese exchanges on the North Pacific islands arrived in Melbourne. From the Australian cable of 18 February the Colonial Secretary had detected 'some uneasiness in the minds' of the Commonwealth ministers, and the purpose of the despatch was to demonstrate that there was 'absolutely no foundation for such an idea.' He revealed – and he provided the essential telegrams, including the telegram of 1 December, to document it – that the Japanese had claimed the right to annex the islands and had asked for British support at the peace settlement. Though the Japanese contribution to the war had to be considered, London had taken the position throughout that 'all the territory taken from the Germans in the Pacific, either by Japan or Great Britain, shall be open for discussion at the conclusion of the war in the terms of peace.'

Harcourt stressed to the Governor-General that the telegrams were of 'such a very secret character' that, while they could be shown to Australian ministers, no copies were to be made and no reference to them was to be allowed to leak out. Finally, he warned, perhaps fearing the worst, that 'no anti-Japanese agitation should, during the progress of the war, be allowed to arise in Australia.' Such untoward action could have the result of causing the Japanese to demand recognition of their claims immediately. Even more, though this was not mentioned, it would

---

[52] Letter, private and personal, Munro Ferguson to Harcourt, 24 March 1915, Harcourt Papers, Bodleian Library MSS. Harcourt 479 and copy of letter, Novar Papers, NLA MS 696/673–74; letter, private and personal, Munro Ferguson to Harcourt, 6 April 1915, Harcourt Papers, Bodleian Library MSS. Harcourt 479 and copy of letter, Novar Papers, NLA MS 696/676–77.

almost certainly have closed off any possibility of securing Japanese assistance in the European theatre.[53] The British Government did play fair and include all the essential telegrams which had passed between Tokyo and London, but they did not disclose what Harcourt had confided to Munro Ferguson when directing him to try to influence his ministers on the topic, namely that, despite their formal diplomatic position, they had tacitly conceded the Japanese case. To this extent the British were still less than candid.

According to Munro Ferguson, when he received the papers, 'I sent for Mr. Fisher & Senator Pearce and read them the Despatch and the copies of the F.O. Cables … I informed the two Ministers that in 24 hours I should destroy the copies of the F.O. cables which no-one but they and myself have seen. This has now been done.' The Colonial Secretary had not asked him to act so officiously. No doubt it pandered to the Governor-General's sense of self-importance to behave in this way. Munro Ferguson reported that Fisher, after scrutinising the documents, agreed to tell his cabinet colleagues only that 'the occupation of German territory in the Pacific by Japan and Great Britain is without prejudice to the final settlement to be arrived at on the conclusion of Peace.'[54]

The Japanese demands for annexation confirmed Fisher in his view that Australia faced a dangerous and uncertain future in the Pacific. After reading the Foreign Office cables he remarked to the Governor-General, with a Pacific fleet in mind, 'I suppose some ships will be coming to us after the War,' and at the Sydney Agricultural Show Dinner that evening he spoke of 'the need for continuous preparation for war', adding that 'cases had been known of seconds falling out after a duel.'[55]

Australia could itself do little to challenge Japan's position in the North Pacific, influence British policy towards Japan or meet possible Japanese aggression. After Fisher had returned from New Zealand and had to confront these seemingly insuperable problems he had continued to press, even if indirectly, for an imperial conference. This appeared to offer the best potential answer for Pacific security. Expressing dissatisfaction with the British Government's arguments against calling a conference, he wrote Harcourt on 15 February:

> I have not been able to convince myself that the reasons you give for postponement are sufficient. My conversations with Mr. Massey in New Zealand gave me a different impression of his Government's attitude on the subject. It should be always in the minds of His Majesty's ministers that Canada and South Africa are in close touch always. Australia and New Zealand

---

[53] Letter, most secret, Harcourt to Munro Ferguson, 23 February 1915, NAA CP78/23 89/68; copy of letter, TNA: PRO CO 418/132/225–27.

[54] Letter, secret, Munro Ferguson to Harcourt, 13 April 1915, TNA: PRO CO 418/132/340–42.

[55] Copy of letter, personal and secret, Munro Ferguson to Harcourt, 13 April 1915, Novar Papers, NLA MS 696/678–80.

The remarks attributed to Fisher by Munro Ferguson are not reproduced in the press reports of the Prime Minister's speech at the Royal Agricultural Society Dinner. See *SMH*, 14 April 1915. Presumably they were excised by the censor. On the other hand the Governor-General wrote his account immediately after the dinner. He had no motive for inventing the words. Given the British authorities sensitivity about Australia's attitude to Japan, the words were likely to stick in his mind.

are far away and their economic policies bring them less before the British public than Newfoundland and Canada.

But, notwithstanding these reservations, he was willing to go along with the decision. He did not want to court an open quarrel in the midst of war: 'We have a policy for this trouble that gets over all difficulties – when the King's business will not fit in with our ideas we do not press them.'[56] Indeed Harcourt used Fisher's loyal words in replying to a question in the House of Commons about the postponement of the Imperial Conference and repeated the promise that 'it is the intention of His Majesty's Government to consult them [the Dominions] most fully, if possibly personally, when the time arrives to discuss possible terms of peace. His Majesty's Government intends to observe the spirit as well as the letter of the declaration.'[57]

Harcourt's public statement, coming just after the Australian Prime Minister had seen the secret telegrams, riled Fisher. In response to Cook's statement in the House of Representatives that 'we in Australia have our own local problems peculiar to ourselves that are already making their appearance on the horizon' and that 'these will need prompt and careful attention immediately the close of war comes and, indeed, before then,' Fisher echoed Cook's sentiments and took issue with Harcourt's attitude towards holding a conference during the war. The Prime Minister contended that, 'The Conference could have dealt with the essential questions at issue between the Dominions and the Mother Country.' When Cook said that a conference would be needed 'later on', Fisher retorted 'A Conference would be valuable now.'[58] Recalling the progress in consultative processes achieved at the 1911 Imperial Conference he voiced his pent-up resentment and commented that Harcourt's statement 'fails to cover the ground opened up by the departure, for the first time in the history of the Empire, in 1911, when the Dominions' representatives were taken into the full confidence of His Majesty's British Government on all important matters of policy carried out by them for the safety and welfare of all.' It might be less than satisfactory but he conceded that it was 'worth something to know that the Dominions will be consulted when peace is restored.'

Dropping his formal pose of loyal deference he made a further and public appeal to the British: 'My advice is, don't wait until that time if an earlier meeting is possible.'[59] Fisher's old leader Chris Watson, who was visiting London, added his voice to the Australian campaign for an early conference. Addressing an imperial parliamentary Association meeting at the House of

---

[56] Letter, Fisher to Harcourt, 15 February 1915, Harcourt Papers, Bodleian Library MSS. Harcourt 463/60.

Fisher was reported as saying that during his visit to New Zealand he had found a feeling in favour of having an Imperial Conference in 1915 and he still thought there would be 'utility' and 'advantage' in holding such a conference. He, however, considered that under war conditions 'our first duty is to support the British Government in any action they may deem it wise to take.' See also *SMH*, 31 March 1915.

Fisher maintained that he would like a conference to be held as soon as practicable but was satisfied that the British in opposing such a conference in 1915 were activated by proper motives; 'What the Imperial Government decides upon, with that will my Ministers agree. What is good enough for the Imperial Government, is good enough for my ministry.' See *SMH*, 3 April 1915.

[57] Great Britain, 5 *Parliamentary Debates* (Commons), XXI, 15–16, 14 April 1915.

[58] *CPD*, 1914–17 session, LXXXI, 2370–71, 15 April 1915.

[59] *SMH*, 16 April 1915.

Commons, Watson urged the British Government to summon an informal gathering of Dominion representatives as soon as practicable.[60] Watson warned Fisher that Australian action was urgent for, 'The point is that, probably some of the terms of peace are being agreed upon now, so if '"twere well 'twere done, 'twere well 'twere done quickly".'[61]

These shrewd suspicions that Britain's peace decisions would not wait for the end of hostilities were not without merit. The British Government, and not least of all the Colonial Secretary, had through March and April been giving some attention to the question of peace terms. In March, as a result of a Russian proposal for the division of the Ottoman Empire, the War Council was forced to consider the general issue. Grey, Churchill, Kitchener and probably Asquith were against the extension of British imperial responsibilities. They wished to leave the German colonies and Turkish territories to be used as pawns at the peace table, either to compensate Germany for losing land in eastern and western Europe or to ensure that Germany would not be too greatly embittered by its defeat and so subsequently seek revenge.[62]

The Colonial Secretary, however, had a very different view. He was closer to the question. He, perforce, understood better than any other minister the Dominions' determination to hold what they had won. In a paper on 'The Spoils', he appraised the position with a hard, unblinking eye. 'It is out of the question,' he wrote, to part with any of the territories now in the occupation of Australia and New Zealand.' And, he continued:

> Japan evidently intends to claim the possession at the end of the war of all the islands she is now occupying with the possible exception of Yap. I fear that this will cause great trouble with Australia, especially as regards the Marshall Islands, the trade of which has been, even under German rule, exclusively with Australia.

---

[60] *Ibid.*, 13 May 1915.

[61] Letter, Watson to Fisher, 11 May 1915, Fisher Papers, NLA MS 2919/1/4.

Indeed a number of Australian leaders visiting London in the northern summer kept up the pressure on the British Government. Sir Edmund Barton, at the Royal Colonial Institute, remaining true to the principles he espoused at the time of Australian federation, spoke out against the idea of an Imperial parliament but nevertheless claimed that 'it would be impossible for the dominions to take a full measure of participation in crises such as the present if they were not given some voice not only in making peace, but in making war.' See *SMH*, 10 June 1915.

R.B. Wise, New South Wales Attorney-General, who was well known to Fisher and shared the Prime Minister's fears of Japan, visited the Canadian Prime Minister in June 1915 and discussed 'Fisher's desire for an informal Conference of Premiers' with him. It is possible that Wise was Fisher's emissary. Borden put the suggestion to the Colonial Office but was given an 'unsatisfactory' reply. Borden considered the British reasons for opposing it to be 'trivial'. On 14 June Borden informed the other Dominion prime ministers that he intended shortly to visit London and implied that if they all came at the one time it would be possible, whether the British Government wished it or not, to hold an informal conference. Fisher, because of the pressure of domestic issues, was unable to join Borden in London. See *Search for Security*, p.177, fn.80; letter, Borden to Bonar Law, 21 June 1915, Bonar Law Papers, House of Lords Record Office; Borden Diary, 9, 11, 14, 15, 17 and 21 June 1915, Borden Papers, LAC.

[62] 'Secretary's Note of a War Council held at 10 Downing Street, March 10, 1915', Asquith Papers, Bodleian Library MSS Asquith 32.

As part of a plan to rationalise the Allies' colonial territories he suggested that if the French were unwilling to give up their share of the New Hebrides condominium in return for concessions in Africa, Britain might offer its interest in the islands to the French in exchange for Togoland and Dahomey. 'This,' he said, 'would be an impossible suggestion in ordinary times of peace owing to Australian prejudice but as Australia is now to acquire a large amount of new Pacific territory she might be induced to agree to it.' Such a swap could be made more palatable by offering to place the British Solomons under Australian administration.[63]

Simultaneously with this survey of post-war possibilities, Harcourt again urged on Munro Ferguson the need to bring Fisher to accept that the islands in the North Pacific must be allowed 'to pass to Japan'. Fisher's acquiescence was important because, 'If he could be brought to such a frame of mind it would greatly ease the situation when the terms of peace have to be settled between the Allies.'[64] A few days later Harcourt, anxious that Australia should not cast greedy eyes on the French South Pacific territories, added to Munro Ferguson's task. He told the Governor-General that the acquisition of New Caledonia was 'absolutely *impossible*' and that the New Hebrides were '*very difficult* and costly on the counter of exchange', and so he would 'therefore be very glad if you could get Fisher and others to take the view that if Australia received the Solomons and Bougainville we might well surrender our share of the New Hebrides condominium to the French.'[65]

By 10 May the Governor-General had received these new instructions and he had begun to apply himself to his new tasks. But by then Fisher had concluded that all the evidence accumulated since December bore out his earlier suspicions of Japan, namely that it was bent on taking advantage of the war to advance its power and interest in the Pacific to the fullest possible extent. Thus Munro Ferguson found that Fisher had 'developed nervousness as to establishment of bases close to Equator'. Now no self-deception was possible. There could be no pretence that the Australians would easily be pacified or made amenable to British wishes. 'You will see' he told Harcourt, 'how difficult it is to give you any definite answer as to what the attitude of "Australia" will be.' Too much had happened. The Australians were wiser and the Japanese more openly menacing. Fisher had 'been made a bit "jumpy" by the Japanese contribution to the Foreign Office correspondence … also by Sir C. Greene's collection of Press extracts from Tokyo; and by the accounts appearing in the Press of Japan's aggression in China.'[66]

---

[63] 'The Spoils', 25 March 1915, signed 'L.H.', Harcourt Papers, Bodleian Library MSS. Harcourt 468.
[64] Letter, private and personal, Harcourt to Munro Ferguson, 24 March 1915, Novar Papers, NLA MS 696/1346; copy of letter, Harcourt Papers, Bodleian Library MSS. Harcourt 479.
[65] Letter, personal and private, Harcourt to Munro Ferguson, 27 March 1915, Novar Papers, NLA MS 696/1325–27.
[66] Cable, secret and personal, Munro Ferguson to Harcourt, 15 May 1915, Harcourt Papers, Bodleian Library MSS. Harcourt 479, 'Islands North of the Equator. Prime Minister is to consult leader of Opposition. Assurance given to Cabinet that nothing conceded until peace settlement. Difficult for Prime Minister to say more without risking publicity. Recent Japanese action has developed nervousness as to establishment of bases close to Equator. French Islands, Prime Minister will consult. He acknowledges French settler difficulty and accepts ruling that New Caledonia is out of the question. Hope to secure more definite pronouncement.'

The British Ambassador, in his first review of Japanese press and public opinion to reach Melbourne, had adjudged that 'there would be popular disappointment mingled with surprise if occupation is not converted into permanent possession', and so confirmed what Fisher already knew.[67] More disturbing had been the news of Japan's ultimatum to China. On 7 May Japan had given China forty-eight hours to accept a revised statement of its twenty-one demands, and two days later the Chinese had submitted and shortly thereafter signed a treaty granting Japan extensive control over their country's affairs. These happenings were reported and discussed in the Australian press,[68] and they could not but compound Australian anxieties. Against this background it is not hard to imagine how the Australian leaders would have responded had they known that the Japanese stand on China had almost brought about the collapse of the Anglo-Japanese alliance and that the British Ambassador in Tokyo had told London, 'as long as the Germans can keep the fighting in the enemy's country, there will, I fear, be some hesitation shown here as to the ultimate issue of the war, and a tendency to "hedge" in appreciating the worth of the British alliance.'[69] Certainly it was understandable that Fisher should be 'jumpy'.

Trying to guide Fisher into the desired path, Munro Ferguson stressed the costs involved in administering so many islands. Moreover he suggested to the Prime Minister that he consult Legge, the Chief of the General Staff, who on 13 May had told the Governor-General that 'if as an Australian soldier he were offered the Islands North of the Line he was not sure whether he would not rather be without them.' Legge thought that they would be both expensive and difficult to defend, that the Japanese would seize them on the outbreak of war and that a potential enemy could not assemble forces in the islands without Australia becoming aware of it. The Governor-General also believed that Pearce was of much the same opinion and assumed that he would be a positive influence. Munro Ferguson, however, could offer no solace to Harcourt on the South Pacific islands; both Fisher and Pearce were disappointed to learn that 'the longstanding wish

---

See also letter, private and personal, Munro Ferguson to Harcourt, 13 May 1915, Harcourt Papers, Bodleian Library MSS. Harcourt 479, and copy of letter, Novar Papers, NLA MS 696/687-90.

[67] Despatch, Sir Conyngham Greene, Tokyo, to Munro Ferguson, despatched 10 March 1915, arrived 10 May 1915, NAA A1 1920/7685.

The despatch had been forwarded through London. Greene had left it to Grey and Harcourt to decide whether it was politic to send his evaluation to the Australians, and they had no objection, See TNA: PRO CO 418/141/168-74.

The Australian Government, in thanking the Ambassador, asked that he 'supply similar information regularly at intervals of not more than three months'. See letter, secret and confidential, Frank G. Tudor, Minister for Trade and Customs, on behalf of Prime Minister, to Munro Ferguson, 31 May 1915, NAA CP78/23 89/68.

[68] *SMH*, 7-10 May 1915; *Age*, 7 May 1915, 'Japan and China. Ultimatum Imminent'; *Age*, 8 May 1915, 'Japan and China. Ultimatum Sent. Reply Required by Sunday. Attitude of America'; *Age*, 13 May 1915, 'No understanding between Britain and Japan over China'.

[69] Cited in Nish, *Alliance in Decline,* pp.152-57, 162.

cherished in Australia to be possessed of New Caledonia and the New Hebrides' could not be realised.[70]

According to the Governor-General, Fisher had at first decided to tell his cabinet colleagues simply that the question of the Pacific islands was to be left over for the peace settlement. If indeed that is what he told the Governor-General, it appears that the Prime Minister some days later had a change of mind and initiated 'an informal discussion in the cabinet on the future of the Islands of the Pacific'. Why Fisher should have changed his mind is not clear. Perhaps on reflection he had decided that the issue was so important politically that he needed to seek his colleagues' advice. It is not likely that he acted at Munro Ferguson's instigation for the Governor-General knew how potentially explosive the issue was; he considered that, if there were a general discussion in cabinet, 'it would be sure to leak out and cause a hubbub.' What Fisher told the cabinet is unknown. Given the restrictions placed on the use of the Foreign Office cables, and the political and diplomatic sensitivity of the issue, it is difficult to believe that Fisher did more than canvass his ministers' views of the 'Pacific Peace Settlement'.

Munro Ferguson on 19 May cabled the Colonial Secretary on the results of this meeting.

> After Cabinet discussion re basis Pacific Peace Settlement Prime Minister reports
>
> (1) he anticipates no effective objection to continued occupation by Japanese of islands North of Line when question raised at end of war;
>
> (2) Australian administrative area including New Guinea, Bismarck Archipelago and possibly Solomons favourably regarded;
>
> (3) continued condominium New Hebrides considered better than our withdrawal as a defensive measure.

And in a further letter to Harcourt on that day he asserted that the Australian Government had adopted a position which:

> followed on lines agreeable your views. There is no doubt that an external administrative area from New Guinea to the Solomons, inclusive, would suit Australia well. All that has recently cropped up respecting the New Hebrides is that the retention of our rights there would, it is considered, be a useful 'point d'appui' should France and Japan at any time combine to annoy us.

New Zealand responded more directly. Perhaps profiting from Fisher's visit earlier in the year it took a clearer and tougher view and one which stressed Australasian solidarity in dealing with the Japanese threat. After digesting the same secret documents, it replied that it 'could not act apart from Australia in the eventual discussion of the issues involved, and should always ask His Majesty's Government to use every effort to prevent the advance of the frontier of Japan in the Pacific.' While it conceded that it might be impossible to insist on Japan surrendering the North Pacific islands, it thought that Japan should agree not to fortify them or to use them as naval bases. Finally it concluded that 'neither Australia nor New Zealand will ever be convinced that in

---

[70] Letter, private and personal, Munro Ferguson to Harcourt, 13 May 1915 and cable, secret and personal, Munro Ferguson to Harcourt, 15 May 1915, Harcourt Papers, Bodleian Library MSS. Harcourt 479; copy of 13 May 1915 letter in Novar Papers, NLA MS 696/687–90.

the future our peril is not from Japan.' If the British were to take the contrary view they 'must be prepared for bitter resentment'.[71]

Even if Fisher did respond to Munro Ferguson's inquiries about Australia's attitude to the post-war settlement in terms approximating the Governor-General's cable of 19 May, it would be utter nonsense to see this, in the words of J. H. Catts in 1919, as 'the most traitorous act that ever occurred in the history of Australia' since, as a result, 'the flood tides of Asia had rushed three thousand miles nearer these shores'.[72] It would, indeed, be nonsense to see it as a surrender of any kind or, even as the Governor-General's letter might suggest, a victory for British diplomacy. What Fisher conceded was that which could not be contested. As the Japanese held the North Pacific islands and, from all the evidence, could only be dislodged by force, Fisher's common sense told him that Australia could raise 'no effective objection' to Japan's annexation of them at the end of the war. Australia might regret, as all its policy deliberations since August 1914 showed it did, the passing of these islands into Japanese hands, but, after the event, it was powerless to undo what had been done. Britain had no leverage it could bring to bear on Japan. Because of the realities of power in the Pacific, Britain had to cultivate Japan's goodwill. Thus the only course open to Australia until the end of the war was to strengthen its own position in the South Pacific. But this acquiescence in what could not be changed did not mean that Australia was any less convinced than New Zealand about a Japanese menace to the security of the Dominions.

Japan presses for a commercial treaty

The Fisher Government felt the impact of Japan's new assertiveness not only in the expansion of its Pacific influence but also more directly and domestically through its persistent efforts to persuade Australia to accept the terms of the Anglo-Japanese Commercial Treaty of 1911. Japan's concerted campaign to achieve this objective, like its claims against the North Pacific islands and its demands on China, began with its naval and military successes at the end of 1914 and its

---

[71] Cable, personal and secret, Munro Ferguson to Harcourt, 15 May 1915, Harcourt Papers, Bodleian Library MSS. Harcourt 479 and copy in Novar Papers, NLA MS 696/6629; copy of letter, Munro Ferguson to Harcourt, 19 May 1915, Novar Papers, NLA MS 696/692–93 has a note on it indicating that a copy was sent to Andrew Bonar Law who became Colonial Secretary in Asquith's Coalition War Government on 25 May.

There are no records in the Fisher Papers of Cabinet meetings held between 21 January and 16 June 1915. See collection of minutes in Fisher Papers, NLA MS 2919 add. ms. 21/8/81, box 12. There are also no references in the press for the period 10–19 May 1915 to a meeting of the Federal Cabinet.

Despatch (secret), Governor of New Zealand, Lord Liverpool, to Harcourt, 13 May 1915, TNA: PRO WO 32/4997. There is no copy of this despatch in TNA: PRO CO 209 (New Zealand – General Correspondence) or TNA: PRO CO 532 (Dominions – General Correspondence) files. An acknowledgment of the receipt of the British secret documents can be found in cable, Liverpool to Harcourt, 21 April 1915, TNA: PRO CO 209/283.

[72] J.H. Catts, an ALP member of the House of Representatives, in 1919, anticipating the irrational kind of accusation which was levelled at the Menzies government over the 'Brisbane line' during World War Two, attacked the Fisher government for agreeing in 1915 to Japan's annexation of the German North Pacific islands. See *CPD*, 1917–19 session, LXXXIX, 12419–38, 12395 and 12628, 17 September 1919.

concomitant awareness of its pre-eminent position in the region. In the same way that they had mounted a three-pronged attack on the *Immigration Restriction Bill* in 1901, so the Japanese in 1914 and 1915 pursued their goal simultaneously in Tokyo through the British Ambassador, in London through the Japanese Ambassador and in Melbourne through the Japanese Consul. Unlike the North Pacific islands issue, however, this was a question over which the Australians had complete control and, having complete control, they used it to keep the Japanese at bay.

In the first week of December 1914 the Japanese Consul in Melbourne had made a 'courteous inquiry as to the status' of his fellow nationals visiting Australia. This was the opening gambit in what was to become a tenacious and sustained diplomatic offensive. By the beginning of January, the Japanese had made it clear to the British Foreign Secretary that they would expect, as a condition for further assistance, greater access to the industrial development of China, a loan of £20 million and an end to discrimination against their nationals in the British Dominions.[73] For Japan, then, the question was of considerable moment, ranking almost with the penetration of China as a war aim.

To this end Japan instructed its Ambassador in London to ask the British Government to use its good offices to persuade the Australians to enter into an arrangement for regulating trade between the two countries. This was 'a matter of supreme desirability'. In the despatch Kato argued exclusively on the basis of an increasing trade relationship: 'the trade relations between Australia and Japan have been steadily growing these last years and, viewed especially in the light of the experience of the months that have elapsed since the outbreak of the present European war, there is every ground for the still marked development in future in this direction.' The lack of a treaty of commerce was a 'source of inconvenience'.

The Japanese were aware that Australia might be reluctant, owing 'to apprehensions in connection with emigration question', but they stated that they had a long-established policy not to send immigrants to Australia and had 'no intention whatever on their part to depart from this policy in any way'. Instead they were willing to give appropriate assurances similar to those given to the United States and Canada. Since the time for adhering to the Anglo-Japanese Commercial Treaty had expired, they intimated that they would be happy to make a special agreement for the purpose. When sending the despatch on to Melbourne, Harcourt tried to smooth the way by observing that Canada had adhered to the treaty on condition that it did not affect its immigration laws and that Article 8 which allowed all Japanese goods to enter the United Kingdom free of duty did not apply to Canada.[74]

---

[73] Letter, Grey to Sir F. Bertie, British Ambassador in Paris, 9 January 1915, Harcourt Papers, Bodleian Library MSS. Harcourt 583. Grey said that he could agree to the first and possibly to the second but he thought that the third would be 'difficult' since it would depend on the Dominions' willingness to accede to Japan's wishes. Since Canada had already reached an arrangement with the Japanese, it was the Pacific Dominions, particularly Australia, that needed to be brought around.

[74] Despatch, confidential, No.2, Kato to Katsunosuke Inouye, Japanese Ambassador in the United Kingdom, 15 January 1915, *Nippon Gaiko Bunsho* (Tokyo: Ministry of Foreign Affairs, 1967), I, '1916', 183; despatch, confidential, Harcourt to Munro Ferguson, 19 March 1915, NAA A981/38(1), 'Japan in the Pacific Islands'.

For Canadian negotiations and agreement, see *Documents on Canadian External Relations*, I, '1909–1918', pp.748–49.

When the Australians did not reply to the London inquiry, the Japanese turned their attention to the authorities in Melbourne. They undertook a 'softening up' process. A visiting Japanese journalist asked his listeners 'most earnestly to disabuse their minds of the suspicion that Japan had any ulterior or sinister objective in view'. Japan did not want 'to take advantage of the present situation to interfere with any part of [Australia's] national policy in the slightest degree'.[75] Japan also sent a naval squadron on a goodwill mission to emphasise to Australians the importance of its naval contribution to the war.

On 10 June the Japanese Consul-General, convinced that the Australian people were 'beginning to show sincere deference towards the Japanese Empire' and that the times were propitious for taking the initiative, had a lengthy interview with Fisher about 'trade and other matters between this country and Japan'.[76] Though receiving little satisfaction for his efforts, Shimizu left with the Prime Minister a 'Brief Statement of Reasons for desiring Australia to join in the Treaty of Commerce and Navigation between Great Britain and Japan'. The paper set out political and commercial grounds for an agreement and presumably summarised the case which Shimizu had presented earlier to Fisher.

> Brief Statement of Reasons for desiring Australia to join in the Treaty of Commerce and Navigation between Great Britain and Japan.
>
> Commercial:-
>
> To remove any doubt as to any hindrances that may be imposed by either Countries [sic] in the future upon the exchange of commodities and shipping, and to assure the parties concerned that the most favoured nation treatment relating to Commerce and Navigation will be given to either side so long as the treaty continues in force at least.
>
> This is important in order to encourage the promotion, or extension, or continuation of the industries which produce goods particularly suitable to the markets of the countries interested; for instance, Wool-tops, Zinc Concentrates, Frozen Meats, etc., in Australia; Woollen and Cotton Textiles, Porcelain and Glasswares, Manure and Cement, etc., in Japan.
>
> Moreover, if the wishes of Australians, so freely expressed at present, to do away with enemy trading, particularly with German-made goods, are to outlive the present war, these measures, which are of mutual benefit, should be adopted, and the sooner it is done the better it will be for all concerned.
>
> Political:-
>
> The harmonious and beneficial operation of the letter and spirit of the Anglo-Japanese alliance, which has received particular attention since the outbreak of the present war, has proved beyond doubt that it is of inestimable value to the British Empire, as well as to Japan, for the maintenance and promotion of their respective and mutual interests. Suspicions once entertained in some quarters of Australia, regarding the faithfulness of Japan, have already been removed, I trust, to a large extent.

---

[75] *SMH*, 25 April 1915. The Japanese Consul-General accompanied the journalist when he spoke to the Millions Club luncheon.

[76] Confidential Despatch No.11, Shimizu to Kato, 18 May 1915, *Nippon Gaiko Bunsho*, I, '1916', 187.

There is no doubt whatever in my mind that all Statesmen, in both Empires, who have their national interests at heart, will wish to take every possible step to strengthen the ties of the Alliance, and if there appears to be anything left undone to consummate this desideratum, I think there should be a strong mutual desire to do it right away.

Should Australia join in the Treaty of Commerce and Navigation between Great Britain and Japan, it would materially contribute towards cementing the amity and cordiality now existing between the two Empires, and undoubtedly help to draw the ties of the Alliance tighter.

If accomplished, this will, in my opinion, show that the present Commonwealth Government has a statesmanlike view, not only of the commercial interests of the Commonwealth, but also of those Imperial considerations which present occurrences show to be so necessary to the solidity and progress of the British Empire.[77]

On the following day Shimizu called on the Governor-General and asked whether the British Government had forwarded the Japanese note to Australia; Fisher had feigned ignorance of the despatch and Shimizu was attempting to check his story. He told Munro Ferguson of Japan's desire that Australia should become a party to the Anglo-Japanese Commercial Treaty and sought his support. The Governor-General, always zealous to protect Britain's constitutional position, gave Shimizu a brief lecture on the powers and functions of the Colonial Office and the Foreign Office which, he claimed, 'no Japanese or Russian consular official seems willing to comprehend.' He complained to the new Colonial Secretary, Andrew Bonar Law that 'the whole consular body are anxious to be regarded as "Diplomatic Agents" and have been given a status in society which is not usually granted to Consular Representatives.' Shimizu was in no way chastened and, after pointing out that there was a precedent for his action in the Ottawa-based Japanese-Canadian negotiations over a commercial treaty, he gave the Governor-General a paper 'which he said reflected his own views as to what a Japan-Australia Treaty should contain.'[78]

Shimizu, a diplomat of considerable resource and enterprise, having failed with Fisher and Munro Ferguson next turned to the Minister for External Affairs and the Secretary of the External Affairs Department. But this tactic proved to be no more successful. Mahon put him off, saying that because of the pressure of business the time was not opportune. Shimizu approached Hunt to find out when 'the time was likely to be more opportune', but all Hunt could tell him was that he had 'no knowledge of the Government's intentions in the matter and no authority even to discuss the question.'[79]

The Japanese motives for pushing this issue so forcefully were probably, as Shimizu's statement suggested, both commercial and political. On the commercial side, it is not at first apparent why the Japanese should accord a treaty so much importance. The Australian tariff discriminated only between goods of British and non-British origins. All that fell within the latter category were subject to the same level of duty. The Japanese were not attempting under the proposed treaty to modify the British preference nor to gain tariff advantages over foreign

---

[77] Fisher note on interview, 10 June 1915, Fisher Papers, NLA MS 2919/6/89 and Shimizu's statement submitted to Fisher at interview, 10 June 1915, *ibid.*, 2919/6/100–01.
[78] Cable, secret, Munro Ferguson to Bonar Law, 11 June 1915, TNA: PRO CO 532/78/36–53.
[79] Letter, strictly confidential, Hunt to Mahon, 17 June 1915, Hunt Papers, NLA MS 52/1516.

competitors. Nevertheless the Japanese had had some indication that Australia might adopt a three-tier tariff, the first, which would have the lowest level, to apply to British goods, the second, which would have an intermediate level, to apply to goods of foreign countries with which Australia had commercial treaties and a third, which would have the highest level, to apply to the goods of all other nations.[80] Japanese trade had increased considerably since the outbreak of the war. The Japanese had been particularly successful in supplying many of the goods which Australia could no longer obtain from Germany. Shimizu had made this point in his statement to Fisher. In addition, when Hunt had sought 'some hint as to the real reasons for the request for this Treaty', Shimizu had said that

> certain Japanese companies were thinking of laying down plant for the purpose of producing goods for the Australian market or for dealing with Australian products (he mentioned specially zinc concentrates), but that having no commercial Treaty with Australia the firm [sic] concerned were uncertain about proceeding as they had no security that our Parliament would not impose some differential tariff prejudicial to the Japanese, or by other legislation, affect their trade rights with this country.

It was known that Australian manufacturers agitating for higher protective tariffs had, as a result of the increase in Japanese imports, made a special plea for protection against Japan. Though on 5 May the Minister of Trade and Customs had announced that the government would not introduce a three-tier tariff, it was understandable that the Japanese should look to a most-favoured nation treaty to safeguard their position.[81]

In his talks with Fisher and Hunt, Shimizu had stressed that his government also had political reasons for seeking a treaty. The Japanese wanted to allay all Australian suspicions of their country. They wished 'to prevent any occasion for utterances by public men of a nature unfriendly to Japan.' Shimizu said that they had particularly resented a speech by Senator Millen, Minister of Defence in the pre-war Cook Ministry, presumably when in denouncing Britain's new naval policy in March 1914 he had cast doubts upon the credibility of the Anglo-Japanese alliance. A commercial treaty would help cement the bonds between Japan and Australia and show that 'good feeling existed between the two countries.'

Shimizu also made it clear that Japan intended to take advantage of favourable political circumstances to achieve its aims. The Japanese Consul stated that if the Commonwealth Government agreed to a trade treaty it would be revealing 'a statesmanlike view … of these Imperial considerations which present occurrences show to be so necessary to the solidity and progress of the British Empire.'[82] Shimizu's explanation seems reasonable. A trade treaty would both secure his country's exports against discriminatory treatment and remind Australians of the British Empire's dependence upon Japan. Moreover it would go some way to remove the greatest cause of offence, namely the application of the White Australia policy to Japanese citizens. It was

---

[80] See speech of Minister of Trade and Customs Frank Tudor, *CPD*, 1914–17 session, LXXV, 1399, 3 December 1914.
[81] Hunt to Mahon, 17 June 1915, Hunt Papers, NLA MS 52/1516.
[82] *Ibid.*, Letter, Shimizu Statement, 10 June 1915, Fisher Papers, NLA MS 2919/100–01; *SMH*, 26 March 1914.

not that the Japanese Government had any desire to encourage migration to Australia. Indeed it was willing to give guarantees, as it had to Canada and the United States, that it would control emigration to ensure that Australia's policy was not in practice violated. And Hunt's judgment was that the Japanese meant what they said. It was his opinion that the ultimate motive was 'not as some might think to attempt to lull us into a false sense of security.'[83]

The Fisher Government, however, was not convinced of the innocent character of the Japanese overtures. Even if the Japanese promise to control emigration could be relied upon, the ministers knew that they would not escape criticism from the hard-line defenders of 'White Australia'. Furthermore, by giving Japan most-favoured-nation treatment, they surrendered their right to protect Australian industry through tariffs that discriminated between foreign nations. Finally, the very fact that the Japanese were pressing the matter at a time when Britain and the British Empire were vulnerable made the Australians question their motives and wonder whether any larger ambition lurked behind the proposal. Since Japan had taken the initiative almost immediately after the betrayal of its pledged word on the North Pacific islands and China, there was a natural reluctance to accept its protestations of good faith at face value. Nevertheless Fisher, very much alive to Australia's weakness, did not directly reject Japan's overtures. He relied on procrastination and obfuscation to prevent the issue from reaching the negotiating table.

By mid-1915 the Australian leaders were very sensitive to the Japanese question. Japan's military dominance, territorial expansion and diplomatic assertiveness was creating a situation which had, in Fisher's words, 'no parallel in our history', and the Prime Minister was determined to avoid giving the Japanese any excuse for pressing even more strongly for their treaty. When Shimizu drew Fisher's attention to the Queensland Sugar Workers' Union threat to call a strike unless all 'coloured' labourers – mostly Japanese as it happened – were sacked, he acted immediately. He wrote T. J. Ryan, the recently-elected Labor Premier of Queensland, warning him of the wider implications of the racial dispute, and he asked Ryan to 'avoid all things that are not paramount if they should give or are likely to give serious offence to the government of Japan.' And he concluded, 'You will keep this letter to yourself and as a request for such action as will best meet circumstances that have no parallel in our history.'[84]

This issue had a history both in Australian-Japanese relations and in Queensland Labor politics. In 1914, at the insistence of Shimizu, the Cook Government had persuaded the then Queensland Ministry to exempt 'coloured' labourers who had worked in the sugar industry for a specified number of years from the racially exclusive provisions of the *Sugar Cultivation Act* of 1913. But the white cane-cutters had remained dissatisfied with this concession to the Japanese, and the Ryan Government had promised that they would revoke all exemptions. As a Queenslander, Fisher appreciated the delicate nature of the issue for his party as well as his country. Nevertheless after consulting cabinet he appealed to Ryan to desist: 'In view of interna-

---

[83] Letter, Hunt to Mahon, 17 June 1915, Hunt Papers, NLA MS 52/1516.
[84] Copy of letter, Fisher to Ryan, 12 June 1915, Fisher Papers, NLA MS 2919/3/282.

tional situation Coml [sic] Govt. recommend State Govt. not to revoke Permits – referred to in your wire June 14th 1915.'[85]

The Commonwealth authorities were equally anxious that no untoward incident should mar the goodwill tour of a Japanese naval squadron, which was taking place just as the Queensland dispute appeared about to erupt. Fisher allowed no sign of Australian uneasiness to show. Indeed he was scrupulous in attending to the formal courtesies associated with the occasion. In response to Admiral Chisuka's statement in Perth that he 'firmly believed the Anglo-Japanese alliance would last until eternity', Fisher lauded 'the honourable way in which it [Japan] had kept its word' under the alliance and hoped that 'peace and amity would exist between them [Australia and Japan] for ever.'[86] At a dinner in Melbourne, at which the Japanese flagship's band played 'What a friend we have in Jesus', Pearce declared that 'the Anglo-Japanese alliance was not being used for territorial expansion, conquest, aggression, or oppression, but was being used to rid the world of a nation which had used its power to make such things a national ideal. Australians were proud to be associated with Japan in an alliance.'[87]

The Australians did not view this demonstration of Japan's naval might primarily as a gesture to the wartime alliance or even to the Anglo-Japanese alliance but rather as a symbolic message of Japan's pre-eminence in the Pacific. The ministers had done their public duty. They believed that Japan had broken its word on the North Pacific islands and China. They saw its wartime policy in Asia and the Pacific as an imperialist adventure. Thus, apart from meeting the forms of diplomacy, their speeches were ironically talking not of the way they knew Japan had acted but of the way they considered it should act under the Anglo-Japanese alliance.

For the Australian Government the developments in the Pacific following the outbreak of war had been very disturbing. The source of Australia's disquiet was not Britain's European enemy but its Asian ally. Japan's expansionist actions in the region, justified by the exigencies of the war, had proceeded unchecked and unchallenged. Given Britain's helplessness, Australia had no way of halting the southward thrust of Japan. Since November 1914, when the Australians learnt that Japan had taken possession of the German North Pacific islands their fears had assumed a palpable form. Dangerous contingencies had to be kept in mind. It was difficult to predict what the Japanese might do if Britain and its Allies suffered severe reverses in the European war. They might require a very high price for their continued support for the Allied cause or, alternatively, they might throw in their lot with the Central Powers. Likewise it was impossible to foresee what peace might bring. If Britain were defeated or had to make a compromise settlement which left

---

[85] Cabinet Minutes, 16 June 1915, *ibid.*, 2919/3/374. The minutes also recorded that 'Question to go to party'.

It appears that on 10 June the Caucus had debated the matter and resolved that 'the Queensland Labor party be requested to take action in connection with the letter respecting coloured labour question.' However, there is no record of any subsequent discussion of the subject. See Weller (ed.), *Caucus Minutes*, Vol.I, pp.403–16.

For the Japanese protest against the proposed discriminatory action of the Ryan government, see *Nippon Gaiko Bunsho*, I, '1915', 209–27.

[86] *SMH*, 8 and 16 June 1915.

[87] *SMH*, 19 June 1915; Novar Diary, Novar Papers, NLA MS696/36, 16 June 1915.

Germany the dominant European power then Japan's hegemonic position in the Western Pacific would be greatly enhanced. Australians could not help but see all these possibilities through the lens of the pre-war 'Australian Crisis' and recognise that should any of these adverse circumstances come to pass Australia's position would be at best precarious.

Fisher, who was most acutely aware of the Japanese danger and fashioned the Australian response to it, was motivated by geopolitical, not racial reasons. From the time of the Russo-Japanese war when he had first been alerted to the Japanese menace he, unlike most Australian leaders, had rarely used racial language in explaining the Pacific problem. While he, of course, supported the White Australia policy he did not enthuse about it; indeed, in his public addresses he only occasionally made mention of it. For him Japan was a potential enemy not because of racial ideology but because of its military power, imperial behaviour and strategic opportunism. In the early months of the war these considerations became even more apparent and ever more pressing, and he reacted accordingly.

To protect Australia's interests Fisher had framed a many-sided policy. He had initially endorsed the proposal of the Naval Board and External Affairs Department that the Australian Government should draw up a statement of its diplomatic and legal claims to the North Pacific islands which could be used to bolster Australia's case at the peace settlement. But when informed by Britain of Japan's intention to keep the islands as war booty, he reacted very sensibly. He did not welcome the prospect of having naval bases on Australia's Pacific island frontier but accepted that nothing could be done to remove the Japanese. He recognised that neither Britain nor Australia could afford to antagonise Japan and so refrained from protesting publicly against its demands. Rather he looked towards consolidating Australia's hold on the South Pacific islands, acquiring the French interests in the New Hebrides and New Caledonia, and preparing Australia's defences, both naval and military, in harmony with New Zealand and possibly other Dominions, to meet the Japanese threat.

Throughout his term in office, Fisher also advocated holding an imperial conference that would enable the Australians to explain their concerns directly to London and to consult Britain and the other Dominions about peace terms and Pacific naval defence. After eight months of seeking vainly to persuade the British to call such a conference, he had become almost bitter about their attitude. At the end of July, when asked whether Australia was being consulted about peace terms, he complained that 'There have been suggestions on these lines but much of our information … comes through the press, in the reports of answers given by the Under-Secretary for the Colonies in Parliament.' Unburdening himself of some of the accumulated resentment, he declared that, 'the British Government does not yet realise to the full the real position of the distant Dominions in matters that very nearly affect us.'[88] The Commonwealth Government felt isolated and had become to some extent alienated by the treatment that it had received from the Mother Country.

For the first fifteen months of the war Australia's defence and foreign policy was pulled in two different directions. On the one hand Australians for strategic and sentimental reasons identified with Britain in its struggle against Germany. They appreciated that at a global level Australia's

---

[88] *CPD*, 1914–17 session, LXXVIII, 5320, 23 July 1915.

survival was linked to a British victory in Europe and so continued to send reinforcements for the AIF. On the other, however, they saw that Japan's rise to power in the Pacific posed a dangerous problem for Australia's immediate security, a problem for which Britain had little sympathy, and this caused them to look to their own defences hopefully supported and sustained by the cooperation of the other Pacific Dominions.

Though Australia, in responding to the war crisis, found itself faced with two distinct and equal strategic threats and developed two distinct policies to meet these contingencies, nevertheless these policies inevitably interacted with one another and faced the Commonwealth with difficult choices. The downward thrust of Japan was alarming, and yet if Australia created difficulties over the North Pacific islands, Japan would be estranged and less inclined to help Britain. It might even be induced to join the Central Powers. Thus the Australian Government was, even if reluctantly, willing at least until the end of the war to give up its claims to Germany's North Pacific insular territories.

The Fisher Government at first thought it probable that the Allies would achieve a victory in 1915 and so, while making a modest a contribution to the Empire's war in Europe, showed little enthusiasm for recruiting men for the AIF. It wished to husband Australia's resources so that its plans for social reform, national development and local defence could proceed without interruption or delay. Thus, in his first statements of government policy, Fisher proposed to build new ships, construct naval bases, establish a strategic railway system, open up the Northern territory to settlement and to press on with the compulsory military training and naval building programs.[89] Indeed for this reason, in early 1915, the government rejected a British request for further troops and approved in principle a more effective organisation of its military forces to meet the possibility of a Japanese invasion.

After it became clear, however, that the Allies were not going to succeed so easily, and after the AIF became engaged in the Gallipoli campaign, pressure to send every available man increased. Strong public sentiment in favour of reinforcing the AIF and of aiding their fellow Britons gave rise after mid-1915 to an orchestrated campaign for conscription. The choices for a sensitive and thoughtful leader like Fisher were narrowing. His support for a more active recruiting policy in the winter of 1915 and for the *War Census Bill* did not satisfy those who believed the very existence of the Empire and Australia was at stake and that duty and efficiency required conscription of the nation's resources. But the government's campaign of moral pressure and the Universal Service League's advocacy of compulsion alarmed other sections of the community who were antagonised by the militarising of society and the prospect of industrial conscription. The result was that Fisher lost control of policy and, in the process, of himself. He was a casualty of the divisive problems, strategic and economic, social and political, which the war

---

[89] The Sydney Conference of Premiers, to which Fisher had invited the New Zealand Prime Minister, 'depressed the P.M. almost to despair.' The Governor-General reported that 'He [Fisher] has at heart the extension of through-railways for defence and for land settlement. The States oppose all his schemes, they break their engagement re loans, they offer to take over the job of recruiting the Federal Army.' Copy of letter, Munro Ferguson to Harcourt, 13 May 1915, Novar Papers, NLA MS 696/687–90.

had brought in its wake, and in October he resigned to take up the post of Australia's High Commissioner to the United Kingdom.

On arriving in England he had not forgotten the problems he had had with Whitehall and he announced that 'I have not come to London to be invited to the counsels. I intend to walk in.'[90] Still smarting from the rebuffs he had experienced from the Colonial Office over the holding of an imperial conference he indicated that he intended by his presence in the Mother Country to make the British authorities more responsive to Australia's concerns about Japan's ambitions in the Pacific. He told a reporter from *The Times* that, while Prime Minister of Australia, 'all the time I have had no say whatever in imperial policy – no say whatever. Now that can't go on. There must be some change.'[91]

---

[90] *SMH*, 3 March 1916.
[91] *Times* (London), 31 January 1916. See also Fisher's speech at the Empire Parliamentary Association's luncheon, *ibid.*, 2 February 1916.

'Our last man and our last shilling'? Loyalty and conscription

For Australia, 1916 and 1917 were the most traumatic and testing years of the war. In these years, the Allies' cause hung in the balance. On the Western front the British and French, though mounting massive offensives against the enemy, were unable to make any progress. In the East, the Central Powers carried all before them as the Russian armies were defeated and demoralised. Italy, which had joined the Allies in May 1915, suffered great losses and became a liability rather than an asset. The German submarines sank great numbers of merchant ships and threatened to cut off vital supplies of food and arms. The Alliance seemed in danger of falling apart – the Russians, having experienced two revolutions, ultimately abandoned the fray. The Japanese commitment, which had been carefully calculated, was suspect. Only the United States entry into the war offered the Allies new hope. Even so, it remained unclear how long it would take this hope to be translated into a significant American military force in Europe.

Under the pressure of these events Britain's role in the war was transformed. At the outset it had taken as its primary task the control of the high seas and the financing of its Allies. While contributing a modest expeditionary force to the defence of France and Belgium, it expected to leave its continental partners to bear the brunt of the fighting. By 1916, however, it had in all respects become the mainstay of the Allies' war effort. It was forced to introduce military conscription and raised great armies to bolster the French position on the Western front. This mobilising for total war subjected British society to great tensions and produced, especially amongst the labour movement, a growing resistance to the warfare state.

Australia also had to reappraise its approach to the war in the light of these developments. It had to decide how far it should go in helping the Motherland and whether it should follow Britain and adopt conscription for the purpose. Because of divisions in the Labour Party, the question was twice put to a popular referendum and in both cases was narrowly defeated. In their rival campaigns where many issues were canvassed, each side was at pains to show – even if very discreetly since it reflected on an ally – that its attitude to the central question offered the safest means by which to protect Australia from Japan and the threat to White Australia. Throughout the turmoil created by the domestic conflict over conscription the national security community continued to give considerable time and attention to the 'cold war' against Japan.

The bitter animosities stirred up by the controversy over conscription tested the ties and sympathies that held the community together. The conscriptionists by taking unto themselves the title of 'loyalists' and denouncing their opponents as 'disloyalists' painted the anti-conscriptionists almost as traitors to the British Empire and Australia. Traduced in this manner labour and Irish Catholic Australians who comprised the public face of anti-compulsion were deeply resentful. The divisions created out of this issue had important and adverse consequences for Australia's defence and foreign policy both in responding to the world crisis of the time and in shaping the debate of the next generation over a greater and even more threatening world crisis.

5

'The Survival of the Fittest': The Crusade for the British Race

On 27 October 1915, when William Morris Hughes succeeded Fisher as Prime Minister, he was faced with a bleak international outlook. The Allies' major assault on the Western Front against the entrenched enemy at Ypres and Loos had, despite high casualties, gained little ground. The Russians had been forced to fall back behind the Vistula River and had lost 2 million men and irreplaceable supplies. In the Mediterranean, the Italian thrust against the Austrians had bogged down, Serbia had been overrun, Bulgaria had joined the Central Powers, Greece had turned its back on the British, and the French and the Allies' retreat from the Dardanelles was only a matter of time. Moreover, doubts about how Japan would behave and whether it would remain loyal to the Allies also contributed to the sombre picture. Hughes knew that critical times lay ahead, and in his first statement to parliament set out the stand which was to mark his approach to government – namely that the war would be 'prosecuted with the utmost vigour until a complete and final victory is assured.'[1]

Single-minded dedication to victory

While making gestures towards continuity with the Fisher administration, Hughes spoke with a new voice, a stridently imperious voice. He was determined that the British cause should triumph, that Australia should do all in its power to assist the Mother Country to defeat the Empire's enemy and that nothing should be allowed to stand in the way of achieving this objective. By both personality and philosophy he was predisposed to take such a view. A gnome-like figure with a potoroo head perched on a wizened frame, he appeared from the arch of his body ready to spring at any enemy who should dare to cross his path or thwart his will. There was something of Shakespeare's Richard III in him. It was as if he had resolved that:

> … since this earth affords no joy to me
>
> But to command, to check, to o'erbear such
>
> As are of better person than myself
>
> I'll make my heaven to dream upon the crown.[2]

But if, like Richard, he could use wit and wile to compass his ends, he nevertheless, in this age of mass nationalism, sought power not only for himself but also for his country and race.

Hughes had almost welcomed the Great War. He had risen to it as though it was his most natural element and he revelled in its challenge. In contrast to Fisher, Hughes was a Social Darwinist who saw human history as the clash of contending races for supremacy. Thus the war

---

[1] *CPD*, 1914–17 session, LXXIX, 6969, 28 October 1915.
[2] *King Henry VI*, Act III, Scene II.

was 'a struggle for the survival of the fittest'. It was the duty of the British peoples to 'demonstrate our fitness, and we must do this by duty and by sacrifice.' His imagination, stimulated by such visions, could contract the great distances separating Australia from the scene of conflict, and leap ahead in time to the consequences of defeat or victory. Australia, integrally allied to Great Britain, was engaged in a struggle 'to the death, calling for the whole energies, personal services and resources of every citizen.' As a subsidiary argument, not clearly connected to the main, he urged that the war was also 'a fight between ideals; between liberty and democracy, and despotism and militarism.' Since the British Empire represented the moral force of mankind, the Royal Navy was the natural 'international policeman' to maintain world peace. As necessity underpinned nationalism, so for him righteousness justified realism.[3]

Given these assumptions, Hughes was never sanguine about the future of international relations. For Hughes, the Great War was never 'the war to end all wars'. Such claims were to his mind fanciful and dangerous. While all might hope, he said, that the Great War would be the last, 'it might not be the last; and if they knew anything of human nature it would not be the last.' And for Australia this had special significance. Shortly before becoming Prime Minister, Hughes had stated rather indiscreetly at the launching of the light cruiser *Brisbane*, that Australia's own naval program would have to proceed:

> for the blindest of men must see that it was in the Pacific that the great problems would have to be faced. There had already ... been a knocking at the door and none but the incurably and hopelessly blind could surely fail to see, though dimly, the problems that lay ahead.

> There could be no salvation for Australia except through defence preparedness.[4]

On the basis of this view of world war and world politics, Hughes offered a clear solution for the issues that had so troubled Fisher. To the questions of how far Australian interest was involved in the European conflict, of how Australia should counter Japan's threat to national security and of how far the Labor Government should pursue its reform program in the light of the war crisis, he gave a very direct and superficially plausible answer. A victory for the British Empire in Europe offered the only certain protection for Australia's future. With that achieved, all else would be added unto Australia. Without it nothing mattered, since Australia would become a vassal state of Japan or Germany. As he told a public meeting in Melbourne in January 1916, 'The duty of all was to bring the war to a speedy and glorious conclusion and everything must be subordinated to that.' Spelling out the implications of this for the Labor Party's reform aspirations, he said that he was 'unable to fight with all his heart and soul more than one battle at a time and for the present he would devote his whole energies to the extirpation of German power and influence.'[5]

From the start of the war, Hughes had made no bones about his desire for the country to be totally committed to the war effort. In August 1914 he had called for a political truce and for the formation of a national war government. As Attorney-General, he had been the chief author of the Labor Government's wartime measures, the *War Precautions Act*, the *Trading with the Enemy Act*

---

[3] *SMH*, 21 January, 3 and 4 February, 1 April and 12 October 1915 and *Daily Telegraph*, 1 April 1915.
[4] *SMH*, 10 October 1915.
[5] *SMH*, 15 January 1916.

and the *War Census Act*. He had, on his own initiative, conducted a strident campaign to rid the Australian mining industry of German influences. For this purpose he had induced mining magnates to establish a metal exchange which would bring the industry under exclusive Australian and British control and give order to the production and sale of Australian ores. He was also associated with the founders of the United Service League, who wished by compulsion to achieve efficiency in both military recruitment and national manpower policy. Indeed, in January 1916, after becoming Prime Minister, he drew on leading figures from this body to create an Advisory Council of Science and Industry, based on a British model. Through the union of business with the universities this council was to exploit Australian technical knowledge in order 'to challenge the scientific prowess of the Teuton warrior'.[6]

Within weeks of assuming office Hughes had placed his stamp on government policy. He abandoned the Labor Party's proposal for a constitutional referendum to give the Commonwealth powers over trade and industry, corporations and arbitration. He announced a new and ambitious plan for recruitment to the AIF. And he indicated his intention of visiting Britain to discuss the conduct of the war and the terms of the peace, and most especially the role of Japan in the Pacific.

The Fisher Government had an electoral mandate to put the constitutional referendum to the people, and the Labor Conference in June 1915 had reaffirmed the need for the Commonwealth to seek the new powers. The referendum had become not only a symbol of Labor's continuing commitment to reform but also a means by which the federal government could acquire authority to deal with the war-induced problems of rising prices and increased unemployment. Since Labor was in office not only in the Commonwealth but also in five of the states, the movement was optimistic that the constitutional amendments would secure the required majorities.

Hughes himself had taken the lead in presenting the case for these reforms in 1910 and again in 1913 when they narrowly failed. At the June conference he had, consistent with his earlier record, been the strongest advocate of the referendum. The concentration of power in the hands of the national government was essential to his notion of socialism, for it enabled the state to control both the economy and the society more completely and more efficiently. In wartime such control was even more urgent, and in a pamphlet he wrote for the expected referendum in October, his central argument for the 'Yes' case was that:

> In order to grapple with the tremendous issues arising out of the war, it is essential that the Government charged with the responsibility should have absolute authority over capital and labour.[7]

After taking up the reins of government, however, he began to regret his earlier enthusiasm for the measure. The Liberal opposition, the Universal Service League, the daily press, and many respectable citizens attacked the referendum as a divisive and partisan issue which would distract public attention from the war. Hughes seems to have accepted this argument. Moreover he begrudged the time and effort he would have to devote to the campaign, especially since the outcome was uncertain. Thus when the state premiers offered, in return for dropping the

---

[6] George Currie and J. Graham, *The Origins of the CSIRO: Science and the Commonwealth Government, 1901–1926* (Melbourne: CSIRO, 1966), p.30.
[7] *Argus*, 26 October 1915.

referendum, to ask their respective legislatures to hand over the same powers to the Commonwealth for the period of the war and six months after, Hughes readily accepted the proposal.[8]

Once more Hughes had made an impulsive judgment. No longer subject to Fisher's restraining hand, he was able to persuade his colleagues to agree to this compromise, an initiative which would return to haunt him. Any careful considerations of the ways and means ought to have warned him of the inevitable outcome. The state legislatures did not pass the enabling Acts. It was evident from the very moment it was adopted that the scheme had little chance of success for, apart from all the other difficulties, the conservative state upper houses were most unlikely to agree to such a measure. As soon as it was apparent that the deal with the states had collapsed, he ruled out all suggestions that he should reopen the question of a national referendum, and the upshot was that many Labor rank and file members, especially in the industrial wing, began to question his leadership of the movement. The federal Executive of the party called him to account for his actions, but in the end were dissuaded from censuring him. Hughes wrote triumphantly of this encounter to the Governor-General: 'the Star Chamber was in fine form and started to make the pace hot but cracked up at the distance and came home limping badly.'[9] In disparaging his own senior party representatives he was showing how far he had separated himself from his social and political roots. It is impossible to imagine Fisher speaking to the Governor-General of his party colleagues in such derogatory terms.

'Call to Arms'

As Britain assumed a greater role in the Allied war effort, the demand for more voluntary recruits and the introduction of conscription grew steadily, and the reverberations from this agitation were felt in all the Dominions. Even though the Universal Service League's campaign had failed, the Australian Government felt obliged to increase their commitment. In the last days of the Fisher Government Senator Pearce, responding to a British Army Council appeal, agreed to increase the monthly reinforcements for the AIF from 10 to 20 percent of establishment – approximately 9500 each month – and to send them in advance. Thus he promised to send 30,000 of the 63,000 who had enlisted in the successful recruiting drive of the previous three months in October and November.[10] But before this recruiting goal could be properly tested, renewed agitation from the British conscription lobby forced the Asquith Government – and, by example, also the Hughes Government – to set even higher targets.

In the last months of 1915, the Asquith Coalition Ministry was rocked by a bitter controversy over conscription. Even though the National Registration had revealed a large pool of available

---

[8] Secret despatch, Munro Ferguson to Bonar Law, 18 November 1915, TNA: PRO CO 418/134/183.
[9] Letter, Hughes to Munro Ferguson, 7 January 1916, Novar Papers, NLA MS 696/2429.
[10] *Argus*, 9 October 1915; secret cable, Sir Ian Hamilton to Pearce, 6 October 1915, Pearce Papers, AWM 3DRL 2222/7. Hamilton, Commander of British Imperial Forces at the Dardanelles, acting on behalf of the War Council, had also stated that 'to meet exceptional demands which are liable to occur a further 10 percent reserves of trained men in Australia would be of great value.' Pearce, perhaps influenced by Fisher, ignored this additional request.

men of military age, enlistments were falling. In order to placate those demanding compulsion, the Prime Minister put Lord Derby, a respected Conservative conscriptionist, in charge of a new voluntary recruiting drive, which was given the impossible task of increasing the army's strength to 70 divisions.[11] On 19 October Derby announced his scheme to raise the soldiers by canvassing, through local committees, all eligible males whose names and addresses were known from the registration lists. It was to be 'the last effort on behalf of voluntary recruiting'.[12]

The Australian Government, under similar pressures, could not ignore the Derby scheme. At his first meeting with the Governor-General after becoming Prime Minister, Hughes had discussed reinforcements. He wanted to know both about British policy in the Balkans, especially the Dardanelles, and the 'requirements likely to be made of Australia in further operations'. Perhaps commenting on the Universal Service League's campaign, he ruled out conscription as a practical proposal until after Britain itself had adopted it.[13]

In the meantime, following the British lead, Hughes looked for a greatly enhanced recruitment program. Having assured the Universal Service League that his government intended to adopt a recruitment plan 'on the lines of Lord Derby's campaign', Hughes persuaded them to give up their public advocacy of conscription. Derby had made loyalty to his scheme identical with loyalty to the Empire. He had sent a message to the Dominions denying rumours of splits in the British ministry and asserting that the government, as well as the country, was united behind him.[14] The members of the United Service League therefore had little choice but that of 'falling into line with Great Britain'. Hughes had argued that to persist with their contentious cause might well compromise its ultimate success. It would seem that Hughes, like Asquith, in part embraced the Derby scheme as a way of preparing the public mind for the necessity of compulsion but, if this were so, Hughes, in contrast to the British Prime Minister, did so with unqualified enthusiasm.[15]

Two days after securing the Universal Service League's cooperation, Hughes announced, with cabinet's approval, his government's acceptance of a new recruiting target of 50,000 men over and above Pearce's 9500 monthly reinforcements.[16] By the end of June 1916, they hoped to have increased the strength of the AIF to 300,000. How the 50,000 figure was arrived at is a mystery. It may have been based on the Army Council's suggestion in October that the Australian Government should plan for monthly reinforcements amounting to 10 percent of establishment.

---

[11] Adams and Poirier, *Conscription Controversy in Great Britain 1900–18*, pp.120–23.
[12] *Times* (London), 18 and 20 October 1915; *Argus*, 21 October 1915.
[13] Cable, Munro Ferguson to Bonar Law, 3 November 1915, TNA: PRO CO 418/134/107A.
[14] *Argus*, 28 October 1915.
[15] *Argus*, 23 November 1915.
[16] Cable, Munro Ferguson to Bonar Law, 23 November 1915, TNA: PRO CO 616/32/325: 'The Commonwealth Government after very careful consideration of the present outlook has decided to raise an additional fifty thousand men for active service to be available in the next few months. These will form new units and are independent of the quota of nine thousand five hundred a month necessary for reinforcements. This further contribution will bring the total number of men supplied by Australia by next June to something like three hundred thousand men.'

Since 96,000 troops had been despatched by the end of October, a six months reserve would equal approximately 50,000.

Yet though this initiative was not the result of a specific British request, it was clearly a response to the Derby scheme, and in implementing their new recruitment policy the Australians copied very closely the Derby procedures. Drawing on the Bureau of Census and Statistics' findings that there were 600,000 'fit' men between the ages of 18 and 44 in the country, the federal Parliamentary War Committee was to approach all eligibles by letter and ask them to complete a card indicating their intentions. Those who refused to join up were required to state 'as explicitly as possible' their reasons, and local committees were given the task of counselling these men. Each municipality or local government district was, moreover, allotted a quota which they were requested to fill. To try to appease those trade unionists and other Labor supporters who objected that the scheme was tantamount to 'compulsory voluntarism', Pearce stated that 'no action of an inquisitorial or persecuting character was to be in any way sanctioned.'[17] Since local committees had considerable autonomy and were pressed to meet specific targets it remained doubtful whether the government would be able to keep this promise. No attempt was made to define the line between reasonable persuasion and inquisitorial intimidation.

Hughes threw himself into the campaign. He appealed to the country in a stirring 'Call to Arms'. Travelling from city to city, his grand theme rang out. The British Empire and its Allies stood on the brink of disaster. As the war remained poised uncertainly between victory and defeat, the nation should be galvanised into action and all its energies applied to meeting the crisis. Hughes's longstanding simple theme was reasserted: 'We are in this war, and we must win or go under. There is no middle course.' No quarter was asked for nor would be given. No thought of a compromise peace could be entertained. In this battle for survival every man that could be mustered had to go into the front line.

Furthermore, taking up the USL cry, he urged that the war required total commitment. The British Empire's and its Allies' resources were superior to those of the Central Powers but, in order to benefit from this, it was necessary to learn from the Germans and organise these resources. Every facet of the nation's life, its finances, its industry, its trade, its technology as well as its manpower, had to be reconstructed under government direction to serve the one end. System and science had to be enlisted not only for the purpose of defeating Germany in the war but also for achieving self-sufficiency for Australia and the British Empire in the peace.[18] These were principles which Hughes had been expounding since the outbreak of hostilities. Now, as national leader, he appealed to the people to support him in giving effect to them.

The Governor-General was full of praise for his new Prime Minister. Shortly after the abandoning of the constitutional referendum he informed the Colonial Secretary that:

> In fighting politics, Mr. Fisher was a diplomat, possibly an Ambassador. Mr. Hughes is a General with an army behind him. The one makes requests, but the other puts forth demands, and only such a man as Mr. Hughes could have made waste paper of the specific orders of the

---

[17] *SMH*, 26 November, 4 and 9 December 1915.
[18] *SMH*, 30 November and 26 December 1915.

Adelaide conference which demanded the amendment of the Commonwealth Constitution, even in the midst of a great war.[19]

Hughes was in nearly every respect superior to Fisher; his 'judgment is better; his insight clear; his capacity for affairs great.' Unlike Fisher who had 'no elasticity of mind' and was 'impervious to other people's ideas', Hughes 'with broader views and sounder judgment was ready to entertain the ideas of others.' It was a mark of the latter's success that he had 'rapidly become popular with the Opposition through his war policy' and had 'already won the confidence of that set of people who ordinarily hold themselves completely aloof from politics and regard the politicians, and especially the Labour [sic] Politicians as anathema.'[20]

Munro Ferguson's assessment of both men was shaped by his view of what Australia's role in aiding the Empire should be. Hughes's attitude towards the constitutional referendum, his adoption of a much larger recruitment target and his call for a more strenuous war effort were taken as evidence of his ability to rise above party prejudice and to learn from wiser counsels. But Munro Ferguson was as mistaken about Hughes as he was about Fisher. Hughes's approach to the war was not the result of a latter-day conversion. It proceeded from long-held Social Darwinist and state socialist beliefs. Of all the national leaders, with the exception of Irvine, Hughes was the most rigid and dogmatic. And he pursued his fixed ideas with a single-mindedness that knew not doubt nor hesitation.

As Hughes's war policy unfolded, however, an ever-widening gap separated the Labor leader from the labour movement. The freeze on wages and the rise in prices of basic commodities, like flour, fed the grass-roots discontent. The failure to proceed with the constitutional referendum, which would have enabled the federal government to legislate to meet the workers' grievances, was viewed as a betrayal. Moreover, Hughes's close ties to the Labor Party's class enemies added to this resentment. Thus many in the movement suspected the new recruiting scheme to be a devious manoeuvre aimed at justifying conscription.

The Brisbane Trades Hall Industrial Council recommended to unionists that they refuse to answer the questions on the recruiting cards which were being sent to all eligible males, and they threatened to advise their members not to support the Labor candidate in the Wide Bay by-election which had been brought on by Fisher's resignation. In a meeting with Hughes they explained their opposition to the cards. They were as much loyal Britishers as Hughes. As 'members of the British nation' they opposed 'veiled conscription'. Since this 'war of attrition' was the product of capitalism which needed to rid itself of surplus value, Australia should not slavishly follow 'the dictates of the Imperial authorities'. The recruitment measures violated Fisher's promises and their enforcement would meet such fierce resistance that it would constitute 'a greater danger to the Empire'.[21]

---

[19] Secret despatch, Munro Ferguson to Bonar Law, 18 November 1915, TNA: PRO CO 418/134/188.
[20] Copy of personal letter, Munro Ferguson to Bonar Law, 8 November 1915, Novar Papers, NLA MS 696/765; secret letter, Munro Ferguson to Bonar Law, 28 December 1915, TNA: PRO CO 418/134/473; copy of personal letter, Munro Ferguson to Bonar Law, 11 January 1916, Novar Papers, NLA MS 696/795.
[21] *SMH*, 10 December 1915.

Hughes, in response, declared that his government stood for 'unionism and advanced democracy' and asked the Council to remember 'the tradition of the race' and the commonsense requirement of fighting the war. It is difficult to gauge how successful Hughes was in appeasing the union leaders, but soon after this confrontation, the seat which Fisher had held with a 9000 majority was lost to the opposition. Hughes was mystified by the Labor candidate's failure. He could not believe that his patriotic crusade would be rejected by the people. It would seem, however, that Labor's defeat was the result of many former Labor voters staying away from the polls. This rebuff was a sign of things to come.

British events compounded Hughes's problems. By the end of December the Asquith Government, working through the predetermined script of the Derby scheme, announced the failure of voluntary recruitment and on 6 January it introduced a bill to conscript single men. This British action confirmed the Australian anti-conscriptionists' worst fears. While Senator Albert Gardiner, an assistant minister in the government, stated categorically that conscription was not necessary in Australia, Hughes was more ambivalent. For him the question had to be seen from 'the point of view alone of victory for the Empire and its Allies'. The British Government was satisfied that the military situation required the measure. He added, however, that he did not think the British attitude would affect Australian policy.[22] The Labor Party's federal executive, which had been convened for the purpose of censuring Hughes over the constitutional referendum, asked him not to bring in conscription without first consulting the federal conference. When Hughes refused to give such an assurance, Senator Thomas Givens, the President of the Senate and Chairman of the federal executive, promised that, if the matter were mooted, he would summon a special meeting of the executive.[23]

The industrial base of the Labor Party was becoming restless. The major labour papers, the Melbourne *Labour Call*, the Sydney *Worker* and the Brisbane *Standard*, all sniped at Hughes for tactics which menaced civil liberties and the rights of unions. His critics were no doubt encouraged by the British Labour Party's action in holding a special conference to condemn the Asquith Government's adoption of conscription.[24] In this atmosphere, discontent in the work place erupted. The coalminers, waterside workers and shearers – in some cases even defying their union officials – struck for higher wages and shorter hours.

Hughes fought to keep control of the labour movement. He bought peace with the strikers by conceding their bread and butter claims. He used his accumulated credit with the unions and the Political Labor Leagues in New South Wales to prevent them from joining the Brisbane Industrial Council's attack on his recruitment policy. With these successes behind him he turned on his adversaries and in major speeches in Melbourne and Sydney denounced those he described as opponents of recruiting. 'Such alien influences', he said 'have nothing in common with Labour or unionism.' They were 'foul parasites attaching themselves to the vitals of Labour'. There was 'between syndicalism – that is its name – and unionism and Labour, as we all know it in this

---

[22] *Argus*, 24 December 1915 and *SMH*, 30 December 1915.

[23] L.F. Fitzhardinge, *The Little Digger, 1914–1952* (Sydney: Angus and Robertson 1979), p.62; *Argus*, 24 and 30 December and 7 and 8 January 1916.

[24] *Ibid.*, 8 and 14 January 1916.

country, a gulf as wide as hell.' Furthermore, he continued, 'Those men know no nationality, no religion or principle.' He then clothed the AIF with the mantle of unionism. He reminded his audience that the Waterside Workers Federation had sent 4000 men and the Australian Workers Union over 20,000 men to the front. Those 'who sneered were not unionists nor socialists but anarchists – enemies not only of society but of all that unionism should stand for.' Foreshadowing future events he asserted that, 'It was no use dealing with them like a tame cat; they only understood force.' This name-calling, which was intended to isolate his enemies and silence his detractors, tended rather to harden hearts and to antagonise many fair-minded members of the party.

Though Hughes said that he was for 'militant unionism' and that at the end of the war the democratic principles exemplified by Australia would triumph in the peace, the burden of his message was directed not to future ideals but to present necessities. Repeating again a familiar refrain he declared: 'The thing to do is to win the war victoriously for ourselves … When you are amid a jungle with wild beasts what is the good of babbling about peace?' In answer to those who claimed that Australia would be no worse off if Germany were victorious, he retorted that the war was 'as much a battle for Australia as Britain', that it might indeed 'find its way to our shore'. Anticipating the argument that he was to employ in August and September 1916 when he himself took up the cause of conscription, he concluded by alluding to the special dangers which Australia would face if Britain were defeated. Australia was 'in deadly peril … Take a map. Look where Australia is. We are five million people and we have challenged the whole Pacific to interfere with us.'[25] It was as close as he dared to go in pointing to Japan as the power which would dominate Australia if the British Empire lost the war in Europe.

In preparing for his visit to England, Hughes had tried to set his Australian house in order, and, on the surface, he had been remarkably successful. The striking workers had been appeased. The Labor Party and the major trade union organisation had been persuaded not to oppose his 'Call to Arms'. He believed that the malcontent minority had been rendered harmless. He had also quieted the pro-conscriptionist forces. The USL had deferred to the authority of the British example and consented to give Hughes's own Derby scheme a fair trial. The Liberal Party's leaders had been swayed by the same arguments. Even the editors of the major daily newspapers had agreed not to publish anything pertaining to conscription during his absence. Leaving as little as possible to chance, however, Hughes had taken additional precautions and instructed Senator Pearce, as defence minister, to ensure that the censors kept out of the press anything which might possibly undermine recruitment. It was, he wrote, 'essential that the public mind should not be disturbed by complaints about hospital treatment, camp troubles or news of the war or opinions in regard thereto.'[26]

---

[25] *SMH*, 14 and 18 January 1916.
[26] Letter, Hughes to Pearce, 4 December 1915, Pearce Papers, AWM 3DRL 2222/3/3; see also letter, Pearce to Hughes, 15 December 1915, *ibid.*, confirming that appropriate action had been taken. Hughes was concerned about the circulation of adverse reports, like that of Ashmead-Bartlett, on the Dardanelles campaign.

Hughes was well pleased with his efforts. On the eve of his departure he wrote to the Governor-General that he had:

> smoothed things out a good deal – And I anticipate no serious trouble of any kind. The Press are unanimous; and all are going to back the present policy without reservation – they say nothing at all about Conscription but back our scheme.[27]

He had persuaded the country into accepting his war policy. Or so it seemed.

The Pacific problem

For Hughes, a very important consideration in deciding to send more men to aid the Mother Country was his fear of Japan. Winning the war in Europe was an essential condition for Australia's security in the Pacific. Until becoming Prime Minister, he had not been directly involved with the Pacific problems. They were the responsibility of Fisher in collaboration with Pearce and Mahon. Hughes had shared the pre-war apprehensions about Japan, and probably while Acting Prime Minister and through general cabinet consultations had gleaned something of the wartime difficulties. However when Fisher, preparing for the handover of the reins of government, took Hughes fully into his confidence, as seems probable, the heir-apparent responded almost too readily to the news of Japan's activities. Two weeks before Fisher stood down, Hughes, echoing his leader's many warnings, made his first public pronouncement on the Pacific peril. Declaring that it was 'in the Pacific that the great problems would have to be faced', Hughes in accordance with the established Fisher doctrine looked to Canadian, Australian and New Zealand naval squadrons joining together in an imperial fleet to patrol the Pacific.[28]

Once Hughes's mind had become fixed on the Japan problem, he treated it in the same way that he had the troop reinforcements, as a vital issue requiring immediate and urgent action. For a solution, he turned to Fisher's idea of an imperial conference to deal with the Pacific. In his first discussions with the Governor-General he had canvassed the possibility of a meeting of British, Canadian and New Zealand Prime Ministers to consider the 'Pacific Settlement'. If it could not be convened in London then, echoing Fisher, he suggested that it should be held in Australia. And a proposal to this effect was cabled to London.

The Colonial Office was no longer so unsympathetic to the idea of consultation. Whitehall, however, still doubted whether the idea of a conference was 'either wise or practicable' as it remained concerned that such a meeting might embarrass delicate relations with Japan and prejudge post-war policy. It was adamant that Germany's colonial territories were 'not open to discussion'. Nevertheless Fisher's persistent criticisms had created a stir; the matter had been raised in the House of Commons. Thus Bonar Law, anticipating Hughes's request, invited the newly installed Prime Minister to visit London for 'an exchange of views', and as an added

---

[27] Letter, Hughes to Munro Ferguson, 20 January 1916, Novar Papers, NLA MS 696/2448.
[28] *SMH*, 10 October 1915.

In early November the Secretary of the Prime Minister's Department prepared a briefing paper showing how the Japanese had come to take possession of the German North Pacific islands, which probably helped to fill out Hughes's understanding of this question. See 'Pacific Islands', NAA A981 MARS2 PART3.

inducement he mentioned that the New Zealand Prime Minister was intending to be in the United Kingdom in January. The two wires had crossed each other. Replying to Hughes on 11 November, Bonar Law repeated the invitation and said it was desirable that the two South Pacific leaders' visits should coincide. The Colonial Secretary was offering Hughes the same courtesy that had been extended in July to Borden, the Canadian Prime Minister, and in September to Fisher. But while it might be possible for Hughes and Massey to consult informally with the British Government about their common Pacific concerns, nothing smacking of a conference, whether formal or informal, was to be tolerated.[29]

Hughes was not so easily deterred from seeking his larger objective. Having accepted the British invitation, he approached the New Zealand and Canadian Prime Ministers to ask them to join him in London and so, in effect, to participate in a conference on Pacific security. Borden was somewhat perplexed by Hughes's news of a Pacific conference. In response to overtures from a leading New Zealand Round Table figure, Borden had written to Massey in September agreeing to take part with Australia and New Zealand in a conference on Pacific defence. But his offer had been rejected. Massey, while supporting the idea of such cooperation between the Pacific Dominions, disowned the Round Table emissary who had acted without authority and endorsed the British position, namely that such questions should be left until the end of the war.[30]

When, therefore, Borden received Hughes's message he asked the British for clarification. The Colonial Office, disturbed by his independent initiative, ordered Munro Ferguson to keep them informed of all Hughes's communications with the other Dominions. Bonar Law wanted to make it clear to Borden that Hughes and Massey were not coming as a result of 'special invitations' and he directed that in the reply there should be no reference to 'the Pacific Islands'. While he tactfully expressed the hope that Borden might be able to come to Britain while the other two leaders were there, he 'did not wish him to think that we considered it necessary for him to come.'[31]

Like Harcourt before him, Bonar Law wanted to manage the negotiations in order to defeat Australia's Pacific conference proposal. In the event, however, it was not the Colonial Office's

---

[29] In the copy of despatch, Munro Ferguson to Bonar Law, 14 October 1915, Novar Papers, NLA MS 696/759 the Governor-General wrote, 'Mr. Fisher is gratified by your message re consultation at home with Prime Ministers of Overseas Dominions. I let him know my personal opinions as to the impossibility of holding a Conference at this stage of the war. He does not himself consider that any Federal Minister could leave Australia for the moment, least of all the Prime Minister, for anything short of a conference.'

See also secret memorandum, J.C.C. Davidson to A. Steel-Maitland, 18 September 1915, J.C.C. Davidson Papers, House of Lords Record Office, box 'World War I, 1914–15'; personal, secret cable, Munro Ferguson to Bonar Law, 3 November 1915, and Colonial Office and Colonial Secretary minutes on the cable, TNA: PRO CO 418/134/106–08; cables, Bonar Law to Munro Ferguson, 5 and 11 November 1915, NAA CP78/22 1915/296, and copy of cable, Bonar Law to Munro Ferguson, 11 November 1915, TNA: PRO CO 532/78/465.

[30] Letter, Richard McBride, Premier of British Columbia, to Borden, 18 August 1915, letter, Percival Witherby to Borden, 10 September 1915, and letter, Massey to Borden, undated, Borden papers, LAC OC 187A.

[31] Cable, Governor-General of Canada to Colonial Secretary, 16 November 1915 and Colonial Office minutes, TNA: PRO CO 532/78/455–80.

manipulations but Canada's and New Zealand's domestic difficulties which frustrated Hughes's scheme. Borden and Massey, because of local political problems, were forced to stay at home. Making the best of the circumstances, Hughes decided, at the request of Borden and Massey, to visit them on his way to Britain and to use the opportunity to discuss not only 'a practical and firm policy' towards Japan and the Pacific but also the future structure of 'Imperial relations.'[32]

During his first three months in office, Hughes's anxiety about the Pacific question mounted. Newspaper accounts of Japan's attitude to Australia and southward expansion, a major Naval Board survey of Japan as a strategic threat, and the Japanese Consul-General's persistent efforts to have the Australian Government accede to a form of the 1911 Anglo-Japanese Commercial Treaty, all contributed to the heightened concern about the problem.

Despatches from the British Ambassador in Tokyo contained alarming intelligence. The new Japanese Prime Minister, Count Shigenobu Okuma, in a speech to the Japanese Emigration Association had observed that because the British navy had 'felt incompetent' in the Pacific and the Japanese squadrons had exhibited 'extraordinary strength' Australians, who had previously discriminated against the Japanese, talked of a Japanese invasion and thought of combining with the United States against Japan, had had 'to minimise the feeling against the Japanese'. The head of the Japanese Government claimed that, as a result of the war, Australia was obliged to make concessions to Japan's preponderant position in the region.

A number of articles in Japanese newspapers were also disturbing. A contributor to the *Asahi* had referred to the Japanese occupied islands in the North Pacific as 'stepping stones to the South Seas' and had remarked that they were 'certainly important and indispensable places for the future Southward expansion of the Japanese.' *Nichi Nichi* carried stories that Britain coveted the islands and, as a result, there was 'absolutely nothing left of the Anglo-Japanese alliance but its body, and it is injurious and unprofitable.' The same writer even hinted that Germany might be a more suitable alliance partner. Ambassador Greene offered no evaluation of these cuttings, and so it is likely that the Australian ministers and officials exaggerated their importance. A series of essays by Dr J. Ingram Bryan in Tokyo which were published in the *Sydney Morning Herald* on such topics as 'Oriental Dilemma: Japan's Control of China' and 'Japan supports Germany in the Pacific' – somehow they escaped the censor's eye – reinforced the impression gained from the Japanese newspapers.[33]

The Naval Board's 17,000 word report, primarily the work of the head of the Naval Intelligence Department, Captain Walter Thring, which evaluated the Japanese threat and set down proposals for Pacific naval defence, was the most substantial strategic appreciation submitted to

---

[32] Letter, Hughes to Munro Ferguson, 22 November 1915, Novar Papers, NLA MS 696/3900 and letter, Munro Ferguson to Hughes, 25 November 1915, NAA CP78/22, 1915/296.

Massey, in explaining his inability to travel to London, suggested that Bonar Law might discuss the possibility of an 'Imperial Minister' visiting New Zealand to hold talks with the Australian and New Zealand governments. See cable, Lord Liverpool, Governor of New Zealand, to Bonar Law, 3 December 1915, Bonar Law Papers, House of Lords Record Office, MS53/6/65.

[33] Copy of despatch, Sir Conyngham Greene, British Ambassador in Tokyo to Munro Ferguson, 14 August 1915 and 11 October 1915 (both initialled by the Defence Minister), NAA MP729/5 393/1/272; *SMH*, 27 November and 4 December 1915.

the Australian Government since Federation. It was intended most immediately to provide the basis for a policy which the Prime Minister could put before a possible Imperial Conference dealing with Pacific naval defence. Presented to Hughes on 21 December it comprised three sections – the first dealing with the problems of Pacific defence, the second with the Japanese danger and the third with Australia's post-war naval policy. Though the immediate impetus for the study had been Japan's actions during the war, the naval authorities drew heavily on Australian leaders' pre-war strategic arguments. In the report, it is possible to discern the influence of the earlier policy debates, the Melbourne Round Table discussions and Eggleston articles (Creswell was a member of the Melbourne Round Table group) and even C. H. Kirmess's 1909 invasion scare novel, *The Australian Crisis*. More specifically the report could be seen as an elaboration of a two-page statement of principles on 'Australian Naval Defence and the Defence of British Interests in the Pacific' adopted by the Naval Board in July 1913.[34]

At the heart of the report lay apprehension about Japan. According to the authors, history showed that Japan was not a satiated power. The record of the previous twenty years bore witness to Japan's aggressive ambitions. Citing Greene's newspaper extracts and Suttor's appraisal of Japan's aims, as well as that country's conduct since the beginning of the war, they concluded that Japan might 'at some future (and not very distantly future) time … put direct hostile pressure on the Commonwealth.' They claimed that 'Japanese residents and visitors to Sydney have lately made extensive purchases of Charts, not only of the equatorial zone of the Western Pacific, north and south, but of the whole Australia coast also', and this was taken as further evidence of Japan's unfriendly intentions.

Japan, the report continued, might have three possible objectives. It might attempt to solve its population problem by colonising 'the half-empty' Australian continent; it might try to compel Australia to modify its White Australia policy so as to remove the affront to its self-esteem; or it might seek to advance southwards and seize the Dutch East Indies which would not only add greatly to its wealth and resources but also bring it 'within reach of absolute predominance in the Indian Ocean' and tempt it to establish a base on Australia's north-west coast. To meet these contingencies, all that Australia had to rely on, for the time being, was the Anglo-Japanese alliance and such respect as the Japanese might have for the British navy, 'which is and for an unknown time will remain concentrated in the Atlantic'. The report, however, evinced little confidence in the alliance for 'it would be foolish after the events of the last two years to lay any stress on treaties in themselves as safeguards against anything.'

Australia was faced by a short-term and a long-term security problem, the former appearing at the end of the war and the latter after the termination of the alliance. The first was the more ominous. Should the Japanese demand as a reward for their wartime services that their citizens be allowed to enter freely any part of the Empire or to settle some parts of northern Australia, then the British might succumb to the pressure. The report was insistent that there were good grounds for these fears. It pointed out that many British politicians and publicists had for some time been criticising Australia's racially-based immigration policy and its failure to develop its tropical

---

[34] *Search for Security*, especially pp.159–63 and 251–60; minutes of Naval Board meeting, 17 and 21 July 1913, NAA MP1049/1 14/0285.

territories. Many influences – 'the diplomacy of Japan, the representations of the Indian government, the interests of high finance, the prejudice of the missionary element and its friends, the ill-informed prepossession of English politicians and press-writers' – would be brought to bear on the British Government to persuade Australia that 'it must accept its fate.' Following Kirmess's plot, the study suggested that Japan might even let their settlers be naturalised as British subjects, as that would 'not really impair their value to her', but would 'go some way to soothe the Imperial Government.'

While Australia was loyally giving extensive naval and military assistance to the Mother Country, the Naval Board was questioning whether Britain could be depended on to protect Australian territory and sovereignty. The authors of the report saw only two ways out of Australia's perceived dilemma. It had either by 'a slow diplomatic attempt' to convince the British that such a Japanese occupation would endanger their interests in India – to convince them that Japan threatened Australia would not be enough – or to issue a 'straightforward declaration ... that the occupation meant war.'

In both the short and long terms the naval officials held that Australia could only be defended adequately if the British Empire established a Pacific fleet along the lines proposed at the 1909 Imperial Defence Conference. Like Fisher and Cook, they attacked what since the 1890s had been the Admiralty's orthodox doctrine, namely that the seas were one and therefore the naval forces of the Empire had to be treated as one. The emergence of Japan as a naval power in the Pacific 'invalidated the "unity doctrine"' and made the Pacific 'a separate problem' from that of the Atlantic. No longer was it possible to consider the defence of Australia and New Zealand 'as a minor and postponable matter' which must remain subordinate to the needs of Britain.

The report contended that 'putting aside ... the question of patriotism' – and it never gave any weight to sentiment – the integrity of the Empire was not equally vital to all its member nations. Canada (sheltered under the mantle of the American 'Monroe Doctrine') and South Africa might well look for protection to some other European power. But for Australia, New Zealand and, indeed, India, imperial cooperation was essential to survival. Without it they would be left 'a prey to any Great Power that cared to annex them'. The preservation of the Empire meant more than maintaining the inviolability of the British Isles; it also included ensuring the safety of the Dominions. The Naval Board attempted to confront the major strategic conundrum in their analysis. They freely acknowledged that, 'Irreparable defeat in Great Britain would break up the Empire at once', but they added that likewise, 'irreparable defeat in Australia would seriously weaken it and would certainly be the first step towards its inevitable dissolution.'

The only satisfactory security for British interests in the Pacific, including Australia, lay therefore in the creation of an imperial Pacific fleet. Giving vent to Australian anger at the British failure since 1912 to accept this view, the report at one point asserted that the cost of such a Pacific fleet would have to be borne by those 'who feel the need of it', by those 'who are exposed' to the Japanese danger and 'who know it'. If carried to its logical conclusion such an argument meant that Australia and New Zealand would have to accept 'the main burden'. However the Henderson scheme, even if supplemented by a New Zealand contribution, would be inadequate to meet the need.

Thus when the report came to consider the particulars it looked to a revival of the Admiralty's 1909 scheme for a Pacific fleet composed of units provided by the British Dominions and territories in the region, 'together with any naval force which the Government of the United Kingdom may see fit to maintain there'. To counter a Japanese fleet of twelve modern battleships or battle cruisers, the British Pacific fleet would require at least nine capital ships, two to be supplied by Australia, one by New Zealand and the British Pacific islands, one by Canada, two by India, Ceylon and the Strait Settlements, and three by Britain 'in respect of Eastern trade and minor possessions'. It was noted that Australia had already acquired one of its battle cruisers, the *Australia*, and that New Zealand and Malaya had already funded one each for the Royal Navy. The practical implication for Australia was that if, during 1916 and 1917, it adhered to the Henderson scheme it would be able to play its part without increasing its anticipated defence expenditure. If, in the short term, Australia and New Zealand were left to fend for themselves, it was recommended that four or five light cruisers carrying sea-planes should patrol the northern approaches from Singapore to Tonga in order to give advance notice of an invasion fleet and so time for the mobilisation of the regional strike force.

On the delicate question of the control of a combined British fleet, the report readily agreed that there should be a unified supreme command. Since, however, what was proposed was designedly a Pacific fleet, it would have to come under the direction of an authority distinct from that governing the Atlantic fleet. This authority would 'require special knowledge of Pacific conditions and problems'. In conclusion the report drew out the Australian Round Table lesson which appropriately followed from such an experiment.

> The gradually acquired habit of joint control in a matter of joint concern – amounting almost to an alliance within the Empire – might well accustom the partners to the idea of joint control in a larger form, and so lead to the creation of a genuinely Imperial Government through which all British communities within the Empire would exercise more direct control over all matters of Imperial concern.[35]

The Naval Board's report assumed that victory would restore the pre-war balance of power in the Pacific and therefore require the adoption of the pre-war solution to the ensuing strategic problems. Positing, as they did, a victory for Britain and its allies, their calculations about the post-war Pacific overlooked the fact that with Germany crushed, the British fleet would be free to come to Australia's assistance in the Pacific. This would make a substantial difference to the geopolitical circumstances which had created the 'Australian Crisis' in the pre-war years. Even if Britain did not station a permanent fleet in the region or join in a Pacific fleet, its capacity to move a superior naval force to counter Japan would act as a strong deterrent. Should Japan be so foolhardy as to attack Australia, the Royal Navy would within a reasonable time be able to break Japanese supply lines and force the invaders to withdraw. As the authors of the report understood

---

[35] Letter, Naval Secretary, G.L. Macandie to Secretary, Prime Minister's Department, 21 December 1915, enclosing the report with a request that 'the Prime Minister may peruse them before his departure for London', Hughes Papers, NLA MS 1538/19/16–55 and copy in NAA MP1049/1 14/0285. The Naval Board approved the paper on 'The Post-Bellum Naval Policy for the Pacific' on 5 October 1915 and the paper on 'The Japanese Danger' on 21 October 1915.

the post-war situation, Britain would only be prevented from playing such a role if new European rivals emerged to pin its navy to the North Sea. That did not seem likely, but the Naval Board's reports did not canvass the issue.

Furthermore, the naval strategists made no attempt to consider the consequences for Australia of Britain losing or drawing the war in Europe, and in late 1915 these were serious possibilities. Either outcome would pose grave problems; in the latter case Japan would become a very formidable threat while in the former Australia would be left at the mercy of Japan. The report did not explain why, at the end of the war, Britain and Canada – both of which had since 1912 refused to contribute to a Pacific Fleet – would be more likely to favour a revival of that plan. One cannot but suspect that, having in the pre-war years settled on a policy which knitted so well imperial sentiment to the national interest, naval authorities were loath to abandon it.

There was an equal lack of logical rigour in dealing with the German North Pacific islands. Though the authors regretted that Japan had been able to seize the islands, they failed to develop a consistent attitude to the problem. While in one section they conceded that since Japan could not be expelled without a violent clash it would have to be left in possession, in another they called for a reassertion of the Australian claims to the islands and included in their naval frontier-patrol scheme proposals for building bases at Yap and Angaur. They could not come to terms with the fact that the war was almost certain to bring into being a new world order, and as a result they did not take this into account in their calculations of Australia's likely post-war circumstances and produce defence recommendations to meet various new possibilities. There is no question that their belief in a Japanese danger and the need for Australia to find a naval strategy to meet such a danger was sincerely held and arose out of the fear of Japan which had informed the thinking of the whole national security establishment for a decade or more.

The report helped to focus Hughes's mind on the subject. It is possible that Hughes had been shown a copy of some sections or had been given a summary of their contents before he made his *Brisbane* launch speech. Certainly as early as October the Governor-General had an inkling of what the Naval Board was about, informing Bonar Law that 'in naval circles' it was believed that 'the whole of the Admiralty's policy in the Pacific, was all along ineffective.'[36] At the end of December Hughes was given a copy of the Navy Department's briefing papers and it may be that the warning he gave in January about Australia's place on the Pacific map was inspired by them.[37]

When within a month or so of taking office Hughes found the Japanese Consul-General on his doorstep pressing Australia to enter into a commercial treaty, he might well have seen in this act a personal manifestation of the more general warnings about Japan expressed in the Tokyo despatches and the Naval Board's report. After the change of government the importunate Shimizu, having failed to move the Fisher administration, lost no time in renewing his campaign. He had begun with the sympathetic Secretary of the External Affairs Department, Atlee Hunt, but this did not help his cause. When Hunt drew his minister's attention to the question the latter said that he was sick of being pestered about the matter and directed that no further time should be

---

[36] Letter, Munro Ferguson to Bonar Law, 29 October 1915, Novar Papers, NLA MS 696/761–64.
[37] Hughes Papers, NLA MS 1538/156/16–55.

spent on the subject. Mahon stated that he had told the consul several times there was 'no probability of our considering the Treaty until the close of war.'[38]

Shimizu would not be put off so easily. He was well aware of the government's policy of diplomatic procrastination. He thus approached the new Prime Minister and, if Hughes is to be believed, was most pertinacious in pressing his case. The consul gave Hughes a document similar to that previously handed to Fisher, and the Prime Minister promised a reply before departing for the United Kingdom. Shimizu, in order to let Hughes know that Japan's representation could not be lightly dismissed, told him that the Japanese Ambassador in London had instructions to pursue the issue with the British Foreign Secretary. Shimizu, in language akin to that used by Okuma, referred to 'the altered conditions after the war and to the admission of Japanese to Australia.'

For Hughes, Shimizu's behaviour smacked of intimidation. Following the interview, Hughes was worried about 'how far the Japanese may put pressure on us during the war to secure the m.f.n. [most-favoured-nation] treatment or even for the admission of coloured races to Australia.' Writing to Bonar Law, Munro Ferguson indicated that 'anxiety was felt as to whether the Home Government would support Australia as against Japan's demands and be in a position after the war to resist them effectively.'[39] The British suggestion that the Commonwealth should withdraw its garrison from Nauru was seen as evidence of the imperial authorities' indifference to Australian interests. The Australians rejected it outright, as such a withdrawal 'might tend to influence steps being taken to secure occupation similar to island north of the equator'. They would not appease Japan further and give it the opportunity to establish itself south of the equator.[40] When the British Government, hoping to obtain additional Japanese naval assistance for patrolling the southern Atlantic, urged on the Australians the importance 'on political grounds of being conciliatory with Japan', Hughes in response agreed only to deal 'civilly but evasively' with the Consul-General.[41]

On 13 January the cabinet considered an External Affairs Department memorandum on Shimizu's representations. Perhaps influenced by the Governor-General, Hunt submitted that since the Japanese might well take a tougher stand and make even greater demands at the peace table it might be wise to reconsider the June 1915 decision to postpone dealing with the Anglo-Japanese Commercial Treaty until the end of the war. Reflecting perhaps the views of the Naval Board and the Round Table, Hunt said that there was 'undoubtedly a considerable feeling among intelligent people in Australia that when the war ends Japan would make demands for much more extensive concessions in the way of the immigration of her subjects to Australia.' For this reason he argued that if Australia entered at once into a commercial agreement with Japan it would

---

[38] Memorandum scrawled in Hunt's handwriting, undated, enclosing copy of letter, Hunt to Mahon, 17 June 1915 and Mahon's scribbled answer, 16 November 1915, Atlee Hunt Papers, NLA MS 52/1515.
[39] Copy of letter, Munro Ferguson to Bonar Law, 22 December 1915, Novar Papers, NLA MS 696/3900.
[40] Copy of cable, Munro Ferguson to Bonar Law, 26 December 1915, NAA CP78/23 and letter, secret, Munro Ferguson to Bonar Law, 19 January 1916, TNA: PRO CO 418/144/44–45.
[41] Copy of letter, personal and secret, Munro Ferguson to Hughes, 6 January 1916, Novar Papers, NLA MS 696/2429; letter, personal and secret, Hughes to Munro Ferguson, 7 January 1916, *ibid.*, 696/2431–33; copy of letter, Munro Ferguson to Bonar Law, 11 January 1916, *ibid.*, 696/793–95.

'probably get a condition from the Japanese Government by which they undertake to recognise all our existing laws both as respect immigration and employment within Australia.' Unless the Australian Government acted quickly it might lose the chance of reaching an amicable settlement.

The cabinet was not persuaded. Hughes was instructed to take up the matter with the British during his visit to the United Kingdom. Meanwhile the consul was to be given 'no encouragement' to expect that Australia would become a party to the treaty 'in the immediate future'. He was to be told that nothing would be done until after the return of the Prime Minister.[42] The Governor-General was not pleased with the outcome. He had failed to win his ministers over to his point of view. Expressing his irritation he told Bonar Law that he hoped an imperial conference would make the Australians consider 'the interests of the Empire as a whole and not merely of a handful of Australians.'[43] On 19 January, Hughes informed Shimizu of the government's decision. He apparently employed his political tricks, most notably his deafness, in order to avoid lengthy explanations or discussions: 'I'm sure he thinks I'm the biggest fool or the deafest one, in all the wide world. Anyhow he got nothing out of me.'[44]

Shimizu reported to Tokyo on his lack of success. Hughes, while admitting that after the war commercial treaties would need to be revised, had said that the Japanese proposals were 'premature'. He would, however, give the matter 'due consideration' if the British should raise the question during his visit to the United Kingdom. Thus Shimizu concluded that the Japanese had 'no choice but to wait until after his arrival in London to persuade the United Kingdom government to take action.'[45] The Japanese were even less pleased than the Governor-General with the result and looked to the British to intervene on their behalf.

Anticipating the coming discussions with imperial statesmen, Hughes sought the Defence Minister's advice on Australia's interest in the Pacific islands. Pearce summarised the conclusions he and Fisher had arrived at by May the previous year. He told Hughes that while the German North Pacific islands were 'not of very great value' to Australia the South Pacific islands were of

---

[42] Memorandum, Atlee Hunt to Minister, 13 January 1916 and minute by Mahon, 13 January 1916, NAA CP717, Prime Minister's Department, Correspondence and Papers, Vol.23, p.580, and NAA CP447/2 SC472(7).
Hughes's cabinet notes of meeting of 13 January 1916 record that on Mahon's motion, 'Nothing was to be done until after the war. P.M. to set out views of Government on Japanese question to British Government', Hughes Papers, NLA MS 1538/112/2.

[43] Letter, secret, Munro Ferguson to Bonar Law, 18 January 1916, TNA: PRO CO 418/144/47.

[44] Letter, Hughes to Munro Ferguson, 20 January 1916, Novar Papers, NLA MS 696/2448.

Despite Hughes's attempt to halt the Japanese diplomatic offensive, it continued during his absence abroad. Hunt in early February reported to Mahon that the Japanese vice-consul in Melbourne had in a 'purely unofficial' way raised with him the treatment of Japanese businessmen and tourists entering Australia. He thought it 'a pity to place Japanese of the merchant and tourist classes in any different position from those of other people'. He asked that the Australian Government should take the subject 'into very serious consideration'. Hunt recommended that 'any very limited restrictions' imposed on their merchants be removed 'without any request coming from the Japanese Government'. See letter, Hunt to Mahon, 9 February 1916, NAA A63/48 J2/3/2.

[45] Cable, Shimizu to Ishii, 20 January 1916, *Nippon Gaiko Bunsho,* I, '1916', 183.

'incalculable value'. Though the islands north of the equator, 'in the hands of another Power' could 'not be of much danger … because of their distance … and intervention of other islands', those south of the line were essential for commercial and strategic reasons. They were 'a shield to the Northern portion of our continent'. Likewise, in accordance with the views adopted by the Fisher Government, Pearce thought that the future of the New Hebrides warranted 'grave consideration'; if France were to transfer its interest in the islands to a hostile power, they would pose a danger to Australian security. It was clear that he had Japan in mind, since he added that the islands were 'important … as forming portion of the shield against an invasion from the north'.[46] Full of the Pacific question, in all its dimensions, Hughes informed the Governor-General on the eve of his departure for England that when he met his Dominion colleagues Massey and Borden, he had 'a quite clear and definite idea' of what he wanted and he regarded it as his mission, 'to make them want it too'.[47]

The Prime Minister's visits to New Zealand and Canada did not achieve all that he had expected. In Auckland Massey was cooperative. Fisher's visit the previous January had prepared the way. Hughes told Pearce that 'I've seen Massey and he agrees with my ideas on a Pacific policy'. Hughes had obviously discussed his desire to unite the Pacific Dominions for the purpose of presenting a common defence policy to the British. For his part Massey, probably on the basis of Borden's September offer to participate in a Pacific conference, thought that the Canadian leader could be 'relied upon to back us up'.[48]

In Canada Hughes met with a more cautious response. Borden shared Hughes's concern that as Britain had declared war without consulting the Dominions, so it might make peace without giving proper attention to the Dominions' interests. But Hughes's desire for Canadian support went beyond this. Perhaps influenced by the Naval Board's report, which he had brought with him, Hughes sought Canadian aid against Japan in circumstances where the German fleet had crippled the British fleet in the Atlantic and left Japan unquestionably dominant in the Pacific. As Borden recorded it in his diary, Hughes was 'very anxious that we should place a fleet unit on the Pacific. Australia great[ly] dreads Japan's future aims. If, in [a] great battle between German and British fleets, the latter although victorious should lose, say one half of its fighting power, Japan would be the greatest naval power.'[49] On this question Borden, though seemingly sympathetic, was non-committal. Canadians, sheltering under the mantle of the United States 'Monroe Doctrine', lacked the spur of fear.

From the available evidence it would appear that Hughes did not discuss in detail the future of the German Pacific islands with Massey and Borden. He might well have accepted Fisher's position that the fact of military occupation would determine the frontiers of the peace. As for his

---

[46] Copy of letter, Pearce to Hughes, 14 January 1916, Pearce Papers, AWM 3DRL 2222/ 1/148.
[47] Letter, Hughes to Munro Ferguson, 20 January 1916, Novar Papers, NLA MS 696/2448.
[48] Letter, Hughes to Pearce, 24 January 1916, Pearce Papers, AWM 3DRL 2222/3/28.
In somewhat less precise terms Hughes told Munro Ferguson that, 'All went well with the Prime Minister of New Zealand; if Borden falls into line I shall be able to do well enough when I reach London'. See letter, Hughes to Munro Ferguson, 4 February 1916, Novar Papers, NLA MS 696/2450.
[49] Borden Diary, 18 February 1916, Borden Papers, LAC; letter, Hughes to Borden, 24 February 1916, Borden Papers, LAC OC 135.

more general defence objective Hughes was no more successful than Fisher. His meetings with the Dominion prime ministers, while it had elicited sympathetic responses, had not resulted in an agreement, not even an informal agreement, on the Empire's 'Pacific policy'.

'To rouse the Empire and put Australia's view'

Arriving in England on 7 March after a brief but disappointing stopover in the United States – he did not meet President Woodrow Wilson who was 'too busy with Washington's Birthday function – or peradventure he was writing another note [to the Germans]' – Hughes set out Australia's claim to be heard and listed the topics he intended to raise with the British authorities. At his first press conference Hughes announced that, among other things, he wished to discuss 'the organisation of trade within the Empire and with our Allies, the question of sea power in the Pacific, and the terms of peace in so far as they affect the interests of Canada, Australia and New Zealand.'[50] He also gave notice that, unlike previous Dominion prime ministers visiting the United Kingdom, he was going to speak out publicly on general issues such as the prosecution of the war and the future of the Empire.

Australian leaders believed that they had earned a right to a say in imperial counsels. Fisher, who had arrived in Britain a month before Hughes, had put his demands rather bluntly. Roiled by the Colonial Office's lack of sympathy for his requests for an imperial conference he had declared: 'I have not come to London to be invited to the counsels. I intend to walk in.'[51] But Fisher did not walk in. He was no longer Prime Minister and the British did not respond to the sick man's somewhat confused and sometimes carping outbursts. Hughes also was intent on making his own mark and so ignored the High Commissioner. Hughes did not, to the best of our knowledge, consult his former leader on any of the issues he took up with the British officials.

Hughes launched himself into an inspirational crusade aimed at rousing the British people to fight the war 'with all their heart, with all their mind and with all their strength'. The gospel that he had preached in Australia was now carried across to the centre of the Empire, and expounded at public meetings in London, Bristol, Edinburgh, Glasgow and other major towns. Suitably dramatised and embroidered for the larger stage it captured national attention. David Lloyd George wrote rather fulsomely in the introduction to the subsequent publication of these addresses that, 'No public speeches of modern times made such an impression on the British public.'[52]

Asquith's critics hailed the Australian as the true voice of the Empire. Hughes had arrived in England already convinced that the Asquith Government with its 'wait and see' policy had failed to grasp the true nature of the war crisis, of this 'life and death struggle' for national survival.[53] The defeat at the Dardanelles, which touched Australia so nearly, was the most recent sign of this lack of direction and decision at the centre of the Empire. Hughes openly attacked what he called the

---

[50] *Times* (London), 8 March 1916.
[51] *SMH*, 3 March 1916.
[52] W.M. Hughes, *'The Day' –and after: War Speeches*, arranged by Keith A. Murdoch, with an introduction by the Rt Hon. David Lloyd George (London: Cassell, 1916), p.V.
[53] Letter, Hughes to Pearce, 21 April 1916, Pearce Papers, AWM 3DRL 2222/3/3.

policy of 'drift' and he was taken up and feted by those who shared the same faith and wished to oust Asquith from office. During his stay in Britain Hughes saw much of Milner and Amery; and of the editor of *The Times,* Geoffrey Dawson; and the great press baron, Lord Northcliffe. In particular, Hughes found himself at one with David Lloyd George, the Liberal Minister for Munitions, who also wanted a strong man running an efficient and whole-hearted war government.[54]

Little time was spent outside business meetings with his official hosts, Asquith and Bonar Law, and he had hardly anything to do with either the British Labour Party or the trade union movement. Indeed the two labour meetings that he addressed in England were organised, one officially and the other unofficially, under the auspices of the British Workers' National League, which Milner had secretly created and funded in order to counteract the influence of the Union of Democratic Control and the Independent Labour Party on the working class.[55] On 10 May, Hughes spoke at the inaugural meeting of the League; and on 22 June, at a meeting arranged by the Dock, Wharf, Riverside, and General Workers' Union and the National Sailors' and Firemens' Union.[56]

The antipodean prophet's rhetoric combined the language of romantic race patriotism with that of scientific social efficiency. It combined J. B. Seeley's pride in an Anglo-Saxon historical community and 'The Expansion of England' with the Social Darwinists' demand for organisation and virility. It offered the British people both a justification for waging total war against Germany and a vision of a pre-eminent and regenerated British Empire in the post-war world.

In accepting the freedom of the City of London, Hughes celebrated the Empire's capital as 'the cradle of our race'. He spoke in national mythic terms, giving the British people a classic teleological history. Thus he declared of the British race that its:

> glorious traditions stretch back into the grey dawn of time; which was before Caesar and his legions came; which has seen Celt, Saxon and Norman merge into one people; which has defied the arbitrary power of kings … which has watched the nation send out its sturdy broods to the furthermost corners of the earth and seen them increase and multiply; whose power for centuries has extended throughout the world.

> The race, as a result of the war, had 'found its soul'. The war had rescued the British from going the way of the Roman Empire.

---

[54] George Allardyce Riddell, *Lord Riddell's War Diary* (London: Ivor Nicholson and Watson, 1933), pp.161–62.

[55] A.M. Gollin, *Proconsul in Politics a study of Lord Milner in opposition and in power* (London: Blond, 1964), p.539.

Milner wanted to imbue the working classes with his race patriot ideals of 'Imperial Unity and Citizen Service.' See J.O. Stubbs, 'Lord Milner and Patriotic Labour, 1914–1918', *English Historical Review*, 87 (October 1972), 717–54.

[56] *Times* (London), 23 June 1916.

Ben Tillett, one of the founders of the British Workers' National League, was a key figure in organising the latter occasion. See J. Schneer, *Ben Tillett: portrait of a labour leader* (London: Croom Helm, 1982).

> The war has done great things for the Empire. Among other things it has saved it. It has saved it from moral-aye, and physical-degeneration and decay; for I firmly believe that we were slipping down with increasing velocity into the abyss of degeneration.

Though primarily a struggle for national survival, the war was also an ideological and cultural conflict: 'Liberty is at stake. Civilisation is at stake. Everything we love is at stake.' History had shown that the 'destiny of the world, the progress of mankind throughout the ages have been decided in the field of battle.' The Battle of Tours in 732 CE where Charles Martel had defeated the Saracens was one such turning point: 'But for this decisive victory, Europe would have been in chains, Christianity trampled in the dust, civilisation smothered in her swaddling clothes, the progress of mankind crushed, and the Western world throttled by the strangling hand of Eastern despotism.' Hughes claimed that the issues at stake in the war against the Central Powers were 'not less vital'. Since Britain stood for 'the highest ideals of civilisation', a British victory would be a victory for 'Right over Might'.[57]

Hughes denounced those who called for a compromise peace or who looked forward to cooperating with the German people at the end of the war. It is even possible that Fisher was one of his targets, for the former Australian Prime Minister, while wishing 'all success' to the 'Fight for Right' movement, had said the Allies should not aim 'to crush the German people – there were nations in Germany who loved liberty as we did and were not free.'[58] Hughes would not allow such a distinction. Germany, he maintained, 'is a military despotism and denies everyone of its citizens, a real right, a living right in the government of the country', whereas Britain was a democracy in which 'the people can, if they do not, govern; the key is in their hands; the political franchise is theirs.'[59] But the German people identified with their government. They had been 'steeped in the poisonous doctrines of [Heinrich von] Treitschke and [Friedrich von] Bernhardi.' They had 'apotheosised Might' and had 'crucified Right'. Hughes asked rhetorically, 'Will any man tell us that we should make peace with a nation which knows no law save that of force, which has trampled underfoot every principle sacred to civilisation and honourable to men, a nation which stands out today as the great international criminal … ?'

Pacificism was the antithesis of patriotism. Those who advocated extending the hand of friendship to the German people were sneeringly dubbed 'internationalists'. Reverting to Social Darwinist vitalism, Hughes decried 'internationalism' as a 'pallid, feeble, sickly and spineless thing'. Patriotism, on the other hand, was 'our inherent gift of virile and resolute men'. Pacificism was a product of the intellect, but patriotism was intuitive 'and springs from the heart'. Patriotism encompassed all the other great human qualities. Freedom itself 'depended upon the spirit of

---

[57] *The "Day" – and After*, pp.25, 51, 60–62, 64, 78 and 133.
[58] *Times* (London), 14 March 1916.
[59] *The "Day" – and After*, p.277.
   H.C.G. Matthews, R.I. McKibbin and J.A. Kay, in 'The Franchise Factor in the rise of the Labour Party', *English Historical Review*, XCI (October 1976), show that by 1914 only 68.1% of adult males were enfranchised in England and Wales. They estimate that 4.8 million males did not have the right to vote in the 1911 elections. By the First World War, Germany had universal manhood suffrage. Of all the major belligerents, only Russia, Hungary and Britain did not have manhood suffrage laws.

patriotism'. Patriotism was 'the supreme reasoning of mankind'. Race patriotism, he might well have said, was the ultimate religious cause.

Bernhardi's oft-cited catch-cry, 'World power, or downfall', had resonance for Hughes. Though the precept was frequently seen as emblematic of Germany's lust for dominion and its responsibility for the war, he embraced it as an apt description of international relations, of the inevitable competition between nations for supremacy. It applied as much to Britain as to Germany. The enemy's military and economic power had therefore to be destroyed completely so that it could never again rise to challenge the *Pax Britannica*.

Drawing upon the greatest work in English religious culture, the King James Bible, Hughes paraphrased Jesus' great question about salvation and asked, 'What must Britain do to be saved?' and, carrying through the metaphor, he told his audience in the spirit of the new religion of nationalism that, 'She must be born again.' As this war was not just as other wars since it 'touches the Empire at every point of its multifarious activities', so the whole of British social and economic life had to be radically restructured. The differences between Celt and Saxon, between upper and lower classes, had to give way before the imperatives of 'the people's war'. The British race had to subordinate everything to the supreme duty of fighting and defeating the foe.

Both for war and peace a new concept of modern statesmanship was required: 'Quite apart from the idea of a self-contained Empire, there is the idea of Britain as an organised nation, and the British Empire as an organised Empire – organised for trade, for industry, for the preservation of the world's peace, and for the protection of the weak against the strong.' For this purpose the British people would have to put aside 'all considerations of party, class and doctrine, and without delay proceed to devise a policy for the British Empire, a policy which shall cover every phase of our national economic and social life.' This new order had to lift up the working class. He told representatives of the ruling classes at Carlton House that, 'You cannot build a great nation when 12 million people are on the very edge of starvation.' It was an 'inexorable law' that when nations had fallen, it was because 'of the failure of the crop of men'. Social efficiency required that the regenerated Britain had to 'lay down conditions for the great mass of the people as will ensure a numerous, healthy and virile race.'[60] This was Hughes's doctrine of national socialism.

If this vision of the future British Empire were to be realised, then imperial relations would have to be reformed. As Hughes well understood, Imperial Federation was a controversial topic in the Dominions. During his voyage to Britain he had consulted Borden and Massey who, while sharing Hughes's general aim, did not seem to have any clear ideas of what should be done. But he was not deterred. Racial, strategic and economic imperatives drove him on. Again and again he indicated that he sought and expected a more highly integrated and organised Empire at the end of the war. In his first public address he told the British Empire Parliamentary Association:

> I hold very decided opinions upon the relations between the Mother Country and the Dominions after the war. I hope you will have a policy which will make the word 'Empire' mean something more than it has meant hitherto. We have the means at our disposal, and we can cement for ever a Federation – Empire – call it what you might – which will ensure the peace of the world.

---

[60] *The "Day" – and After*, pp.2–3, 5, 7, 10, 22–23, 40, 44–55, 78, 80–81, 112–13, 119, 128–29.

But he shied away from proposing any specific scheme. From London he wrote to Pearce about 'Imperial Relations' that:

> Something must be said on this vitally important matter before I go … What I propose to say in effect is this. That the present system: under which the Parl of Gt Britain determines our destiny – we having no voice, [cannot] continue. I shall not say what form the change should take.[61]

As he had made it his first word so he made it his last. In his farewell address he once more canvassed the problem of the Dominions and their role in the Empire. To the British dignitaries who had come to praise him, he declared that, 'For all practical purposes, save one, the Dominions are really independent nations, bound to Great Britain only by the ties of kinship, of self interest and of common ideals.' On questions of peace and war, however, the Dominions had no voice:

> 'This war is made for the Dominions by a government which they do not elect, a parliament in which they are not represented. The Dominions because of their involvement in British wars were being burdened with heavy financial commitments and, it was implied, being subjected to taxation without representation. Thus he concluded, 'I shall not pretend to say anything of the nature of this change … It is sufficient to say that there must be a change, and it must be radical in its nature.'[62]

A British Imperial autarky

While reluctant to prescribe for constitutional change, he was not reticent about offering advice for restructuring the trade and industry of the Empire. The most persistent single theme running through his addresses was the need to make the British Empire economically self-sufficient and to free the economies of the British Empire and its Allies from German influence.[63] Hughes believed that economic and political power were closely connected and that Germany's aim in going to war was as much to achieve economic as political dominion over the world. The Germans 'saw in war a short and safe road to those luscious commercial pastures, occupied by decadent nations, grown flabby by luxurious living.' According to this argument Germany had, prior to the war, penetrated and manipulated other countries' economies, and it was the first task of the British Empire and its Allies to rid themselves of this 'cancer'. To this end Hughes urged the British to follow Australia's example and remove German influence over business activity, and when he spoke of Germans he defined them racially, including Germans who were naturalised British subjects.[64] Hughes did not provide evidence to show that existing controls over enemy interests in the British economy were inadequate. Nor did he cite cases to support his aspersions on the loyalty of naturalised Germans.

---

[61] Letter, Hughes to Pearce, 21 April 1916, Pearce Papers, AWM 3DRL/2222 3/3.
[62] *The "Day" – and After,* pp.174–76.
[63] See letter, personal and private, Munro Ferguson to Bonar Law, 29 October 1915, Novar Papers, NLA MS 696/762: 'Apart from the operations at the Front the matter that excited the deepest interest is the exclusion of Germany … after the War from the Commerce of the Empire … I find myself in harmony with the policy of Mr Hughes.'
[64] *The "Day" – and After,* pp.2 and 9.

But the lack of reasonable grounds did not trouble him. The religion of race patriotism was itself justification enough.

Hughes viewed the rooting out of German economic influences not just as a war measure but also as a prerequisite for the post-war restoration of the British Empire's global supremacy. Before the war the Germans had taken advantage of Britain's free trade policy to advance their economic position and achieve their wider ambitions. Thus Hughes urged that in the post-war era the British Empire should seek to attain economic self-sufficiency. He renounced his former belief in free trade and asserted that, in planning for the future, the British Empire would have to cast aside 'the shibboleths of economic doctrine'. The Empire would have to accept a role for government in the managing of the economy. Though he was 'not necessarily' advocating 'tariff reform', he admitted nevertheless that it 'probably will, immediately follow'. On 25 May in the Manchester Free Trade Hall, the ideological home of Britain's laissez-faire economic policy, he advocated the organisation of trade and industry so as to ensure 'Britain's national safety and our future industrial and commercial welfare', and he was given a rousing reception.[65]

This call for a declaration of economic war against Germany was timely. The Allies were planning a conference in Paris to consider improved measures for controlling trade with the enemy. Following the setbacks suffered in 1915, the British and French governments desired to make the Allied war effort more effective, and they agreed to hold military, political and economic joint talks for this purpose. On the British side the impetus for the economic conference came from W. A. S. Hewins, a noted Tariff Reformer, and his associates in the Unionist Business Committee, and on the French side from Étienne Clémentel, the visionary Minister of Commerce. Both wanted the Allies to cooperate against Germany in peace as well as in war. They hoped, through properly coordinated policies, to free the Allies from any form of dependence on Germany. Thus on 22 December, Clémentel informed the British that the French Government intended calling a conference to discuss economic cooperation against Germany during the war and after the war.[66] Since this conference was to deal with matters which profoundly affected the future of Australia and the Empire, Hughes claimed the right to participate.

The British Prime Minister had misgivings about the French proposal. What the French had in mind seemed to be at odds with his own and his party's free trade principles. It might prove to be politically divisive and a threat to his Coalition government. Consequently when the British Cabinet first discussed the French invitation on 24 February, Asquith attempted to postpone a decision by appointing a committee to examine the matter. Reporting to the King he even used the imminent arrival of Hughes as grounds for delay; the government needed to seek his advice.[67]

---

[65] *Ibid.*, pp.138–48.

[66] Marc Trachtenberg, '"A New Economic Order": Etienne Clémentel and French Economic Diplomacy during the First World War', *French Historical Studies*, X (Fall, 1977), 318–22; Robert E. Bunselmeyer, *The Cost of the War, 1914–1919: British Economic War Aims and the Origins of Reparations* (Hamden, Connecticut: Archon Books, 1975), pp.35–36; copy of letter, Paul Cambon, French Ambassador to the United Kingdom, to Sir Edward Grey, 22 December 1915, TNA: PRO CO532/86/195; cable, Pearce to Hughes, 24 February 1916, NAA A3934 SC11/6.

[67] Report to the King of cabinet Meeting, 24 February 1916, Asquith Papers, Bodleian Library, MSS Asquith 8.

On 9 March, following a meeting of the cabinet attended by Hughes, Asquith announced Britain's willingness to take part in the conference. At the meeting Hughes had learnt of the Allies' inability to devise a strategy for defeating the Central Powers. Neither an assault on the Western Front nor an invasion of the Balkans were thought to have much chance of success, and in these circumstances the British had agreed to the French suggestion for greater Allied cooperation at every level. Seizing the opportunity, Hughes stressed the importance of the Allies taking joint economic measures against the enemy.[68] Asquith still remained suspicious of the French intentions and warned that a vindictive peace might hurt the British as much as the German economy. He insisted that the conference should neither commit the British Government nor limit its freedom to decide its own fiscal policy.[69]

Asquith did not look with favour on Hughes attending the conference. Since Hughes espoused the view that Germany should be excluded from the Empire's trade and commerce at the end of the war, he might well embarrass the British Government. Consequently Asquith at first rejected Australian representation. He pointed out that Dominion leaders had never previously been represented at major international conferences and that, in any case, it would be invidious to allow only the Australian Prime Minister to attend. To allay Dominion fears that the conference might reach conclusions touching on their trade interests, he assured their governments that no decision would be taken at Paris on post-war trade arrangements. Hughes, for his part, did not seek any such assurance. Rather he wanted to see a clear and comprehensive policy established at the conference. Thus he was disappointed by Asquith's attitude and told Pearce that though the British Government was against Dominion representation he was 'opposing vigorously'.[70]

The British delegation for the Paris Conference grew 'like Topsy'. The process of its selection was quintessentially Asquithian. At first he named W. R. Runciman, the Liberal President of the Board of Trade, as Britain's representative. Then, following protests from the Conservative protectionists in his cabinet, he added Bonar Law. Next, after agitation in the press and parliament, he set aside all his earlier objections and agreed to include Hughes. Finally, at the end of May, when Sir George Foster, a Canadian minister and a free trader, arrived in England, Asquith added his name to the team. The British Prime Minister in nominating Hughes had given in to the demands of those race patriots who acclaimed the Australian as the chief spokesman for imperial unity and total victory. Bonar Law, in justifying the British Government's turnabout, told the Canadian Prime Minister that 'public pressure has precipitated the matter and made it unwise to delay further.' Nevertheless he explained that Hughes would go to Paris 'not as specially representing Australia but as … one of the representatives of the British Government.'[71] Asquith

---

[68] *Ibid.*, 9 March 1916.

[69] UK, *Parliamentary Debates* (House of Commons), LXXX, 1771–74, 9 March 1916.

[70] Letter, Bonar Law to Asquith, 13 March 1916, TNA: PRO CO532/85/339; cable, Bonar Law to Munro Ferguson, 16 March 1916, NAA CP447/3 SC11/5; cable, Hughes to Pearce, 16 March 1916, *ibid.*; cable, Bonar Law to Lord Devonshire, Governor-General of Canada, 20 March 1916, Bonar Law Papers, House of Lords Record Office MS53/6/65.

[71] Copy of cable, Bonar Law to Devonshire, 8 April 1916, *ibid.*, 50/2/3.

no doubt hoped that since Hughes was to be a member of the British delegation and the British delegation had to vote as a unit he would not prove troublesome.

The Paris Conference, which was at first scheduled for the end of March, did not meet until 14 June. Though Hughes, growing impatient at the delay, suspected a British conspiracy to put off the event until after his departure for Australia, it nevertheless seems clear that the postponements were caused by the need to await the arrival of the Japanese delegation and to accommodate the Italians who were facing a domestic political crisis.[72]

The British and French collaborated in preparing for the conference. On 1 May Runciman, meeting with Clémentel, agreed that the agenda should, as the French had earlier suggested, cover cooperation both in war and peace. The ultimate aim was to free the Allies permanently from dependence upon German trade and commerce. Runciman had, however, insisted that the conference should confine itself to resolutions and not draw up a binding treaty. Subsequently he met with Bonar Law and Hughes to discuss the form of the resolutions.[73] As the appointed time for the conference drew nearer, Runciman, responding to public demands and French requests, extended the range of the draft resolutions. What part Hughes may have played in this is not known, but it would appear that he was, on the whole, content with the proposals which the British brought to Paris. When the conference met, the British and French – with one minor exception – put a common set of resolutions before the delegates. It was a credit to the careful Anglo-French planning that the conference was, within the space of three days, able to adopt unanimously a program for action.

While all other delegations were restricted to one spokesman, Clémentel, as President of the conference, had ruled that the Dominion representatives, though remaining part of the British delegation for voting purposes, could also take part in the discussions. Hughes did not take great advantage of this opportunity, but when he did it was always with the intent of tightening the resolutions to make them more comprehensive and more effective.

Hughes's opening salvo occurred during the debate on the first section of the first resolution which aimed at cutting off all trade with the enemy. It was the only paragraph in the packet of resolutions where the British and French offered alternative versions. The French wording sought a straightforward prohibition on all trade with enemy subjects wherever they resided, while the British required the Allies to compile a combined list of banned firms. Hughes, who spoke as though he knew the Germans better than their European neighbours, protested, according to the French account, that 'the Germans are past masters in the art of contraband' or, according to Hughes's own record, that 'the Germans have carried the business of evasion to a fine art.' As a result, he contended that the Allies had 'to meet every subterfuge with laws so drastic that by no means at all can they trade.' He declared that 'I have yet to learn that it is possible to go too far with an enemy like the Central Powers.' But the British and French would only go so far with Hughes. They settled their own differences by integrating the substance of their drafts and appeased Hughes by spelling out the implications of the British blacklist. The final form of the

---

[72] Letter, Bonar Law to Grey, 2 May 1916, TNA: PRO FO 800/91and letter, Bonar Law to Hughes, 22 May 1916, NAA A3934 SC11/6.
[73] TNA: PRO CAB37/147/3; letter, Hughes to Runciman, 11 May 1916, NAA A3934 SC11/5.

resolution forbade trading with 'persons, firms and companies whose business is controlled wholly or partially by enemy subjects or is subject to enemy influence and whose names are included on a special list.'

At the same meeting Hughes had circulated copies of the *Australian Enemy Contracts Annulment Act* and proudly trumpeted its virtues. Under this legislation the Commonwealth could cancel not only contracts with enemy citizens but also with persons and firms who in the opinion of the Attorney-General were carrying on business for the enemy's benefit or with his capital or help in any way. By means of this legislation the Australian authorities had removed from company registers every shareholder of enemy origin, whether naturalised or not. He called on the Allies' delegates to adopt equally drastic measures. The other delegates, however, were not impressed by this Australian model. Bonar Law would not agree to break all contracts without compensation. Hughes had to be satisfied with wording that cancelled unconditionally only those contracts that were 'injurious to the national interest'. Though he scribbled a draft amendment to apply the Australian rules to shareholding, it was ignored and never reached the conference table.

The next day Hughes addressed the weakness he saw in the resolutions governing the treatment of the Central Powers during the period of post-war reconstruction. For him a military victory was not enough. The Germans were already planning with their Austro-Hungarian allies an 'even more implacable' economic campaign for the post-war era and, since their 'capacity for organisation ... is greater than ours', sterner action was needed to counter 'this peril'. He criticised the proposed restrictions on the Allies' trade with the enemy powers. It was inadequate merely to prohibit the dumping of goods or other unfair trade practices. By definition there could not be fair competition with the Germans, and he therefore wanted all trade and commerce with the defeated enemy outlawed.

Likewise he complained – and this incorrectly – that the discriminatory provisions were to stay in force for only two years. Instead he stated his preference for an earlier draft which set no time limit. So overwhelmed was he by his sense of the German menace, that he misconstrued the provisions he attacked. The conference resolution placed restrictions on German trade – 'la durée devra être au moins de deux années' – for a minimum of two years. It was open-ended so that the term could be subsequently extended. On the other hand the wording which Hughes advocated left the period to be determined; that is, it could be even less than two years. Clearly for his purpose the resolution, as it stood, was more satisfactory. Nothing was done, however, to prolong the period of the trade ban. Rather Bonar Law who had thought the two year period too inflexible, used Hughes's confusion to reinstate the original words 'during a number of years to be fixed by mutual agreement'. In this way it might be suggested that Hughes had actually helped to weaken the punitive conditions governing post-war trade with Germany.

Hughes's only other contribution to the proceedings came at the end of the conference. Fearful that the Allies' determination might dissolve with the departure of the delegates, he moved – and the conference unanimously agreed – that the delegates should urge their governments to take all steps, without delay, to give effect to the resolutions.[74]

---

[74] NAA A3934 SC11/5, especially 'Procés-verbal, Conference Economique Des Gouvernements Alliés' and typed record in English of Hughes's remarks to the conference on 14 June 1916.

The conference was celebrated by Hughes as a great triumph. The Allies' representatives had agreed to take harsh measures against enemy interests and trade during the war and in the immediate post-war period and also to adopt permanent policies for 'mutual assistance and mutual cooperation' which would render their countries independent of the enemy in raw materials and manufactured articles as well as financial, commercial and maritime services. As Hughes summed it up, the Allies had been engaged in 'the task of formulating the terms of an economic treaty which would absolutely revolutionise not only the trade relations between their respective countries, and with those of the Central Powers, but also the entire economic fabric of the Allied nations.' Thus the conference had 'not only … done good work but great work.' If the resolutions were put into effect promptly they would become 'a most effective weapon against our enemy during the war, shortening its duration, assuring to the Allies the fruits of victory, their economic independence after the war, and a lasting peace.'[75]

Hughes's motives in supporting the Paris resolutions were as they appeared. Though the Australian Government in suggesting that Hughes seek to attend the conference had acted at the behest of export industries, there is no evidence that he was at all influenced by domestic economic concerns. In some ways this might seem surprising since he spent so much time in Britain trying to sell Australian wheat and minerals as well as to find ships in which to transport these products to Europe. But not one of his amendments to the Paris resolutions served specific Australian trading interests. Similarly, of the whole package of resolutions adopted at Paris, only Part II of the 'Permanent Measures', under which the Allies agreed to facilitate their 'mutual trade relations', could be seen as possibly having direct benefits for Australia. This provision, which Hughes had no part in formulating, might be seen as favouring Australia, along with other Allied primary producers, against neutrals such as the United States and Argentina. Even so, the proposed assistance was limited to improving transport and communications. Hughes at Paris was not primarily interested in seeking advantages for Australia. His great aim in fighting to achieve Allied economic cooperation was, as his philosophy of international relations dictated, the crushing of Germany and the restoration of the British Empire's position in the world.

The Paris resolutions did not fulfil Hughes's high hopes for them. The resolutions did not constitute a treaty. Each government was left free to decide for itself whether and how they would be implemented. The British had to take the lead in order to persuade the other Allies to act. Yet, after the cabinet approved the resolutions in principle, the Asquith Government referred them to a parliamentary ways and means committee which took over eighteen months to report and when it did its recommendations fell far short of Hughes's expectations.[76]

'Japan was and is most keenly interested in Australia'

While Hughes's public addresses were directed towards invigorating Britain's war effort, urging closer imperial ties and attacking German economic influence, his private diplomacy was taken up – apart from his efforts to sell Australia's primary products and to obtain freight in which to

---

[75] *Times* (London), 21 June 1916.
[76] Letter, Asquith to King George V, 14 July 1916, TNA: PRO CAB 41/37/26; *Times* (London), 19 July and 3 August 1916 and 27 April 1918; see also Bunselmeyer, *The Cost of the War, 1914–1919*, pp.40–45.

export them – with the question of Japan. As he had indicated before leaving Sydney, his most pressing aim was to consult the British about Japan and its ambitions. In particular he wanted to discuss the future of the German Pacific islands and the prospects for Pacific naval defence.

By the time Hughes arrived in London Anglo-Japanese relations had reached a delicate stage. Britain had been disturbed almost as much as Australia by the reports from its embassy in Tokyo. Though Japan had signed the London Agreement under which all the Allies had promised not to make a separate peace with the enemy, its public criticisms of the British for failing to recognise its position in China raised doubts in the minds of Whitehall officials.[77] Towards the end of 1915 the British Ambassador was informing London that the Japanese, as a result of their success in East Asia, had become arrogant and even questioned the value of the Anglo-Japanese alliance. He cabled the Foreign Secretary that the 'touchstone of Japanese feeling as exhibited in the daily press is self-interest combined with overdeveloped national ambition', and he added that Japan was assuming an 'attitude of overlordship in all matters concerning the Far East'.[78] Subsequently Greene informed London that the Japanese had come to see the Anglo-Japanese alliance as an obstacle standing in the way of their of their expansionist aims. They believed that it had prevented them from taking full advantage of their 'opportunity for action in China', and he cited articles in the press that were urging 'an immediate revision of alliance'.[79]

At about the same time British authorities were disturbed to learn that the Germans were offering the Japanese a free hand in China, control of the Dutch East Indies or, more generally, hegemony in East Asia and the Pacific as an inducement to withdraw from the conflict. Despite the fact that the Japanese had informed London of these approaches, the British were worried by Germany's attempt to divide the Allies. On all sides – in Japan, Italy, Russia and even France – the failure to achieve a quick and easy victory was producing disaffection. Japan had the least reason to stay loyal to the Allies. It had the most to gain from a rapprochement with Germany. The head of the Far Eastern Department of the British Foreign Office commented that:

> We cannot exclude the possibility of an alliance between Japan and Germany after the war, for a reconstruction of the situation in the Far East … The quarrel between Japan and Germany is not a deep one, and owing to present conditions in Europe, Germany is Japan's least dangerous competitor in the Far East.

Sir Arthur Nicolson, the permanent Under-Secretary at the Foreign Office, minuted that 'there is a good deal of Oriental mystery in the whole of this question which leaves one with an uneasy feeling.'[80]

---

[77] Nish, *Alliance in Decline*, pp.166–70.
[78] Cable, Greene to Grey, 8 December 1915, PRO FO 410/65.
[79] Cable, Greene to Grey, 14 February 1916, *ibid*.
[80] Very secret cable, Grey to Greene, 24 January 1916, TNA: PRO FO 371/2690/82–83; cable, Sir A. Johnstone, British Ambassador to the Hague, to Grey, 19 February 1916, TNA: PRO FO 410/65; despatch, Sir E. Howard, British Ambassador to Stockholm, to Grey, 1 March 1916, *ibid*; and minute on cable, Johnstone to Grey, 19 March 1916, TNA: PRO FO 371/2691/61–62.

For an overview of German approaches to Japan during the war, see F.W. Iklé, 'Japan-German Negotiations during World War I', *American Historical Review*, LXXI (1965), 62–76.

Grey appreciated the weakness of Britain's position. He knew that if Japan were to be kept from defecting to the German side and to be persuaded to contribute more to the Allies' cause, then the British would have to show more understanding of its Asian and Pacific interests. From the moment of Japan's entry into the war, the British had been beholden to the Japanese. Adverse European developments had strengthened the need for appeasement. At the very time that Grey heard of the German overtures to Japan, he was, at the instigation of the Admiralty, asking Japan for a cruiser squadron to patrol the Indian Ocean and for a small destroyer force to guard the Malacca Straits.[81] When in return the Japanese sought concessions – in particular that Australia and Canada should accede to the Anglo-Japanese Commercial Treaty and the Straits Settlements allow qualified Japanese doctors to practice in the colony – Grey sent an encouraging reply. After pointing out that the Canadians had already signed the treaty, he promised to urge the Colonial Office to make concessions on the Straits Settlement question – which it did – and to discuss Australia's adhesion to the treaty with Hughes during his visit to the United Kingdom.[82]

As a result, when Hughes took up 'Japan and the Pacific Question' with Asquith, Harcourt, Bonar Law and Grey, he was immediately on the defensive. The picture was grimmer than he had expected. While the Foreign Office may not have shared with Hughes their bleak evaluation of the European alliance, they were very frank about Japan. They may even have exaggerated the position somewhat in order to make him more conciliatory. It was very disquieting. Hughes had come to London to push his Pacific concerns, including the control of the German Pacific islands ('the line of division – British and Japanese') and Pacific naval policy (especially cooperation between the Dominions and Britain), but in the event found himself fending off Japanese pressure for concessions.[83]

After four weeks in which he had several long conferences with Bonar Law and Grey about 'the Japanese problem: in its threefold aspect (1) abolition or modification of our alien restriction legislation, (2) Commercial Treaty, (3) control of the Pacific', Hughes wrote Pearce of his grave foreboding. This letter was the fullest account of his London discussions that he ever penned. In it, he told Pearce that 'all our fears – or conjectures – that Japan was and is most keenly interested in Australia are amply borne out by facts.' Hughes noted that the 'Foreign Office was … much concerned about the attitude of Japan.' Grey had tried to reassure Hughes that Japan could be relied upon and that it would 'stand behind Britain', but had had to admit that there was 'a large and growing party in Japan who look askance at the alliance and with favour on Germany.' It seems highly probable that Grey had enlightened Hughes about the German inducements to the Japanese, including the offers of the Dutch East Indies and supremacy in the Pacific. Hughes had not unreasonably concluded that it was 'quite clear that in the event of even a temporary reverse

---

[81] Letter, Grey to Katsunosuke Inouye, Japanese Ambassador to London, 10 February 1916, TNA: PRO FO 800/67.
[82] Despatch, very confidential, Grey to Greene, 21 February 1916, TNA: PRO FO 410/65.
[83] Cable, Hughes to Pearce, 16 March 1916, NAA A63/48 J2/3/2.
For the list of subjects, see under heading 'Pacific', NAA A981 Japan 38, Pt.I General.
In June the New Zealand Government, unaware of the problems facing Hughes, belatedly informed London of their support for the Pacific policy which Hughes had discussed with them in January, see despatch, Liverpool to Bonar Law, 24 June 1916, TNA: PRO CO 209/287.

to the Allies, the Japanese Government might not be able – even if they so desired – to keep Japan behind Britain.'

The Foreign Secretary had explained that the British request for Japanese naval assistance had 'aggravated' the position, since the Japanese demanded 'some evidence of Britain's friendliness towards her in order possibly to justify her action or placate the opposition.' Furthermore, he had indicated that Japan saw Australia's unwillingness to make territorial concessions, to change its immigration policy or to sign a commercial treaty, as obstacles to continued cooperation. While Hughes appreciated the need to keep Japan on side, he remained adamant that there could be no compromise on the White Australia policy; 'Australia would fight to the last ditch rather than allow the Japanese to enter Australia.' On the question of the German Pacific islands he was, however, willing to be more flexible. Following the pragmatic attitude adopted by Fisher, Pearce and the latter's military advisers, Hughes told Grey that 'as to the control of the Pacific after the war' the Australian Government 'were prepared to consider favourably the Equator as a line of demarcation.'

A commercial treaty posed more complex problems. Since the Japanese had singled out this particular issue above all others as the basis for a *quid pro quo* it had to be considered seriously. Though the Australian Government had repeatedly rejected the Japanese Consul-General's representations on the point, Hughes under pressure from Grey relented a little. He was aware of the dire consequences for Australia if Japan withdrew from the war and made its peace with Germany. Thus he told the British Foreign Secretary that 'if he considered it was of vital importance to securing the further aid … of Japan in this war … we would consider the question of giving Japan the same rights under the Tariff we gave to any other of our Allies.' Even so, Hughes insisted that Japan 'would not enjoy the same preference as Great Britain or any other part of the British Empire' and that Australia 'would not consider the question of adhering to any other parts of the Commercial Treaty.'[84]

Though at the end of March the Japanese waived their precondition and without further ado sent a naval squadron to the Indian Ocean, they continued their campaign for a commercial treaty. Indeed the Japanese, in ceasing to haggle over the British request, probably saw that the extension of their naval power into the region might give them more leverage, and they asked Grey to inform the Australians that a Japanese naval force would be operating off their coasts.[85] Whatever the reason for their change of tactics, the Japanese did not resile from their efforts to have Australia sign a treaty, and Grey used his good offices to try to persuade Hughes to accept the Canadian formula and so reach a settlement.

Throughout the negotiations Hughes held firm to the principles he had laid down in the letter to Pearce. On no account would he accept the terms of the Anglo-Japanese Commercial Treaty. When, at the beginning of April, Hughes learnt Grey had told the Japanese that the Australian Prime Minister was willing 'to negotiate for adhesion of Australia to our commercial treaty', provided that he received adequate guarantees against Japanese immigration and that trade between Australia and British Pacific possessions was reserved for Australian and British vessels,

---

[84] Letter, Hughes to Pearce, 21 April 1916, Pearce Papers, AWM 3DRL2222/3/3.
[85] Cable, Grey to Greene, 28 March 1916, TNA: PRO FO 410/65.

he denied emphatically ever acquiescing in such an arrangement. He would place Japan on a '"favoured nation" basis in any tariff the Commonwealth may make, and his promise began and ended there.'[86] It was made clear that this offer did not affect Australia's right to grant tariff preference to British Empire countries. Brought up short, Grey assured the Australian leader that if the Japanese wished for more than the tariff concession he would tell them that he could 'say nothing until Mr Hughes has been consulted.'[87]

Australian obstinacy was a major impediment to improved Anglo-Japanese relations. Consequently, at the beginning of May, Grey put it to Hughes that Australia should become a party to the Anglo-Japanese Treaty on the same terms as Canada. But Hughes flatly refused, maintaining that if such a treaty were presented to the Commonwealth Parliament 'it would be exceedingly difficult to get it through.' The whole twenty-seven clauses would be 'examined and debated line by line.' Australia would not in any way relinquish its control over the entry of Japanese citizens. Hughes offered instead a one clause treaty which would grant Japan most-favoured-nation tariff treatment and that alone. He would consent to nothing which touched Australia's immigration policy.[88]

When Grey brought the Australian Prime Minister and the Japanese Ambassador together on 9 June, direct diplomacy achieved no more than the previous arms-length exchanges. In the presence of the British Under-Secretary of State for Foreign Affairs Hughes reaffirmed his position. He told the Ambassador that while he would support the extension of the most-favoured-nation tariff regime, the British Empire nations excepted, to Japan he could not agree to apply the same principle to the entry of Japanese nationals into Australia. He was willing to admit Japanese students and tourists, 'leisured classes', for temporary residence on the same basis as Europeans but all other Japanese, businessmen as well as labourers, would have to 'submit to the same restrictions as at present'. On this latter point he was 'emphatic'. Why Hughes was unwilling to treat merchants in the same way as students and tourists is not clear. Perhaps he believed that merchants might seek to establish long-term residence and therefore be a greater threat to White Australia or even more likely that they would use the privilege to put Australian burgeoning industries out of business.

For the Japanese the general principle was the nub of the matter. The Ambassador explained that, above all, his government wished to remove the discriminatory handicaps under which Japanese laboured in conducting commerce and attaining residence in Australia. He pointed out 'in a friendly way' that all Australians, 'as to travel and residence, would be on a footing of absolute

---

[86] Cable, Grey to Greene 23 March 1916, TNA: PRO FO 800/91 and TNA: PRO CO 532/86/368–69; letter, M.L. Shepherd, Hughes's private Secretary, to J.C.C. Davidson, Bonar Law's private Secretary, 5 April 1916, TNA: PRO FO 800/91 and TNA: PRO CO 532/86/364.

For Hughes's rejection of Grey's terms, see Hughes's scribbled note, undated, on letter Davidson to Hughes, 1 April 1916, containing copies of cables, Grey to Greene, 23 and 25 March 1916, NAA A981, Japan 38, Pt.I General.

[87] Minute by Grey on letter, F.G.A. Butler to E. Drummond, Grey's private Secretary, enclosing Shepherd's letter of 5 April 1916, 6 April 1916, TNA: PRO FO 800/91.

[88] Cable, Grey to Greene, 11 May 1916, FO Confidential Print 92475, Harcourt Papers, Bodleian Library MSS Harcourt 589; despatch, Grey to Greene, 11 May 1916, TNA: PRO FO 410/65.

of equality with all other foreigners' in Japan.[89] Australian-Japanese negotiations had again reached an impasse. Hughes had kept faith with his government and remained true to his and his people's racial vision of their country. At little cost to British diplomacy and the Allied war effort he had managed to keep the Japanese at bay.

Hughes's mission to London had mixed results. In the short term he was very successful or appeared to be very successful. His crusade to rouse the British people to a more whole-hearted struggle against the Hun had met with a favourable reception from much of the press, many of the politicians and large sections of the general public. At the Paris Economic Conference his view that the conflict was as much economic as military or political was acknowledged, and the Allies had passed resolutions to coordinate economic measures against Germany, not only for the duration of the war but also in the peace which would follow. More specifically, he had managed to sell Australian wheat, wool and metal, and had obtained shipping wherewith to transport these products to Europe; to circumvent British controls over shipping he had purchased a number of merchant vessels which became the nucleus of a Commonwealth shipping line. In dealing with Japan he had steadfastly refused to consent to any modification of the White Australia policy.

These achievements were superficial or ephemeral. As he told Pearce, he had intended to have the issue of peace terms and the Peace Conference 'quite thoroughly thrashed out' before he left the United Kingdom, but there is no evidence that these topics had even been broached. The British did not discuss their peace aims with him. It would appear that Hughes knew nothing of the House-Grey Memorandum of 22 February which was the focus for much British diplomacy in the first half of 1916. Under this 'agreement', as President Wilson's emissary Colonel E. M. House called it, the American Government intimated that if France and England proposed a Peace Conference and peace terms 'not unfavourable to the Allies and Germany rejected either, then the United States would probably enter the war against Germany.' The memorandum and how it should be used was keenly debated among senior cabinet ministers as they pondered various contingencies.[90] But there are no British or Australian records suggesting that Hughes was drawn into this debate or even made aware of it. Similarly, though he had hailed the results of the Paris Economic Conference, seeing in them a vindication of his war philosophy, the resolutions ultimately proved to be little more than pious expressions of Allies in search of unity at a critical point in the war. The explanations for most of these failures lie not so much with him personally as with the difficult war circumstance that faced the Empire and dictated British policy.

Hughes's much-vaunted campaign to stir up the British Government and public left no lasting impression. Lloyd George at the time might write a very flattering preface to Hughes's published collection of speeches – speeches which served Lloyd George's own political purposes –

---

[89] Letter, Arthur Nicolson, British Under-Secretary of State for Foreign Affairs, to Grey, 9 June 1916, TNA: PRO FO 371/2688/305–06.

For the Japanese report of the meeting, see cable, Katsumasuke Inouye, Japanese Ambassador to United Kingdom, to Kikujiro Ishii, Japanese Foreign Minister, 11 June 1916, *Nihon Gaiko Bunsho*, I, '1916', 202–03.

[90] Arthur S. Link, *Wilson: Confusions and Crises, 1915–1916* (Princeton, New Jersey: Princeton University Press, 1964), pp.130–36; David French, *British Strategy and War Aims, 1914–1916* (London: Allen and Unwin, 1986), pp.192–95.

but in his *War Memoirs* the British statesman only mentions in passing Hughes's visit to Great Britain.[91] As the time for his return to Australia drew near rumours abounded that he had been invited to stay in Britain and to take a seat in the House of Commons or the House of Lords and so become a member of the British Cabinet. At his farewell banquet, though Hughes was surrounded by well-wishers such as Bonar Law, Churchill and Lord Northcliffe, only Earl Grey, the President of the Royal Colonial Institute, suggested that Hughes should have a permanent place in British political life. Grey claimed that any of Britain's 600 constituencies 'would be delighted to claim him as its representative.' He welcomed the idea that Hughes might become:

> a member of His Majesty's Government, leading the way and guiding the Councils of Empire, so as to secure the advantages of absolute unity in such a way that the men of Australia and other Dominions would have the same influence in Imperial affairs as had the men of Northumberland and of Devonshire.

But Grey, an aging apostle of Imperial Federation, carried no political weight. As his critics alleged, he was 'too much inclined to allow his enthusiasm to get the better of his judgment'.[92] Bonar Law's assessment of Hughes's visit to Britain has more merit:

> The psychological time at which he came here helped to magnify his importance, for ... he was able to express his view with freedom from responsibility, which would have been impossible to any British politician ... If he had been compelled to translate his eloquence into definite proposals he would not have found his position here so easy.[93]

---

[91] David Lloyd George, *War memoirs of David Lloyd George*, 6 vols (Boston: Little, Brown and Company, 1933–36), Vol.IV, pp.17–18.

Indeed Lloyd George's only recorded statement about Hughes's participation in the councils of the Empire was to say that he along with the other Dominion leaders might be able to make a valuable contribution to the British War Committee if they could stay in the country for at least six months. Of all the Dominion leaders Lloyd George was most anxious to have the advice of South Africa's General Smuts of whom he spoke 'very highly'. *Lord Riddell's War Diary, 1914–1918* (London: Ivor Nicholson & Watson, 1933), p.166.

[92] *Times* (London), 24 June 1916.

Fitzhardinge in *The Little Digger* (p.146) confuses Earl Grey with Sir Edward Grey who was created Viscount Fallodon the following month, and thus gives this appeal much more importance than it deserves.

On Lord Grey, see letter, private and personal, Munro Ferguson to Bonar Law, 7 March 1916, Davidson Papers, House of Lords Record Office MS3/35; 'Lord Grey is a man ... But his capacity for enthusiasm sometimes impairs his judgment.'

Amongst the broader public the most fervent and organised efforts to keep Hughes in Britain and 'to get Mr W.M. Hughes on to the Inner War Council of the Empire' came from the Women's Social and Political Union, a suffragette movement which, after the war had broken out, renamed its journal, *Britannia* and committed itself to an ultra patriotic campaign for the war and Empire. Its two major figures, Emmeline Pankhurst and her daughter Christabel, on the eve of Hughes's departure for Australia, organised a procession with banners proclaiming 'We Want Hughes', and 'Hughes The People's Choice'. See David Mitchell, *Queen Christabel; A Biography of Christabel Pankhurst* (London: Macdonald and Jane's, 1977), pp.256 and 260.

[93] Copy of letter, Bonar Law to Lord Buxton, Governor-General of South Africa, 17 August 1916, Davidson Papers, House of Lords Record Office MS4/103.

By the end of his stay in England, Hughes had assumed the mantle of the Empire statesman, the representative of Greater Britain. He looked to the other Dominions for support in reforming imperial relations. He had already sounded out the New Zealand and Canadian Prime Ministers, and on his way home to Australia, responding to appeals from Imperial Federationists, he hoped to confer with the South African Government and to convert it to the cause. Such a visit was, however, anathema to Louis Botha, the South African Prime Minister. Lord Buxton, South Africa's Governor-General, urged Bonar Law to dissuade Hughes from pursuing his plan. Buxton wrote:

> I am confident … in existing circumstances it would do more harm than good, would tend to accentuate not diminish racial feeling …
>
> However tactful Hughes's speeches were they would of necessity play into the hands of the British citizens and other ultra-loyalists who do more harm than the rebels … Just now the less tub thumping, flag flapping Empire federation and trade propaganda the better.

Though Hughes was alerted to these problems, he did not heed the warning. He even allowed press statements to the effect that he was going 'to discuss matters of importance' with Botha. The South African leader did not look forward to the prospect. To escape embarrassment he journeyed to East Africa to consult General Smuts about further operations against the German colonial forces in Tanganyika. The Governor-General stated that the 'desire of a decent excuse to avoid Hughes' had caused Botha to make the trip.

The worst fears of Botha and Buxton were confirmed by the event. In four days Hughes made ten speeches. Though the Governor-General had asked him 'to avoid Imperial Federation and fiscal after the war questions', Hughes towards the end of his stay 'talked much Imperialism' and stirred up the ire of the Afrikaners. After Hughes sailed for Australia, Buxton reported to Bonar Law that 'Hughes appeared to be totally unconscious that his visit was not very welcome and that his speeches were not helping to cement the Empire.'[94] Hughes was indeed oblivious to the effects of his addresses. His crusade was a religious one. Having absolute faith in his mission to save the British Empire and to unite the British race against the German challenge he was incapable of understanding how other members of the Empire might view his campaign.

Nationalism had found in Hughes with his profound sense of insecurity a most apt disciple. From the late-nineteenth century, Australians were particularly open to the siren song of nationalism which throve on the *anomie* of mass societies. They were even more open to its influence than the people of the British Isles. These transplanted Europeans had cut themselves free from traditional ties and patterns of social order which many of the British in the British isles had carried with them into the era of modern nationalism. Suffering from the trauma of mobility and anonymity associated with rapid modernisation the Australians had created for themselves a collectivist fraternal democracy; from almost the beginning of colonial self-government they had manhood suffrage and from the beginning of the Commonwealth universal adult suffrage. They needed a new language of identity and loyalty in order to connect to one another, a need which was intensified by anxieties about their proximity to an alien Asia. And, as in other modernising

---

[94] Cable, Buxton to Bonar Law, 9 May 1916, copy of cable, Bonar Law to Buxton, 10 May 1916, cable, Buxton to Bonar Law, 8 July 1916, cable, Buxton to Bonar Law, 19 July 1916 and letter, Buxton to Bonar Law, 25 July 1916, *ibid.*

Western countries, it was nationalism rather than its contemporary competitors, socialism or internationalism, which gained their prime allegiance. Nationalism was best equipped to meet the psycho-social crisis since its myth linked the past which was lost to the unsettling present and so made them one. The myth, which Hughes had so eloquently expounded during his visit to Britain, gave people a sense of belonging to a historic community which from immemorial times had shared a common cultural and biological heritage. It made him a national hero and yet, as Bonar Law pointed out, nationalism was not policy and when Hughes attempted to translate it into policy he found himself caught in bitter conflicts which divided the nation and compromised his leadership.

The absolutist view of nationalism which Hughes embraced was his undoing. This simple all-encompassing answer to war's dangers and uncertainties did not fit the social realities. It did not take into account the social and intellectual complexities of Britishness, that there were other views of Britishness and other social loyalties, even if subordinate ones. While in the United Kingdom Hughes, for good reasons, neither took his crusade to Ireland nor attempted to win over the mainstream labour movement. During his stay in Britain, apart from more general considerations, he should have been warned of the limitations of his nationalist message by the Easter Day rebellion in Dublin and the Trade Union Congress's opposition to conscription. Many English liberals also resisted this authoritarian nationalism. What would the liberty for which Britishness stood mean if Hughes had his way? What would happen to the rights of individual citizens? What to the ideal of an international community free from war and injustice? What to their ideal of free trade? Liberal suspicion of the executive's tendency to abuse its power would not easily accept the fusion of state with nation. Hughes's answer to all these difficulties was that such dissidents had to be converted or suppressed. But as he was to find when he returned to Australia and tried to apply his nationalist creed to conscription, the people there also would not follow him or, at least, not all the way. Since nothing less than 'all the way' would satisfy the demands of his nationalism, the British Empire – which he had imagined and for which he gave so much of himself – necessarily eluded him.

6

The War and the Home Front: Japan and the Defence of Australia

While Hughes was in England rousing the British to their responsibilities, learning of the dangerous stalemate on the European fronts and having all his worst fears of Japan confirmed, the Australian Government in Melbourne was wrestling with war issues on the home front which had gained a new life during the Prime Minister's absence. Fresh reports of Japan's Asian and Pacific ambitions intensified concern for national security and Britain's adoption of conscription revived the acrimonious debate of late 1915.

The Japanese spectre

At the very time Hughes was being briefed by the Foreign Office in London about Japan, Acting Prime Minister Pearce in Melbourne was receiving news from Osaka and Tokyo which lent support to the Naval Board's assessment of Japan's intentions. In March Pearce read Suttor's analysis of Japanese views about 'Expansion to the South', 'the Anglo-Japanese alliance' and 'Commercial Supremacy and Control of Ores and Metals'. Suttor wrote that the question of Japanese southward expansion was 'receiving greater attention than hitherto'. He was 'convinced that the desire for expansion is deep-rooted, and that the south and China offer the most interesting fields'. A translated article from the influential journal *Yuben*, which, Suttor asserted, expressed 'what Japan would really like to do', claimed that 'Japan's destiny lies in Java and Sumatra.' Suttor maintained that 'New Zealand and Australia might also be added, and were doubtless eliminated purposely by the author.' Since Japan lacked raw materials, including 'indispensable metals', it not only sought commercial supremacy over China and Korea, but also looked with ambitious eyes on Australia and India. He believed that Japan's large-scale naval-building program was directed to 'some great objective'. The Anglo-Japanese alliance had lost favour and, if Britain's naval power should 'become in any way weakened as a result of the war', Suttor predicted that Japan might well seek other allies who would be more sympathetic to 'Japan's aspirations to dominate Asia and the South Seas'.[1]

At the end of April further intelligence from Tokyo reinforced this warning. The British Ambassador reported that the Japanese Diet had passed resolutions urging their government to bring to an end 'anti-Japanese actions in the British South Seas', seeking the abolition of special restrictions on Japanese businessmen and recommending the establishment of a regular steamship service to the South Pacific islands and to Northeast Australia. The chief proponent of

---

[1] Letter, W.A. Holman to Pearce, 7 March 1916 enclosing copies of letters from the Commercial Commissioner for NSW in the East, 24 and 31 January 1916, NAA MP729/5, 393/1/272. It was minuted 'seen' by 'G.F.P. 20 March 1916'.

the resolutions had complained that Australia humiliated Japanese by treating them like Chinese and Indians and had demanded that all barriers to Japanese immigration and trade in the South Pacific islands be removed. 'It is an urgent need of the day', he had declared, 'that Japanese should devote themselves to emigration and the promotion of foreign trade.' Even more disturbing for the Australians, Japanese Minister for Foreign Affairs Baron Ishii had echoed these sentiments. He had claimed that 'the Government have long been endeavouring to find room for the development of our compatriots, having regard to the increase of population in the Empire and to the present conditions of expansion abroad.' Ishii had assured the parliament that:

> We are accordingly striving to remove as far as possible any impediments to the development of our emigrants. The difficulties connected with the admission of our labourers to the territory of our ally have been engaging the anxious attention of the government for years past. On this point … we have since the opening of hostilities further explained our point of view to the Colonial Governments and on the other hand in England, and these conversations are now progressing.[2]

Other evidence seemed to give colour to these sentiments. The officer-in-charge of the Wireless Station at Nauru, who had travelled through the Marshall and Caroline groups at the British Admiralty's request in order to become acquainted with Japanese activities, repeated Burns Philp's earlier complaint that they had entrenched themselves in the islands and were encouraging the trade and industry of their own merchants. Some officials even suggested that Japan intended to 'use its utmost endeavours' to acquire Nauru and its phosphate resources.[3] Suttor, on leave in Australia in April, maintained that the:

> great objective of the Japanese is to take every advantage of the conditions occasioned by the result of the war to further their own interests in regard to the industrial progress of Japan by controlling the production of ores and metals formerly exported to England, Europe and US.

He had been confidentially informed that a representative of Osaka Shosen Kaisha, a leading shipping company, was on his way to Australia for the purpose of inaugurating a steamship line.[4] These reports, followed by Hughes's letter from London, convinced Pearce that the Japanese campaign to secure the Commonwealth's adherence to the Anglo-Japanese Commercial Treaty and equal opportunity for trade in the South Pacific masked an imperial design to destroy White Australia and establish Japan's economic and military hegemony in the region.

---

[2] Letter, George Steward, Official Secretary to Governor-General, to J.H. Starling, Acting Secretary, Prime Minister's Department, 17 April 1916 enclosing despatch, British Ambassador to Munro Ferguson, 1 March 1916, *ibid*. It was minuted 'Seen' by 'G.F.P. 28 April 1916'.

[3] Memorandum, Colonel S.A. Pethebridge, Administrator, late German New Guinea, to Acting Secretary. Defence Department, 17 March 1916 enclosing notes of wireless officer on the SS 'Pukaki', NAA CP78/23 89/258 and CP447/2 SC 472 (7).

[4] Letter, H.G. Hoyle for New South Wales Premier, to Pearce, 27 April 1916, enclosing letter Suttor to Holman, 25 April 1916, NAA MP729/5 393/1/272, minuted 'Seen', by 'G.F.P. 3 May 1916'.

Moreover the Japanese by protesting against the *United States Immigration Bill* of 1916, which excluded all Asian migration, showed that they were determined to resist all such discriminatory measures. See *SMH*, 24 April 1916.

Accordingly when the authorities learnt that the Japanese intended to send another naval squadron to visit Australia's major ports in May and June they greeted the news with reserve, if not alarm. The Japanese in 1913 and 1915, on the occasion of earlier visits, had approached the Australians through the British Admiralty and had given them two months notice. By contrast the Australians first learnt of the proposed 1916 tour from the Japanese Consul-General on 9 May just a few days before their expected arrival. Though Shimizu attributed the successive visits to war conditions which 'naturally circumscribe the possible area of a squadron voyage, because of the inconvenience – to say the least – of visiting neutral ports', the Australians remained highly sceptical. Shimizu's further argument about the 'advisableness of keeping the vessels in regions where their presence might be useful' had a double edge to it. In the light of all that they knew of Japan's ambitions, the Australians could not but wonder whether Japan might be using the occasion to demonstrate its naval dominance of the Pacific and so make Australians more amenable to its demands.[5]

The Australian ministers were, as Pearce confided to the Governor-General, 'much concerned over the visit of the Japanese Training Squadron'. They had noted that 'the ships are large and one of them over 10,000 tons and each of them has a complement of over 700 men'.[6] The Australian Government conveyed its misgivings to the British. It could not accept the Japanese explanation for the frequent visits. The Colonial Office was informed that the Australians 'know of no reason why presence of these warships in Australian waters is needed at the present moment'. Even the Japanese request for secrecy was thought to have dangerous implications. It was pointed out that no secrecy had been observed during the 1915 visit.[7]

The British, wishing to avoid offending the Japanese, reassured the Australians. Inside the Foreign Office it was agreed that though the Japanese visits seemed 'unnecessarily frequent' they could 'hardly object during the war'.[8] The Admiralty in their official reply stated that the Japanese, in saying that their presence in Australian waters might be useful, meant only that their ships could act as a deterrent to German raiders. It noted that Japan's naval presence in the region accorded well with Britain's earlier request for aid. Furthermore it observed that if Australia rejected visits by Japanese ships, 'Australian transports will not be convoyed by them'. The cloak of secrecy was ascribed merely to the need to keep information from the enemy during wartime. The Admiralty concluded that they could 'see no cause for alarm'.[9]

Yet, despite this British response, there were good grounds for the Australians to believe that the Japanese intended the naval visit to play a role in their diplomatic offensive. From the first the Japanese had shown themselves to be unwavering in their efforts to have Australia accept the terms of the Anglo-Japanese Commercial Treaty. They had sought to bargain further naval assistance in return for Australian compliance with their wishes. After they had agreed to undertake patrol duties in the Indian Ocean, they had specifically asked the British Government

---

[5] Letter, Shimizu to Munro Ferguson, 9 May 1916, NAA CA12 and 'Papers Relating to Visit of Japanese Training Squadron, 1913–16', NAA CP103/11.
[6] Letter, Pearce to Munro Ferguson, 17 May 1916, Novar Papers NLA MS 696/3175.
[7] Cable, Munro Ferguson to Bonar Law, 15 May 1916, TNA: PRO FO 371/2693/195–96.
[8] Ibid., 197–203.
[9] Cable, Bonar Law to Munro Ferguson, 23 May 1916, NAA CP103/11, minuted 'seen' by G.F.P.

to inform Melbourne of their enlarged role. Moreover, the decision to send a naval squadron to Australia corresponded very closely in time to the final stages of the Japanese-Australian negotiations in London. Indeed Pearce had cabled Hughes about the Japanese visit. Even so the news clearly did not shake Hughes's resolve to resist all pressure to modify the White Australia policy.

Since the Australians could not afford to rebuff Japan they made the best of the situation. The visit itself went off quietly. As in 1915 pleasantries were exchanged. Pearce and the press praised Japan for its part in the war effort. Pearce accepted that 'the destinies of both nations were woven together.' In rather ambiguous terms he associated Australia with Japan: 'To us in Australia Japan has a particular interest all her own. Her island base is closer to us than our own homeland of origin in Europe.'[10] Probably Henry Boote, the editor of the Australian *Worker*, expressed the general public's attitude when he wrote to his brother: 'Great fêting of visiting Japanese in town. Crowds of them are in the streets. Australians will never mix with them. One look at those Japanese in the streets today is enough to spoil the blend.' No doubt many would also have agreed with him when he concluded that 'he would sooner have the Kaiser here than the Mikado.'[11] A socialist and anti-conscriptionist, Boote was at one with Hughes in his racial view of the world.

Given all these ominous portents, the government recognised that it had to have more accurate and complete knowledge of Japan and to be able to prepare its defence cadres for the possibilities of future conflict with that country. Suttor had warned of the difficulties of penetrating and interpreting the Japanese mind:

> The esoteric working of the Japanese brain is always more or less clouded in mystery ... The uppermost idea, both in private and political matters, is always self interest; and it is really only by a knowledge of the language of the country that one can get an insight into the secret working of the Japanese mind, and form an estimate of the future aspirations of the people.[12]

The government took this advice to heart. They had to unravel the mystery at the core of this alien civilisation. The European idea of 'Orientalism' as applied to the Japanese had acquired a sinister connotation. Just as the Commonwealth authorities, following the first signs of trouble, obtained independent information on Japan's attitude to Australia and the Pacific, so, after learning from these very sources of Japan's growing hostility and expansionist aims, they sought the services of a linguist and scholar who could train military officers in Japanese, translate intercepted Japanese communications for the censor and, more generally, explain Japan to Australia's national security officials.

On 24 April 1916, the Acting Prime Minister sent a minute to the Chief of the General Staff recommending such an appointment. Further reports from Japan as well as Hughes's letter from London helped to strengthen Pearce's determination to act. Disguising the real motive he cabled the British Ambassador in Tokyo that 'in view growing commercial relations between Japan and

---

[10] *SMH*, 16 June 1916.
[11] M.E. Lloyd (ed.), *Sidelights on Two Referendums, 1916–1917* (Sydney: William Brooks, 1952), p.43.
[12] Letter, Holman to Pearce, 7 March 1916, enclosing copies of letters, Suttor to Holman, 24 and 31 January 1916, NAA MP729/5 393/1/272.

Australia' the government proposed to establish a lectureship in Japanese at an Australian university, and he requested names of suitably qualified candidates.

At the same time the University of Sydney was approached in order to provide an acceptable cover for the appointment. Sydney was the most appropriate location for the lectureship. It was closer than any other university to Duntroon Military College where the successful candidate was expected to spend the greater proportion of his time. Moreover, Brigadier-General Hubert J. Foster, the Chief of the General Staff, had been the first director of the University's Department of Military Science and was well acquainted with the University authorities. For its part the University was happy to cooperate with the Commonwealth. At its meeting on the 12 June the University Senate had responded favourably to an approach from the Newcastle Chamber of Commerce to found a chair of 'Eastern languages'. But when, at the Senate's meeting on 3 July, the Chancellor announced that the Commonwealth Government was 'engaging a British teacher in the Japanese language' and 'would be prepared to allow the University of Sydney to appoint this gentleman as its lecturer and to pay his salary,' it set aside its earlier plans and accepted this proposal with alacrity.

Whether the Senate was informed that the Defence Department would require the use of the lecturer's services in Canberra is not known. However, in offering the post to James Murdoch, a distinguished scholar who had migrated from Scotland to Australia in 1881 and subsequently moved to Japan where he had lived with only one short break for 27 years,[13] the Commonwealth Government made it plain that he would be required 'to necessarily visit Royal Military College and to translate Japanese letters for censor.'

At a meeting of Foster and the University authorities with Murdoch on 28 April 1917 it was agreed that Murdoch would only attend at Sydney University on Mondays and Tuesdays during term and for the rest of the time he would teach Duntroon military cadets Japanese language, politics, sociology and economics. The Commonwealth was to pay his salary of £600 per annum and the University to pay £150 to defray the cost of travelling between Sydney and Canberra. The Defence Department was anxious that Murdoch's appointment should be that of a university lecturer since, as Foster explained to the Registrar, 'it is not considered desirable that it should be known that he was brought down from Japan especially to teach Japanese in a Military College.' The University happily served the state in establishing the lectureship. It accepted that national security not commercial intercourse was the justification for the government action. It agreed to the terms imposed by the Defence Department. And without further inquiry it appointed the person selected by the Commonwealth to the post. Ironically the *Japan Advertiser*, in its report on

---

[13] For an excellent account of Murdoch's life and career, see D.C.S. Sissons, 'Australia's First Professor of Japanese, James Murdoch (1856–1821)', unpublished manuscript, 1985, David Sissons Papers, NLA MS 8230/58.

the appointment, interpreted the University's action as a sign of improved relations following the 'success' of the Japanese squadron's visit to Australia.[14]

The Commonwealth Government also heeded Suttor's warnings about Japanese activities in the Dutch East Indies and the Philippines, and decided to seek first hand information by stationing their own officials in these islands. On 25 June Pearce cabled the Colonial Office that because of 'the considerable intelligence, shipping and other interests which Australia has in East Indies as a whole', his government wished to attach naval officers to the British Consulate in Batavia and Manila. Though the British rejected this request, Pearce, responding to further reports of Japanese interest in Java, again pressed the matter. If London considered naval officers inappropriate, Melbourne was willing to employ civilians for the purpose. Having received a copy of a despatch from the British Consul-General in Batavia to the Foreign Office which outlined 'Japan's anticipated move in the East', he stressed the importance of being regularly supplied with such information.[15]

The British were not moved. The Admiralty argued that intelligence material gathered by Australian officials would be incomplete and therefore difficult to assess. It insisted that, 'For the efficient working of the general scheme of Naval intelligence it is essential to avoid anything in the nature of an independent organisation.' The Australians did not find this reply convincing. If the Admiralty, as it promised, gave Australia all relevant material which came into its hands then the Commonwealth could analyse the reports from its own agents in the light of the broader perspective. More likely the Admiralty's opposition followed from its concern that Australia might use its independent sources to develop a policy at odds with what London deemed to be 'imperial' interests. The British would only agree to send copies of those despatches which might be 'likely to prove of interest' to Australia. They allowed that the Commonwealth might, if it wished, appoint civil officials to collect commercial information. From the Australian standpoint this was an unsatisfactory outcome but, short of challenging the diplomatic unity of the Empire, they had no alternative but to go along with the British decision.

---

[14] For the University of Sydney's acceptance of the Defence Department's proposal, see Senate Minutes, University of Sydney, University of Sydney Archives, G1/1/14, 12 June and 3 July 1916 and letter, Warden and Registrar, the University of Sydney to T. Trumble, Acting-Secretary, Defence Department, 4 July 1916, NAA A3688 488/R1/55.

For the subsequent correspondence, see NAA CP78/22 1916/65 and NAA A3688/R/55.

For the arrangements about Murdoch's services see 'Report in reference to the Commonwealth Instructor in Japanese', 30 April 1917, University of Sydney Archives, G3/13 and letter, Trumble to Warden and Registrar, University of Sydney, 7 May 1917, *ibid.*

Japan Advertiser, 12 September 1916.

[15] Cable, Munro Ferguson to Bonar Law, 25 June 1916, TNA: PRO CO 418/145/108–11; cable, Bonar Law to Munro Ferguson, 17 July 1916, TNA: PRO CO 418/151/137; letter, Atlee Hunt to Trumble, containing extracts from correspondent in Java, 14 July 1916, minuted 'Read with interest' by 'G.F.P. 21 July 1916', NAA MP729/2 box 2 175/3/10; despatches, Munro Ferguson to Bonar Law, 2 and 22 August 1916, TNA: PRO CO418/245–47 and 323–26; letter, W.R.D. Beckett, British Consul-General, Batavia to Munro Ferguson, 16 October 1916, enclosing copy of despatch, 16 October 1916 and letter, Beckett to Munro Ferguson, 20 October 1916, enclosing despatch to Foreign Office, 20 October 1916, NAA CP78/22 1916/149.

Defence planning and renewed calls for conscription

These growing anxieties about Japan had implications also for the Commonwealth's defence planning. As the movement for conscription gathered strength, the question of how far Australia should go in stripping itself of its military age men returned to trouble policy-makers.

Despite the fact that Hughes, before leaving for London, had persuaded the Universal Service League, the Liberal opposition and the press to hold their peace on conscription during his absence, the continuing British controversy kept the topic in the public eye and ultimately propelled it into the centre of the political stage. The British debates over conscription which led to the introduction of compulsion for single men in January and to general compulsion in May had their repercussions in Australia. Pearce, on becoming Acting Prime Minister, recognised that the Australian Government would, as a result of British action, have to face the issue and he foresaw that it might well destroy the labour movement. Writing to Fisher in February he noted 'a distinct growth of Public Opinion towards Conscription'. While he expected that 'our party will give it', he was also convinced that 'it will throw the party back five or ten years. About twenty percent against compulsory service and they are our men most Stalwarts with vague, perhaps crude ideas of Liberty but they will stand firm and go out fighting.'[16] There was good reason for Pearce's gloomy outlook for, within days of Hughes's departure, the Australian Workers' Union, the largest union in the country, had condemned conscription for overseas service and shortly thereafter the Queensland Labor-in-Politics Convention had also gone on record against the principle of compulsion.[17]

From the end of March, as British agitation for a more thoroughgoing conscription law increased, the tempo of the Australian debate picked up. The Australian Natives Association at its annual conference called on the government 'to fully utilise the services of every citizen and the resources of the Commonwealth.'[18] In response, the Vice-President of the Melbourne Trades Hall Council denounced conscription as destructive of the liberty of the working class and warned that, 'If such a thing happened there would follow a serious revolution.'[19] Two weeks later the Victorian Political Labor Conference rejected the conscription of human life, whether for home or overseas defence, and instructed party branches and affiliated unions not to preselect pro-conscriptionist candidates. After Asquith, on 2 May, bought down a Bill making all 18 to 41-year-old men liable for military service, the NSW Political Labor League Conference followed its Queensland and Victorian comrades and committed themselves to fight 'conscription of human life for service abroad', and, like their Victorian counterparts, threatened to withhold endorsement from pro-conscription candidates.

The President of the Political Labor League, J. D. Fitzgerald, a founder of the NSW Labor Party and a man of broad interests, struggled against the anti-conscriptionists. He defended his position as vice-president of the Universal Service League, declaring that he was a 'Democratic Socialist' who believed in the 'organisation of society in peace, war and all the time.'

---

[16] Letter, Pearce to Fisher, 14 February 1916, Fisher Papers NLA MS 2919/1/195.
[17] *Argus*, 29 January 1916.
[18] *Ibid.*, 23 March 1916.
[19] *SMH*, 10 April 1916.

The survival of Australia's industrial liberty depended on the British Empire defeating Germany. Universal service would contribute not only to protecting Australia against Germany but also, if necessary, against Japan. But his arguments were to no avail. The labour tide was running too strongly against conscription. An interstate trade union congress meeting in Melbourne pronounced its 'uncompromising hostility to conscription' and enjoined all sections of the labour movement to work for the defeat of conscriptionists both within their own ranks and within the country as a whole.[20]

Cabling Pearce from London, Hughes warned that the British decision to adopt compulsory military service 'must be felt Commonwealth and through all Empire.' He knew that the British initiative would 'brace public opinion Commonwealth and other Dominions so as to make action imperative' but he wanted the issue postponed until his return.[21] Pearce, though willing to do so, was unable to comply with Hughes's wishes. Circumstances conspired against him. He had to contend with not only the British introduction of compulsory service but also the failure of the 'Call to Arms' to reach its extremely ambitious target. Recruitment figures had declined from over 22,000 in January to less than 10,000 in April. Voluntarism was scarcely raising enough men to meet the reinforcement quota. By the end of April the federal Parliamentary War Committee, with five Labor members absent, had agreed that 'Australia was not adequately represented at the front' and, if a prescribed number did not enlist by a date to be set, then the whole question of voluntary service should be revived.[22] This was the same political strategy that the British Government had pursued in bringing in conscription. Pearce, taking his cue from Asquith, tried to seize control of the explosive debate by calling a secret session of parliament. He appealed to both sides to wait until Hughes could personally report to them about the European situation. Furthermore, in order to quieten the conscriptionists, he explained that, even if more men were available, they could not be sent to the front since there was great difficulty in obtaining shipping.[23]

The British action had, however, so 'braced' the advocates of compulsion that they were unwilling to hold off any longer. The agreement which had been reached with Hughes was set aside. The Liberal opposition and the Universal Service League returned to the fray. Cook, in responding to Pearce, insisted that Australia follow the British lead in order 'to strike a decisive blow as soon as may be'. Since there was a majority in the parliament for compulsion, he demanded that the government should act immediately.[24] On 22 May the Universal Service League, sweeping aside the solitary protest of Fitzgerald, resumed its campaign, and on 6 July the Liberal Party's National Conference committed itself to the principle of compulsory overseas service.[25]

As the controversy proceeded, the issue of Japan – despite the wartime alliance and the instructions of the censors – entered more and more into the argument. Political leaders some-

---

[20] *Ibid.*, 9, 11 and 12 May 1916; Australian Council of Trade Unions, *Australian trade unionism and conscription: being report of proceedings of Australian Trade Union Congress, together with the manifesto of the National Executive* (Melbourne: Labor Call Print, 1916).
[21] Cable, Hughes to Pearce, 1 May 1916, Pearce Papers, AWM 3DRL 2222/2/3.
[22] Copy of letter, Pearce to Fisher, 29 April 1916, Pearce Papers, AWM 3DRL 2222/1/2.
[23] Copy of letter, Pearce to Hughes, 11 May 1916, Pearce Papers, AWM 3DRL 2222/3/3.
[24] *CPD*, 1914–17 session, LXXIX, 7770–72, 10 May 1916.
[25] *SMH*, 23 May and 6 July 1916.

times appeared almost recklessly determined to defy the censors in talking about the Japanese danger. Sometimes the danger was hinted at and at other times it was explicitly spelt out. Irvine in supporting Cook in parliament had claimed that 'the safety of Australia calls for immediate compulsion. If the British Empire did not win, within a few years of such a peace of exhaustion we would no longer control the oceans ... and our possession of the continent would last no longer than that control.'[26] Senator P. J. Lynch, a Labor conscriptionist, was more forthright: 'The present ... is the most perilous and momentous hour in the history of our country ... Australia today is menaced ... What has happened in Russia from successful Japanese attack may happen here.'[27] J. E. Fenton, a Labor anti-conscriptionist, said that as Irvine had ignored Pearce's plea for restraint he felt free to speak frankly. What Japan had done 'since the termination of her war with Russia' in establishing great naval and military arsenals, Australia should also have done. Australia could not spare more men for the Western Front.[28] The debate showed once more the profound impact that the Russo-Japanese war had had on the Australian political imagination.

J. H. Catts, a Labor anti-conscriptionist who was both Director of Recruiting for New South Wales and a member of the federal Parliamentary War Committee, produced the most alarmist and extensive exposition of the Japanese danger and its relation to conscription. On the basis of his reading of 'the speeches of Japanese members of Parliament, and articles in their papers' he composed a memorandum on 'Australia's Peril and Australia's Need' which he sent to Pearce. It outlined 'the dangers with which we are surrounded' and set out the steps which should be taken to prepare Australia to repel invasion.

In the submission, which was subtitled 'Compulsory Training for Home Defence: Voluntary Enlistment for Empire Service', he gave an account of Japan's wartime aggression, ambition and deception, from its attempt to assert its suzerainty over China to its betrayal of the Anglo-Japanese alliance and its demand for the reform of the White Australia policy. He noted that Japan had entered into an alliance with Russia which at the end of the war might be turned against Britain if it attempted to deny Japan its territorial spoils. He pointed out that in December 1915 the Japanese Government had begun a new naval building program. Though Japan had quarrelled with the United States, it was more likely that its strike force would be used against Australia. Australia was closer to Japan, was relatively defenceless, having a population of only 5 million, and was 'a more tempting prize'. Japan had differences with Britain over the peace settlement, most particularly 'the Marshall and other Islands'.

Australia should learn from Britain's mistakes. It was Catts's view that the Mother Country had failed to grasp the meaning of Germany's military preparations and had 'nearly come to destruction'. And he asked rhetorically, 'Shall we do absolutely nothing, whilst the rumbling of war (with the Pacific as its theatre) are being anxiously canvassed by every interest in the Pacific but Australia?'

The code of silence on the subject had to be broken. Australia was 'prepared for sacrifice to any extent both physical and material for home defence, if a realistic government will declare and inform the people of its necessity'. He concluded that, 'The manhood of Australia should be

---

[26] *CPD*, 1914–17 session, LXXIX, 7777–79, 10 May 1916.
[27] *Ibid.*, 7799, 11 May 1916.
[28] *Ibid.*, 7897, 13 May 1916.

trained and armed at once for home defence and at least given an opportunity to strike a blow for itself.' In order to begin the process of public education and to bring pressure to bear on the government he gave copies of his memorandum to the press. On the day after he sent the letter to Pearce, the *Sydney Morning Herald* reported Catts saying that Japan not Germany was the real enemy, and that Australians should be 'trained and armed at once for home defence'.[29]

Pearce needed no lectures on the Japanese menace. It was a theme with which he was very familiar. He had been a leading Japanophobe since 1905. Yet, though he understood the added danger that the European conflict meant for Australia's own security and shared Catts's fears about Japan's intentions, he considered that Catts's call for general mobilisation went beyond what was necessary. Thus he replied privately that the government was 'not neglecting its duty in respect of possible dangers which may arise from any quarter' and publicly that there was no good reason to call out the home defence.[30] Pearce did not believe that Australia was in imminent danger from Japan and, given the difficult choices that had to be made, he considered Australia's security best served by doing everything possible to win the European war and restore Britain's naval supremacy.

Nevertheless the government took preliminary steps to put Australia in a position to deal with any post-war difficulties. In addition to appointing Murdoch to teach Japanese to the military cadet officers, Pearce reinstituted compulsory military training for home defence, which had been suspended at the end of October the previous year in order to free officers to meet the demands of Hughes's 'Call to Arms'. In November he announced the formation of an Australian Army reserve which would be made up of those who had completed their military training, returned soldiers, retired members of the permanent forces, and members of rifle clubs, and at the end of the war their ranks would be expanded still more by the addition of the returning members of the AIF. He expected that by twelve months after the end of the war the reserve would number 50,000–200,000 men.[31] This substantial military force was not being raised to meet an attack from Germany on Australia, to prepare to take part in future imperial wars or even to suppress a rebellion at home. Rather it was intended to meet the possibility of a Japanese invasion.

More far-reaching still, Pearce and the cabinet endorsed a proposal originally put forward by Captain Thring for a substantial reconstruction of the Council of Defence. Thring had submitted this scheme to the federal Munitions Committee. It was a follow-up to the agitation about Japan which had developed in the first half of 1915 and the Navy Department's briefing paper about the 'Japanese danger' at the end of that year. His plan was intended to make the council a more effective, integrated and authoritative instrument for policy-making. In particular it was to act as a continuous source of strategic intelligence and analysis. In other words it was to be a kind of national security council. On the basis of this report Pearce set up an inquiry into the existing 'moribund' Council of Defence which, following Thring's scheme, made two key recom-

---

[29] Lloyd (ed.), *Sidelights on Two Referendums*, pp.41–42; letter and memorandum, Catts to Pearce, 29 May 1916, NAA IA 16/15272; *SMH*, 30 May 1916; see also J.H. Catts article on 'Australia's Peril – Home Defence Compulsion – Voluntarism for Empire', *Sydney Sun*, 14 June 1916.
[30] Letter, Pearce to Catts, 2 June 1916, NAA A1 16/15272; *SMH*, 1 June 1916.
[31] *SMH*, 19 November 1916 and 7 February 1917. The military reserve was to be 'purely a home defence institution'.

mendations – firstly the appointment of a secretary to the council who would 'keep in mind continually the probability of war with foreign powers'; and secondly the creation of subcommittees to cover every aspect of defence planning. The secretary was to be charged with responsibility for collecting information 'on all matters essential to the well-being of the Commonwealth likely to be effected during the progress of the war' and, after sifting and assessing it, reporting all matters of importance to the council. The subcommittees were to deal with strategy and combined naval and military operations; exports, imports and trade; intelligence; inventions; economic subjects and transport; and censorship. Australia was to be as 'self-supporting as far as may be'. Pearce presented this report to Hughes on his return to Australia, but since conscription almost immediately came to absorb all political energy the proposals were set aside to await a more propitious times.[32]

For most of these Australians, these suspicions about Britain's ally, Japan, were not prompted primarily by insular isolation, colonial ignorance or racial antagonism. Such mistrust was a commonplace of the nation-state system. Indeed the Allies, even as they were fighting alongside one another against the Central Powers, were giving thought to post-war possibilities and their likely meaning for a future balance of power. In August 1916 the British, buoyed by the prospect of victory on the Somme, were anxious that neither France nor Russia should replace Germany as the dominant power in Europe.[33] The American Government likewise shared Catts's view that the Russo-Japanese alliance might enable Japan more easily to extend its hegemony over China and the Western Pacific. President Wilson, in resisting pressure to enter the European war, told his cabinet in February 1917, 'If he felt, in order to keep the white race or part of it strong to meet the yellow race – Japan for instance, in alliance with Russia, dominating China – it was wise to do nothing, he would do nothing.'[34] Even if Australians' racial views of the world and world politics caused them to exaggerate the danger of Japan, their basic rationale was strategic, namely Japan's pre-eminent position in the region, its evident intent to expand its influence in East Asia and the Western Pacific, its pressure on the Commonwealth to modify its racially discriminating immigration policy and its diplomatic efforts to seize every advantage from the European war crisis.

---

[32] Letter, Pearce to J.A. Jensen, Minister for the Navy, 6 April 1916, and Minute, Creswell to Secretary of the Department of Defence, 31 January 1917 and Minute by Creswell, 28 August 1917, NAA A9791/1 1; letter, Pearce to Hughes, 10 August 1916, Hughes Papers NLA MS 1538/117/3.

See also a Navy Department paper, drawn up in the Intelligence Branch, which on the basis of a study of Japanese and other countries' newspapers, concluded that Japan had adopted a policy of 'penetrating all the islands of the Pacific and the Eastern Archipelago' and was intent on seizing the opportunity of its naval dominance in the region to demand 'the unrestricted admission of Japanese to all countries in the British Empire'. Letter, Naval Secretary, Macandie, to Secretary, Department of Defence, 16 September 1916, NAA A2219, Vol.6.

[33] French, pp.210–16.

[34] David F. Houston, *Eight Years with Wilson's Cabinet,* 2 vols, (Garden city, New York: Doubleday, 1926), Vol.I, p.229.

7
'The Greatest Crisis in our History': The Conflict over Conscription

Hughes's homecoming was a personal triumph. The fame which he had acquired abroad flattered the Australian ego and made him a popular hero. Just as the Anzacs had put Australia's name on the military honour roll of history, so the 'Little Digger' had, as the press reported it, brought great credit to his country and caused Britain and its Allies to treat Australia as a valued partner in the common endeavour. He had become an imperial statesman and through his speeches 'over there' attracted much public acclaim. The people took pride in their leader and basked in his reflected glory. Even the music hall celebrated his international renown. In J. C. Williamson's Sydney production of the 'Mother Goose' pantomime the song of 'Little Billy Hughes' was a great hit.

Little Billy Hughes

REFRAIN

Oh! the man Australia's proud of is little Billy Hughes.
We love to read his speeches and to listen to his views;
And what Billy asks old England we know she won't refuse,
For all Australia's right behind our Little Billy Hughes.

VERSE 1

There's a little pocket Statesman, his name is Billy Hughes,
His speeches in the papers are crowding out the news;
And the whole world listens to him, especially the Hun,
For Billy's on the warpath and he's only just begun
He's the idol of the Allies, he's fighting German trade
He hits out from the shoulder and he calls a spade a spade
And King George is so delighted he sends him "Billy Doos,"
Saying come and stop at Windsor with me Little Billy Hughes.

VERSE 2

Billy's shaken up old England he's stirred up things a treat,
They've loaded him with honors, they've dined him on the fleet
And for freedom of their cities he freely gives them speech
He tells them just to strangle all the German trade in reach
And he says the British Empire's for Britain and their friends
The Germans and their cheap goods to Hades Billy sends
'Our chance is now or never the day has come to choose
If Britain's still to boss the world!' says Little Billy Hughes.

The coming of the conscription crisis

From 31 July when he landed in Fremantle until 22 August when he reached Sydney, the Australian Prime Minister progressed through the southern capitals being greeted along the way with rapturous enthusiasm. No public figure returning from overseas had ever been accorded such a welcome. Not only civic dignitaries but also large crowds of ordinary people paid homage to the man. After Hughes's boat arrived at Outer Harbour, waterside workers, ignoring protocol, broke into the official party and shook the hand of the founding president of their Federation. At Port Adelaide the train taking Hughes to the formal reception was stopped to allow him to speak from an improvised platform, and he was 'cheered to the echo' in this Labor stronghold. In the evening 7000 people packed into Adelaide's Exhibition Building for what was 'probably the greatest indoor meeting ever held in the city'.[1]

Sydney surpassed its sister-cities in acclaiming its favourite son. After driving in a motorcade through streets thronged with people, Hughes attended an Eight Hour Day banquet given in his honour by the labour movement. The Labor Lord Mayor, addressing an audience which lacked 'tall hats or frock coats or other such marks of class distinction', set the tone of unqualified adulation. Hughes was, he said, 'not only the most colossal personality that the public life of Australia had produced, but … one of the greatest men in the British Empire.' The following evening, to cap off all that had gone before, the Prime Minister was tendered a civic dinner which brought together the most eminent personages from nearly every section of public life. The distinguished company included the leading members of the federal government and opposition and of the New South Wales Government and opposition, the chief justices of the High Court and the New South Wales Supreme Court, the Anglican and Roman Catholic archbishops, the Presidents of the New South Wales Political Labor League and the Trades and Labour Council, the Presidents of the New South Wales Employers' Federation and Chamber of Commerce, the Japanese Consul-General, and the list went on and on. This was the high point in Hughes's popularity and political career.[2] Almost the whole country, as it seemed, lay at his feet.

Yet it was not long before half the cheering stopped. Behind this demonstration of national unity lurked the vexed issue of conscription. Both sides to the debate looked to the Prime Minister to take their part and settle the issue in their favour. The conscriptionists, after Hughes's 'Win-the-War' campaigns in Australia and Britain, confidently expected him to espouse compulsion. The anti-conscriptionists, more sceptically, hoped that Hughes, as leader of the Labor Party, would respect the clearly expressed view of the labour movement; the Sydney *Worker* greeted him with the banner headline 'Welcome Home to the Cause of Anti-conscription.'[3] Thus when at the end of August Hughes declared himself for conscription the rather unnatural harmony instantly collapsed and the paeans of praise were replaced by partisan catchcries and bitter recriminations. While to the conscriptionists he was a statesman who put Empire above party, to the anti-conscriptionists he was a turncoat who had betrayed his own class and country.

---

[1] *Advertiser*, 7 August 1916; *Register*, 7 August 1916.
[2] *SMH*, 22 and 24 August 1916.
[3] *Australian Worker*, 31 July 1916.

For Hughes, the decision to support conscription was logical and natural. Though, as he had told the Governor-General at his first interview as Prime Minister, it would be impossible to justify Australia taking this step until Britain itself had acted, nevertheless his conviction about its necessity was not determined by the British example. It is true that after the British had in May adopted a comprehensive conscription law he had no doubt but that Australia must follow suit: 'this action of British Government makes non-committal attitude impossible and will brace up public opinion so as to make action imperative.'[4] Nevertheless he did not blindly follow the British. Rather, his commitment to conscription derived from his long-held beliefs about racial survival, national efficiency and state socialism, all of which were closely interlinked. More immediately it came from the war philosophy he had been expounding since 1914. As the war was a climactic episode in the history of the British Empire and 'the greatest crisis in our history', so the will to win required national organisation and personal sacrifice. The future of the British peoples and their heritage of liberty were at stake. In particular, Australia's own security was dependent on an Allied victory in Europe. Defeat would mean either German or Japanese control of the Pacific and a stalemate would still leave Australia in great danger.

Hughes had learnt from discussions in the British War Cabinet and with Grey, Lloyd George, Sir William Robertson, the Chief of the Imperial General Staff, and other British officials about the gravity of the Allies' position and how the Japanese were exploiting it for their own advantage. The permanent head of the Foreign Office, Arthur Nicolson, had told him that 'in early spring we should be entering into the "last lap"' and he had warned that since 'Germany was fighting for her existence as a great nation she would therefore make a stiff fight for it.'[5] Thus Hughes had returned to Australia strengthened in his conviction that the British Empire had to marshal all its resources to achieve a speedy victory. Australia in its own interest as well as in the interest of the British race as a whole had to be prepared to give its last man and its last shilling to the cause.

Arriving home, Hughes had been apprised by Pearce and the Treasurer, W. G. Higgs, among others, that the labour movement in the Eastern states was strongly opposed to conscription, Pearce seeing it as an obstacle to be overcome and Higgs as a viewpoint entitled to respect. Consequently the Prime Minister refused to allow himself to be drawn on the issue until he could meet face to face with Cabinet and Caucus. In the intervening three weeks he hoped that his great public reception would both enhance his stature as national leader and create such a climate of opinion that the Labor Party would be forced to let him have his way.

Laying the groundwork, Hughes took every opportunity to awaken the public to the true meaning of the war. In every capital city he expatiated on the magnitude of the task facing the Allies and the dire consequences for Australia should they not prevail. In addition to the general arguments about the loyalty owed Britain and the British race, he raised the spectre of the threat to 'White Australia'. Despite British admonitions against offending Japan, despite the inexpediency of expressing open distrust of an ally and despite his own government's banning of the publication of such statements, Hughes at every port of call hinted not very subtly that a defeat for the British Empire would expose Australia to an Asian invasion.

---

[4] Cable, Hughes to Pearce, 1 May 1916, Pearce Papers, AWM 3DRL/2222 3/3.
[5] Letter, Nicolson to Munro Ferguson, 20 March 1916, Novar Papers, NLA MS 696/8328.

In speech after speech he lambasted those who failed to see how Australia's future in the Pacific was tied inexorably to the outcome of the Great War:

> There are some people who are so short-sighted that they cannot see the danger in which Australia stands. They seem to imagine that because we are remote from the battlefront, because the blood red waves of war have not reached our peaceful shores, we are not in danger, that we are not even directly concerned.

On the contrary, he assured his audiences of the 'utter helplessness of Australia to arrest her downfall if Germany triumphs', and explained graphically, using familiar images and phrases, Australia's particular peril:

> Let me give my fellow-citizens a much-needed warning. Have those who think Australia remote from the world which hatches dangers and wars ever looked at the map? It is well that we should all do so. So far from being far removed from the busy hive of men we live almost within hail of its greatest populations. We have nailed 'White Australia' to the top-mast. Yet we are but a tiny drop in a coloured ocean. We are five million white people claiming to hold inviolate a great continent, which would maintain 100 million and we live almost within coo-ee of a 1000 millions of coloured people who jostle one another for want of room. It is well that we should remember this and comfort ourselves accordingly.

The conclusion was that Australians could not afford to be complacent about their right to dwell in and enjoy their land:

> The old life of jogging along without any set purpose must make way for the narrow life by which we must all endeavour to do something by organised effort for each other and for the country.[6]

At the Sydney civic dinner, held on the eve of the federal Parliamentary Party Meeting, Hughes spoke 'as a man inspired' or, perhaps more aptly, as a man possessed. In the presence of the Presidents of the New South Wales Trades and Labour Council and the Political Labor League, he ended his address by proclaiming, 'We have a plain duty to perform ... I shall do my duty ... and ask you to believe that I am prepared to do whatever is necessary to save Australia from its enemies of all sorts and kinds.' And within the phrase 'enemies of all sorts and kinds' he included not only Germans and Japanese but also those Australians who dared to oppose conscription. He was aiming his shafts most immediately at those who, during his absence, had gained control of the party machine and organised anti-conscription demonstrations of upwards of 60–100,000 people in the Sydney Domain.[7]

The spirit informing the invocation stirred the audience. The Labor Lord Mayor, who was a member of the Universal Service League, openly encouraged Hughes to declare himself: 'The Prime Minister has said he will follow the light. If he is prepared to do so we are prepared to

---

[6] Perth speech, *SMH*, 2 August 1916; Adelaide speech, *Advertiser* and *Register*, 7 August 1916. The censor in Sydney cut these indirect references to Japan from the Sydney report of the Adelaide speech but they were published in full in all other cities; Melbourne speech, *SMH*, 15 August 1916; Sydney speech, *SMH*, 22 and 24 August 1916; see also Pearce echoing the same sentiments in his address at the Eight Hour Day Banquet in Sydney, 'dangers confronting them on all sides', *SMH*, 22 August 1916.
[7] *SMH*, 24 August 1916.

follow'. The New South Wales Labor Premier, likewise a foundation member of the Universal Service League, endorsed these sentiments: 'Tell us what Australia is to do and the undaunted democracy of Australia will rally round the leader, will not flinch until the task has been completed.' The leader of the state's Liberal opposition, asserting that Hughes had united all classes behind the war effort, joined in the appeal. He expressed the hope that 'out of these great days would arise a great new party in the Commonwealth.' All those present at the gathering understood that a great political crisis was imminent. When, however, a voice cried out, 'Say the word', Hughes would not. He contented himself with impassioned appeals to duty, honour and self-interest, and kept his formal declaration for the Caucus meeting.

By this time the labour movement, especially in the Eastern states, had committed itself to anti-conscription. Hughes's public addresses had been counter-productive. Just as his militant oratory had given heart to the conscriptionists, so it had the effect of galvanising the anti-conscriptionists. He had lost all feeling for the dynamics of the labour movement. He had forgotten what Fisher so well understood. Though Labor leaders might be elected to political office and introduce measures to alleviate the lot of working people, employees still depended for their employment and livelihood on the same masters. They could never in the same way or to the same extent as the business, professional and official classes regard the state and society as their own.

By comparison with Britain and other European countries, Australia was an egalitarian democracy. Unlike the 'old World' it had no pre-modern ruling caste which could still command deference from many in the working class. In Australia leaders frequently came from the working class and out of the union movement. At the outbreak of war, the leaders of both the Liberal and the Labor parties had been coal miners with little formal education. They had to appeal to an electorate in which nearly all adult British subjects had the right to vote. This social egalitarianism was evident in the AIF myth about mateship and indiscipline. These characteristics were a frequent source of British officers' comment and complaint. General Bridges had explained to General Birdwood, the British Commander of the AIF that:

> among the ranks of the Australian soldiers were men who probably belonged to the strongest of socialist communities in the world – men who a few weeks before had looked upon it as an absolute degradation to humanity that they should salute any other man, or call any man 'Sir' …

And he added that:

> The greatest difficulty in this respect was the matter of officers. Officers in the vast majority of cases came from exactly the same class as the men, and it was therefore very difficult for them to exercise proper command or to command respect from their men.[8]

The labour movement overwhelmingly identified with the British race and Empire, and had contributed proportionally its share of men to the AIF. But this loyalty remained qualified by social condition. Since the creation of the Universal Service League and the passage of the *War Census Bill*, grass roots resentment of the government's war policy had gathered momentum. The abandonment of a reform program, the failure to make the rich share more equitably the cost of

---

[8] Letter, Birdwood to General Sir A.J. Murray, 25 February 1916, Murray Papers, BL Add 52461.

the war, the rising cost of living, the militarisation of civilian life, the defence authorities raids on trades hall offices, the censorship of labour newspapers and the prosecution of labour and socialist speakers and writers had spread disaffection. This new authoritarianism for which the most vulnerable in society paid the highest price induced a reaction. And anti-conscription thus became the focus and symbol for a broader spirit of discontent. The disaffected could do little to influence the administration of the *War Precautions Act* or to force the Labor Government to implement the party's platform. The cause of conscription for overseas service, which was enthusiastically pushed by employers, military officers, conservative politicians and professional men, called for a further and novel expansion of state power over the lives of ordinary people. Conscription of this kind challenged the voluntary principle enshrined in the *Commonwealth Defence Act*. The anti-conscriptionists could claim to be fighting to preserve the Federation's defence policy. It was an appropriate and timely issue around which workers and trade unionists could rally in order to vent their accumulated frustrations.

Irish Catholic anger at Britain's ruthless suppression of the abortive Easter rising in Dublin gave further impetus to the anti-conscriptionist cause. Though most Irish Catholic leaders had initially denounced the Irish Republican Brotherhood's nationalist insurrection – to use the words of the Archbishop of Melbourne – 'as an outburst of madness, an anachronism and a crime', nevertheless by the end of May the summary court-martialling and execution of the captured rebels had brought about a change of heart. The Irish Catholic community, including the hierarchy and the press, began to question whether the British Government was serious about Home Rule and to wonder whether their previous unqualified support for the British Empire and the war was justified. With the breakdown in negotiations over Home Rule in July these attitudes hardened. Some Irish Catholics expressed sympathy for the reinvigorated Sinn Fein Party's demand for complete independence. Many more, however, found an outlet for their sense of grievance in opposing conscription.[9] Since most Irish Catholics were working class people they did not so much swell the ranks of the anti-conscriptionists as give to the movement a more fervent tone.

When therefore, at the beginning of the winter, encouraged by the British example, the Universal Service League and its allies started to campaign for compulsion, the labour organisations in the Eastern states not only restated their opposition to conscription but also made opposition to conscription a test of loyalty to the Labor Party. They entered the lists against

---

[9] Alan D. Gilbert, 'The Conscription Referenda, 1916–17: The Impact of the Irish Crisis', *Historical Studies*, 14 (October 1969), 60–64.

It may be that Irish Catholic Labor supporters who had in 1914 and 1915 mounted a major but unsuccessful campaign for state aid to Catholic schools found in anti-conscription a cause through which they could express their resentment. Though the two matters were not directly linked in the debates it may well be that since those calling for conscription for the defence of the British Empire were also responsible for their failure to obtain public funding for parochial schools this gave them a further reason to support the anti-conscription cause.

For the Catholic campaign to secure state aid, see Celia Hamilton, 'Catholic Interests and the Labor Party: Organised Catholic Action in Victoria and New South Wales, 1910–1916', *Historical Studies*, 9 (November 1959), 62–73.

the conscriptionists, organising mass meetings and demonstrations. In response to a Universal Service League announcement that it was sponsoring a rally at the Sydney Town Hall, New South Wales trade union leaders and the Political Labor League executive joined with other anti-conscriptionist bodies, such as the Australian Socialist Party, the Australian Freedom League and the Industrial Workers of the World, to hold a meeting on the Sydney Domain.[10] From that time the two sides competed vigorously for public support, and this competition stirred fierce passions and bred mutual hostility. Newly enlisted soldiers as well as returned soldiers frequently attempted to break up the anti-conscription meetings, and the anti-conscriptionists retaliated in kind. The confrontation was straining the bonds of civil society.

After Hughes's return, the labour movement left him in no doubt as to where they stood. The eastern states' organisations defiantly reaffirmed their earlier decisions. Incensed by the demands for conscription which began to issue from the press, the pulpit and the platform and by the military censors' harsh treatment of anti-conscription publications, they reacted strongly. On 13 August the New South Wales Political Labor League for the first time sponsored its own protest on the Domain. It attracted a crowd of 100,000 – to that point by far the largest demonstration against conscription.[11] The Labor Party was itself taking the lead. Hughes's own West Sydney federal Labor Council passed a formal resolution against conscription.[12]

For Hughes the omens were not good. He knew that he had to contend with formidable odds in trying to win his colleagues over. Writing to his confidant, Keith Murdoch, an Australian journalist who acted as his personal representative in London, Hughes admitted that:

> All or nearly all the Labor organisations – political and industrial – my own league included – have passed strong resolutions against compulsion. A large majority of our party in the Parliament are frightened out of their lives – many of course dare not call their souls their own. I'm not sure even of the *Cabinet*!

But he indicated that he was 'neither hopeful nor hopeless' and that, at all events, he 'was resolved to go on.' Acknowledging the possibility of failure he refused to allow it to deflect him from his course. Regardless of the opposition from labour movement and the Labor Party organisations he was unshakeable in his determination to proceed. He averred defiantly 'I shall do what I think right.'[13] Hughes knew that winning over the Labor Party was the key to achieving his objective and so delayed his announcement until parliament was recalled and he could meet formally with his Labor colleagues. On 25 August at a meeting of the Caucus Hughes finally declared himself and called for support for the cause of conscription.

In urging his case Hughes's hand was greatly strengthened by a cable from the British Army Council which arrived on the morning of the Caucus meeting and requested a very high rate of reinforcements to replace the AIF's heavy losses in France. The British military authorities stated that to prevent the break up of the Third Division, Australia should in September provide a special draft of 20,000 men in addition to the normal monthly reinforcements, and in the three

---

[10] *SMH*, 19 June and 3 July 1916.
[11] *SMH* and *Daily Telegraph*, 14 August 1916.
[12] *SMH*, 13 August 1916.
[13] Letter, Hughes to Murdoch, 15 August 1916, Murdoch Papers, NLA MS 2823/23.

following months increase the level of reinforcements to 25 percent of establishment or 16,500 men for each month. The cable's arrival was so fortuitous that it seems not impossible that Hughes either directly or indirectly solicited it.[14]

Certainly the circumstances surrounding the despatch of the cable suggest that it was concocted for an ulterior purpose. Firstly, the request itself was unprecedented; never before had the British Government asked Australia to raise a precise number of troops. Secondly, the nominated level of reinforcements was extremely large and not clearly related to the casualty rate.[15] And thirdly, it seems a remarkable coincidence that the request arrived on the very day Hughes was announcing his support for conscription to the Caucus. Indeed scholars agree that the timing of the cable was politically motivated.[16] It seems likely that British military and political officials may have conspired with Colonel Robert M. M. Anderson, the Commandant of the AIF's Administrative Headquarters in London, to use the reinforcement question to assist the Prime Minister's conscription campaign.

The British authorities were at this time under great pressure to raise more divisions for France. Britain's own resources were fully stretched. The summer campaign on the Western Front

---

[14] Cable, Bonar Law to Munro Ferguson, despatched 6.15pm 24 August 1916, Hughes Papers, NLA MS 1538/20/1.

No direct reference to this cable could be found in the British archives. Neither the Army Council minutes and associated papers in the War Office files nor the papers of the Chief of the Imperial Guard Staff and of his Adjutant-General contain a copy of the cable or any allusion to it. (See Minutes and Precis of Army Council minutes, 3 February–27 December 1916, TNA:PRO WO 32–33; War of 1914-1918, Correspondence and Papers of Military Headquarters, TNA:PRO WO 158; Army Council Secretary Minutes TNA:PRO WO 163; Papers of Field Marshall Sir William Robertson and of Lt. General Sir Launcelot Edward Kiggell, Liddell Hart Centre for Military Archives, King's College, London). Even more remarkable, the Colonial Office records, which are normally so meticulous and complete, do not contain a copy of the cable or any direct reference to it. (TNA:PRO CO 418/144–146, 155 and 156; TNA:PRO CO 532/82–84, 88; TNA:PRO CO 616/63–67).

Colonel Robert M. M. Anderson, the Commandant of the AIF's Administrative Headquarters in London, who was an old friend of Hughes, had worked with British official to produce the cable. He had been a successful shipping and timber merchant and probably met Hughes during the Sydney waterside workers' strike of 1908. Subsequently he became Hughes's investment adviser and bought and sold shares on his behalf. (Letter, Anderson to Hughes, 29 June 1913 Hughes Papers, NLA MS1538/1/40–43). During his stay in London, Hughes had insisted that Anderson be appointed head of the AIF's Administrative Headquarters in London. Anderson was a man whom Hughes could trust to do his bidding. It is possible that Hughes, responding to an earlier Anderson cable which reported that the War Office was going to draw on the Third Division in England for reinforcements for the AIF in France, had urged Anderson to act as he did or it may simply be that Anderson, intuitively knowing Hughes's mind on the matter, had taken the initiative himself.

[15] See Scott, *Australia during the War*, p.360; Bean, *Official History of Australia during the War*, Vol III, 'The A.I.F in France 1916', p.888; Fitzhardinge, *The Little Digger*, p.183.

[16] Scott in his treatment of the topic points out that the numbers that the Army Council sought were at least double what that body considered necessary after the failure of the conscription referendum and accepts that the anti-conscriptionist critics of the Army Council's figures were correct. (Scott, *Australia during the War*, p.359).

had taken a very heavy toll. On the day before the despatch of the cable, Lloyd George, as War Minister, had declared in the House of Commons that:

> We are fighting a very great military power in gigantic resources … We shall need more men … and we shall need the courage and the endurance of our race in every part of the world in order to convert the work which has begun … into a victory which will really be a final and complete victory.[17]

The War Office and the Army Council were preoccupied with this problem. Field Marshal Sir William Robertson, Chief of the Imperial General Staff, despaired of being able to maintain the British army in France at full strength and looked to the Dominions for increased reinforcements. He also hoped to extend the application of conscription to Ireland and recognised that each Dominion which followed the British lead added moral force to his case.[18] Anderson, a long-time confidant of Hughes, who courted political leaders and men of influence, believed that personal relations were more important than institutional forms. In a later letter to Robertson he reminded him that this was the best way of working in Australia.

> May I urge you to take special note of this: that any communication on Army matters, as far as possible communicate with Australia direct. The usual long-winded official channel is so attenuated as to lose force; they know you, and that is the reason I have always tried to get you into direct personal touch with them, as you know how easily difficulties have been solved when you did that.[19]

Accepting Hughes's view of the necessity of conscription Anderson had no compunction in using his position to advance that objective. Anderson was in London at the centre of the controversy over reinforcing the AIF and, as Fitzhardinge has concluded, 'he saw an opportunity to help the cause of conscription in Australia.' On 22 August Anderson informed Hughes that the Army Council 'at my request cabling you through Colonial Office estimated reinforcements required and exact position.'[20]

Despite the prestige accrued from his overseas trip, despite his success in selling Australia's wheat, wool and metals to the British and despite the Army Council's cable giving precise numbers of reinforcements required to maintain the existing AIF divisions – numbers which, it was maintained, voluntary enlistments could not supply– Hughes faced great difficulties. A substantial majority of Caucus members were opposed to conscription, some out of conviction, some out of loyalty to the movement and some, no doubt, out of fear for their preselection. Hughes realised this and also the consequences for the party if he put the principle directly to Caucus. Ever resourceful, he offered a compromise. A national referendum on conscription would be held on 28 October and, in the meantime, unless enough men volunteered to meet the Army

---

[17] Great Britain, 5 *Parliamentary Debates* (Commons), LXXXV, 2555, 23 August 1916.

[18] Copies of letters, Robertson to General Sir Douglas Haig, 14 and 25 August 1916, Robertson Papers, Liddell Hart Centre for Military Archives MS1/22/68 and 70.

[19] Letter, Anderson to Robertson, 28 April 1917, Robertson Papers, Liddell Hart Centre for Military Archives MS1/37/5.

[20] Fitzhardinge, *The Little Digger*, p.184; cable, Commandant, AIF Headquarters to Defence Department, Melbourne, 22 August 1916, Hughes Papers, NLA MS1538/20/1.

Council's target for September, 'sufficient men' were to be called up for training under the *Defence Act* to await the people's will. He hoped to achieve his end by other means. That is, he hoped by showing that the country overwhelmingly favoured conscription to convince the party to accept the inevitable. After a bitter Caucus fight lasting four days and nights, enough of the waverers were won over and the proposal was narrowly approved.[21]

The referendum campaign and the issue of Japan

Hughes believed that his scheme guaranteed the acceptance of conscription and so would enable Australia to despatch the requested troops to the Western Front in time for the 1917 summer offensive. It was impossible for him to imagine that Australians, as a British people, would refuse what the survival of their race demanded. It was impossible for him to entertain the idea that British Australians would not follow the lead of their kith and kin in the British Isles and New Zealand.[22] He was 'quite certain' the voters would approve conscription and, after informing parliament of the government's plan, he cabled the Army Council on 31 August that Australia would 'send a special draft of 20,000 men immediately' and 'thereafter 16,500 per month.'[23] In giving this assurance, the Prime Minister went beyond what had been sought and promised the figure of 16,500 – not merely for the ensuing three months but for the indefinite future. 'We may assume,' he claimed in the House of Representatives, 'although we are not told, that the demand for reinforcements thereafter [after the first three months] will continue on that scale; that is to say at the rate of 16,500 a month.' His calculations about future needs were made on that basis. Australia by the end of March 1917 would supply 131,500 additional men, that is 32,500 for September and 16,500 for each of the six succeeding months.

At first glance it is difficult to understand why Hughes should have committed himself to go beyond what the British had asked for and promise to continue the higher levels of reinforcements into 1917. The explanation would seem to be that once the authorities had looked into the matter they had found that, given the number of reinforcements Australia could supply from accumulated voluntary enlistments, a case for conscription based on the Army's Council's numbers could not be sustained.

The Defence officials, before making allowance for the completion of the Third Division and for wastage from illness and misadventure, had estimated that there were in England, in transit and in camp 103,023 men and, after making allowance for the above, 73,000 immediately available which was more than enough to meet the Army Council's targets. Down to the end of January 1917 the Australians would draw on the troops already available in Australia and England, including the

---

[21] Weller, (ed.), *Caucus Minutes*, Vol.I, pp.434–35.
[22] For New Zealand, see Paul Baker, *King and Country Call: New Zealanders, Conscription and the Great War* (Auckland: Auckland University Press, 1988), especially chapter 3. In New Zealand, following an overwhelming vote in the parliament, conscription became law on 1 August 1916.
[23] Cable, Hughes to Murdoch, 30 August 1916, Hughes Papers, NLA MS 1538/20/1; Scott, *Australia During the War*, p.538. It is worth noting the Commonwealth did not despatch 20,000 men 'immediately' or indeed during September for they did not have the shipping available for more than 12,500.

Third Division, for reinforcements. Thereafter the September recruits, following three months training in Australia and a month's sea voyage, would feed into the system.

To overcome this embarrassing problem Hughes with the cooperation of Pearce, the Minister of Defence, manipulated the figures. Hughes asserted that by the end of January only 3000 of the original 103,000 would be left as reinforcements for February. On this basis, if the Third Division were to be reconstituted and the new level of monthly reinforcements maintained – that is, 16,500, instead of 12,500 a month – it would be necessary for Australia to supply 33,500 men from September enlistments. Hence Hughes declared that unless 32,500 volunteered in September then the difference would be made up from single men who would be called up under the *Defence Act*. These conscripts would be undergoing training during October so that after the referendum they could be sent overseas at the end of December and land in Europe by the end of January. This arithmetic was, however, an exercise in obfuscation. It seemed to be devised so as to arrive at the foreordained conclusion. It arbitrarily assumed that the increased level of reinforcements would be needed. And, in calculating the number of reinforcements available in Europe, it did not take account of 'the large proportion' of the ill and wounded – between the middle of July and the end of August 13,754 in this category had returned to active service – whom the Defence Department advised would 'probably resume duty in due course.'[24] For the purpose of securing conscription a British request for reinforcements had been converted into a demand for maximising recruitment.

The decision to supply 16,500 reinforcements each month for the duration of the war exceeded what the British had requested and what was necessary to keep the existing five divisions of the AIF in the field, even according to Hughes's figures. All that he said by way of justification was that 'no man is to put a period to this war, and it would be criminal folly to assume any such thing. We would rather prepare for another complete year of war than anticipate any premature peace.' It may well be that Hughes and Pearce planned on adding a sixth division to the AIF. Birdwood claimed to know that the Australian Government wished through conscription to raise a sixth division for the AIF, writing a friend after the referendum had failed that, 'Australia had contemplated sending us out a 6th Division, but the Defence Minister now tells me he has had to give up all hope of this.'[25]

Little attention was given to the manpower consequences of Hughes's reinforcement proposal. The Defence Minister stated that the Commonwealth on 9 June had 152,910 'fit' single men between 18 and 44 who had not enlisted. After making provision for those who had volunteered by the end of August (approximately 14,000), and for the 18 to 21 year olds who were exempted from conscription (approximately 21,000), the government would have no more than 118,000 single men left to meet the recruiting target which by March 1917 would amount to 131,000. Long before this, since many of the single men would be excused under other categories, the government would have to turn to the approximately 300,000 married men in the eligible age group who remained in the country. Pearce at one point claimed that as 72,000 of the 131,000

---

[24] 'Summary of casualties that have occurred in Europe', 19 July–30 August 1916, Hughes Papers, NLA MS 1538/20/1.
[25] Letter, Birdwood to Rintoul, 12 Nov 1916, Birdwood Papers, Imperial War Museum.

men required by March were already available, only 60,000 single men would be needed to make up the balance. But this was misleading. Both Hughes and Pearce had made it clear that the government's policy was to obtain 32,500 new recruits in September and 16,500 for at least the following six months – that is 131,000 new recruits in all just for this period.

It seems that the government's scheme was intended to serve Hughes's wider war policy. Convinced by his visit to Europe that the war had reached a critical stage and that the fortunes of the British Empire depended on its outcome, he was determined that Australia should contribute as many men as possible in order to help win a victory over the enemy in the 1917 spring and summer offensive on the Western Front. He endorsed Lloyd George's call for a 'knock out blow'. A compromise peace would bring 'only fearful apprehensions of and feverish preparations for a new and more deadly struggle.'[26]

Fired by this conviction Hughes threw himself into the referendum campaign. 'I am going into the referendum campaign', he said, 'as if it was the only thing for which I lived.'[27] For the sake of conscription he was putting at risk his party's unity and thereby his own political career. The succeeding eight weeks were the most exhausting and exhilarating of his whole life. Immediately after announcing the government's policy in parliament, he set about trying to convert the majority of Labor parliamentarians and state organisations to the cause. But in both cases his appeals fell on stony ground. Only the Western Australian and South Australian parties agreed to allow members the freedom to espouse a 'Yes' vote. In the Eastern states the labour movement stood firm, and on 15 September, the day after Hughes had publicly declared his intention to lead the 'Yes' campaign, the New South Wales Labor League expelled him from the party.[28] As a result, when he opened the referendum campaign in the Sydney Town Hall on 18 September, Hughes led a 'Yes' coalition comprising nearly all the country's respectability against a 'No' organisation based overwhelmingly on the labour movement.

He took the full burden of winning the referendum upon himself. Cut off from the Labor and trade union organisations he barnstormed the nation, supported only by his newly-appointed private secretary, Percy Deane, who was his speechwriter, adviser, companion and comforter. Deane, who was only 27 years old when he obtained the post, had compressed much into his early life. He had begun his working life as a committed Methodist lay preacher and then moved to journalism at which time he had become contemptuous of egalitarian democracy. As an admirer of Thomas Carlyle he looked to great men, an 'aristocracy of talent', to govern nations and save their souls.[29] Invalided back from Egypt where he had served as Quartermaster in the First AIF General Hospital, he found in Hughes a masterful statesman who was the very image of Carlyle's hero. He threw himself into the conscription campaign, not sparing himself in the service of his leader. And from that time until Hughes's fall from power in 1923 he remained by the Prime Minister's side through all his political campaigns and his overseas trips.

---

[26] *CPD*, 1914–17 session, LXXIX, 8402–04, 8408–15, 8421–27, 30 August and 1 September 1916; *SMH*, 2 October 1916.
[27] *CPD*, 1914–17 session, LXXIX, 8425, 1 September 1916.
[28] *SMH*, 16 September 1916.
[29] *Brunswick Star*, 29 October 1909.

In the ensuing debate over rights and duties, liberty and loyalty, unionism and militarism, the issue of Australia's hot and cold wars was also to the fore. Security in the Pacific, especially the threat from Japan, was a pervasive theme, often appearing in various disguised forms. Hughes's homecoming addresses had already alluded to the Japanese problem. Subsequently, when speaking off the record to a secret session of the Commonwealth Parliament and to the New South Wales Trades and Labour Council and the State Labor Party executive meetings he was more explicit. It seems likely that he shared with them something, suitably embroidered, of what he had learned about Japan while in London. One parliamentarian later recalled that the Prime Minister had warned 'of the dangers to which Australia was exposed by her close proximity to the hordes of the coloured races, with particular reference to Japan, who although our Ally in the then World War, might at some future time be our enemy.' A member of the New South Wales Political Labor League executive reported him as saying, in a similar vein, that:

"Australia was but a few days' steam etc."

"The whole course of evolution in the Pacific had catastrophically come to a head!"

"There was an ambassador in London!"

"He said to me … ! I put him off."[30]

During the referendum campaign Hughes was more discreet both because he did not wish to offend an Ally and because he did not wish to give ammunition to his opponents who turned the White Australia argument against him. While contending that 'this life and death struggle in Europe and Asia is a struggle in which our lives and our liberties are being determined' and that 'in this great struggle in Europe, defeat writes our national epitaph', he named Germany only as the enemy who would claim Australia as a prize. To counter the anti-conscriptionists' exploitation of the Japanese threat he declared that keeping Australian soldiers at home 'in order to protect Australia against Germany and any other predatory Power is, to speak mildly, humbug.' Even if every citizen rallied to the defence of Australia, 'once Britain is beaten we are doomed men.'[31]

Yet Hughes remained fearful of Japan and for this reason approved of close military and naval intelligence surveillance of Japanese in Australia. In October, after reading a naval officer's report on a Japanese fisherman living in Oyster Bay, Western Australia, who was suspected of espionage simply because he seemed to do little fishing and possessed old clothes of a better class than an ordinary fisherman, Hughes scribbled an instruction, 'This man must be carefully watched.'[32]

But he was unable to keep Japan out of the referendum campaign. Both sides alluded to the threat of Japan to bolster their respective positions, though the anti-conscriptionists, possibly because they saw that it worked more directly for them and cared less about offending an ally, made more of it.

The issue of Japan was most prominent during the passage of the *Military Service Referendum Bill* which came before parliament in the third week of September. Though the Bill's purpose was

---

[30] D.C.S. Sissons, 'Attitudes to Japan and Defence, 1890–1923', MA thesis, (University of Melbourne, 1956), chapter 3, fn.23; *Australian Worker*, 6 February 1917.

[31] *SMH*, 19 September 1916.

[32] Letter, M.L. Shepherd, Secretary, Prime Minister's Department to G.L. Macandie, Secretary of the Department of the Navy, 17 October 1916, NAA CP447/1 SC252.

to authorise the referendum, the debate was focused not on the plebiscite but on conscription itself. It was here that pro- and anti-forces faced each other and engaged each other for the first and last time. It was here that the rival camps presented their most considered statements and attempted most seriously to meet the arguments of their opponents. The Labor politicians, in particular, were anxious to justify their individual stands both to the party and the people. More than half the members of parliament spoke to the Bill – thirty-seven from the House of Representatives and twenty-five from the Senate and in doing so many touched upon the relation of conscription to White Australia and the challenge of Japan.

This topic was undoubtedly more important than the official record might suggest. Hughes, at the outset, had warned the parliamentarians against using language insulting to the British Empire or its Allies. The censor had also been instructed to take special care during the referendum campaign to suppress any publications which might have that effect.[33] Many members, especially those who supported conscription, thus felt reluctant to speak about the problem of Japan. Even those who did speak out would sometimes preface their remarks with phrases such as, 'I can't say all that I would like to say on this matter', or, on broaching the subject, would be met with interjections such as, 'You are about to give the censor a lot of work' or 'Is it wise to go into this question?'[34]

Those opposed to the referendum as well as conscription were the most uninhibited. Of the nine speaking against the Bill in the House of Representatives, seven in one way or another raised the spectre of the threat from the north. A majority of these did not object in principle to compulsory military training or even conscription for overseas service but they maintained that what the government sought would leave Australia's defenceless before a potential Asian foe. As J. F. Hannan put it, 'Geography makes a great deal of difference ... If we were confronted with a crisis tomorrow, we could not do justice to ourselves.' Frank Anstey, a leader of the no-conscription campaign, amplified this theme. Insisting that he was not against conscription for overseas service if that contributed to Australia's safety, he denied that the government's proposal satisfied this test. 'No country', he claimed, 'is situated geographically and economically as we are.' He rejected conscription for the Western Front because it was 'inimical to the future development of Australia as a White Man's country'. J. E. Fenton similarly explained his refusal to accept overseas conscription in term of the post-1905 'Australian Crisis' orthodoxy, namely that 'As a matter of fact Australia and New Zealand occupy the most dangerous outposts in the Empire.'

Only two members, Dr W. R. N. Maloney, who had been one of the first to raise the alarm after the Russo-Japanese war, and J. H. Catts, who had since 1915 become the most outspoken advocate of the Japanese threat and was shortly to head the anti-conscription organisation in New South Wales, named Japan and elaborated on the character of the menace from the north. Maloney, asserting that his views were widely shared, maintained that one could 'hear whispers on the street corners, "Be Careful of Japan"'. People feared that some day the Pacific would be 'under the domination of Japan', and at that time it would be 'better to go to America cap in hand

---

[33] *CPD*, 1914–17 session, LXXIX, 8554, 14 September 1916.
[34] *CPD*, 1914–17 session, LXXX, 8806, Senator J. Mullan, 21 September 1916; *ibid.*, LXXIX, 8593, J.F. Hannan, 21 September 1916; *ibid.*, LXXX, 8702–03, Sir Robert Best, 20 September 1916.

than perhaps bend some day in sackcloth and ashes under an Eastern race.' He could not blame the Japanese for seizing their opportunity but that opportunity menaced Australia. It was therefore necessary to retain every man in Australia.

Catts offered the most defiant and most precise Japanese argument. To those who urged caution upon him, he answered on the subject:

> I do not want to say anything derogatory to another great Power, which has very great interests in the Pacific. We are told that we should refer to this matter with bated breath although the newspapers are full of information and comment on the subject.
>
> Why should it not be discussed here? It is being openly discussed throughout the length and breadth of America. It has been openly discussed in every street in Japan.

He substantiated his points, citing for the first an article in the *Sydney Morning Herald* entitled 'Warning to Australia' and for the second Japanese newspapers. It was his considered opinion that there were 'nations in the Pacific that have their eyes on Australia ...' It was well-known that, 'There have been instances in previous wars where allies fighting together one day have fallen out among themselves on the cessation of hostilities.' His research had revealed that there was 'ample evidence of the dangers surrounding the country'. The Japanese were openly demanding a dominant position in China, access to India and South Seas trade and the abolition of racial discrimination in the immigration policy of Australia and other British possessions as conditions for the renewal of the Anglo-Japanese alliance. The former New South Wales recruiting director reaffirmed the views he had earlier put to the Defence Minister. Australia had sent enough men overseas. In the light of the Japanese danger, Australia's pre-eminent task was to use compulsion to prepare for an invasion from the north.

In the Senate a similar number of those opposed to conscription voiced the same concerns. Senator John Mullan, feeling himself restricted by Hughes's admonitions – 'I can't say all that I would like to say on the matter' – cleverly turned the Prime Minister's own words against him. Surely the latter's public statements could not embarrass the British Empire? And so Mullan repeated the key phrases from Hughes's capital city speeches: 'We have nailed White Australia to our mast, yet we are but a tiny drop in a coloured ocean', and so on. These sentences, he said, were 'worth a thousand against conscription.' He would not send a single man out of Australia 'because the question of home defence is of supreme importance.' Harking back to Fisher's defence policy he wanted Australia to concentrate on constructing strategic railways, unifying the railway gauges, building seaplanes and thousands of aeroplanes as well as dirigibles. He would erect the most up-to-date arsenals and honeycomb Australia with bases for the Australian fleet. Senator John Barnes employed the same artful tactic in speaking in favour of home defence and Senator James Long, citing the same authority, echoed Mullan's contention that Australia had 'a more serious menace than that of Germany'.

Only three or four of the pro-conscriptionists were willing to answer the 'anti's' in these terms. Since many on this side of the question, both Liberal and Labor alike, had earlier expressed fear of Japan, it is probable that the great majority shared Hughes's belief that a quick victory for the Allied cause in Europe was the best way of safeguarding Australia in the Pacific. Even if most heeded Hughes's warning that they should not air the subject publicly, the few who did speak out nevertheless spoke to the point. G. H. Wise, a Labor-leaning independent member who was an heir to the Deakin liberal tradition, openly acknowledged the reality of the Yellow Peril. Like Hughes he cloaked concern about Japan inside the language of racial conflict:

> Every man with any capacity for thinking at all must have realised that sooner or later the great Armageddon must come – when the white and the coloured races of this world meet in conflict. At present, the white races are engaged in destroying their manpower, leaving the coloured race untouched. This makes it all the more necessary that the war be brought to an end as quickly as possible, in order that our nation, at any rate, may not be absolutely exhausted when peace comes about.

The welfare of Australia could be secured 'only by a decisive victory for the Allies in the quickest possible time'. W. H. Laird Smith, a Labor conscriptionist, also urged the necessity of compulsion in order to save Australia: 'If we experience a set back on land or if Great Britain's naval supremacy should be upset, we might be threatened with an invasion of Australia. But I question whether it would be a German invasion.'

In the Senate, Thomas Givens, also a Labor conscriptionist, took the unusual step for the president of that house of intervening in the debate, and in a very comprehensive and compelling speech, which defended compulsion as a defence of land and liberty against a German thrust for world power, discreetly rebutted the 'anti's' case on the Pacific issue.

> There is another argument that we have something to fear at the hands of other alien enemies. It is very true that there are constant dangers and menaces threatening Australia, and it would be idle to deny the fact. But one way to secure safety and immunity is to win the present war. We could then defy all the danger and menaces from any direction whereas if the enemy wins the war, there is nothing we can do … that can save us.[35]

The threat from Asia, either in the specific form of Japan or the broader one of the Yellow Peril, was a pervasive issue in the referendum campaign, and, as in the parliamentary debates, the anti-conscriptionists made most of it. Censorship and the fear of censorship limited the publication of what Maloney had claimed was being whispered on street corners but, even so, a great deal of evidence remains to show its importance. The 'No' campaigners, citing as an example a shipload of Maltese migrants headed for Australia, stressed that coloured labour would take the jobs of the Australians sent overseas. But the 'anti' organisations in Victoria and New South Wales went much further than this. In Sydney, the Political Labor League Manifesto asserted that under Hughes's scheme, '200,000 men would be shipped to the shambles of Europe in 12 months. We cannot stand such strain upon our vital strength …' And it asked voters, 'Are you prepared to break down the barriers that keep Australia white?'[36] Boote's *Australian Worker* also made the preservation of White Australia the main theme of its attack on conscription. In Melbourne, the *Labor Call*, the chief organ of the labour movement and the anti-conscription campaign, gave as its first reason for urging a 'No' vote, 'keeping Australia a white man's country'. It had no doubt that the next war would be 'fought in the Pacific between the white and yellow races'. Australia

---

[35] *Ibid.,* pp.8614, 8674, 8739, 8752–53, 8692, 8699–703, 8713, 8731, 8806, 8844, 8922, 8952, 14–22 September 1916.
[36] *SMH*, 24 October 1916.

therefore should not send its youth 'to far off battlefields as we must prepare for the racial war to come.' The paper hinted that it was a Japanese invasion that they had in mind. It held 'the conviction that Australia's undue weakness in men might be an invitation to an unrevealed enemy.' The editorial writer added that, 'In spite of the war across the seas ... I cannot prevent a feeling of the insecurity that this country is in from the dangers not lying at the other end of the world.'[37] Through the thinly veiled euphemisms and circumlocutions the message was clear. Deane, who had accompanied the Prime Minister as he campaigned across the country, declared that 'the poster most prominent on the hoardings was "Vote No and keep Australia White".'[38]

When, in the week before the poll, the Minister for the Navy, J. A. Jensen, finally declared himself for conscription, he justified his decision by repeating Hughes's Asian arguments. Perhaps influenced by the senior naval officers who had drawn up the alarmist report on Japan in 1915 he stated that:

> In the event of the defeat of the Empire we are in the most precarious position of a people on the earth ... With densely populated countries immediately to the north of us we aspire to retain this comparatively empty continent exclusively for our own people. In this way we have hitherto been supported by the power of Great Britain, our Mother country. Must not such exacting demands on our part be backed up by everything we can do to give effect to them.[39]

Pearce, likewise, on the eve of the poll, ignoring his leader's words, threw caution to the winds and wound up his pro-conscription campaign in Fremantle expressing similar sentiments.

> The white Australia Act would not have been worth a snap of the fingers but for the might of the British Navy ... What in the circumstances was Australia's best course in order to make its position clear? The best course was to help with all the forces at its command to give Germany the knock-out blow, and thus have the British Navy free to come to these shores if need be. The shortest way to Australia's safety was to win the war as speedily as possible.[40]

The importance of the Japanese issue was not lost on overseas observers. Lionel Curtis, the British Round Table's chief ideologue, who was in Australia for the purpose of promoting his scheme for Imperial Federation as set out in 'Problems of the Commonwealth', complained to the editor of the *Round Table* journal in London of the difficulties he had in spreading the message. The conscription issue was consuming public attention, and 'the Pacific problem here is very acute, much more so than most people realise.'[41] The Japanese Consul-General was also aware that his country was an issue in the referendum campaign, and he took unprecedented action to allay

---

[37] *Labor Call*, 26 October 1916.
For the widespread appeal to racial imagery and the migratory and military threat to 'White Australia' in the anti-conscription campaign in Queensland, see Raymond Evans, *Loyalty and Disloyalty: Social Conflict on the Queensland Homefront, 1914–18* (Sydney: Allen and Unwin, 1987), pp.96–97.
[38] Letter, Deane to Dr James Barrett, 2 November 1916, Barrett Papers, University of Melbourne Archives.
[39] *Advertiser*, 25 October 1916.
[40] *West Australian*, 25 October 1916.
[41] Letter, Lionel Curtis to Philip Kerr, 5 October 1916, Round Table Papers, Bodleian Library MSS. Eng. Hist. 798/292.

such fears. He publicly complained that Japan was 'frequently referred to by the public speakers both for and against the conscription proposal'. Slightly confused, as well he might be, about the respective positions of the two sides, he thought that the 'Yes' faction wanted conscription 'in order to defend Australia from Japanese aggression' and the 'Nos' opposed it out of concern that there would be 'an influx of Japanese labour into the Commonwealth'. He, however, denounced all such talk as 'baseless' calumny.[42]

The defeat of conscription

On 28 October the people decided against conscription by a narrow majority of 72,476 in a poll of 2,308,600. To Hughes and his fellow conscriptionists the result was a great shock. Hughes had gathered behind him a seemingly invincible coalition. The 'Yes' campaign had been backed by nearly all major newspapers, public institutions and national organisations. The pro-conscriptionists numbered in their ranks the Prime Minister, three other federal ministers, some federal Labor parliamentarians, the whole of the federal Liberal opposition, five out of six state premiers, including three Labor premiers, opposition leaders in five out of six states, and the great majority of local government bodies. Moreover all the Protestant churches, with the exception of the tiny Society of Friends, gave the cause their blessing. Though the Roman Catholic coadjutor Archbishop of Melbourne, spoke out on two occasions against conscription, the Archbishop of Perth declared himself in favour and the rest of the hierarchy stood on the sidelines. In addition nearly every professional, business and civic organisation, such as the Employers' Federation, the Farmers and Settlers Association, the Chambers of Commerce, the Returned Soldiers Association, the Australian Natives Association, the Young Men's Christian Association, the Australian Women's National League, the Women's Christian Temperance Union, the National Council of Women and even the Red Cross, endorsed the call for a 'Yes' vote. Finally, at the urging of Hughes, all the former Commonwealth Prime Ministers, including Barton who was a justice of the High Court but excluding Fisher who had pleaded his office as high commissioner, had joined in an appeal on behalf of conscription. This was a very impressive array of political, religious, business and civic authorities.

The anti-conscriptionists, by contrast, had the support of one former federal minister, a group of federal Labor parliamentarians, the Queensland Premier and government, numerous state Labor politicians and, in a very modest way, Archbishop Daniel Mannix of Melbourne. The only significant institutions to identify themselves with the 'anti' group's position were the trade unions and five of six state Labor organisations. Given this disparity, Percival Deane wrote that 'from an arm-chair it looked a cinch; it almost seemed the Government were wasting money in taking a vote.'[43]

Many explanations for the defeat of conscription, based on the 'anti's' case against conscription or on class or communal interests hostile to compulsion, have been put forward. None, however, convinces. The issue of 'White Australia' and 'Japan' was among the most popular

---

[42] *Argus*, 21 October 1916; *Advertiser*, 23 October 1916.
[43] Letter, Deane to Dr James Barrett, 2 November 1916, Barrett Papers, University of Melbourne Archives.

arguments advanced in the 'No' campaign, but it is difficult to see how it could have been a decisive influence. It was drawn upon by both factions and, even if the 'anti' campaigners made more of it, nevertheless they lost some ground because of it. Neither could the 'No' majority be attributed to the discontent of the working class. The working class Labor vote, had it remained intact, was not of itself able to provide the required numbers. Since so many Labor notables, among whom were founders of the party and union leaders, favoured conscription, some Labor voters undoubtedly followed these leaders into the 'Yes' camp and thereby reduced further the potential working class 'No' vote. Likewise since the Irish Catholic community comprised only about 23 percent of the population and was largely working class, it could not in its own right have contributed the decisive element in the defeat of conscription.[44]

It would seem that what Hughes called the 'selfish' vote made the difference. As Hughes astutely observed in one of his more clear-eyed moments, the conscriptionists would have won 'in spite of the official Labor organisations being against us, in spite of the Irish vote, in spite of the shirkers, if the farmers and Conservatives had stood by us.'[45] Many farmers, small businessmen, mortgaged homeowners and other individuals, who normally voted Liberal, probably felt that conscription would destroy their private hopes and plans. It was a motive that they could not, of course, publicly declare. Moreover Hughes, though he sought conscription ostensibly to keep the existing AIF divisions in the field and promised generous exemptions, had by the very conduct of his campaign exacerbated these fears. Hughes's impassioned appeals for Australia to send as many men as possible, his commitment to maintain reinforcements at a monthly level of 16,500 beyond December and his decision to call up 21 to 35-year-old single men under the *Defence Act* at the end of September raised suspicion that conscription was likely to touch everyone, depriving farmers of labour to bring in their harvests and extending its compass to married men with family and business responsibilities. Perhaps Hughes's bullying style and his intolerance towards opponents added to this impression and alienated some fair-minded citizens.

Even if ultimate explanations for the failure of the referendum must be based on conjecture, a comparison of voting patterns in the 1914 federal election with those of the conscription poll lends support to the 'selfish' explanation. It would seem highly likely that at the time of the referendum many voters had switched allegiances. That is, some who had voted Labor in 1914 followed Hughes and many Labor political notables into the 'Yes' camp, while even more of those who had formerly voted Liberal defied their leaders and party and put 'No' on the ballot paper. Indeed an examination of electoral behaviour in the referendum suggests the critical factor in producing the majority against conscription was that a considerable number of the 'middling sort' deserted their old loyalties and voted 'No'.

---

[44] Ian Turner in *Industrial Labour and Politics: The Labour Movement in Eastern Australia, 1900–1921* (Canberra: Australian National University Press, 1965), chapter 4, has a good account of the evolution of working class attitudes to conscription in 1916.

Alan D. Gilbert in 'The Conscription Referenda, 1916–17', pp.71–72, shows clearly how Irish Catholic views of the Empire and war changed and became lukewarm or even hostile after Britain's execution of the Sinn Fein rebels who had been responsible for the Easter rising.

[45] Letter, Hughes to Bonar Law, 6 November 1916, Bonar Law Papers, House of Lords Record Office MS53/4/15.

In New South Wales and South Australia – the two states with the largest majorities for 'No' – this pattern is most evident. Nearly all rural and suburban electorates, gave a higher proportion of their vote to 'No' than they had given to Labor in its great victory of 1914. In eleven New South Wales country seats there was an average swing to 'No' against the 1914 Liberal vote of 17 percent. In the Sydney suburban seat of Lang which the Liberals had won in 1914, there was a swing of 7.5 percent to 'No', and 'No' received 54 percent of the votes cast. And in a similar seat, Parkes, which the Liberals had also won in 1914, there was a swing to 'No' of 5.7 percent. Of the Liberal seats in Sydney only the most blue-ribbon of all, North Sydney, showed an increase for 'Yes' over the 1914 Liberal vote and that was very marginal. By contrast, in all solid inner city working class seats there were only modest gains for 'No' over the 1914 Labor vote. In West Sydney, perhaps because of Hughes's personal influence, the 'Yes' result actually exceeded the Liberal vote of 1914 by 4 percent.

In Victoria the pattern of voting was somewhat different. In the rural seats there was much less of a swing to 'No', and in three seats – Indi, Corio and Gippsland – there were swings to 'Yes' against the 1914 Labor vote. In Melbourne itself both Labor and Liberal held seats voted strongly for 'Yes' as against the Labor vote of 1914. It has been surmised that the behaviour of the Victorian country electorates was influenced by the more generous decisions of that state's exemption tribunals for farmers and farm workers, and that the result in all Victoria's electorates was affected by a Protestant sectarian backlash against Archbishop Mannix's intervention. But Victoria's difference only qualifies the generalisation about the national pattern. It does not overturn it.[46]

Whatever the precise reason for the 'No' vote it is impossible to treat it as a triumph for local nationalism, radical socialism or peace at any price government. Apart from the Industrial Workers of the World and a few prominent Labor figures in the 'No' campaign (such as Senator Myles Aloysius Ferricks who expressed suspicion about British motives and declared that 'he did not believe in the war'),[47] anti-conscriptionists were happy to affirm their loyalty to the British Empire and their desire to see an Allied victory. Indeed, many proudly boasted that they had sons, brothers or union mates in the AIF. Indeed, when the National Party, composed of Labor pro-conscriptionists and Liberals, went to the polls in May 1917 on a 'Win-the-War' policy, it trounced the 'No Conscription' Labor Party.

Regardless of the reasons for the outcome of the referendum the conflict over conscription was a signal event in the history of Australia's relations with the world. The political animosities and personal antagonisms generated by the issue were to have lasting and detrimental consequences for the country's defence and foreign policy.

---

[46] I am indebted for this analysis of the 'inward' factor in the Australian response to the conscription referendum to T.A. Metherell, 'The Conscription Referenda, October 1916 and December 1917: An Inward-Turned National War', PhD thesis (University of Sydney, 1971).

[47] *CPD*, 1914–17 session, LXXX, 8857, 22 September 1916.

8
'Loyalty' and Empire: The Nation Divided

By the end of 1916 the great struggle for the mastery of Europe had reached a critical point. The war was placing a great strain upon the whole British world and victory seemed as elusive as ever. The Australian Government understood Britain's precarious position and shared its anxieties, and in both countries the race patriots who had from the outset embraced the war as a struggle for national survival and supremacy took control. In Britain, Lloyd George, after calling for a 'knock-out blow' against Germany, had ousted Asquith from office and constructed a Coalition Government centred on the Milnerites and those Conservatives who had demanded a more energetic prosecution of the war and a more purposeful leadership of the Empire.[1] In Australia, Hughes, having being expelled from the Labor Party along with the other conscriptionists, led his followers into an alliance with the Universal Service League, the Referendum Council and the Liberal Party, and formed a 'Win-the-War' administration.

The Imperial War Cabinet

On taking office in December 1916 Lloyd George was confronted by a daunting prospect. The Somme offensive which cost the British Empire over 500,000 casualties had not achieved the long-sought-for breakthrough on the Western Front. In Eastern Europe the Allied position was desperate. Romania had fallen into German hands, the Balkans were dangerously exposed and Russia was on the verge of collapse. The Allies were suffering from the exhaustion of attrition. Britain itself had reached the end of its resources. Its merchant navy lay at the mercy of German U-boats. Its supply of vital foodstuffs was endangered. Its manpower had been repeatedly culled for recruits to meet the demands of the generals. Its finances were stretched to breaking point. Britain was heavily in debt to the United States and had no more assets which could be pledged for loans.[2]

Though Lloyd George had no hesitation in rejecting American and German peace overtures, he had little idea of how to 'carry the fight to a decisive finish' and was willing to grasp at any stratagem which might compass his ends. Thus he responded readily to the suggestion of Milner and his Round Table disciples that Britain should look to the Empire for greater assistance and in return draw the Dominions into the centre of imperial policy-making. Such a move was needed to counter what the retiring Colonial Secretary warned was a growing spirit of disaffection in the

---

[1] Robert J. Scally, *The Origins of the Lloyd George Coalition* (Princeton: Princeton University Press, 1975), especially chapter 12.
[2] Paul Guinn, *British Strategy and Politics, 1914 to 1918* (Oxford: Clarendon Press, 1965), pp.170–87; Kathleen Burk, *Britain, America and the Sinews of War, 1914–1918* (Boston: Allen and Unwin, 1985), especially chapters 4 and 5.

Dominions. Writing to Walter Long, Bonar Law's successor at the Colonial Office, Lloyd George explained his conversion to the new imperialism simply in terms of British needs:

> The more I think about it, the more I am convinced that we should take the Colonies into our counsel in a much larger measure than we have hitherto done in our prosecution of the war. As we must receive even more substantial support from them before we can hope to pull through, it is important that they have a share in our councils as well as our burdens. We want more men from the Colonies.[3]

Earlier in the war Asquith had refused the requests of both Fisher and Hughes for an imperial conference, fearing that the Dominions might restrict Britain's freedom of action in negotiating war aims with its Allies or peace terms with its enemies. Since Lloyd George had committed himself to securing victory at all costs, he was no longer held back by these considerations. Indeed, on the contrary, he was willing to give the Dominions a share in imperial decision-making and thereby have them accept a more complete responsibility for the Empire's cause. For this reason Lloyd George adopted much of the program of the Round Table men who advocated 'organic union', and, 'largely on Milner's initiative', he invited the Dominion leaders to a 'special and continuous meeting' which would not be an ordinary imperial conference but an expanded session of the British War Cabinet. It was to deal with the great issues of peace and war, including trade, defence and foreign policy.[4]

At the end of 1916, however, the Australian Government, despite its longstanding desire for an imperial conference, was in no position to accept Lloyd George's invitation. Though the British Prime Minister seemed to be conceding all that Hughes had sought during his stay in England, the initiative came at a most inopportune time. Hughes was embarrassed by Lloyd George's proposal. The Australian Prime Minister had an uncertain hold on office and was faced with civil unrest. After leading the conscriptionists out of the federal Parliamentary Labor Caucus he had formed a minority government which depended on Liberal support in the House and lacked a majority in the Senate. In these circumstances he would only consider leaving Australia if he were assured that the Dominions would have a real say 'in shaping policy'.

---

[3] 'Things are not going well in the Dominions, and there is especially an ugly spirit in Australia', copy of letter, Bonar Law to Lloyd George, 11 December 1916, Bonar Law Papers, House of Lords Record Office MS50/2/19; letter, Lloyd George to Walter Long, 12 December 1916, Long Papers, WRO 947/568/61.

A more guarded statement of this new approach to the Dominions can be found in Lloyd George's announcement in the House of Commons, Great Britain, 5 *Parliamentary Debates* (Commons), LXXXVIII, 1356, 19 December 1916.

[4] Letter, Lionel Curtis to Bonar Law, 1 November 1915, Bonar Law Papers, House of Lords Record Office MS51/5/1. Curtis wrote of his work 'The Problem of the Commonwealth', which contained the British Round Table's conclusions about the future of the British-settled Empire, 'As you said, in our last interview at the Colonial Office, there is no solution but organic union, and the object of this volume is to show what the inescapable conditions of organic union are'.

See also Maurice Hankey, *The Supreme Command, 1914–1918*, 2 vols (London: Allen and Unwin, 1961), Vol.I, pp.657–60 and Minutes of Meetings of British War Cabinet, 20, 22 and 23 December 1916, TNA: PRO CAB 23/1.

The new Colonial Secretary, Walter Long, in trying to convince Hughes that he should come to London, repeated what Lloyd George had said in his invitation, namely that what was contemplated was 'not a session of the ordinary Imperial Conference, but a special War Conference of the Empire'. For this purpose the Dominion prime ministers would:

> attend a series of special and continuous meetings of the War Cabinet in order to consider urgent questions affecting the prosecution of the War, the possible conditions on which, in agreement with our Allies, we could assent to its termination, and the problems which will then immediately arise.

The Dominion prime ministers were to be members of the War Cabinet and therefore have an equal say with the British Prime Minister in determining imperial policy. Long stressed that it would be 'a serious misfortune' if any Dominion were not represented.

These assurances were very encouraging. Hughes saw that, if the meeting were to have these powers, then he ought to try to attend. To clear the path, that is to overcome the constitutional requirement that an election be held in 1917, the Senate would have to join the House of Representatives in petitioning the British parliament to suspend the Australian constitution and extend the life of the Australian Parliament until the end of the war. Since he did not control the Senate that course of action, as things stood, was not likely to succeed. If the Irish question could be resolved and 'Home Rule' conceded then he believed that the Irish Catholics in the opposition might be separated from the labour radicals. He would only agree to leave Australia if the Imperial Conference would place the Irish question at the centre of its deliberations and so enable him to appease that element in Labor's ranks. 'For this I would go', he told the Governor-General. But, in the given circumstances, he knew that he had no alternative but 'to stay here and put the country straight'. As a result of the conscription crisis Australia's Pacific and imperial interests had to be subordinated to those of securing a loyal order at home.[5]

Deeply concerned about the question, Hughes broke protocol, side-stepped the Governor-General and the Colonial Secretary, and cabled Lloyd George directly about his problems. There was 'no immediate prospect' of being able to leave Australia. His own Labor followers were engaged in 'a war to the knife' with the official Labor Party. Even if his supporters were to enter into a formal coalition with the Liberals, they would still be frustrated by the Senate. The Labor majority could prevent 'any Government from carrying on or at all events from taking action necessary to vigorous prosecution of the war.' Hughes confessed that, 'As things are, recruiting is practically at a standstill and considerable section more or less hostile to war and beginning to definitely demand peace.' Of the two major elements responsible for this, the 'Syndicalists' and the Irish, the latter held the key to the restoration of Australia's war effort. The anger over British actions in Ireland 'makes recruiting, voluntary or compulsory, almost all impossible, hamstrings effective Government and imperils future Imperial relations.' The Irish question was 'now an imperial question and to be so treated.' In 1914 with the promise of Home Rule the Irish Catholic community had loyally supported the war and the Empire. If a mutually acceptable form of Home

---

[5] Cable, Long to Munro Ferguson, 24 December 1916, NAA CP 78/23 89/512 and copies in Hughes Papers, NLA MS 1538/16/1665 and TNA: PRO CO 532/85/225; letter, Hughes to Munro Ferguson, 26 December 1916, Novar Papers, NLA MS 696/2575.

Rule could be agreed upon, he believed that they would return to their allegiance and British race unity would be restored in Australia.

What was necessary was that Lloyd George should convince his Conservative Unionist colleagues that 'a disaffected Ireland not only makes ideal [of] imperial unity impossible but … prevents empire putting forth maximum manpower and strength generally.' If this were done, then it was likely that 'an immediate settlement could be effected.' In Australia the settlement of the Irish question would have a profound effect: 'We could get reinforcements; we could prosecute vigorous war policy, the air would be cleared; we should be a really united people and Australia could speak with one voice. The syndicalists and peace propagandists would be driven into their holes.' Concessions over Home Rule would appease Irish Catholic Australians and bring them back into the fold. Unless the British Government conceded self-government, Hughes saw no possibility of being able to leave Australia before an election in April or May: 'To leave here would be to ensure disaster. The people who support your policy here look to me to lead them and I must not fail them.'[6]

In January 1917, as Hughes's National Labor and Cook's Liberal followers were moving towards the formation of a National Government, the question of Australia's attendance at the Empire's War Cabinet became more urgent. Irvine, one of the chief architects of the 'Win-the-War' coalition, regarded Lloyd George's proposal as 'the most important constitutional development since the grant of self-government'. There were to be no more imperial conferences for the mere discussion of issues. What was being proposed was 'for the first time an Imperial Cabinet in the fullest sense.'[7] Under pressure from his new political partners, Hughes cabled Keith Murdoch, his special agent in London, to ask for his 'candid opinion' about 'the whole matter generally in its relation to the war, the Empire and Australia.' In particular, he wanted to know whether the Prime Ministers' meeting would be 'shaping policy', whether it would deal with the topics most important to Australia, namely Ireland and the peace terms.[8]

After consulting Lloyd George and Milner, Murdoch reaffirmed what Long had already told Hughes about the importance of the occasion. The gathering was to mark a momentous step forward in the development of the Empire. The Dominion prime ministers were to be 'temporarily members War Cabinet with plenary powers [to] decide all questions of policy.' They would act as 'a super Empire Cabinet' having responsibility for the 'whole vast sphere of war and peace'. On Ireland there was a division of opinion. Milner and the Tories considered it a domestic question but Lloyd George thought this special Empire Cabinet might handle it. Hughes's presence was necessary to give substance to the constitutional innovation and to protect Australia's interests, not least of which being the fate of the German colonies in the Pacific. There would be an opportunity to complete what he had begun in 1916, especially in 'Imperial trade development which has been wholly neglected since your visit.' Lloyd George, no doubt prompted by Murdoch's inquiry, replied to Hughes's earlier cable also urging the necessity of Australia being

---

[6] Cable, Hughes to Lloyd George, 29 December 1916, Lloyd George Papers, House of Lords Record Office F32/4/14.
[7] *SMH*, 10 January 1917.
[8] Copy of cable, Hughes to Murdoch, 15 January 1917, Hughes Papers, NLA MS 1538/117/1.

represented. Even as the British leader set out the intractable nature of the Irish problem, he insisted that the meeting would cover matters 'vital to AUSTRALIA and Empire'.[9] Hughes could no longer doubt the significance of what was proposed. And the agenda, arriving hard on the heels of these cables, reinforced this view. Among the topics to be discussed, in addition to 'Increased effort in men, money, transport', was 'Policy with reference to Peace Proposal on territorial changes' and 'immediate problems arising out of peace'.[10]

Within the government and among its supporters there was a growing belief that it was imperative for Australia to send a representative to London. Hughes passed on to the public a suitable summary of what he had learnt from Murdoch and Lloyd George. It was, he said, 'quite clear that the representatives of the Dominions sitting as members of the War Cabinet will deal with matters absolutely vital to the welfare of Australia as well as that of the Empire.' Cook added that Australian representation was necessary not only because the Imperial Cabinet was to deal with war policy, peace terms and imperial relations but also because, 'We have our own peculiar Pacific problems which are involved in the war and its settlement.'[11] The Naval Board, alert to the possibilities of such a meeting, reminded Hughes of its 1915 'Report on Australia and the Pacific'. It told him that from the Australian point of view the topics of:

> the creation and establishment of a Navy for the Pacific by the cooperation of the Mother Country with the Dominions sufficient to ensure the safety of Australia and all British Dominions and Dependencies bordering on that ocean [were] some of the most important … of the matters which are likely to be considered by the Conference.[12]

Yet Hughes's hopes were not realised. He could not control the events which controlled his decision. Unable to induce the Senate to pass a resolution favouring an extension of the life of the parliament, he had to admit to Lloyd George that it was unlikely he would be able to attend the War Cabinet.[13]

L. S. Amery, who had admired Hughes since their first meeting in 1907 and found in him a soul mate during his visit to Britain in 1916, joined Lloyd George, Long and Murdoch in appealing to the Australian Prime Minister to come to London. At Milner's instigation Amery had become a member of Lloyd George's War Cabinet secretariat and had taken a special interest in the proposed imperial gathering. In a letter which reached Hughes on 17 February Amery wrote that the Dominion prime ministers were to be members of an enlarged version of the War Cabinet which would be composed of the 'strongest men in the Empire' and be charged with the responsibility 'first, of winning the war, and then of not allowing that victory to be thrown away in

---

[9] Cable, Murdoch to Hughes, undated probably 19 January 1917, Hughes Papers, NLA MS 1538/16/2578-80; cable, Lloyd George to Hughes, 18 January 1917, Hughes Papers, NLA MS 1538/16/1690-91.

For an account of Lloyd George's political difficulties with Irish Home Rule, see John Turner, *British Politics and the Great War: Coalition and Conflict, 1915–1918* (New Haven and London: Yale University Press, 1992), pp.176–79.

[10] Cable, Long to Munro Ferguson, 26 January 1917, NAA CP290/15/2.

[11] *SMH*, 29 January 1917.

[12] Letter, G.L. Macandie, Naval Secretary, to Shepherd, Secretary, Prime Minister's Department, 3 February 1917, NAA CP447/2 SC472(7).

[13] Cable, Strictly Personal, Hughes to Lloyd George, 12 February 1917, Long Papers, WRO 947/624/15A.

the peace negotiations'.[14] Yet though Amery spoke to Hughes's deepest convictions about imperial government, war policy and peace aims, the Australian Prime Minister could not find a way to take part in this great experiment.

Hughes's problems were made more intractable by the animosities generated in the conscription debate. The conscriptionists and subsequently the 'Win-the-War' alliance had defined loyalty to mean an unquestioning commitment to the Empire and the war effort. They had taken unto themselves the title of 'National', in the National Labor Party, the National Federation and eventually the National Party. During the conscription campaign Hughes and many of his supporters had charged those who opposed them with being traitors or dupes of traitors. Most of those who had advocated 'No' resented deeply the way that Hughes had behaved towards them, especially attaching the stigma of being 'disloyal'.

The reconstructed Labor Party shared, to different degrees, the British Australian ideal, but since the conscriptionists had clothed themselves in imperial patriotism Labor's leaders were uncomfortable with that language and what it might signify. They had no other concept of loyalty that they could set against the Crown, the Union Jack and the national anthem, that is against a British race identity. 'Australia first' gained no traction among the great majority of the anti-conscriptionists. All that their leaders could do was to debate what loyalty to the Empire meant for Australians. The charge of disloyalty was resented. The country, if not polarised, was deeply divided. During early 1917 mutual distrust grew. Thus Labor, suspicious of Hughes's motives, would not give him a free hand in dealing with either imperial or world affairs. After Hughes's betrayal of the party and his campaign of vilification they would not trust him on any question. Hughes was never again able to go to London as a representative of the whole nation.

The Labor Party, unlike its British counterpart, refused to join in a coalition government. Having no confidence in Hughes his former comrades would do nothing to help him attend the imperial gathering. At a special conference of the party, which had met in Melbourne in early December 1916, the delegates, anticipating Lloyd George's initiative, had passed a resolution that 'any proposal for Imperial Federation involving the slightest surrender of her [Australia's] self-governing powers in return for a voice in the Empire's foreign policy would be disastrous for Australian ideals and should not therefore be entertained.' Since the only form of Imperial Federation that they could envisage was one in which Australia's interests would be subordinated to those of the Mother Country, they would have none of it.

---

[14] Letter, Amery to Hughes, 8 January 1917, arriving Melbourne in the second week of February, John Barnes and David Nicholson (eds), *The Leo Amery Diaries*, 2 vols (London: Hutchinson, 1980), Vol.I, p.139.

Hughes might have made this final attempt to arrange to go to the Imperial Conference out of concern for Japan's latest move to secure permanent control of the German North Pacific islands. On 1 and 5 February the British Government had cabled Melbourne seeking Australia's consent to a Japanese proposal that the British should support Japan's claims at the end of the war to the North Pacific islands in return for Japan supporting the British Empire's claims to the South Pacific islands. Hughes, while accepting the necessity of falling in with Japan's wishes, nevertheless stated that if he were able to attend the conference he would 'lay before you the views of the Commonwealth Government on this matter at length'. See cable, Munro Ferguson to Long, 7 February 1917, TNA: PRO CO 532/91/215. For further treatment of this Japanese proposal and the Australian response see chapter 11.

The Labor parliamentarians saw the proposal for an 'Imperial War Cabinet' in these terms. They were not hostile to the Empire as such. They were not republicans and did not offer, as an alternative, an exclusive Australian nationalism. W. G. Mahony, while denouncing the plan as a move towards Imperial Federation, was content that the ties of Empire should be sustained 'by race and sentiments'. Political union threatened Australia's national security. Australia's unqualified support for the British cause had obliged it to abandon its own naval-building program, which was 'a suicidal policy'. In order to counter 'the danger lurking ahead' Australia needed to speed up naval construction 'to the uttermost limits'. Similarly James Mathews maintained that if Hughes went to London he would 'win the war and damn Australia'. It was impossible to predict what this novel imperial institution might do. He feared that it might attempt to impose conscription and, if such an attempt were made, he had no doubt that Australia would respond as the American colonists had at the time of the Boston Tea Party.[15]

Rebuffed by Labor, Hughes had no choice but to call an election in the hope that the country would legitimise his government and give it a mandate to rule. Hughes did not like being driven to this expedient. He had wanted to go to London and he was uncertain about the outcome of an appeal to the people. On 23 March, just a week after the dissolution of parliament, believing still that Ireland was the chief stumbling block to Australia's returning to a wholehearted allegiance to the Empire, he again exhorted Lloyd George to take up the question. The Senate had seemed to confirm Hughes's view when it voted by 29 to 2 for a resolution in favour of Irish Home Rule.

Once more he told Lloyd George that the real strength behind the anti-conscription and anti-imperial movement was 'the organised Irish determined at all costs to force Home Rule.' The decline in Australia's military contribution to the Empire's war effort, the fact that recruitment was 'practically at a standstill' was the 'effect of present position in Ireland'. If the election went ahead it would 'intensify bitterness'. A Labor victory would be disastrous for the Empire. If Lloyd George announced that the British and the Dominion prime ministers would negotiate a settlement with representatives of Irish Nationalists and Ulster Loyalists, and simultaneously ask for the Australian election to be postponed, it was likely that parliament would grant the request. Hughes might then be able to attend the conference.[16]

Hughes was clutching at straws. His belief that a public declaration by Lloyd George would appease Irish Australians was mistaken. The British and Australian Governments by their own actions had made it impossible for a return to the halcyon days at the outbreak of the war when John Redmond's Irish National Party and John Gavan Duffy and the Australian hierarchy had given unqualified support to the British cause. The gulf which Hughes and conscription had opened up between the National and Labor camps could not be bridged by a formal gesture of goodwill from London. Moreover, as Lloyd George had earlier explained, he was not free to take such a bold step. By the time Hughes's message reached London, the British Prime Minister had already decided that the Imperial Cabinet and Conference should begin its deliberation on 20

---

[15] *Argus*, 9 December 1916; *CPD*, 1914–17 session, LXXXI, 10357–59 and 10569–72, 8 and 22 February 1917.

[16] Cable, Hughes to Murdoch, 12 March 1917, Lloyd George Papers, House of Lords Record Office F/28/2/1 and Murdoch Papers, NLA MS 2823/23.

March, thus making it impossible for Hughes to take part in its proceedings. Of all the Dominions, Australia alone was not represented at this meeting of imperial leaders. Australia, which had more vital interests at stake in the war and the peace than any other Dominion, had to forego this unprecedented opportunity to contribute to the making of the policies which would determine the Empire's role in the evolving world crisis.

Conscription as a test of 'loyalty'

Labor's hostility to Hughes's going to London was a manifestation of a more general sickness afflicting the body politic. The issue of conscription had poisoned the wellsprings of national life. It had destroyed the consensus that had marked Australia's entry into the war. By the time of the referendum the bitterness and rancour generated in the campaign had caused recruiting, the war and the Empire to become symbols of domestic division and strife.

Both sides of the conscription debate had had reasonable arguments to advance. The dynamics of the dispute, however, locked the contending parties into a spiral of mutual recriminations. In the face of claims by the authorities that conscription was the test of loyalty to the country and Empire, dissenters expressed a determination never to yield and made anti-conscription the test of loyalty to the labour movement. The conscriptionists saw this as recalcitrance and the accompanying appeals for civil disobedience as nothing less than a seditious conspiracy.

For the conscriptionists, the war had brought out the true meaning of British race patriotism for Australians. To their mind the war had also shown that the defence of Britain was in every way the defence of Australia. Those who openly resisted the compulsory enlistment of men for the service of the Empire endangered the survival of the British race and betrayed Australia. Since the conscriptionists had assumed the mantle of the guardians of British Australia this definition of Australia's central cultural myth put their opponents on the defensive. Despite Syndicalist advocacy of international working class solidarity and some few Irish Catholic assertions of an 'Australia first' principle, the great body of anti-conscriptionists had no alternative myth to put in place of Britishness, of which indeed 'Australia first' was only one of the weaker forms. Indeed those who wanted to put 'Australia first' were never able convincingly to accuse their detractors of disloyalty to their country. The British race myth was all-pervasive. Before the conscription crisis, South Australia, while under a Labor Government, had introduced a 'National Salute' or pledge of allegiance for public school students who in daily ceremonies were required to swear:

> I love my country, the British Empire,
>
> I honour her King, King George the Fifth,
>
> I salute her flag the Union Jack,
>
> And I promise cheerfully to obey her laws.[17]

The labour movement was therefore always on the defensive in the argument over loyalty.

---

[17] E.H. Kwan, 'Making "Good Australians": The Work of Three South Australian Educators', MA thesis (University of Adelaide, 1981), pp.198 and 254 and Elizabeth Kwan, 'Making "Good Australians"', *Journal of Australian Studies*, 29 (1991), pp.44–45.

When the self-proclaimed apostles of British patriotism made conscription the measure of civic loyalty and used their control of the state to censor and harass those who differed from them, many of the anti-conscriptionists, instead of buckling under, began to air doubts about the war and about the Empire. Since it was claimed that conscription was required to win the war and was the test of loyalty to the Empire the more militant anti-conscriptionists were provoked into considering the wisdom of the war and the character of Australia's relation to the Empire. The mainstream of the movement did not seek the withdrawal of Australia from the war or the Empire, but many of them nevertheless began to press for a compromise peace and for greater autonomy within the Empire.

Though the potential for a rupture had been present from the end of 1915, it was Hughes's decision to push willy-nilly for conscription and to steamroll all opposition which led, through a spiral of provocations, to the breaking of the bonds of mutual trust. His action, which ignored the strongly expressed views of a majority of labour organisations, hardened hearts and steeled resolve and his authoritarian and vindictive referendum campaign intensified these feelings.

The calling of men into camp before the referendum results were known seemed an arrogant prejudgment of the people's will and a gross abuse of the *Defence Act*'s 'emergency' provisions. It incited the labour militants into industrial protests and other acts of defiance. Such resistance was for Hughes and the conscriptionists the final proof that the opponents of compulsion were enemies to Britain and Australia. And so they put half the nation outside the pale, vilifying those who would not surrender to the necessities of war and Empire as disloyalists or fellow-travellers with the disloyal.

On 24 September 1916, at the beginning of the week when the government was expected to summon all eligible men into camp, a trade union conference in Melbourne decided that stop-work meetings should be held on the day of the announcement. Five days later, following the Governor-General's proclamation, John Curtin, the secretary of the Interstate Trades Union Congress, duly named 4 October as the day for the protest. Though, apart from the mining, metal and railway industries, the unions' response was lukewarm and the strike meetings that were held passed only moderate resolutions,[18] Hughes and many of his co-conscriptionists began to deny the legitimacy of the opposition. They declared that the war effort and the British cause were being subverted by domestic enemies, which included not only Australians of German descent but also Syndicalist anarchists and Sinn Fein Republicans.

The conscriptionists became more intolerant of those they saw as the enemy of the British race. G. H. Knibbs, a Round Table scientist who was head of the Commonwealth Bureau of Census and Statistics, was enraged by the replies which 'Australian-born residents of Queensland and German parentage' had given in their War Census cards. Writing to Pearce on 5 October he cited the answers of six young men who refused to enlist because they had 'relations in the Prussian army' and, as one put it, did 'not want to go and shoot my father's brothers and sisters sons.' These men were, Knibbs declared, 'Germans at heart'. While he believed Australia should

---

[18] Ian Turner, *Industrial Labor and Politics: The Labor Movement in Eastern Australia* (Canberra: Australian National University Press, 1965), pp.108–09.

For Brisbane strike meetings, see *Daily Standard*, 4 October 1916.

mobilise its human and material resources for the war he considered that, if this were to 'result in providing – for the enemy within the gate – a secure means to increase and multiply and replenish the stricken land with the race which has been responsible for the cataclysm, a crime will have been committed against our people.' Since 'the saying "he who is not with me is against me" is as true today as it was 1900 years ago', he urged that these men should not be allowed to sabotage the sacred cause of the British Empire and should therefore be 'treated in all respects as enemies'.[19] Even though in early 1917 the Defence Department admitted that they had no evidence of German spying, sabotage or sedition, the defeated conscriptionists increased the virulence of their attacks on the loyalty of German-Australians and Hughes, prior to the May election, took away the right of naturalised Australians who were born in enemy countries to vote.[20]

More insidious and subversive, however, were the Industrial Workers of the World who, it was believed, exercised an increasing influence among trade unionists and Catholics. The IWW was an apocalyptic, millennial syndicalist movement. Its very existence was a celebration of rebellion against authority and an incitement to direct, even violent, action. Its members stirred up class hatred and encouraged direct and indirect resistance to the capitalist bosses. One member had been implicated in the murder of a policeman in a New South Wales coal town and others were accused on good, if not conclusive, evidence of forging banknotes and setting fire to business houses in Sydney. They had great success in popularising their creed. They understood well the art of propaganda, the value of the eye-catching phrase, the pithy dramatic image. They knew that dodgers and posters, placed anonymously on telegraph poles and in railway carriages and public buildings, had great effect in giving heart to the angry and alienated and in terrifying the powers-that-be.

Their anti-conscriptionist literature declared that the working-class had no interest in the war and exhorted the workingman, if called up, to refuse to go. One widely distributed leaflet appeared under the heading 'Defiance: The Only Way to Deal with Hughes' stated:

> THE ONLY WAY TO DEFEAT THIS PROPOSAL IS TO REFUSE TO ATTEST. Simply ignore the order of Hughes the HUN.
>
> Be sure of this: HUNDREDS OF YOUR COBBERS ARE GOING TO REFUSE.
>
> Your only hope is to defy the military order. ONCE YOU ARE IN CAMP YOUR SLAVERY IS HOPELESS.
>
> REMEMBER IRELAND: THE TOILERS IN IRELAND DIED WITH ENGLISH BULLETS IN THEIR BRAIN ON YOUR BEHALF: LET HUGHES AND HIS BLOODTHIRSTY MOB GO TO HELL BEFORE YOU BETRAY YOUR CLASS.

---

[19] Letter, Knibbs to Pearce, 5 October 1916, Hughes Papers, NLA MS 1538/117/3. In 1921 Hughes appointed Knibbs Director of the Commonwealth Institute of Science and Industry.

[20] Michael McKernan, *The Australian People and the Great War* (Sydney: Collins, 1980), pp.157–70.

C of A 8 of 1917, *Commonwealth Electoral (Wartime) Act*, clause 10 exempted from the general disenfranchisement provision those whose fathers, brothers or sons had volunteered to join the AIF and thus proved their loyalty in the only acceptable way.

Another pamphlet which was sponsored by what they named the 'Anti-Hun Society' – one of the ironic touches the IWW delighted in as they turned the moral language of their opponents against them – added intimidation to agitation, warning that enlistment would bring retribution:

> Every man who dons the khaki will be a scab on his mates, and when the chance comes he must be SHOT and that time will come as sure as Judas is dead.[21]

The trade union day of protest, set against this background of IWW agitation, rang the alarm bells for the conscriptionists. Their leaders, supported by the major daily newspapers and Protestant churches, condemned not only the strikers but all anti-conscriptionists. The *Sydney Morning Herald* on 28 September for the first time took this line and headed its editorial 'The Anti's: Anti-British at heart'.[22] Hughes, on the eve of the strike, also took up this theme, a theme which came naturally to him and which dominated the rest of his term as Prime Minister. He had never suffered opposition easily. Convinced of the necessity of conscription in order to preserve the British race he could not tolerate those who dared to stand in his way. It was therefore no great leap for him to interpret the union protest against the call-up as a syndicalist plot to foment a general strike and to destroy the basis of society. Those responsible were trying to 'create conditions under cover of which they hoped something approaching civil war could be engineered.' He urged the great mass of unionists not to allow themselves to become tools in the hands of 'radical extremists and secret enemies of Britain who wished her to be defeated'.[23]

From this point he then moved to define the core issue in the referendum as one of loyalty to the Empire. At a conscription rally in the Brisbane Exhibition Hall he set out his case in Manichean terms. 'Are you for the Empire or against it?' he asked. 'This is the question which must be put to every man and woman.' At a meeting of 10,000 women at the Sydney Town Hall he accused the anti-conscriptionists of being 'against the war, because they are against Britain', and then proceeded to claim that, 'They are the agents of Germany.'[24] In Hobart he hinted that the anti-conscription forces comprised an unholy alliance between Irish Catholics and atheistic Wobblies: 'Opponents of the government's proposals were recruited from a section of the people who have nothing in common except hatred of Britain.'[25]

The defeat of conscription at the polls did nothing to restore harmony and goodwill. The anti-conscription activists, having been pilloried for their principles, feared that the

---

[21] NAA MP729/2 2021/1/40.

[22] *SMH*, 28 September 1916.

The *Age* on 27 October 1916 described anti-conscriptionists as 'the off-scourings of crime, disloyalty, pro-Germanism, meanness of spirit and hatred of England.' See *Age,* 27 October 1916.

The *Church of England Messenger*, reflecting a widespread view among the Protestant churches, asserted that 'the Empire is fighting the battle of Christ against Satan' and 'every loyal Britisher in our land ought to vote Yes.' See *Church of England Messenger* (Victoria), 20 October 1916.

The New South Wales Presbyterian General Assembly passed, almost unanimously, a resolution urging a 'Yes' vote. See *SMH*, 3 October 1916.

[23] *Daily Telegraph*, 4 October 1916.

[24] *Daily Telegraph*, 5 and 7 October 1916.

[25] *Daily Telegraph*, 13 October 1916 and *SMH*, 15 October 1916.

conscriptionists would refuse to accept the verdict and would use their control of the state's machinery to impose their will industrially as well as militarily. They did not trust the government or the conscriptionists who were allied with it. At a meeting of the Anti-Conscription League in the Sydney Domain on 6 November some speakers urged strike action to try to force Hughes from office and so head off any attempt to overturn the people's decision. Others declared against compulsion even for home defence, arguing that the enemies of labour might well take advantage of any form of military compulsion to introduce overseas service as well as industrial regimentation. Despite many trade unionists' long standing antagonism to the IWW and its methods, there was considerable sympathy for its members who had been charged with forgery and arson. It was believed that since the Wobblies had been the most outspoken and uncompromising critics of conscription, the government had made an example of them. These men came to be regarded as martyrs to the cause.[26]

The referendum campaign restructured Australian politics. Just as some in the labour movement drew closer to the IWW and pacifist organisations, so it seemed natural that the pro-conscriptionists should come together in a permanent alliance. When, following the failure of the referendum, Hughes lost control of the Parliamentary Party and led his supporters out of the Labor Caucus, a group of senior figures from the National Referendum Council – 'some of those concerned were original members of the Universal Service League' – began to work for a coalition of Hughes's newly formed National Labor Party with Cook's Liberal Party. This National Federation, as the alliance was initially called, would have as its twin pillars, the prosecution of the war and the unity of the Empire.[27] The National Federation had as its moral inspiration the leitmotif of the Round Table scientists, the Universal Service League and the Referendum Council, namely the organisation of the nation for service to the Empire. Its proud boast was that it put issues of party and class aside in the broader interest of achieving social efficiency for the good of the British race. Its immediate goal was to concentrate all national energies for the purpose of achieving victory.

These pro-conscriptionists took their defeat hard. Irvine, perhaps the most extreme advocate of compulsion, even suggested to the Governor-General that the British Parliament might 'properly have decreed conscription for the Empire' and so compelled Australia's selfish democracy to do its duty.[28] Heedless of the referendum result, Irvine declared his willingness to take whatever steps were necessary to introduce conscription. None of his colleagues however, were willing to adopt such a stance. Following the defeat of the referendum they accepted that such a course would be politically untenable.

---

[26] *Daily Telegraph*, 7 and 10 November 1916; the very brief, censored accounts of the meeting in the *Telegraph* only recorded the resolution which demanded that the will of the people be respected. The more complete account is found in the report of the secret service that Hughes subsequently used in order to condemn the meeting. See Ian Turner, *Industrial Labour and Politics*, pp.131–33.
[27] Hume Cook Papers, NLA MS 601, 'Man and the Hour', pp.49–50.
[28] Letter, personal and private, Munro Ferguson to Stamfordham, 29 February 1917, Novar Papers, NLA MS 696/270; see also Novar Diary, 20 February 1917, 'We agree pretty much on everything – though he carries his view of the propriety of the Imperial Parliament legislating – i.e. on conscription – too far.'

Hughes too was shaken to the depths of his being by this rejection. The people's verdict was a great blow. He had been convinced that conscription was essential to the survival of the British race. His reception after returning from England had reinforced his sense of being a man of destiny. Convinced that race nationalism was the most powerful force underpinning democracy he had believed that he was the voice of the people and that they would accept his leadership. He had given more of himself to the cause than to any previous political battle. For him the call to sacrifice was almost as much about national regeneration as it was about national security. Hughes had difficulty in understanding how so many had put their private interests before the honour of the nation. Deane, who was by the Prime Minister's side throughout the campaign, had his contempt for the masses confirmed by their action. Commenting on the outcome of the referendum he wrote that 'Never was there a clearer illustration of the danger of democracy. Demagogues by the most impossible lies sought to stampede the people and succeeded.' In Australia, 'the foremost Democracy in the world', the referendum had represented 'a big test for Democracy – and Democracy failed.'[29]

The result was humiliating as well as bewildering. It was particularly galling that only a small majority of Hughes's ideal Australians, the AIF volunteers, had voted for conscription, with something like three quarters of those in the trenches on the Western Front voting against. The great crusade to save the Empire now seemed hollow. The rejection of conscription had made a nonsense of his lectures to the British about following Australia's example and creating a true people's democracy in which all would unite to serve the race. It hurt particularly that the British labour movement had submitted to the law of the land, accepted conscription and even allowed their representatives to continue to serve in the War Cabinet.

From this time, in confiding his thoughts to his intimates, he developed a self-mocking, heroic language and imagery to describe the great events, most of them setbacks, with which he had to contend. Reporting the results of the 1916 referendum to Keith Murdoch, he wrote:

> The Ides of March have come and gone and Caesar still lives! But he lives as Cicero said of his friend Cataline on sufferance – or at least in doubt! Before this pathetic epistle reaches you the cypress may droop over his political grave: may indeed – for threats of the 'happy despatch' fall thick as autumn leaves on Vallombrosa – wither on his tomb!

> We have lost by a head! Ah! that head. How little yet how much. And when I think what turned on victory I can hardly forebear to rail at the Anzac vote which could and it would have pulled us through.[30]

---

[29] Letter, Deane to Barrett, 2 November 1916, Barrett Papers, Melbourne University Archives.
[30] Letter, Hughes to Murdoch, 4 November 1916, Murdoch Papers, NLA MS 2823/23.
  It is striking that throughout the referendum campaign Hughes does not seem to have given any thought to how, if he should secure a narrow – as he wrote to Murdoch a 'little' – majority, he would enforce conscription against a hard core of anti-conscriptionists who were determined not to yield and who would be able to rely on the sympathetic support of almost half the country. The point of the referendum was to give him a moral authority to bring in conscription and so cause his opponents in the Labor Party and labour movement to fall in with his plans, but, if this were the case, then the way he

No doubt the exaggerated pathos helped salve the wounds and quiet the hurt. But what it could not do – indeed the very style denied it – was to restore his faith in the Australian people and his mission on their behalf to the British Empire and the world. After this defeat, though he continued to fight for the same ends, he was never quite the same person.

Preparing to meet a civil uprising

Even as he reluctantly submitted to the people's will, he could not but see those who were primarily responsible for the betrayal of their race as enemies of the state. To his mind the fiery speeches of the victorious anti-conscriptionists proved that there was more at stake than opposition to military compulsion. It was evident that there was in the country:

> a number of persons who are opposed to this war, who are against the Empire and who will do all that they can to prevent Australia doing her duty as part of the Empire. The strikes and upheavals, political and industrial, we see around us are the manifestation of a deliberate policy which aims at destroying society as it now exists.

Once again identifying the enemy as a coalition of IWW anarchists with Irish Republicans, he declared that 'Anarchists [were] assisted for their own purpose by a certain section which … are against the Empire.'[31] The labour movement had been captured by this disloyal combination. They had revolutionary aims and were a menace to the state itself.

Since October Hughes and Pearce had become alarmed at the prospect of social unrest and industrial sabotage. HMAS *Brisbane* had suffered damage at the hands of workmen at Cockatoo Island in Sydney Harbour. Aggrieved by the guilty verdicts on twelve IWW members who had been tried for arson and sedition, militant unionists were attempting to bring about a general strike. The intelligence services reported that in every part of Australia the IWW and their sympathisers were fomenting strife and inciting rebellion. During the referendum campaign rumours were abroad that the IWW were encouraging members to enlist in the AIF, especially as cooks, 'in order to spread sedition in the camps', and Pearce ordered discreet inquiries to be made. These investigations, however, uncovered only a single suspect, 'One Man Found Working At Construction New Camp Newcastle Which Is NOT Yet Occupied', and the Commander of the New South Wales military district, Brigadier-General G. Ramaciotti, assured his minister that the man, presumably without any chance to clear himself, would be 'discreetly disposed of'. Is it possible that this was World-War-One-speak for 'terminated with extreme prejudice'? It is a question.

In November the government learnt of a more serious case of the IWW's revolutionary activity. Two sergeants who had been sent to apprehend AIF deserters reportedly working on the railways on the north coast of New South Wales, blamed the IWW's influence for their inability to carry out the task. They believed that 'the prevalence of the IWW spirit in this district' was the result 'of the large number of Railway navvies employed on the New Construction'. These roughly

---

conducted the campaign only served to alienate further the party's organisations and the trade unions, and ensure the opposite result.

[31] *Daily Telegraph*, 10 November 1916.

2500 railway workers were 'of the most violent IWW type', corrupting the locally employed who joined the railway gangs. They were 'spreading revolutionary and anarchist doctrines among the people', and thereby 'stopping recruitment'. These men were 'absolutely opposed to everything military, and military defence, and made no secret of harbouring deserters, and preaching non-compliance with Regulations issued by the Government.' Though some of the men still wore military uniforms, brazenly flaunting the fact of their desertion, the local constabulary advised the military police against making any arrests 'as we should have been kicked to death.' Indeed, even without attempting to apprehend deserters the sergeants were 'subjected to the grossest insults … the vilest language'. They were informed that incendiarism was rife and these fires were 'practically recognised as the work of the IWW'. At Coffs Harbour they claimed that they had direct experience of this tactic when the Billiard room adjoining the hotel where they stayed was burnt to the ground.[32]

Consequently, in early December, when the IWW and radical labour leaders tried to organise a general strike in protest against the conviction of twelve Sydney 'Wobblies' for arson, the government, when setting these reports against their general belief in widespread disaffection, concluded that the country was on the brink of revolution. On the day the IWW members were sentenced a meeting of the 'Militant Propagandists of the Labor Party' in the Melbourne Trades Hall called on the labour movement and the Labor Party to recognise 'the critical condition confronting Organised Labor of Australia'. They urged the labour movement to take 'combined action in the interest of working class Solidarity and Progress' to force the immediate release of the twelve men who had been 'so severely and unjustly sentenced'. On 4 December the Broken Hill miners' leaders called on Trades and Labour Councils to join in a 'general strike from December 12 until industrialists … released.'[33]

In all these specific instances of defiance and disobedience – whether substantiated or not – the fevered imaginations of Hughes, Pearce and their officials discerned the phantasmagoria of a violent uprising. Since October their military and intelligence advisers had been cultivating this impression and recommending that the government take firm action to suppress the IWW,

The Chief of the Counter Espionage Bureau, Major George Steward, who also served as the Governor-General's Private Secretary, argued that since the organisation preached sedition, sabotage and treason 'in its most vicious form' the government should give it short shrift. He proposed, as a first step, that he should meet the representatives of the state police forces for the purpose of forming a plan 'for dealing with the IWW as a whole.'

About the same time Brigadier-General Ramaciotti had described the IWW as an organisation 'frankly formed to wage war against the existing scheme of civilisation' and openly

---

[32] Confidential Minute, Pearce to Quarter-Master General, 4 October 1916, NAA MP729/3 2021/1/40; Report, 'Re Activities of IWW in North Coast District', 2 December 1916, NAA MP729/2 1997/1/139.
[33] Copy of letter sent by Mary Francis, Secretary, Militant Propagandists of Labour to Mr N.G. Grant, Secretary, ILC (in memo, Deputy Chief Censor to Acting Secretary, Department of Defence, 15 December 1916), 6 December 1916, posted 14 December 1916, NAA MP729/2 1997/1/136; copy of censored cable, W.D. Barnett to 'Secretary, Labor Council, Sydney, Victoria, Adelaide, Newcastle, Queensland, West Australia', 4 December 1916 and copy of censored cable, Barnett to A.C. Willis, Secretary, Coal Miners' Federation, 4 December 1916, NAA, MP729/2 1997/1/121.

committed to achieving its aims by illegal attacks on society. Moreover, he stated that the group was suspected of 'being deliberately used by pro-enemy persons to handicap the Government in the present crisis', though he had to admit that there was 'no absolute proof of this'. It was his view that the Commonwealth should proceed to outlaw the IWW.[34]

These warnings fell on receptive ears. On 15 December Hughes introduced the *Unlawful Associations Bill* which was intended to proscribe activities that undermined the war effort. It was directed particularly at what Hughes called 'an association known under the sonorous and imposing title of the Industrial Workers of the World'. In defending this restriction on civil liberty Hughes repeated the case he had made out against the IWW in 1908. For him 'Anarchy and Socialism are the negative of one another. One put the State above everything, and the other made war on the State in order to destroy it.' The IWW's methods were incompatible with representative government. In Australia, where the workers ruled, the government rested on the will of the majority of the people as expressed through law.

Hughes affirmed that he, unlike the IWW, was 'a believer in Democracy, and regarded the welfare of the State as the supreme good.' Furthermore the IWW denied that 'the spirit of nationality [was] a good thing'. Its members were, as a result, engaged in an 'open declaration of war against society'. Their violent methods amounted to 'treason itself against the State'. Agents reported that at their meetings 'every man was armed with a pistol.' Though this foreign excrescence during its first ten years in Australia had made little progress, the war had afforded it an opportunity to poison 'a considerable portion of the body economic in the country'. Finally, he said that since most of its members had foreign names, a fair number of which were German, it suggested, 'if it does not do more' that the organisation was being used against the Allies.[35]

There is no doubt that the government believed that the country was faced with grave civil disorder, even an insurrection. Three days after the passage of the *Unlawful Associations Act* the Defence Minister instructed all military districts to take 'SECRET precautionary measures' against the possibility of both a 'sudden emergency' of a minor kind and of '*Riots* or civil disturbances of a more serious nature.' To deal with the lesser danger a special force of 900 men was to be equipped, trained and armed to act immediately against such behaviour, and in each capital city it was to be supplied with a machine gun and ammunition. For the purpose of meeting the greater and more general outbreak each district commander was told to draw up a scheme for the creation of 'small mobile forces, if possible of all arms'. While the officers and men were to be 'carefully selected', presumably for their political reliability, they were not to be informed beforehand of their precise function.

All district commanders, despite some doubts and difficulties, did their best to comply with these orders. South Australia had problems. The Commanding Officer reported that there was a poor response to the advertisement for the guard and that they could not provide all the arms since there were no machine guns and only three field guns in the state – and two of the latter

---

[34] Letter, secret, Steward to Pearce, 1 November 1916, NAA MP729/5 216/1/2112; letter, secret, Ramaciotti to Secretary, Department of Defence, 3 November and 6 December 1916, NAA MP729/3 216/1/2122 and NAA MP792/2 1997/1/139.
[35] *CPD*, 1914–17 session, LXXX, 10097–103, 18 December 1916.

were doing duty at the AIF training camp. However, he showed willing, assuring his superiors that his office was preparing a training manual to cover 'street fighting, defence of buildings, attacks on fortified houses etc'.

The Western Australian Commander seemed bemused by the instruction and even queried its necessity: 'From the light of past experience and in view of present indications the possibility of riots on a large scale is very remote, as at present there is no set of circumstances existing which would give rise to such contingencies … Civil rioting is not anticipated.' He considered that the only kind of problem that might be envisaged, such as attacks on 'Greek shops' in Perth or the goldfields, would be 'of a very minor nature' and could be handled 'efficiently' by the existing military police and guards. Such complacency was rejected out of hand and Western Australia was required, along with all the other states, to prepare for an uprising.

Melbourne, the seat of government, took the matter most seriously and produced the most comprehensive plan for meeting civil disorders or a mass uprising. To combat 'Riots or Civil Disturbances of a more serious nature', the Victorian military authorities had at their disposal, in addition to a Reserve Company and the District Guard which was on call, a mobile force comprising an AIF infantry battalion, two 18-pounder guns, two machine gun sections and fifty light-horsemen, and in the last resort the citizen militia would be drawn upon. This force was to be supplied with and supported by the most modern weapons. Even two aeroplanes were to be made available:

(a) To overawe rioters by their presence in the air,

(b) To cooperate with the Artillery,

(c) To assist in dispersing the rioters by the use of machine guns and revolvers and by dropping bombs or hand grenades.

The military planners thought that 'the use of aeroplanes would have a great moral effect.' By the beginning of February 1917 all was in place and ready for the day.[36]

The government's decision to prepare the military to maintain internal order was highly significant. It breached the constitutional conventions which since Federation had underpinned a broad political consensus on defence. Since 1903 successive governments had given assurances that the defence forces would not be used to keep the peace. This had been a condition of the labour movement's support for compulsory military training and the raising of the AIF. The violation of this undertaking, to which Hughes and Pearce themselves had been parties, symbolised the extent of the breakdown in national community. Those responsible were the heirs of a liberal parliamentary tradition and by these standards no reasonable assessment of anti-conscriptionist or IWW behaviour could justify the view that the country faced armed resistance

---

[36] Letter, secret, Adjutant-General, Brigadier-General V.C.M. Sellheim, Department of Defence, Melbourne to Commandants, All Military Districts, 18 December 1916; letter, Commandant, 5th Military District, Perth to Secretary for Defence, 19 January 1917; letter, Acting Commandant, 3rd Military District, Melbourne to Secretary, Department of Defence, 2 February 1917; NAA B197 1887/1/52.

to lawful authority, and therefore the government's preparations to turn soldiers' rifles against their fellow citizens.

It is true that the IWW preached a revolutionary doctrine of class conflict and direct action and some of its members had engaged in isolated attacks on authority and property, but their number was small – no more than 2000 scattered across Australia – they had little influence among the working-class and did not control the anti-conscription movement. The Labor Party had voted for the *Unlawful Associations Act*. The appeals by the IWW and other radical labour leaders for a general strike had fallen on deaf ears. And, even if this had not been the case, a general strike did not in itself constitute an armed rebellion.

The government had no evidence of a plot to overthrow the constitutional order. They had no evidence that the IWW, the Irish nationalists, German sympathisers or any other disaffected group were accumulating arms. There was a report that each IWW member attending meetings in Sydney carried a revolver. But the report lacked confirmation and, even if it were true, the numbers involved were small and the arms inadequate to mount any attempt at a coup. In Broken Hill the miners in response to the threat of compulsion had formed what they called the Labor Volunteer Army. In effect, it was, however, no more than a rhetorical device; it possessed no arms, no discipline and acted merely as another anti-conscription organisation.[37] The Western Australian Military Commandant, no friend of civil disorder, had the measure of the matter, and not only for Western Australia. This was not, however, a time for common sense, calm judgment or broad sympathies. Hughes and Pearce and those who stood with them, their officials and advisers, the Referendum Council and the Universal Service League, considered that they were the guardians of Australia's British heritage. They saw the war as a cosmic struggle of races for survival and were intolerant of those who would not accept their prescription for meeting the war crisis. Resistance meant, at least potentially, rebellion. As a result, they were willing that British liberty should be subordinated to British loyalty.

Creating two Australias

Out of the tensions created by the imperious demands of the authorities that all should unite for the good of the Empire and be ready to lay down their lives for the common cause there arose an irreconcilable conflict between two Australias. On the one hand there were those who required submission to the will of the state as the embodiment of the British race and on the other those who refused to surrender their British liberties to the state. The conscriptionists, their racial instincts intensified by the experience of the war, came to regard the principle of compulsory service not just as a preferred measure for achieving victory, but also as the test of loyalty to state and empire. They denounced their outspoken critics as disloyalists and their silent opponents as selfish dupes. They had no compunction in enlisting the power of the state to curb and control these supposed enemies of the Empire.

---

[37] P.J. Rushton, 'The Industrial Workers of the World in Sydney, 1913–1917; A Study of Revolutionary Ideology', MA thesis (University of Sydney, 1969), especially pp.71–82; Ian Turner, *Sydney's Burning* (Melbourne: Heinemann, 1967); Ian Turner, *Industrial Labour and Politics*, pp.133–35.

It might be said that democracy in Australia worked in contrary ways to create out of conscription an issue which would fundamentally divide the country. While on the one hand mass democracy had made many Australians more absolute in identifying with the British race and the British Empire, on the other it also made some citizens, especially in the labour movement, more self-confident in the assertion of collective rights against the state. When during the war the first group, insensitive to the other, put the question of conscription to the people, these opposing tendencies of Australian democracy confronted each other, split the nation and, because of the passions aroused by the controversy, prevented both the government and the opposition from being able to deal with defence and foreign problems on their merits or, more precisely, on the basis of Australia's national interests.

From the end of 1916 Hughes and his National Labor and Liberal colleagues treated the Labor Party, the labour movement and all others who did not cooperate with their 'National' government's war policy as suspect. To their way of thinking the Labor Party had revealed its true colours by expelling all conscriptionists from its ranks and making anti-conscription the key test of party orthodoxy.[38] Similarly its refusal to join in a National Government, its unwillingness to agree to a party truce to allow Hughes to attend the Imperial War Conference and Cabinet, its questioning of the Allies' war aims and its lack of enthusiasm for voluntary recruitment were taken as signs of disloyalty or, at the least, signs that the party was under the influence of disloyal elements.

When Hughes, on behalf of the Nationalists, called an election for 5 May, he set out the issues in terms of the images of loyalty and disloyalty which had since the referendum come to dominate the political discourse of the conscriptionists. The National Federation presented itself as a movement dedicated not to partisan interests but to national ideals. At a public meeting in January to mark the installation of the National Government the presiding officer, H. Y. Braddon, (Past President of the Associated Chambers of Commerce of Australia, part-time lecturer in business practices and principles at the University of Sydney, member of the Round Table and a founder of the Universal Service League) praised Hughes and Cook for standing together under the one banner on which was emblazoned 'Loyalty to the Empire'.[39] In announcing his National Cabinet to parliament, Hughes had also stressed that it was, like Lloyd George's War Cabinet, a government of national unity. It was 'not a rich man's government, not a poor man's government' but 'the people's government', a government committed single-mindedly to winning the war, preserving the White Australia policy and maintaining Empire solidarity. Implicitly drawing an analogy between the European monarchs' threat to the French Revolution, which had produced Robespierre's Reign of Terror, and the German threat to the British Empire, he proclaimed that his National Government was 'a Committee of Public Safety'.[40]

---

[38] *SMH*, 7 December 1916.

[39] *SMH*, 27 February 1917.

[40] *SMH*, 24 January, 23 and 27 February 1917; *CPD*, 1914–17 session, LXXXI, 10569, 22 February 1917. Hughes probably took this historical reference from L.S. Amery who in a letter to Hughes had described Lloyd George's new War Cabinet as a 'Committee of Public Safety'. It was certainly an image which comported well with his own view of wartime government. See letter, Amery to Hughes, 8 January 1917, Barnes and Nicholson (eds), *Leo Amery Diaries*, Vol.I, p.139.

During the election campaign these themes were developed further. At meeting after meeting Hughes iterated that his government and supporters stood 'openly and frankly for the Empire'. They were for the Empire because they were for Australia; 'We are loyal to the Empire first and foremost because we are of the British race.' It was a specious argument to try to draw a distinction between the interests of Australia and the Empire. Not unmindful of many farmers' failure to vote for conscription, Hughes pointed out how rural interests were tied to the British market. The British had bought the whole of the 1915–16 and the 1916–17 wheat harvest for a record price. They had also bought the whole wool clip for a record high price and had agreed to purchase the total output of the base metal industries. Britain, moreover, had advanced Australia £150 million which was enough to cover Australia's war debt. Not only was the Empire 'at once our sword and our shield' and 'the greatest guarantee of the world's peace' but also the source of the nation's material prosperity.

By contrast the Labor Party was, he contended, 'made up for the most part of men either hostile to or lukewarm on the war, indifferent to the Empire or openly opposed to it, and who put other interests before those of their country.' To its shame 'the great organisation of Labor has been captured by a narrow-minded, disloyal section who wish to serve their own selfish purposes.' Expanding on this he continued:

> Some are violently hostile to Britain, sneering at the Empire and all that it stands for. Some consider it to be possible to be for Australia yet indifferent, if not hostile, to the fate of the Empire. Some openly revile everything we hold sacred and dear, declaring themselves as having no God, no country, no flag, save the red flag of revolution. Some mistakenly put sectional interests before those of the country in which they live and the country to which they owe everything.

Hughes allowed that Frank Tudor, his successor as leader of the Labor Party, and many more in the party were loyal. This was a difficult concession to avoid since the Labor leader had declared in opening his campaign that it was Labor policy to remain true to the policy adopted by the party since 1914 and if elected to office to pursue Australia's war effort 'with vigour and determination' and to send every man willing to serve to the front.[41] But Hughes asserted that these well-meaning Labor men were manipulated and controlled by disloyalists. The nature of the party could be gauged from the fact that every disloyalist looked to the ALP 'as his champion, as his hope'. And he rhetorically asked: 'Is there one IWW man who will not cast his vote for the Tudor party … ? Is there one enemy of Britain who will not do so? Is there one man of German descent and who has a vote who will not vote for them?' The power behind the parliamentary party, the state executives, were, for the most part, hostile to Britain: 'They hate her, and see in her danger their opportunity for personal advancement.' Thus the Labor Party was not a loyal opposition but a creature of the unholy trinity of the IWW, the Sinn Feiners and German-Australians, all of whom sought to bring about the downfall of the British Empire.

In summing up the National Party position, Hughes claimed that, by contrast, they stood for a British heritage of 500 years which had given the British people self-government and the Australian working classes 'conditions the like of which are unknown in any other country'. The

---

[41] Scott, *Australia During the War*, pp.394–95; *Argus* and *Age*, 30 March 1917.

British Empire was the product of the genius of the British race. He could not understand why Labor and Liberal should be at each other's throats. Were they not of the one race? 'Does not the same blood flow in Mr Cook's veins as in mine?' What was at stake was 'British civilisation and British liberty'. Support for the war was 'a matter of life and death, material and spiritual'.[42]

The National Party interpreted their triumph at the polls, where they achieved overwhelming majorities in both Houses, to mean that the country had endorsed their creed of British race patriotism. And this was both true and untrue. Clearly in October 1916 a majority of Australians had rejected compulsion for overseas service and had by so doing placed limits on the sacrifices which they would make for the Empire. Hughes, wisely recognising this, had during the election qualified his government's commitment to the war by promising not to introduce conscription without first putting the question to the people. As a result, those who had voted 'No' in the referendum to protect their private interests were free to consult their public principles. Influenced by the government's depiction of Labor as racially disloyal and socially dangerous, many of them voted as their cultural identity dictated – for law and order, war and Empire.

Buoyed by its great electoral success, the National Government assumed it had a clear mandate to suppress the domestic enemy. Millen, the Vice-President of the Executive Council, concluded that, 'Australia has put its foot down on those who are disloyal to the Empire.' Hughes affirmed that the 'junta supported by disloyalists and extremists has been taught a lesson that it will not soon forget.'[43] There was no magnanimity in the hour of victory, no Lincoln-like gesture to try to heal the wounds in the body politic. During the remaining months of the war the divisions in the country became ever sharper. The Nationals were haunted by a spectre largely of their own creation and by adopting a stand based on the image of an embattled bifurcated society they almost brought it into being. As the voices of dissidence grew louder and greater numbers took up radical positions on war and peace, capitalism and socialism, Hughes and the Nationals resorted to increasingly harsher measures in an attempt to crush 'the enemy within the gate'. They proceeded to show what a loyal government, acting as a 'Committee of Public Safety', could do to silence the traitors in their midst.

[42] *SMH*, 28 March and 5, 6 and 9 April 1917.
[43] *SMH*, 7 May 1917.

9
'The Enemy within the Gate': The Attack on National Community

During 1917 the warring world was at war with itself. Apart from the United States, which entered the fray in April, all the belligerents were suffering from the stress imposed upon the bonds of community by the drawn-out conflict. On the battlefields, generals had to contend with mutiny and disaffection in the ranks, and on the home front, governments had to face much greater industrial turbulence and social unrest. In the most extreme case, a revolution toppled the Czarist Empire and forced Russia to withdraw from the war.

Although Australia was never threatened by revolution, nevertheless it too was increasingly troubled by political, industrial, communal and sectarian discord. Centring on the conflicts over conscription, this discord assumed a vindictive and unforgiving character. As a result, the earlier consensus about war and Empire and about military reinforcements and peacemaking had broken down. Such issues became symbols of the broader internal divisions. The conscriptionists became obsessed with the problem of how to contain and control the enemy within the gate.

Dealing with the dissidents

Flushed with victory at the polls, Hughes's 'Win-the-War' government in its determination to rout the trouble-makers first tackled the labour movement. During the first half of 1917, labour's political and industrial organisations had responded to loyalists' language by adopting an increasingly radical rhetoric which in turn fed the government's paranoia. Through newspaper and intelligence reports the Commonwealth authorities were alerted to this growing trend. They read accounts of Political Labour League and Trades and Labour Council meetings where delegates declared themselves 'opposed to the war', claiming that it had been 'engineered for the enslavement of the workers'. They were informed that statements, such as 'the day the Government proclaimed conscription or military service of any description unionists should down tools', drew great applause. The Russian Revolution was praised and ex-senator Rae, who had sons in the AIF in France, boldly averred that he would take whatever steps were necessary to resist conscription, 'even to the extent of joining in revolutionary action'.[1]

Attributing much of this inflammatory talk to the influence of the IWW, the government, in order to impress its supporters and intimidate the opposition, brought down legislation which went far beyond the *Unlawful Associations Act*. It gave the authorities power to declare associations unlawful, to make membership in the named associations an offence and to seize the property of such associations. Hughes in speaking to the Bill justified this harsher measure on the

---

[1] *Argus*, 6 June 1917; letter, Pearce to Hughes, 12 June 1917 containing a secret agent's report of the Sydney Political Labor League Conference, Hughes Papers, NLA MS 1538/117/1.

ground that the 1916 Act had proved unable to cope with the IWW, 'this great menace to society' which was 'still very actively at work in Australia'. Its doctrine of sabotage was antithetic to 'the very principles of, not only Liberty and Democracy … but of Socialism also.' Quoting from an IWW pamphlet, 'Industrial Efficiency and its Antidote' in which 'go slow' was recommended as 'sabotage on the job' and in which it was said that 'scientific management must be met with scientific sabotage', Hughes retorted that 'industrial efficiency is the means whereby alone we can save the country.' Once again the Labor parliamentarians, fearful of being branded as IWW sympathisers, went along with what was proposed. After Hughes accepted an amendment exempting registered unions from its provisions Labor joined the National Party in voting for the Bill.[2] The government then proceeded to destroy the IWW, seizing its assets and imprisoning its members. The leading historian of the movement has written that by the end of September the IWW 'was out of business'.[3]

Almost simultaneously with the passage of the Bill, a great strike broke out in New South Wales – a strike which was to become 'the biggest industrial upheaval ever experienced in Australia'.[4] It spread to Queensland and Victoria, lasted almost twelve weeks and involved overall about 100,000 workers from the transport, mining, waterfront and associated industries. It began when the Railway Commissioners announced that they were going to introduce a 'card system' to cost individual jobs and thereby to check workers' efficiency. The engineers who were the first group to be subjected to the new procedures refused to cooperate, and on 2 August almost 6000 other railway and tramway workers came out in sympathy. From that point the strike spread bushfire-like up and down the East coast states.

The New South Wales and federal governments saw the hand of the IWW in this struggle over 'industrial efficiency'. From their perspective the unionists had embraced the IWW's ultimate tactic of a 'general strike'. A week after the engineers and their sympathisers downed tools the New South Wales Premier denounced the strike:

> The enemies of Britain and her Allies have succeeded in plunging Australia into a General Strike. For the time being they have crippled our Country's efforts to assist in the Great War. AT THE BACK OF THIS STRIKE LURK THE IWW AND THE EXPONENTS OF DIRECT ACTION. Without realising it, many Trades Unionists have become the tools of Disloyalists and Revolutionaries.[5]

The Commonwealth agreed. The strike was the work of the enemies of Britain and the Allies. It was aimed at Australia's ability to contribute to the war effort. It was a challenge to the 'Win-the-War' government. Here was an opportunity to destroy the subversive elements in the labour movement.

The two governments eschewed all overtures for negotiations and cooperated with the employers to break the strike and the strikers. The Commonwealth used regulations under the *War Precautions Act* to arrest the leaders of the 'Strike Committee'. It deregistered striking unions,

---

[2] *CPD*, 1917 session, LXXXII, pp.230–480, 16–26 July 1917.
[3] Ian Turner, *Industrial Labor and Politics*, p.135.
[4] *Ibid.*, p.141.
[5] Cited in *ibid.*, p.146.

denying their members the protection of the arbitration system and opened the way for these unions to be named as unlawful associations. Both governments worked closely with employers to enable non-union labour and volunteers to take the place of the strikers.

The strike and the governments' response to it were clear evidence of the ill-will and distrust which by this time pervaded Australian political and industrial culture.[6] In 1916 when the New South Wales Railway Commissioners had first introduced the card system, the Labor Government in office at the time, under pressure from the unions, had withdrawn it. In 1917, however, union protests were ignored and those affected by the innovation regarded it as a provocation. There was no IWW conspiracy.[7] The strike was not a calculated design by militant leaders to take control of the workplace. On the contrary all evidence suggests that it was, like a similar strike in Britain, a grassroots reaction to specific circumstances. The strikers acted without waiting for union guidance and IWW influence was marginal, most unionists having little time for the nihilism of the romantic revolutionary. A 'Strike Committee' was brought into being only after the strike was well under way. Indeed the strike's very undisciplined character contributed to its defeat. The 'card' system would seem to have provided the occasion for an expression of workers' disillusionment with authority and its arbitrary uses.

The loyalists won the trial of strength. By early October all the strikers were forced to capitulate. The union leaders were unable to obtain any concessions for their members. The Loyalist strike-breakers were given preference in employment. Those who were allowed to return to their jobs were totally at the mercy of their employers. The vanquished carried from the experience a deep sense of grievance that alienated them further from the dominant culture.

Simultaneously the Irish Catholic community, which was well represented in the labour movement – and increasingly so since the Labor Party split – began to air its own complaints. As 1917 wore on, their ire was roused by the British failure to offer satisfactory terms for Irish self-government and by reports of the British repression of Sinn Fein, which had taken over the leadership of the nationalist movement and was calling for complete independence. It seemed to many that the British had reneged on the 1914 promise of Home Rule. As a result, their antagonism to conscription was strengthened and some began to express doubts about Britain's war aims.

Though Irish Catholics had a number of representative organisations, such as the Hibernian Australasian Catholic Benefit Society and the Catholic Federation, they lacked any broadly-based

---

[6] It is worth noting that the British Government in May had to deal with a widespread strike by 200,000 unionists in twenty major industrial centres. It was, like the New South Wales strike, a work-place based spontaneous movement. The British War Cabinet, instead of using confrontationist tactics, set up a Commission to Inquire into Industrial Unrest, and when the Commission reported sympathetically on the strikers' grievances – the members of the Commission had gone to the workplace and listened to the workers' complaints – the government adopted most of its recommendations, which addressed these complaints, and the strike was amicably brought to an end. See David French, *The Strategy of the Lloyd George Coalition, 1916–1918* (Oxford: Clarendon Press, 1995), pp.88–89.

[7] Verity Burgmann, *Revolutionary Industrial Unionism: The Industrial Workers of the World in Australia* (Melbourne: Cambridge University Press, 1995), pp.174–77.

institutions which could express their more general social and political concerns.[8] On these issues they looked to the Catholic clergy and press for leadership. In this way Archbishop Daniel Mannix became the much-admired hero and symbol of the Irish cause and, through it, of the anti-conscription movement. During 1917, whenever he spoke, the faithful, supplemented by other anti-conscriptionists, often came in their tens of thousands, even sometimes in their hundreds of thousands, to hear him and to demonstrate their solidarity against those who denounced them as disloyalists.

For Mannix, as for many of his followers, Ireland was as much the occasion as the cause of antagonism towards conscription. Prior to coming to Australia from Ireland as coadjutor Archbishop of Melbourne in 1913, he had shown little interest in either Home Rule or the Gaelic Renaissance. In the new country, Mannix's first objective was to obtain state funds for Catholic schools. He thought it most unjust that, unlike Ireland, public monies should only be used for the support of public schools.[9] After three years of unavailing efforts to change government policy he felt frustrated. Since it was the same Protestant majority that defined loyalty to mean loyalty to the British Empire as discriminated against Catholic education he expressed his resentment by opposing conscription and taking up the Irish cause. His passion for Ireland as well as his appeal to put 'Australia first' lacked substance. It would seem that his stand on these matters, at least in their origin, were a by-product of his sense of inequity over the education question. In his speeches on Ireland and conscription – which were often delivered at the opening of a new school – he would almost invariably connect his remarks to complaints that Catholics were being 'robbed wholesale' and being 'ground down and persecuted'.[10]

The Ireland issue did not loom large until 1917. During the latter part of 1916, the Catholic press had criticised Britain's actions in suppressing the Dublin rising and had come out against conscription but nearly all the bishops had remained silent. The Archbishop of Perth had come out in favour of conscription and Mannix himself only twice entered the fray declaring that 'Australia had done enough'. In September Irish Catholics from the pro- and anti-conscriptionist camps could still join together to appeal for funds for Irish relief and to reaffirm the principle of Irish Home Rule.[11] When, however, Hughes and others blamed Irish Catholics for the defeat of conscription and accused them of disloyalty, the lines were drawn more sharply and Mannix responded in kind.

Thus in January 1917, perhaps emboldened by the 'No' victory, he – for the first time – attacked Britain's treatment of Ireland and cast doubt on Britain's motives in going to war. Opening a parish school at Brunswick, he declared that, though they had heard much about how the war was being fought for the rights of small nations, it was nevertheless 'simply a sordid trade

---

[8] The Irish National Association which had been established in 1915 in Sydney 'to assist Ireland to achieve her national destiny' never had more than 1500 members, and the Irish troubles of these years did little to increase the popularity of the association.

[9] Walter A. Ebsworth, *Archbishop Mannix* (Armadale: H.H. Stephenson, 1977), pp.76–89; *ADB*, Vol.XII, p.399.

[10] *Advocate*, 3 February 1917 and 23 June 1917.

[11] Gilbert, 'The Conscription Referenda 1916–17: The Impact of the Irish Crisis', pp.62–63; *SMH*, 5 September 1916.

war'. The phrase stung loyalists to the quick and they took it as a public confession of treason. In one sense Mannix – and this was a mark of his rhetorical cunning – was merely repeating Hughes's own statements that because Germany had attempted to conquer the British Empire through conquering world trade it would be necessary to prevent Germany from ever again challenging the Empire's commercial supremacy. But there can be no question that Mannix chose his words for the very purpose of suggesting Britain's hypocrisy and so taunting the race patriots.[12]

As attacks on anti-conscriptionists' loyalty mounted, Mannix became ever more outspoken and partisan. During the federal election campaign he cast doubt on Hughes's promise that, if returned to office, his 'Win-the-War' government would not attempt a further referendum on conscription without some extreme deterioration in the Allies' fortunes:

> As they previously said that conscription was necessary then they, if elected to power, would find the very ready excuse that conscription was still necessary and would put a referendum to the people again.

Mannix hoped 'it would not be found necessary to send any more troops from Australia either volunteers or conscripts.'[13]

By this time Mannix was asserting that Australians should put Australia first and was investing his campaign against the conscriptionists with an appeal to a supposed separate Australian loyalty. This appeal, however, was not based on anything that could be called Australian nationalism, whether of culture or interest. Mannix, like most anti-conscription leaders, never considered what would happen to Australia if Germany defeated the Allies. This debate over loyalty took place within a Britishness framework. The anti-conscriptionists did not have a distinctive Australian myth to put in the place of the British race story. In so far as Mannix tried to provide Irish Catholics with a separate national story it was not an Australian but an Irish one. But his audience, who were more fully Australian than Mannix, understood that this could never supplant the idea of Britishness. The loyalists in this sense were in an unassailable position. The clerical 'new chum' merely used 'Australia first', in this battle over loyalties, as a means of giving his people who felt themselves persecuted as workers and Catholics, seemingly respectable, even if implausible, grounds for challenging the Australian and British Governments' abuse of their war powers.[14]

---

[12] *Argus*, 29 January 1917. The Catholic *Advocate*, 3 February 1917 gave a more moderate version, namely 'The war was just like any other war – just an ordinary trade war.' Michael Gilchrist in *Daniel Mannix: Priest and Patriot* (Blackburn, Vic: Dove Communications, 1982), p.39 judges this to be an attempt to take some of the sting out of the offending words.

[13] *Argus*, 23 April 1917.

[14] In an early article dealing with the question of loyalty and conscription, Alan Gilbert argued that Mannix's idea of 'Australia first' inspired Irish Catholic resistance to conscription. Citing Emile Durkheim's notion that social change occurs when divergent ideals defining a society ('that which has the authority of tradition and that which has the hope of the future') confront one another, he sees in this political conflict 'incipient nationalism'. He sees in these appeals to 'Australia first' an 'incipient nationalism' that 'grew up alongside the imperial ideal'. Thus for him the struggle over ideas of society. symbolised by conscription, was one between an old Protestant Australia armed 'with the authority of tradition' which saw loyalty as

When in May Mannix succeeded Archbishop Carr as Archbishop of Melbourne, his new responsibilities in no way curbed his combative instincts. He became, if anything, more outspoken in challenging Australia's Protestant ascendancy, stressing the Irishness of Australian Catholics and defending the Irish cause against British oppression. In a panegyric sermon at St Patrick's Cathedral to honour his predecessor, Mannix attempted to give Australia's Irish Catholics an identity by giving them a history. It was 'the invincible, unconquerable Faith of the Irish exiles' that had, despite prejudice and persecution, established Catholicism in Australia and enabled it to flourish. A century later Irish Catholics were still denied their due place or proper influence in public and political life. They had 'resisted the temptation to accept the state Godless schools' and had been refused justice in education. Even as Irish Catholics became more Australian they could 'not afford to part with any of these inherited Irish qualities which have made us what we are.'[15]

The self-proclaimed guardians of the British faith were infuriated by these suggestions that Australians might have dual or alternative identities. Mannix's barbed shafts, which mocked those demanding an unquestioning allegiance to the British race, contributed further to the loyalists' belief that the country was being destroyed from within. As a result, they began to organise not only against the IWW and militant industrialists but also against the Irish Catholics. In July, a Protestant Federation was formed in Victoria and by November it had recruited 100,000 members.[16]

Though Hughes and the National Government were convinced that Mannix was a traitor who was subverting the loyalty of Irish Catholics and undermining Australia's war effort, they were at a loss to know how to handle him. Certainly some of Mannix's speeches were not very different from those of others who had been gaoled for prejudicing recruitment. The authorities

---

centred on Australia as an integral part of the British Empire and another championed by Irish Australians, who freed by their Irishness from the thrall of this tradition were able to look to the future 'by putting Australia first and the Empire second'. Gilbert, however, fails to show what was the substance or content of this supposed 'incipient nationalism'. See Gilbert, 'Protestants, Catholic and Loyalty: An Aspect of the Conscription Controversies 1916–17', *Politics*, 6 (May 1971), pp.24–25.

But this attempt to create a teleological Australian nationalism out of the conscription crisis and so to give the vague idea of Australian independence – which was beginning to take form at the time he was writing the article – a historical pedigree, neither fits with the way the Irish Australians responded to the notion of 'Australia first' at the time or the way their view of conscription and loyalty was understood in the intervening generations. Mannix himself in defining his own identity and that of Irish Australians did not put Australia first. He was intent on giving these Australians an Irish identity. In speaking in England in 1920 to an audience made up predominantly of Irish expatriates he used classical nationalist terms in defining himself. 'I was', he said 'an Irishman before I was an Archbishop, and I remain an Irishman today in spite of the fact that I am an Archbishop. If Ireland's cause is a just and holy and sacred cause, as I believe it to be then … the Irish people have a right to look to me … for something better than lip-service. For I am bone of their bone and flesh of their flesh.' Cited in Michael Gilchrist, *Daniel Mannix, Priest and Patriot*, p.97. Mannix never spoke in a similar way of the Australian people or nation.

[15] Ebsworth, *Archbishop Mannix*, pp.163–66.

[16] Alan D. Gilbert, 'Protestants, Catholics and Loyalty: An Aspect of the Conscription Controversies 1916–17', p.22.

could not, however, treat an Archbishop as they had the IWW and recalcitrant union leaders and haul him before a magistrate for transgressing WPA regulations. Consequently they turned to diplomacy, hoping, through the intervention of Rome, either to have him silenced or removed from Australia.

The Prime Minister therefore in July suggested to the British Government that 'Rome be asked exercise control over Cardinal [sic – probably a decoding error] Mannix lest trouble ensue as deserves internment.'[17] Hughes's hostility to Mannix derived not from anti-Catholicism as such but rather from Mannix's criticism of Britain and the British cause. It offended Hughes's British race religion. He had always supported 'Home Rule' for Ireland within the British Empire as a just solution to the problem. Mannix's seeming endorsement of the Sinn Fein and independence outside the Empire went beyond the pale, and his willingness to use any means, including the war itself, to achieve this made him and his following almost as dangerous as the syndicalist anarchists.

The British sympathised with the Australian request. A. J. Balfour, the British Foreign Secretary, thought that the Pope, in issuing his peace initiative on 1 August, was pro-German and working closely with the Austrians.[18] But the Foreign Office was still uncertain about how to respond to Hughes. The Foreign Office thought that Mannix's attitude was 'perhaps not worse than that of certain Bishops in Ireland', and it would 'not be easier for the Vatican to go for him than to go for the Irish Bishops.' Moreover, at the very time when they were considering the matter, Cardinal Bourne, the senior Roman Catholic prelate in England – than whom there was 'no one more competent to give advice on the best procedure' or 'be more helpful generally' – was absent from London. The English Catholic hierarchy did not share their Irish co-religionists' interest in Irish national independence. Thus, while awaiting Bourne's return, the British asked the Australian Government to forward more detailed evidence of Mannix's disloyal utterances and information about any action which might be taken against him – seeing in the latter a lever which might be used to prise concessions from Rome.[19]

There was no difficulty in furnishing the requested material. Since July Mannix had added to the catalogue of his sins. Hughes reported that he 'sympathises openly with Sinn Feinn [sic] and is himself its protagonist.' He endorsed the Pope's peace proposals 'mainly because they seem to hit Great Britain and to help Germany.' Not content with taking up Irish and Catholic causes, he also weakened Australia's war effort by backing striking workers, 'stirring up strife sectarian industrial class'. His intent was clear, that is 'to hamper recruiting … and prevent despatch of food etc, shipping to Britain and her Allies.' Hughes told Lloyd George that he was trying to make up his mind whether he should prosecute Mannix, 'a Sinn Feiner', for statements hindering recruitment or deport him. But by 4 September when formally replying to the British it would appear that he

---

[17] Cable, Munro Ferguson to Long, 15 July 1917, TNA: PRO CO418/158/323.

[18] French, *The Strategy of the Lloyd George Coalition*, p.143.

[19] Letter, P.F. Dormer, Foreign Office to A.F. Batterbee, Colonial Office, 10 August 1917, and copy of cable, Long to Munro Ferguson, 14 August 1917, TNA: PRO CO418/158/317–26.

had ruled out both possibilities. The government was reduced to seriously considering dismissing him from his post as Chaplain-General of the AIF.[20]

The British Government decided that they could no longer delay approaching the Vatican. Hughes's detailed account of Mannix's activities was accepted at face value. The Foreign Office agreed that Mannix's 'reputation as a Sinn Feiner is notorious in Catholic circles here too', and it decided to protest to Rome about the Archbishop of Melbourne's 'anti-British attitude'. Cardinal Bourne's representative had advised 'taking advantage' of the return of the Australian Apostolic Delegate, Monsignor Cerretti, to Rome to press the issue. It was thought that Cerretti would be helpful since on leaving Australia he had assured Munro Ferguson that he shared the government's disquiet about Mannix and intended to have the Vatican send Mannix 'a letter of reproof'.[21] The British Minister in Rome was instructed to ask the Vatican 'to induce the Archbishop to moderate his utterances' lest the Commonwealth Government should 'find it necessary to take action against him under the *Defence of the Realm* [sic – citing the British equivalent of the *War Precautions Act*] *Regulations*'.[22]

The revival of the conscription issue

While, however, the wheels of this three-cornered diplomacy continued to turn according to the laboured measure of its kind, the question of loyalty and disloyalty gained a new intensity with the revival of demands for conscription. The Nationalists had been returned to office on a 'Win-the-War' platform and, as such, recruitment policy was at the centre of their program. The government took as its minimal objective the maintenance of five AIF divisions.[23] Hughes announced on 29 June that Australia would need to raise 7000 men a month to keep the five divisions in the field. As Mannix was quick to point out this number was much less than the

---

[20] Letter, Hughes to Lloyd George, 17 August 1917, Lloyd George Papers, House of Lords Record Office F/28/2/2; cable, Munro Ferguson to Long, 4 September 1917, TNA: PRO CO418/159/12.

[21] Notes by C.F. Drummond to Lord Robert Cecil, 23 August and 11 September 1917, TNA: PRO FO 371/2994/162738 and 176152; despatch, Munro Ferguson to Long, 8 May 1917, TNA: PRO CO418/158/27.

[22] Copy of letter, W. Longley, Foreign Office to Count de Salis, British Minister to the Vatican, 20 September 1917 in letter, Long to Munro Ferguson, 29 September 1917, NAA, A1606/1 8C F42/1.

[23] Though Pearce and Birdwood, following the rejection of conscription in 1916, had agreed that a sixth division could not be formed, the British Army Council in February 1917, in their desperate search for men ('Operations of current year will be of supreme importance to ultimate issue of war'), asked the Australians to consider raising 'a sixth Australian Division' which, if ready to take the field by July, 'could be invaluable'. In contrast to the estimates given the previous August they now stated that only 11,500 men would be required each month to keep the existing five divisions up to strength and this figure included the recuperating sick and wounded. Pearce, despite his rejection of a sixth division following the defeat of the referendum, nevertheless urged Hughes to attempt to meet the Army Council's wishes. However the government, probably because of the election, seems to have decided against it. See cables Long to Munro Ferguson, 1 and 8 February 1917 and letter, Pearce to Hughes, 12 February 1917, Hughes Papers, NLA MS1538 20/277–78.

16,500 specified at the time of the conscription referendum,[24] and by implication he threw doubt on the new target.

Well might Mannix be suspicious. It would appear that in May the Army Council, responding to an Australian request, had stated that the minimum reinforcements required to maintain the five divisions at full strength was only 20,000 men for five months or, as the Governor-General noted, less than a third of the August 1916 estimate. According to the Colonial Office, what the Army Council sought was '5000 a month for three months – June to August – and 2500 for the last two months [that is, October and November]'. Why then did the government set 7000 as the necessary level of reinforcements? Certainly the Governor-General found the Army Council's figures embarrassing. He feared that, if they became public knowledge, it would put 'an additional damper on recruiting and render impossible the resurrection of any idea of national service'.[25] Almost certainly the government shared Munro Ferguson's concerns. It might even be surmised that they could not allow the voluntary system to be seen to be satisfactorily serving the needs of the Empire since such a view would make nonsense of their rationale for the conscription campaign and the 'Win-the-War' government. Furthermore they believed that Australia should do more than simply reinforce its existing divisions. 'Loyalty', as they had defined it, required that Australia should be made to feel guilty for refusing to accept conscription for the cause of empire. Arguments about the fate of Britain and Australia, should the Allies be defeated, no longer entered into the considerations underpinning recruitment policy.

Not surprisingly, the government's inflated target was never reached. Even with the increased moral and material suasion brought to bear on the eligibles – for example, the agreement by Sydney's major retail stores to sack all 'shirkers'[26] – the number of enlistments rather than growing, fell away, declining to 2460 in September and 2761 in October. Not only were the workingmen made jobless by the great strike unwilling to heed the government's call, but also many conscriptionists refused to cooperate with the voluntary system, regarding it as morally bankrupt. In September, when the Queensland Premier, T. J. Ryan, an avowed anti-conscriptionist, took part in a recruiting rally in Brisbane, he was heckled by conscriptionists who broke up the meeting.[27]

Against this background of industrial strife, Irish Catholic assertiveness and the seeming failure of the voluntary principle, conscriptionist sentiment revived and the more fanatical loyalists began to organise for the purpose of forcing the government's hand. Though those who assumed leadership of the movement made passing reference to the difficulties on the Eastern Front and the disorder in Russia, their arguments were not primarily strategic. Indeed, the campaign had taken off well before the Bolshevik Revolution and even before the press began to report that the Central Powers had achieved 'a startling success' at Caporetto in Italy. They emphasised the duty that Australians owed the Empire and the troops at the front and how

---

[24] *SMH*, 30 June 1917.
[25] Letter, personal and confidential, Munro Ferguson to Long, 4 June 1917 and note, H. Lambert, Colonial Office, to Long, 20 August 1917, Long Papers, WRO 947/624.
[26] *SMH*, 9 July 1917.
[27] D.J. Murphy, *T.J. Ryan* (St Lucia: University of Queensland Press 1975), p.279.

shameful it was that Australia had refused to follow the example of the United Kingdom, New Zealand, Canada and the United States and adopt conscription. In the middle of October, at the first public meeting called for the purpose, the speakers made the case that the failure of voluntarism 'put into peril our gallant fellow-countrymen at the front and the performance of our duty to the Empire at large.'[28] This second campaign for conscription would seem to have been primarily motivated by the desire of the loyalists to impose their sense of duty to the British race on the domestic enemy, both open and hidden.

The call for a second referendum was accompanied by a more virulent attack on disloyalty of every stripe. Not only were steps taken against striking trade unionists and dissident Irish Catholics but also against those of German origin. As Gerhard Fischer has pointed out it was at this very time that the persecution of German residents, naturalised Germans and Australians of German extraction reached its height.[29] These German-Australians, unlike the Irish Catholics and trade union leaders, had not criticised Britain or the British Empire's war aims. It was enough that the blood of the enemy should flow in their veins. In this atmosphere of frustration and hysteria, the Anti-German League, many of whose members were also involved in the new call for conscription, held a monster meeting at the Sydney Town Hall for the purpose of reducing 'to a state of impotence ... the immense power of evil of the enemy within our midst'. The very well-attended gathering decided to approach the Commonwealth to seek protection for their life and property from 'attacks by enemies and disloyalists'. Despite the fact that no substantial evidence was produced to show how the loyalists' life and property were threatened, their proceedings carried considerable weight. The Acting Premier expressed his sympathy for the objects of the meeting and Sir Joseph Carruthers, a former premier, moved the main resolution.[30]

A few days later a deputation, led by Carruthers, waited upon the Minister for Defence and urged him not only to disenfranchise naturalised Germans but also Australian-born citizens of German parentage. They were of the same mind as the Prime Minister in believing that naturalisation was 'merely a cloak to hide their deeds'. Among a number of cases of German-Australians who, despite complaints to military intelligence, were still at large, they singled out Edmund Resch, the founder of Resch's brewery, who was alleged to have made it possible for a Mr Agar Wald to secure a licence for a Sydney hotel frequented by Germans and who, it was rumoured, had been heard 'slinging off at British and Australian statesmanship'.[31] Pearce was almost embarrassed by the enthusiasm of the ultra-loyalists, but he promised that the government would seriously consider disenfranchising all Australians of German origin. Shortly afterwards Resch, an almost blind 71 year old man who had contributed generously to patriotic funds and

---

[28] *SMH*, 19 October 1917. See also the supporting editorial, 'these obligations are owing to the men at the front, to this country and to the Empire as a whole', *SMH*, 20 October 1917.

[29] Gerhard Fischer, *Enemy Aliens: Internment and the Homefront Experience in Australia 1914–1920* (St Lucia: University of Queensland Press, 1989), p.130.

[30] *SMH*, 29 October 1917.

[31] 'Record of Meeting of Minister for Defence with Australian Anti-German League (New South Wales Branch)' on 2 November 1917, NAA A2/1 17/4096 Part 2.

whose firm had encouraged its employees to enlist and was supplementing the military pay of sixty employees, was arrested and interned.[32]

Yet, as the Anti-German League itself acknowledged, the German question was only one part and that not the most important part of the problem of disloyalty. Indeed the Lord Mayor of Sydney had suggested that the League transform itself into a National Vigilance League in order to create a state-wide body of loyal citizens who would be 'banded together to take observations of and to report to the authorities any suspicious movements of the people.' Similarly in their conference with the minister the deputation had made it clear that they 'aimed at the suppression of all disloyal people'.

With the crushing of the eastern states' strike and the gaoling of the IWW members, the conscriptionists recognised Mannix and the Irish Catholics as their most formidable enemies. Mannix was considered to represent the twin evils of the Sinn Fein and the IWW, and many thought of him, in the words of Robert Gordon Menzies, a young Melbourne law graduate, as 'a cunning, sinister and national menace'.[33] No stone should be left unturned in order to limit his influence. When, therefore, the Loyal Orange Institution and the Protestant Alliance Friendly Society learnt that Mannix was to be the keynote speaker at an Irish independence demonstration to be held in Melbourne's Exhibition Hall on 5 November, they – with the backing of the Victorian Premier, the city's Lord Mayor, the *Age* and the *Argus* – prevailed upon the trustees of the hall to withdraw their permission.[34]

The organisers of the demonstration, however, rose to the challenge. The sponsors, the Young Ireland Society, joined by other Irish Catholic bodies, persuaded John Wren, a wealthy Catholic who had risen from the back lanes of working class Collingwood to become a gambling and horse-racing magnate, to offer the Richmond racecourse as an alternative venue. Loyalist persecution was greatly resented, and an enormous crowd – variously estimated at from 30 to 100,000 – turned out to bear witness to their community's solidarity and to honour their hero. It was reported that when Mannix appeared the roar of approval that went up from the crowd resounded throughout all the surrounding suburbs.

Mannix made the most of his moral position. Deeply affected by the treatment meted out to his people, he replied in kind, for the first time unequivocally identifying himself with Sinn Fein and Irish independence. He castigated those who called on Australia to rush to the rescue of small nations but wished to stifle any discussion of the wrongs of Ireland. Ireland's scars, he said, were 'deeper than Belgium's scars'. The condition of Ireland was 'a reproach and standing disgrace to the British Empire'. He declared that men and women of Irish extraction everywhere were tired of being told to be patient, and he urged the Irish people to exploit the opportunity of the war. His own advice 'would be to say, "Now or never"'. Casting aspersions on Britain's good faith, he assured his listeners that if the Irish could not obtain their goal during the war they would have 'very faint hope of getting it when England has got out of her present difficulty'.

---

[32] *SMH*, 27 November 1917; NAA A3201 TE1372.
[33] Letter, Menzies to F. Corder, 18 September 1917, quoted in Gilchrist, *Daniel Mannix: Priest and Patriot*, p.49.
[34] *Age* and *Argus*, 27–31 October 1917, and *Argus*, 1 November 1917.

The immediate occasion for the demonstration was the British Government's attempt to find a solution to the Irish question through a Convention which, though ostensibly made up of representatives of all parties – British and Irish, Catholic and Protestant – excluded the Sinn Fein. Mannix was very scathing of this British initiative. He thought it was merely a sop to America – 'the price, or part of the price that America made them [the British] pay for coming into the war'. He did not expect anything to come of it. The Convention did not represent Ireland. The British had been driven to this expedient by 'the driving power of the Convention' which was located 'out in the country, on the hillside of Ireland.' With this remark Mannix aligned himself with the Sinn Fein which desired that 'Ireland should be ruled by Irishmen according to Irish eyes and the interests of Ireland.' He believed that Australians would sympathise with these Irish aspirations since they too were Sinn Feiners and, like the Irish, put their own country first and the Empire second. The Sinn Feiners sought to 'wrest from English hands the government of their country and to set up in Ireland a government with Irish ideals and for Irish interests.' As a result of the martyrdom of the Easter week rebels 'a new soul had entered her body.' Ireland stood 'erect, more self-reliant, more nation-like than before'. Ireland should not be cut into pieces to please an unworthy and disloyal faction in Ulster. Sinn Fein properly laid claim to the whole of Ireland.[35] Ironically Mannix was seeking for the Catholic majority in Ireland the same right to define loyalty for the Protestant minority that the Protestant ascendancy in Australia were claiming for themselves in relation to the Irish Catholic community. Neither side evinced much tolerance for the other. Once the drawbridge had been pulled up no quarter was asked or given.

Mannix's words and the great reception he had received at the demonstration elicited even more savage Protestant and Loyalist denunciations. The *Argus* described Mannix as 'an arrogant Irish ecclesiastic, openly vaunting his disloyalty in the most intensely loyal dominion.'[36] In Sydney an enthusiastic meeting was held to form a League of Loyalty to combat Mannix and all his works. The chairman, in opening proceedings, considered it strange that Mannix was still at large. 'Where', he asked, 'was the justice of committing John Jones to prison for expressing IWW sentiments, and permitting a man like Archbishop Mannix to go scot free (Applause).' The Rev. J. L. Rentoul, master of Ormond College within the University of Melbourne and Presbyterian Chaplain-General to the AIF, assured his listeners that Victorians were 'not a bit afraid of Archbishop Mannix'. He refuted Mannix's claim to speak for Ireland. Rentoul was an Irish migrant and was as much an Irishman as Mannix. Irish farmers were prospering as never before but 'the Irish priests would not allow them to fight for the flag that sheltered them.' He urged conscription as the only means of ensuring that all did their duty by the Empire. Loyal Australians must demand of their 'Win-the-War' government that it act: 'Nothing could win the war except

---

[35] *Argus*, 6 November 1917; Catholic *Tribune*, 8 November 1917.

It would appear that there was some substance to Mannix's charge that the British Government saw the Irish Convention simply as a public relations exercise intended to appease the United States and the Dominions. See letter, Maurice Hankey, Secretary to the British War Cabinet, to J. St Loe Strachey, 2 August 1917, cited in John Turner, *British Politics and the Great War*, pp.243–44.

[36] *Argus*, 7 November 1917.

conscription ... If the Government declares for conscription the nation will surely rise behind it (Applause).'[37] This was the loyalist answer to Mannix and his ilk.

On the very next day, 7 November, the Prime Minister announced that the government would hold a second referendum to seek the people's approval for the introduction of conscription.[38]

Hughes and his senior ministers had not reached their decision easily. They had grave doubts about the wisdom of this course. Certainly until the middle of October, Hughes had thought that any attempt to revive conscription would have been impractical, even counter-productive. In August, when the British had pleaded for more Australian reinforcements and hinted at the desirability of conscription, Hughes had replied that 'to make the desired change at present would under existing domestic conditions be most unwise.'[39] What told against conscription was not so much the great strike in the eastern states or Mannix's hugely popular meetings as the belief that no new appeal to the people was likely to be successful. Moreover, Hughes, recognising the importance of the injection of American forces onto the battle field, probably agreed with the Governor-General's judgment that 'It would take nearly a year to get troops for the field in appropriate numbers' and by that time the war would be over. If such were the case, then it was doubtful whether it would be 'worthwhile to throw the country into turmoil'. The Prime Minister told Munro Ferguson that he would only feel bound to try to carry conscription again if the British War Cabinet insisted that there was an urgent need for men. As late as 13 October Hughes remained convinced that conscription was 'quite impossible'. He conceded that 'Australia had lost her great opportunity for spiritual regeneration.'[40] Hughes at this point had seemingly lost faith in his country and its willingness to do its duty by the Empire.

The other members of the government voiced similar doubts and misgivings. Millen, Minister for Repatriation, commented on the New South Wales conscriptionists' plan to collect 100,000 signatures for a petition, that it would be of 'no avail' since 356,000 from that state had voted 'No' in the previous year. Navy Minister Cook, under pressure from interjectors at a public meeting, maintained that since the people had already rejected compulsion 'the way at present is full of difficulty', and he added that the available shipping could not handle the large numbers of volunteers who were awaiting embarkation for Europe. Pearce, facing the same demands at public meetings, 'even expressed the opinion that the voluntary system had not had a fair show, owing to the disturbing effect of the strike.'[41] As practical politicians they suspected that the people were no more inclined to support conscription in 1917 than they had been in 1916, and that a second campaign followed by a second rebuff would undermine the government's authority and possibly bring it down.

Why then did the government set aside its better judgment and call a second referendum? The answer is not to be found in either of the triggers named by Hughes at the time of the May

---

[37] *SMH*, 7 November 1917.
[38] *SMH*, 8 November 1917.
[39] Copy of cable, Munro Ferguson to Long, 27 August 1917, Pearce Papers, AWM 3DRL 2222/3/3.
[40] Novar Diary, 26 September and 14 October 1917, Novar Papers, NLA MS 696/36. See also despatch, private and personal, Munro Ferguson to Long, 5 October 1917, Novar Papers NLA MS 696/968.
[41] *SMH*, 26 and 31 October and 1 November 1917.

general election, that is a marked deterioration in the Allies' strategic position or the British insistence on the urgent need for reinforcements. Rather it was the mounting pressure from within the National Party's own ranks which forced his hand. By early November the government could not but be impressed by the rapid growth of the pro-conscription agitation. When giving public addresses, ministers were being harassed by their own people. By 31 October the New South Wales branch of the Universal Service League had thrown its weight behind Sir William Irvine's call to the government to dissolve the House of Representatives and to go to the people on the sole issue of conscription.[42] Associated with this there was a plot to oust Hughes from the leadership of the party.[43] The pressures were so great that Hughes had to interrupt a holiday and summon a cabinet meeting where his ministers agreed that if they did not bend before the storm they might lose control of the government. Just as domestic electoral considerations had at first held them back so domestic party considerations ultimately forced them to act. Hughes on 7 November when explaining the decision to Murdoch stated that 'the fate of the Government hangs in the balance.'[44]

This time, in taking charge of the 'Yes' campaign, Hughes stressed less the strategic imperative and more the need to be true to the British race and to compel national loyalty. In a speech at Bendigo on 12 November where he outlined the government's proposal, he went through all the forms of arguing the case in strategic terms. He maintained that the condition which he had earlier laid down for calling a second referendum had been met, namely the tide of battle turning decisively against the Allies. It was his view that 'never since the war began has the position been graver.' During the previous two weeks, the collapse on the Russian front and the retreat of the Italian army had produced such a reversal in the Allies' fortunes that the government felt justified in seeking approval for conscription in order to keep Australia's five divisions in the field. Hughes further claimed that, in reaching this conclusion, he spoke with all the authority of 'a member of the Imperial War Cabinet' to whom all the information at its disposal was communicated.[45]

There is no reason, however, to believe that the strategic argument was any more persuasive for the government than it was for those who had revived the conscription issue. Firstly there is no extant record of Hughes receiving any intelligence appreciation, which suggested that the Allies faced the gravest military crisis of the war.[46] Secondly, in evaluating the strains being placed upon the Allies by the Italian collapse at Caporetto and Russia's possible withdrawal from the war,

---

[42] *SMH*, 1 November 1917.
[43] Letter, Deane to James Barrett, 4 January 1918, Barrett Papers, Melbourne University Archives. Deane wrote that 'a certain gang of politicians were at the time launching a big conspiracy to "out" Prime Minister Hughes'. Deane had 'got wise to it, and aware of its extent, by a proposition made to me quietly in the form of a "feeler".'
[44] Letter, Murdoch to Birdwood, 7 November 1917, Birdwood Papers, AWM 3DRL 3376/27.
[45] *SMH*, 13 November 1917.
[46] Memorandum, Pearce to Hughes, 10 November 1917, Hughes Papers, NLA MS 1538/20/324. Pearce in summarising the arguments for conscription made his case exclusively on the grounds of the numbers of enlistments necessary to keep the existing five divisions in the field. Should Australia fail to do this the only adverse consequence would be the 'great disappointment and bitter feeling among the troops'.

he failed to take into account the massive American reinforcements that would reach the Western Front before any Australian conscript could arrive. By the summer of 1918 the number of American forces expected in France would more than match any advantage that Germany gained by the withdrawal of Russia from the war. Moreover, since at the time of the Australian Government's decision to hold the referendum the Bolshevik revolution had not occurred, Hughes could not know what the future role of Russia in the war might be.[47]

Once they had cast the die, Hughes and his ministers, sharing as they did the frustrations and resentments of those who had initiated the movement, treated the referendum as a plebiscite over loyalty which would empower the government to discipline the disloyal. Hughes set the tone for his side and concentrated on the issues of loyalty and subversion. In his opening address the Russian and Italian reverses were attributed to internal enemies akin to Australia's own. In Russia a revolutionary government 'composed of just that type who tried to secure the reins of government in Australia, who were responsible for the recent strike, who are enemies of the Empire', had seized power. It was these very same elements in the ranks of labour, 'Dreamers, theorists, anarchists, pro-Germans', who had gained control of the government and stabbed the Allies in the back. Similarly in Italy:

> They, upon whom Italy relied, betrayed her. Treachery, mark that word, and apply it to our own circumstances. The agents of Germany within the gates of Italy, and not the valour of German arms, brought about the Italian debacle. As it had been in Russia and in every one of the Allied countries, it is in Italy an insidious propaganda worming itself into the very fibres of the Italian people, playing upon their prejudices, their ignorance, fostering class hatred, using Italian socialism as a tool to destroy Italian liberty. A campaign of lies whispered in the ears of people about Britain, about France, peace notes inspired from Berlin, all these had done their deadly work in Italy.

Hughes was warning that the same forces which had wreaked such havoc in Russia and Italy were also at work sapping the morale of Australian society.

Indeed Hughes asserted that it was these very forces which were responsible for the failure of voluntary recruiting. He averred that the voluntary principle had not produced the required numbers 'because of a systematic campaign of poisonous doctrines insidiously disseminated throughout the country.' Though those responsible for purveying such doctrines were still the unholy trinity of Germans, IWW radicals and Sinn Feiners, it was the Sinn Feiners rather than the IWW who in 1917 were the chief villains in the moral drama. The Sinn Fein was a 'sinister and disloyal' movement that sought an independent Ireland. It openly avowed its hatred of Britain and the British Empire, and 'gloats over every success by Germany'. Mannix's assertion that Australians were 'Sinn Feiners' was an insult to the men of the AIF who had 'gone forth to battle for the Empire'.[48]

---

[47] *SMH*, 10 November 1917. This contains the first report of the Bolshevik revolution. Hughes, in commenting on the report, said that 'it seems to be pregnant with even more possibilities than the Italian debacle', and he hoped that 'later communications may qualify the disquieting news.'
[48] *SMH*, 12 November 1917.

Acutely aware of the difficulties in his way Hughes this time was more cunning in devising the proposal which was put to the people and more ruthless in dealing with his opponents.

The conscription scheme was much more modest than that put forward in 1916. It was intended to keep intact the majority that had voted the 'Win-the-War' government into office in May. The monthly reinforcement target was set at 7000, which was 9500 less than that of 1916, though 2000 more than either the Army Council in June or Legge, the Chief of the General Staff, in October had sought. The government would only conscript single men and then only enough to make up the numbers of voluntary recruits to the required figure.[49] In contrast to 1916 the government offered liberal exemptions for workers in essential industries. Furthermore, to ensure that the disloyal and the shirkers bore the brunt, the first call for conscripts was to fall upon those families who had not sent a volunteer to the front. Trying even more directly to lock in the National Party's electoral majority, Hughes pledged the very existence of his government to the cause. He stated that he would not be able to govern without the power to conscript and he would not attempt to do so.[50]

Since the government identified conscription with loyalty they had no scruples about using the machinery of state against their opponents. Hughes was adamant that the disloyal should be made to submit:

> I say to them the sun shall move from its course, the heavens may be o'erturned, but so sure as God lives and we are here tonight, they shall do their duty.[51]

This justified employing whatever expedient was necessary for the purpose. Australians of German extraction were a natural target. Against the background of the Anti-German League's representations the Commonwealth Statistician, who had during the 1916 referendum denounced German-Australians as enemies of the British race, wrote Hughes that:

> Whether naturalised or not, the average German is so strongly pro-German that he *cannot* (and in many cases his children cannot) give a patriotic (Australian) vote on 'conscription' or any other 'defence question'.[52]

---

[49] On 8 October 1917 Legge had told his minister that Australia would need to despatch 4650 reinforcements each month to keep the AIF in France and Palestine up to strength. Since 8–10 percent of recruits for various reasons never left for overseas, he advised that the government's reasonable recruiting target should be 5000. Copy of report, Legge to Pearce, 8 October 1917, L.E. Groom Papers, NLA MS 236/2/1811–12.

Apparently on 18 and 29 October the government had received cable messages from, respectively, the Army Council and General Birdwood which stated that the number of reinforcements required each month to maintain the AIF at existing strength was 6100. Adding 10 percent to cover those enlistees who never reached Europe Pearce concluded that the monthly recruitment target was 6710, and 'therefore the figure of 7000 fixed by the government is essential to keep the units up to strength'. Memorandum, Pearce to Hughes, 10 November 1917, Hughes Papers, NLA MS 1538/20/324. I was unable to find any copies of these cables in the Pearce papers, or in the Defence Department or British War Council files.

[50] *SMH*, 13 November 1917.

[51] *Argus*, 11 December 1917.

[52] Letter, Knibbs to Hughes, 7 November 1917, Hughes Paper, NLA MS 1538/20/310.

Agreeing with this sentiment the government issued a WPA regulation disenfranchising not only naturalised citizens of enemy origin but also native-born Australians whose fathers were born in enemy countries, exemptions only being allowed for those that had proved their loyalty by serving in the AIF or by having half their sons in the AIF.[53]

The Prime Minister also used the government's secret service to spy upon the 'No' campaigners, and he widened the censorship net to ban statements which were deemed to be false or misleading as well as those considered prejudicial to recruiting or offensive to allies. Since the government was the judge of all such statements, no 'Yes' utterance – no matter how deceitful or divisive – was ever censored. Resident censors were placed only in the offices of the anti-conscription press.

The Queensland Labor Government, the only anti-conscriptionist government in the country, was subject to the most unconscionable exercise of these powers. Premier Ryan, an inheritor of the Fisher tradition, openly espoused the British cause and spared no effort in encouraging voluntary recruitment. He attacked conscription not only as an abuse of government authority, but also as a divisive measure which impaired the nation's ability to aid the Empire.

Ryan found himself in trouble when at a public meeting in Brisbane he argued, from published official statistics, that, if the AIF required 7000 men each month, then, without taking into account future voluntary recruitment, there already existed over a year's supply of reinforcements available from troops in Europe and Australia, and therefore the grounds advanced in defence of conscription were spurious. The censor not only refused to allow Ryan's speech to be published in full but also cut it so as to make it appear that he favoured conscription. Ryan defiantly read out the forbidden extracts in the Queensland Legislative Assembly, included them in Hansard and printed several thousand copies of his speech for distribution. On learning of this ruse the censor seized one batch at the post office. Hughes, who happened to be in Brisbane at the time, led a small raiding party of soldiers and censors to take possession of the remaining copies from the government printer. When Ryan took up Hughes's challenge and repeated his words outside parliament, Hughes had Ryan charged with breaching the WPA regulation which made it an offence to publish misleading information. Since the prosecutor at Ryan's trial had to admit that the Labor leader had based his case on official figures the magistrate had no choice but to dismiss the case. Nevertheless this bizarre persecution of Ryan exemplified the intimidatory malice with which the National Government pursued anti-conscriptionists. They would not concede that on such an issue as conscription there could be a loyal opposition.[54]

---

[53] *SMH*, 7 December 1917.

[54] Murphy, *T.J. Ryan*, pp.313–36.

See also for a suggestion that the Queensland Cabinet considered using the police and, if necessary, armed trade unionists, to resist further Commonwealth interference with the right of the state parliament to publish, uncensored, its proceedings, Evans, *Loyalty and Disloyalty*, pp.106–09.

Fitzhardinge's judgment that 'censorship was applied more strictly to the opponents of the proposals than to their supporters ... but there is no evidence that Hughes himself was responsible' is a grotesque distortion. No pro-conscriptionists' statements are known to have been substantively censored. On the evidence there is a very good case to be made that Hughes's explanation of reinforcement numbers was false and misleading, certainly a much better case than that made against Ryan But no censor ever

Yet though Ryan emerged from the incident as the nationally recognised leader of the 'No' campaign, it was Mannix who was perceived as the more dangerous and radical spokesman for that side of the referendum issue. For the conscriptionists he was a much more rewarding target. Unlike Ryan, Mannix neither stressed his commitment to the British cause nor called for volunteers to come forward. Mannix threw himself into the campaign, and in the battle over conscription found an outlet for his hostility towards the 'Win-the-War' patriots and their attitude to Catholic education. In expressing his revulsion at the British treatment of Ireland, he went far beyond Ryan and maintained that Australia had done its share: 'it was nonsense to say that Australia had not done enough.'[55]

Once more he made the point that Australians should not be asked to sacrifice everything for the Empire. They should, like the Irish, put their country first. He had no hesitation in raising, in language not unlike Hughes's but adapted for the anti-conscription purpose, the Asian danger to White Australia: 'The sun never sets upon the Empire, with its many-coloured races. But we, a handful of whites in a huge continent, insist on a White Australia policy. Our Coloured fellow-citizens of the Empire ask for an entry. But no, not even for the Empire's sake do we lift the embargo.' Similarly he alluded, in a suitably disguised manner, to the military threat of Japan: 'There are enemies nearer to Australia than Germany, and the day may not be too far distant when Australians will be required to defend their own interests at home.'[56]

Finally, Mannix repeated his doubts about Britain's motives. While Britain was justified in going to war to save Belgium or to protect itself, it ought not to be supported if its aim, as the Prime Minister hinted, was 'the economic domination of the world'.[57] If Britain was so concerned about the rights of small nations, 'How was it that a certain small nation could not get justice from that power?' He suggested that the time might have come 'to get out of the war' and to seek through the Pope's good offices a compromise peace. Moreover, by casting doubt on the binding nature of a 'Yes' majority, should that be the result, he seemed to be inciting civil disobedience.

All this was grist to Hughes's conspiratorial mill. Mannix enraged the loyalists in a way that Ryan could never do. Hughes, replying to the Archbishop's charge that he was the country's 'greatest sectarian', castigated Mannix for allegedly declaring that 'if he were to have his way there

---

considered that question. Fitzhardinge's further assertion that Hughes's regulation forbidding 'dissemination of falsehoods calculated to deceive the electors' was in itself not unreasonable is equally partisan (Fitzhardinge, *The Little Digger*, p.297). Who was to decide what was a falsehood? Political controversies such as those surrounding conscription necessarily involve conflicts about the interpretation as well as the truth of information. The censors were the creatures of the conscriptionists. That one side should be in a position to determine what should be censored made a mockery of freedom of speech and fair play in the referendum campaign and served to harden further the bitter divisions which were bedevilling the country.

[55] *Argus*, 9 and 29 November 1917.

[56] Ebsworth, *Archbishop Mannix*, pp.194 and 209. In 1916 he had been even more explicit on this point: 'A Certain Oriental Power, that we one day must surely fight, is finding Australia a happy hunting ground, and is dumping goods of every kind into our warehouses in prodigious quantity. The same money is probably building up warboats against Australia's day.'

[57] *Argus*, 12 November 1917.

would be no Protestants in Australia.'[58] As the campaign hysteria gathered pace the more militant Protestants attacked Mannix, and pro-conscription meetings passed resolutions condemning 'disloyal and seditious utterances of prelates of the Roman Catholic Church' and urged the government to take whatever steps might be necessary to suppress them.[59]

Hughes regretted that Mannix's status as a leader of a major Christian church prevented the government from taking action against him. Hughes had thought of refusing to allow the Catholic leader to be issued with the formal commission appointing him a Chaplain-General to Australia's military forces. On 25 October the Defence Department had sent the nominees of the four major denominations to the Governor-General. When a month later the department urged that the commissions 'be completed at the earliest possible date' the Governor-General forwarded those for the Protestant churches but explained that, at the Prime Minister's behest, Mannix's was being held over. After the Defence Department explained that a conference of the Protestant churches had agreed the chaplains-general should be appointed on the recommendations of their governing bodies and that the Roman Catholic bishops had nominated Mannix, Hughes was forced to give in and allow the appointment to proceed.[60] It was galling for the Prime Minister who had to content himself with denouncing Mannix as a representative of disloyal elements and an enemy of Britain. In Brisbane on 25 November Hughes declared that Mannix was 'the spokesman of Sinn Fein' who encouraged Irish people to take advantage of England's difficulties 'to stab her in the back'.[61]

The second referendum campaign took place in a highly charged atmosphere. The lines between the two parties were more settled and clear cut than had been the case in 1916. From the outset, the protagonists had not shown any interest in debating rationally the cases for and against conscription. Both sides resorted to simple slogans. The 'anti' groups in response to the pro-conscriptionists' cries of honour, duty and loyalty declared that what was sought would bring about the triumph of militarism, the end of unionism and the destruction of 'White Australia'. How Australia would fare if Germany won the war was little discussed. The 'anti's' still cited Japan as an issue. But this time the censorship was more efficient and intelligence agents attending 'anti' meetings ensured that any adverse comments on Japan were not published in the press. Since 1916 J. H. Catts had made the fear of Japan his major argument against conscription. While on a tour through northern New South Wales he spoke again and again of the 'deadly menace of Japan' to White Australia, of Japan's attempt during the war to dominate China, of the Japanese people's pro-German sympathies and their belief that Germany would win the war.[62] Indeed Catts's persistence caused Hughes to tighten up the WPA regulation forbidding adverse references to Allies since 'the present position is such that an insult to Japan might send her over to the other

---

[58] *Argus*, 21 November 1917.

[59] *Argus*, 27 November 1917; *SMH*, 2 and 20 November, 3 and 19 December 1917.

[60] Letters, Acting Secretary of Defence Department to Secretary, Prime Minister's Department, 23 November and 6 December 1917, NAA A1606/1 SC F42/1.

[61] *Argus*, 30 November 1917.

[62] Copy of a military intelligence officer's account of Catts's speech at Armidale, New South Wales, 20 November 1917, enclosed in letter, E.L. Piesse, Director of Military Intelligence to James Murdoch, 5 June 1918, NAA A2219, Vol.1, Pt.2.

side and so utterly destroy us.'[63] Hughes shared Catts's suspicions of Japan, but recognised that it was impolitic to allow such views to be aired; not only would they antagonise an ally but they also would give powerful support to the anti-conscription cause.

The heightened feelings led to mutual intolerance and organised efforts to break up opponent's meetings. When the 'pro's' sang 'Red, White and Blue', the 'anti's' would reply with 'Solidarity Forever' – the latter never found a distinctive Australian song with which to counter their detractors' charge of disloyalty to the British Empire, and indeed no such generally accepted song was available. Retaliating against conscriptionists attempts, often through the agency of returned soldiers, to silence those who dared to defy what loyalty demanded, anti-conscriptionists began to disrupt pro-conscriptionists' demonstrations. By the end of the campaign the 'anti's' had gained the upper hand. At a grand conscriptionist rally at the Melbourne Cricket Ground on 10 December which attracted 100,000 people, the 'anti' groups turned out in force, assailed the speakers with eggs, rocks, blue metal and other missiles, and forced the conscriptionists to withdraw from two of the three platforms.[64] By contrast when Ryan arrived in Sydney on 15 December to address the final 'No' meeting he was greeted by a crowd of 100,000 to 200,000 who cheered him on his way as he processed to the Domain where they hailed him as their hero.[65]

Social tensions had reached a dangerous level but the animosities thereby created never erupted into murderous oppression or bloody revolution. The violence was kept within understood limits. No-one was killed. The police, for the most part, acted with restraint and even-handedness in trying to protect the rights of both parties to free speech and free assembly. Much to the surprise of the authorities the voting on polling day took place in a peaceful and orderly manner.

The referendum results confirmed the worst fears of Hughes and his ministers. The 'No' majority in a turn out of almost 2,200,000 voters was 166,588 or 94,112 greater than in 1916. In all states except South Australia where the 'No' tally fell by approximately 13,000 – probably as a result of the disenfranchisement of German-Australians – the anti-conscriptionist vote had risen and Victoria moved across to join the ranks of the 'No' states. As Hughes had surmised, the National Party's victory in the May election had not meant a change of heart by those conservatives who had voted against conscription in 1916. Moreover, on this occasion, it was more difficult to show that the British Empire was facing defeat, and Hughes's promises about the limits on numbers and the exemptions of individuals were more suspect. Probably, even more than in 1916, there was a reaction to the government's heavy-handed and discriminatory treatment of its opponents. At the least such authoritarianism must have strengthened popular concerns about the conscriptionists' intent and their promise of liberal exemptions. On this occasion also since the conscriptionists did not raise White Australia or Japan it is probable that

---

[63] Copy, cable, Sydney censor to Deputy Chief Censor, Melbourne, 22 November 1917, plus Pearce's note recommending reference of Catts's behaviour to Hughes and the possibility of prosecution, 28 November 1917, Hughes Papers, NLA MS 1538/21/86–87, and Dorothy M. Catts, *James Howard Catts* (Sydney: Ure Smith, 1953), pp.77–79 and 202–08.

[64] *Argus*, 11–12 December 1917. For further examples of attempts to break up meetings, see *Argus*, 17, 22, 26, 27, 29 November and 1, 4, 5–8, 10, 11, 13, 18–20 December 1917.

[65] *SMH*, 17 December 1917.

Australia's Pacific peril counted more decisively for the 'anti's'. Keith Murdoch, in trying to explain why the AIF, like the rest of Australia, had shown less enthusiasm for conscription in 1917 than in 1916, told General Birdwood that:

> It should be recognised, although it is not pleasant, that Australia and Australians do not and cannot feel the same towards the war as Englishmen. They are prepared to go on helping all they can, but the instincts of self-preservation and all the old frontier feelings which fire the English in this war do not come into it as regards the Australians ... They have nearly all been away from home now for two years or more, striving against an enemy who is not to them nearly as great an object of enmity and dread as the Japanese.[66]

Defeat of the second referendum and the loyalists' revenge

The conscriptionists, even as they resigned themselves to the outcome, refused to accept the people's verdict. If anything their moral indignation was greater after the 1917 defeat. Once again the respectability, the parsons, professors and professionals, had lent their prestige to the cause. It was for them a transcendent crusade, even more a vindication of British civilisation in Australia than a *sine qua non* for the survival of Britain and Australia. The failure of the masses to endorse their betters' judgment could only be explained away as the 1916 result itself had often been explained away, namely through the existence of sinister and alien forces at work within the country. Hence the need to identify, isolate and punish scapegoats.

Among the loyalists Mannix had assumed the status of a *bête noire*. He was the demon above all others who needed to be exorcised. On the very day of the referendum defeat, Dr Rentoul, a founder of the Loyalty League, wrote to Hughes urging that Mannix, this 'evil-minded man', who had brought 'an excitable and hysterical ignorant population ... to the very verge of civil war', should be 'damped out or transported out'.[67]

Such attitudes, in their most extreme form, were present at the very centre of the national security establishment. Steward, the head of the Secret Intelligence Bureau, informed his British counterpart not only that Mannix and the Irish Catholics caused the defeat of conscription but also that Mannix had as his 'chief object ... a cherished dream of the Roman Catholics to one day see this country under the rule of Rome.' This man of Intelligence could personally vouch for the truth of the Popish plot. During his twenty-seven years in Australia he had observed that, 'without exception, Roman Catholic churches, monasteries, nunneries and other buildings peculiar to this organisation, occupy all the highest, literally, and best positions.' This was the totality of the evidence, which even in itself was clearly false, that he adduced in support of his conspiracy theory. The passions unleashed by the conscription controversy allowed the head of Australia's secret service to give credence to one of the most absurd myths circulated by anti-Catholic sectarians.

In accounting for the rejection of conscription, Steward allowed that there were 'several other small items', such as the women's vote and the Labor vote, which 'possibly contributed a share, or a small share, to this unfortunate result'. In analysing the role of the different disloyal elements he

---

[66] Letter, Murdoch to Birdwood, 27 December 1917, Birdwood Papers, AWM 3DRL 3376/27.
[67] Letter, Rintoul to Hughes, 20 December 1917, NAA A1606 SC 42/1.

discounted the Germans altogether: 'I have not the slightest reason to believe that there was any enemy money in this campaign.' Similarly he denied that the extreme radical organisations had 'any influence whatsoever on the result'; he was able to boast that 'We killed absolutely the IWW. Everyone of its leaders is in gaol … The IWW is a thing of the past.' It was therefore his considered conclusion that:

> The conscription referendum was undoubtedly lost through the Roman Catholic hostile vote which was clearly and most forcibly applied through Dr. Mannix's leadership throughout the Commonwealth.

Mannix was the core of the problem: 'He has been the most disturbing element this country has ever seen.' He was 'clever, cunning and untrustworthy', and hoped 'to force England into giving Ireland Home Rule' and to bring Australia 'under the rule of Rome'. While criticising conscription the Archbishop 'openly and publicly, in fact in every possible way, announced that he was a Sinn Feiner, indeed an absolute rebel.' The experience had left Steward with an uneasy feeling. 'I am', he concluded, 'very conscious and disturbed by things generally here, but the whole of this unrest is, I am quite satisfied, locally produced and locally maintained.' It was evident that he saw Mannix as the source of this incipient rebellion.[68]

Hughes shared fully the prejudices of the loyalists both inside and outside the government. He too believed that the conspirators who had engineered the defeat of conscription would not be content with that victory. For Hughes, as for his fellow race patriots, it was Mannix who, above all others, symbolised this spirit of disaffection which was directed against the British character of Australia. The Irish question, which in the United Kingdom appeared in many different guises, assumed in Australia a simple, monolithic form which divided the nation into the loyal and disloyal.

Mannix and the Irish Catholic community did not hesitate to give colour to the loyalists' apprehensions. They exulted in their triumph over their enemies. At a Catholic Federation picnic on Boxing Day, Mannix castigated Hughes and the loyalists for their 'sectarianism and social hatred', and 50,000 voices joined in the singing of 'God Save Ireland'. On 16 March 1918, the St Patrick's Day procession through Melbourne's streets was deliberately provocative. The floats were decked in the Sinn Fein green and gold. The Archbishop who took the salute made no attempt to remove his biretta when 'God Save the King' was played but bared his head when the Young Ireland Society's tableau representing 'The Men of Easter Week' passed before him.[69]

The loyalists, so taunted, replied in kind. In a counter-demonstration in the Melbourne Town Hall, Mannix was described as 'that man of foreign extraction, that man who hated the very name of England'. He was anathematised as an agent of the Sinn Feiners who stood 'shoulder to shoulder with the Hun and the hosts of Satan'. A large deputation from the meeting pressed the

---

[68] Letter, Steward to Frank Hall, assistant to Colonel V.G.W. Kell, head of MI5, 30 January 1918, NAA A8911/1 240.

For more considered analyses of the referendum poll, showing how many National Party voters deserted their leaders and voted 'No', see Metherell, 'The Conscription Referenda', chapter 9 and a report on 'The Failure of the "Liberal" Vote at the Referendum', Hughes Papers, NLA MS 1538/20/511.

[69] Gilchrist, *Daniel Mannix: Priest and Patriot*, pp.61–62, 66; *Age*, 18 March 1918.

Prime Minister to ban disloyal processions and speeches and to expel the Archbishop from the country.[70]

The government was stung into action. New regulations were issued under the WPA to make it an offence to incite disloyalty to the British Empire, whether by word or deed, or to display flags or emblems which were symbols of an enemy country or of those disaffected from the British Empire. Hughes himself believed that since Mannix and 'the bulk of the Roman Catholics of Irish descent are unreservedly disloyal', he might have 'to face the difficult question of deporting Mannix'.[71] Though Hughes once again decided that it was too politically explosive to touch the prelate, he nevertheless authorised raids on the Irish National Associations in Brisbane, Melbourne and Sydney, the seizure of their papers and the subsequent arrests of a number of their leading members.[72] Hughes had become so suspicious of the Catholic Church that when the Vatican requested the usual diplomatic courtesy for its Apostolic Delegate to use a cipher when communicating with Rome he would only agree on condition the Vatican consented to restrict its communications to ecclesiastical matters and to give copies to the Governor-General.[73]

Mannix, by his extreme statements and open involvement in domestic politics, had become a problem for the universal church. The Apostolic Delegate to Australia, concerned by Mannix's role in the second conscription referendum, had already moved to pre-empt state action against Mannix and, as a result of representations to Rome, the Vatican had sent the Archbishop a mild rebuke. In a letter of 3 April the Sacred Congregation of Propaganda had reminded Mannix that 'the office of a Pastor is to pacify souls, to allay discords and to prevent their arising or becoming embittered'. The Apostolic Delegate in May followed this up and at a meeting of Australian archbishops discussed 'the best means of re-establishing calm and avoiding further cause of trouble'. Seemingly submitting to Rome, Mannix moved a resolution which urged the clergy 'to use prudence and caution in dealing with public questions', especially conscription, recruiting, Ireland and matters related to the war. The clergy were to be enjoined privately to avoid words or deeds that could 'give cause for the accusation against Catholics of disloyalty to the Empire'.

Unaware of these developments the Australian Government had resumed their complaints to the British about Mannix's behaviour and the British Foreign Office had passed on these complaints to Rome. In his reply, the Vatican Secretary of State informed the British of the

---

[70] *Argus*, 22 March 1918.
[71] Secret despatch, Munro Ferguson to Long, 2 April 1918, TNA: PRO CO 418/160/272–73.
[72] In a secret 'Report on the Activities of Sinn Fein and Seditious Irish Societies', dated 23 April 1918, the heads of Naval and Military Intelligence reviewed all the evidence, including the material seized in raids on the Irish National Association. They were able to show that a small number of the members of the Association, among whom were 'leading executive officers', were secret members of the Irish Republican Brotherhood and that this small group expressed not only sympathy for the Sinn Fein aim of total independence for Ireland but also a willingness to support armed rebellion and to help Germany for the same purpose. Since, however, the IRB members – in so far as they indicated an inclination to take up arms – spoke only of returning to Ireland to take part in the struggle, the authors of the report could not find that they plotted rebellion against the Commonwealth or that they had collected arms or formed an organisation which threatened the peace of the Commonwealth. NAA CP106/1/1 BUN 1.
[73] Cable, Long to Munro Ferguson, 5 April 1918, TNA: PRO CO418/169/291A and NAA A1606 SC L42/1.

substance of the 3 April letter to Mannix but added that there were extenuating circumstances, namely that he had been subject to 'personal attacks on the part of various newspapers and certain political personages'.[74] After Hughes arrived in London for an Imperial War Cabinet meeting the Foreign Secretary consulted him about further action. Balfour was convinced that 'the Vatican would view with the extremist disfavour any action on the part of the Archbishop which brought him within reach of the law.' Rather than allow this to happen they would 'probably take the strongest steps … to prevent it'. And so Balfour asked Hughes again whether he could supply any relevant evidence which could be passed to Rome.

In private talks, Hughes intimated that he was 'most anxious' that the Vatican should recall Mannix – 'nothing less, in his opinion, is sufficient' and he accordingly supplied Balfour with a seven-page memorandum which set out Mannix's activities 'in proper perspective' and a schedule of his most objectionable statements.[75] Transmitting this to the Vatican Balfour told the British envoy, 'The strength of the case seems to me to be in the fact that the Archbishop should have been arrested or deported, owing to what he has said had it not been for the ecclesiastical position he holds.' The Foreign Secretary warned that the Australian Government would be 'forced to allow the law to take its course unless the Vatican recalls him'. At Balfour's suggestion Hughes agreed that in return for Mannix's recall he would drop the requirement that copies of the Vatican's cipher communications had to be given to the Governor-General.[76]

The Vatican was unwilling to take such a drastic step and inquired informally whether a 'strong reprimand' would suffice. Hughes, however, would not compromise. He was 'quite clear that this would not meet the case'.[77] The Vatican too would make no concession. Gasparri, in his reply, pointed out that the Sacred Congregation of Propaganda had in April sent a cautioning letter to Mannix and that it would be premature to take further action against him until it could be seen whether the Archbishop heeded the Vatican's advice. At the same time Gasparri allowed that Mannix had himself some reason for complaint, and it was suggested that the Australian Government might try to induce the Sydney and Melbourne press to cease accusing Catholics of sympathy for the Central Powers on the 'absurd ground' that they had promised to restore the Pope's temporal power. And he added that he had 'learned from an unimpeachable source' that 'a

---

[74] Letter, Cardinal Pietro Gasparri, Vatican Secretary of State, to Count de Salis, British Minister Plenipotentiary to Vatican, 24 June1918, TNA: PRO FO 371/3229; despatch, Munro Ferguson to Long, 2 April 1918, TNA: PRO CO 418/160/272–73.

[75] Letter, Hughes to Balfour, 24 July 1918, TNA: PRO FO 371/3229. In the accompanying memorandum, 'Sinn Fein in Australia: Its Growth and Objects: The Part of the Church', it was asserted that Mannix was the acknowledged leader of the Sinn Fein in Australia who had openly confessed that 'he was a Sinn Feiner and was proud of the fact.'

[76] Letter, Balfour to de Salis, 29 July 1918, *ibid*.

[77] Draft cable, Balfour to de Salis, 14 August 1918, *ibid*.

high political personage of Australia' had been spreading the selfsame story. It was clear to whom Gasparri was referring.[78]

Hughes was again frustrated. The Foreign Office suggested he could bring the matter to a head by sending an ultimatum to the Vatican stating that unless the Archbishop was recalled within a specified time he would be arrested and tried. But they did not recommend this course of action since if the Vatican refused to comply the Australian Government would be obliged to carry out the threat and bear its consequences. Hughes thus had for the time being no alternative but to let the matter drop while he collected more current evidence of Mannix's disloyalty.[79] The imperious Hughes, like Henry II, might well have asked despairingly, 'Who will rid me of this turbulent priest?', but unlike that Plantagenet monarch he found no-one to solve his problem.

Since the first conscription defeat the National Government and many of its supporters had believed that the country was in danger of being convulsed by a violent uprising. Those who appeared indifferent to the fate of the Allied armies on the Western Front, who questioned British motives in going to war, who urged the pursuit of a compromise peace, who sided with Irish rebels in their demands for independence and who initiated strikes and so sabotaged the war effort were considered to have renounced their allegiance to Australia as an integral part of the British Empire. As a result, Hughes and the loyalists held that they were justified in using all the resources of the state against these enemies of the British race. In the 1917 referendum campaign Hughes, inspired by the fear of a coming civil war, not only created a Commonwealth Police Force to compel recalcitrants, like the Queensland ministers, to submit to federal authority but also instructed the commandants of all military districts, as a matter 'of the utmost importance', to ensure that the plans drawn up in the previous December to put down riots and insurrections were 'in working order' and able to be 'put into force with the smallest delay'.[80]

Hughes also had no scruples about using the intelligence organisations, especially the Counter Espionage Bureau, which since January 1917 had been renamed the Special Investigative

---

[78] Letter, Robert Cecil, Parliamentary Under-Secretary for Foreign Affairs, to Hughes, 2 September 1918, containing letter, Gasparri to de Salis, 22 August 1918, TNA: PRO CO 537/1143 and NAA A1606/1 SC F1/42.

De Salis cabled the Foreign Office that in the Vatican's view 'personal hostility to Archbishop is not unconnected with action of Prime Minister of Australia who does not appear to have their confidence'. See cable, de Salis to Balfour, 21 August 1918, TNA: PRO FO 371/3229.

[79] Letter, Cecil to Hughes, 27 August 1918, TNA: PRO CO 527/1143; letter, Balfour to de Salis, 30 September 1918, TNA: PRO FO 371/3229.

[80] Adjutant-General, Brigadier-General V.C.M. Sellheim, to Commandants of all Military Districts, 10 December 1917, NAA B197 1887/1/52.

For the Commandants' responses, especially the Queensland Commandant's reply in which he claimed that in addition to the military 'a body of 500 Returned Soldiers can be made available by the Returned Soldiers' Association', see *ibid.*, 1887/1/45.

In justifying a *War Precautions Act* regulation setting up a Commonwealth Police Force, which was approved at an Executive Council Meeting on 2 December, Hughes told the Governor-General that state police forces, especially in Queensland where the 'present position' was 'one of latent rebellion' and where the police were 'honey-combed with Sinn Feiners', could not be relied on. Draft cable, Hughes to Munro Ferguson, Hughes Papers NLA MS 1538/20/418.

Bureau, to spy on his political opponents. National security had to be protected from domestic as well as foreign enemies. This intelligence agency, set up in January 1916 to suppress the activities of enemy agents in Australia, had by the time of the first conscription crisis extended its function to include the surveillance of internal subversives including the IWW, pacifists, leaders of the labour movement and the Irish Catholic community.

In 1917 Steward cooperated closely with Hughes and on the latter's instructions spied upon the National Party's political opponents. The Governor-General was very concerned that his private secretary's duties as 'Detective-in-Chief for the Commonwealth Govt [sic]' might compromise the position of the King's representative. In a 'secret and personal' letter to Long, he explained that Steward was 'specially engaged in unravelling the schemes of the IWW and following the doings of various malefactors of this type' and that in the process members of parliament did 'not entirely escape' the secret service's attentions. Munro Ferguson could not view with complacency the presence of 'Detectives, Informers and such like persons' in Government House nor that Steward took his orders directly from the Prime Minister or the Defence Minister. Though he had overlooked Hughes's violation of constitutional proprieties on earlier occasions because he had regarded Hughes as the country's most able war leader, nevertheless the Prime Minister's use of the secret service disturbed him. Hughes, he admitted, was 'By nature and by training … prone to catch at any expedient by which he can compass his ends', hinting that material obtained by secret agents might be used against anti-conscriptionists and the Labor Party. The Prime Minister was 'in constant touch' with Steward 'and seemed to extend to him a greater measure of his confidence than to anyone else.' Munro Ferguson proposed to demand that Hughes give guarantees that Steward would not be involved in any activities which might embarrass the Crown.[81] By August Munro Ferguson's anxiety about the misuse of the secret service had reached such a pitch that he told Hughes to replace Steward as head of the SIB and to remove the headquarters of the secret service from Government House.

Hughes was unwilling to end such a useful relationship. Since Steward himself was loath to give up his post, the Prime Minister conspired with him to deceive the Governor-General. Though in November Steward formally relinquished his connection with the SIB, he remained in practice its chief, and, during the last year of the war, he continued to help both Hughes and the National Government to impose their loyalty program on the country. In cooperation with Military Intelligence, the SIB placed under surveillance and investigated not only Irish nationalists and labour leaders but also Labor parliamentarians.

In the midst of the conscription campaign, probably as a result of Ryan's clash with Hughes, the Queensland Premier was subjected to the most thoroughgoing scrutiny. Every aspect of his

---

[81] Letter, secret and personal, Munro Ferguson to Long, Long Papers, WRO 947/625/49.

In his first circular letter of February 1916 Steward had defined the task of the CEB as 'the widest possible interchange with the British Government of confidential intelligence, bearing especially upon the activities of rival secret service agents throughout the Empire', but following the alarm about the Japanese later in the year, Steward on 16 August told Pearce that the CEB's function had been broadened to include 'Enquiries into movements of Japanese settlers etc. on the North West and North East Coasts of the Commonwealth'. See NAA MP1049/1 16/104 and letter, Steward to Pearce, 16 August 1916, Hughes Papers, NLA MS 1538/21/2–26.

public life, his speeches, his associates and his stands on recruitment, the war and the Empire, was put under the microscope. The subsequent report on Ryan reveal very clearly the partisan character of the intelligence service. The report concluded that:

> Although Mr. Ryan's attitude in connection with the war can be described as the attitude of a disloyalist, it is almost impossible to find anything in his speeches which might be construed as direct disloyalty to the Crown, or as favoring [sic] the Germans or Republican Extremists … His utterances whenever he has referred to the Empire have always been loyal – and more fervently so since the outbreak of the war.

It further stated that since:

> it is a very difficult matter to connect him in any way with disloyalty, out of his own mouth … the only possible line to take with a view to connecting him with disloyal sentiments and pro-Germans is to prove his association with disloyalists and subservience to the Labor organisations, which have often shown themselves openly disloyal.[82]

The point of the report then was to find evidence to impugn Ryan's loyalty and enable the authorities to charge him with subverting the war effort. It was assumed, presumably because he opposed conscription and objected to the unreasonable use of censorship powers, that he was disloyal, and therefore, if he could not be condemned out of his own mouth, 'the only line' to take would be to prove guilt by association.

The Australian Protective League

The National Government and the intelligence agencies were so incensed by the attitude of many in the Irish Catholic community and the labour movement to the war, recruitment and the Empire that they set about establishing an Australian Protective League, a secret organisation made up of loyal citizens who would report on any suspicious or disloyal behaviour. Hughes had given R. D. Elliott, a Melbourne businessman who was to visit the United States in late 1917, a letter of introduction to the American Protective League, which was thought to be a possible model for Australia. Elliott had met in Washington the 'Head of the Citizen Section of the United States Secret Service, known as "The American Protective League" – the Organisation responsible for the quietness of the German and Irish sympathisers of the Central Powers – our enemies.' On his return to Australia he sent the Minister for Defence a copy of the constitution of the Chicago branch and in his covering letter to Pearce explained the structure and function of the League. It was organised on quasi-military lines, the captain of each subdivision enlisting members who were 'loyal to the country and the employers.' The members were pledged to secrecy and obedience, and their task in their respective industries was to 'promptly report … any and every

---

[82] Report on 'Mr Ryan's Associations', undated but most probably, from internal evidence, in November or December 1917, NAA MP729/2 2021/1/270.

The only National Party member that the CEB investigated was T.A. Bavin, a prominent conscriptionist who after the 1917 referendum defeat had wanted Hughes to be true to his pledge and resign as Prime Minister. Steward recommended to Hughes that in the light of that stand Bavin should not be considered for an appointment as a Naval Intelligence Officer. See letter, Steward to Hughes, 12 February 1918, Hughes Papers, NLA MS 1538/118/4.

case of disloyalty, industrial disturbance or any other matter likely to injure or embarrass the Government of the United States', and this report was then forwarded to the Justice Department.[83]

Pearce's initial reaction had been positive, but, since the government was embroiled first in the conscription referendum and then in a political crisis over Hughes's pledge to resign, a decision had to be delayed. Following the St Patrick's Day celebrations and the Loyalist protest against Mannix in March 1918, the cabinet had referred the proposal to the newly-constituted Council of Defence which duly recommended the formation of an Australian Protective League on the American pattern. Taking up the recommendation the Acting Prime Minister, W. A. Watt, then called a meeting of community leaders for 29 May to consider the formation of such a body.[84]

At this meeting there were three representatives of the government, the Acting Prime Minister, who presided, Senator Pearce and Major-General Legge, Chief of the General Staff, and sixteen private citizens. The latter were hand-picked for the purpose. Pearce had consulted Herbert Brookes, the retiring President of the Victorian Chamber of Manufactures and the major force behind the Loyalist and Protestant associations in Victoria, about the men who should be invited to attend. Those selected were already closely associated with the Referendum Council and other Loyalist bodies. They included not only leading members of professional, commercial and manufacturing organisations, and academics from the University of Melbourne; but also the Lord Mayor of Melbourne, a stalwart of the Protestant Association.[85]

In his opening remarks Pearce, after outlining the function of the SIB and Military Intelligence, stated that the government believed that these official channels were inadequate to meet the gravity of the problem. The government wanted to link up with 'bodies throughout the Commonwealth, such as bankers, mining societies, members of the Commercial Travellers Association, insurance agencies, doctors, legal practitioners and even the clergy for the purpose of bringing to notice anything of a suspicious character.'

It was generally agreed that the country was facing unprecedented danger from a subversive conspiracy. Archibald T. Strong, head of the Department of English at Melbourne University, declared that 'the enemies within our gates had been working with subtleness and thoroughness … since the first two or three weeks of the war.' Following the last referendum,

> these enemies had … been increasingly earnest to wreck the war organisation … and as the work was underground the country could not learn the evil effects of it. If ever there came a big national crisis it would be found that forces had developed which we had not touched.

---

[83] Letter, R.D. Elliott to Pearce, 29 November 1917, NAA MP792/2 1851/2/43.

[84] Minutes of Cabinet Meeting, 27 March 1918, Hughes Papers, NLA MS 1538/112/2; letter, Pearce to Watt, 2 May 1918, NAA MP729/2 1851/2/43; minutes of Council of Defence meetings, 23 April and 1 May 1918, NAA A9787/2 2.

[85] Letter, Herbert Brookes to Pearce, 2 May 1918, NAA MP729/2 1851/2/43.

See also copy of circular letter from Herbert Brookes, 25 March 1918, inviting people to attend 'the preliminary meeting of the Citizens Loyalty Committee' on 27 March. The Committee was to help plan a public demonstration against the 'subversive and seditious' activities of Mannix and the St Patrick's Day procession. Brookes Papers, NLA MS 1924/21/2–24.

> That is to say that there was a big wave of Bolshevism and the only way to overthrow it was by organising a counter wave.

Though no specific evidence was advanced to back up these very broad and alarming allegations Legge echoed these sentiments, assuring the meeting that an Australian Protective League was 'necessary'. 'Speaking confidentially', he referred to the probable dangers and the Defence Department's existing methods of surveillance. It was his view that 'the only thing to do was to get everybody loyal to organise and [he] suggested that badges denoting loyalty be worn.'

They were acting in the name of the Australian people, and they therefore 'assumed that the majority of the people were not hard or disloyal'. Moreover, Legge urged – rather surprisingly given the make-up of the meeting – that 'there should be "no class" in this, [for] if there were, the whole effect would be gone.' In the same vein Strong was firmly of the opinion that 'a non-party man' should be appointed director of the organisation. Otherwise people would say 'that both the man and the organisation had been appointed in order to exalt the National Party.' Despite the nature of the origins of this organisation and the lack of any union or Labor Party representatives on the founding committee it was still necessary for them as the guardians of the British race in Australia to believe that they were acting not for a class or a party but for the nation.

It was unanimously concluded that they should set up a 'Citizen Bureaux of Intelligence and Propaganda'. Watt told them that they should 'come to the Government for whatever they wanted, and the Government would give it.' He indicated that there had already been positive soundings made in Queensland and New South Wales, and he looked forward to them thinking along 'National lines'. Convenors were appointed to summon a further meeting which would give the organisation a more precise definition.[86] Despite this initial burst of enthusiasm, it would appear, however, that differences among the loyal citizenry and between them and the security authorities prolonged the process of setting up the new body, and with the coming of the peace the government eventually lost interest.

At the Council of Defence meeting in August, E. L. Piesse, the Director of Military Intelligence, reported that the issue of an 'Australian Protective League' was still under consideration, and on 28 October Brookes, who had become the recognised spokesman for the loyal citizens, met with Watt and Pearce. According to Brookes's own account, the ministers accepted the outline of a structure for the bureau which he placed before them.

Brookes, more than any other, believed that there was a paramount need for such an organisation. Herbert Brookes, in addition to being a successful businessman who treated his workers well, was a philanthropist, a patron of the arts and a worthy citizen who gave a lot of his time to public service.[87] But what at bottom gave meaning to his life was an idealisation of the British race which was fused with his ideas of fair play, culture and liberty, and it was this which made him an implacable, indeed fanatical, enemy of all those who did not give unqualified loyalty

---

[86] 'Notes In Connection With Meeting Held At The Prime Minister's Office. Melbourne, On the 29th May, 1918, To Consider The Matter Of The Formation Of An Australian Protective League – And Of A Propaganda Bureau In Connection With The War', NAA MP729/2 1851/2/43.

[87] Alison Patrick, 'Herbert Brookes' *ADB* (1891–1939), Vol. VII, pp.425–427; Rohan Rivett, *Australian Citizen: Herbert Brookes* (Melbourne: Melbourne University Press, 1966).

to the British Empire. He had gone to much trouble to prepare his case, and he presented it with conviction and in great detail. To prove his *bona fides* he pointed to his role as the founder and financier of the Loyalty League. Furthermore he already had agents 'working at Trades Hall', 'among the One Big Union crowd' and in 'the State Police Dept.' These men were selected from the Masons, Loyalty leagues, the Soldiers and Sailors Fathers Association, and the National Federation. They were 'Vigilantes' whose task was to report disloyal behaviour and help break up disloyal gatherings.

Then he laid down the principles he considered should be the basis for the citizens' security bureau. Firstly, it should be secret. Secondly, he was opposed to the May meeting's idea of giving the organisation a constitution. The 'prime movers' should have a freehand in choosing their team. For his part, Brookes made it clear that if he were to be involved he would want complete control, for he would 'hesitate to form any committee for important work that I did not have a hand in selecting.'

Thirdly, the organisation was to be directed by 'a secret centre of three': the Minister of Defence who would be chairman; a departmental head who would be in charge of the federal police and secret service; and a representative citizen whose qualifications he described in such a way as to make himself the most logical candidate. That is, the citizen member should be someone who had 'access to all sorts and conditions of organisations and associations and … had experiences of organisation work in many spheres.' This person would be the link between the committee and the voluntary bodies that cooperated in the task 'of combat [sic] ing and extirpating disloyalty in all forms in our midst'. The citizen member with the consent of the committee would appoint the deputies for each state 'to whom alone his existence is known'. Brookes wanted to run the League on the principle of secret centralism. In submitting names for the deputy posts in each state, he recommended that because Queensland was to be 'the field of operations which will cause the most concern', the State's Police Commissioner, Frederick Urquhart, should be made the permanent head of the combined federal Police and Secret Service in Queensland or put in charge of Queensland and New South Wales, or of all the states 'immediately under the permanent federal head'.

Fourthly, this inner committee was to have the power to decide whether individuals accused of disloyalty should be prosecuted. Perhaps still smarting from the government's failure to charge Mannix and others, Brookes wished to ensure that political expediency should not stand in the way of national security. It would be a mistake in his view 'to let this final decision rest with a Minister who from the very nature of his profession must be consciously or unconsciously biased by political considerations.'

Finally, in order to protect the organisation's clandestine character Brookes suggested that, if the government had to justify public expenditure on the organisation, they could pretend that there was 'a grave necessity to counter German Post-War Secret Trade methods'. They would 'concentrate on the other enemies in our midst under cover of this screen if such were necessary'.[88]

---

[88] 'Rough Notes Conference with Acting Prime Minister and Minister of Defence and Self. Oct 28/18 when this Suggested Scheme was adopted'. Brookes Papers, NLA MS 1924/17/38–49.

Despite Brookes's claim that Watt and Pearce had accepted his scheme, it would appear that for very good reasons they viewed it with some misgivings. Apart from being asked to hand over so much authority to a private citizen, they must have been concerned by the obsessive intensity of his approach to the question of loyalty. Though they shared to some extent his fear of subversion and suspicion of Roman Catholics, Brookes's extreme views must have troubled them. Nevertheless, the ministers did not dismiss the scheme out of hand. They asked Steward and Piesse to meet with Brookes and Urquhart to draw up an agreed constitution.

It would seem that the intelligence heads did not see eye to eye with Brookes. Piesse reported to his minister that they had agreed to establish what they called 'A Federal Investigation Authority' which would:

> detect, prevent and suppress all attempts to subvert ... the constitution ... or to impede the preservation of the peace, or to hinder, embarrass or retard His Majesty's subjects in the pursuit of their lawful occupations ... or to establish anything in the nature of a combination or super-authority having for its object the overriding, impeding or embarrassing the equal ... administration of the law for all classes.

This 'Department' was to comprise the Special Intelligence Bureau, some officers from Naval and Military Intelligence and some from the federal police force. It was the majority contention that this body should be able to build up an effective voluntary arm which since it would be 'in alliance with an acknowledged public Department will not bring upon itself any suspicion which could not be avoided if the organisation was a purely voluntary one.'

The report was at odds with the plan that Brookes had put to the ministers. Piesse explained that this latest scheme was 'a compromise between different views'. Though he maintained that all four had agreed to it, he did admit that they were not of one mind about 'the best means of linking the permanent organisation with the voluntary'. To make his position clear Brookes enclosed with the report a modification of his earlier plans for the League. Under this proposal a central committee made up of representatives from various 'Loyalist' bodies would form a central executive committee, and it would have 'the greatest freedom of action and methods'. The Department should be 'elastic and unarbitrary [sic]' in its relationship with the League. In order to help further secure its autonomy, the League might from its own resources pay an organiser or organisers.[89]

At a subsequent conference on 3 December of Steward, Piesse, Urquhart and Brookes with Pearce, Brookes amplified his critique of the proposed 'Voluntary Arm' and demonstrated how unhappy he was with the intelligence chiefs' determination to keep close control of the League. What they had proposed was 'not a true voluntary arm'. It would never be:

> permitted to become a self-governing, self-determining organisation because it might become ... even dangerous to the power ... and position of the Director and even to the Ministers.

---

[89] Report, Piesse to Pearce, 29 November 1918, Brookes Papers, NLA MS 1924/17/2–5.

Piesse, in writing to his wife, mentioned another meeting of Pearce, Brookes, Steward and himself on 16 November, and told her that he was 'very dubious of what is proposed' and that 'the Minister took a view rather nearer to mine than I had expected.' Letter, Piesse to Christine Piesse, 17 November 1918, Piesse Family Papers, NLA MS 882.

He told Pearce the government would:

> not get the real useful volunteers unless you trust them truly. The type you *will* get, who are willing to submit to the tyranny of the Director and Co. will be a servile woolly type.

It should be prepared 'to run the risk of having to submit to pressure from the voluntary arm.' Indeed for Brookes this was 'its greatest recommendation' since it was important to have a body which could 'exercise considerable pressure upon the ministerial head and cabinet'. The voluntary arm should be able to prevent 'backing down in a genuine and important matter from political considerations'. In essence he was saying that these private citizens acting out of pure motives of loyalty were more to be trusted to protect the country against its internal enemies than the elected government and its officials, and that therefore their secret society should be given greater authority to act than the government itself. It should in essence be a secret state inside the constitutional state. He concluded that unless his plan for the voluntary citizen organisation were accepted, they would 'court the same failure that has been experienced already.'

At the meeting Brookes warned Pearce that if he adopted the Steward-Piesse version of an 'Australian Defence League', which was nothing more than 'an arm of the government service under its direct supervision and created and controlled by it in the person of its Director', then he would have to take it to the cabinet and such a course would be 'dangerous and will condemn itself from the outset.' If Pearce were to proceed this way Brookes, still assuming the role of the master-strategist in the cause of national security and the voluntary league, advised Pearce that there should be 'only faintest reference to a proposed voluntary arm'. It was important that he did not mention Brookes's name – '(speak to Mr. Watt beforehand so that he will not ask any questions)'. Brookes further counselled that, if the voluntary organisation were discussed, 'two of your colleagues G and R [Glynn and Russell – the only Roman Catholics in the cabinet] will at once suspect it and have it investigated.' Indeed Glynn and Russell would ensure that 'certain R.C. organisations are admitted to this Defence League with what results you can guess.' The advantage of Brookes's proposal for a relatively autonomous body was, as he explained it to Pearce, that

> the minister 'need say nothing or next to nothing to the Cabinet of the Voluntary side.' Pearce 'need only say that *if found necessary* voluntary assistance may be called in and let it stop at this. We the voluntary army will do the rest.' What Brookes was here proposing was that this secret organisation should under his control play a central role in protecting the integrity of the nation against subversion and that since it represented loyal Australia its existence and operation should be kept even from some ministers, that is colleagues of Watt and Pearce, whose loyalty was already compromised by their religion.

Brookes appealed to Pearce not to put off a decision any longer. He was impatient with 'the paper schemes' and with Steward who was:

a maker of constitutions by nature – and a believer in a volunteer army so long as it can be *forced compelled conscripted* in all its activities from its inception to its disbandonment.[90]

But nothing was done. Undoubtedly Brookes's monomania, his absolute confidence in his mission, his antagonism to the senior intelligence officers, his desire for a completely free hand in running the 'Volunteer army' and his conspiratorial cast of mind must have helped to cool Pearce's ardour for setting up an Australian Protective League. Yet probably even more important in bringing the government to abandon the project was the end of the war. In 1921 when the Defence Department was tidying up its paper work, the 'Australian Protective League' file was sent to the Chief of the General Staff, Major-General C. B. Brudenell White, who, after consulting the Prime Minister's Department, was told that 'this matter appears now to be dead.' White accordingly minuted that 'this branch does not propose further action.'[91]

In 1918 the National Government had become hysterical about loyalty. The crisis of the war had given notions of British race patriotism an absolute value. It had tested for the first time the full meaning of nationalism. After 1915 the rulers and the respectability, acting in the name of the people, required total submission to and sacrifice for the common cause. For these Australians, conscription was the ultimate symbol of the collective commitment and therefore of the loyalty to the state and race. The preservation of British Australia was inextricably connected to that of Britain and the British Empire as a whole. By this line of argument anti-conscriptionists could not be loyal. They were necessarily disloyal or the dupes of disloyalists and under the influence of Germans, Syndicalists or Sinn Feiners. The pattern was clear. Those who came out against conscription were the same people who incited internal disorder, called for Irish independence, questioned British war aims, backed a compromise peace and even discouraged voluntary recruitment. Such attitudes amounted to a conspiracy against the nation and presaged a social upheaval.

Consequently the Commonwealth authorities had no compunction in denouncing anti-conscriptionists as traitors, in censoring their speeches and publications, in prosecuting them under the *War Precautions Act* regulations, in using the intelligence service to spy upon them and in preparing to put down a mythical uprising by military force. By 1918 the government considered the threat to be so urgent that they took steps to establish a secret organisation of loyal citizens, similar to the American Protective League, which would assist the intelligence services to uncover sedition and subversion. Employers would report on workers, businessmen on customers, professional people on clients, clergy on parishioners, neighbours on neighbours. One half of the country with the backing of the state was to be set against the other.

---

[90] 'Conference, Senator Pearce, Sir George Steward, Major Piesse, Mr. Urquart and Self', 3 December 1918. Brookes Papers, NLA MS 1924/17/26–36.

Brookes's preoccupation with a world-wide Catholic plot to overthrow the British Empire was evident also in his Loyalty League's resolution, passed on the eve of the Armistice, which called on the Allies to place their representatives in the German and Austrian archives so as to prevent the destruction of documents, 'more especially all such as have passed between the Vatican on the on hand and the Kaiser and the Emperor on the other.' At Brookes's request Watt cabled the resolution to Hughes, asking him to 'Give matter your consideration.' Cable, Watt to Hughes, 11 November 1918, NAA CP360/18 B1/2.

[91] NAA MP729/2 1851/2/43.

At the Governor-General's recruiting conference of 12–19 April 1918 this collapse of national consensus, of mutual trust and confidence, was most dramatically evident. Following the defeat of conscription, enlistments had fallen off. In the first three months of the year, the average monthly number of men coming forward had dropped to less than 2000 – the lowest figure for the war. The conscriptionists felt no enthusiasm for a system of recruitment which they believed, was flawed and had failed. Similarly many anti-conscriptionists were so alienated that they would not support recruitment in any form since their persecutors used it to traduce those they labelled 'disloyal'. Sir William Irvine, again refusing to accept the result of the referendum, had urged parliament to legislate for conscription; but the National Government understood fully that such an action would be politically disastrous and it gained no support.

Thus in March when the British Government – alarmed by the massive new German offensive on the Western Front – appealed to Australia, along with the other Dominions, to 'reinforce their heroic troops in the fullest possible manner, and with the smallest possible delay',[92] Munro Ferguson took it upon himself to seek a resolution to the problem. He was aghast at the failure of voluntary recruiting – 'A tremendous recruiting rally last night – result one man'[93] – and recognised that nothing would be achieved unless the country could 'arrive at some harmonious working on the part of all classes.' With this in mind he invited to the conference leaders of the federal government and the opposition, the leaders of the state governments and opposition parties, the heads of the National Party and Labor Party organisations in each state, and the presidents of the employers' associations and trade union bodies in both the Commonwealth and the states.

When the conference assembled, the auguries were not good. The Queensland Industrial Council and the Tasmanian Trades and Labour Council refused to take part. They both declared themselves against sending additional troops to Europe. Furthermore, in response to the Governor-General's request at the opening of the conference that the members should pass a motion which would commit all participants to agree about the necessity 'to secure adequate reinforcements', the labour representatives would not discuss this principle before their grievances had been aired and addressed. Many delegates referred to 'disharmony', 'discord', and a 'split in the community'.

The federal Labor leader, Frank Tudor, complained of how he and his supporters had been vilified by their opponents in the conscription campaign. And he showed the hurt: 'I take it that I am as good an Australian citizen as any other man in the community. I realise my duty to Australia as a part of the Empire to which we belong.' Ryan, who also could speak from experience, criticised the way in which recruiting committees had declared that the voluntary system was dead merely in order to justify conscription. He insisted fairly that 'the charging of anti-conscriptionists with disloyalty militated against recruiting.' He also protested at the way the

---

[92] Scott, *Australia During the War*, p.445; Adams and Poirier, *Conscription Controversy in Great Britain*, p.229. See also cable, Long to Munro Ferguson, 31 March 1918, Hughes Papers, NLA MS 1538/16/2021–25, which contained a message from Lloyd George seeking immediate reinforcements.
[93] Novar Diary, 30 March 1918, Novar Papers, NLA MS 696/36.

government had used censorship and WPA regulations to stifle criticism and gain political advantage.

Union leaders, for their part, did not think that peace could be achieved at home until the government put an end to the sacking of men of eligible recruiting age from business houses and government departments, and took steps to reinstate workers who had lost their jobs in the great strike of 1917. The President of the New South Wales Federal Council of Labour went as far as to say that 'a worse condition, under our bitterest enemy, could hardly exist than obtains at present in some industrial circles in Australia.' Labour spokesmen reiterated that what they sought was not revolution but a 'return to the days of harmony that characterised the early years of the war.'

Against this background Tudor and Ryan drafted a statement of conditions which would have to be met if harmony amongst all sections of the community were to be restored and Australia thereby enabled 'to discharge its duty during the present grave crisis'. To this end they required the Commonwealth Government to give assurances that conscription had been 'finally abandoned', that neither public nor private employers would pursue a policy of 'economic conscription', that all punitive measures taken against striking unionists in 1917 would be rescinded, that the partisan application of the WPA regulations, including that evident in censorship and political and industrial prosecutions, would cease and that those imprisoned as a result of such prosecutions would be released.[94]

The Governor-General was disconcerted by the drift of the debate. He feared that the conference would become bogged down in argument about the labour movement's grievances, and would lose sight of his original objective. In despair he urged Hughes, who because of illness had missed the first two days, to take charge and return the conference to its central purpose. Munro Ferguson had no sympathy for labour's litany of complaint. As he wrote Hughes:

> Our whole effort should be to get a promising recruiting scheme – and then let the onus of the collapse of the Conference rest upon those who, though having agreed to it, refuse for party reasons to support it.[95]

Entering the fray, Hughes denied that there were reasonable grounds for the criticisms but promised, in a manner that suggested that it was an unwarranted and almost meaningless concession, that the Commonwealth and State governments were prepared to make such changes in their policy as would substantially satisfy the labour leaders and so remove any objection they might have to taking part in formulating a recruitment policy. Hughes's bluster did not, however, kindle confidence in those who had many reasons to doubt his word. When he proposed to read the latest cables from London to illustrate the seriousness of the military position, he was stopped by an interjector who cried out 'We've had enough of your forgeries.'[96] Consequently during the remaining days of the conference the labour side pressed Hughes for detailed clarification of his assurances. They raked over all the burning issues from the 1917 conscription campaign. The

---

[94] 'Report of Proceedings of the Conference Convened by His Excellency the Governor-General at Federal Government House, Melbourne, April, 1918', *CPP,* IV, '1917–1918', 657, 667 and 695.
[95] Copy of letter, personal, Munro Ferguson to Hughes, 14 April 1918, attached to letter, Munro Ferguson to Long, 22 February [sic – April] 1918, Long Papers, WRO 947/625/101.
[96] 'Report of Proceedings …', *CPP,* IV, '1917–1918', 695.

labour leaders were keenly aware that their people would not be easily persuaded to cooperate with the National Government, that vague words from Hughes would not satisfy them.

Both sides for different reasons desired that a resolution should issue from their deliberations. Labour wished to avoid giving the impression that they were opposed to the war and voluntary recruiting while the Nationalists and employers were anxious to bind the labour leaders to a strong resolution which would oblige them to combat anti-war and anti-recruiting elements among their supporters. On the last day, in the interests of attaining unanimity, the Nationalists and employers settled for a weak resolution. Contrary to the wishes of the Governor-General it contained no recruitment plan. The labour delegates would not accept 'victory' as an aim of the war and recruitment. Hughes also had to give up his ambition to have the labour leaders commit their respective organisations to the principle of securing 'an immediate and continuing increase' in the number of voluntary recruits for the AIF. At the end, the conference agreed, over Hughes's objections,

> to make all possible effort to avoid defeat at the hands of German militarism and [to] urge the people of Australia to unite in a whole-hearted effort to secure the necessary reinforcements under the voluntary system.[97]

It was not surprising that the conference did very little to restore goodwill and trust in the community. The conference had not been designed for the purpose of healing the wounds in the body politic. The Governor-General's intent, as he reported it to the Colonial Secretary, was to try to meet the 'Home Govt's' appeal for more men.' From almost the beginning of the war Munro Ferguson had intervened to encourage the despatch of the greatest number of men possible. During the conscription crises he had been equally partisan and had allowed his 'little dictator' a great deal of constitutional licence because he believed Hughes was 'head and shoulders above the rest of his colleagues in vigour, intellect and reasonableness' and was the leader best able to bring in compulsion and so maximise Australia's military contribution to the Empire. After the failure of the second referendum Munro Ferguson had petulantly advised Long that:

> it being now plain beyond doubt that Australia declines to take her full share in the war, the Home Gov't can when dealing with questions of purchases, shipping, loans, and military discipline consider only the interests of the Empire as a whole in the prosecution of the war.[98]

The faithless Australians should no longer be indulged by the Mother Country. Munro Ferguson also shared the loyalists' hostility to Mannix, the Irish Catholics and the labour movement. With his high hopes for the conference thwarted he condemned Ryan, the most moderate of the labour representatives, as 'a rebel at heart like Mannix'; there was something about the man 'which treachery itself cannot trust'.[99]

The Commonwealth Government in its approach to the conference also evinced no desire for a genuine reconciliation. Even as they met with the labour leaders in Government House, the same ministers were proceeding with secret plans to establish an Australian Protective League

---

[97] *Ibid.*, 700 and 807–12.
[98] Letter, Munro Ferguson to Long, 27 December 1917, Long Papers, WRO 947/625/85.
[99] Letter, personal, Munro Ferguson to Long, 22 February [sic – April] 1918, *ibid.*, 947/625/101.

which would organise loyal citizens to spy on the labour movement and the Irish Catholic community. Though Tudor and Ryan, in the month after the conference, acted in the spirit of the resolution and helped raise the May enlistments to almost 5000, the government remained convinced that they faced a national conspiracy against constituted authority and pressed ahead with the formation of the League. Implicitly the government was acting on the assumption that an unbridgeable gulf had opened up between the two Australias, the loyal and the disloyal, and that it was involved in a battle at home to defeat 'the enemies within the gate'. The liberty for which Hughes had proclaimed that Australia and the Empire were fighting had been made subservient to the state and the imperative of British race patriotism it embodied.

'Annexation and Indemnity': Australia's War Aims

From the beginning of 1917 the issues of peace and peace terms moved to the centre of the international stage. Even as the belligerent governments steeled themselves for yet another throw of the dice on the battlefield, they found it necessary to answer their liberal and socialist critics who, disillusioned by the great human costs of the war, demanded that the rival parties publish their aims and seek a negotiated settlement.

The two great events of that year, America's entry into the war and the Russian Revolution, helped to strengthen these concerns. President Woodrow Wilson, espousing the doctrine of liberal internationalism, had stated that America was fighting not the German people but the German militarists, that Americans sought nothing for themselves but only 'to make the world safe for democracy'. Similarly the Russian Soviets had called for a peace of 'no annexation and no indemnity', and the Bolsheviks, after seizing power, had revealed the Allies' secret agreements and reaffirmed this stand. The Bolsheviks' decision to withdraw Russia from the conflict was a great blow to the Allied governments and encouraged their more militant domestic critics. As a result, in January 1918, the British Prime Minister and the American President, in separate speeches, committed their countries to a liberal peace based on national self-determination, the destruction of militarism and the formation of an international organisation to prevent future aggression.

The Australian Prime Minister, however, had no time for these sentimental peace proposals and saw no point in trying to curry favour with dissidents. He would not contemplate anything less than total victory, and he defiantly asserted that the Allies were entitled to a peace of 'annexation and indemnity'. He was scathing in his attacks on the labour and Irish Catholic leaders who were half-hearted in their attitude to the war and dared to raise doubts about the British Empire's motives. Furthermore he would not allow that the United States, which only belatedly entered the war, had any right to lay down peace terms for the Allies. He had only contempt for President Wilson's sermonising.

For Hughes the British Empire was engaged in a struggle for survival in which the enemy's forces had to be routed. Germany was an international criminal and as such was liable for the full cost of the war. It had to be crippled economically and militarily, and so deprived of the capacity to engage in further aggression. The British Empire was entitled to the fruits of victory. The peace settlement should draw the British peoples closer together, restore the Empire's global supremacy and so safeguard Australia against the might of Japan. In the meantime Australia, without conceding anything substantial, had to make some concessions to the Japanese and so prevent them from abandoning the Allies. From early 1918 when Hughes left Australia for Washington and London, he single-mindedly pursued these aims.

10
The Attack on Peacemongers and the Appeasement of Japan

The Labor Party's war aims

As in all other belligerent nations, popular discontent in Australia led to questioning of the war and agitation for a negotiated peace. In Australia this movement had gained impetus from the bitter political divisions over conscription. Both labour and Irish Catholic leaders in the rancorous atmosphere created by the dispute expressed misgivings about Australia's participation in the war and the British Government's purpose in prolonging it. Reviled by the conscriptionists, the reformed Labor Party began to qualify its support for the Empire. A special ALP conference in December 1916, in addition to expelling conscriptionists from the party, called on Britain and its Allies to state their war aims and so pave the way 'for an early and honourable peace'. In contrast to the 1915 conference the delegates did not pass a resolution of loyalty to the Crown.[1] Likewise, in a different venue, Mannix, articulating Irish Catholic grievances, asked how Britain could maintain that it was fighting for the freedom of small nations while at the same time it was oppressing the Irish people. By declaring that Britain was engaged in 'a sordid trade war' he brought into question the moral legitimacy of the Empire's cause.

During 1917 labour was encouraged by the European socialists' appeals for a peace 'without annexation and indemnity' to believe that an early end to the conflict might be possible. The Labor Party, at all levels, took a firm stand against the 'Win-the-War' government's demand for total victory. The New South Wales conference in June resolved that peace would only come through the cooperation of the workers of the world. They congratulated the Russian people on their revolution and looked to an international settlement which would end hostilities. The Victorian conference, while narrowly defeating a call for an immediate peace 'without annexation and indemnity', endorsed its northern comrades' actions, and the South Australian and Queensland conferences followed suit.[2]

The National Government's uncompromising attitude towards the great strike of August-September and its malicious and oppressive tactics during the second conscription referendum intensified this anti-war feeling. While the more militant members of the Labor Party openly welcomed the Bolshevik government's decision to take Russia out of the war and seek a peace of 'no annexation and no indemnity', the mainstream embraced the British and American liberal peace programs as enunciated in January 1918 by Lloyd George and Woodrow Wilson.

In January 1918, at a picnic to celebrate the defeat of the referendum, Melbourne anti-conscriptionists endorsed the common elements of these peace declarations, namely the right of

---

[1] *SMH*, 7 December 1916.
[2] Ian Turner, *Industrial Labour and Politics*, pp.172–74.

small nations to political independence, the application of self-determination in disputed territories, the end of secret diplomacy and the creation of a 'world-wide parliament' for arbitrating international disputes. The Labor Party's leader, Frank Tudor, in supporting the motion, said that the ALP's position on the peace differed little from that of the British and American leaders. He considered that it was 'not beyond the statesmanship of the Allied countries to bring about an acceptable peace' based on these principles.[3]

When in the same month the Queensland Labor-in-Politics Convention adopted the New South Wales branch's peace resolution, the President of the ALP Central Executive maintained that there were 'strong signs of growing war-weariness' in all the belligerent countries. He attributed the rejection of conscription to 'the growing desire for peace'. The Russian Revolution with all its 'possibilities for a world-wide democracy' had caused the warring powers to revise their peace terms. Total victory would mean 'human annihilation'. And he concluded that it was the duty of all labour movements to unite in extirpating imperialism, 'whether German, British or any other which was the root and cause of all wars'.[4] In February the Labor Party for the first time joined with the Peace Society, Australians for Democratic Control, the Anti-Conscription League, the Australian Socialist Party and the Women's Peace Army to sponsor a meeting at the Sydney Town Hall which resolved that Britain and its Allies should begin peace talks without delay 'on the basis of no annexations and no indemnities' and the right of all peoples to choose their own governments.[5] While in 1914 and 1915 Australian labour had been more united than its British counterparts in supporting the war, by 1917 the reverse was the case. The labour movement had not changed its view primarily because its members had come to know more about the shortcomings of British policy or the evils of war than British workers. Rather the vicious campaigns conducted by Hughes and the conscriptionists had had the effect of making the Empire, the war and recruitment symbols of domestic division and partisan politics.

Labour's opposition to the war continued to develop step by step with its hostility to the National Government. At the Governor-General's recruiting conference Labor's parliamentary leaders not only sought the cancellation of the WPA regulations which had been used against strikers and anti-conscriptionists but also demanded concessions on war aims and peace terms. Much to Hughes's annoyance the labour representatives refused to accept a resolution for increased voluntary recruitment for the purpose of achieving victory. They would only agree to an appeal for 'necessary reinforcements for the AIF.' They understood well the increasingly angry mood among their people.

The Commonwealth Labor Party Conference in June exemplified most strikingly this feeling of alienation and militancy. In the preamble to a peace resolution the delegates drew on a mixed

---

[3] *Argus*, 29 January 1918.

[4] *Daily Standard*, 29 January 1918.

The Labor Party may have taken their lead from a British Trade Union special conference on 28 December which had adopted a Wilsonian liberal peace program similar to that subsequently espoused by Tudor. See reports on that conference, *SMH* and *Argus*, 31 December 1917. See also K. Robbins, *The Abolition of War: the Peace Movement in Britain, 1914–1919* (Cardiff: University of Wales Press, 1976), pp.152–53.

[5] *Australian Worker*, 14 February 1918.

bag of liberal and socialist orthodoxies to justify their desire for an end to the European conflict. They blamed all the European governments equally with their 'class rule' and 'Silent [sic] diplomacy' for the bloodshed. The international system, as it stood, inevitably stirred up commercial rivalry, territorial greed and dynastic ambitions. Since the ruling classes had made huge profits out of the war they had no interest in looking for ways to bring about peace. Only through the cooperation of workers in all the belligerent countries could the senseless slaughter be stopped. Against this background they welcomed the Russian Revolution and the Russian people's efforts 'to abolish despotic power and class privilege' – it is not clear whether this was meant to refer to the Bolshevik Revolution alone – and they exhorted workers in other countries who suffered from the same oppression to follow the Russian example.

In formulating specific peace proposals, however, they left the socialist critique behind. Here they made no mention of ruling classes, working classes or profiteering capitalists. Instead they adopted a liberal program, one which Andrew Fisher might well have been proud of, calling for popular self-determination in territorial settlements, open diplomacy, abolition of armaments, freedom of the seas and 'a world-wide parliament as advocated by President Wilson'. Their only distinctive inclusions, reflecting local politics, were 'the right of small nations (including Ireland) to political independence' and 'the abolition of conscription in all countries simultaneously'.

The conference took a hard line only on recruitment. The conference asserted that Labor's attitude to aid for Britain remained what it had been at the outset of the war, namely 'assistance to Great Britain, under the voluntary system', to protect 'liberty and democracy and the independence of small nations'. Reflecting the movement's distrust of the Allies' motives and Japan's intentions it was proposed that Labor should cease to support further campaigns for voluntary recruitment until the Allies declared their willingness to enter into peace negotiations on the basis of 'no annexations and no penal indemnities' and there had been an inquiry into Australia's manpower needs both for 'home defence' and industrial purposes. There was also a move to make opposition to recruitment, like opposition to conscription, a test of loyalty to the party. But more moderate counsels prevailed, and it was agreed that a ban on participation in recruitment rallies would be postponed until after a plebiscite of members approved it. The war ended before the vote was completed and, as a result, the issue disappeared and the party was saved from another bloodletting.

Some members regarded even compulsory military training as an anti-worker militarising of society and wished the Labor Party to take a stand against it. The majority, however, influenced by Catts's and other Eastern states delegates' view that 'effective steps should be taken for a more adequate defence of Australia against a probable invasion be [sic] Japan', defeated this proposal.[6]

---

[6] *Report of the seventh Commonwealth Conference of the Australian Labor Party opened at Perth, June 17, 1918* (Perth: The Party, 1918), pp.23ff.; *Argus*, 21 June 1918; memorandum, Captain Reginald Hayes for Deputy Chief Censor to Chief of the General Staff, 24 June 1918 enclosing copies of resolutions 'not published in full' from an intercepted letter, NAA A2219, Vol.1A; letter, H.E. Jones, Assistant Director of the Counter Espionage Bureau to Pearce, 5 August attaching report of Seventh Commonwealth Labor Conference by Don Cameron to 'Officers and Delegates, Metropolitan District Council A.L.P.', 31 June 1918, Pearce Papers, NLA MS 213/3 and 213/10/5–14; for Labor's continuing fear of Asia see also letter, W.H. Demaine, President of the Central Political Executive of the Queensland branch of the Labor Party to

As Catts subsequently explained in parliament these resolutions were not directed against Britain, but were based on the view that aid to the British cause should not be at the cost of Australia's own survival.

> I am with Britain up to the hilt, subject only to the condition that the interests of my native land, Australia, shall not be sacrificed. I will do all I possibly can to help Britain in this struggle, but for the last couple of years I have wanted to know whether my native land was being sacrificed, and that is what the Perth Labour Conference wanted to know.[7]

And Catts in taking this stand gave voice to the position adopted at the 1918 Labor Party conference when it declared in its fighting platform that, while opposed to Imperial Federation, it looked to 'complete Australian self-government as a British community'.

The National Party's war aims

The Nationals treated the demands for peace negotiations and the reservations on recruitment as further evidence of Labor's disloyalty to Australia and the Empire. The 'Win-the-War' government repudiated such views and condemned those who held them. Hughes in May 1917, responding to a report of a British parliamentary debate on the new Russian Government's peace program, had proclaimed his belief in a peace of 'annexation and indemnity'. In taking this position he was reacting not only to the Russian Soviets and German socialists who had popularised the slogan of 'no annexation and no indemnity' but also to President Wilson who had rejected any territorial or other selfish aims. Hughes averred that the Allies had every right 'to annex such territory as will safeguard the future of civilisation' and to exact the full cost of the war from those responsible for initiating it. In particular, Australia's future depended 'upon the control of the Pacific being in the hands of the Empire and its Allies'.[8] Indeed this slogan summed up neatly the policies which Hughes unwaveringly pursued in the debates in the Imperial War Cabinet and at the Paris Peace Conference.

Hughes was alarmed by a Russian-Dutch-Scandinavian socialists' proposal for an international conference in Stockholm that would bring together representatives from both the belliger-

---

Andrew Fisher, 6 October 1917, Fisher Papers, NLA MS 2919, 'and we want no fooling with White Australia and I am afraid that the present Imperial game is in that direction. I favoured your taking the High Commissionership for one reason, viz., that you would stand against any fool notion of closer unity and uphold a White Australia to the bitter end and I look to you to stand by your guns if need arises.'

An inflammatory article by an ultra-nationalist writer, Kazan Kayahara which attacked the White Australia policy and announced that Australia was 'destined for the Japanese by God' was circulated at the conference – probably by Catts – and had a significant part to play in persuading some members, against their branches' instructions, to support the retention of compulsory military training Extensive passages from the article were cited by one delegate in a debate in the South Australia House of Assembly shortly after the conference. See South Australia, *Official Reports of the Parliamentary Debates* (Session 1918), pp.50–52, House of Assembly, 31 July 1918.

[7] *CPD*, 1917–18 session, LXXXV, Pt.2, 6383, 25 September 1918.

[8] *Age*, 18 and 19 May 1917. For Australian reports of Russian and German socialists' peace activities see *SMH*, 16 and 25 April and 8 May 1917. For an account of the Russian Soviet and German Socialists' peace program see Stevenson, *The First World War and International Politics*, pp.149–55.

ent and neutral countries to discuss the making of peace on the basis of 'no annexation and no indemnity'. He believed that it would endanger the Allies' cause and urged Lloyd George not to allow British labour delegates to attend. It was his contention that British representation at Stockholm would be 'most undesirable and calculated to hamper Allies in prosecution of war and in deciding terms of peace'. In keeping with his belief that all such proposals by their very nature must be subversive and the work of the enemy, he asserted that the conference would be nothing more than an occasion 'at which peace cranks of all countries including Britain and secret agents of Germany masquerading as pacifists and friends of labour will be gathered together.' It was 'a cunning trap to catch loyal British labour representatives and through them organised labour now supporting war.' Hughes was critical of Lloyd George's indecisiveness. From the Australian leader's standpoint what had to be done was simple and straightforward. His government would refuse passports to labour leaders seeking to travel to the conference and, through the exercise of its censorship powers, would also prevent the labour movement from sending messages of support to Stockholm.[9]

There should be no truck with a compromise peace no matter from what quarter the idea emanated. These schemes were part of a conspiracy directed against the British race. When at the end of November Lord Lansdowne, a former British Conservative Foreign Secretary, published a letter urging the Allies to give up the ambition of crushing Germany and appealing for an end to the war 'in time to avert a world-wide catastrophe', Hughes was more forthright than Lloyd George in denouncing the defeatist sentiments. Speaking in the midst of the second conscription referendum campaign he regretted that Lansdowne had given the impression that the Empire was wavering at the very moment when 'Every man of British race worth his salt had determined that the hour had come when a supreme effort must be made to achieve a decisive victory.' Lansdowne should not be taken seriously. He was speaking only for 'himself, a clique of doctrinaire pacifists and pro-German agents who are striving to repeat in Britain what they have accomplished elsewhere.'[10]

Though Hughes had pronounced ideas about what constituted a good peace, he had had no part in making British policy. He had not been able to attend the 1917 Imperial War Cabinet meeting where peace terms had been discussed. He had not been privy to the British Government's peace negotiations with enemies or Allies. Nor had he been consulted about Lloyd George's January 1918 speech, which was the most complete and authoritative statement of British war aims. Lloyd George had, two days before the event, informed Hughes of the address and assured him that it contained 'no change of policy'. The British leader in undertaking this *demarche*, which contradicted previous promises and Imperial War Cabinet undertakings, did not

---

[9] Copy of cable, Munro Ferguson to Long, 10 August 1917, Novar Papers, NLA MS 696/2661 and NAA CP78/34 8/27 and copy of cable, Munro Ferguson to Stamfordham, 27 August 1917, Novar Papers, NLA MS 696/295.

For a general account of the Stockholm Conference see David Kirby, 'International Socialism and the Question of Peace: The Stockholm Conference of 1917', *Historical Journal* 25 (1982), pp.709–16.

[10] *SMH*, 3 December 1917; for Lloyd George's response, see John Turner, *British Politics and the Great War*, pp.249–50.

give Australia any chance to contribute to its formulation. He took the Dominions' assent for granted.

This speech, delivered at a Trades Union Congress, was intended to quieten murmurings in the ranks of radical and labour dissidents. Unlike Hughes, Lloyd George met domestic dissent with conciliatory gestures.[11] After dismissing the published peace terms of the Central Powers, he denied that the British Empire sought to destroy Germany or the German people, and outlined a settlement based on liberal principles. In the statement he promised to respect international law and treaties, to support the application of self-determination to territorial disputes and to help establish an international organisation that would 'limit the burden of armaments and diminish the probability of war.' There was no mention of a 'knock-out blow' or of fighting on until victory had been won.

This was an embarrassment. Lloyd George seemed to give credibility to peace terms that the Australian Government had attacked as dangerous and disloyal. Indeed a number of labour leaders, including the leader of Labor's parliamentary party, publicly associated themselves with the British Government's proposals. Hughes made the best of it by trying to turn the speech into what he believed it ought to be, and he hailed it as 'a great and statesmanlike declaration of the views of the Empire and its Allies' which was 'proof of the resolution of the Allies to continue the war until victory is achieved'.[12] President Wilson's Fourteen Points address, delivered three days after Lloyd George's speech, was even more difficult to reconcile with Hughes's call for annexation and indemnity. Hughes resented this latecomer to the war presuming to dictate to the British Empire and its Allies. There can be no question but that he already felt hostility towards Wilson and his peace principles. Yet though Wilson's peace principles received as much press coverage as Lloyd George's Hughes refrained from commenting on the Fourteen Points. Since the American President did not commit Australia, Hughes was under no obligation to respond. Rather than offend this new great ally he held his tongue.

Anxiety about Japan's war aims

Hughes's attitude towards the peace derived not only from fears for the future of the British Empire but also from concerns about Australia's position in the Pacific. When insisting on a peace of annexation he had especially in mind Australia's desire to keep the German South Pacific islands and to prevent the Japanese from extending their influence into the region. These islands were to provide a protective barrier against the downward thrust of Japan. Despite being preoccupied throughout 1917 with industrial and political crises, he still had time to give attention to the mounting evidence of Japan's activities. His suspicions of Japan, which had been strengthened during his visit to London in early 1916, continued to grow.

Since returning from Europe he had received a stream of intelligence dealing with Japanese expansionism. The Navy Department in September had sent him Japanese press extracts that contained attacks on the White Australia policy and support for 'a policy of steady penetration' in

---

[11] For Lloyd George's placatory attitude to labour unrest, see Chris Wrigley, *David Lloyd George and the British Labour Movement: Peace and War* (New York: Barnes and Noble Books, 1976), chapters X-XIV.
[12] *SMH*, 6 and 19 January 1918.

the Pacific. Shortly after this, the British Consul-General in Batavia had reported that the Japanese seemed intent on securing a foothold in the Dutch East Indies. Simultaneously the New South Wales Trade Commissioner in Kobe, in forwarding further newspaper cuttings, had repeated his earlier warning that Japan aspired to dominate Asia and the Pacific; 'The real objective is south, and, although the articles specially refer to Java and Sumatra, for diplomatic reasons Australia and New Zealand are not included.' Suttor stressed that Australia was Japan's ultimate objective.[13] Munro Ferguson told the Colonial Secretary that 'The really anxious matter here, apart from the state of chaos presently prevailing in Recruiting and Industry, is the situation in the Pacific', notably 'the peaceful penetration by Japan, which may at any time develop some aggressive form.'[14]

When, therefore, the British Government on 1 February 1917 informed Australia that Japan wished to secure British backing for its claims to the German possessions in the North Pacific at the end of the war, Hughes was little surprised. From the end of 1914 the Australian authorities had recognised that the Japanese would be difficult, if not impossible, to evict. They understood that Japan was bent on exploiting the European conflict to consolidate its dominance of the region. At every stage of the war the Japanese had behaved exactly in this manner. They had taken advantage of their Allies' preoccupation to enhance their long-term position.

The Japanese had responded to British requests for naval assistance in the Atlantic and Mediterranean as they had a year earlier by asking for a *quid pro quo*. They intimated that their cooperation would depend upon Britain giving a pledge, similar to the one it had given Russia and Italy for their territorial ambitions, that it would at the peace settlement support their right to retain their Asian and Pacific conquests. The British Government was reluctant to consent to such a deal, but the Admiralty's need for reinforcements was so great that they felt obliged to accede to Japan's wishes.[15]

Since London was aware of Australian and New Zealand apprehensions about Japan and had previously assured them that no decision would be made about the future of the German Pacific possessions until the Peace Conference, it wanted to obtain their approval before entering into any agreement. In putting the Japanese proposition to the Australians the British explained that they had hoped to discuss the future of Germany's Pacific colonies at the forthcoming Imperial War Cabinet but Japan had forced their hand. They noted that the British Empire was not being asked to give up anything that they could expect to acquire at the end of the war. Japan occupied

---

[13] Memorandum, George L. Macandie, Naval Secretary to Shepherd, Secretary, Prime Minister's Department, 16 September 1916, NAA 63/48 J2/24/4; despatch, W.R.D. Beckett, British Consul-General, Batavia, to Sir Edward Grey, 14 October 1916, transmitted to the Prime Minister's Department, 8 November 1916, NAA MP729/2 1877/5/54; letter, H.C. Hoyle, Secretary, New South Wales Premier's Office, to Hughes, 1 November 1916, NAA A981 JAP38, Pt.1.

[14] Personal despatch, Munro Ferguson to Bonar Law, 7 December 1916, Davidson Papers, House of Lords Record Office 3/53; see also secret letter, Munro Ferguson to Long, 3 January 1917, TNA: PRO CO 418/157/6.

[15] Letter, Secretary to the Admiralty to Under-Secretary of State, British Foreign Office, 18 December 1916, TNA: PRO ADM 116/1702; cable, Greene to Balfour, British Foreign Secretary, 27 January 1917, TNA: PRO FO 371/3236; Minutes of British War Cabinet Meeting (51), 1 February 1917, TNA: PRO CAB 23/1.

the North Pacific islands and it would be 'practically impossible to induce her to surrender them'. Sweetening the pill the British told Hughes that they would insist on Japan giving a reciprocal assurance of support for the Empire's retention of the South Pacific islands. In a supplementary cable the British explained that, though the Japanese had in the event agreed to the Admiralty's request without receiving the desired promise, it was still important that Japan's wishes should be met. It was necessary to appease Japan both to ensure its continuing naval cooperation and to frustrate Germany's efforts to detach it from the Allied camp. The Colonial Secretary warned that 'Any answer which could be interpreted as unfavourable to the Japanese aspirations would inevitably react on their general attitude and have the most unfortunate effect on the general course of the war.'[16]

Hughes, like Fisher before him, could not avoid the constraints that the war had placed upon Australia's choices. As a result of his visit to Britain he had grasped the 'importance and delicacy' of the Japanese question, and he assured the British that Australia would 'carefully abstain from doing or saying anything likely to strain or make difficult' relations with Japan. In this spirit he replied that 'Australia would not object to Japan's occupancy of islands North of Equator except one or two small ones on or near the borderline, of which Nauru and Ocean Islands are typical.' Hughes, however, wanted to leave the British in no doubt about Australia's anxieties, and he promised that if he were able to come to London for the next Imperial Conference he would spell out 'at length the view of the Commonwealth Government'.[17]

The British were not satisfied with this answer. It was legal title not 'occupancy' that was at issue. Moreover the reference to the Nauru and Ocean islands was puzzling since both islands were south of the equator. Perhaps Hughes in making this odd qualification had in mind the earlier British suggestion that Australia should withdraw from Nauru, a suggestion which the Australians had construed to mean that the British wanted to hand over the island to the Japanese. Perhaps he had confused Nauru and Ocean islands with the Greenwich atoll which lay just north of the equator: in October 1914 the Japanese Navy during its sweep across the North Pacific had hoisted a flag on the atoll even though it was leased to a British subject and quite distant from the Carolines. London, endeavouring to clarify the matter, inquired again of Hughes whether Australia would agree that the British Empire should commit itself to support Japan's annexation of the North Pacific possessions in return for a Japanese promise to support the British Empire's claims to the South Pacific islands. So pressed Hughes replied that Australia would have 'no objection'.[18] Hughes had bowed before the necessities of the time and accepted the Japanese *fait accompli* in the North Pacific. On 14 February the British informed the Japanese Government that they were willing to enter into the proposed arrangement.

---

[16] Cables, Long to Munro Ferguson, 1 and 5 February 1917, NAA A981 MARS2 Part3; see also Hughes Papers, NLA MS 950/5/40 and NAA CP78/23 89/316.

[17] Cable, Munro Ferguson to Long, 7 February 1917, TNA: PRO CO 532/91/215.

[18] Cable, Long to Munro Ferguson, 8 February 1917, NAA A981 MARS2 Part 3. As was Hughes's custom the draft reply was scribbled in Hughes's handwriting on the cable.

See also cable, Munro Ferguson to Long, 9 February 1917, TNA: PRO CO 532/91/232.

The Anglo-Japanese agreement, formal notification of which reached Australia in May, did nothing to allay Australian fears about Japan. Quite the contrary. And throughout 1917 accumulating evidence of Japanese aims and actions in the region added further to these concerns.

In February and March Hughes received two reports that painted pictures of a predatory Japan extending its influence into every part of the Western Pacific. Colonel Robert Sands, whom Hughes had sent to the Far East to investigate Japanese activities, concluded that 'the clutching yellow hand … is busy gradually placing stepping stones for its countless millions to walk over when the time is propitious.' He maintained that it was 'the united opinion of all the leading diplomats and businessmen in Japan today … that Australia is the ultimate objective.'[19] Walter Henry Lucas, Island Inspector for Burns Philp, in his 'Notes on Western Pacific and Australian Interests Therein. Actual and Potential', stressed the danger from Japanese competition. Unlike Sands, Lucas identified a number of possible post-war commercial rivals, including the Dutch, French and Americans. But, nevertheless, it was Japan, 'gradually creeping Southwards', that posed the greatest threat to Australian interests. To bring home the point he recounted how the Japanese had used their occupation of the North Pacific islands not only to oust the Germans but also to concentrate the island trade in their own hands.[20]

In the first half of 1917 the Australian Government had to consider the future of the Pacific against this background. Following a petition from the Australian Associated Chamber of Commerce the Minister for Defence asked the Chief of the General Staff, Brigadier-General Hubert Foster, to assess the importance of the German Pacific islands, both north and south, to national security. Foster, a seconded British officer who deferred to the War Office authorities, did not share Australian fears of Japan and he offered the government advice consistent with the British optimistic assessments. While he thought it 'decidedly desirable' that the British Empire should keep the South Pacific islands, he rejected the notion that Japan's retention of the North Pacific islands would constitute a danger to Australia. He denied that Japan would be able to establish naval bases in the Marshalls, Carolines and Ladrones. And he insisted that, in mentioning this, he did not wish it to 'be taken as implying the probability of any attack on Australia by our present Ally'. Similarly his support for holding the South Pacific islands was based not on strategic grounds but administrative convenience, namely that it would 'round off the British Possessions of Papua, and the Solomons'.

Pearce was not impressed by Foster's advice and he wrote the Prime Minister that 'in view of importance of these islands to Australia and especially in view of the fact the Commonwealth was not represented at the recent Imperial Conference … strong representations should now be made to the British Government to the affect [sic] that the Commonwealth would strongly object' to the South Pacific islands 'being either handed back to Germany or to any other foreign power'. With either Germany or Japan in possession these islands would pose a grave threat to national security. Two weeks later cabinet, for the first and last time before Hughes left for London in 1918, discussed 'peace terms', and while approving the British Government's position as laid down by

---

[19] Copy of Sands' Report in private and personal despatch, Munro Ferguson to Long, 7 February 1917, TNA: PRO CO 418/157/241.
[20] NAA A981 Japan 38, Pt.1, General.

Asquith and Lloyd George agreed that these terms had to include the 'annexation of Pacific Islands South of the Equator'.[21] Accordingly on 13 August Hughes drafted a message for London which, taking over Pearce's words, stated that 'Ministers now desire to emphasise that the islands in question south of the Equator should not be returned to the Government of Germany nor handed over to any foreign power.' But four days later he thought better of it and cancelled the cable.[22]

During 1917 Hughes felt the impact of Japan's new-found confidence. The Japanese resumed their campaign to persuade Australia to sign a commercial agreement. The Japanese Consul-General had been informed of the discussions that had taken place in London and he had been instructed to take up the case again in Melbourne. Shimizu told Hughes that he was 'aware of the views ... set forth by you in the conversation you had with the Japanese Ambassador in London last year', and he assured the Prime Minister that 'the difficulties to which you then referred may be overcome without any great trouble by a frank exchange of ideas and opinions.' Shimizu intimated that Hughes could no longer plead his uncertain hold on government as an excuse for refusing to enter into negotiations. Since, after the May election, the National Party had a commanding majority in both houses the government's decision would 'meet with a minimum of opposition'.[23] But once more Hughes gave the Japanese no satisfaction.

The Australian Government had become convinced that Japan, as the reports from Batavia and Kobe had agreed, was bent on a course of 'peaceful penetration'. Having conceded that they could do nothing to prevent Japan from dominating the North Pacific, Hughes and Pearce were determined to do all in their power to shut Japan out of the South Pacific. In February the Australian Government, for the first time, had imposed restrictions on the entry of Japanese into German New Guinea. Following an inquiry from Shimizu Hughes stated that his government thought it 'undesirable to encourage any immigration into the territory' and that therefore they would only admit female relatives of Japanese males already resident in New Guinea. In order to make it appear that this was a non-discriminatory policy based on military considerations, Hughes assured Shimizu that the same rules would apply to Australians. When Shimizu

---

[21] Despatch, Long to Munro Ferguson, 2 March 1917, forwarded to Hughes, 16 May 1917, NAA A981 MARS2 PART3. Hughes noted on the despatch that, since Japan had reneged on part of the naval assistance, namely the destroyer flotilla for the Mediterranean, the British and Australians had good reason to question the reliability of Japan's reciprocal promise for the British Empire's claims to the South Pacific islands.

Letter, J.W. Vasey, President of Associated Chambers of Commerce of Australia, to Hughes, 15 April 1917, NAA MP1049/1 14/0285; note, Pearce to Secretary, Defence Department, 10 May 1917, *ibid*.

Report by Foster on 'German Possessions in the Pacific', 23 May 1917, NAA A981 MARS5 and CP 447/2 SC 472(7) and 63/48 J2/3/2. Brigadier-General S.A. Pethebridge, Administrator of German New Guinea, cautioned against accepting Foster's 'rather sweeping' downplaying of the value of the North Pacific islands to Japan. See letter, Pethebridge to Acting Secretary, Defence Department, 27 June 1917, NAA MP1049/1 14/0285; letter Pearce to Secretary, Defence Department, 30 May 1917, *ibid*.; Minutes of Cabinet Meeting, 12 June 1917, Hughes Papers, NLA MS 1538/16/688.

[22] Draft cable, Hughes for Munro Ferguson, 13 August 1917, NAA A981 MARS2 PART3.

[23] Letter, Shimizu to Hughes, 3 July 1917, NAA CP 447/2 SC472(7); see also secret letter, Munro Ferguson to Long, 3 January 1917, TNA: PRO CO 418/157/6.

complained that this policy unduly hampered Japanese firms engaged in shipbuilding, coconut plantations and fishing who employed more than sixty workers, Hughes modified the rule to allow Japanese employees who took leave in Japan to return to New Guinea and to permit the firms to replace those who did not return. In making this concession, however, it was stipulated that the number of Japanese in the former German colony would not be allowed to exceed the number resident at the time of Australian occupation.[24]

The Australian Government was so set on keeping Japan out of the South Pacific that it was willing to surrender Burns Philp's established right to trade in the North Pacific islands. After the Japanese had taken possession of the Marshalls and Carolines, Burns Philp had encountered difficulties in carrying on business there. Even though the Japan authorities in December 1915 had put Burns Philp on an equal footing with Japanese firms in the islands under their control, they insisted that this was conditional on Australia conceding equal rights of access to the South Pacific islands. In October 1916 the Japanese placed further restrictions on foreign traders when they announced that 'owing to military necessity' only foreign companies with pre-existing rights would be allowed to trade in the Japanese held islands and that 'foreigners generally', even in that case, would be accorded the right only 'in so far as there is no military impediments.'

Burns Philp, which had established rights to trade from the time of the German administration, found that the Japanese frequently put obstacles in their way. In December 1916 one of their trading ships was refused entry into Jaluit, the chief port of the Marshalls. When at roughly the same time the company attempted to open an office in Jaluit and to establish ten trading stations elsewhere in accordance with the terms of a pre-war arrangement the Japanese refused to allow it until Japanese firms received reciprocal treatment in the islands under Australian control.[25]

Burns Philp's attempt to expand its trade in the Marshalls embarrassed the Australian Government. When the Japanese conditions were brought to their notice, Hughes and Pearce were troubled by their implications. Thus they informed the British that they trusted the Japanese condition of 'same treatment to Japanese as to British subjects … means and is limited to those facilities to trade that we ask for Burns Philp and does not mean that in exchange for these facilities Japanese subjects are to have same treatment as British subjects in all other matters within captured German territories under our control as this would mean giving to Japanese subjects something we have not asked for British subjects in captured possessions under Japanese control.'[26]

---

[24] Letters, Shimizu to Pearce, 27 January 1917, Hughes to Shimizu, 12 February 1917 and Hughes to Shimizu, 31 March 1917, NAA CP 447/2 SC472(7).
[25] Copy of despatch, Grey to Munro Ferguson, 17 February 1916 enclosing copy of letter, Kikujiro Ishii, Japanese Minister for Foreign Affairs to Greene, 14 December 1915, and copy of despatch, Greene to Ishii, 15 December 1915, NAA CP 447/2 and 472(7); copy of despatch, Greene to Viscount Motono, Japanese Minister for Foreign Affairs, 19 December 1915 and despatch, Greene to Balfour, 27 January 1917 enclosing copy of letter, Motono to Greene, 26 January 1917, TNA: PRO FO 371/2949/28–30.
[26] Cable, Munro Ferguson to Long, 20 May 1917, TNA: PRO FO 371/2949/43 and copy in NAA CP 447/2 SC472(7).

The Australian Government's concerns were justified. The Japanese in inquiring about Australian policy in the South Pacific had sought to know whether established Japanese firms would be permitted to bring in Japanese workers over and above the numbers necessary to replace those returning to Japan.[27] The British, in passing on the Japanese query, advised the Australians that they should let sleeping dogs lie. They told the Australians that it was 'undesirable' to press the Japanese further on what they meant by equal treatment and that the Commonwealth should in the interim assume the phrase referred only to trade facilities. For the Foreign Office, Australia's clear intent to apply the White Australia policy to New Guinea posed an awkward problem. The British recognised that if this were openly admitted there would be 'a howl in Japan and the whole immigration question will be raised at a moment when neither we nor the USA are in a position to withstand Japanese pretensions.'[28] The Australians followed the British suggestion, and in their reply avoided the issue of workers and averred that they were unaware of any difference in the treatment of Japanese and British traders in the South Pacific. They only wanted equal trading access to Japanese held islands and were prepared to grant 'reciprocal advantages' for such purposes in the islands they held.[29]

The Japanese were not deceived by the answer. On 23 July Shimizu, at the direction of Tokyo, wrote Hughes that since the Japanese had accorded equal treatment to British subjects in the North Pacific islands they expected that Japanese subjects would be able to enjoy the same rights in the South Pacific islands, and he asked Hughes to reconsider the ban on the entry of additional workers into New Guinea. But this appeal, like all its predecessors, fell on deaf ears. The Australians were immovable. As Munro Ferguson confided to the Colonial Secretary, 'So long as he [Hughes] maintains ante-bellum status quo rights of trade in all the late German possessions either side of the Equator, he is on safe enough ground. If, on the other hand, he presses for new trade privileges north of the line, then he must concede them to the south of the line. This being done, then Japan will expect equal facilities with those enjoyed by British traders throughout the British Pacific Dependencies.' Hughes skirted around the problem and merely expressed regret that his government was unable to meet Japanese wishes. And there the matter rested. At the time the number of Japanese in German New Guinea was estimated to be 230; by 1919 there were only 92 left in the territory.[30]

The Australian Government was also adamant that Japanese merchants should as far as possible be kept out of the South Pacific. When the Nan'yo Boyeki Kaisha applied for permission to be allowed to trade with the Solomons Islands the British, in forwarding the request to Melbourne, stated that as the Japanese had agreed to equal treatment on a reciprocal basis the only ground that could be used to justify a refusal was 'military impediment'. The British warned that, if Australia rejected the application, the Japanese might well retaliate against Australian firms. This in no way deterred Hughes. Australia had little to lose. Since nearly all Australia's

---

[27] Cable, Greene to Balfour, 12 June 1917, TNA: PRO FO 371/2949/57.
[28] Cable, Long to Munro Ferguson, 21 June 1917, NAA CP 447/2 SC 472(7) and TNA: PRO FO 371/2949/56–57.
[29] Cable, Munro Ferguson to Long, 10 July 1917, NAA CP 447/1 SC 472(7).
[30] NAA A3934, SC 472(7); *CPP*, 1920, No.49, 'Report of Royal Commission on late German New Guinea', pp.16–19.

merchant ships had been requisitioned for war service, the Japanese, if given the opportunity, would be able 'to monopolise the whole of the inter-island trade of those islands under British control'. The Australians saw in Japan's move a further step towards the 'peaceful penetration' of their sphere of influence. Burns Philp still dominated trade in the South Pacific and the Australian Government was determined to protect its privileged position. Trade policy served strategic interest. The Australians acknowledged that they had to abandon their claims on the North Pacific islands. They were, however, resolved to preserve their Monroe Doctrine for the South Pacific. Therefore Hughes replied to the Japanese that it was 'not considered advisable for military reasons to grant request'. He turned the Japanese phrase back on them. The Japanese could not fail to understand its meaning, but having employed it themselves they had no choice but to submit to what they could not change.[31]

All this activity on the part of the Japanese renewed anxieties about home defence. The Inspector-General, Major-General Legge, ever alert to the Japanese danger, warned Pearce that 'preparations for Home Defence should not be neglected.' Indeed preparations were 'urgently necessary, because experience has shown that ... peace between original combatants has often been only a prelude to further conflict between new combinations of belligerents.' Australian authorities could 'not anticipate what demands may be made at the final settlement, and some may be such as Australia would resist to the last man.'[32]

---

[31] Copy of despatch, Long to Munro Ferguson, 7 November 1917 and copy of cable, Munro Ferguson to Long, 28 March 1918, NAA A3934 SC 472(7).

Munro Ferguson, after meeting the senior officers from a Japanese squadron which visited Australia in October 1917, realised that the Japanese fully understood how the Australians viewed them. He informed the Colonial Secretary that 'These Japs, while frankly disliking and distrusting the Australians, are under no illusions as to the sentiment being reciprocated. they [sic] think they are being used for the moment and discount all friendly overtures'. The Governor-General was pessimistic about Australia's ability to defend itself against Japan for, as he put it, 'The more one comes in contact with the Japanese the more one recognises their efficiency and the helplessness of Australia if left alone in the Pacific.' See personal dispatch, Munro Ferguson to Long, 25 October 1917, NLA MS 696/970–72.

[32] 'On the Preparation of Australia for Home Defence', Memorandum, Legge to Pearce, 19 June 1917, and letter, Hughes to Pearce, 10 July 1917, NAA B197 1856/4/392. Pearce read it with 'keen interest and appreciation' and passed it on to Hughes who also read it.

11
Manoeuvring for the Spoils of War: American Consultations and Imperial Councils

Looking out on the war and the world at the end of 1917, Hughes felt disturbed and frustrated. Apart from the collapse of the Eastern Front and the stalemate on the Western Front, developments inside the Allied camp itself were disquieting. Following America's entry into the war and the overthrow of the Czarist regime in Russia, American liberals and European socialists began to have increasing influence on the Allies' peace terms. It seemed to Hughes that the British Empire might be deprived of the fruits of victory which ought to encompass both the destruction of Germany and the restoration of the Pax Britannica. Moreover, Japan – its power greatly increased – might at the end of the war expand further into the Western Pacific and menace Australia's safety. Thus when he saw that the Allies were giving more attention to defining their peace terms he was anxious to go to Britain to join in these discussions and so put things right.[1]

Accordingly when in January 1918 the British Government invited the Dominion premiers to a second Imperial War Conference and Cabinet, Hughes welcomed the chance to rouse the Empire to demand a peace of annexation and indemnity. Cook, who was to accompany Hughes on his trip to London, shared in broad terms his leader's vision. On the eve of departure he told the Millions Club that he would 'stand behind him [Hughes] while he urges that we should retain these islands [The German islands in the South Pacific] to the last gasp. They are vital to our future security here.' 'For the rest', he added 'we shall go on believing in our hearts that we shall best serve the interests of Australia by trying to keep together the mighty British Empire in trust for the whole of civilised mankind.'[2]

Wooing America

To achieve his objectives, especially his Pacific objective, Hughes recognised the importance of gaining America's cooperation. It was evident that the United States, having entered the war, intended to play a pivotal role in the peace, and with this in mind he was intent on visiting the United States on his way to London. He hoped to convince President Wilson and other key figures in the administration to adopt a punitive attitude to Germany and to support Australia's claim to the South Pacific islands.

---

[1] Private and personal despatches, Munro Ferguson to Long, 5 and 13 October 1917, Long Papers, WRO 947/75.

[2] *SMH*, 25 April 1918. On 13 February Hughes, having settled his difficulties with the National Party, which had insisted that Cook accompany him to London, accepted the invitation.

Cable, Long to Munro Ferguson, 15 January 1918, Hughes Papers, NLA MS 1538/16/II (1)/22; cable Long to Munro Ferguson, 31 January 1918, *ibid.*, 1538/16/1938; cable, Munro Ferguson to Long, 13 February 1918, *ibid.*, 1538/133/4.

In America, though Hughes made speeches celebrating a common Anglo-Saxon heritage, he did this primarily as a rhetorical device intended to suggest shared values and purposes. He resented the fact that the United States had taken so long to join the Allies and to recognise its responsibility to help thwart the German menace. Following America's declaration of war Hughes had expressed no gratitude for this belated assistance. Its intervention was overdue; 'America has at length seen what its duty was and is determined to do it.'[3] And that duty was to help the British Empire vanquish its enemies. He despised President Wilson for his earlier advocacy of American neutrality and his boast that the United States was 'too proud to fight'. Wilson's liberal ideology and peace principles were anathema. He saw, moreover, that in the post-war period America would contest the Empire's naval and commercial supremacy. When in early 1917 the British Treasury, having come to the end of its own resources, had suggested that Australia might raise a loan in America, Hughes was 'much disturbed'. It was, he told the Governor-General, 'wrong in principle'. If Australia had to turn to America it would 'strike a vital blow at relations between Britain and Australia'. Once Australia became financially dependent upon America its trade and industry would follow. It would give the quietus to Hughes's ambition to create a self-sufficient autarchic Empire that would embody the aspirations of the British peoples.[4]

Even before Hughes reached America he had antagonised the leading figures in the administration. Since the British had commandeered the merchantmen that in peacetime normally transported Australian exports to Europe, Hughes, in May 1917, had ordered fourteen ships from America. On learning only two months later that the United States was proposing to seize these vessels, along with all other vessels being built for foreigners, he was greatly indignant. It was a sign of America's coming challenge to *Pax Britannica*. His first thought was to ask the British Ambassador in Washington to present Australia's protest to the State Department. The Governor-General, however, who was a stickler for proper procedure and had little sympathy for Australia's problem – the ships in his eyes were simply to be used 'to market her produce for her own profit' – insisted that the request should be sent through the Colonial Secretary. Impatient with such roundabout methods of communication and fearing that such a delay might be fatal to the cause, Hughes approached Lord Northcliffe who had just been appointed head of a British War Mission to Washington. Hughes had high hopes of obtaining Northcliffe's assistance as he had met the press baron while in England in 1916 and found him to be sympathetic and supportive.[5]

---

[3] *SMH*, 5 April 1917.
[4] Letter, Hughes to Munro Ferguson, 10 January 1917, Novar Papers NLA MS 696/2587; cable, Munro Ferguson to Long, 13 January 1917, Long Papers, WRO 947/507; letter, Munro Ferguson to Long, 10 January 1917, Novar Papers, NLA MS 696/891; Novar Diary, *ibid.*, NLA MS 696/36, 12 January 1917.
[5] Minutes of Cabinet Meetings, 24 May 1917 and 11 June 1917 Hughes Papers, NLA MS 1538/16/679–85; letter, Munro Ferguson to Hughes, 17 July 1917, Novar Papers, NLA MS 696/2647; letters, Hughes to Munro Ferguson, 17 July 1917, *ibid.*, 696/2651–52; personal despatch, Munro Ferguson to Long, 18 July 1917, Long Papers, WRO 947/624/634; cable, Northcliffe to C.J. Phillips, Special Representative in Foreign Office for Long, 16 August 1917, TNA: PRO CO 418/164/232; letter, Phillips to Long, 14 September 1917, enclosing copy of cable, W.J. Young, Australian Government representative in the United States, to Hughes, 'I am doing my best with Northcliffe to save ships', TNA: PRO CO 418/164/347.

Northcliffe duly obliged and passed on Hughes's memorandum of complaint to Colonel House, the President's confidential adviser and 'alter ego'. The document was, as House called it, a 'remarkable communication'. It was a mixture of Australian special pleading and British race arrogance. Hughes had, in his haste, allowed his feelings to show. On the one hand he asserted that Australia was 'for all practical purposes an independent nation' which had 'done great things in the war', and that the ships being built for the Commonwealth were to be employed exclusively on war work carrying wheat and flour to Britain and its Allies. On the other, however, he warned that Australia would regard the seizure of its ships as an 'unfriendly act' against a country which had been 'fighting gallantly for three years'. He rejected out of hand even the suggestion that the vessels might be leased to the United States. This was unthinkable, since 'to carry American flags and crews' would be a 'blow against the naval and maritime supremacy of the British Empire'.

The language of the message gave great offence. The reference to Australia's war record was a reflection on America's tardy decision to take up arms. 'Unfriendly act' was one of the strongest phrases in the diplomatic vocabulary, often a prelude to a declaration of war. Moreover the appeal to the British Empire's right to 'naval and maritime supremacy', especially after the Anglo-American disputes over neutral rights on the high seas, could only serve to alienate and infuriate the Americans. Even if Hughes did not want Northcliffe to hand the memorandum to the Americans – and there is little reason to think that this was not his intent – it is clear that he wished the substance to be conveyed to them. House was outraged by it and not unreasonably concluded, in sending the message to Robert Lansing, the Secretary of State, that Hughes was 'unfitted for the place he occupies & Northcliffe is unfitted for the one he has.'[6]

Seemingly unaware of how his memorandum had been received Hughes looked forward to winning American approval for the annexation of the South Pacific islands and the containment of Japan. Before leaving Australia he had discussed with the Governor-General the idea, first advanced by Deakin in 1909, of having the United States extend its Monroe Doctrine to the South Pacific as a 'Possible shield against Japan'.[7] Since this seemed impracticable, Hughes decided to take the opportunity while in America to proclaim an 'Australasian Monroe Doctrine for the South Pacific'. He hoped to establish at least the appearance of an Australian-American 'entente cordiale' in the Pacific.

Hughes was no doubt prompted to give his plans this specific form by reports that Viscount Ishii, Japan's envoy to the United States, during negotiations with the Wilson Administration, had announced a Japanese 'Monroe Doctrine in the Far East' – a policy that at the end of 1917 was tacitly embodied in the Lansing-Ishii Agreement.[8] Japan loomed large in Hughes's thinking as he prepared for his overseas trip. Munro Ferguson recorded that his Prime Minister was 'most anxious to see President Wilson in order to persuade him that the Democracies of the Pacific

---

[6] Cable, Northcliffe to House, 13 August 1917, enclosing Hughes memorandum, House Papers, Yale MS 466; House Diary, 15 August 1917, Vol.XI, p.241, *ibid.*; Lansing Desk Diaries, Vol.I, 16 August 1917, Lansing Papers, LC mm 78029454.

For Northcliffe's response to Foreign Office and Colonial Office criticisms, see cable, Northcliffe to Lloyd George, 21 August 1917, Lloyd George Papers, House of Lords Record Office F41/7/13.

[7] Novar Diary, 12 January 1918, NLA MS 696/36.

[8] *SMH*, 2 October and 7 November 1917.

must stand by one another.' Hughes spurned the advice of Dr G. L. Morrison, the Australian-born former China correspondent for the London *Times*, who had recommended that Australia in order to avert 'the Japanese peril' should follow Canada's example and make a 'gentleman's agreement' with Japan to regulate immigration. For Hughes, Australia was best protected by great and powerful white race friends who could be coaxed or cajoled into accepting that Australia's interests were their interests.[9]

Arriving in the United States, Hughes travelled to Washington where he met the President and the Secretary of State. On 29 May, accompanied by Cook, he lunched with Lansing at the British Embassy, and then, under the watchful eye of the British Ambassador, had a brief audience with Wilson in the Oval Office at the White House. Wilson, it would appear, did most of the listening. Keenly aware that what he sought was at odds with the President's peace principles, Hughes exerted all his powers of persuasion, couching his arguments in language that might earn Wilson's sympathy.

As the British Ambassador, Lord Reading, reported it to London:

> Mr Hughes impressed on the President that it was vital to the security of Australia that Germany should never be allowed to take any part of New Guinea or the Islands of the Pacific. Mr Hughes made plain that Australia was not seeking all these Islands for herself that she had sufficient territory but that her life would be menaced if Germany with her predatory designs held any of these Islands and he emphasised the necessity of these belonging only to the British Empire and friendly Powers.

Though according to Reading, 'The President was sympathetic' Wilson's only response was to say that he would communicate the substance of Hughes's talk to 'those to whom he had entrusted the study of these and similar questions', meaning a group of scholars called the Inquiry.[10] After this poor beginning Hughes met with some members of the Inquiry, but he did not make any better impression on them than he had on the President.[11]

---

[9] Personal letter, Munro Ferguson to Long, 1 April 1918, Long Papers, WRO 947/625/100; Novar Diary, 27 March 1918, NLA MS 696/36.

[10] Cable, Reading to Balfour and Long, 2 June 1918, Balfour Papers, BL Add 49741, folio 200.

For Hughes's account, see W.M. Hughes, *Policies and Potentates* (Sydney: Angus and Robertson, 1950), pp.229–30. Written thirty years after the event this version of the meeting was dressed up in the mock heroics and self-serving hyperbole which habitually coloured Hughes's stories. Almost certainly his recollections were also affected by his unhappy encounter with President Wilson at the Paris Peace Conference.

If Wilson had known of the Anglo-Japanese agreement of February 1917 he might have viewed Hughes's arguments as a defence of a secret treaty serving not only British imperial but also Japanese imperial interests. The question as to whether Wilson had been informed by the British of this agreement is assessed judiciously by Ian Nish in *Alliance in Decline*, pp.214–15. That Secretary of State Lansing was told of its contents is, however, certain. See cable, Sir Cecil Spring Rice, British Ambassador to the United States, to Balfour, 13 August 1917, TNA: PRO FO 371/2954/485 and 489A.

[11] Laurence E. Gelfand, *The Inquiry: Preparations for Peace, 1917–1919* (New Haven: Yale University Press, 1963); James T. Shotwell, *At the Paris Peace Conference* (New York: Macmillan, 1937), p.11.

It is hard to believe that what Reading described as 'sympathy' was anything more than formal courtesy masking personal antipathy. Even if Wilson had not read Hughes's 'remarkable' memorandum which challenged Washington's right to requisition the ships being built for Australia in the United States, it is likely that House or Lansing would have acquainted him with its contents. That a Prime Minister of a small, remote British colony should have the effrontery to address the American Government in this manner was not to be suffered. In the sweltering heat of a Washington summer the President had given Hughes a cool reception. Imperial aggrandisement masquerading as national security grated harshly against liberal internationalism sublimating national power. Two days after Hughes's interview Wilson told the congregation of Washington's Central Presbyterian Church that, 'there would be a renaissance of higher ideals and better lives after the war ... the spectre of twenty nations battling against the forces of evil was startling evidence that Christ still reigns in the hearts of men.'[12] This first meeting of the two men probably confirmed the disdain that each felt for the other. Here were the seeds of a personal and philosophical antagonism which was to run through the entire peacemaking process.

Conscious of the difficulties of persuading Wilson and his officials, Hughes took his message to an influential section of the American public. He did not need Murdoch's warning that he might have 'trouble with Wilson over the German Pacific islands if there is no propaganda' and that it might pay to 'do a little speaking in USA'.[13] Hughes was able to take advantage of an Anglophile movement that had sprung up at the end of the nineteenth century in reaction to the mass migrations from southern and eastern Europe. It stressed America's British origins and had its base in East Coast academic, professional and financial circles. It founded organisations such as the Pilgrims' Society and advocated closer ties between the British Empire and the United State and closer Anglo-American cooperation in world affairs.[14] In this spirit the Pilgrims arranged a dinner at the Union League Club in New York to honour the Australian Prime Minister and to enable him to address the issues of the hour.

Making most of this opportunity Hughes proclaimed an Australasian Monroe Doctrine for the South Pacific. In the speech he tailored his introductory remarks to the prejudices of his audience. He flattered the Americans telling them that the United States entry into the war was 'the final and exclusive evidence of the justice' of the cause in that 'the greatest of democracies' had answered 'the cry of democracy in peril'. After asserting that only a complete victory over the enemy would be acceptable, he then came to the nub of the matter. He declared that America, Australia and New Zealand had 'common interests in the Pacific' and that Australia looked to America, 'the elder brother ... to stand by her around the peace table'. Australia had to have 'guarantees against enemy aggression in the future'. Drawing on the classic phrase from the American foreign policy tradition he said that this had to involve an 'Australasian Monroe Doctrine in the Southern Pacific'. The archipelagos which lay to the north and east of Australia guarded or menaced its coasts 'according as they are held by friend of foe'. And he asked the

---

[12] *New York Times*, 1 June 1918.
[13] Letter, Murdoch to Hughes, 22 November 1917, Murdoch Papers, NLA MS 2823/33.
[14] Bradford Perkins, *The Great Rapprochement: England and the United States, 1895–1914* (New York: Atheneum, 1968).

Americans rhetorically, 'what would your attitude be towards any predatory power that claimed territory as near to your own shore?' It was 'inexorable circumstances' which had caused the Commonwealth to adopt the doctrine of 'Hands Off the Pacific'. Australia did not seek empire but security 'against all predatory nations'. Australians would give effect to this doctrine 'to the last ounce of effort at our disposal'. In carrying out this task they looked to America for its 'steadfast and wholehearted cooperation and aid.'[15]

The Prime Minister here went far beyond what he had said to the President. As his speech was interpreted in Australia, Britain and Japan as well as America, Hughes wanted American support not merely to rid the South Pacific of the German presence but also and more importantly to counter Japan's ambitions in the region. It was evident to all that when he said Australians would defend the principle of 'Hands Off' the Pacific 'against all predatory powers' he had in mind Japan as much as, if not more than, Germany.[16] Hughes, in seeking American endorsement for an Australasian Monroe Doctrine for the South Pacific, might well have been angling for an informal understanding to balance the Lansing-Ishii agreement that had seemed to concede to the Japanese the right to a Monroe Doctrine in the Northeast Pacific.

This visit to the United States helped to bring home to Hughes the importance of Australia's relations with the principal Pacific powers. Anticipating Prime Minister Robert Menzies's action in 1939, he concluded that Australia should have its own representatives in the key countries of the region, in the United States as a potential friend and in Japan as the potential foe. Shortly after arriving in North America he had proposed to Acting Prime Minister W. A. Watt, that Australia should appoint an 'attaché' to Tokyo. But Watt, Pearce and other senior ministers, perhaps more sensitive to the proprieties, thought that Hughes 'should consult British authorities and advise us

---

[15] *New York Times*, 1 June 1918.

The next day Hughes repeated his message to the Association of Foreign Correspondents in America. *New York Times*, 2 June 1918.

[16] The Governor-General, no doubt after reading an account of Hughes's speech in the local press (*SMH*, 1 June 1918), wrote to Long that Hughes 'wishes to obtain through his persuasive influence the support of America to the White Australia Policy and to a restriction of Japanese activity south of the Equator.' Munro Ferguson believed that Hughes was 'animated by a real imperial patriotism', but the Governor-General was 'not without fear lest in his zeal for Australia's safety he be inclined to turn to America and seek a very close and direct understanding with her.' Personal letter, Munro Ferguson to Long, 5 June 1918, Long Papers, WRO 947/625/109.

For examples of the Japanese view that Hughes's speech was aimed at Japan, see *Japan Chronicle*, 6 June 1918 and *Osaka Asahi Shimbun*, 7 June 1918. Suttor in reporting the Japanese reaction wrote that the Japanese believed Hughes was 'anxious to court the friendship of America by way of blocking the progress of Japan to the South'. Letter with enclosures, Suttor to W.A. Holman, New South Wales Premier, 7 June 1918, forwarded to Watt, NAA A2219, Vol.1A. A few community leaders, such as Sir William McMillan and Senator Herbert Pratten, disturbed by the Japanese reaction to Hughes's speech, joined with the Japanese Consul-General in founding a 'Hands Around the Pacific club' which published as its objective 'the cementing [of] the British, French, Australian and Allied interests in the Pacific, both internationally, socially and commercially.' See *SMH*, 12 July 1918. But this initiative gathered little support and was still-born.

their views before we do anything'.[17] Hughes himself had rejected a similar suggestion from G. E. Morrison in January 1918.[18] It is possible that J. G. Latham, Cook's private secretary, may have used the long voyage across the Pacific to convince Hughes to take this initiative. Commander Latham, as Director of Naval Intelligence, shared with Major E. L. Piesse, the Director of Military Intelligence, the conviction that British officials in the Far East did not appreciate Australian concerns about Japan and that therefore Australia should have its own official relations with that country.[19] Frustrated by his colleagues, Hughes let the matter drop.

The need for an Australian representative in the United States was a matter of greater urgency. During his brief stay in America in 1916 Hughes had suggested that Australia should have a Defence Department official attached to the British Consul General's staff in New York 'in order to watch Australian interests in America',[20] but overwhelmed by the conscription controversy he had not at that time pursued the question. This later experience had brought home to him even more the imperative need for Australia to have its own representative in the country. Making the case to Watt he pointed out that Australia's image and interest suffered by comparison with 'every small Twopenny ha'penny South American Republic', all of which had their envoys in Washington. The British Foreign Service was not adequate. They acted 'for us in a casual sort of way'. These British diplomats 'haven't the remotest idea of what Australia is like nor of its importance, and even with the best of intentions they are unsatisfactory'. As he envisaged it Australia would have a trade representative in New York and on the West Coast, and a diplomatic representative in Washington. Summing up he concluded that Australia found itself greatly disadvantaged 'in national prestige, in opportunities of trade, in every way through its failure to have adequate representation'.[21]

This time Hughes's colleagues in Melbourne raised no objections. There was, however, some confusion over the precise status and role of the appointee or appointees. Hughes had indicated that he wished the Washington representative to have political as well as commercial functions

---

[17] Cable, Watt to Hughes, 24 May 1918, NAA CP360/8 B1/1; see also copy in Hughes Papers, NLA MS 1538/23/82 dated 28 May which may be the day on which the British Embassy relayed it to Hughes.

[18] Copy of personal despatch, Munro Ferguson to Long, 1 April 1918, Munro Ferguson Papers, NLA MS 696/102–23.

[19] Copy of letter, Latham to Piesse, 3 September 1918, Latham Papers, NLA MS 1009/20/796.

Australian naval and military intelligence had for some time been urging the Commonwealth Government to appoint 'a suitable representative ... to Japan who could report on current events'. Captain Walter Thring, who had succeeded Latham as head of naval intelligence, wrote that Suttor, the New South Wales Trade Commissioner in Kobe, had acted in this capacity but had found that 'the work ... interfered with his other duties'. In a formal paper in May 1918 he raised the issue again and recommended that the Australian appointed to Tokyo should have 'a good knowledge of Eastern affairs, be on friendly terms with Japanese who could give him inside information'. And he noted that there was 'now in Australia a man, who, I believe, possesses all these qualifications and I suggest that his appointment should be considered.' He clearly had in mind James Murdoch who had been brought to Australia by the Defence Department as a lecturer in Japanese to teach at Sydney University and Duntroon Military College. See Intelligence Report by W.H. Thring on 'Japan', 23 May 1918, NAA MP1587/1 184J, which was sent to Latham in London.

[20] Despatch, Bonar Law to Munro Ferguson, 24 July 1916, NAA CP78/22 1916/133.

[21] Cable, Hughes to Watt, 3 June 1918, NAA CP360/9/1.

but he had not explained how the Australian official would be related to the British Embassy. The Australian Government selected Henry Yule Braddon, the head of Dalgety and Company and a former President of the Associated Chambers of Commerce, for the post. Watt applied to the Governor-General for a letter of introduction to the British Ambassador for the 'Commissioner for Australia to represent the Commonwealth in the United States'. Munro Ferguson, ever watchful for colonial encroachments on imperial prerogatives, demanded to know 'the scope and character of his mission'. He would not be a party to anything that smacked of independent diplomatic representation. After discussion it was agreed that Braddon would have the title of 'Commissioner representing the Commonwealth of Australia in the United States of America'. He would – though formally restricted to fostering trade relations, disseminating information and supervising government business dealings – still be able to 'furnish reports at regular intervals on any matters which are likely to be of interest to the Government'. On these terms Braddon took up his post in New York in October.[22]

At the end of his stay in America Hughes had little to show for all his efforts. While he had met many notable figures from politics, business, labour and the military and had received courteous treatment from the Pilgrims and their friends, the administration had given him no sign of encouragement. No doubt he enjoyed his visit with Theodore Roosevelt, the former president who in 1908 had sent the Great White Fleet to the South Pacific to show solidarity with Australia and New Zealand and who since 1914 had been a vocal advocate of America's entry into the European war. Hughes might boast to the Governor-General that he had done 'some useful work in America on the Pacific Island question' and that he was sure he had taken 'the right line in seeking to enlist the sympathy of Uncle Sam', but it is difficult to see how his sojourn in America had produced any worthwhile results.[23]

Campaigning for a reorganised Empire

In Britain Hughes assumed a more familiar role. Here he became the champion of the British race. Here he was among his own people. As the tribune of his fellow Britons, he had no compunction in calling for a punitive peace that would restore the British Empire's global supremacy and, as part of that process, allow Australia and New Zealand to annex the German South Pacific islands. Encouraged by the proceedings of the 1917 Imperial Conference and Cabinet Hughes looked forward to making his mark. The Dominions and the United Kingdom would 'meet on equal terms' and Australia, along with the other Dominions, would have a voice in the councils of the Empire.[24]

Hughes, like most Australians of his time, thought of both the British Empire and Australia as his nation, the first the nation of cultural identity and the second the nation of political community. Addressing the British Empire League he referred to the Empire as 'a nation such as

---

[22] Memorandum, Shepherd to Steward, 29 August 1918 and note by Steward, 29 August 1918, NAA CP78/22 1918/234; copy of letter, Watt to Braddon, 13 September 1918 and copy of letter, Munro Ferguson to Long, 26 September 1918, NAA CP78/22 13/234.
[23] Letter, Hughes to Munro Ferguson, 10 July 1918, Novar Papers, NLA MS 696/2722.
[24] *SMH*, 15–16 June 1918.

ours, with traditions such as ours'. Yet at a British Empire Parliamentary Association welcome to the Dominion prime ministers he praised the Empire as a 'league of free nations'.[25] Speaking to Australian troops in France Hughes spelt out the meaning of the latter idea of 'nation', when he told them that before the war:

> We were a people isolated ... We made laws about a White Australia irrespective of the fact that within a stone's throw of us there were a thousand million people who coveted our land. There is but one way in which we who hold Australia can keep it: And that is the way you have chosen.[26]

Despite Australians' desire that the two nations might be one they had, because of the two countries' very different geopolitical circumstances, been forced to accept that British and Australian interests were not easily reconcilable. Since the end of the nineteenth century Australians, for this reason, had refused to accept any form of imperial federation in which Britain would have had the dominant say and so been able to subordinate Australian interests to its own. The Great War had served to highlight this dilemma.

Hughes had an acute sense of this problem. The war had convinced him that the only solution was to be found in the reorganisation and reintegration of the Empire. During his visit to Britain in 1916 he had preached this doctrine throughout the land. Two years later he was an even more fervent believer. The war had brought on a crisis for the Empire. It had uncovered weakness deriving from a lack of unity, a weakness that had sapped the Empire's energy and weakened its will. He was particularly disheartened by the British Government's failure to give effect to the Paris Economic Conference resolutions. Thus no sooner had he set foot on British soil than he resumed his campaign to win hearts and minds for his peace of annexation and indemnity. As he traversed the country from London to Glasgow and from Cardiff to Manchester, he sought to rouse the public and so bring pressure on the Imperial War Conference and War Cabinet to adopt his vision of the post-war world.

Of all the Dominion leaders Hughes alone had a simple, clear and absolute answer to the problem of the Empire's future, especially its economic future. Murdoch, writing to Hughes while he was still in America, had tried to alert him to the difficulties he would encounter if he chose to press the matter. Murdoch cautioned Hughes that 'The best opinion here is that the country is not ripe for strong work on the Paris resolutions.' There were, he added, many opposed to them. Lloyd George had 'never been strong on the Paris resolutions, indeed ... he was definitely against or at least lukewarm.' Nevertheless Murdoch, knowing his man, flattered Hughes that the country would respond to his message; it would 'rally to a man who can state its issues and its problems plainly.'[27] Certainly nothing that Murdoch had said caused Hughes to deviate from his predetermined course.

In his first major speech he reminded the London Chamber of Commerce that when last in Britain he had called for 'organisation – economic, financial, general' and he reaffirmed that the

---

[25] *Times* (London), 20 June 1918; *SMH*, 24 June 1918; see also *Times* (London), 22 June 1918 which cited Hughes describing the Empire as a 'veritable Commonwealth of Nations'.
[26] *Times* (London), 20 August 1918.
[27] Letter, Murdoch to Hughes, 3 May 1918, Hughes Papers, NLA MS 1538/23/38–39.

future of the Empire 'depended absolutely on such organisation.' He expressed his dissatisfaction with the lack of progress in giving effect to the Paris Economic Conference resolutions: 'But as yet no definite general policy, fiscal or economic, has been declared, no national agreement established, no machinery created.' It was his view that these things 'ought to be done without delay'. The kind of organisation he envisaged was not a socialist but a nationalist scheme. He offered Australia as a model. On his initiative manufacturers and producers in every industry had formed associations and elected councils which acted as executives for each industry. When problems arose which the councils could not solve, they appealed to the Central Council of Industry. The Central Council could then make recommendations to the government for financial aid, bonuses, tariffs or other forms of support.[28]

Hughes took on his detractors, especially the Liberal and labour free traders and internationalists who had formed a 'Radical Council' to contest his autarkic chauvinism. Taking advantage of the friendly platforms afforded him by the British Empire's Producers' Association, the Imperial Commercial Association and the British Empire League, he denounced 'muddling through' and 'laissez-faire'. He derided the critics of the Paris resolutions who advocated a more open and cooperative international order; the Germans had revealed their economic aims in the harsh terms that they had imposed on the Russians in the Brest-Litovsk treaty. He renewed his demands for the eradication of German influence from the British economy and expressed amazement that 'a firm like Merton & Co. are still here in the citadel of the Empire.' He declared himself 'sick of the humbug about internationalism'. His appeal was to the British people throughout the world. It was his proud claim that he 'preached the development of the heritage of the Empire'.[29]

As Australia's Prime Minister, Hughes was particularly interested in having the market for the Empire's raw materials organised on a long-term basis. Since, as a result of the war, Australia had a large national debt, the securing of assured markets for its primary products was an urgent matter. Moreover the various producer associations had lobbied Hughes for this purpose. The Copper Producers' Association, for example, had told Hughes that they wanted fixed contracts based on current prices for the period of the war and ten years after. Yet, despite Hughes's best efforts, the British refused in nearly all cases – wool being the major exception – to offer long-term contracts at fixed prices. Hughes reported back to Melbourne that 'Re … COPPER, GLYCERINE, TALLOW, BUTTER, WHEAT, HIDES, LEATHER, MEAT, RABBITS', the difficulties were 'very great'. The British were hostile to 'any suggestion for long contracts'. They preferred, he said, to buy from America. While Hughes had found Bonar Law sympathetic, the Chancellor of the Exchequer was 'apprehensive of political effects of buying goods which he cannot ship and which may slump after the war'.[30] Yet, though Hughes's crusade for an organised, self-sufficient Empire might have been influenced by Australia's special interests, he was primarily driven by a

---

[28] *Times* (London), 28 June and 25 July 1918; see also Hughes's speech on the subject of Australia's national organisation, *SMH*, 5 November 1917 and 13 February 1918.
[29] *Times* (London), 11 and 25 July and 2 August 1918.
[30] Cables, Hughes to Watt, 24 June, 2 July, 2 and 21 August 1918, NAA CP360/8 B1/1.

For the need to have assured markets in order to pay off war debts, see Hughes's speech of 4 November 1917 in *SMH*, 5 November 1917.

conception of empire that he had held for over a decade. Unlike Lloyd George who was a political chameleon, changing his policies to suit the circumstances, Hughes pursued his vision with a chilling consistency.[31] If need be he would appeal to the British people over the heads of their government.

Though it was often found difficult in practice to maintain the functional distinction, the British Empire's leaders met formally, as they had in 1917, under two headings; in an Imperial War Conference chaired by the Colonial Secretary to deal with internal Empire matters, and in an Imperial War Cabinet chaired by the British Prime Minister to deal with war and peace, defence and foreign policy. Hughes had cabled ahead that he wished to have two general and two specific issues considered: in the Imperial Cabinet – 'post-war problems including trade and tariffs', and 'the Pacific question'; and in the Imperial Conference – reform of the Privy Council and of the channels of communication between the Dominion and British Prime Ministers.[32]

The 1917 Imperial Conference and Cabinet had passed resolutions that had gone some way to meet Hughes's wishes on both economic organisation and the Pacific. The Imperial Cabinet had appointed two committees to consider post-war policy. One had recommended the annexation of all German territory in British hands and the other the control of the Empire's material resources in order to make it self-sufficient. Lloyd George, however, recognising the difficulties involved in adopting these fixed positions, surrounded them with suitable qualifications. On the first, he persuaded his colleagues to accept the wording merely as a guide since its feasibility depended both upon the fortunes of war and the consent of Britain's Allies. And on the second, he modified the language so that the conference agreed that, 'having due regard to the interests of our allies', all parts of the Empire would accord 'specially favourable treatment' to each other's products.[33] Yet even in these watered down versions, the resolutions showed that British race patriotism was a dynamic force in the shaping of the Empire's approach to the peace.

The members of the 1917 Cabinet Conference had agreed that the British Empire, through vanquishing its enemies and marshalling its resources, should be restored to its former glory. In the interest of its post-war security they believed that the Empire should keep its conquests and develop its economy so as to be independent 'in respect of food supplies, raw materials and essential industries'. They also doubted whether a League of Nations would be a reliable substitute for the Royal Navy.[34]

---

[31] L.S. Amery summed up Lloyd George's political style well when he wrote of him, 'I never knew a man who lived so entirely by spontaneous reaction to his environment … He was not deliberately inconsistent or untruthful. But living entirely in response to the immediate stimulus, he had no clear memory either of past events or of his own former motives. I always felt that if Lloyd George had been confined in an empty whitewashed room he would have just faded into thin air, like a similar character in one of Henry James's stories.' See Amery, *My Political Life*, Vol.II, p.95.

[32] Cable, Munro Ferguson to Long, 22 March 1918, TNA: PRO CO 532/110/93; cable, Munro Ferguson to Long, 6 May 1918, TNA: PRO CO 532/110/356.

[33] Minutes of 1917 Imperial War Conference Meeting, NAA CP290/15/2 1917/19/26.

[34] Minutes of the Imperial War Conference, 26 March–24 April 1917, TNA: PRO CO 532/97/585–618 and 864–66.

At the 1917 conference meetings New Zealand, in the absence of Australia, had taken the initiative in pressing for Pacific naval defence, that is for an imperial force which could protect the South Pacific Dominions against Japan. The New Zealanders complained of the failure of the Admiralty to honour its 1909 commitment to contribute to a Pacific fleet. They clearly identified Japan as the object of their concern. Prime Minister Sir Joseph Ward, citing Frank Fox's *Problems of the Pacific*, said that the great question for the future would be 'whether the White Race or the Yellow Race' was to predominate in the Pacific. He urged that the 1909 scheme should be revived, and the Imperial War Conference resolved to ask the Admiralty to prepare a plan which would provide 'for the Empire's future security'.

During the 1918 Imperial War Conference and Cabinet meetings these issues were revisited. Hughes took an active part in the deliberations, speaking up for a peace which would destroy Germany as a world power, guarantee the economic self-sufficiency of the British Empire and provide for Australia's security in the Pacific.

When the Colonial Secretary at an early meeting of the Imperial Conference introduced a motion, intended to implement the 1917 decision, which stated that it was 'desirable' to control certain essential raw materials produced within the Empire, Hughes supported the principle. But since such controls were 'absolutely essential for the welfare, and even the economic existence of the Empire', he was adamant that this objective was not just desirable but 'absolutely necessary'. Repeating his familiar theme that at the end of the war there would be 'a struggle between the two races … for economic domination or supremacy', he insisted that the measure was 'necessary for the economic stability or greatness, or development of Great Britain and the Empire after the War.' He had his way and 'necessary' replaced 'desirable' in the resolution. He was contemptuous of 'pious expressions of opinion' and was impatient for action. He wanted to include a plan which would give effect to the principle. But much to his chagrin the conference left the execution to future consultations between governments and producers.[35]

As part of his campaign to eliminate all German influence in the Empire Hughes also gave his backing to a New Zealand proposal that Britain and the Dominions should for a period after the war refuse naturalisation to citizens of enemy countries and prevent them from acquiring 'political rights', land titles or mineral rights. It was a measure after Hughes's own heart. It spoke to his deepest convictions about loyalty and identity. In his Manichean way he maintained that there was 'no middle way … You have either to be for your own race or against it.' He candidly explained that his government had 'disenfranchised native-born Germans in Australia because we know from experience … that blood is thicker than water.' Reiterating the argument he had advanced at the time of the adoption of the *War Precautions Act*, he said that those who were of German ethnic origin 'directly war comes … are for Germany, just as we, if we were in Germany and had lived there twenty years, when war broke out, would be for Britain, naturally.' For him the proposal did not go far enough. He wanted it to cover German influence in the Empire's economy as well; 'the main thing we have to do is to prevent the Germans, the enemy, getting control of our industrial and financial life by holding shares in our companies.' As in the case of control over raw materials Hughes took a more extreme stand than any other British Empire leader. Indeed the

---

[35] Minutes of the Imperial War Conference, 19–26 June 1918, pp.5–45, NAA A2939/1 SC76.

Canadian and South African representatives were disturbed by the injustice that would be done to those of German descent who had proved their loyalty during the war. When New Zealand pressed for a vote Hughes, seeing that nothing better could be attained, voted for the motion, and it was carried with South Africa and Canada abstaining.[36]

A war strategy for peace-making

The Imperial War Cabinet absorbed the greater part of the Dominion leaders' energies. Lloyd George had proclaimed it to be a 'real cabinet', an extension of the British War Cabinet, ostensibly an executive for the Empire, responsible for imperial defence and foreign policy.[37] In 1918 its meetings were primarily concerned with the immediate problems of war and peace. Between 11 June and 15 August there were sixteen full meetings of the Imperial Cabinet and thirteen meetings of the 'Prime Ministers Committee' – the 'inner executive' Hughes dubbed it – and the discussions ranged over a wide field, covering such issues as military strategy, Japan and an Eastern Front, post-war security and a League of Nations as well as the terms of peace both generally and for the Pacific.

In June, when the Imperial Cabinet began its work, the Allies were facing their most perilous moment of the war. In March the German high command had launched a great offensive on the Western Front aimed at overwhelming the British and French forces before substantial American reinforcements could arrive to turn the tide. By the time Hughes reached London the Germans, after inflicting heavy casualties on the Allies, had crossed the River Marne and advanced to within 90km of Paris. It was natural therefore that the cabinet should attend first to war policy and military strategy.

At the initial meeting of the Imperial War Cabinet Lloyd George and the Chief of the General Staff, Sir Henry Wilson, offered a detailed overview of the Allies' grave position. They reported on the huge losses that had been sustained and on the fragility of the defensive line to which their forces had retreated. The Empire's political and military leaders were agreed that the best they could hope for was 'lasting out for the next couple of months' until the Americans arrived in

---

[36] *Ibid.*, 22 July 1918, pp.175–91.

[37] Minutes of Imperial War Cabinet Meeting, 2 May 1917, TNA: PRO CAB 23/40; UK, *Parliamentary Debates*, Vol.XCIII, cols 1790–92, 17 May 1917.

Lloyd George's acceptance of the Imperial War Cabinet as the body responsible for determining imperial defence and foreign policy was more apparent than real. In response to the military crisis, he had begun, even before the Dominion prime ministers had arrived in London, to meet informally with the Minister for War and the Chief of the Imperial General Staff to discuss war strategy and to decide military policy. During the period in which the Imperial War Cabinet was in session he continued this practice, holding these meetings a half hour before the meeting of the Imperial Cabinet. Neither the existence of nor the decisions made by these secret meetings were brought to the attention of the Dominion prime ministers. Lloyd George pursued a similar style of decision-making, often bypassing the British War Cabinet as well as the Dominion leaders, when he formulated Britain's armistice terms for Turkey, Austria and Germany. See Stephen Roskill, *Hankey: Man of Secrets* (London 1970), 2 vols, I,'1877–1918', 546–618. Hankey kept a special 'X' and 'A' Series of 'Notes of Conversations' and '(Very Secret) Draft Minutes' covering these meetings. For these records, see TNA: PRO CAB 23/17 and 23/14.

strength. Wilson allowed that 'for another two months we have got a very, very anxious time.' He could not predict what might happen. Lloyd George even felt it necessary to give some thought to what Britain should do if France fell, and he ruminated on the possibility of a joint British Empire-United States blockade of the Continent, along the lines of Britain's blockade of Europe during the Napoleonic wars.[38]

The Dominion prime ministers held the generals responsible for the setbacks on the battlefield. They demanded to know why after the sacrifices of 1917 and 1918, including substantial Canadian, Australian, New Zealand and South African casualties, the Allies found themselves in such dire straits. Hughes joined Borden in placing the blame on defects in planning and preparation as well as organisation and leadership. He also complained that, despite the contribution made by the AIF, Australia had never received any explanation for the reverses, 'never a scratch of a pen'.[39]

Lloyd George, who was himself unhappy with the generals' failure to deliver a 'knock-out blow', set up a committee of the Prime Ministers to look into the reasons for the debacle and to canvass new strategies. He doubted 'whether it would be necessary … to consider once more the question of peace aims'. These had been dealt with in his speech of 5 January, or at least he hoped that the Dominion leaders would agree that this was so. The major task before the Empire was to find a way to win the war without incurring further great losses. It was of utmost importance that they should still have 'a great army next year not merely in order that the Empire may be able to claim its fair share in the victory' but also so that 'if ever we came to a Peace Conference the fact we have great forces behind us will count when we come to a settlement.'[40]

During June and July at the meetings of the Imperial War Cabinet and the committee of the Prime Ministers, Hughes stressed as their first priority the need to achieve a complete victory on the main battlefield, the Western Front. Ever conscious that the war was a life or death struggle, Hughes argued that only total victory would restore the Empire's global supremacy. He contended that they had 'to reach a position where the Military power of Germany was broken.' The Empire could 'only get what we wanted by giving them a thrashing.'[41]

Lloyd George understood Hughes's point quite well for in a way it was his own. He was, however, loath to see the British Empire's forces frittered away in a costly new offensive in France. As a member of every British ministry since the outbreak of the war, he had heard generals give repeated assurances that each new attempt to break the German lines would bring the promised victory. But, as he bitterly noted, all they had brought were huge losses that sapped the foundations of British power. For this reason he believed the Empire's army should not be risked in another such frontal attack. In answering Hughes, Lloyd George maintained that if the Empire's army were gravely weakened the Americans would be left dominant in the field and would be able to impose their will upon the Allies. Hitting Hughes where it hurt most, he suggested that:

---

[38] Shorthand Notes of Imperial War Cabinet Meetings (15 and 18), 11 and 18 June 1918, TNA: PRO CAB 23/43.
[39] Shorthand Notes of Imperial War Cabinet Meetings (15 and 19), 11 and 20 June 1918, *ibid.*
[40] Shorthand Notes of Imperial War Cabinet Meetings (15), 11 June 1918, *ibid.*
[41] Draft Minutes of Prime Ministers' Meeting, Imperial War Cabinet (27A), 31 July 1918, TNA: PRO CAB 23/44A.

> When Australia said she wanted the Pacific Islands … President Wilson would look down his nose and say that he had entered the war with quite different ideas in view, he would say he had his 120 divisions ready to continue the war, and he would ask what assistance we could give.

With this in mind the British Prime Minister wanted to avoid another futile blood-bath on the Western Front and to accomplish Germany's downfall by attacking its vulnerable allies, Austria-Hungary, Bulgaria and Turkey.

Hughes was not indifferent to these considerations. Above all he prided himself on his hard-headed 'realism', that is, his appreciation of the relation of economic and military power to political influence. But he insisted that if the Germans were to be beaten they had to be beaten in France, and it behoved the British Empire to be in at the kill. Only then could they be certain of having their proper say in the peace-making. It was true that 'if the British Empire won a victory on the field of battle but bled to death in the process and then had to go to a Peace Conference, we should have gained the shadow but lost the substance.' Moreover the Empire would have also lost its competitive edge in the post-war world: 'If we use our manpower at the rate we are doing, whether we win or lose we are done … In two years … your chances as a competitor with America or with Germany will be very small.' Nevertheless he remained certain that 'the Power that had the largest force at the end of the War would probably exercise the greatest influence on the terms of peace.' Hughes could offer no satisfactory way to square the circle. Though he thought that their war policy should be devised so as to prevent 'America or anybody' – and America loomed large in his consideration of the subject – from being able to dictate the peace and to compel the British Empire 'to accept crumbs from the table', his only suggestion for conserving manpower which would not lead to an abandoning of a major role on the Western Front was to make better use of military technology, especially tanks and aeroplanes.[42]

All agreed that the most satisfactory solution to the problem would be the reopening of the Eastern Front in Russia. It would take the pressure off the Western Front and provide a barrier against German penetration of the Middle East. Lloyd George 'could only see one thing that would make the difference, namely if Russia could so far recover as to become a formidable menace and compel the Germans to detach the necessary superiority composed of good, fighting divisions … to crush it.'[43]

While the logic of this preferred strategy was in the abstract impeccable, the British leaders could find no way of bringing it about. Since the Bolsheviks' seizure of power and their unilateral withdrawal from the war and humiliating surrender to the Germans, Russia lacked any significant rallying point around which pro-war forces could unite. When Hughes asked whether there was 'some man or some men who have the capacity of leadership, who can get a sufficient force of men who will fight and who will wake these dreamers up', Balfour offered no hope of salvation

---

[42] Draft Minutes of Prime Ministers' Meetings, Imperial War Cabinet (27A and 27B), 31 July and 1 August 1918. TNA: PRO CAB 23/44A; Shorthand Notes of Imperial War Cabinet Meeting (22), 28 June 1918, TNA: PRO CAB 23/43.

[43] Draft Minutes of Prime Ministers' Meeting, Imperial War Cabinet (27A), 31 July 1918, TNA: PRO CAB 23/44A.

from that quarter; 'all that central flat part of Russia [not yet conquered by the Bolsheviks] ... had never produced a great man, and ... apparently is totally without inherent or internal vigour.'[44] Lloyd George in search of a suitable Russian leader had interviewed Kerensky, the first leader of the Russian Revolution, who after being deposed by the Bolsheviks had fled to England. But when Kerensky, after declaring that 'Russia was ripe to take up arms against Germany', asked what Britain could do to help, the sceptical Lloyd George had replied that he first wanted to know what the Russians were prepared to do for themselves.[45]

Disappointed by the Russians, the British tried to persuade the Japanese and the Americans to mount an expedition through Vladivostok into Siberia. Balfour told the Imperial War Cabinet that the European Allies believed that Japan 'should go as far west as to be a threat to German domination.' Since the Japanese were unwilling to act without the Americans, Britain had urged President Wilson to cooperate with them in this undertaking. The Americans, distrusting the Japanese, had, however, refused. They argued first that the 'yellow races' would be 'unpopular in a white country' and would drive the Russians into the arms of Germany, and second that it was foolish to expect that an allied contingent in Vladivostok would be able to affect the German front which was 8000 kilometres distant.[46]

Despite the reasonableness of these American objections the British continued to pin their hopes on this strategy, and the Imperial War Cabinet spent some time discussing how President Wilson could be won over. Hughes, having just come from Washington, put himself forward as an expert on American policy. During his visit he had met 'the Committee on Foreign Relations', a body which, he claimed, had been entrusted with the responsibility of advising the President on this question. It would seem that he was here alluding to the Inquiry. The members of this 'Committee' had given him 'the impression – in fact they said so plainly – probably that arose out of what I said about Japan – that they were not in favour of Japan operating herself' but were 'in favour of a joint operation'. Here Hughes mentioned a 'Doctor Schlesinger'. The problem, as Hughes assessed it, was that the Americans had not considered intervention in Siberia to be a question 'of the first importance'. It appeared to have 'no greater urgency' than the other Pacific questions that he had discussed with them. According to Hughes this committee was considering both items together and was due to present an 'Interim Report in a day or two'. Pleased with his rather dramatic contribution to the cabinet's deliberations, he concluded that it was 'of the utmost

---

[44] Shorthand Notes of Imperial War Cabinet Meeting (19), 20 June 1918, TNA: PRO CAB 23/43.

[45] Secretary's Notes of Prime Ministers' Meeting, Imperial War Cabinet (19B), 24 June 1918, TNA: PRO CAB 23/44A.

It would appear that both Deane and Hughes actually met Kerensky and talked to him about the Russian problem. Deane maintained that Kerensky was 'a great man – a good sociologist, a fine dreamer – but he lacks force. Billy's got him skun [sic] a mile'. Letter, Deane to Ruth Deane, 27 June 1918, Deane Papers, University of Melbourne Archives.

[46] For the American attitude to intervention in Russia, see Betty Unterberger, *America's Siberian Expedition 1918–1920: A Study of National Policy* (New York: Greenwood Press, 1955) and George F. Kennan, *Soviet-American Relations, 1917–1920* (Princeton: Princeton University Press, 1958), Vol.II, 'The Decision to Intervene'.

importance to get into touch with this Committee, because, after all, the President will follow what they say.'

The British Foreign Secretary was puzzled by this news. Knowing a little more about American foreign policy procedures, he inquired of Hughes whether he was referring to the Senate Committee on Foreign Relations or a cabinet committee, to which Hughes replied that it was a cabinet committee. Balfour, eager to exploit any opportunity to secure American assistance, then obtained Hughes's consent to take up the matter with the British Ambassador in Washington.[47] The Ambassador, responding promptly, even if rather testily since Hughes's assertions implied a dereliction of duty on his part, stated that there was no cabinet committee on foreign relations, that the name, Dr Schlesinger, was unknown and that the President was fully seized of the importance the Allies attached to intervention in Siberia. The Ambassador seems not to have been aware of the existence of the Inquiry.

Faced with this rebuttal Hughes tried to exonerate himself by blaming Hankey, the Secretary of the Imperial War Cabinet, for misreporting his remarks. Hughes scribbled over his copy of Balfour's cable:

> This does not correctly set out what I said. (a) I did *not* say that I met the Cab. Committee on Foreign Relations. I said I met *a* Committee etc. (b) Dr. Schlesinger is unknown to me. I never heard of him, let alone met him. I did meet a Dr. Slosser.[48] (c) I am quite sure the men I met were in close touch with Colonel House & were men of high standing considerable influence. (2) I did not say that the Committee thought the Allies did not attach much importance to intervention. What I did say was: that I thought the matter was not being pushed enough.[49]

The Australian and New Zealand Prime Ministers agreed that not only from an Allied perspective but also 'from an Australasian point of view, there were considerable advantages in encouraging Japan to devote her energies to intervention in Siberia' rather than to the South Pacific. They, nevertheless, shared the general feeling in the Imperial War Cabinet that Japan should not act alone. When in early July President Wilson decided to send a military contingent to Siberia the British problem seemed to be solved. But the Allied forces dispatched to Vladivostok had no effect on the strategic situation in Europe, and in the end the intervention only tended to exacerbate

---

[47] Shorthand Notes of Imperial War Cabinet Meeting (19), 20 June 1918, TNA: PRO CAB 23/43.

[48] Probably this is a reference to Dr Peter Slosson who was a twenty-five year old historian attached to the Inquiry. See Gelfand, *The Inquiry*, p.64.

[49] Hughes's comments on cables, Balfour to Reading, 24 June 1918 and Reading to Balfour, 27 June 1918, Hughes Papers, NLA MS 1538/23/1039 and 1104–05. While Hankey did allow himself a little latitude even in the shorthand notes of the Imperial War Cabinet discussions, his reputation for accuracy had rarely been challenged. It is very difficult to believe that Hankey could have so egregiously misreported Hughes. More probably Hughes, realising after the event that his vanity had led him into making statements that he could not substantiate, tried to cover himself by claiming that he had been misquoted.

tensions between the Bolsheviks and the Western countries and between the Japanese and the Americans.[50]

Imperial communications

Hughes, in addition to taking an active interest in the conduct of the war, also brought before the imperial gathering matters relating to the structure of the Empire.

He had proposed a procedural reform for communications between the British and the Dominion governments. He wanted Dominion prime ministers to be able to communicate directly with the British Prime Minister without the interposition of the Governor-General and the Colonial Office. On his return to Australia in 1916 Hughes had found the established methods irksome. This was especially the case after Lloyd George, with whom he had formed a certain rapport, became British Prime Minister. The war had brought home the need for immediate exchanges of views between the British and Australian Governments and Hughes grew impatient with anachronistic procedures, a legacy of Australia's previous colonial status, which delayed the resolution of problems and weakened the impact of Australian representations. Indeed, partly for this reason, he had arranged for Keith Murdoch, his journalist confidant in London, to act as a personal emissary to Lloyd George.

Moreover Hughes resented the cumbersome and circuitous process. Revelling in power he was wont to brush aside obstacles that stood in the way of its free exercise. The Governor-General, though admiring the little man's 'Imperial patriotism', had felt obliged to rebuke him from time to time for his tendency to ignore constitutional conventions. Hughes for his part resented the Governor-General's insistence on the scrupulous observance of vice-regal prerogatives. Hughes had been frustrated by the Governor-General's refusal to let him use the official cipher to communicate directly with the British Ambassador in Washington when protesting the American decision to commandeer the Australian ships. He had had to endure Munro Ferguson's complaints about sending messages through Murdoch to Lloyd George. Indeed, just before leaving on his overseas trip Hughes's anger had boiled over when Munro Ferguson called him to account over a personal message about Ireland which he had sent to Lloyd George, and he charged the Governor-General with wanting to act as a 'supervisory power' and as 'the *de facto* Government of the Commonwealth which under our Constitution and that of Britain he is not'.[51] It is possible that brooding on this as he steamed across the Pacific, he was led into placing the item on the Imperial Conference's agenda.

---

[50] Secretary's Notes of Prime Ministers' Meeting, Imperial War Cabinet (20A), 26 June 1918, TNA: PRO CAB 23/44A.

For Wilson's attitude on intervention, see Betty Miller Unterberger, 'Wilson and the Bolsheviks; The "Acid Test" of Soviet-American Relations', *Diplomatic History*, 11 (Spring 1987), 82–88 and Victor M. Fic, *The Collapse of American Policy in Russia and Siberia, 1918: Wilson's Decision Not to Intervene* (New York: Columbia University Press, 1995).

[51] Letter, Hughes to Munro Ferguson, 8 February 1918, Novar Papers, NLA MS 696/2604; see also for summary of the Ireland incident, Munro Ferguson to Long, 25 July 1918, TNA: PRO CO 532/111/120.

The proposal was timely. The creation of the Imperial War Cabinet with its implied right for the Dominions, and therefore for their Prime Ministers, to have an equal say in the making of imperial policy provided a fitting opportunity for a review of communication procedures. From the 1907 Imperial Conference when the then Australian Prime Minister, Alfred Deakin, had suggested that the British Prime Minister should take over responsibility for Dominion affairs, dissatisfaction with the existing machinery had grown apace. Borden and Smuts shared Hughes's wish for change though, unlike Hughes, they were more influenced by a desire to bring constitutional forms into harmony with ideas of equality of status rather than by a concern to acquire an equal voice in policy-making.[52]

Before the issue reached the Imperial Conference and Cabinet there was much manoeuvring behind the scenes. Both the Round Table Imperialists and the Colonial Office traditionalists had a strong interest in the matter. Amery, on behalf of the former, commended the proposal to Lloyd George. Amery had nothing but disdain for the Colonial Secretary and the Colonial Office. As he saw it, they obstructed progress towards the new empire. He wrote the Prime Minister:

> From the point of view of Imperial unity no less vital is a complete change in the Colonial Office. Fiddes [permanent head of the Colonial Office] whom Long follows blindly is a fatal influence, pedantic and narrow and suspicious of any Dominion public men who come in contact with him, even across the cables.

He considered that the Dominion leaders' proposal once adopted would have 'a great effect on making them feel the Imperial Cabinet is a reality'. His own preference was that all correspondence from the Dominion prime ministers should go to the Imperial War Cabinet office or, in the case of 'personal and private communications', direct to the British Prime Minister.[53]

The Colonial Secretary, on the other hand, was hurt by this criticism of himself and his department. He saw no need for change. After Borden had informed Lloyd George of the Dominions' wishes, Long tried to warn his Prime Minister about the bureaucratic difficulties which would be attendant upon such alterations to established procedures. Long contended that the Dominions had 'no knowledge of the value and extent of the work' which was carried out by the Colonial Office and which would become the responsibility of the Prime Minister if the Dominions had their way.

As a compromise Long suggested that the Dominion prime ministers should be able to communicate directly with the British Prime Minister 'on certain special occasions' on issues of 'pressing and vital importance'. Likewise he was willing that inside his Department Dominion business should be separated from that of the Crown Colonies and should be placed under a Secretary of State who would have a seat in the British Cabinet. But these innovations should be

---

[52] Borden Diary, 19 June 1918, Borden Papers, LAC.
[53] Letter, Amery to Lloyd George, 8 June 1918, Lloyd George Papers, House of Lords Record Office F2/1/24–25; Memorandum, 'Imperial Relations 1918', 24 July 1918, NAA A981 IMP 104.
According to his diary Hankey had persuaded Long to accept this compromise after an hour's conversation at the Colonial Office on 10 July. See Hankey, *Supreme Command*, Vol.II, p.833.

left until the end of the war. Since Hughes's resolution 'must lead to a very strenuous controversy', he thought it would be best to procrastinate and for the moment to 'avoid any decision'.[54]

In introducing his resolution at the Imperial Conference, Hughes asserted that the existing methods were not appropriate for the new constitutional order represented by the Imperial War Cabinet. The great principle underpinning his reform was that the Dominions were 'no longer Colonies in the old sense, but self-governing nations'. Since the British Empire had become 'a League of Free Nations', the formal structures should be adjusted to fit this new reality. The other Dominion leaders backed Hughes's stand, the Canadian and South African stressing that the forms should reflect the growing national consciousness in their countries. Long was unable to prevent a decision. At the Dominions' insistence it was accepted that there should be a change in the 'Channels of Communication' which would bring the British and Dominion governments 'more directly in touch with each other'. Significantly it was left to the Imperial War Cabinet where the British Prime Minister presided to devise suitable machinery for the purpose.[55]

Hughes repeated his arguments in this second forum. He wanted 'a formal but real recognition' that 'The Dominions were participants in the councils of the Empire on a footing of equality'. In response to a query from Lloyd George, he agreed that the Dominions leaders were seeking a level of communication comparable to that which the French and Italian Prime Ministers enjoyed with the British Prime Minister. Hughes said that this was particularly important for Australia and New Zealand because, 'There was always the danger of peace coming suddenly, and long before Mr. Massey and himself could arrive in this country, the pourparlers might have committed the Empire irrevocably.' Without having direct access to the British Prime Minister, 'they might arrive, in fact, to find the principle of the League of Nations, or the Freedom of the Seas, accepted and the Empire no longer, as a reality, in existence.'

Taking into account both Long's and Amery's advice – and perhaps draft wording prepared by Hankey – Lloyd George suggested that the Dominion prime ministers should be able to communicate directly with the British Prime Minister on questions of 'Cabinet importance', and the Dominion leaders accepted this compromise which met the substance of their demand. Simultaneously Lloyd George, fearing that at the end of the war imperial feeling might dissipate, had at Amery's prompting proposed that the Dominions should be able to appoint either resident or visiting ministers who would sit in the British Cabinet between regular meetings of the Imperial Cabinet and that the Imperial War Cabinet should set up a committee to consider 'permanent machinery for Imperial cooperation'. The Dominion prime ministers endorsed the first; Borden saw it as a positive step forward but Hughes, having little confidence in his ministers, while he went along with this decision, never took advantage of it. The second, the idea of reviewing the imperial structure while the war continued, was rejected. There was a general

---

[54] Borden Diary, 27 June 1918, Borden Papers, LAC; letter, Borden to Lloyd George, 28 June 1918, Lloyd George Papers, House of Lords Record Office F5/2/11; letter, Long to Lloyd George, 15 July 1918, enclosing memorandum, 16 July 1918, *ibid.*, F33/1/7; copy of letter, Long to Lloyd George, 28 June 1918, Long Papers, WRO 947/651/1.

[55] Minutes of Imperial War Conference, 18 July 1918, NAA A2939 SC76.

For Hankey's authorship of the final draft, see his diary entries for 25 and 28 July 1918 in Hankey, *Supreme Command*, Vol.II, p.833–34.

feeling that they should wait until the peace when, as had been foreshadowed at the 1917 Imperial War conference, a special conference would be held to consider the Empire's constitution.[56]

Peace terms

Though the Imperial Cabinet had been preoccupied with war policy, Hughes did not wish it to disband before it had an opportunity to consider peace terms. For him the most important benefit deriving from the setting up of the Imperial War Cabinet was the acknowledgment of the Dominions' right to an equal say in the making of the Empire's peace terms. He had very definite ideas about what those terms should be. As time had passed he had become ever more certain that a peace based on Wilson's Fourteen Points would be disastrous, and he feared that some of the British leaders, including Lloyd George, were too willing to appease the Americans. His most immediate purpose in gaining the right to communicate directly with the British Prime Minister had been to ensure that he would have a say in the peace. When therefore towards the end of July it seemed that the Germans had lost the initiative and were being driven back across the Marne, Hughes proposed that the Imperial War Cabinet, before it concluded its business, should try to arrive at a 'clear basis' for peace. As a result, the final sessions of the cabinet from 13–15 August were given over to a discussion of the Empire's peace objectives.

In the event Hughes took little comfort from the ensuing discussion for it exposed the members' divergent viewpoints. Some of these derived from differences in expectations about the outcome of the conflict and others from differences over the principles which should inform the peace. These deliberations failed completely to meet Hughes's desire that the British Empire's aims should be 'settled definitely, so that we know where we are on all these matters'. The British Foreign Secretary outlined Britain's commitments and interests. The Foreign Secretary declared that, with regard to Wilson's Fourteen Points, Britain would leave it to the Allies to make any concessions they thought appropriate to placate the Americans. The Foreign Secretary was reluctant to acquire more territory for Britain, apart from that necessary to ensure its hold over the rich oil reserves in the Middle East. He agreed that Germany should not recover any of its colonies, that Australia, New Zealand and South Africa should retain the colonies that they had occupied, and that Japan should, as promised, be supported in its claims to the German North Pacific islands.

On the question of the South Pacific islands Hughes was uncompromising. While the British ministers and the Canadian Prime Minister professed support for Australia's right to annex the islands, he detected a willingness on the part of some to make concessions to President Wilson. Lord Reading, the Special British Ambassador to the United States who was present at the meetings, did not think that 'the President would fall in with the view of Australia taking possession' of these islands. For the benefit of these temporisers Hughes defiantly declared that 'If you want to shift us, come and do it. Here we are – "J'y suis, j'y reste"'. Having seemingly forgotten about the February 1917 Anglo-Japanese agreement, he also challenged Balfour's statement

---

[56] Letter, Amery to Lloyd George, 9 July 1918, Lloyd George Papers, House of Lords Record Office F2/1/26; Shorthand Notes of Imperial War Cabinet Meetings (26–28), 23, 25 and 30 July 1918, TNA: PRO CAB 23/43.

concerning the promise to Japan. He was 'pretty sure' that Australia never assented to the agreement, implying perhaps that Australia might well wish to reopen the question. To abort such a troublesome possibility Lord Robert Cecil promised to have the Foreign Office prepare a memorandum setting out what had happened and Australia's part in it.[57]

Hughes was most unhappy with the proceedings. His interjections were often tart and testy. He found the rather vague, inconclusive discussion frustrating. When he was informed that the British Government had in principle approved a League of Nations and had commissioned a group of scholars to draw up a report about the form it might take, he refused to be bound. He despaired that the British Government should give any credence to President Wilson's League of Nations when no-one knew what it was or how it would work, and he opposed publication of the report until the Imperial War Cabinet had an opportunity to pronounce upon it. The spectre of Wilson hovered over the Empire's deliberations, and from Hughes point of view it was an ominous presence, distracting the cabinet from pursuing its true course.

At the end of the great imperial confabulation, Hughes had failed to win over his colleagues, despite the energy he had invested in his crusade for a peace of annexation and indemnity – a peace which would restore the economic and political pre-eminence of the British Empire. So strong was Hughes's conviction about race and blood, about war and power, that he had been prepared to stand almost alone in fighting for his cause. There was almost an air of heroic recklessness or, some might say, egotistical perversity about his advocacy. But, as in the conscription campaigns, his simple-minded certainties tended to alienate more than to persuade. When these certainties had to confront the complexities of the British Empire's circumstances, when it was evident that his public campaign exacerbated divisions in Britain and troubled Britain's relations with its allies, instead of learning from this experience he became, if anything, more recalcitrant. Similarly, when in the Imperial War Cabinet he had to consider war and peace not from the distance of Australia but at the centre of the Empire where hard choices, governed by the limits of military power and dependence on allies, had to be made, he became not reasonable and accommodating but querulous and quarrelsome. His only clear success had been a procedural one, the right to direct communications with the British Prime Minister.

In the evening, after the final session of the Imperial War Cabinet, Hughes had gone from the confusion and division of that forum to the public platform where, in a sympathetic environment, he could give order and purpose to the British Empire. He spoke under the auspices of the British Empire League, and it was reported that here they hungered for his message; 'Hundreds had to stand – many were unable to gain admittance.' Here he freely gave vent to his feelings. He denounced his critics, those 'who held out the right hand of fellowship to the Hun, these pacifists, these defeatists, these little Englanders, these little Navy men', and demanded that the Empire adopt 'some policy, some organisation which will ensure a market here for our raw materials'. Since national greatness and national security depended in the last analysis upon economic prosperity, it was vital that the British Government take the decision necessary to guarantee the

---

[57] Shorthand Notes of Imperial War Cabinet Meetings (30–32), 13–15 August 1918, TNA: PRO CAB 23/43. The New Zealand Prime Minister acknowledged the arrangement which had been made with the Japanese in February 1917 and 'was content to abide by the agreement.'

Empire's future. Yet the decision he sought was brought no nearer. As in 1916 his public posturing even troubled some British leaders who were otherwise well-disposed to the general thrust of his argument; Long, an ardent Imperialist, thought Hughes's campaign to be 'rather rash'.[58] His greatest problem, however, was that, by contrast with his earlier visit, his crusade did not attract the support of major political figures. Indeed those who had lionised him on the earlier occasion were now themselves in office and so the targets, even if indirectly, of his tirades.

During his stay in Britain Hughes's behaviour had done much to antagonise the leaders of both the British and the Dominion governments.[59] Following the end of the Imperial War Cabinet meetings, an article by Keith Murdoch, which was published in the Melbourne *Herald*, fuelled further distrust. While the article spoke of the affection that Lloyd George and Hughes felt for each other, it also hinted at their rivalry for the highest office in the British Empire. It claimed that, when he was in Britain in 1916, Hughes's reputation had overshadowed that of Lloyd George since it was Hughes who had 'rallied the British public full-throated behind him'. Hughes had then 'missed the chance that would have made him [British] Prime Minister'. In the meantime Lloyd George had 'risen to almost absolute ascendancy'. Murdoch stated that Britain still looked 'as keenly as ever to the great man [that is, Hughes] to save her'. Moreover he asserted that Hughes was 'unquestionably master of the economic question' and that Lloyd George still differed from Hughes about imperial preference and post-war organisation. He then proceeded to justify Hughes's demand for the Dominions' direct access to the British Prime Minister by pointing both to the new status Australia had achieved as a result of its wartime sacrifices and to the 'crusted, procrastinating, bureaucratic inefficiency and ineptitude of the Colonial Office'.[60]

The article caused 'a great scandal' in Whitehall. Long, having been apprised of its contents by Munro Ferguson, tackled Hughes who expressed regret. He said he did not understand it since Murdoch had 'always spoken so highly of C.O. & yourself'. Knowing that Murdoch was privy to Hughes's innermost thoughts Long and Lloyd George probably took Hughes's reassurance with a grain of salt; Hughes's behaviour since arriving in Britain was tantamount to a challenge for the leadership of the Empire. Lloyd George joined with Long in deploring the article and agreed that the British Government should issue a public rebuttal citing commendations of the Colonial Office from Hughes himself as well as other Dominion leaders.[61]

---

[58] *Times* (London), 16 August 1918; copy of letter, Long to Munro Ferguson, 17 August 1918, Long Papers, WRO 947/625/111.

[59] Borden was 'irritated' with Hughes as he 'rambled', was 'late and did not read papers' for meetings. See Borden Diary, 14 August 1918, Borden Papers, LAC.

[60] *Herald* (Melbourne), 7 September 1918.

[61] Cable, Munro Ferguson to Long, 8 September 1918, and Long's Minute, 13 September 1918, letter, Long to Lloyd George, 11 September 1918, and cable, Long to Munro Ferguson, 13 September 1918, TNA: PRO CO 532/111/309–35.

When a copy of the full article arrived by seamail in October the Colonial Office expressed its disgust that Murdoch who had been privileged to entertain Lloyd George and Hughes had so betrayed the trust that been placed in him. Long ordered that the article should be sent to Lloyd George and that Murdoch be refused any further 'information or courtesies'. Minute by Long, 26 October 1918, Long Papers, WRO 947/625/123.

Hughes's absolutist campaign had isolated him. He had offended, for no good reason, not only the British Prime Minister but also the American President, who rightly perceived in Hughes the arch-enemy of his new world order. Indeed Wilson was so affronted by the reports of Hughes's public agitation for a peace of annexation and indemnity that, on learning of the Australian's intention to return home through the United States, he gave instructions that the Ambassador in London should refuse the Prime Minister a visa. It was an extraordinary step to deny the head of an allied government entry into the country in time of war. Though State Department officials, more aware of the diplomatic implications, persuaded the President not to persist in this course of action, Wilson nevertheless wanted the British to be informed that, if Hughes made speeches in the United States similar to those he had given in Britain, then the American Government would 'feel obliged to state publicly that the United States entirely dissociates itself from Hughes's policy.' The President was firmly resolved that Hughes should not be able to spread his noxious doctrine of 'economic mastery and retaliation' in America.[62]

---

[62] Letter, Wilson to Lansing, 29 August 1918, and letter, Lansing to Wilson, 31 August 1918 enclosing draft cable, Lansing to American Embassy, London, sent 3 September 1918, NARA RG 59 033.4711/18; copy of letter, Gordon Auchinloss to Wilson, 31 August 1918, Arthur S. Link (ed.), *The Papers of Woodrow Wilson* (Princeton: Princeton University Press, 1985), Vol.49, pp.408–09; cable, Sir William Wiseman to Lord Reading, British Ambassador to the United States, 31 August 1918, TNA: PRO FO 800/225/84.

During July and August 1918 American journalists in London who shared Wilson's liberal ideals, such as R.S. Baker and Walter Lippmann, sent the President extensive accounts of speeches by British leaders who sought to re-establish the Empire's commercial supremacy by control of access to raw materials, the raising of imperial preference and the imposition of a harsh and discriminatory peace on Germany. See Laurence W. Martin, *Peace Without Victory: Woodrow Wilson and the British Liberals* (New Haven: Yale University Press, 1958), pp.178–82. For Wilson's reaction to the reports of these speeches, see W.B. Fowler, *British-American Relations, 1917–1918: The Role of Sir William Wiseman* (Princeton: Princeton University Press, 1969), pp.212–13.

Moreover Hughes's speeches were summarised and criticised in some leading American newspapers. See, for example the *New York Times*, 30 August 1918. It contrasted the British mission of Samuel P. Gompers, the President of the American Federation of Labor, who was 'a powerful apostle of union' with that of Hughes. Hughes, the Australian 'premier', had come to Britain as 'theoretical apostle of disunion'. He had come 'certainly not as representing its people', but 'at the interested invitation of a British financial clique'. Hughes was using his 'eloquence ... to set factions by the ears over a problem which he has not the capacity to understand, but upon which he is held to be capable of stirring up by his declamations excitement enough to sway to the side of his backers the general election they seek to engineer.' It reported that, as part of this electoral strategy Hughes had made a 'vehement speech' in Glasgow in favour of 'protection as an after-the-war measure necessary to safeguard the Empire'.

12
'The Very Threshold of the Promised Land': Joining Battle over the Armistice Terms

Unlike his Canadian and New Zealand colleagues, the Australian Prime Minister did not return home at the conclusion of the Imperial War Cabinet meeting. In writing to Watt – who had grown impatient with Hughes's long absence – he offered very practical reasons for delaying his departure, the need to sell Australian primary products and to obtain home leave for the veterans of the Gallipoli campaign. Moreover, after the great debates in the Prime Ministers' committee, he still doubted whether Lloyd George had solved the problem of military policy. He wanted to ensure there would be no more Passchendaeles.[1] But most of all he suspected that the conflict was in its last stages and he was determined to have a say in the shaping of the armistice and the peace upon which depended the future of the British peoples.

Hughes was acutely sensitive to the tide of battle. Since July when the Central Powers had been forced onto the defensive the omens had looked increasingly favourable. Fresh American troops were arriving in great numbers and there was growing evidence of low morale in the enemy camp. Hughes had good reason to question the military authorities' view that the Allies would have to wait until the spring of 1919 before they could achieve victory. By the final week of September all the signs were there that the end was in sight, and he told the Governor-General that the Allies were on 'the very threshold of the Promised Land' and that he would stay on for the peace settlement.[2]

Events rapidly overtook expectations. On 4 October the German and Austrian governments approached President Wilson to parley an armistice which would lead to a peace based on the Fourteen Points. After satisfying himself that the new German Government was acting in good faith Wilson sought the consent of the European Allies to his terms. With two reservations they accepted the American conditions for ending hostilities, and on 11 November the armistice came into effect and the fighting ceased. But Hughes was bitterly disappointed. This was not the armistice or the peace that he had envisaged. He himself was not consulted about the conditions. The British and French had capitulated to Wilson and had essentially accepted his *Diktat*, his right to lay down the principles upon which peace was to be made. In Hughes's view this was a selling of the pass into the 'Promised Land', a betrayal of all that they had fought for. It put at risk the future security of the British Empire and Australia. As a result, from the first moment that he became aware of the German overtures, he pursued with all his customary pugnacity a lonely struggle against Wilson's peace principles.

---

[1] Cable, Hughes to Watt, 27 August 1918, NAA CP360/8 B1/1.
[2] Letter, Hughes to Munro Ferguson, 28 September 1918, Novar Papers, NLA MS 696/2731.

Confronting President Wilson's armistice principles

The American President took pride in the fact that the Central Powers had approached him to seek an armistice. From the moment that he had taken the United States into the war he had kept America's moral distance. America was only 'associated' with the Allies, not one of them. He was resolved to prevent America from being tainted by too close an identification with the corrupt Old World. In setting out America's prescriptions for peace, he made it clear that he did not believe the Allies shared his vision of a 'world made safe for democracy'. He was suspicious of the Allies' motives. Consequently when in the last week of September he, like Hughes, realised that the time for negotiations was at hand he had publicly expressed his distrust of their governments and stated his determination to impose America's peace by appealing, if necessary, over the heads of the statesmen to their people.

On the very day Hughes had written home that the enemy was on the run and the fight for the peace was about to begin, Wilson had again set forth the principles of his Fourteen Points address and asserted that these American principles were the principles of all peoples everywhere and the only just basis for the peace. In accordance with this Americanised liberal philosophy he had maintained that the war had become a people's not a politician's war and, as such, the people would compel their reluctant leaders to accept his peace. 'Plain workaday people' understood Wilson's ideals. They were demanding that their leaders eschew balances of power, secret alliances, territorial arrangements and 'selfish economic combinations'; and seek only 'broad-visioned justice' which hinged on the acceptance of collective security in a League of Nations that was 'the most essential part of the peace settlement'. In a not too subtle message to his European colleagues, Wilson had warned that, 'Statesmen must follow the clarified common thought or be broken.' He had repeated these sentiments in an address to the Senate where he declared that the people of the world were 'looking to the great, powerful, famous Democracy of the West to lead them to the new day for which they have long waited.' America was the national embodiment of the ideals of humanity and Wilson himself was the personal embodiment of the ideals of America.[3] Wilson thus had in view a very different 'Promised Land' from that which had captured Hughes's imagination.

In private conversations with friends Wilson spoke freely of his distrust of the Allied governments. He told Thomas Lamont, the proprietor of the *Evening Post*, that, while he believed 'the peoples of Great Britain and France are with me, just as well as America', it did 'not necessarily mean that the existing governments are of precisely the same mind.' In particular, he cited British Empire leaders' agitation for the restoration of the British Empire's commercial power and for the acquisition of German colonies, the very issues that Hughes, above all, had made his own. 'For instance,' Wilson said 'you may have noticed that in their plans for an after-the-war trade, the British have appointed a lot of committees, made up of men who are anxious to maintain Great Britain supreme commercially all over the world'; the latter phrase could have been adapted from Hughes's protest against the takeover of the Australian ships being built in America. Similarly, on

---

[3] *The Papers of Woodrow Wilson* (Princeton, 1985), Vol.51, pp.127–33 and 158–59.

the colonial question the President complained that 'Great Britain has certain ideas which she would like us to fall in with, but which we cannot.'[4]

When therefore the Germans and Austrians asked Wilson for an armistice he ignored the advice of House, who urged him to 'at once confer with the Allies', and proceeded through a series of exchanges to assure himself of the Central Powers' commitment to his peace principles. Only after he became convinced that this was so, did he approach the Allies, thereby presenting them with what was essentially a *fait accompli*.

The President handled the negotiations with the Germans in a very naïve manner. He had given no thought of how to connect his peace terms to the armistice. At first he seemed to require merely that the Germans should give up the occupied territory in France and Belgium and retreat behind their own frontiers. Following warnings from the Allied governments and his military advisers, he stipulated, in successive notes, ever harsher conditions. From insisting that the Germans should guarantee 'the present military supremacy of the armies of the United States and of the Allies in the field' he moved to demanding that they 'leave the United States and the powers associated with her in a position to enforce any arrangements that may be entered into and to make a renewal of hostilities on the part of Germany impossible.'[5] Initially, after the reformed Berlin government accepted his peace principles, he was willing to allow the Germans an armistice which would not render them impotent or unduly humiliate them. By the end he required what was tantamount to unconditional surrender. It was, as he confessed to one of his officials, that he 'work(ed) along with hardly more than instinct for a guide.'[6]

The Allied leaders were angered by the high-handed attitude of the American President but Hughes, being equally arrogant and dogmatic, was the most incensed. He could hardly contain his fury. At first, however, when speaking about the armistice negotiations, rather than attack Wilson directly he remade the American leader's messages to suit his own purpose. He denounced the German overtures and approved what he called Wilson's rejection of this trick. The Germans with 'this canting whine of peace' would not escape the 'penalty of their crime'. Hughes, like Wilson, wanted an enduring peace but, unlike the Americans, he saw this as only possible after Germany had been completely defeated and deprived of its war-making capability: 'until we have drawn the teeth and claws of this tiger the people of the civilised world say there shall be no peace.' Thus the right course was for the Allies 'to gird up our loins, and with unfaltering purpose press resolutely on. In this way, and in this way only, will come the peace we are resolved to have.' Total victory had to precede total peace.

Addressing the Tariff Reform League, Hughes was even more emphatic about the price Germany would have to pay. Again he pretended that Wilson's second note had endorsed his views. The Germans had received 'the answer they deserve'. He maintained that 'those who had suffered so much were not to be tricked out of the fruits of victory.' And he averred that Germany would not be readmitted to the family of nations until it had restored the Allies' economies to the position they had enjoyed before the outbreak of the war. Since the Germans' territory had not

---

[4] *Ibid.*, pp.222–24.
[5] *Ibid.*, pp.333–34 and 418.
[6] Letter, Wilson to Bainbridge Colby, 26 October 1918, *ibid.*, p.453.

been invaded they would emerge from the war economically more intact than any of their European victims. Germany consequently should be required to restore the infrastructure of France and Belgium and to hand over its mercantile fleet to the Allies. Until their economies had recovered Germany should be deprived of access to raw materials. Turning to the Empire's post-war policy he once more called upon Britain to buy Australia's raw materials and for the Empire to become as far as possible self-sufficient. The achievements of the Empire in war if now adapted to the tasks of peace would 'give us still greater victories, which shall endure throughout the ages – an organisation national in extent, Imperial in its purpose.'[7]

In private Hughes made no secret of his hostility to Wilson and his principles. He derided the Fourteen Points and took every opportunity to encourage the British and French to reject them. The stakes were high; in the settlement of this great world war 'a thousand great and conflicting interests' were in the balance. As he explained to Watt, he was fearful that 'in the negotiations our interests to say nothing of those of the Empire, may suffer.' Hughes was as convinced as Wilson that the people's will should be done. He was, however, equally certain that it was he, not Wilson, who spoke for the victor nations. He assured Watt that, even if their leaders should waver in resisting the Fourteen Points, 'the people of Britain and France are very determined that the fruits of victory shall not be taken from them.' And he continued, suggesting what would happen to the Wilson formula; 'There will probably be twenty-four, or maybe sixty-four points before we have done.' The most objectionable, especially points two, three and five – those that most affected Australia and the Empire – which dealt with 'freedom of the seas', control over trade and tariffs and the disposal of the German colonies, would 'wholly disappear or be so changed that no-one will know them.'[8]

Lloyd George shared in large part Hughes's dislike of Wilson and had serious reservations about his peace principles. Hankey reported in his diary that the British Prime Minister was 'irritated with Wilson' because of his failure to consult, his vagueness about armistice conditions and his attempt to compel the Allies to go along with his peace terms. The British were greatly annoyed by Wilson's actions, for 'in asking if the Germans accept his Fourteen Points, he almost seems to assume that we do accept them (although as a matter of fact we totally reject the doctrine of the freedom of the seas)'.[9] But, in contrast to Hughes, Lloyd George recognised the practical difficulties of Britain's situation. He could not afford to alienate President Wilson, create divisions in the Allies' camp and risk jeopardising the military victory that promised a favourable peace.

During the preceding months Lloyd George's impatience with Hughes's uncompromising stand had grown apace. Through 'back channels' he had learnt of Wilson's personal antipathy to Hughes.[10] The British Prime Minister resented the Australian's public campaign for a harsh peace,

---

[7] *Times* (London), 10 and 17 October 1918. Wilson's New York speech was reproduced in *Times*, 28 September 1918.
[8] Copies of cables, Hughes to Watt, 11 and 16 October 1918, Hughes Papers, NLA MS 1538/23/228.
[9] Hankey, *Supreme Command*, Vol.II, p.854 and Riddell, *Lord Riddell's War Diary*, pp.366–67.
[10] Cable, Reading to Wiseman, 12 September 1918, TNA: PRO FO 800/225/20. Reading reported to Wiseman that he had 'told the PRIME MINISTER of the President's views respecting HUGHES'S and that 'the PRIME MINISTER understands and will deal with it.'

his attacks on trade policy and his obstreperous conduct in the Imperial War Cabinet. More immediately he took umbrage at Hughes's scarcely veiled attack on the imperial authorities for failing to ready themselves to make the most of Germany's defeat. On 9 October Hughes in a speech at the Baltic Exchange had suggested that the Empire was not prepared for the peace.

> Are we prepared for peace when it comes, as it must come? Who can say that we are? Have we rooted out the German cancer in our midst? Have we organised on a great national basis to grapple with any of those great problems, Imperial in their nature, affecting the whole Empire and on the satisfactory outcome of which the very existence of the Empire as such will depend? … Is Britain to be one of the main markets for the raw materials produced within the Empire? If she secures the raw materials, can she use them profitably? Her organisation which will ensure the control of markets, home and overseas, in which to sell her manufactured goods, maintain and enlarge the volume of her trade, and secure the well-being of her mercantile marine by carrying those raw materials to Britain and goods to overseas. And only on such foundations is the defence, and so the existence, of the Empire possible …
>
> The decisions of the Peace Conference are going to have a profound influence on the future of this Empire, and indeed on the whole world. Have we a clear concept of the conditions necessary for the safety of the Empire and for the economic and general welfare of its citizens? What is our Policy?[11]

All these questions were aimed at Lloyd George and his inaction, specifically his failure to consult Hughes.

At an Imperial War Cabinet meeting summoned two days later to hear Lloyd George's report on talks with the French and Italians about the armistice, Hughes set out his position. Since it would be impossible because of war weariness to resume hostilities to enforce peace terms he supported the military authorities' demand that the 'armistice must approximate to the basis of the conditions of peace'. Germany had to be disarmed at the time of the armistice so that it would be powerless to resume the struggle should it not find the final peace conditions to its liking. He pressed for the insertion of a 'dragnet clause' in the armistice agreement that would allow the Allies to do whatever they considered necessary to safeguard their interests.[12] The victors had to have a free hand at the Peace Conference in imposing whatever terms were necessary for achieving the interests of the Empire and safety of the world.

A few days later in Paris Hughes did his best to stir up the French. At a lunch at the British Embassy he was 'very free in his criticism of Wilson's action'. Lord Derby, the British Ambassador, informed the Foreign Secretary that Hughes was 'in a very pugnacious mood with regard to Wilson.' The Australian had said that there was 'not a single one of the latter's articles of faith that he agreed with and that if England agreed to them it would mean her absolute ruin.' Derby begged Hughes not to attack Wilson or America when he met the French ministers, and claimed that Hughes had agreed. Derby warned the French Premier, Georges Clemenceau, about Hughes, and, according to Derby, Clemenceau said he had no intention of speaking to Hughes.

---

[11] *Times* (London), 10 October 1918.
[12] Minutes of War Cabinet (484) and Imperial War Cabinet (35), 11 October 1918, TNA: PRO CAB 23/42.

Whether Hughes and Clemenceau did give Derby these assurances or whether, if they did, they honoured their word is not certain. Hughes would seem to have taken the opportunity of meeting the French to share with them his view of the American peace proposals. After returning to London he cabled Watt that he had 'had conference with several Ministers French Cabinet as well as with Clemenceau, and discussed Wilson's Fourteen Points.' He stated that they held the same opinion as himself and that he had 'strongly urged them to let the voice of France to be heard.' Derby saw in Hughes a meddlesome troublemaker, and the Ambassador told Balfour that when he asked whether the Australian intended to return to Paris, he had replied, much to Derby's discomfiture, that, 'Yes, he should certainly come if there was any Conference to discuss the questions of peace.'[13]

Lloyd George could not abide the Australian leader's wayward behaviour. He had come to see Hughes as a dangerous demagogue and conniving troublemaker and resolved to exclude him from the armistice discussions. Hughes was therefore invited neither to the British ministers' informal consultations nor to the War Cabinet meetings of 14, 15, 17 and 21 October. Hughes's status, however, created problems for the British Government. Lloyd George had no proper grounds for sidelining the Australian. With the establishment of the Imperial War Cabinet it had come to be accepted that when the British War Cabinet was considering imperial defence, trade or foreign policy the Dominion prime ministers had a right to join in its deliberations; in these circumstances the British and Imperial Cabinets were one. According to the minutes of the 11 October meeting, which Hughes had attended, it was both a British and an Imperial War Cabinet meeting.

When Derby, alarmed that Hughes was claiming to speak as a member of the War Cabinet, inquired whether this was so, Balfour had replied that he was 'not a member of the War Cabinet, but of the Imperial War Cabinet' though 'the distinction is perhaps somewhat fine.' Imperial War Cabinet meetings were held when 'matters of the highest importance are to be discussed.' For such purposes 'Any Dominion ministers who happen to be in London are usually invited to attend', and he cited the example of 11 October.[14] This was, in general, a fair summation of the new practice adopted in conjunction with the Imperial War Cabinet. The point of the new practice was that the British Prime Minister no longer had a discretionary power to decide whether Dominion leaders could or could not sit in the War Cabinet when questions of importance to the Empire were on the agenda.

Nevertheless the Imperial War Cabinet was not what it seemed. It was not a cabinet but 'a cabinet of cabinets'. Perhaps cabinet was the wrong word altogether. By drawing this analogy with the cabinets of Britain and the Dominions the Milner imperialists, who had fathered this new institution, wished to suggest that it was a policy-making body for the whole Empire. It, by its

---

[13] Letters, Derby to Balfour, 13 and 14 October 1918, Balfour Papers, BL Add 49744; copy of cable, Hughes to Watt, 16 October 1918, Hughes Papers, NLA MS 1538/133/4.

During the visit to France President Raymond Poincare bestowed the Grand-Croix de la Légion d'Honneur on Hughes and in the ensuing discussion Poincare 'was very forceful in regard to peace terms ... [and] said France wanted no armistice until a real victory had been achieved.' See letter, Deane to Ruth Deane, 12 October 1918, Deane Papers, University of Melbourne Archives.

[14] Copy of letter, Balfour to Derby, 16 October 1918, Balfour Papers, BL Add 49744.

nature, however, could not act in the manner of a national cabinet. It was not accountable to one parliament. Decisions could not be arrived at through majority vote; they had to be unanimous. Its chairman did not choose its members nor could he sack them. And there was no principle of collective responsibility; Hughes himself felt free to take issue with his colleagues' views on public platforms.[15] That the Imperial War Cabinet idea proved unworkable was not surprising since, apart from its inherent political problems, its members differed not only over questions of national interest and policy priorities but also over the nature of the Empire itself.

Lloyd George had the unenviable task of trying to give effect to this grand experiment while simultaneously holding his Coalition Government together, managing relations with Britain's wartime partners and ensuring that Britain's own interests were not sacrificed to those of the Dominions. As a master of improvisation, he was not inclined at this critical juncture to allow constitutional niceties to stand in the way of achieving his objectives. When Hankey on 17 October suggested that Hughes ought to be invited to a cabinet meeting which was to deal with the armistice and the peace, Lloyd George retorted that in order to avoid this he would hold 'an informal conference of ministers.' Though some British ministers complained about these practices and the Colonial Secretary protested about the exclusion of Hughes, Lloyd George remained unmoved.

According to Hankey's minutes, Hughes was invited to the cabinet meeting of 24 October which was to deal with the British response to Wilson's proposed armistice terms. But, if this were so, notice must have been sent to Hughes after he had left for a speaking tour of the north of England. Indeed Hughes, anticipating skulduggery – he himself was a master of such tactics – had sent Hankey a detailed itinerary from York, his first stop, so that he could be recalled immediately to take part in any cabinet discussions on the armistice. On 25 and 26 October when the British Cabinet held further meetings on the armistice no serious attempt, it would appear, was made to invite Hughes. Hankey, as was his wont, had tried to find a way to square the circle and so reconcile Lloyd George's wish to exclude Hughes with the conventions of the Imperial War Cabinet.[16] But he had clearly failed.

The upshot was that Hughes had no say in the British response to Wilson's armistice terms, and Lloyd George's action precipitated a clash with Hughes which, setting aside the personal element, brought into question the nature of the Imperial Cabinet and the meaning of imperial

---

[15] H. Lambert of the Colonial Office, commenting on this, remarked that if Hughes were to 'sit as an equal with British Ministers at the Cabinet table ... he must if it is a Cabinet at all, be content to be overruled on occasions.' Hughes's behaviour in causing a public controversy seemed to be 'a repudiation of the Imperial Cabinet system' since it implied that he considered himself free to protest as though he were not a member of the cabinet. See TNA: PRO CO 532/118/18–19.

[16] Roskill, *Hankey*, Vol.I, pp.615–18; letter. Hankey to Lloyd George, 18 October 1918, Lloyd George Papers, House of Lords Record Office F/23/3/17; copy of cable, Hughes to Hankey, 24 October 1918, Hughes Papers, NLA MS 1538/23/238; minutes of War Cabinet Meeting (490), 24 October 1918, TNA: PRO CAB 23/8.

It is worth noting that when Hughes later protested that he had not been consulted about the armistice terms neither Hankey nor Lloyd George claimed in their defence that they had invited Hughes to the 24 October cabinet meeting.

unity. It was a clash that had immediate repercussions in Britain and Australia and long-term consequences for the evolution of the Empire. It brought to the fore the contradiction in Australia's two views of nation.

From the beginning of the armistice process, that is from the time that the British Government began negotiating with Bulgaria and Turkey, Hughes's suspicions had been aroused. Indeed he cabled Watt that he did not think Lloyd George had taken any ministers other than Balfour, Bonar Law and perhaps Milner into his confidence. Hughes felt that the Imperial War Cabinet meeting on 11 October would be merely asked to ratify arrangements already worked out with the French and the Italians. By the time of Wilson's approach to the Allies, Hughes was aghast at what was happening and enraged at being omitted from the armistice talks. He told Watt, 'I feel there are powerful influences working assiduously beneath the surface for a peace other than a dictated peace.' He believed that 'British party politics ignore Imperial interests.' The Dominions had been abandoned. He had been left completely in the dark. There was 'no Imperial Government in this great crisis, although there may be an Imperial War Cabinet.' Within the limited role allowed him he was trying 'to do what I can to hold up Australia's end here and to prevent any peace that does not guarantee peace of the world and safeguard our interest in Pacific and elsewhere.'[17]

While Hughes was in York and Hull and Leeds pouring vitriol on the Germans and scorn on liberals and socialists and urging the people to oppose the 'Peace babble centred on President Wilson's points' which was 'designed to rob the Allies of victory',[18] the British War Cabinet debated its answer to the American President. Lloyd George welcomed the tougher line of the third Wilson note for if Germany accepted Wilson's conditions then it 'would be equivalent to military surrender.' He was, however, less enthusiastic about the Fourteen Points as a basis of the peace. Britain had never been consulted about them. All ministers were adamant that Britain should not be bound by Point Two, the 'freedom of the seas', since the navy was Britain's chief and indispensable defence weapon. It was agreed that Lloyd George should reserve Britain's position on that question. There were also some misgivings about the economic provisions, which were referred to the Treasury. A Foreign Office committee was requested to look at the other points to see how they might affect British interests.[19] When on the 28 October Lloyd George left for Versailles to join representatives of the United States, France and Italy in framing armistice terms his only instruction was to make it plain that under no circumstance would Britain accept the principle of 'freedom of the seas'. Hughes's oft-stated concerns about the extent of reparations, the right to impose discriminatory tariffs, the disposal of the German colonies and the desirability of a League of Nations were ignored.

Encouraged by all the signs of a German collapse on the battlefield the Supreme War Council, composed of representatives of the United States, the United Kingdom, France and Italy, after two

---

[17] Copy of cable, Hughes to Watt, 11 October 1918, Hughes Papers, NLA MS 1538/23/228 and copy of cable, Hughes to Watt, 23 October 1918, *ibid.*, 1538/23/233. The originals are missing from the collection of Hughes-Watt cables in NAA CP360/8 B1/1.
[18] *Times* (London), 25, 26 and 29 October 1918.
[19] Minutes of War Cabinet Meetings (490, 491A and 491B), 24, 25 and 26 October 1918, TNA: PRO CAB 23/8 and 23/14.

days of intense bargaining, came up with an agreed statement that the American President was to convey to the Germans. The military and naval arrangements were arrived at with comparative ease. President Wilson had directed House, whom he had nominated as his representative, to obtain terms which, while preventing the Germans from renewing hostilities, would be 'as moderate and reasonable as possible'. He considered that 'too much success or security on the part of the Allies' would 'make a genuine peace settlement difficult if not impossible'[20]. The military and naval conditions, however, made nonsense of this distinction. The Germans were required to withdraw behind the Rhine and to surrender their submarines and battle fleet. Lloyd George was a little troubled by the French insistence on the former but was willing to appease them in return for their support for the latter. House seemingly accepted these conditions without demur.

On the Fourteen Points there was more argument, and to help remove some of the confusions, two journalists in Wilson's confidence – Frank Cobb and Walter Lippmann – were asked to draw up an explanatory memorandum. This gloss, which Wilson approved, went some way to meeting the Allies' concerns. However, on the points that most concerned the British and the French – namely numbers 2 and 8 which dealt with the 'freedom of the seas' and reparations – the Cobb-Lippmann document offered few concessions. The memorandum declared on Two, which called for 'absolute freedom of navigation upon the seas … alike in peace and war', that it was not applicable to a war in which the League of Nations took action against an outlaw country. It said that the point was aimed at maintaining the rights of neutral shipping and commerce, which should 'be clearly and precisely defined in the law of nations', against belligerents in conflicts where the League of Nations was not involved. On Eight, it stated that France could not claim the cost of the war, only the damage done to territory occupied by the Germans; the British Empire, by implication, would have little or no right to reparations.[21]

On 30 October, at a preliminary conference with House and Clemenceau, Lloyd George agreed to accept the Fourteen Points as a basis for the peace, subject to two reservations. True to his instincts and instructions, the British leader refused to be bound by Point Two in any form and would only accept the reparation principle on the understanding that reparations would cover compensation 'for all damage done to the civilian population of the Allies, and their property … by land, by sea, and from the air.' By extending the meaning of reparations in this way the British would be able to make some claims and the French would be able to increase theirs considerably. Clemenceau backed Lloyd George. House's only quarrel was with the reservation on the 'freedom of the seas'.[22]

When Hankey reported these developments to the War Cabinet in London some ministers were upset that Lloyd George had not also taken exception to Points Three and Five which dealt with 'removal of all economic barriers' and 'the impartial adjustment of colonial claims'. On the latter point, the Colonial Secretary declared that, if the Dominions were unable to keep the German colonies they had captured, then 'there was likely to be very serious trouble.' Following these discussions the cabinet sent a message to the Prime Minister asking him, if it were no longer

---

[20] Cable, Wilson to House, 28 October 1918, *The Papers of Woodrow Wilson*, Vol.51, p.473.
[21] *Ibid.*, Vol.51, pp.495–504; for Wilson's approval see cable, Wilson to House, 30 October 1918, *ibid.*, p.511.
[22] Cable, House to Wilson, 30 October 1918, *ibid.*, Vol.51, pp.515–17.

possible to add further reservations, to inform the other powers, firstly that Britain could not be committed 'to grant of "most-favoured nation" treatment to enemy nations which would prevent fulfilment of our obligations to assist in restoration of allied territories, and prejudice our own economic policy in future', and secondly that the claims of the Dominions to the German territories in their possession could 'not possibly be waived'.[23]

By this time Lloyd George had concluded that any further reservations might cause America to seek a separate peace. In private talks with House he indicated that South Africa and Australia would have to keep the colonies that they had occupied respectively in Africa and the Pacific, and that unless this were done Great Britain would be confronted by a revolution in those Dominions.[24] But he made no attempt to insert a provision in the draft agreement to protect the Empire's position either on the colonies or the most-favoured-nation principle. All his diplomatic skills were directed towards ensuring that the British reservation on the 'freedom of the seas' was included in the response that the Allies made to the Germans. This lay at the heart of British national security. Lloyd George knew that Wilson's point was directed at limiting Britain's ability to employ the Royal Navy against neutral shipping in time of war and so at its ability to use its most potent weapon to full advantage.

Wilson, on hearing from House of the British leader's intransigence, was infuriated. He, like Hughes, suspected a secret plot by evil men to overturn his peace. For the American there could be 'no real difficulty about peace terms' if the Allied statesmen had 'no selfish aims of their own.' If they sought 'to nullify my influence' he ordered House to 'force the purpose to the surface' and he would place the issue before world opinion. He said that the British should not have a problem with 'freedom of the seas' since the setting up of the League of Nations underpinned this, as every other, point in his program. 'Freedom of the seas' was special for Wilson. It arose out of his anger at the British treatment of American ships and goods when the United States had been neutral. This alone can explain his inflexibility on the matter. If the League of Nations were to create a new international order that would be able to use all sanctions against aggressors, including controlling neutral trade with the aggressor, as had been the case with Germany after America entered the war, then America should have no problem with Britain's use of the Royal Navy against neutrals' trade. The 'freedom of the seas' provision was somehow to right a wrong of the past in terms of the past. After January 1918 he had, nevertheless, committed his own moral prestige to compelling the malefactors, the navalists as well as the militarists, to give up their evil ways.

Wilson thereupon authorised House to inform Lloyd George that America would not 'take part in a peace which did not include the freedom of the seas'. All he wanted, he cabled House, was acceptance of the principle. He was willing to agree that it 'needs careful definition and is full of questions upon which there is need of the freest discussion and the most liberal interchange of views.' He wanted a rhetorical resolution that could be portrayed as a moral victory for his new diplomacy. To achieve this he even suggested that if the British would not concede the principle 'they can count upon the certainty of our using our present great equipment to build up the strongest navy our resources permit.'

---

[23] Draft Minutes of War Cabinet Meeting (495A), 1 November 1918, TNA: PRO CAB 23/14.
[24] Cable, House to Wilson, 30 October 1918, *Papers of Woodrow Wilson*, Vol.51, p.514.

In the end, however, he had to be content with much less than he had hoped for. All that House could extract from Lloyd George was the quite innocuous statement that, 'We are quite willing to discuss the freedom of the seas in the light of the new conditions which have arisen by reason of the war.' The agreed reply to the Germans stated that the Allies reserved 'complete freedom on this subject when they enter the Peace Conference'. Faced with Lloyd George's obduracy, the Americans recognised that they had to appease the British or negotiate a separate peace and give up their claims to world leadership. Unwilling to allow that he had settled for rather less than his master had required, House flattered Wilson that 'we have won a great diplomatic victory in getting the Allies to accept the principles laid down in your January eighth speech.'[25] At the subsequent Peace Conference the Americans did not raise the issue of the Freedom of Seas in the negotiations over either the Peace Treaty or the Covenant of the League of Nations.

The clash with Lloyd George over the armistice terms

Returning to London Lloyd George gave an account of the Supreme War Council meetings and decisions to the 5 November Imperial War Cabinet, at which Hughes was present. The British leader knew that he had been less than honest with Hughes and that he might well have to face the Australian's wrath. In order to give the impression that he had conceded nothing on the peace terms, the British Prime Minister spoke of the Versailles proceedings as though they had been limited merely to working out the military and naval conditions for the armistice. When Hughes, referring to a letter he had sent to Lloyd George, said that nothing should be done to allow the Japanese to keep the North Pacific islands, Lloyd George, playing fast and loose with the truth, assured the Australian that 'these questions had not been discussed.'

Hughes, as a result of Lloyd George's explanation, thought that the armistice had not dealt with peace terms and so stressed 'the importance of entering a *caveat* in time that the Fourteen Points were not our Terms of Peace'. He said that he 'declined to be bound to the chariot-wheel of the Fourteen Points, especially those dealing with the League of Nations.' Lloyd George tried to prepare a case in advance of the time when Hughes would grasp the full picture. Thus he asserted that the peace terms were not limited by the Fourteen Points but by all the addresses that President Wilson had delivered since January 1918. He had scrutinised them carefully and he 'could not find a single point which we wanted that was not amply covered, with the exception of the points regarding the freedom of the seas and indemnities, and of our position in regard to these matters notice had been duly given.'[26]

---

[25] Cable, Wilson to House, 31 October 1918, *ibid.*, p.533; cables, House to Wilson, 3 November 1918, *ibid.*, pp.568–69; cable, Wilson to House, 4 November 1918, *ibid.*, p.575; cable, House to Wilson, 4 November 1918, *ibid.*, pp.581–82; cable, House to Wilson, 5 November 1918, *ibid.*, p.594. For Hankey's fractured account of the Versailles conference see Roskill, *Hankey*, Vol.I, pp.624–28.
[26] Minutes of Imperial War Cabinet Meeting (36), 5 November 1918, TNA: PRO CAB 23/42.

The storm burst the following day. Having overnight read the *process-verbaux* of what had transpired at the Supreme War Council, Hughes realised that Lloyd George had sold the pass.[27] All Hughes's worst fears, as he had expressed them to Watt, were confirmed. Thus at the Imperial War Cabinet next day the Australian Prime Minister unleashed an impassioned assault upon Lloyd George and the Versailles agreement. It was 'quite clear that the Peace Terms had been practically settled', and that the British Empire was saddled with Wilson's Fourteen Points, subject only to the reservations about the 'freedom of the seas' and reparations. He had come fully armed for the fray and effectively took over the meeting, mounting an extensive and detailed argument against this betrayal of the Dominions and their right to consultation on the peace terms.

Addressing the failure to consult the Dominions, Hughes charged that what had been done was 'a breach of the plain declaration that had been made to them'. Despite assurances to the contrary, the Dominions were still being treated as subordinate colonies. Just as the British Government had gone to war without giving the Dominions a say, so they were settling the peace without reference to them. The procedure adopted in the settling of the armistice made a mockery of the Imperial War Cabinet.

He confessed he did not understand precisely what the functions of the Imperial War Cabinet were supposed to be. Certainly its functions were not executive, and they could hardly be called consultative. At the last three meetings, Dominion representatives had been told of what were accomplished facts, without having been given an opportunity of expressing their opinion beforehand. Meetings of the Imperial War Cabinet had become merely occasions for informing overseas delegates, after the event, of the British Government's decisions.

Hughes then turned to the peace principles that had been incorporated in the armistice. While he congratulated the government on having retained complete freedom of action on point two, he did not think that the reservation on reparations went far enough. It 'did not cover the ground'; neither Belgium nor France nor the British Empire would receive the reparations to which they were entitled. He was especially concerned with Points Three and Five, and he rehearsed all the objections that he had advanced on the public platform and in previous cabinet discussions. On the former he feared that it might 'shut the door on differential tariffs and, perhaps, even on preferential trade within the Empire.' He asseverated that, 'Australia meant to reserve to herself complete liberty after the war to deal with tariffs as she thought fit.' Moreover he was troubled that under this point the League of Nations might attempt to control the distribution of raw materials, which would affect the plans for imperial self-sufficiency. Germany had to be restricted in its access to raw materials after the war. On Point Five Hughes expressed regret that the British Government had restricted itself to insisting that Germany should not recover its colonies. The Dominions expected that those they held, they would keep. On the League of Nations itself, Hughes repeated his familiar criticism. He was against a scheme which was 'so nebulous and which might be fraught with danger to the Empire'. If it were intended to usurp the right of the British Empire to govern and defend itself, he was 'absolutely opposed to it'.

---

[27] See the 'Notes of a Conversation, Oct 29th. 1918', between House, Lloyd George, Clemenceau and Giorgio Sonnino, the Italian Foreign Minister, and Hughes's critical comments and underlinings, Hughes Papers, NLA MS 1538/23/326–342.

Finally, Hughes demanded that Australia should be represented at the Peace Conference. At Versailles when representation at the Peace Conference had been discussed, he observed that Lloyd George had urged the claims of the Japanese because they were a 'very sensitive people'. Hughes pointed out that 'Australians were also a very sensitive people, and further, throughout Australia, Japan was regarded as a daily menace.' The Japanese had made no sacrifices; 'the number of the Australian dead was actually greater than the army Japan had in the field in Siberia where she was looking after her own interests.' And he asked, 'What sacrifices had Japan made which were in any way comparable with those of Australia?' In effect, he wanted to know how Lloyd George could be so solicitous on behalf of the Japanese while ignoring Australia and its interests.

Lloyd George mounted a spirited defence. His leadership was being challenged. Hughes's charges were serious and substantial. They could not be easily brushed aside and Lloyd George was put on his metal in replying to them. He denied that the Dominions had not had a chance to discuss the peace terms. At both the 1917 and 1918 meetings of the Imperial War Cabinet these issues had been canvassed. Nothing had been done at Versailles that was contrary to decisions reached at these meetings. Lloyd George claimed that it was not his fault that Hughes had not been consulted about the armistice since when he was invited to attend an Imperial War Cabinet meeting for the purpose – presumably the meeting of 24 October – it was found that he had gone to York. At this point Bonar Law who had presided at the War Cabinet meetings during Lloyd George's absence added that he had telephoned Hughes twice to invite him to attend – the second probably being the 1 November meeting which discussed the progress in negotiating the armistice terms – only to find that he was unavailable. To try to show his good intentions Lloyd George stated that he had 'urged very strongly' upon both Clemenceau and House that the Dominions were entitled to representation at the Peace Conference.

Responding to Hughes's criticisms of the Fourteen Points, Lloyd George maintained that nothing had been decided at Versailles 'which ruled out what had been agreed upon at the Meetings of the Imperial War Cabinet.' Since Lloyd George's conduct of these meetings had ensured that there would be no decisions he was, strictly-speaking, correct. He reaffirmed what he had earlier said about the German colonies, namely that he had told House that Britain would not consent to the return of the German colonies or to the surrender of any colonies conquered by the Dominions. Moving on to Hughes's specific arguments he declared that they had not sought a war indemnity, that is the full cost of the war, because, after paying full reparations, Germany would not have the means to pay more. Lloyd George expected that reparations would amount to somewhere between £1000 to £2000 million. If Germany was to be squeezed it could not pay in gold and if it paid by exporting its manufactures then it would have to have access to raw materials. This was the beginning of the case that Lloyd George was to build over time against Hughes's persistent demand that Germany should pay the full cost of the war.

Lloyd George was less sure in dealing with Point Three. While he felt certain that President Wilson understood that preferential tariffs inside the Empire were 'a purely domestic question' – which was not the case at all – he did think that if Australia intended to impose a higher tariff on Japanese goods, which Hughes had indicated, as opposed to those of other foreign countries then that 'would not be compatible with President Wilson's own interpretation of his Clause 3.' Bonar

Law tried to help out by assuring Hughes that the British and French representatives had agreed that 'the terms of Clause 3 were so vague that we could really place any interpretation upon them that we liked.' To which Hughes retorted, quite aptly, that 'if this could be done … Clause 3 was only worth what it was – three lines of print.' He was not convinced that, apart from the 'freedom of the seas', all the other points were open to any construction the Allies chose to place upon them, and that therefore the acceptance of the Fourteen Points did not limit what the Empire might seek at the peace table.[28]

The Australian Prime Minister remained unappeased, and the more he reflected on the answers he had received the more irate he became. After the meeting he wrote Lloyd George rejecting the latter's claim that because he had been out of London he had been unavailable for consultation over the armistice and peace terms. Anticipating that these questions might come to the fore while he was away he had left the details of his itinerary with both Hankey's and Long's private secretaries so that he could be contacted and return post-haste for the purpose. Since the Allies had not sent their reply to Wilson until 4 November there had been ample time 'during which I as the representative of Australia could have been asked to express the views of the Dominions on the Peace terms.'[29]

There were reasonable grounds for complaint. Hughes had, as he said, left his addresses with the officials, and no-one had informed him of the Versailles meeting and recalled him so that he might have his say. On the other hand Hughes had set out on the 24 October and had therefore been unable to attend the War Cabinet meeting on that day. Perhaps he could have been summoned back the following day for the crucial meeting which had given Lloyd George his instructions; though, even if a message had reached him, it is doubtful whether he could have reached London in time. The point, however, is that no serious effort was made to locate him and extend an invitation to him. There were further meetings of the War Cabinet on 26 October and again, in Lloyd George's absence, on 1 and 4 November, none of which Hughes attended.[30] The meeting of 1 November was particularly important for at that meeting the British ministers considered Lloyd George's report on the proposed terms of the armistice. According to Bonar Law, who had presided on that occasion, Hughes had been invited but had replied that he was unavailable, and Hughes did not answer this claim. Even if Bonar Law's explanation for the 1 November is accepted, he remained silent about the 4 November meeting. Regardless of these claims and counterclaims there is no doubt that Lloyd George and his closest confidants among the British ministers wanted to prevent Hughes from participating in the armistice negotiations.

Lloyd George had slighted Hughes not because he was a colonial – Smuts had been consulted and had attended all the War Cabinet meetings that discussed Wilson's proposed armistice terms

---

[28] Draft Minutes of Imperial War Cabinet Meeting (36A), 6 November 1918, TNA: PRO CAB 23/44A. It was perhaps because of the acrimonious and explosive nature of the meeting, a meeting which questioned the whole idea of the Imperial War Cabinet, that these minutes were never given a formal status and not included in the official series CAB 23/42.

[29] Letter, Hughes to Lloyd George, 6 November 1918, Lloyd George Papers, House of Lords Record Office F28/2/8.

[30] Draft Minutes of Meetings of War cabinet, 26 October and 1 November 1918, TNA: PRO CAB 23/14 and Minutes of Meeting of War cabinet, 4 November 1918, *ibid.*, CAB 23/8.

– but because he had been so uncooperative and obstructive. If allowed to take part in the negotiations over the armistice, Hughes might have wrecked any chance of reaching an accord with the Americans. Division in the Allied camp would only serve Germany's cause and possibly prolong the war. The inter-allied diplomacy over the armistice needed wise counsel and delicate handling.

It was almost as though Hughes had courted this confrontation, as though in part he had contrived to produce an incident that would bring his differences with Lloyd George to a head. The next day he took his complaint into the public arena and, in an address to the Australasian Club, launched what was a thinly veiled attack on the British Prime Minister. The speech which was widely reported in the British and Australian press highlighted his dissatisfaction with the lack of consultation over the terms of peace and his belief that the Fourteen Points endangered Imperial and Australian interests.

Lloyd George could not ignore this challenge and on 9 November the British Press Bureau published an official answer. It was a public relations version of the case that Lloyd George had advanced in the Imperial War Cabinet. It recognised the right of the Dominions to an 'equal voice with the United Kingdom in the settlement of the terms of peace.' But it contended that the Dominions had been consulted about peace terms in the 1917 and 1918 Imperial War Cabinet meetings and that nothing had been done which was 'inconsistent with the general conclusions arrived at in those discussions'. The British Government had every intention of associating the Dominions with itself 'at every stage in the future discussions of the terms of the peace'. It had summoned the Dominion leaders back to London for the purpose of seeking their advice and having them represented at the coming Inter-Allied Conference which would 'consider in detail the practical application of the general principles of the peace settlement.'

Hughes was no more satisfied with this than with the explanations offered at the Imperial War Cabinet meeting. In another public address that same evening he countered all the British Government's assertions. It was his view that the statement missed the point at issue. Though Wilson's Fourteen Points had never been accepted by the British or the Dominion governments the armistice terms had fixed the principles of the peace. Moreover what discussions there had been in the Imperial War Cabinet had taken place in the midst of war, and what was discussed then had the character of war aims rather than peace terms. Despite promises given in time of war, the Dominions were presented with terms of peace that had been 'definitely settled'. Hughes was mystified by this. He could not understand how it could have happened. He was available in England for consultation and the other Dominion leaders could have been consulted by cable. Once again he protested about the absence of assurances that Australia's interests would be protected. He wanted to know why the British delegates had not reserved the Empire's position on the future of the German colonies and the control over tariffs in the same way they had reserved their position on 'freedom of the seas'.[31]

Lloyd George's reply to Hughes's letter added little to what had been said in the published statement. Once more he set forth his specious arguments. It was again stated that there was a great difference between the armistice and the final terms of peace. The Fourteen Points had been

---

[31] *Times* (London), 8 and 9 November 1918 and *Morning Post*, 9 November 1918; *SMH*, 11 November 1918.

accepted because it was believed that their language was broad enough to cover everything that it was 'intended to raise when the issue of peace came to be dealt with.' Neither Australia's control over tariff policy nor its claim to the Pacific islands had been compromised. Had the British delegation attempted to debate all these issues the armistice conference would have become a long, drawn out Peace Conference, and by implication it was suggested that the armistice would have been unduly delayed. Lloyd George offered Hughes an olive branch. He attached a coda in his own hand expressing his regret that 'the universal joy in the Victory achieved for the cause of freedom should be marred by the least misunderstanding', and he assured Hughes once again that 'The Dominions have by their heroic efforts won a place in the Great Council which will settle the destiny of the world for ages to come.'[32]

Immediately after the fiery exchanges at the Imperial War Cabinet Hughes sent Watt a cable asking for his Australian colleagues' support. Summarising his grievances he told Watt that 'the peace terms have been in effect settled, that Australia has not been consulted nor had any opportunity to state its views and that, although formal peace Conference will follow, we shall be limited to Wilson's 14 points, with such qualifications as are here set out.' There were only two clear qualifications – the 'freedom of the seas' and reparations for damages inflicted by the Germans – both of which had been specifically inserted into the final document. He added that Lloyd George claimed to have told House that the German colonies would not be returned and that the Dominions would keep those they had captured, but since House had not assented to these terms the outcome was still uncertain. For the rest the Allies were bound by Wilson's Fourteen Points, which meant that Australia and the British Empire would be committed to the League of Nations, with whatever that might entail for sovereignty and self-government. He said that Cook 'entirely agrees with my view and thinks that we have been treated very badly.'

The Australian Cabinet did not, however, give Hughes the unqualified endorsement that he sought. While they were considering their reply they had been 'greatly embarrassed' to read about Hughes's speech to the Australasian Club. Watt had thought that Hughes would have waited to hear from his colleagues before going public. The Acting Prime Minister feared for the political fall-out in Australia. Hughes's precipitate action was the beginning of a serious breach with Melbourne. Watt had been growing restless with Hughes's failure to consult his cabinet before taking decisions. He felt towards Hughes something of the same sense of being taken for granted that Hughes felt towards Lloyd George.

Though the cabinet shared Hughes's 'surprise and indignation' that the peace terms should have been decided without consultation with the Dominions – a 'painful and serious breach of faith' – they were less than wholehearted in their response to Hughes's criticisms of the armistice terms and his reading of the Fourteen Points. As they pondered the matter, they had not only the Hughes cable before them but also one from Lloyd George giving his side of the story, and this undoubtedly influenced their deliberations. Watt reported that the cabinet members were unanimous in refusing to accept any interpretation of the Fourteen Points which 'would limit her [Australia's] right to deal with her tariffs as she thinks best', which suggested that they were not

---

[32] Letter, Lloyd George to Hughes, 11 November 1918, Lloyd George Papers, House of Lords Record Office F/28/2/10.

convinced that Hughes's fears about Point Three were altogether justified. Moreover they appreciated the 'resolute attitude' that Lloyd George had adopted on the question of the Pacific islands. They approved his statement to House that the British Government 'had no intention of handing them back to Germany or of calling upon the Dominions which had conquered them to surrender them,' quoting back to Hughes the words from Lloyd George's cable. They believed that such a policy was 'essential to the future safety of Australia and British interests in these isolated seas'. Hughes was authorised to convey these views to the Imperial War Cabinet.[33]

There was little comfort here for Hughes. In order to persuade his colleagues that he had good grounds for taking his public stand he repeated to Melbourne the arguments he had set out in his letter to Lloyd George, namely that the Imperial War Cabinet had never discussed the Fourteen Points or the peace terms as such and had had every opportunity to consult him during the Versailles negotiations. What rankled especially was that Japan had been present at Versailles and Australia had not; 'we who have fought for four years as equals are treated like lackeys.' Using Watt's words he agreed that this was a 'painful and serious breach of faith'. He was sure that his colleagues would see that the British answer was a 'palpable evasion of position'. He disputed Watt's assertion that Lloyd George had taken a resolute stand on the Pacific islands. The British Prime Minister had merely expressed a view in an informal conversation. Why, Hughes wanted to know, did not the British delegates insist upon Australia's right to these islands being 'guaranteed in the Peace terms in same way as France's rights to Alsace-Lorraine is guaranteed?' Hughes regarded the Imperial War Cabinet as 'a farce and a sham'. As a result of the way he had been treated, he had lost confidence in this body as the representative council of the Empire that would, through the combined deliberations of the British and Dominion leaders, decide imperial defence and foreign policy. 'Emphatic protest' was the only means by which Australia could obtain 'the terms to which she is entitled'. He reaffirmed that 'Australian feeling here is unanimous.'[34]

And so Hughes continued with his 'emphatic protest'. Never reluctant to use whatever instruments were to hand, he then tried to persuade the state governments through their Agents-General in London to join his campaign. To this end on 15 November at a luncheon hosted by the Agents-General he gave an address that brought together all aspects of his case. Cook, whom Hughes had ignored ever since arriving in the country, was also present and stated that he was in 'absolute agreement' with his Prime Minister.[35] But, in reporting on this to Watt, Hughes had to

---

[33] Cables, Hughes to Watt, 6 November and Watt to Hughes, 8 November 1918, NAA CP360/8 B1/2; *SMH*, 9 November 1918.
[34] Cable, Hughes to Watt, 13 November 1918, NAA CP360/8 B1/2.
[35] *Times* (London), 15 November 1918.
  According to Latham, Hughes and Cook had 'met on business for a few hours only since leaving Australia.' Hughes had little use for Cook for whom he had nothing but disdain. Cook for his part seemed willing to allow Hughes a free hand in policy as it left him free to enjoy the pleasures of his public position. Though the former Liberals in the National Government had sent Cook to keep a watchful eye on Hughes, there is no evidence that Cook either officially or privately communicated with his colleagues about Hughes's or Australia's role in imperial affairs. Latham, who disliked and distrusted Hughes, urged Cook to assert himself and insist on being consulted, but without much success. See letter, Latham to Cook, 2

acknowledge that here too he had received less encouragement than he had expected. He claimed that while the Agents-General personally supported him the state governments refused to commit themselves.[36]

Even before learning of this latest outburst the Australian Cabinet had become alarmed at Hughes's public agitation, and Watt had sent Hughes a cable expressing their disquiet at the Prime Minister's attack on Lloyd George and what it meant for the unity of the Empire. At the very time that Hughes was embarked on yet another lambasting of the British Government, Watt was warning him that 'a continued or extended public criticism of imperial authorities on consultation issue might easily reflect injury on interests of Dominions and bonds of Empire.' Watt reminded Hughes of the 'loyalty' problem in Australia and intimated that 'a slight mistake concerning such delicate and important relationships might seriously prejudice yourself and the Government.' In this context Watt, made anxious by Hughes's dismissive attitude towards the Imperial War Cabinet, reported that his colleagues, while agreeing Australia had an 'imperative necessity and absolute right' to be consulted, especially about Points Three and Five, did not think this implied a right, 'either express or inferential', to be represented on the Supreme War Council at Versailles or at the Peace Conference. If Hughes was thinking in these terms he was asked 'to reconsider this phase very carefully'.[37]

Four days later the Australian Cabinet reviewed the whole question again and Watt sent Hughes a further cable setting out their reservations even more plainly. In their deliberations they were able to take into account both Hughes's speech to the Agents-General and Long's cabled reassurances which challenged Hughes's interpretation of the armistice terms and pledged Britain to fight for Australia's interests. Watt outlined to Hughes what he called the 'Points of agreement' and the 'Points of disagreement'. Under the former they accepted first that the British Government had failed to honour its promise to consult the Dominions about the peace terms, second that Australia could not 'forfeit or limit her right to deal with fiscal or other economic questions as she thinks fit' and third that, since the German Pacific islands were 'so important … to the future safety of Australia', Australia's right to annex them should to be a condition of the peace.

More points were listed under the 'disagreement' heading. Cabinet denied that the terms of peace had been settled by the armistice arrangements. They did not think that Point Three 'prejudged' Australian powers over either tariffs or raw materials. They considered that Australia should pursue its interests not by public protests or complaints but by 'strong representations' to the British authorities. Expanding on this they said that public criticism amounted to 'hanging British family linen on the line for the information and amusement of other nations, including enemies.' This practice was likely to injure, even break, Empire ties. Finally they declared that any claim for Dominion representation either at the Supreme War Council or the Peace Conference 'cannot be supported by Cabinet'. Watt told Hughes that it would be impossible to pass a

---

September 1918, Hughes Papers, NLA MS 1538/23/2079. How Latham's critical letter came to be in Hughes's papers is difficult to understand.

[36] Cables, Hughes to Watt, 14 and 16 November 1918, NAA CP360/8 B1/2.
[37] Cable, Watt to Hughes, 14 November 1918, *ibid.*

resolution in parliament in favour of Dominion representation. This cable was intended to make Hughes reappraise his approach to the British Government as well as the peace. Watt urged him to 'give due weight' to their disagreements and to 'advise on result'.[38]

The cabinet, in taking issue with Hughes, was responding as much to the political climate in Australia as to the armistice terms themselves. Unlike pre-war Liberal leaders cabinet members did not feel able to rebuke the British authorities publicly for failing to honour their commitments. Ever since the conscription crisis the National Party and its supporters had castigated and condemned their opponents for disloyalty to Britain and the Empire. To admit that Britain had betrayed Australia would be to destroy the legitimacy of the National Party and all it stood for. It would play into the hands of the domestic enemy. Hughes, who was the chief author of the ideology of loyalism, had for six months been living in another world – an imperial and international one – and was reacting to that world. Watt had no time for Wilson or his Fourteen Points, 'the source of all trouble', and conceded that Lloyd George had violated the promises made to the Dominions about consultation, but he was adamant that Australia's protests should not be aired on the podium or in the press, and so allowed to threaten the legitimacy of the Nationals and the unity of the Empire.

Watt and his colleagues were greatly influenced by the local political ethos. They could not but heed the hostile editorials appearing in the major city dailies and the rumblings of discontent from their own backbench. Watt, indeed, had to head off a motion from one of the latter that called on the House of Representatives to repudiate Hughes's claims about British neglect of Australia's interests.[39] Following these cable exchanges Watt was made anxious by Hughes's silence. He no doubt feared that Hughes might ignore the cabinet and cause a crisis in the government. As a result, on 23 November Watt sent an urgent appeal to London, stating that the 'matter is extremely dangerous', that he had only been able to stall Hughes's enemies in the parliament and that he needed Hughes's 'prompt and frank' answer.

Pearce, Hughes's old Labor comrade and close political associate, seeing that conservative enemies in the National coalition were using this issue to undermine his leadership, added his voice to that of Watt. He cabled Hughes, pressing him to heed the cabinet's wishes and to cease public criticism of the British Government. There was dissension in the coalition's ranks and the disaffected were trying to use the loyalty issue to bring him down. He counselled Hughes to give up any idea of seeking separate representation for Australia and to content himself with putting Australia's view to the War Cabinet.

Hughes in reply assured Pearce that he had 'never claimed or sought publicly or in War Cabinet representation for Australia' either at the Versailles Council or the Peace Conference. He understood the motives of those who maligned him and asserted that he had done 'more for the Empire than 10,000 such men'. But true to the Australian tradition he maintained that 'Britain is

---

[38] Cable, Long to Munro Ferguson, 15 November 1918, Novar Papers, NLA MS 696/5130 and personal letter, Munro Ferguson to Long, 16 and 18 November 1918, WRO Long Papers, 947/625/131; Cable, Watt to Hughes, 19 November 1918, NAA CP 360/8 B1/2.

[39] *SMH,* 13 November 1918 and *Argus,* 19, 20 and 21 November1918; *CPD,* 1917–18 session, LXXXVI, 8100–09, 20 November 1918; cables, Watt to Hughes, 22 and 23 November 1918, NAA CP 360/8 B1/2.

not the Empire.' His immediate task was 'to protect Australia's interests'. He needed help, and he looked to members of the National Labor and National parties to back him. Hughes's frustration with those who dared question his leadership vented itself in petulant sarcasm. How, he wanted to know, was it that 'when I speak up for Australia I am told I ought not to have protested and that our interests are safe in the hands of Downing Street'? And he concluded with a nice flourish, 'Does experience support such view, and if it does why should Australia be represented at all but leave her interests in matters to Downing Street?'[40] He expected that Pearce, above all others, with his long service as Minister for Defence would know the correct answer to that question.

Hughes answered Watt in similar terms, even if in more measured language. He quoted for the first time from the records of the Allied leaders' conversations at Versailles to try to show that Lloyd George had committed the Empire to a peace based on the Fourteen Points with the sole exceptions of 'freedom of the seas' and reparations. To justify his public actions he declared that when at the Imperial War Cabinet he had learned 'what HAD BEEN done', he saw that the only way of influencing the British Government was to alert the British people to the 'danger to Britain and to whole Empire through unsatisfactory terms of peace'. He was 'quite sure that as a result of my action public opinion here will make British representatives to Peace Conference much more insistent upon points to which I referred.' He did not explain, however, how they would be able to save the day when, as his interpretation would have it, they were already and irretrievably locked into a Wilsonian peace. In answer to his colleagues' other major concern he denied that he had ever, either in public or in the Imperial War Cabinet, suggested that the Dominions should be represented at the international gatherings that would determine the peace – which was less than the whole truth. Others had raised the issue, and he hoped that Watt would not say anything 'which would support the view that if British Govt [sic] is desirous of giving Dominions representation, Australia is not to be represented along with the other Dominions.'[41]

This brought to an end Hughes's dispute with Melbourne. He gave up his public denunciations of Lloyd George and his crusade to rouse the British people against their government. As the Dominion leaders assembled in preparation for the Peace Conference Hughes returned to the Imperial War Cabinet and carried on the campaign for his peace of annexation and indemnity behind closed doors.

This pronounced difference of views between Hughes and his cabinet was not primarily one between an egotistical nationalist and his more conservative Imperialist colleagues. It was more fundamentally a difference between Australians who had different perspectives on the problem of Empire, between Australians who experienced the Empire at first hand in London or who imagined it from a distance in Melbourne. From Melbourne the Nationalists who, during the conscription controversy, had defined Australia's Britishness as an unquestioning loyalty to the

---

[40] Cable, Hughes to Pearce, 26 November 1918, Pearce Papers, AWM 3DRL 2222/3/3/70.

[41] Extract from cable, Hughes to Watt, 25 November 1918, Hughes Papers, NLA MS 1538/16/2078–79. This extract is found in the 'Precis of Cables to and from Australia' prepared for Hughes to help him defend himself from Watt in parliament in 1921. The original is missing from the collection of Hughes-Watt cables in NAA CP360/8 B1/2 and no copy could be found in the Hughes Papers.

For the Hughes rebuttal of Watt's charges see *CPD* (House of Representatives), 1920 session, XCIV, 5817, 20 October 1920.

Empire and justified their very existence in those terms, could not tolerate the notion that the British Government had been disloyal to Australia. Hughes's public dispute with Lloyd George not only challenged their own identity but also gave comfort to 'the enemies within the gates', those whom they had anathematised as 'disloyal'. From London Australians saw Lloyd George's behaviour over the armistice question as symbolic of the British Government's disregard of the rights of loyal Australian Britons and of its often cavalier treatment of Australian interests, and therefore they were united behind Hughes and his public criticism of the British Prime Minister. British-based representatives of major Australian financial, mining and grazing interests quietly lent their support to Hughes,[42] and not only Cook but also the other major figures on the Australian delegation sympathised with their leader. Even Fisher privately expressed his dismay at Lloyd George's by-passing of the Dominions. It was what he had campaigned against for the whole of his career as Prime Minister. Lloyd George's behaviour was a further example of the short-sightedness and arrogance of the British. On this he was at one with Hughes. Writing to his wife, he declared that 'The failure to include a Dominion Representative at the Council which prescribed the terms of surrender (or rather the conditions of armistice) is very regrettable and cannot be repaired by subsequent actions. The great point missed was the place of the growing Dominions in future Empire difficulties.'[43]

---

[42] Hughes, recognising that Australian criticism undermined his standing in London, appealed to the Australian businessmen, whose commodities he was attempting to sell, to use their influence with the conservative politicians and press barons to silence his detractors. As a result, on 27 November, R.G. Casey, the head of Mt Morgan Gold Mining Company, sent a cable on behalf of 'leading land and financial companies', to W. Riggall, a well-connected Melbourne lawyer who carried weight in the National Union, the Victorian branch of the National Party, calling on the National Union to 'loyally solidly' support Hughes. Casey said they should 'trust Hughes … and endeavour stop these depreciatory press cables from your side which weaken his hands.' He assured Riggall that he need 'not fear any friction with Imperial Government as result his policy.' Casey and his backers thought that Hughes should receive 'active support' from 'Your press and Parliament', and he recommended that Riggall pass on their views to Sir Lachlan Mackinnon, the proprietor of the Melbourne *Argus* and the *Australasian* and to Sir James Fairfax, the proprietor of the *SMH*. See Copy of cable, R.G. Casey to W. Riggall, 27 November 1918, Hughes Papers, NLA MS 1538/118/4.

It is not altogether clear why these London-based Australian business magnates threw their influence so strongly behind Hughes. Hughes had been working very hard to persuade the British Government to buy Australian commodities on long-term contracts at good prices and to find shipping at reasonable rates which could carry the Australian raw materials to Britain. This was of fundamental importance to these Australian financial, agricultural, pastoral and mining companies. Hughes's efforts in this direction, including discussions with Casey representing the Copper Producers' Association, are well documented in Hughes's cables to Watt. See cables, Hughes to Watt, 7, 11, 16, 24, 27 and 30 November and 16 December 1918, NAA CP360/8 B1/2. Hughes also listened sympathetically to a deputation of 'Australian interests' who complained about Australia's war profits super tax and sought to bring it in line with Britain's more lenient treatment of excess profits, and he suggested to Watt that the government accede to their request. See cable, Hughes to Watt, 1 November 1918, *ibid*. The issues at stake between the Australian and British Governments over the sale of wool, wheat, zinc, lead and copper are set out roughly in letter, Hughes to Bonar Law, 21 November 1918, Hughes Papers, NLA MS 1538/23/257.

[43] Letter, Fisher to Margaret Fisher, 7 November 1918, Fisher Papers, NLA MS 2919/1/482.

The trial of Imperial Union and Dominion representation at the Paris Peace Conference

The Anglo-Australian controversy was very hurtful to those new Imperialists who had seen in the Imperial War Cabinet the institutional means whereby their grand ambition for Greater Britain would be achieved. The Imperial Cabinet would, with the consent of the British and Dominion leaders, fashion a common defence and foreign policy for the whole British race. This new institution, created out of the emergency of the war years, would both put an end to British paternalistic treatment of the Dominions as subordinate colonies and counter the centrifugal forces that encouraged a more complete form of national autonomy. The chief officials, attached to the Australian delegation in London, John Latham, Cook's private secretary and R. R. Garran, Hughes's Solicitor-General, shared this view. They had been founding members of the Melbourne Round Table moot and were deeply shocked by Lloyd George's failure to consult Hughes and the other Dominion leaders at the time of the armistice negotiations. It was in their eyes a great blow to this ideal of uniting all the British peoples in facing up to the world.

Latham protested to Philip Kerr, who was both Lloyd George's Private Secretary and a senior member of the Round Table movement. Though Latham was no great admirer of Hughes and thought his public attack on Lloyd George 'undiplomatic and made too much of the personal aspect', he nevertheless was much concerned by the implications for the future of the Empire. He wrote to express his:

> deep regret that Great Britain accepted Peace Terms without in any manner consulting the Dominions. It would have been so easy to do it by a short cable. Every motive of loyalty and every consideration of good faith required that the opinion of the Dominions should have been asked before Great Britain became bound.

And he added:

> I am unwilling to think that the course taken was deliberately adopted. I prefer to believe, as long as I can, that the omission to do what was clearly necessary was due to carelessness ... In any case, the people of the Dominions will be justified in believing that they cannot safely trust the leaders of Great Britain.
>
> The consultative principle embodied in the Imperial War Cabinet is supported by no legal or even conventional sanctions. It depends upon an assumed basis of common loyalty and good faith – the existence of which but few have hitherto even professed to doubt. A basis of the same character, but even more substantial would be essential to any closer unity. The events of the past few days have shown that either that basis does not exist or the leaders of Great Britain have not the Capacity and breadth of view, despite their past utterances, to realise the grave significance of these events ...
>
> The neglect to consult the Dominions at this critical juncture whether due to design or to indifference, causes me the most grave apprehension as to the future of the Empire.

He wished the British to understand that his complaint was not simply a response to the treatment meted out to Hughes. It was the general principle which exercised him; 'The course pursued would have been equally disastrous had no representative of any Dominion been in

England.'[44] Latham sent copies of this letter to two other members of the British Round Table and, as a result, a special meeting was called to discuss the issue. According to Latham he at first encountered some resistance, but after the British Round Table members had heard him out they came around to his point of view. There was 'a general admission that "someone has bungled"'. Though Garran, who was also present, gave a similar account, the official minutes of the meeting do not bear this out. Only one British representative supported the Australians. Numerous members spoke in defence of Lloyd George. Some maintained that since Wilson's January speech setting out the Fourteen Points, the Dominions had had many opportunities to express their views on these peace terms. Others argued that the peace had come 'like a thief in the night' – a rather unfortunate image – and required the British Government to act without delay. And yet others declared that the armistice terms could be interpreted in many ways and thus would not prevent the Dominions from obtaining any of their objectives. Lionel Curtis 'in conclusion' summed up the problem by pointing out, as he had in his book, that 'such incidents were bound to occur' unless and until the Dominions demanded the 'organic reconstruction' of the Empire.[45] It would seem that Latham and Garran allowed their hopes to colour their impressions of what had been achieved.

The Australian protests, even if they failed to exact an apology from British leaders, heightened British sensitivity to the question of Dominion participation in the peace. The apostles of the new Imperialism were alarmed, especially at Hughes's public denial that there was 'any such thing as an "Imperial Government"'. Amery, who had himself been at Versailles as a member of the British delegation, was convinced by Hughes that the Dominions had been treated badly and he feared that the dispute boded ill for the future unity of the Empire. Amery told Balfour:

> I don't suppose any of us realised at Versailles the other day that in giving a sort of second reading adhesion to President Wilson's 14 commandments we were settling the terms of the peace. But an hour's talk I had the other day with Hughes has convinced me that the case which he made out against the British Government is technically at any rate a pretty strong one, and that with a quarrelsome and vain person like our little friend, and with a very touchy and possibly swollen-headed public behind him … mischief may be caused if the breach is allowed to continue.

Amery was sure that 'this question of the effective representation of the Dominions in the forthcoming Peace settlement is one of supreme importance, a very "articulus standis aut cadentis imperii"', and he sent Balfour a memorandum setting out what needed to be done to avert the disintegration of the Empire:

> The extent to which the Dominions are given a really effective voice in the Peace Settlement will determine their whole outlook on Imperial questions in future. If they consider that they

---

[44] Latham diary, 7 November 1918, and copy of letter, Latham to Kerr, 9 November 1918, Latham Papers, NLA MS 1009/20/909A and 1009/19/23–25.

[45] Letters, R. Coupland to Latham, 11 November 1918, and Latham to Coupland, 13 November 1918, Latham Papers, NLA MS 1009/19/24–25; Round Table Moot Notice for meeting, 21 November 1918, *ibid.*, 1009/19/27; Latham diary, 21 November 1918, *ibid.*, 1009/20/909A and Garran diary, 21 November 1918, Garran Papers, NLA MS 2001/3/21; minutes of a 'Moot' held at Lionel Curtis's home at 23 Cambridge Square, Hyde Park, 21 November 1918, Lothian Papers, NAS GD40/17/477.

have been treated in the full sense of the word as partners and have had an equal voice in the decisions not merely of such questions as affect them locally but in the whole peace settlement, they will be prepared to accept the idea of a single foreign policy for the British Commonwealth directed by the machinery of an Imperial Cabinet.

The public furore stirred up by Hughes was 'a significant warning of the possibilities of troubles'. The only answer to the problem was to ensure that the Dominions were given direct representation on the British delegation at the Peace Conference.[46]

Once the Dominion prime ministers had reassembled in London to prepare for the Peace Conference and the Inter-Allied Conference that was initially planned to precede it, the question of Dominion representation, which lay behind Hughes's attack on Lloyd George, came to the fore. Borden, on behalf of Canada, had taken the initiative on the matter. He cabled Lloyd George as soon as he had received his summons that 'The press and people of this country take it for granted that Canada will be represented at the Peace Conference.'[47] This Canadian demand was made prior to the Hughes-Lloyd George confrontation and was independent of it. Lloyd George knew that the Dominions would require some form of representation, and at the Versailles Conference he had told House when discussing the size of the great powers' Peace Conference delegations that they should be large enough for him to be able to include in the British delegation a 'man from the colonies and a labour representative.'[48]

From this time until the opening of the Paris Peace Conference in early January 1919, the questions of whether and how the Dominions would be represented was debated both inside and outside the Imperial War Cabinet. The very idea was novel. The Dominions had never been represented at an international conference which dealt with foreign policy, unless Hughes's membership of the British delegation at the Paris Economic Conference in 1916 counted. The issue was further complicated by the uncertainty over whether they were considering a preliminary Inter-Allied Conference or a formal Peace Conference, and, if the former, whether the conference would be conducted by the great powers with the small allied powers only in attendance where their interests were concerned or whether it would have plenary sessions at which all allied powers would be present.[49] Above all, however, the question was clouded by the need to satisfy a variety of different and, in some respects, divergent aims. While Hughes wanted representation in order to achieve an effective voice in decision-making, especially as it affected Australia, Borden's objective was a matter of status, to gain recognition for Canada as an equal of other small powers. All, however, were agreed that whatever was done should not destroy the unity of the Empire.

---

[46] *Times* (London), 9 November 1918; letter and memorandum, Amery to Balfour, 14 November 1918, Balfour Papers, BL Add 49775, ff.189–94.
[47] Copy of cable, Borden to Lloyd George, 29 October 1918, Borden Papers, LAC box 336. In a letter to Lloyd George of 2 November 1918 Borden developed this notion further. See Lloyd George Papers, House of Lords Record Office F/5/2.
[48] Cable, House to Wilson, 6 November 1918, *Papers of Woodrow Wilson*, Vol.61, p.606.
[49] This question was not resolved until the leaders of the 'Big Five' powers met in Paris in early January and decided that the preliminary Inter-Allied Conference should become the definitive Peace Conference.

A number of specific solutions were advanced. The Canadian Prime Minister as soon as he arrived in London was engaged in discussions with the British Government. Lloyd George and Bonar Law said that they thought the best answer would be to include Borden as a member of the British delegation. But there was some doubt whether the other Dominions, especially Australia, would be happy with this arrangement.[50] Subsequently Smuts prepared a memorandum which was intended to meet the two distinct Dominion aims, on the one hand, by taking the Imperial Cabinet to the Peace Conference so that the Dominion prime ministers could be continuously consulted 'on all the principal questions', and, on the other, by allowing the Dominions to fill one spot on the British delegation on a rotation basis and so give them a formal representation standing at the conference.[51]

At the first meeting of the reconvened Imperial War Cabinet both Borden and Lloyd George urged that the Dominion leaders should make their cases for annexation of the colonies under their control to the 'Inter-Allied Conference, which is a thing that matters'.[52] Two weeks later, after the Imperial War Cabinet had met with the French and Italian Prime Ministers, the Allied leaders agreed to give the Dominions the same rights as other small powers attending the Inter-Allied Conference. The Dominions, in common with Belgium and Serbia, would be able to present their point of view at the conference when the leaders of the great powers were considering questions that specially affected them.[53]

On reflection Borden, however, saw that this would not satisfy Canada. As he explained to Hankey, Canada was not specially affected by any specific questions and therefore would not have any reason to be represented at the Inter-Allied Conference. Borden had just received a cable from Ottawa informing him that his cabinet colleagues were 'even more strongly of opinion than when you left that Canada should be represented' at the Peace Conference, even though 'in any final decision' the Empire 'may find it necessary to speak with one voice.' If Canada could not obtain independent status then, as a second best option, Borden 'should form one of whatever delegation represents the British Commonwealth.'

Impelled by this message, Borden told Hankey that if the Allied leaders' solution to the problem was to be consultation by interest he might well have 'to pack his trunks, return to Canada, summon Parliament, and put the whole thing before them.' Lloyd George tried to placate Borden by raising again the possibility of including him in the British delegation. He told Borden that Hughes was unlikely now to protest about being omitted since he had accepted the Allies' formula. But Long and Hankey warned Lloyd George that Dominion jealousies being what they were Hughes would not accept exclusion. To circumvent this Borden backed Lord Curzon's suggestion that the British Empire should be represented at the conference or conferences

---

[50] Borden diary, 17 and 18 November 1918, Borden Papers, LAC.
[51] 'Dominion Representation at the Peace Conference (Note by General Smuts)', 25 November 1918, Hughes Papers, NLA MS 1538/23/2458.
[52] Shorthand Notes of Imperial War Cabinet Meeting (37), 20 November 1918, TNA: PRO CAB 23/43.
[53] Copy of cable, House to Wilson, 5 December 1918, House Papers, Yale MS 466.

determining the peace by three named delegates together with two others selected from a panel of British ministers and Dominion prime ministers.[54]

The matter was not taken up again until after President Wilson had arrived in Europe and the Peace Conference was imminent. On New Year's Eve the Imperial War Cabinet, prompted by a cable from the British Ambassador in Paris containing French proposals for representation at the coming conference, resumed the debate. From the Dominion point of view the French scheme was a rebuff. The French had seemingly resiled from the concessions they had made at the London Conference earlier in the month. Under this latest regime the great powers were to have five plenipotentiaries each: lesser states recognised as allies were to have two; states in formation, one; and neutral states, one. The great powers were to be represented at all sittings and committees, and the smaller allied powers were to have the right to be present at all sittings at which questions concerning them were discussed. Nothing at all was said about the Dominions.

The Dominion leaders were greatly concerned by this omission. Both Hughes and Borden condemned the French proposal. It was intolerable that neutral countries, like Sweden, or puny allies, like Portugal, should be represented and the Dominions not. Hughes declared that Australia had put more troops into the field than Belgium and therefore deserved as much representation at the conference. It is, however, difficult to ascertain what precisely Hughes had in mind in demanding representation. In making his claim for representation he had argued that the League of Nations would be 'one of those questions at the Conference which would most vitally concern the Dominions', and had added that in twenty-five years the white population of the Dominions would equal that of Britain. Australia had a right to have its voice heard as much as Belgium, but whether he meant this to be achieved through distinct national representation or membership on a British Empire delegation or a combination of the two methods is uncertain. Whatever he meant, Hughes acted contrary to the assurances he had given his colleagues in Melbourne; he was not a passive observer waiting on the sidelines to benefit from the work of others.

Borden's intent was also rather obscure. Perhaps he, like Hughes, had not taken in fully what the French plan implied. In accord with the messages from Ottawa, which seemed to have a very different object from those that Hughes had received from Melbourne, he maintained that 'There was no question on which the people of Canada were more insistent than their claim to Representation at the Peace Conference.' The Dominions should be entitled to as ample representation as Belgium or Holland. But, having made that point, he then proceeded as though the French were still offering the London Conference terms, the same right for the Dominions as for the small allied powers to be consulted where their interests were affected. He complained, as he had earlier to Hankey, that 'To provide that Canada should be called in only when her special interests were in question would be regarded as little better than a mockery' since Canada had no special interests which were likely to be at issue at the conference. Then he put forward the answer which he had come upon after the London Conference, namely that the 'British Empire' should have a delegation which would in part be selected from 'a panel, upon which each Prime Minister

---

[54] Borden Diary, 25 and 26 November 1918, Borden Papers, LAC; Roskill, *Hankey*, Vol.II, pp.29–30; cable, Sir Thomas White, Acting Canadian Prime Minister, to Borden, 4 December 1918, *ibid.*, box 336; letters, Borden to Lloyd George, 5 and 6 December 1918, Lloyd George Papers, House of Lords Record Office F/5/3.

from the Dominions should have a place, and that one or more of those Prime Ministers should be called from time to time ... to sit in the delegation representing the whole Empire at the Conference.'

When, however, Lloyd George replied that it would be impracticable to persuade the leaders of the victor nations to give the British Empire a delegation made up of five British representatives plus three more from the Dominions and India, at Borden's instance it was finally agreed that they should press for dual representation for the Dominions and India at the Peace Conference. The Imperial War Cabinet decided that Dominion representatives and India 'should in all respects be on an equal footing at the conference with Belgium and other smaller Allied States' and that 'The Prime Ministers of the Dominions and representatives of India should be placed on a panel from which part of the personnel of the British Delegation could be filled according to the subject for discussion.'[55] Because of the Canadian problem it was agreed that, in addition to the Smuts proposals, each of the Dominions should be represented on the same basis as the other small belligerents even though this created some ambivalence about the international status of the Dominions and the Empire.

This was not the end of the matter. The other great powers had still to be convinced. When the Allied leaders assembled in Paris in early January 1919 to begin the work of peace-making this was the first question under consideration. At the initial meeting of the leaders of the 'big five' in the so-called Council of Ten, which was to become the executive body for the Peace Conference, Lloyd George moved that the four major Dominions and India be allotted two representatives each on the same basis as Belgium and Serbia, and Newfoundland be granted one. President Wilson objected, asserting that 'those who did not know the full facts' – and perhaps he was thinking of his fellow Americans – might well think that the British Empire's representation was unduly large for 'in any question affecting the Dominions which might also affect the rest of the world ... Great Britain and the Dominions between them would have 10 or 12 votes.' As a compromise, he suggested an enlarged British delegation and an extensive use of a panel system.

Lloyd George responded that the Dominions were 'entirely autonomous' and had interests of their own which were quite separate from those of Britain. Furthermore the Dominions' contribution to the war was such that it would be impossible to seat Siam at the Peace Table while at the same time excluding them. And he observed that, since it was agreed that decisions were to be reached by consensus and not by voting, the number of representatives granted to the British Empire was immaterial. The Dominion representatives would only have the same rights as the lesser allied powers, namely the right to attend the Council of Ten 'on questions which affected them'. As a compromise, Wilson agreed that each Dominion should be entitled to one representative, that is half the number which Belgium and Serbia had been allotted.

Lloyd George recognised that he would have to refer this to the Dominion leaders, and the following day called a meeting for the purpose. Though they had all bound themselves to insist on representation 'equal to that of the smaller Allied powers', they, with the grudging consent of their Canadian colleague, accepted Wilson's offer on the understanding that a fair method of selecting the British Empire's five delegates was adopted.

---

[55] Minutes of Imperial War Cabinet Meeting (48), 31 December 1918, TNA: PRO CAB 23/42.

Even so, sensitive to the pressures from home, Borden remained dissatisfied and continued to belabour Lloyd George with his misgivings. Borden was certain that this discriminatory treatment would be badly received in Canada. Consequently, when the Council of Ten resumed their deliberations, Lloyd George put forward again the Dominions' original claim to be placed on an equal footing with the lesser allies. Though, after making his case, Lloyd George said that he would not press the point 'if ... a greater representation of Dominions would create a bad feeling', Wilson without further ado proposed that Canada, Australia and South Africa should have two representatives and New Zealand one. Much to Borden's annoyance Belgium and Serbia were subsequently awarded a third representative. But the battle had been essentially won. The Dominions, for the first time, were to be represented in their own right at a major international conference dealing with war and peace. In addition, they would be members of the British Empire delegation and so be able to have an influence unavailable to other small powers.[56]

Why had the Dominion leaders sought to break with precedent and seek representation at the Peace Conference? What did this push for distinct recognition on the international stage signify? The conventional wisdom has been that it was an expression of an incipient Dominion nationalism, that it was a step on the path to complete national independence. But this is too simple and imposes on the past a teleological intent fashioned out of the future. This explanation finds the cause in the consequence. It is true that the Canadians, in some of their statements, seem to look upon Dominion representation as the beginning of a process which would free them from the last vestiges of subordination to Britain. Borden, on 1 December, had noted in his diary that 'Canada must in the end assume full sovereignty.'[57] The Canadians were convinced that their contribution to the war required that they should be given the same degree of international recognition in the making of the peace as that accorded to Belgium or the other lesser allies.

This, however, was only half the story. Borden, like Hughes, was very close to the Round Table movement and was sympathetic to its goal of reintegrating the Empire.[58] He, like Hughes, wanted the Dominions and the Mother Country to share equally and collectively in the making of a common defence and foreign policy. For both leaders these views were a natural consequence of their attachment to a British racial and cultural identity and their belief that their nations' interests and the world's peace were best secured by a strong and united Empire. Borden in his *Memoirs*, writing of his approach to these questions at the Peace Conference, declared that he had 'a profound belief in the integrity of the Empire, in its future destiny, and in its influence for good.'[59] What he desired, as he put it in the debate over representation, was an Empire based on equal nationhood and an equal voice in foreign relations. It was the reformed Empire which the

---

[56] Minutes of the Meeting of the Council of Ten, 12 and 13 January 1919, *FRUS*, 1919, 'Paris Peace Conference', Vol.III, pp.483–87 and 531–38 and 604; Minutes of the Meeting of the British Empire Delegation at the Paris Peace Conference, 13 January 1919, TNA: PRO CAB 29/28; cable, White to Borden, 4 January 1919, Borden Papers, box 336 and Borden Diary, 15 and 18 January 1919, Borden Papers, LAC.
[57] Borden Diary, 1 December 1918, Borden Papers, LAC.
[58] *Search for Security*, pp.236–37.
[59] Henry Borden (ed.), *Robert Laird Borden: His Memoirs* (London: Macmillan, 1938), 2 vols, Vol.II, p.879. He believed that 'upon the basis of equal nationhood and adequate voice in external relations the salvation of the Commonwealth could be worked out most surely.'

Imperial War Cabinet was meant to exemplify that shaped his vision of the future. For Borden, separate representation at the Peace Conference did not mean that Canada wished to pursue its own path independently of the Empire. Rather he hoped that through the Imperial War Cabinet and its successor body, the British Empire Delegation at Paris, the British and Dominion leaders, would reach a consensus that they would present to the conference as the views of the Empire.

Hughes had both a simpler and a more complex attitude. He had welcomed the creation of the Imperial War Cabinet and its promise to give all the British peoples, the Dominions along with the Mother Country, an equal say in the making of a trade, defence and foreign policy for the whole Empire. It retained the idea of the unity of the Empire but of an Empire that took into account Dominion as well British interests. That is, Britain acknowledged that the Dominions were sovereign political communities which were united with the Mother Country through race and culture in a common empire and as a result would face the world as one. He had come to Britain in 1918 with high hopes for achieving much through the new imperial machinery. But he could not impose his will upon it. The members' interests were too diverse for common culture to mediate the quarrels which arose between the sovereign entities. He was most unhappy that his colleagues in the Imperial Cabinet would not adopt his peace aims, and that under Lloyd George's chairmanship their discussions never arrived at any conclusion. The British Prime Minister found the 'cabinet of cabinets', that is, the practice of governing through a council of governments, even if governments closely and intimately associated by history and culture, excessively time-consuming and very troublesome. As the leader of a world power he was not prepared to allow its foreign policy to be controlled by what he considered, especially in Hughes's case, to be the perversity and ignorance of the Dominions. Consequently he tended to bypass the Imperial Cabinet where crucial British interests were at stake or circumstances required immediate decisions. To this extent Hughes's disillusionment was understandable.

With the war coming to an end and the interrelated questions of the armistice and the peace looming ever larger, Hughes had told Watt that 'British politics ignore Imperial interests' and that there was 'no Imperial Government in this great crisis, although there may be an Imperial War Cabinet.' Frustrated, he dismissed the Imperial War Cabinet as 'a farce and a sham'. The British leaders had subverted the idea of a collective government for the Empire that would act on behalf of the whole and for the good of the whole. As he had during his Northern tour expressed it to the good citizens of Hull, they had given the quietus to his vision of Empire.

> The bulk of the Empire's white population was now in Great Britain, but in fifty years the bulk would be overseas. The future of the Empire depended on the policy adopted now, Upon the people of today rested the responsibility as to whether the Empire could be a 'real Empire', and whether we could be participators or not.[60]

On learning that Lloyd George had, without a word to the Dominion leaders, negotiated the terms of the armistice, Hughes had lost confidence in the Imperial War Cabinet.

It was neither an executive nor a consultative body. Rather 'the meetings of the Imperial War Cabinet had become merely meetings of the War Cabinet when overseas delegates were informed of a *fait accompli*.' For Hughes, Britain was 'not the Empire', a distinction which it seemed that the

---

[60] *SMH*, 28 October 1918.

British leaders, for the most part, were unable to make. Since the Imperial War Cabinet did not work he decided he had no choice but to speak out about 'the danger to Britain and the whole Empire' as well as to Australia's own interests. Indeed he held that Australia's interests properly understood were an integral part of the Empire's interests.[61]

In principle Hughes continued to hold that the interests of Britain and the Dominions could be reconciled and that some form of Imperial Government, if operated in the spirit of equality and mutual respect, was feasible. He could not see, indeed would not see, that his problem was not simply with Lloyd George, and that Britain, regardless of who might lead it, would never allow the Dominions a veto right over decisions which affected the United Kingdom's vital interests. His commitment to the idea of the British race united as a cultural community in a Greater Britain prevented him from recognising that the notion of a 'cabinet of cabinets' was inherently flawed or that he himself by his own actions had helped to contribute to its failure. Thus, even while Hughes's prime reason for seeking Australian representation in its own right at the Peace Conference was his conviction that the British could not be relied on to fight for his country's interests, he nevertheless could not abandon this cultural myth and so was concerned to achieve a good peace for both the Empire and Australia. Despite his reservations about the British attitude to the Dominions, in the weeks leading up to the meeting of the Allied and Associated Powers in Paris, he spared no effort in pursuing these twin objectives in the Imperial War Cabinet. As an Australian cocooned in a British race culture, he had to believe, despite disappointments and setbacks, that his two nations could still be made one.

---

[61] Extract from cable, Hughes to Watt, 23 October 1918, Hughes Papers, NLA MS 1538/16/275; draft Minutes of Imperial War Cabinet Meeting (36A), 6 November 1918, TNA: PRO CAB 23/44A; cable, Hughes to Watt, 13 November 1918, NAA CP 360/8 B1/2; cable, Hughes to Pearce, 26 November 1918, Pearce Papers, AWM 3DRL/2222 3/3/70; extract from cable, Hughes to Watt, 25 November 1918, Hughes Papers, NLA MS 1538/16/2078–79.

'Not a Good Peace': The Making of the Treaty of Versailles

Australia had entered the world stage at a climactic point in history. The Great War had encompassed the whole globe. It had been a war of mass nationalism, of peoples against peoples. The belligerents' economies and societies had been mobilised for total war and science and technology had been enlisted in the struggle. All of these ingredients mixed together had brought death and destruction to civilians and combatants on a scale never before seen.

In reaction many liberals and socialists had come to perceive this great human tragedy as the war to end all wars. It was to be the precursor to the Enlightenment dream of international peace and harmony, an apocalyptic moment which would, in President Wilson's words, 'make the world safe for democracy.' He had set out in his Fourteen Points address America's principles for a new diplomacy and it was these principles with a British reservation on 'Freedom of the Seas' and a French reservation on the meaning of reparation which were accepted in the armistice terms as the basis for the peacemaking.

The Australian Prime Minister, who represented the most democratic nation in the New World, denounced Wilson's liberal shibboleths and embraced the realpolitik of the Old World even more fervently than the French. The Fourteen Points challenged outright his policy of 'annexation and indemnity' and in the months preceding the Paris Peace conference Hughes at Imperial cabinet meetings urged, unsuccessfully, the empire leaders to fight against a Wilsonian peace for Germany. Unshakeable in his own certainties he carried his campaign into the conference itself, and at Paris where these contrasting ideologies came face-to-face Hughes confronted Wilson, pressing for a peace which would crush Germany, restore the British Empire's global power and protect Australia against Japan. For this purpose he demanded that Germany should pay the full cost of the war, Australia should be able to annex the German South Pacific islands and Japan be prevented from including a racial equality principle in the League of Nations Covenant. He had no faith in Wilson's nebulous League of Nations and did not want it incorporated in the peace treaty. For Hughes it was the British Empire, based on ties of race and history, which was the only sure foundation for preserving and policing a civilised world order.

At the end, however, despite his defeat of the Japanese over the racial equality question, he conceded that he had lost the battle, and it was his judgment that the outcome inscribed in the Treaty of Versailles was not a good peace either for Australia or the Empire.

13
Preparing for the Paris Peace Conference

The Fourteen Points and the League of Nations

When Lloyd George summoned the other Dominion prime ministers back to London to prepare for the Peace Conference, Hughes seized the opportunity to try to commit the Empire to a peace of 'annexation and indemnity'. Sensing that the critical moment for shaping the peace had arrived, he threw himself with great energy and urgency into the Imperial War Cabinet debates. He denounced Wilson's 'Fourteen Points' and pressed for peace terms more in harmony with his own philosophy of international relations. It was a lonely and stressful role that he had chosen for himself. But though he could do no other it came at a cost. Deane, his trusty confidant, bore the full burden. As he complained, 'I've not had a day away from W.M. since I left Australia. Just imagine tied up with him as his fortunes ebbed and flowed, as my nerves sang or sagged! We've fought, argued, sulked.' Nevertheless Deane remained loyal to his hero through it all and was able to write, 'We always get back – I'm his only pal – all the other swine run when anybody yells.'[1]

At the end of the summer of 1918, when it appeared that the Germans were faltering, Hughes had insisted that before the Dominion leaders returned to their homes the Imperial War Cabinet should consider the question of the peace. He argued that though Australia approved of Britain's entry into the war in 1914, the decision was made without consulting the Dominions, and to ensure complete support in the future it was 'vital we shall have some opportunity of moulding the foreign policy of this country before it is made.' Most immediately he had in mind the conditions of the peace which would frame the new world order. At the mid-August Imperial War Cabinet meetings which were devoted to this subject, Hughes repeated that it was 'essential ... that there should be complete agreement in the Imperial War Cabinet as to what the attitude of the British delegates at the Peace Conference should be'. Australia 'should have a voice in the settlement before it was made'.

Of the Dominion prime ministers Hughes was the most assertive in claiming a say in the Empire's overall peace policy and in calling for binding decisions to be made there and then. Australia had not only a particular interest in the future of Germany's Pacific island territories, but also a general interest in the future safety of the Empire. To his dismay the representatives of the other Dominions, following the lead of Lloyd George and Balfour, were content to engage in a discursive exchange of views on the issues. Though frustrated, Hughes nevertheless stressed that when the time came Australia should be consulted.[2] He was determined that the British Empire should win the peace as well as the war. During September and October, as we have seen, he became increasingly critical of Wilson's peace proposals. Indeed it was in large part for this very reason that Lloyd George had sidelined the Australian when the armistice negotiations took place.

---

[1] Letter, Deane to Ruth Deane, 6 December 1918, Deane Papers, Melbourne University Archives, 76/74.
[2] Shorthand Notes of Imperial War Cabinet Meetings (30–32), 13–15 August 1918, TNA: PRO CAB 23/43.

After the armistice terms were revealed Hughes had protested both against the lack of consultation and the acceptance of Wilson's 'Fourteen Points', even as modified by reservations on 'Freedom of the Seas' and 'Reparations', as the basis for the peace. At the Imperial War Cabinet meeting on 5 November when Lloyd George gave an evasive and misleading report on the Allies' armistice conditions, Hughes emphasised 'the importance of entering a *caveat* in time that the Fourteen Points were not our Terms of Peace.'[3] When, by the following day, he had grasped the full significance of what had occurred he did not mince words. The reparations provision still would not allow for indemnities; that is, for Germany to pay the full cost of the war. Point Three would prevent states from levying differential tariffs and might outlaw imperial preference. Point Five seemed to contradict all that Australia, New Zealand and South Africa had particularly insisted on, namely the annexation of the German possessions under their control. Yet of all the points, the most obnoxious was the proposal for setting up a League of Nations. This 'nebulous' scheme 'might be fraught with danger to the Empire'. Hughes had declared that if it were intended to usurp the right of the Empire to govern and defend itself then he was 'absolutely opposed to it'.[4] Kerr subsequently had tried to allay Hughes's fears and, repeating Lloyd George's leitmotif, had told the Australian that the 'Fourteen Points' were 'mostly verbiage and have to be interpreted in fact by the light of the situation and the determination of the different parties concerned.'[5] But Hughes remained unconvinced by these soft words.

During the Imperial War Cabinet meetings summoned to prepare for the Peace Conference, Hughes remained true to his philosophy of international relations. At the meeting on 20 November when the question of bringing Kaiser Wilhelm II to trial was discussed, he opposed the suggestion. Making war was not a crime. It was a natural part of international life. The Kaiser could not be indicted for plunging the world into war. Hughes contended that '85 percent. of the German people are as bad as the ex-Kaiser, and are as deserving of death.'[6] It was not that he had any sympathy for the German Emperor, but rather that he felt it impossible to single him out for punishment. All, or nearly all, Germans, being equally culpable for the war, were equally deserving of death.

At subsequent meetings Hughes resumed his attack on the 'Fourteen Points'. He was the only member to offer a general review of the whole question. After countering those points which affected the Empire most closely, he set out a program for action. On the 'Freedom of the Seas', he thought that there was 'a considerable difference between what President Wilson wants and what this Empire is prepared to accept'. The issue was one on which the Empire could not make concessions. Yet since it was 'bound up with League of Nations' they had to consider the possibility that Wilson would be obdurate. On the banning of discriminatory tariffs, he urged that the British delegation should adopt an interpretation which left 'each nation with the same powers that it had before the war', and so make the point nugatory. On reparations, he similarly urged that the meaning of the term should be extended to include indemnities for the cost of the war.

---

[3] Minutes of Imperial War Cabinet Meeting (36), 5 November 1918, TNA: PRO CAB 23/42.
[4] Draft Minutes of Imperial War Cabinet Meeting (36A), 6 November 1918, TNA: PRO CAB 23/44A.
[5] Letter, Kerr to Hankey, 13 November1918, Lothian Papers, NAS GD 40/17/57.
[6] Shorthand Notes of Imperial War Cabinet Meeting (37), 20 November 1918, TNA: PRO CAB 23/43.

On the captured German colonies he was pleased to note that the Imperial Cabinet had intimated its support for the Australian, New Zealand and South African claims. Taking up a suggestion of Borden's he agreed that on that question it would be best for the individual Dominions themselves to put their respective cases to the Americans so that it might not appear that the acquisition of these colonies was adding to the territory of Great Britain. He conceded that though this might be 'quite a wrong distinction' it would be a good tactic.

The League of Nations as a plan for remaking the world was the most dangerous and objectionable part of the 'Fourteen Points'. Hughes was opposed 'altogether to President Wilson's scheme'. As he construed Wilson's meaning, the League was intended to be 'some sort of world-State, in fact a Utopia, in which all nations would have to surrender some of their self-governing rights.' There would be international police and military forces. In Hughes's view this was a nonsense:

> But it will not bear an examination for ten minutes. It is a very obvious thing that no country will allow for a moment its vital interests to be decided by anyone but itself. I speak with some considerable experience of what nations will do in that direction, and those who shout loudest for international arbitration will stand most rigidly on their own rights when a vital interest is threatened [A barb aimed at the United States]. Let us ask ourselves if Great Britain would agree to interference by any Council of Nations as regards the size of her navy. Certainly not.

He then proceeded to show hypothetically how such a body might affect Australia. Given that Australia was capable of carrying a population of 100,000,000, and that its population was only 5,000,000, the League of Nations might well uphold the 'moral right' of overcrowded Asian nations, like China and Japan, to settle their peoples in Australia, a prospect which Australians would never countenance. The White Australia policy would 'come up' and 'whilst she had a leg to stand on Australia would fight' to resist such incursions.

Instead of this utopian league of abstract principles, Hughes favoured an organic league based on ties of blood, history and purpose: 'If America and Great Britain were to stand together, the peace of the world would be assured.' Since Britain's power was waning Hughes, echoing Henry Parkes Centenary vision, was willing to 'have a great Anglo-Saxon Empire', acting as a global peacemaker. The British Empire's other wartime allies, France and Italy, could also be associated. He allowed that there would be 'great rivalry between the United States and ourselves', especially over trade, but he was hopeful that the bonds of consanguinity would prevent a 'keen trade war' and enable the two peoples to cooperate in maintaining the peace.[7]

It is difficult to know how serious Hughes was about this alternative solution to the problem of world order. America was the chief threat to his vision of the peace and peace terms. In the making of the peace Hughes consistently expressed great resentment that America should

---

[7] Shorthand Notes of Imperial War Cabinet Meeting (38), 26 November 1918, TNA: PRO CAB 23/43.

Parkes's similar appeal to Anglo-Saxonism in 1888 looked forward to the day when 'these two great countries [Australia and America] will stretch out their hands again to the mother country and all in one great empire to govern the world.' New South Wales, Legislative Assembly, *Debates*, Vol.35, p.602, 21 November 1888.

presume to replace the British Empire as the pre-eminent economic and naval power. Perhaps here he was putting forward a scheme which might placate those members of the Imperial Cabinet, including the Canadian Prime Minister, who did not wish to offend the Americans.

When in December the Imperial War Cabinet learnt that President Wilson, who was leading the American delegation to the Peace Conference, was shortly to be in England for informal discussions the British leaders became even more focused on the problem of the peace terms. Lloyd George thought it important that when he and Balfour met Wilson they should be able 'to rightly interpret the Imperial War Cabinet's views'. Hughes, taking his cue from Lloyd George, insisted that it was essential that the cabinet should decide 'what line they were going to take on the Fourteen Points'.[8]

At the 24 December meeting, just four days before Lloyd George and Balfour were to meet Wilson, Hughes once again took up the issue of the League of Nations as the basis of the post-war world settlement. Once again it was Hughes who made the running. He was the only member of the cabinet to offer a critical overview of the question. This time instead of attacking the League directly he defined it to suit his own assumptions about international affairs. Perhaps he was induced to take this tack as a result of Lloyd George's announcement that the British Government had agreed to the establishment of a League of Nations. Hughes might also have calculated that, if Wilson was granted his wishes in this respect, he might be more inclined to give ground on the substantive issues. Thus Hughes, while admitting that 'some organisation for the control of international affairs was essential', on this occasion, instead of stressing the desirability of an Anglo-Saxon League, praised what he called Wilson's 'more moderate scheme' – that is, more moderate than the plan put forward by Smuts which seemed to suggest some form of international executive[9] – which depended on the 'organising moral force of mankind' and merely called for a year's discussion of a dispute before nations resorted to arms.

Hughes maintained that what he was proposing was 'just such' a plan as that which had been adopted at the 1915 ALP Conference. Yet though Hughes had on that occasion moved the resolution on a future structure for keeping the peace, there had been nothing in the resolution about an Anglo-Saxon hegemony as the basis for future world order. See *Official Report of sixth Commonwealth Conference of the ALP, held in Adelaide, 31 May–7 June 1915* (Sydney: Worker Trade Union Printery, 1915).

Wilson had anticipated that Hughes and his fellow reactionaries in Britain might come up with such an alternative to the League of Nations. As he crossed the Atlantic on board the George Washington en route to Europe he told the other members of the American delegation that any scheme for world order based on the British and American navies jointly patrolling the seas would be 'only another form of militaristic propaganda'. Cited from the Charles L. Swem papers, in William Reynolds Braisted, *The United States Navy in the Pacific, 1909–1922* (Austin: University of Texas Press, 1971), p.430.

[8] Shorthand Notes of Imperial War Cabinet Meeting (43), 18 December 1918, TNA: PRO CAB 23/42.
[9] J.C. Smuts, *The League of Nations: A Practical Suggestion* (London: Hodder and Stoughton, 1918).

Copies of Smuts's plan had been circulated to all members of the Imperial War Cabinet. Smuts believed that his blueprint for 'a new stage in world Government' would have been adopted by the Imperial War Cabinet 'but for the objection of W.M. Hughes.' See letter, Smuts to M.C. Gillett, 27 December 1918, W.K. Hancock (ed.), *Selections from the Smuts Papers* (Cambridge: Cambridge University Press, 1966), Vol.IV, p.34.

Afraid that Wilson might attempt to make his league a form of world government Hughes urged Lloyd George not to commit the Empire to a League of Nations which went beyond the moral sanctions of arbitration. It was his opinion that 'if compulsory force were to be supplied, let it reside in the four nations that had fought this war.' Britain's wartime allies, with the exception of Japan, could be trusted to maintain the world which the victors were to create and which they all would have an interest in preserving. It is noteworthy that once Wilson had arrived in Europe the notion of an exclusive Anglo-Saxon alliance had lost something of its appeal, if ever it did have an appeal. France and Italy were seen as equally valuable partners for the kind of peace that the British Empire needed. Again Hughes ended with his fundamental principle that 'Nothing should be done to impair our right to maintain and to control exclusively such navy as was essential to our safety.'[10] At bottom the British peoples, like all peoples, could only rely on themselves and their own naval and military power. The absolute integrity of the nation was axiomatic. National sovereignty was an inviolable principle.

Hughes's canvassing of the issues, while it elicited a range of individual responses, nevertheless failed to lead the cabinet towards a consensus on the Empire's peace aims. Hughes might wish the Imperial War Cabinet to arrive at clear decisions about the peace but Lloyd George was not to be pinned down. The British Prime Minister with his practical politician's philosophy of life, namely 'follow your nose',[11] understood that in the peace negotiations there would have to be much hard bargaining and inevitable compromise. Therefore until all the parties met and the time for decision-making arrived it was necessary to keep options open. Hughes failed to persuade the British Empire to take a stand against a Wilsonian League of Nations.

Japan and the future of the German Pacific islands

The one specific interest that Australia had in the peace settlement was keeping Japan at bay. As Hughes put it, 'Whatever else the people of Australia differed on, they were united on two things: firstly, their attitude towards Japan and the White Australia policy and secondly, the retention of the Pacific islands that they had seized from the Germans.'[12] And these two aspects of Australia's approach to the peace were intimately connected.

From the first months of the war Australians had been deeply concerned about the German Pacific possessions and their future. They had, at Britain's urging, expected to capture them all. But because of the accidents of naval strategy, the Japanese had occupied the North Pacific islands before an Australian expedition could reach them and the Japanese had then made it clear that they had no intention of relinquishing them. Since the Fisher and Hughes governments had no choice but to accept this reality, they had at that time resigned themselves to Japan holding the North Pacific islands. In early 1917 at a time when Britain was anxious to keep Japan's goodwill, Hughes had given his consent to an Anglo-Japanese Treaty guaranteeing British support for Japanese claims to annex these islands at the end of the war. Nevertheless, as the end of hostilities

---

[10] Shorthand Notes of Imperial War Cabinet Meetings (43 and 44), 20 and 24 December, TNA: PRO CAB 23/42.
[11] Riddell *Lord Riddell's War Diary*, p.345.
[12] Shorthand Notes of Imperial War Cabinet Meeting (47), 30 December 1919, TNA: PRO CAB 23/42.

drew near and the need to placate Japan no longer seemed so compelling, Hughes reopened this question.

Australia's interest in the future of the German Pacific Empire derived from its long established fear of Japan's southward expansion. While in London Hughes had received cables from Melbourne warning of Japanese claims to hegemony in the region and of their plans for capturing the trade of the South Pacific and for gaining control of the nickel deposits in New Caledonia. On 16 July Watt had sent Suttor's report showing that the Japanese understood Hughes's 'Monroe Doctrine' for the South Pacific speech was aimed at them. The Japanese press not only complained that the proposal excluded Japan but also recognised that it was aimed against Japan. Two days later Watt informed Hughes of an intercepted message to the Japanese Consul-General in Sydney which stated that the Japanese Government was despatching four engineers to New Caledonia to investigate the supposed great iron ore deposits in those islands. Watt also revealed that the Consul-General had told Tokyo that the Japanese through their traders were seeking 'to control the cotton business in the New Hebrides'. The Australian Government was concerned that the French, after learning of Japanese designs on New Caledonia's nickel resources, had apparently taken no action to frustrate them and during a visit to Paris later that month Hughes spoke to M. Henri Simon, the French Minister for Colonies, concerning Australian anxieties about Japan.[13]

Simultaneously John Latham, official secretary to Cook, had begun to examine the implications of Japan's growth in power for Australian defence. In his previous role as Chief of Naval Intelligence he had become aware that the Navy Department viewed Japan's occupation of the North Pacific islands as a threat to Australia security. Ignorant of the Anglo-Japanese agreement of February 1917 the department had never conceded Japan's right to keep these islands at the end of the war. It stuck to the position that the government had taken in January 1915, namely that Australia had, at the outset of the war, been invited to take possession of all Germany's Pacific islands and that the German surrender at Rabaul had included both the north and south Pacific archipelagos. Latham had also digested the 1915 secret report on the Japanese danger, and while crossing the Pacific he had read Frank Fox's 1912 'Australian Crisis' work entitled *Problems of the Pacific*, which only served to reinforce his concerns about Japan.[14]

Thus throughout July and August Latham busied himself with writing a series of papers arguing that Japan should not be allowed to retain the North Pacific islands. In the two papers fundamental to his case he postulated that Japan's continued possessions of these islands had 'a most important bearing on the problem of the defence of Australia.' It was in his judgment '*scarcely too much to say that ... the possession of these islands would make it ... necessary to double the strength of the Australian naval and military forces; and the number of days necessary for mobilisation would probably be halved*' and the '*annual increase in cost to Australia would amount to many millions of pounds*' [Latham's emphasis]. So desperate would Australia's position be that the 'possession of these islands by Japan might even make it impossible to defend all parts of

---

[13] Cables, Watt to Hughes, 16 and 18 July 1918, NAA CP360/8/B1/1 and A981 Japan 101, Pt.1 and Control of N/Hebrides 24.
[14] Latham Diary, 13–17 May 1918, Latham Papers, NLA MS 1009/20/909A.

Australia by any force whose provisions would be financially possible.' He also rehearsed Australia's diplomatic and legal claims to the islands, and, referring to a report in the London *Times* of 7 July which suggested Japan was installing a civil administration in the North Pacific islands, he concluded that 'action should be taken to secure strict adherence to the terms of surrender by which Japan, as well as the British Empire, should be absolutely bound.'[15]

Latham discussed these matters with Hughes and, with the approval of Cook, sent the Prime Minister the briefing papers on the North Pacific islands question.[16] Latham's arguments helped focus Hughes's mind on the problem. Coming just after Watt's reports about Japanese economic interest in the South Pacific these arguments spurred him into laying claim to all Germany's Pacific islands. As a consequence, at the Imperial War Cabinet on 13 August, Hughes protested when Balfour set out the Empire's peace commitments. Balfour stated that in addition to the Dominions keeping the German territories they had occupied, Japan had been promised the North Pacific islands. Hughes wanted to know the nature of the promise. He denied that Australia had consented to this. He was 'certain that the Commonwealth Government were not consulted.' Much confusion ensued. The agreement had not made a deep impression on the British ministers. Balfour thought the promise had been given before he came to the Foreign Office. Lloyd George felt that it had been negotiated by the Asquith Government. Bonar Law thought that Hughes had 'quite definitely agreed' to the Equator division when he had been in the United Kingdom in 1916. All were in error. But Hughes's query had opened up a potentially embarrassing problem for Anglo-Japanese relations, and the Foreign Office was instructed to examine the record and report back to the cabinet.[17]

During the following two months Hughes was further alerted to Japan's ambitions and his suspicions about Japanese intentions grew, almost to paranoia. On 11 September he forwarded to Balfour a cable from Watt asking for advice on an application from a Japanese merchant to ship pearl shells and copra from Rabaul to Japan. As the Australian Government's policy was to purchase all such products for war purposes, the merchant was approaching the Japanese Government for its support. Hughes saw this as yet one more demonstration of the Japanese conspiracy to penetrate and dominate the western Pacific. The cable, he wrote, 'speaks for itself'. It was clear that, 'These people are everywhere: and working assiduously.' As additional evidence of this deep-laid plot he cited the presence of some thousands of Japanese in the Philippines. They were 'waiting for the Americans to go' and 'then they'll promote a row & step in to maintain law & order.' The British race too 'must work in like fashion or return like our ancestors from the fat plains to the lean and rugged hills'. And he ended with an ironic flourish, 'Banzai!!', a mock salute to the putative enemy.[18]

---

[15] 'The Importance to Australia of German New Guinea and the Islands (Lately German) North of the Equator' and 'Surrender to Australian Forces and Occupation by Australian and Japanese Forces of German Possessions in the Pacific', both 11 July 1917, NAA MP 1049/1 14/0285. See also Latham diary, 9 July 1918, NLA MS Latham Papers, 1009/20/909A.

[16] Latham diary, 23 and 25 July 1918, *ibid.*, 1009/20/909A.

[17] Shorthand Notes of Imperial War Cabinet Meeting (30), 13 August 1918, TNA: PRO CAB 23/43.

[18] Letter, Hughes to Balfour, 11 September 1918, TNA: PRO FO 800/203/354–55; copy of cable, Watt to Hughes, 7 September 1918, NAA CP360/8 B1/1.

Latham was on a mission. He had little help from his minister who down to the end of July had rarely spoken with Hughes, except at public functions.[19] Cook seemed slothful and self-indulgent and content to leave business in the hands of his forceful and dynamic leader. Likewise he was happy to give Latham more or less a free hand in pressing his cause. Not willing to let his case go by default, Latham had approached Hughes directly and had his ear – the good one. The arguments in the briefing papers spoke to the Prime Minister's deepest convictions. Latham, having received an 'essay' on 'Japanese Expansion and Ambitions' from his friend and colleague, E. L. Piesse, the Director of Military Intelligence, took the opportunity on 3 October to resume lobbying Hughes. Though Piesse's report was merely a thoughtful survey of information gleaned from British representatives in East Asia and Japanese and Western newspapers, there was enough material in it – especially dealing with 'Pan-Asianism' and 'Nan'yo' or 'South Seas' expansion' – to give further colour to Latham's campaign. On the following day he forwarded Piesse's report to Hughes and urged that the British authorities be approached 'for an effective interchange of intelligence affecting the Pacific'.[20]

On 30 October, when the Australians read a report from the *Times* correspondent in Tokyo, the issue came to a head. The *Times* quoted the views of Shigenobu Okuma, who had been Prime Minister at the outbreak of the war, on Japan's attitude to the peace. In an article for the *Kokumin Shimbun*, Okuma indicated that while on questions affecting Europe Japan would follow the lead of its Western allies, it considered its claims in its own region 'must be settled in a way satisfactory to Japan at all costs.' In particular he stated on the Marshall, Caroline and Ladrones [Marianas] islands that Japan 'must continue in possession of them'.[21] Cook, probably at Latham's instigation, went to see Hughes about the report, and on his return told Latham that he would have 'plenty of work to do', especially with the German islands north of the equator. Hughes asked for a succinct account of Australia's case to acquire them. The next day he informed Watt, 'We shall have to watch our interests very closely … I shall never feel satisfied that Pacific and White Australia policies are safe until Peace Treaty which guarantees them is signed.'[22]

In a nine page draft letter Latham summarised all the arguments that he had advanced in his earlier papers: legal – the islands had been formally surrendered to Australian forces in Rabaul; diplomatic – the Japanese had promised in late 1914 to hold them only provisionally; and strategic – the islands in the hands of an enemy would be very dangerous to Australia. But of the three it was the strategic aspect that was given the most extended treatment. Several of the islands

---

[19] Letter, Latham to Ella Latham, 29 July 1918, Latham Papers, NLA MS 1009/1.

See also letter, Latham to Cook, 2 September 1918, Hughes Papers, NLA MS 1538/133/5 in which Latham stressed that Hughes was 'dealing with all sorts of important subjects' and exhorted Cook to seek to 'confer with him [Hughes] frequently'. How this letter came into Hughes's possession is a mystery.

Cook was not quite as slack as Latham indicated. On 25 July, following a dinner at Brooks's club, he had spent an hour with Milner and Amery 'making a lot of fuss about the Japanese having the islands north of the Equator.' *The Leo Amery Diaries*, I, '1896–1929', 229.

[20] Letter plus enclosures, Latham to Percy Deane, Hughes's Private Secretary, 4 October 1918. NAA MP1587/1 184J.

[21] *Times* (London), 30 October 1918.

[22] Cable, Hughes to Watt, 31 October 1918, Hughes Papers, NLA MS 1538/16/2088.

had harbours capable of holding very large fleets. If the British Empire held these islands they could use planes based there to harry an enemy fleet a good distance from Australian shores and to gain information about the direction of the invading fleet, the probable date of its arrival on Australia's coasts and the strength of the invading force. If, on the other hand, the Japanese kept the islands they could serve as points for secret concentration of hostile forces. If a potential enemy possessed the islands, it would 'probably halve the number of days available to Australia for mobilisation and make it necessary to maintain a larger and more expensive defence.' Since therefore these islands were of the 'highest value and importance' the letter recommended that 'every possible step should be taken by pressing these considerations upon the imperial authorities and if opportunity offers, upon America, to secure British control of the whole of the German Islands North of the Equator, as well as those South of the Equator.' Cook for some inexplicable reason had all direct references to Japan removed from the letter, but with these omissions he sent it to Hughes. [23]

The time for action had come. The armistice was being negotiated. Peace was in sight. And the Japanese were putting their cards on the table. Acutely aware of this Hughes sent Lloyd George an emphatic protest 'against Japan's right or even claim to the islands mentioned by Marquis Okuma, viz, the Marshalls, Caroline, and Ladrones.' In the letter to the British Prime Minister he set out almost word for word Latham's arguments. In the previous week the Foreign Office had furnished him with a detailed record of the British Empire's commitments to Japan, including the February 1917 agreement, but he would not allow that Australia had assented to them and even suggested that they were no longer binding on the British. Since the 1917 agreement had been signed 'much water had run under the bridges' and, moreover, Japan's attitude to the Empire in the war, namely its failure to send aid to the European theatre, would justify Britain refusing to honour the arrangement. Japan was a fair-weather ally. It was manifest that had the German offensive in March 1918 been successful 'we could hardly have looked for much help, to put the case at its best, from Japan.' In summing up he reminded Lloyd George 'once more that Australia profoundly distrusts Japan, that its national welfare and its trade alike are seriously menaced by Japan.'[24] Japan was on his mind. He was always very conscious of how small Australia's population was in comparison with that of Asian countries – especially Japan, and how that made Australia an inviting target for these envious, alien peoples. Australia should build up its white British stock. He cabled Watt that, 'If we are to hold Australia and develop its tremendous resources we must have numerous population.' The coming demobilisation of the British army offered 'a unique opportunity of securing right type of immigrant'. He urged the government to treat this as a matter 'of vital importance'.[25]

In taking Lloyd George to task over the armistice terms, Hughes pursued his xenophobic campaign against Japan. At the Imperial War Cabinet on 5 November Hughes, referring to the

---

[23] Latham diary, Latham Papers, 30 and 31 October 1918, Latham Papers, NLA MS 1009/20/909A and copy of letter, Cook to Hughes, 31 October 1918, Cook Papers, NLA MS 2212.

[24] Letter, Hughes to Lloyd George, 4 November 1918, Lloyd George Papers, House of Lords Record Office F/33/1/44A.

[25] Cable, Hughes to Watt, 5 November 1918, NAA CP 360/8 B1/1.

letter on the Japanese question he had sent Lloyd George, declared that 'it would be most unfortunate if such a claim were admitted.' To this, Lord Robert Cecil, Parliamentary Under-Secretary at the Foreign Office, replied that the paper setting out the history of commitments to Japan, which had been distributed to members of the cabinet,[26] had shown that 'no steps whatever had been taken without full consultation with and the approval of the Australian Government.' Hughes was reluctant to concede the point and scrawled over his copy of the minutes, 'This is not true.'

Hughes, moreover, objected to the Japanese participating in the armistice discussions. That Lloyd George out of sympathy for this 'very sensitive people' had taken the initiative in inviting them to Versailles was especially grating.

> Japan could certainly not claim admission on the ground of having made great sacrifices in this war. The number of Australian dead was actually greater than the army Japan had in the field in Siberia where she was looking after her own interest ... Australians were also a very sensitive people, and, further ... throughout Australia, Japan was regarded as a daily menace ... Did anyone dispute that, had the tide turned against us in the course of the war, we could have been certain of Japan's continued adhesion?

Australia had as much right to a voice in the making of the armistice as Japan.[27]

Yet, despite his best efforts, Hughes could not rally any support for wresting the North Pacific islands from Japan's grasp. The British would not, even if they had thought it practicable, renege on their side of the bargain. His own cabinet also could not be convinced. While Latham had been pressing the issue with the ministers in London, the Council of Defence had been making the same case to the Australian Government in Melbourne. In a submission to Watt, the Standing Committee (Operational), which included Rear-Admiral Sir William Creswell, and Major-General J. G. Legge, had asserted that the retention of the German Pacific colonies South of the Equator was necessary for the defence of Australia and that the German islands North of the Equator 'would be of great use to any enemy threatening Australia.' Since Legge had replaced Foster as Chief of the General Staff, the army and the navy had come to share the same view of the importance of the North Pacific islands. The committee, employing the same arguments as Latham, recommended to the government that it should take steps to ensure that Australia kept the South Pacific islands and that 'those North of the Equator be also retained or held by an International authority.'[28] Since they did not hold the islands they meant 'retained' only in the legal

---

[26] For Hughes's copy, see Foreign Office Memorandum G.T. 6078 dated 15 October 1918, enclosed in letter, Hankey to Hughes, 26 October 1918, Hughes Papers, NLA MS 1538/25/240.

[27] Minutes of Imperial War Cabinet Meeting (36), 5 November 1918, TNA: PRO CAB 23/42 and Draft Minutes of Imperial War Cabinet Meeting (36A), 6 November 1918, PRO CAB 23/44A; Hughes Papers, NLA MS 1538/111/4.

[28] Report of No.1 Standing Committee (Operational), Council of Defence, 27 November 1918, NAA B197 1851/2/81.

The Defence Committee, like Latham, had no knowledge of the Anglo-Japanese agreement of February 1917. It would appear that Hughes had told neither his ministers nor the Defence and Navy departments about his consent to this arrangement, and as a result all the Navy Department papers which Latham had brought with him to London and all his advice to Hughes were compiled without any knowledge of this

sense that they had been formally surrendered to Australia by the German Governor at Rabaul. The cabinet, however, rejected this second recommendation. Perhaps Watt had been alerted by Piesse to the existence of the 1917 treaty and, like Fisher in 1915, he and the other ministers simply recognised that any attempt to eject the Japanese would necessarily fail and only serve to court their ill-will. Watt in forwarding the substance of the report to Hughes informed him of the cabinet's decision.[29]

In the light of this reaction from London and Melbourne Hughes then abandoned the cause. At the Imperial War Cabinet meeting Hughes said, 'for the purpose of the record', that 'Australia could not regard herself as responsible for the position which Japan now held in the North Islands.' As for the February agreement, Hughes tried to explain away Australia's part in it:

> … the then Colonial Secretary had informed the Commonwealth that it was vitally important not to offend Japan, that Japan was in possession of the islands anyhow and that nothing we could say would affect this occupation. That was the real position – Australia simply accepted the inevitable.

Cook, intervening for almost the first time in the cabinet's proceedings, backed up his leader and expressed the anxiety felt by the Australian national security community. It was 'a serious matter that Japan should be brought to within striking distance of Australia.'[30] This too was an empty, 'for the record', protest at the very moment when the Australians were conceding defeat.

Why, it might be asked, did Hughes, Cook and their naval and military advisers believe that Japan could be persuaded or compelled to hand over the North Pacific islands either to Australia or an international authority? They knew how strongly the Japanese felt about the islands, and they were in occupation. Moreover after the Foreign Office had in October presented Hughes with the evidence that Australia as well as Britain had consented to the February 1917 Anglo-Japanese arrangement, it is difficult to understand why he should have persisted. It was neither an ambit claim that was meant to ensure the British would stand behind Australia's demand to keep the South Pacific islands nor a bargaining chip which could be used against Japanese requests for

---

treaty. Piesse, however, had discovered the exchanges with London in the Governor-General's papers and may have alerted Watt to the existence of the agreement. See letters, Piesse to Latham, 2 December 1918 and Latham to Piesse, 21 February 1919, Piesse Papers, NLA MS 882/5/4 and 882/5/8.

[29] Cable, Watt to Hughes, 9 December 1918, NAA CP360/8 B1/2.

Certainly Hughes had support in parliament for his desire to keep Japan out of the North Pacific islands. In the House of Representative debate on the South Pacific islands resolution Watt had carefully avoided saying anything about the North Pacific islands but a majority of speakers, about equal number from both sides of the house had, in one way or another, expressed their concern about Japan being left in control of the North Pacific islands. One Labor member, James Mathews, had openly stated that he 'would as soon have the Germans holding the islands in the Pacific as I would have the Japanese' at which the Speaker had intervened, commenting that it would be 'ill-advised' for Mathews to pursue the subject. When Mathews attempted to do so he was ruled out of order, and he complained that he was only trying to point out 'another menace to Australia'. See *CPD*, 1917–18 second session, LXXXVI, 7833–75 and 7936–43, 14 and 15 November 1918.

[30] Minutes of Imperial War Cabinet Meeting (44), 20 December 1918, TNA: PRO CAB 23/42.

trading rights in the South Pacific.[31] There is not a skerrick of evidence for such an explanation. Rather what impresses is the seriousness with which they all envisaged the Japanese danger. The fear of Japan, which had been heightened by the war, derived from a history that they all shared. Looking back at Japan's imperial expansion, its attempts to dominate China, its pressure on Australia to enter into a commercial treaty and its exploitation of the European conflict to expand its interests throughout the region the threat seemed palpable. The sense of racial menace, of the Asian masses pressing down on Australia, gave an added, almost hysterical dimension to their strategic anxieties.

Hughes's belief that there were sinister forces 'working assiduously beneath the surface', to deny the British race the fruits of its victory over Germany and to help further Japan's designs upon Australia drove him on.[32] Thus rational calculation was overborne by an emotional conviction that the British race should be entitled to obtain at the peace table whatever was needed to ensure its survival. For him the Japanese were the 'Huns' of Asia, the enemies of the British race in the Pacific. That is, while there were prudential grounds for keeping a watchful eye on Japan and for being anxious about the southward expansion of its territory, Hughes, as was his wont, transformed these concerns into an all-encompassing conspiracy. He, however, more than any of his advisers knew the full diplomatic picture, namely that Britain would not back a move to wrest the North Pacific islands from Japan and that the Japanese were as determined as the Australians to keep what they held. The notion that Australia through Britain could somehow bring the Japanese to give up what they controlled was a fantasy.

For almost two months the Foreign and Colonial Offices had been engaged in putting together a reply to Hughes's 4 November letter to Lloyd George. They had agreed to a draft which asserted that the honour of both Britain and the Australasian Dominions was pledged to the Japanese. Should the British Empire break their word it would be a 'breach of faith'. It was also pointed out that, if they were successful in denying the North Pacific islands to the Japanese, then the principle of 'no annexations' might have to be applied to the South Pacific islands. After the Australian retreat, however, this argumentative response was set aside. Lloyd George merely promised that the British Government would do 'their utmost to safeguard the interests and security of Australia and Empire'. Concluding, he said that the British would therefore go to the Peace Conference pledged to support Japan's claims to the North Pacific islands – 'a pledge', he added 'to which the Australian Government was a consenting party.' Hughes in seeking the last word agreed that there was no need to revisit the arguments about the vital importance of those islands to Australian security, and, responding in kind to Lloyd George, he expressed his confidence that the British Government would 'use every effort' to ensure that the Peace Conference would 'deal with this matter satisfactorily'.[33] Hughes could not leave the subject without rebutting the charge that he had consented to the Anglo-Japanese agreement. And he

---

[31] Cf. Fitzhardinge, *The Little Digger*, p.350.

[32] See cable, Hughes to Watt, 11 October 1918, Hughes Papers, NLA MS 1538/2/228 and letter Hughes to Balfour, 11 September 1918, TNA: PRO FO 800/203/355.

[33] Letter, Long to Kerr, 12 December 1918 containing the amended Foreign Office draft letter, and copy of letter, Lloyd George to Hughes, 31 December 1918, Lloyd George Papers, House of Lords Record Office F/33/1/45; Foreign Office draft reply to Hughes letter, TNA: PRO CAB FO 371/3236/382–85.

referred to the defence he had offered at the October meeting of the Imperial War Cabinet, namely that Australia had merely accepted the inevitable, and he cited Bonar Law's minuted confirmation that 'Mr Hughes had acquiesced in that which was already done.'[34]

During all these meetings Hughes had said little specifically about the German South Pacific islands. The basis for Australia's case for annexation was built into the argument for Australia's right to the North Pacific islands. Britain, at least since 1917, had never contested Australia's right to keep the islands which were under its control. Balfour at the 13 August meeting of the Imperial War Cabinet had, in setting out Britain's attitude to the peace, accepted that Australia, New Zealand and South Africa should 'obtain the colonies' that were 'adjacent' to them. Moreover under the Anglo-Japanese compact of February 1917 the Japanese, in return for British support at the Peace Conference for their right to hold the North Pacific islands, had promised to back the British Empire's claims to the South Pacific islands. The Japanese Ambassador visiting Hughes on 28 November assured him that Japan had no interest in the islands south of the equator. Hughes was resolute that the islands which Australia had captured should remain in its hands. Hughes had made it clear that: 'If you want to shift us, come and do it: here we are – "J'y suis, j'y reste."'[35] Curiously he had not seen that the Western powers, even if they had wished to do so, would have had the same problem in forcing the Japanese out of the North Pacific islands.

The only fly in the ointment was Wilson's peace principles. Wilson's peace program was opposed to territorial annexation. He wanted to bring all the German colonies under some form of international supervision. In meeting this challenge Hughes had spoken out in blunt terms: 'As to the restoring of the German colonies, so far as the Pacific was concerned, the safety of Australia imperatively demanded our retention of these islands.'[36] It was probably Hughes's complaints about Wilson's Fourteen Points that led Watt to introduce a Resolution in parliament supporting Australia's claim to keep the occupied islands.[37] The cabinet in Melbourne fully agreed with Hughes that these South Pacific islands should be taken over by the British Empire and come under Australian administrative control.[38]

It was Wilson's imminent visit to Britain that caused Hughes to push the South Pacific islands to the front of his agenda. Two days after Lloyd George announced that Wilson was coming to London to discuss the peace terms, the Imperial War Cabinet, as part of its general discussion of British peace aims, considered the future of the German colonies. It had already been agreed that the captured territories were not to be returned. The issue before the meeting was what was to be done with them. Borden, in the interests of Anglo-American harmony, urged that all the colonies with the exception of the territories adjoining Australia, New Zealand and South Africa, should be placed under League of Nations mandates. Hughes reinforced this distinction. It was his view that since these territories were 'in the immediate neighbourhood' of Australia, New Zealand and South Africa, 'the differentiating of their occupation from that of the adjoining Dominions, would

---

[34] Copy of letter, Hughes to Lloyd George, 7 January 1919, Hughes Papers, NLA MS 1538/23/312.
[35] Shorthand Notes of Imperial War Cabinet Meetings (30 and 31), 13 and 14 August 1918, TNA: PRO CAB 23/43; cable, Hughes to Watt, 29 November 1918, NAA CP360/8 B1/2.
[36] *Times* (London), 10 October 1918.
[37] *CPD*, 1917–18 second session, LXXXVI, Part 2, 7833, 14 November 1918.
[38] Cable, Watt to Hughes, 30 November 1918, NAA CP360/8 B1/2.

create insuperable difficulties in respect to customs, laws, coastwise trade.' He had made it clear to President Wilson when he had met him at the White House that 'the demand' for these islands was 'put forward in the interests of Australian security'.[39]

Lloyd George was not going to allow himself to be committed in any way. Hankey, in a note prepared for the Prime Minister before the meeting, had stated that it was 'generally agreed' that the South Pacific islands 'should fall to Australia and New Zealand' and that 'everyone' was agreed that South-West Africa should be 'annexed' to South Africa. Hankey, who wanted to make the Imperial War Cabinet work and therefore wished to find a solution to the problem, spent the following day negotiating with the Dominion leaders. As a result, he produced draft resolutions that spelt out in more detail the principles which seemed to have had general support in the Imperial War Cabinet. That is, the resolutions allowed that, with the exception of the German colonies in the South Pacific and South-West Africa, all the captured territories were to become mandates of the League of Nations. He wanted the Imperial Cabinet 'to give their strong and unqualified support to the claims for the incorporation of [these adjacent territories] with the Dominions.'

Hankey was disappointed by Lloyd George's response. The Prime Minister did not want the resolutions brought before the Imperial War Cabinet. As Hankey reported it in his diary: 'Lloyd George flatly declined even to discuss the question of the German colonies. The fact is that he didn't mean to be bound in any sort or kind of way in his conversation with President Wilson.'[40] Lloyd George who had ultimate responsibility for negotiating the peace with the leaders of the other great power victors wanted to keep as free a hand as possible. For him the fate of the German colonies, whether those held by the Dominions, Britain or Britain's allies, was not in itself a fundamental issue.

Thus the ground was moving under Hughes's feet. Recognising this, he decided rather belatedly to build a case which would meet Wilson's Point 5 and its requirement that in determining the future of the captured colonies the interests of the peoples concerned had to be given 'equal weight', and so he asked the Melbourne authorities to collect all the evidence they could of German mistreatment of the natives of New Guinea and associated islands.[41] At the opening of the Peace Conference the auguries did not seem favourable. Hughes had to admit that the North Pacific islands were lost, and he could not but be dismayed that the British Government had failed to back the Dominions' claim to annex the South Pacific islands.

Indemnity and reparations

From the first time that Hughes had thought about the peace he had held that Germany should pay an 'indemnity' for engaging in war. Until it was clear that Germany was collapsing, the word

---

[39] Minutes of Imperial War Cabinet Meeting (43), 18 December 1918, TNA: PRO CAB 23/42.
[40] Minutes of Imperial War Cabinet Meeting (44), 20 December 1918, TNA: PRO CAB 23/42; Hankey note, 'Item 1 of Agenda Captured Colonies', 19 December 1918 and note, Hankey to Lloyd George, 21 December 1918 enclosing draft resolutions, Lloyd George Papers, House of Lords Record Office F/23/3/30–31; Roskill, *Hankey*, Vol.II, pp.37–38.
[41] Cable, Hughes to Watt, 18 December 1918, NAA CP360/8 B1/2.

had been undefined. It was an ideological weapon aimed at those – especially socialists and liberals – who, denouncing 'indemnities' as they had 'annexations', called for a generous peace. It was used as a menacing metaphor for the righteous revenge which the British Empire would take against the defeated foe. It was a symbol of the British race's intent so to crush Germany that it would never again be able to rise up against the *Pax Britannica*. When in mid-October the Germans had sued for peace and President Wilson had offered them armistice conditions based on his Fourteen Points, Hughes had joined jingoist figures such as Leo Maxse, editor of the *National Review*, and Horatio Bottomley, editor of *John Bull*, in demanding that 'Germany's punishment must be such that no nation would dare to make a similar war again.' Germany had to pay 'the price of her bloody crimes'.[42]

It was not, however, until he was presented with the agreed terms of the armistice that he was compelled to think what an indemnity might mean and how it might work, and indeed how it might affect Australia's right to a share of the financial spoils. At the Supreme War Council where the terms had been settled, the French Premier, Georges Clemenceau, assisted by Lloyd George, had insisted on a clarification of Wilson's formula in Points Seven, Eight and Eleven which covered the restoration of invaded territory and were the only points referring to financial claims that might be made against Germany. In the final terms presented to Germany it was stated that by 'restoration' they understood that compensation was to be made 'for all damage done to the civilian population of the Allies and their property by the aggression of Germany by land and sea and from the air'. At the Imperial War Cabinet meeting on 6 November where Hughes had protested against the terms themselves as well as the lack of the consultation, he stressed the inadequacy of this reservation. He believed that under the Fourteen Points 'it would be impossible for Belgium and France and the British Empire to get the reparations to which they were entitled.'[43]

In his subsequent denunciations of the armistice pact Hughes developed this theme. At the Australasian Club on 7 November and then at the lunch with the State Agents-General a week later he said that, among other reasons, he opposed the terms of peace 'because they do not provide for indemnities'. And here he distinguished between reparations and indemnities. While he admitted that some provision had been made for restoration and reparation none was made for indemnity. That is, while France and Belgium and other countries which had been physically invaded would be able to claim for damage to civilians and property, the Empire and Australia, 'staggering under a load of debt', would not be entitled to any compensation for the cost of the war. Australia had a war debt of £300 million, and Hughes, refusing to accept the exclusion of indemnity from the peace negotiations, asserted that 'We must see that the aggressor pays.'[44]

At the Imperial War Cabinet meeting on 26 November the issue of indemnity came to a head. Hughes made much of the reparation question. If, as it seemed, President Wilson's principles, which were built into the armistice agreement, precluded an indemnity then it would create an

---

[42] Speech on 16 October to Tariff Reform League in Central Hall, Westminster, *Times* (London), 17 October 1918.
[43] Draft Minutes of Imperial War Cabinet Meeting (36A), 6 November 1918, TNA: PRO CAB 23/44A.
[44] *Times* (London), 8 and 15 November 1918.

'invidious distinction between a country like Belgium and, say, a country like Australia or even England.' Belgium would recover a lot of its losses while 'We shall get nothing.' To meet this Hughes contended that every effort should be made 'to stretch the interpretation of the clause, as far as it will go, and show that there is no distinction of kind between indemnities and payment for damages done.'

Lloyd George was in a quandary. He had read a Board of Trade Memorandum on 'Economic considerations Affecting the Terms of Peace' which included a report on indemnities written by Professor William Ashley and John Maynard Keynes of the Treasury, and this had brought home to him the great difficulties in requiring Germany to pay the full cost of the Allies' war effort, estimated at more than £20,000 million. Britain's own share of this was £8000 million, £1000 million of which was owed to the United States. Thus he challenged Hughes to show how Germany could pay this sum. Over and above seizing movable property such as shipping and rolling stock and assets held in foreign countries, this could only be done by handing over gold – and the best estimate of German holdings amounted in value to no more than £200 million – or by exporting goods to the world and so earning foreign credit. But this latter method would mean Germans dumping their cheap products in overseas markets, and no nations were likely to permit this since it would destroy their industries and cause their workers to lose their jobs. Moreover Lloyd George pointed out that Hughes wanted to raise tariffs against German goods in the post-war era and to deny the Germans access to the raw materials necessary for manufacturing their products. Yet, as the British general election campaign gained momentum, the British politician recognised the increasing public clamour for a harsh peace and so he did not want to be seen to be unsympathetic to Hughes's argument.

The British Prime Minister's answer was to establish an inquiry into the matter, and he cleverly manoeuvred Hughes into accepting the chairmanship of the committee. Hughes had for a long time been a thorn in Lloyd George's side. Indeed Hughes's first response to the invitation to join the committee was that, 'I much prefer to remain free so that I can criticise.' To this cantankerous answer Lloyd George retorted that it was 'not quite playing the game'. He then pressed the Australian to take the chair. No doubt the wily Welshman hoped through this means to prevent Hughes from speaking out on reparations and indemnities during the rest of the election campaign. The British Prime Minister might also have thought that the experience would be educational and that Hughes might emerge from it with a more sophisticated understanding of the problem.

But Hughes was not interested in understanding the problem and he used his position as chairman to ensure that the report reflected his preconceived ideas. As the first step in that direction, he influenced the choice of the other members. With the exception of Sir George Foster, the Canadian Minister for Trade and Commerce, all the members of the committee – Sir Walter Long, the Colonial Secretary and stalwart of the Conservative Party; W. A. S. Hewins, a leading figure in the Tariff Reform movement; Lord Cunliffe, a former Governor of the Bank of England; and the Hon. Herbert Gibbs, a City of London banker – shared to one degree or another Hughes's determination that Germany should pay the full cost of the war.

Assuming 'that the enemy ought to pay an Indemnity', as their instructions put it, the committee was charged with the task of investigating 'the amount of Indemnity to be paid; the amount of Indemnity which it would be possible to exact; and the subsequent effects on the Allied countries of Germany having to pay such an Indemnity.'[45] The last two questions followed from Lloyd George's doubts about an indemnity and were meant to test its practicality. The committee was required to report its findings speedily. They were needed for an Inter-Allied Conference to be held in London from 1 to 3 December and also for the Imperial Cabinet as it prepared for President Wilson's arrival in Europe. During all the meetings, the first four from 27 November to 1 December which led up to the preliminary report and then the following seven from 3 to 11 December which produced the final report, Hughes never allowed the questions of Germany's capacity to pay or the possible effects on the economies of the Allied countries to stand in the way of achieving his objective. It was his committee and he was determined that it should express his view; 'Everything is practicable to the man who has strength enough to enforce his views, and we have that strength.' In response to suggestions from Foster, Keynes and Sir H. Llewellyn Smith of the Board of Trade that Germany's capacity to pay should be seriously considered, Hughes answered that the committee's task was to calculate what Germany ought to pay, and, after that it would be the Germans' responsibility to show that they were unable to meet the bill.

Both the preliminary and the final reports, which were essentially the same, contended that Germany was liable for the full cost of the war. It would appear that Hughes and Hewins drew up the reports – copies of the drafts with extensive amendments in Hughes's handwriting are in the Australian archives. The reports ignored the Board of Trade's judgment that reparations themselves would be so great that 'no useful purpose would be served by putting forward a claim for an indemnity proper unless it be thought to be expedient to do so for bargaining purposes.' While they argued, as Hughes had done in the Imperial War Cabinet and in the Indemnities committee, that 'in all essential respects Indemnity is identical with Reparation', they accepted the Board of Trade's distinction between reparation for damage done to persons and property caused by aggression and indemnity for the cost incurred in repelling aggression. They indicated that they used the word 'indemnity' not in the German 1871 sense as a punishment but in the narrower sense as the obligation to pay all expenses incurred as a result of the war, and in this latter sense they held that the enemy should 'indemnify the Allied Powers for the cost of the war'.

This distinction may have been adopted for the purpose of meeting Wilsonian objections but, even if this were the case, the substance of the report made little of it. The summary conclusions made this clear. The enemy was to pay the Allies the full cost of the war which it was thought might amount to £24,000 million. It was to be paid in 'cash, kind, securities and by means of a funding loan'. Since Germany's total wealth was only reckoned to be £15–20,000 million and the gold, securities and movable property would only amount to about £1000 million, a funding loan or bond issue was to be the major means of extracting the indemnity; it was to be for the maximum of ten years and to pay interest on the total sum at 5 percent per annum, that is £1200 million each year.

The reports denied that this indemnity would have adverse effects on the economies of the Allied countries. Rather 'with their manpower seriously reduced, their territory laid waste, their

---

[45] Shorthand Notes of the Imperial War Cabinet Meeting (38), 26 November 1918, TNA: PRO CAB 23/43; minutes of Imperial War Cabinet Meeting (38), 26 November 1918, TNA: PRO CAB 23/42.

industries paralysed and burdened with a huge load of debt …' they would, without the indemnity, 'be unable to compete successfully in the markets of the world'. They asserted that '*No army of occupation should be required*' [Report's italics] to make the Germans carry out such an agreement. The committee, in defending this comforting assurance, merely remarked that should the problem arise the Allies had 'sufficient resources at their command to compel them to fulfil their obligations.' Once again there was no thought given as to how in practice these resources could be marshalled so as to achieve the purpose. The reports did not consider whether the Allies would be likely, as time went on, to have a common interest in employing force or to have the political will to do so. Nor did they give any thought as to how, if the Allies did act, the German people could be coerced into paying these obligations and what would be the ensuing costs in every sense of an occupation.

Finally the reports posited that 'the enforcement of an Indemnity' would 'operate as a deterrent to future aggression and be a substantial guarantee of the world's peace'. In the text the meaning of this was made more explicit. In quintessential Hughes language it was maintained that, if an indemnity were not imposed, the Allies:

> would be left staggering under a load of debt that would retard their industrial and social development, and impair their powers to meet new aggression; whilst Germany, escaping the penalty of defeat, would be in a stronger position, not only to organise her industries, which have been unravaged by war, but also to re-equip her army and navy and try again.[46]

Unless the British Empire insisted on exacting the full cost of the war, it would emerge from the conflict gravely weakened.

In a covering letter to Lloyd George, Hughes explained that, in a world where nations struggled for survival and supremacy, an indemnity was necessary not only to meet the future competition of Germany but also that of the United States. Indeed he said it was the committee's view that 'the great menace to the trade of the British Empire comes from the USA.' He gave voice to all his accumulated resentments about the Americans and their behaviour in the war. America's war expenditure was less than half that of the British Empire 'which had been pouring out great streams of blood and treasure during the whole period of the War.' From being a great creditor nation, the Empire had become a debtor nation. America had become 'predominant both financially and industrially; and if there are to be no indemnities it is impossible to say that in the course of time British trade may not be completely ruined by American competition.' Thus he concluded that, 'An indemnity recovering the whole cost of the war … would go far to restore the

---

[46] Draft Minutes of Committee on Indemnity Meetings, 27 November to 11 December and Reports of the Committee on Indemnity, p.38, 3 and 11 December 1918, TNA: PRO CAB 27/43. See also for Hughes's drafts and amendments to Reports, NAA A981 IMP 104 and CP 351/1/1 Bun1/8.

Keynes in 'Notes on an Indemnity' which he sent to the Chancellor of the Exchequer on 2 November had calculated that the maximum that Germany could pay, without crushing Germany, would be £1000 million, made up of £500 million of movable property and £500 million of kind and cash paid over a period of years; and, with crushing Germany, £2500 million. See Elizabeth Johnson (ed.), *The Collected Writings of John Maynard Keynes* (London: Macmillan St Martin's Press, 1971), Vol.XVI, 'Activities 1914–1919; the Treasury and Versailles', p.342.

relative position of the two countries.'⁴⁷ The rightful position of the British race in the world was at stake. This Carthaginian-like economic peace would both prevent the resurgence of Germany and hold off the challenge of America.

Hughes was proud of his achievement. He believed, as was his wont, that he was fighting against a conspiracy. There were 'very strong influences working against Indemnity – pro-German International Finance Jew and Gentile men trading with Germany, and lastly extreme labour, who do not want Dear Brother German crushed.' But he boasted to Watt that 'Despite many efforts [to] sprag wheel [of the] committee we are presenting report today in favour Germany paying whole cost of war.'⁴⁸

The Inter-Allied Conference had found the reparations question too hard to deal with, and, following the British example, had decided to set up a Commission on Reparation to study how much the enemy countries should and could pay and what form such payments might take. When the Imperial War Cabinet was informed of this, Hughes, in line with his report, insisted that the Commission consider an indemnity as well as reparations, and he at first had his way. The French and Italian leaders accepted the amendment without demur and the Imperial War Cabinet agreed that Hughes and his Committee on Indemnity should nominate the British members of the Inter-Allied Commission.⁴⁹ The Americans once again frustrated him. Colonel House, who had been suffering from influenza and not attended the Inter-Allied Conference, when he learnt of what had been done demanded that the Commission should limit itself to investigating the issue of reparations.⁵⁰

---

⁴⁷ Letter, Hughes to Lloyd George, 10 December 1918, Lloyd George Papers, House of Lords Record Office F28//2/16.

Herbert Gibbs had provided an initial 'Note' on this topic which, for obvious reasons, could not be included in the report and so Hughes rewrote the note substantially, giving it its more cosmic dimension and vivid language, before sending it separately to Lloyd George. Hughes had for a long time sympathised with these views and even expressed something of the kind in his protest to the American Government when it was threatening to seize merchants ships being built in the United States for Australia. Compare draft of the note and Hughes scribbled amendments with the letter sent to Lloyd George, NAA A981 IMP104.

Hughes undoubtedly had also read and noted the Admiralty's warnings about the American challenge to Britain's mercantile supremacy. In August the Admiralty had informed the War Cabinet that the Director of the United States Shipping Board, which was responsible for building an American merchant fleet, had said that 'the new American mercantile marine is to be the largest in the world ... The more vigorously we fight the war, the more tonnage we shall have at our disposal when peace is declared. I believe that wise foresight now, in utilising this tonnage after the war, to develop our own world trade, and develop trade and industry in other countries ... will be a direct help to winning the war', and it angrily asked whether the Britain was 'to go on losing ships in our Allies' immediate interests, and repairing ships for them while they overtake us in their Mercantile Marine.' See Memoranda, Sir Eric Geddes, First Lord of the Admiralty for War Cabinet, 2 and 24 August 1918, Geddes Papers, TNA: PRO ADM 116/1809.

⁴⁸ Cable, Hughes to Watt, 9 December 1918, NAA CP360/8 Bl/2.

⁴⁹ Minutes of Imperial War Cabinet Meeting (40), 3 December 1918, TNA: PRO CAB 23/42.

⁵⁰ Cable, House to Wilson, 6 December 1918, Link, *Papers of Woodrow Wilson*, Vol.53, p.325.

Lloyd George, however, saw that Hughes's views on reparations, while they could cause trouble with the Americans, also could be used to his advantage in the British election. As polling day drew near the press and the populace were calling for a vengeful peace. Sir Eric Geddes, the First Lord of the Admiralty, who was at heart a sceptic about the desirability of harsh reparations, had learnt of this mood in the electorate the hard way when he had aired these views in his Cambridge constituency. Confronted by shrill criticism he had quickly adapted his words to the prevailing wind so that by 10 December he was calling for Germany to pay the full cost of the war. And he came around to promising that, if the government were returned to office, the Germans would 'be squeezed as a lemon is squeezed – until the pips squeak.'[51] Lloyd George had also felt the same public pulse and he appealed to Hughes to hasten on the final report so that he could demonstrate how draconian the government's attitude towards Germany would be.

Hughes was only too willing to oblige and on 10 December gave Lloyd George a copy of the report and a draft for the speech which the latter was to deliver at Bristol the following night, just three day before the people went to the polls. The draft speech was a classic Hughes exercise. He had turned the dry report into a hard-hitting and unequivocal defence of an indemnity. He apologised to Lloyd George that, while he had not been given any other 'raw material for your Bristol Speech', he had 'hacked out something' but had 'not had much opportunity to polish it'. Yet though Lloyd George was grateful for the assistance and on the night took over some of the phrases and used much of the material he nevertheless gave the argument a more subtle rendering. That is, even as he assured his audience that the government proposed 'to demand the whole cost of the war', he also laid it down that the indemnity must neither be accompanied by the dumping of German goods on the British market nor require the stationing of an army in Germany to enforce its collection.[52] This 'get tough' oratory caught the mood of the moment, and on 14 December when the results were announced, Lloyd George's Coalition was returned with an overwhelming majority. No doubt Hughes saw this great electoral victory as proof that the people were with him and shared his vision of the peace.

On Christmas Eve, a few days before Wilson's arrival, the Imperial War Cabinet dealt with the Indemnity Committee's report. At the meeting on the previous day Bonar Law had distributed a Treasury Memorandum on 'The Indemnity Payable by the enemy powers for Reparation and Other Claims', which was substantially the work of Keynes. Its conclusions were completely at

---

[51] Robert E. Bunselmeyer, *The Cost of the War: British Economic War Aims and the Origins of Reparations* (Hamden, Connecticut: Archon Books, 1975), pp.154–56.

[52] Letter with draft speech, Hughes to Lloyd George, 10 December 1918, Lloyd George Papers, House of Lords Record Office F/28/2/13; *Times* (London), 12 December 1918.

Hughes presented the Report to Lloyd George as the unanimous views of the committee. This was not the case. When the Indemnity committee met on the 11 December Foster, who on the previous day had signed the report – no doubt under strong pressure from Hughes – in order to help Lloyd George, wished to place it on record that he did not believe the evidence placed before the committee had been 'sufficient to enable any definite sum to be fixed that could be exacted from the enemy Powers.' But Hughes backed up by Long ruled that since such a codicil would contradict the report, (it would not as it happened), it would place both Lloyd George and Hughes in a 'false position'. The committee agreed and Foster was forced to acquiesce. See Minutes of the Committee on Indemnity, 11 December 1918, NAA CP351/1/1 BUN1/18.

odds with those of Hughes's document. While it agreed that the total cost for the Allies of the war, excluding the cost of inter-allied loans, was approximately £25,000 million, it calculated that Germany's capacity to pay would fall short of the probable reparations claim, and therefore 'a claim for the general costs of the war, in addition to reparations, could not be met, even in part.' When at the meeting the discrepancy between the two reports was pointed out, Bonar Law merely commented that he thought it 'proper to give the Imperial Cabinet the opportunity to read it.'[53] More probably he was alarmed by the extraordinary sums which Hughes's report was demanding as an indemnity.

Whatever the reason, Hughes was unmoved and reaffirmed his committee's arguments. There was 'no just distinction' between indemnity payments for the cost of the war and reparation payments for damage to property. Drawing selectively and misleadingly on the Ashley-Keynes paper, which had been before his committee, he maintained that the experience of the Franco-Prussian War showed indemnities were not harmful to the countries receiving them. He cited Lord Cunliffe's authority for their finding that Germany could pay at least £1200 million a year towards an indemnity. But whatever the actual amount he repeated his oft-stated maxim that Germany should be required to prove that it could not pay such a figure. When Milner interposed that the most certain way of 'Bolshevising' Germany would be to place an excessive burden upon it, Hughes retorted that, 'A salutary course of industry was the best cure for Bolshevism.'

Hughes asked the cabinet to instruct the British delegates on the Inter-Allied Reparation Commission 'to secure the greatest possible indemnity which Germany could pay without danger to our own finance and industry and without danger to the peace of the world.' It was obvious that he had sounded out other members of the cabinet before the meeting and realised that he could not obtain a blanket endorsement of the committee's conclusions. Even so, Lloyd George insisted on a further qualification, namely that whatever was asked for must be achievable without the need for an army of occupation. Thus the final wording directed that the delegates should endeavour to secure 'the greatest possible indemnity ... consistent with the economic well-being of the British Empire and the peace of the world and without involving an army of occupation in Germany for its collection.'[54]

In this period of preparation when the Empire's leaders were gathered together to establish their collective position, Hughes, more than any other Dominion leader, had urged the Imperial War Cabinet to reach agreement on all the issues which affected the future security and prosperity of the Empire and Australia. Yet he had had little success in winning over his colleagues. Despite his opposition, the British Government had made it clear that they were committed, at least in principle, to the setting up of a League of Nations. Likewise, while the Imperial War Cabinet accepted that the German colonies were not to be returned, it would not give cast iron support for their annexation. On the matter of an indemnity Hughes might appear to have achieved more – the cabinet had approved his committee's central principle – but its decision was still hedged around with conditional clauses. Lloyd George who had managed the diplomacy producing this

---

[53] Johnson, *Collected Writings of Keynes*, Vol.VI, pp.358 and 382; Minutes of Imperial War Cabinet Meeting (45), 23 December 1918, TNA: PRO CAB 23/42.
[54] Minutes of Imperial War Cabinet Meeting (46), 24 December 1918, TNA: PRO CAB 23/42.

overall result had acted in anticipation of the difficult negotiations which lay ahead, first when he met President Wilson and then when he took part in the diplomacy at the Peace Conference itself.

The visit of President Wilson

The American President's visit to Britain made Hughes realise even more sharply the great gap that existed between the peace terms which he advocated and those that Wilson seemed determined to impose on the Allies. In coming to Europe Wilson remained profoundly suspicious about the Allied leaders' intentions. Like Hughes, he smelt a conspiracy. As he sailed on the *George Washington* towards the war-torn Old World, he called together the senior members of his Inquiry team, and in an emotional chat told them that the Americans 'would be the only disinterested people at the Peace Conference' and that the statesmen with whom they had to deal 'did not represent their own people.' It was a recapitulation of earlier speeches, put in starker language, which justified the American delegation's right to lay down the terms of the peace settlement. Placing a League of Nations at the centre of his peace plans he indicated that on major issues the Americans were going to encounter opposition. Referring to the Inter-Allied Conference's commission on reparations, he declared that 'under no conditions would he assent to the imposition of indemnities beyond the damage actually suffered.' He was equally adamant that, despite European desires to share out the spoils, the German colonies should become the responsibility of the League and be given to smaller states to be administered as mandates of the League.[55]

Wilson envisaged having the greatest difficulty with the British Empire. During the British elections a number of ministers had publicly taken positions which were at odds with his peace principles. Churchill, the former First Lord of the Admiralty, had stated that while he was not opposed to a League of Nations it could not be a substitute for the British fleet. Wilson in informal talks on the *George Washington* said that if England held 'to this course' America would make a separate peace and build 'the greatest navy in the world'. Showing how deeply he had felt the humiliation of the Royal Navy's blockade practices when the United States had been a neutral country, he recalled how near he had come to having a showdown with the British. As he put it, 'if it had not been for his realisation that Germany was the scourge of the world, he would have been ready to have it out with England.'[56]

---

[55] Diary of William Christian Bullitt, 9[10] December 1918 and Memorandum on the Remarks by the President to Members of the Inquiry on December 10, 1918 by Isaiah Bowman, Link, *Papers of Woodrow Wilson*, Vol.53, pp.350–56; Diary of George Louis Beer, 10 December 1918, Beer Papers, LC mm 79004954.

See also cable, Wilson to House, 28 November 1918, Link, *Papers of Woodrow Wilson*, Vol.53, p.249. 'Papers indicate that Lloyd George is about to consult Clemenceau about peace proposals … Do you think there is any danger of their anticipating me? I should be afraid of their formulations.'

[56] Diaries of Dr Cary Travers Grayson and of Edith Benham, 8 December 1918, *ibid.*, Vol.53, pp.336–38 and 341.

Indeed Wilson when he first met Clemenceau in Paris told the French Premier that 'the American people were anti-British and that the easiest thing in the world would be to get them to build a navy larger than the British Navy.' See *ibid.*, p.446.

Two days after the birthday of the Prince of Peace and a day before the birthday of the President, Lloyd George and Balfour met with Wilson for an exchange of views, and on the following day they summarised the discussions for the benefit of the Imperial War Cabinet. Lloyd George reported that the President had given the impression that the League of Nations was his foremost concern and that he was anxious that it should be the first issue settled at the Peace Conference. The two British leaders saw nothing dangerous in the plan and suggested that by placating Wilson with the League he might be made more malleable on other matters.

On the questions which Hughes had made his own, German colonies and reparations, Wilson had stood firm. He had been insistent that the German colonies should be placed under League of Nations mandates. When Lloyd George had suggested that an exception should be made for the contiguous territories which the Dominions had conquered, naming as an example South Africa's claim to South-West Africa, Wilson, while he did 'not seem prepared to contest that contention', had 'of his own accord retorted that the position of Australia with regard to the Pacific colonies was not quite the same.'

When Lloyd George and Balfour had pressed the security grounds for annexation, Wilson had responded that similar cases could be made for all the colonies. Again, when they pointed out that Japan had been promised the North Pacific islands and that if Japan was to be allowed to keep those islands it would be impossible to deny the South Pacific islands to Australia and New Zealand, Wilson had made it clear that he was not bound by the treaty and intimated that he was not even sure that Japan should be allowed to hold the mandate for those territories. Wilson, as he had done earlier in discussing Siberia, appeared to be 'strongly anti-Japanese' and he remarked that he regarded it as one of his functions 'to act as a buffer to prevent disagreeable things, such as the Japanese retention of the Islands, being carried out.' There can be no doubt that the British ministers, knowing the depth of antipodean feeling, had done their best to move the President from this position, but to no avail.[57]

On the surface it seems curious that Wilson was willing to waive his rule for a remote territory in Africa while at the same time remaining a stickler for principle in dealing with these small far-off Pacific archipelagos. It might be suggested that the explanation is personal; that is, his admiration for General Smuts and his loathing of Hughes. But there is more to it than that. The American President had long perceived Japan as a strategic threat. As we have seen, it was perhaps the most important reason why in early 1917 he had delayed calling for a declaration of war against Germany. The experience with the Japanese in Siberia had strengthened his conviction that the Japanese were bent on imperial expansion.

What seemed to have weighed most with Wilson, was his naval advisers' warning that if Japan annexed the North Pacific islands it would endanger America's security. Just before Wilson had left for Europe the Secretary of the Navy, Josephus Daniels, had given him a Memorandum, prepared under the direction of the Chief of Naval Operations for the General Board, which posited that Japan was the only power which posed a serious threat to America. In reviewing the future of the German islands it urged that the United States should seize the opportunity 'to better secure our strategic position in the Pacific'. Japan's annexation of the Marshalls, Marianas and

---

[57] Minutes of Imperial War Cabinet Meeting (47), 30 December 1918, TNA: PRO CAB 23/42.

Carolines was 'opposed to the interest of the United States'. Therefore since Japan could not be forcibly ejected from these territories it recommended that all the German colonies in both the north and south of the Pacific should be internationalised. This would prevent Japan from fortifying the Northern islands or using them as naval bases. The report recognised that Japan would not accept mandates for the islands it occupied unless the same principle was applied to the South Pacific islands. Admiral W. S. Benson, Head of the United States Advisory Naval Staff at Paris, reaffirmed these findings. In a note to the President on the 17 December, Benson stated that the United States should seek to ensure that all the Pacific islands were held under international conditions by which the power in possession would have to agree, among other things, not to fortify the territory. As he explained:

> The value of these islands lies principally in their situation, and in the possibility of their military and naval use for the control of the Western Pacific. They would be particularly valuable to Japan should she be engaged in war with the United States.
>
> The solutions we have offered are intended to strip the islands of their principal strategic importance while still assuring to Japan possession of these islands.[58]

It followed from this that, since the circumstances were analogous, Australia and New Zealand should not be allowed to annex the South Pacific islands.

On indemnity the President had been 'stiffer than on any other question'. The most that he seemed willing to consider, as Lloyd George reported it – and he certainly wished to put the best gloss upon the subject – was that after reparations had been tabled other claims might subsequently be looked at. Lloyd George had pointed out that under this proposal France and Belgium would 'practically get everything and the British Empire hardly anything.' It was unfair that the British people who had accumulated a war debt of £6000 million, which was much greater per capita than that of Germany should receive practically no recompense. Lloyd George had told Wilson that Australia owed £75 for every man, woman and child and that that war expenditure was as much a loss due to the war as houses destroyed by the enemy in France or Belgium. But nothing would shake the President's determination to apply strictly the wording of the Fourteen Points as embodied in the armistice agreement.

Even though the Australian Prime Minister should have expected nothing less from Wilson, the news infuriated him. All his preparations for the Peace Conference had become exercises in futility. Hughes had never been able to understand why the Allies agreed to base the armistice on the Fourteen Points, but as a result they had become, as he wrote the Governor-General, the 'Law

---

[58] Letter, Josephus Daniels, Secretary for the United States Navy, to Wilson, 2 December 1918, enclosing Memorandum for Admiral C.J. Badger, Chief of Naval Operations and Chairman of the Executive Committee of the General Board, Wilson Papers, LC mm 73046029 VIIIA. While Link includes Daniels' letter in the *Papers of Woodrow Wilson*, Vol.53, p.312, he only provides a brief summary of the Memorandum and the summary omits that part which treats the problem of Japan and the North Pacific islands.

'Recommendations of the United States Navy advisory Staff on the Disposition of German Islands in the Pacific', signed by Admiral Benson, 17 December 1918, Wilson Papers, LC mm 73046029 VIII. This document is not included in Link's *Papers of Woodrow Wilson*.

of the Medes and the Persians'.[59] Having invested so much of himself in seeking a very different peace, especially on the Pacific islands and reparation questions, he could not but protest in the most forthright manner. Replying to Lloyd George he launched into an extensive and bitter critique reminiscent of his 6 November attack on the armistice itself. On this occasion, however, the verbal shafts were aimed not at Lloyd George's perfidy but at Wilson's pretensions.

If the British leaders 'were not very careful they would find themselves dragged quite unnecessarily behind the wheels of President Wilson's chariot.' The Americans had not earned the right to dictate the peace. They had come late into the war. They had profited greatly from the years of neutrality. Their losses of men did not even equal those of Australia. America's contribution did not entitle Wilson to be 'the god in the machine at the Peace Settlement'. If 'the saving of civilisation had depended on the United States, it would be in tears and chains today.' It was 'intolerable' that Wilson should demand that the peace should be made on his terms. Hughes hoped that the British and French Prime Ministers, who represented the two great powers which had borne the heat and burden of the war, would stand firm and ensure that 'their sacrifices had not been in vain'. They should not let their future be decided by someone who did 'not even speak for his own country', and here he was alluding to the American electorate's rejection of Wilson's appeal for a vote for the Democrat Party in the November mid-term Congressional elections. Lloyd George, having won a landslide victory on this issue, would have not only the whole country behind him but also half of the American people. By implication Hughes was insisting – as he had from the beginning – that it was he and not Wilson who spoke for the people of the world. If Britain and France acted together, they could defy Wilson and 'settle the peace of the world as they liked.'

Turning to the particular issues which had been discussed with Wilson, Hughes repeated that it would be a mistake to give primacy at the Peace Conference to the League of Nations. As he had stated earlier, the only international organisation which would work would be one, like the British Empire, which was based on 'historical associations and practical needs'. Wilson's proposal based on abstract principles was neither feasible nor efficacious. He had offered no detailed scheme to show how it would operate. The League was to him 'no more than a toy was to a child'. It had become an expression of the President's own vanity. He wanted to return to America waving a piece of paper, so to speak. Hughes did not believe that, if a league were established, all other problems would fall neatly into place. To rely on such an international body 'would mean giving up the substance for the shadow.' What he wanted was that first of all the Empire should obtain the 'necessary guarantees' for its own security and development. These guarantees should include the unrestricted power of the Royal Navy – an interpretation of Freedom of the Seas 'as we mean to have it' – and reparations and indemnities. After that he was willing that 'a properly constituted' League of Nations, might be left 'to handle other matters'. As for Australia, Hughes repeated that the people of the Commonwealth were agreed on two interconnected topics which affected their very survival, namely Japan and the White Australia policy and the retention of the German islands in the Pacific. Since New Guinea was only 130 kilometres from Australia's northern coasts, it was clear that Wilson 'was talking of a problem which he did not really understand'.

---

[59] Letter, Hughes to Munro Ferguson, 14 December 1918, Novar Papers, NLA MS 696/2752.

This sweeping condemnation of Wilson followed from the view of international relations which Hughes had embraced in the early years of Federation and which he had drawn upon to make sense of every foreign crisis that had subsequently threatened Australia or the Empire. The war itself had been a culminating point in the struggle of the nations. Each country could only look to itself for its salvation. Only the restoration of the Empire's economic and military power could ensure the safety of the British peoples and their role as the guardians of order and liberty. It was these material factors not vague principles which would determine their future. If the British leaders surrendered to the self-indulgent and woolly-minded preaching of Wilson they would be inviting the destruction of their Empire. Hughes's understanding of the world and history, even as it was, like Wilson's, coherent and in its own terms persuasive, was also ironically, like Wilson's, one dimensional, absolute and in the end self-defeating.

Though, as Lloyd George's memoirs would have it, 'the Cabinet were impressed with the critical powers of the Hughes speech', nevertheless the latter's lambasting of Wilson and his peace principles caused division in its ranks. While Curzon, Long and Churchill from one aspect or another expressed sympathy for Hughes's position, Borden, Reading and George Barnes, a Labour member of the British War Cabinet, disassociated themselves from his attack on Wilson and the concomitant suggestion that Britain should stand with France against America. Borden was willing to support the British Empire's claims to the Pacific islands and indemnities, but regretted the animosity shown towards Wilson. He made it clear that Canada would not approve collaborating with a European power against the United States.

Lloyd George with his acute sense of the possible saw a way through the impasse which would keep his government together, unite the Empire and achieve a peace in cooperation with the United States. There were practical limits to what Britain could reasonably expect to obtain. Certainly he was not willing so early in the negotiations to adopt Hughes's confrontationist diplomacy. He recognised that this would cause unnecessary friction. He was not pessimistic about reconciling Wilson's principles with the British Empire's desiderata. Answering Hughes he repeated that it was only on indemnities that Wilson had manifested 'a really hard resistance' to British wishes. On the League of Nations he was 'by no means extreme' and on the Pacific islands the difference between annexation and mandatory control might not prove to be significant. If he were given his League of Nations he might well be reasonable on the other questions. Lloyd George assured the Imperial War Cabinet that the British Empire's representatives at the Peace Conference would not leave 'without securing the things that mattered most to them'.[60] Unlike

---

[60] Minutes of Imperial War Cabinet Meetings (30 and 31), December 1918, TNA: PRO CAB 23/42; David Lloyd George, *The Truth about the Peace Treaties* (London: Gollancz, 1938), 2 vols, Vol.I, pp.201–02. Lloyd George wrote about Hughes's speech at the Imperial War Cabinet meeting on 30 December, 'It was fine specimen of ruthless and pungent analysis of President Wilson's claims to dictate to the countries that had borne the brunt of the fighting. I wish there had been a verbatim report which would reproduce the stabbing sentences in the form in which they were delivered.'

Hughes's own attitude towards Japan was no doubt strengthened further by a cable from Watt in which the latter summarised an article on Japan's ambitions in China, probably written by Morrison, in which it was asserted that if Japan's demands were conceded it would 'become immediately one of the most powerful and menacing of the world's powers.' Watt had commented that 'Japan's aid has been well paid by

Hughes and Wilson, Lloyd George was not an ideologue. Lloyd George signalled to Hughes that he should accept inevitable compromises over both the language and terms of the peace. But Hughes, being who he was, was unmoved by this appeal to reason and good sense.

In taking the position he did on the peace Hughes was expressing, even if in an hyperbolic manner, an Australian view of the war and the world. Australians, as democratic colonists making a new life for themselves in an Asian world, felt the insecurities which bred nationalism far more intensely than their kinsfolk in the British Isles. During the Commonwealth Parliament's debate over a resolution affirming Australia's right to keep the South Pacific islands, speakers representing both parties, used the same language to define Australia and the Asian threat to its survival. One Liberal Nationalist was at a loss to know how 'The Greater Britain of the southern Seas' could be 'retained as part of the British Empire to be peopled by the British' unless Britain and America controlled the islands. A Labor member had declared that if the war had 'brought the British peoples together … it may prove a very useful and satisfactory event.' Another maintained that Australia was 'one of the great homes of the white race' but he was alarmed that 'all … the Anglo-Saxon-Celtic race had done so far' was 'to embroider its borders with splendid cities.' The vast emptiness of the interior invited invaders. Watt in introducing the resolution adjured the British to see that Australia, as 'a great country for the White people', had a chance to work out its destiny 'without fear and trembling'.[61] Hughes, because of his own emotional needs, embodied these anxieties more completely than any other Australian leader, and he had converted them into a monolithic theory of race and power. Thus throughout the Peace Conference he fought defiantly against all odds and held to his unilateral course.

---

enormous commercial gains and not comparable with Australia's loss of manhood and heavy debts.' See cable, Watt to Hughes, 16 December 1918, NAA CP360/8 B1/2.

[61] See Sydney Sampson, William Finlayson, Dr W.R.N. Maloney and Watt, *CPD*, 1917–18 second session, LXXXVI, Part 2, 7839, 7863, 7875 and 7936, 14–15 November 1918.

14
'Absolutely Unbearable': The Defeat of Hughes's Vision for the Post-War World

On 18 January 1919 the first plenary session of the Paris Peace Conference was held in the 'Peace Rooms' at the French Foreign Office in the Quai d'Orsay. Hughes and Cook, representing Australia – along with delegates from Great Britain, the other Dominions, India and twenty other countries, great and small – took their seats to begin the official process of settling terms with Germany and creating a new world order. Hughes, reflecting his personal and philosophical prejudices, reported that Wilson made 'a clever, concise, but cold speech' and Clemenceau, who presided, was 'full of fire and energy'. The conference was to become, as Hughes facetiously described it, 'the Greatest Show on Earth'. And it was true that the eyes of the whole world were focused on Paris and this grand global conclave. It was here that the world was to be remade, and Hughes believed that the Australians could 'hope for much' and expect to 'get – not all – but most of what we want.'[1]

Though for the first time Australia was present in its own right at a major international conference, this did little to enhance its role or give it more influence. While the plenary session was the formal body for approving the Peace Treaty it was the great powers that fashioned the terms of the treaty. Even before the first meeting of the whole body of delegates, the Supreme War Council, transforming itself into the Council of Ten, made up of two representatives each from the British Empire, France, Italy, the United States and, more peripherally, Japan, had taken charge. Through this body these powers selected the nations to be invited to the conference, set the number of their delegates and drew up the agenda for the plenary session. They renewed the armistice with Germany and took responsibility for enforcing its conditions. They took under their purview the whole range of world problems arising out of the war, including the Bolshevik Revolution and the future of Russia, the territorial settlements in Eastern Europe, the control of the Arab lands and their great reserves of oil, the nature and extent of reparations, the limitations to be imposed on Germany's frontiers and armaments and the disposition of the former German and Turkish colonies. They gave meaning to the Fourteen Points, the armistice principles governing the peace. When, as the conference progressed, some of these issues became ever more contentious and difficult of resolution, the Council of Ten, often became Four – Lloyd George, Clemenceau, Wilson and Vittorio Orlando of Italy; or just Three – Lloyd George, Clemenceau and Wilson. But whatever form the peacemaking process took it was the Big Three or Big Four who in nearly all cases made the running and ultimately determined the outcome.

---

[1] Letter, Deane to Ruth Deane, 18 January 1919, Dean Papers, University of Melbourne Archives; letter, Hughes to Munro Ferguson, 17 May 1919, Novar Papers, NLA MS 696/548.

On the eve of the first meeting of the plenary body Hughes set out, in a press interview, Australia's 'demands' for the peacemaking. Summing up the terms which he had been advocating since his arrival in Europe he was reported as saying that:

> Australia wants the German islands in the Pacific, and the exaction of indemnities from Germany.
>
> She favours the League of Nations, but does not want promiscuous immigration, and claims to make whatever economic arrangement she pleases.
>
> She opposes the 'freedom of the seas' and limiting of Great Britain's naval supremacy.
>
> She opposes intervention in Russia but is in favour of military support for Poland.[2]

This statement was made without consulting Melbourne and Watt, with the armistice crisis in mind, again complained to Hughes about taking stands on policy which resulted in the government learning about his views from the press. While endorsing in broad terms the other policies Watt dissociated the cabinet from the implied claim to the North Pacific islands. He seemed to be particularly worried by Hughes's provocative anti-Japanese outburst when he told a reporter that his compatriots 'would regard with suspicion any geographical advance by Japan toward Australia.'

Hughes's reply was a blustering defence. He noted that the cabinet agreed with him on all but one point. He denied he had said he 'would strenuously oppose' Japan's annexation of the North Pacific islands but nevertheless stated that if he could have stopped the Japanese getting them he would have certainly done so. On the broader question of how to deal with Japan he was even more assertive: 'I am not here to represent Japan, but Australia … I have said nothing but what is not only true but what position and interests of Australia demand.'[3] This did nothing to placate Watt. Having been Victorian Premier for three years he was, unlike most other ministers, unwilling to allow Hughes to treat the cabinet as a cipher. This exchange marked the beginning of a continuing effort by Watt to enable cabinet to have a say in the making of Australian policy at the Peace Conference, especially on Japan.

Since the great powers had taken effective control of the peacemaking process Hughes's ability to achieve Australia's aims was limited. Even on those topics which he had made his own, namely reparations and indemnities and Japan and the Pacific islands, he was often frustrated or bypassed. On most others he could only have an influence through the Imperial War Cabinet which for the purpose of the conference had been transmuted in Paris into the British Empire Delegation (BED). And here he was dependent on Lloyd George's willingness to bring the issues to their meetings.

The first substantive subject which came before the Council of Ten, was the attitude to be adopted towards the Bolsheviks and the Russian civil war. While it involved most directly the question of whether Russia should be represented at Paris, it also raised the more general issue of whether the Allies should intervene in the civil war. When Lloyd George consulted the BED about

---

[2] *Argus*, 20 January 1919.
[3] Cable, Watt to Hughes, 24 January 1919, NAA CP 360/8 B1/2; cable, Hughes to Watt, 10 February 1919, *ibid*.

the Russian question Hughes seized the occasion to air his hostility to its revolutionary doctrine. He had always believed that Bolshevism was one of the great enemies of the British race. Writing to the Governor-General about the difficulties of the post-war era, he had admitted that he 'always regarded Syndicalism as the greatest danger to civilisation.' Syndicalism did not differ from Bolshevism. Both preached anarchy. All other forms of government would keep a country together and give order to society. Even Socialism was acceptable since 'its ideal was the state.'[4] Thus at the BED meeting he described how he had a direct experience of a kindred movement, the IWW, during the battle over conscription and the ensuing political and industrial agitation. These movements rejected the state as the basis of political order and spurned nationalism as the core of social solidarity. And he translated his criticisms of the IWW to the world stage and the upheaval in Russia. Nevertheless Hughes, while opposing the recognition of Lenin's regime and its right to sit at the peace table, spoke out against intervening in the internal affairs of the nation. According to his idea of nationalism, each people was unique and sovereign and thus the Russians had to be left to work out their own destiny. But Bolshevism's expansion should be resisted. It knew no country. Hughes agreed with Lord Reading that it 'must inevitably die if confined within the borders of Russia.' This, he believed, was the way to handle the problem. He was an early advocate of the containment doctrine.

Hughes was also anxious that the British Empire should not be drawn into an unwinnable war in Eurasia where its already depleted resources would be drained further. Engaging in such an enterprise would divert Britain's attention from the defence of the overseas Dominions. When pressed by Lloyd George, who himself was opposed to military intervention, Hughes joined with Borden in declaring that the Dominions would not provide troops to put down the Bolshevik revolution. Lloyd George was under pressure from some senior members of the British Cabinet – especially Milner and Churchill – to assist the anti-Bolshevik forces in Russia, and no doubt the British leader found the Dominions' support for his position politically useful. With this backing he was able more confidently to join with President Wilson in the Council of Ten in rejecting appeals for more military aid to the anti-Bolshevik armies and in proposing that representatives of all the warring parties be brought together to see whether they would agree to halt hostilities and form a coalition government.[5]

The Australian delegation and the League of Nations

During the long five months of the conference, the Australian delegation had the unenviable task of helping the Prime Minister to accomplish his aims. The formal Australian contingent at the conference was very small. In addition to Hughes and Cook, it comprised Garran, Latham,

---

[4] Letter, Hughes to Munro Ferguson, 14 December 1918, Novar Papers, NLA MS 696/2749–50.
[5] Minutes of the Plenary Session of the Plenary Conference, 18 January 1919 and Notes of a meeting of the Supreme War Council, 12 January 1919 and Secretary's Notes on Conversations held in the Quai d'Orsay (hereafter Minutes of Council of Ten Meeting), 12–22 January 1919, *Foreign Relations of the United States*, 'Paris Peace Conference 1919'(hereafter *FRUS*, 'PPC', 1919'), Vol.III, pp.157–59, 472–73, 490–91, 496–97, 577, 589–93, 629–40, 655–68, 676–79; Minutes of British Empire Delegation Meetings (1 and 2) (hereafter BED), 13 and 20 January 1919, TNA: PRO CAB29/28.

Frederic Eggleston – a friend of Garran's and Latham's and a prominent member of the Australian Round Table – and Percy Deane.

For Garran, Latham and Eggleston, their time in Paris afforded an opportunity not only to participate in the most important international conference in history but also to enjoy the vibrant and venerable culture of the city and the country. Latham wrote to his wife about the Australians' life in Paris: 'there is more of interest here than I can tell you.' They resided with the other British Empire delegations in the Hotel Majestic, 'the home of most of the leaders of our race', which, as Latham commented, being 'justly named' allowed them to live 'in magnificence'. As the chief officials in the Australian delegation the three friends shared with the senior staff of the other British delegations the privileges of their status, including being able to take their meals in the 'restaurant' instead of the 'dining room'. Even Lloyd George, Balfour and Bonar Law who had their own flats would often eat in the 'restaurant'. Because of their position, the Australians were able to meet and mix with a wide range of eminent British and Imperial figures, such as Colonel T. E. Lawrence, Lord Robert Cecil, Lord Reading, Lord Hardinge, the head of the Foreign Office, the chiefs of the British navy, army and air force, E. S. Montague, the Secretary of State for India, and the Indian, South African, Canadian and New Zealand representatives. [6]

Garran, Latham and Eggleston, having musical, literary and historical interests, were much excited by the great riches of Paris as a centre of arts and entertainment. On the first night in the city Latham had accompanied Hughes and Deane to the Folies Bergère and a fortnight later had with Garran and Eggleston enjoyed Hector Berlioz's opera, 'La Damnation de Faust'. From that point the accounts of their cultural exploits multiply. Sometimes sitting in the President's Box, they either singly, together or in company with others went to the *Opéra Comique, Comédie-Française, Grand Guignol, Théâtre Française, Odéon, Vaudeville*, classical concerts, and, in the case of the more mystical Eggleston, to hear Gregorian chants and admire the ritual of a Russian Orthodox church. Again, either singly or together, they visited the Versailles Palace, the Louvre, the Pantheon, the Latin Quarter, Montmartre and other famous sites. Latham and Eggleston took a trip to Chartres to admire the cathedral and Eggleston visited Rouen, the ancient capital of Normandy from which, as he noted, William the Conqueror had set out to win the crown of England. They also occasionally dined at the *Ritz*, the premier hotel in the French capital.[7] It helped that they all had a smattering of French; however it would seem that Hughes, who had won a prize for French at school and had paid a brief visit to Paris before emigrating to Australia, was the most fluent member of the delegation.[8]

But all was not pleasure. The Australians had important work to do. The three officials took their responsibilities seriously and prepared extensive briefs for the Prime Minister on the Pacific islands, reparations, White Australia, the League of Nations and the future world order. Hughes,

---

[6] Letter, Latham to his wife, Ella Latham, 21 January 1919. Latham Papers, NLA MS 1009/21/1423.

[7] Garran diary, 12 and 18 January, 5, 7 and 21 February and 26 March 1919, Garran Papers, NLA MS 2001/3/22; letters, Latham to Ella Latham, 26 January, 24 February and 10 March 1919, Latham Papers, NLA MS 1009/21/1426, 1431 and 1433; Eggleston diary, 31 January, 2, 14 and 23 February and 3 and 9 March 1919, Eggleston Papers, NLA MS 423/6.

[8] L.F. Fitzhardinge, *William Morris Hughes: A Political Biography*, 2 vols (Sydney: Angus and Robertson, 1963), Vol.I, 'A Fiery Particle, 1862–1914', pp.5 and 11.

however, paid them little heed. As Eggleston rather caustically and not altogether unjustly remarked, Hughes 'has made his mind up about everything and does not want advice.'[9] This was Hughes's style of leadership. He continued to ignore Cook, the other Australian plenipotentiary. Cook was not consulted on any of the matters that Hughes fought for at the conference. Hughes neither invited Cook to accompany him when visiting the Australian troops who remained in France, nor to join the party which went to Lyons to celebrate a specially declared 'Australian Day'. While both Latham and Eggleston were highly critical of Hughes, they had little sympathy for Cook's indolence and lack of spirit which played into Hughes's hand. Latham and Eggleston were willing to concede that Hughes had some admirable qualities. Latham admitted that he was 'able ... and often a good companion', but at the same time found 'his methods, almost always and his objects, very frequently to be most objectionable'. Eggleston was impressed with his ability to tell a story graphically and 'his knowledge of literature and his taste for the best', even while regarding him as being 'quite unfitted for diplomacy'. Hughes lacked subtlety; 'His only idea was fight.' He was 'the leader of the most extreme chauvinists'.

Inside the Delegation there was a degree of friction between the official advisers and Hughes's intimate circle of Deane, Keith Murdoch[10] and Henry Gullett, a press liaison officer. These latter three flattered Hughes and danced to his tune, or at least Deane and Gullett did. By the middle of the conference Murdoch – taking his cue from Lord Northcliffe, his patron – had begun in his columns in the Melbourne *Herald* to denounce Hughes's ultramontane stands, especially on reparations. Latham and Eggleston suspected that Hughes's confidants asked 'sly questions' to try to test the their loyalty. Latham believed that they carried 'false stories of his views to Hughes'. Eggleston could not abide their crude cynicism. Garran who had been a public servant for twenty years and had for many years served Hughes as his Solicitor-General was more circumspect than his friends. Indeed he had a sophisticated view of Wilson which helped to keep him in Hughes's camp. Garran considered Wilson to be 'a dangerous man, an idealist who believes in himself and his mission, determined to the point of obtuseness'. Of course, in this respect he could equally be speaking about Hughes except that Hughes was a 'realist' and, unlike Wilson, represented a small power, and so the damage he could inflict was accordingly limited. Garran further repeated Hughes's reasonable point that Wilson 'had no scheme for the League of Nations' and was trying 'to make a patchwork out of other men's ideas'. Eggleston, as a British race patriot and a liberal internationalist, was troubled that Hughes's actions, though not intended to do so, might weaken the unity of the Empire and 'mar all the efforts of the Best [sic] English, American and European statesmen to create the beginnings of a better order'. He resented Garran's unwillingness to pass on to Hughes the elaborate papers he had written on these subjects.

In Hughes's entourage, opposition to Wilson and the League of Nations was the test of loyalty. Eggleston, though not an unbiased witness, recounts how, on the day there had been an attempt

---

[9] Eggleston diary, 15 February 1919, Eggleston Papers, NLA MS 423/6/12.

[10] Murdoch adapted his views to suit his different masters. When his newspaper proprietor mentor ceased to call for harsh peace terms and became critical of Hughes, Murdoch danced to the new tune and wrote Northcliffe that 'Hughes has disappointed Australia. He is pursuing an utterly reckless mischievous line of policy, and will not listen to his colleagues.' Letter, Murdoch to Northcliffe, 15 March 1919, Northcliffe Papers, BL Add 62179, Vol.XXVII.

to assassinate Clemenceau, Hughes, in his inimitable style, told an American journalist that he wished the assassin had 'got Wilson instead'. He had then expanded on this by saying that he did not know how Providence had allowed Wilson, on his passage across the Atlantic, to escape the numerous mines still floating about. Though this was Hughes's form of jocularity it nevertheless carried meaning. It expressed Hughes's personal antipathy to the man. Indeed, so that there could be no mistake, Hughes told the journalist, referring to the Australian delegation, that they were 'an anti-League of Nations table'.[11]

As it happened, it was the proposal for forming a League of Nations that was the first major topic to come before the Peace Conference, and as much as Hughes wished to postpone consideration of the matter or to block it altogether he found himself effectively sidelined.

At the first meetings of the Council of Ten the American President pressed the issue of the League of Nations and, at the bidding of the Big Four, the subsequent plenary conference appointed a commission under Wilson's chairmanship to draw up a draft covenant. Lord Robert Cecil and Smuts who were known supporters of the League were nominated as the British Empire's representatives. Hughes had no say in the matter. At the plenary session setting up the commission he had inquired whether members would be able to discuss the scheme when complete, and Clemenceau, who was in the chair, assured him that that was so.[12]

Wilson had identified Hughes as the chief enemy of his League of Nations and his crusade for a new diplomacy. He knew what Hughes's query portended. And Hughes made no secret of his views.[13] Thus when towards the end of the conference, the question of whether the final draft of the covenant should be submitted to a plenary session was mooted, the President came out against it. As he said 'emphatically' to one of his confidants:

---

[11] Eggleston diary, 24 and 29 January, 9,10,15 and 19 February and 9 March 1919, Eggleston Papers, NLA MS 423/6; letter, Latham to Ella Latham, 21 February 1919, Latham Papers, NLA MS 1009/21/1429; Garran diary, 6 February 1919, Garran Papers, NLA MS 2001/3/22. Hughes's statement to the press at the beginning of the conference that Australia 'favours' the League of Nations was probably intended by giving Wilson his 'toy' to make the American more malleable when it came to dealing with substantive issues of the German colonies and reparations. Even in making this concession, which went against the grain, Hughes surrounded it with conditions.

[12] Record of the Second Plenary Session, 25 January 1919, *FRUS*, 'PPC, 1919', Vol.III, p.186.

Apparently Hughes had been prepared to speak to the substance of the matter. Frederic Eggleston, who was not at all sympathetic towards Hughes, recorded that 'as usual ... Hughes got up his case at the last moment ... He is the great apostle of Reality today, the Big Stick man, and the League of Nations has his support as long as it is a League of nations with a big stick. He is most scornful [of Wilson's proposal].' But since the plenary session was restricted to formal speeches from the Big Four leaders and to setting up a commission to draft the League of Nations Covenant Hughes held his fire. Eggleston diary, 26 January 1919, Eggleston Papers, NLA MS 473/6/72.

[13] In an interview with the Reuters Paris correspondent Hughes deplored Wilson's demand that the League of Nations Covenant should be incorporated in the German Peace Treaty: 'Indeed to delay this preliminary peace agreement – sufficiently difficult in any case – by including any subject not vital to it is to invite disaster.' For him the league in some limited form might have to be accepted but it was not urgent or essential and therefore should not be allowed to hold up the peace settlement. *Evening Standard* (London), 18 March 1919.

No, we cannot have it. It would only give old Hughes of Australia an opportunity to talk and object. We must have it signed by everyone. If Hughes refuses to sign we shall simply have to let him go.[14]

Hughes, unlike Lloyd George and Clemenceau, did not wish to indulge Wilson and wait to see what the commission produced. He did not heed Amery's advice that it might 'be worthwhile conceding a good deal to the Professor in the way of "pet toys" if only we can get the essentials.'[15] The moralistic grandstanding and self-delusion of the American leader[16] challenged Hughes's own equally absolute certainties about how the world should be saved. Hughes's fundamentalist 'realism' which gained its moral authority from the civilising power of the British Empire stood in stark contrast to Wilson's fundamentalist abstract 'liberalism' and the redemptive crusade of America's missionary nationalism. Hughes was at one with Milner who, after being appointed Colonial Secretary in January, wrote that he was 'an out and out Imperialist of the modern school, who regards the British Empire as the only veritable "League of Nations".'[17]

Having failed to win the backing of the other members of the BED, Hughes had little opportunity to influence the debate over the League of Nations Covenant. After the commission, following quiet Anglo-American negotiations, had produced a draft covenant he put his criticism down on paper and circulated them to the BED. In this document he focused on what he had seen from the beginning to be the great danger in Wilson's scheme – namely that the League might aspire to be an international superstate. Hughes pointed out that in the covenant's provisions there was much confusion over whether the League was to be an executive or a consultative body, and he urged that all suggestions of the former kind be expunged and that each member's national sovereignty and freedom of decision in responding to acts of aggression be left unimpaired.[18]

---

[14] Diary of Ray Stannard Baker, 2 April 1919, Link, *Papers of Woodrow Wilson*, Vol.56, p.543.

Wilson, however, could not avoid having to place the revised Covenant before a full meeting of the conference, and after it was over and all went well, House noted in his diary that 'Hughes of Australia never got an opportunity to make the speech which he had been threatening to make all the winter against the Covenant.' See House diary, 28 April 1919, *ibid.*, Vol.58, p.186. The Americans were haunted by an image of Hughes as the great disturber of their peace.

After Wilson's presentation of the draft Covenant to the Plenary Conference on 14 February, he expressed his anxiety about Hughes, confiding to Dr Cary Grayson about the 'difficulties with Premier Hughes of Australia … indicating that he [Wilson] regarded Hughes as one of the troublesome obstacles at the conference – reactionary.' See diary of Dr Grayson, 14 February 1919, *ibid.*, Vol.55, p.160.

[15] Letter, Amery to Hughes, 11 January 1919, Hughes Papers, NLA MS 1538/24/9.

[16] Even Cecil, who of all the members of the British Empire delegation was the greatest enthusiast for the league, found Wilson personally unpleasant. See Cecil Diary, 6 February 1919, Link, *Papers of Woodrow Wilson*, Vol.54, p.514: 'Now that I have sat for two or three days with the President I am coming to the conclusion that I do not personally like him. I do not know what it is that repels me: a certain harshness, coupled with vanity and an eye for effect. He supports idealistic causes without being in the least an idealist himself, at least so I guess, though perhaps I misjudge him.'

[17] Letter, Milner to Hughes, 18 January 1919, Hughes Papers, NLA MS 1538/24/16.

[18] 'Notes on the Draft Convention for the League of Nations, 1 February 1919, TNA: PRO FO 608/243 and 'League of Nations: Notes on the Draft Covenant by Rt Hon. W.M. Hughes', 21 March 1919, *ibid.*, CAB 29/9.

There was much to be said for this criticism. Wilson and the liberal internationalists glossed over this problem. Lloyd George shared Hughes's disquiet, but since the League Council could not make any decision without the unanimous consent of the great powers, the British leader, for the sake of maintaining Anglo-American cooperation, was willing to wear it. Hughes lacked such political discernment. Though he found it difficult to reconcile himself to the idea of a league he did not persist with his objections. Among the Dominions it was Borden who took up the cudgels to limit national responsibilities for collective action under the covenant. And it was Borden similarly who took the lead in fighting for the right of the Dominions to have representation equal to those of other small powers both in the Assembly and the Council of the League.[19]

Hughes could rail as much as he wished against the League and its apostle, but since the great powers were all agreed to allow Wilson his 'toy', there was little that the Australian could do to frustrate the American. He had to be content to restrict his fight against the Fourteen Points to those issues where he had some influence, such as the disposition of the German Pacific islands, the Japanese desire to include a 'racial equality' commitment in the League Covenant and reparation claims against Germany. His major objectives during the conference were thus to contain the territorial and racial expansion of Japan and prevent the economic and military resurgence of Germany.

Pacific Security and the containing of Japan

Shortly after arriving in Paris Hughes gave the *New York World* an interview in which he publicly declared Australia's attitude towards Japan:

> The Japanese are a highly intelligent people, but their ways are not our ways. We would regard with suspicion any geographical advance by Japan towards Australia.[20]

At the Peace Conference, with this as his theme, Hughes sought to keep the German islands in the South Pacific as a barrier against Japan and to block Japan from inserting any form of words in the League Covenant which might challenge, even faintly, the White Australia policy.

Very soon after the conference had assembled the question of the future of the German colonies came to the fore. The Council of Ten, having set up commissions to draft a League of Nations covenant and to look into the matter of reparations, turned its attention to the disposal of the colonial territories which had been captured from the enemy.

On 23 January, Lloyd George had proposed that while the commissions continued their work, the council might deal with 'the Oriental … and Colonial questions' which were 'less involved' than many others. Clemenceau and Sonnino agreed, and though Wilson suspected that the European Allies wanted to take up this issue in order to settle the matter before the League of Nations had come into being, he went along with the majority view.[21] In the following week the

---

[19] George W. Egerton, *Great Britain and the Creation of the League of Nations* (London: Solar Press, 1977), pp.121–24, 126, 143, 159–60, 165–67. See also Minutes of BED Meetings (26 and 27), 21 April 1919, TNA: PRO CAB 29/28.
[20] *Herald* (Melbourne), 23 January 1919.
[21] Minutes of the Council of Ten Meeting, 23 January 1919, *FRUS*, 'PPC, 1919', Vol.III, pp.699–700.

great power leaders and their advisers became engaged in a tense and sometimes acrimonious debate over the future of these territories – most especially over whether they should be handed over to the countries that had occupied them or whether they should become mandates under the League of Nations.

In this debate the Dominions played a central role. Lloyd George was acutely aware of the Australian, New Zealand and South African feelings on the matter. In introducing the topic at the beginning of the conference he no doubt hoped to clear this question out of the way. And so on 24 January he brought the Dominion prime ministers to the Council meeting so that they could plead their own cases. To ease the path and placate Wilson he announced that Britain was happy to accept the mandate principle for all the enemy territory that it had seized. At the same time, however, true to the commitments he had made to Australia, New Zealand and South Africa he argued that since the German colonies which the Dominions had captured adjoined their territory they should be allowed to annex them.

The Dominion prime ministers were then invited to put their own cases. Hughes led off. At the core of his claim for annexation was Australia's need for security in the Pacific. He had brought a large coloured map, approximately three metres by one and a half metres – probably supplied by Latham – to illustrate the geographical importance of New Guinea and its associated island groups to Australia's defence. He asserted that 'Strategically the Pacific islands encompassed Australia like a fortress.' In front of Baron Makino, who was representing Japan, he pointedly remarked that 'friends in one war were not always friends in the next.' Australia had 'a right to be free from the menace of any enemy such as had weighed upon her before this war.'

Hughes's argument against placing these islands under a League of Nations mandate was rather weak. Observing that the south-eastern portion of New Guinea was already an Australian territory he maintained that making the German section a mandate would lead to administrative confusion. He was also happy to assure the council that Australia would protect the rights of the native people. He did not explain why, if Australia held the mandate for New Guinea, its defence concerns would not be met. His only reference to a mandatory power seemed to assume that Australia would not be the trustee, for he declared that 'in the Mandatory Power established in New Guinea … Australia would see a potential enemy.'[22] It was a brief and not a very good speech. He was handicapped to some extent by the fact that Wilson had not yet made clear how he thought the mandate system would work and how the mandates would be distributed.

Three days later, at the next meeting of the Council of Ten, Wilson made reply. For him the desire to put the former German colonies under League of Nations' mandates arose out of 'a feeling which had sprung up all over the world against annexation'. Taking South-West Africa as an example, he said that if South Africa were to become the mandatory power under the League of Nations it would be able to 'administer it as an annex to the Union so far as consistent with the interest of the inhabitants.' As long as the mandatory power carried out its duties to the people in its care, the League would have no reason to interfere. If successful administration of the territory led the people to seek union with those to whom it had been entrusted he would be 'the last to object'. Wilson at the same time poured scorn on Hughes's security-based claim for annexation.

---

[22] Minutes of Council of Ten Meeting, 24 January 1919, *FRUS*, 'PPC, 1919', Vol.III, pp.718–22.

The argument reminded him of the story of the man who when asked why he kept buying up real estate said that 'he would never be satisfied so long as anyone owned land adjoining his own.' Australia's fears showed 'a fundamental lack of faith in the League of Nations'. Under the League they would 'rally the whole world against an outlaw'. Once the organisation had been established there would no longer be any need for states to seek protection by annexing territory.

Hughes, having mastered a paper drawn up at his request by Latham, had come better prepared for this meeting[23], and he tackled Wilson's views head on. For Hughes the most direct form of government was best, and therefore the mandatory principle had to justify itself in each case, and he went on to deny that it was appropriate for German New Guinea. Australia already had experience in governing New Guinea. Australia was a democracy which would not 'tolerate the ill-treatment of the people'. Setting aside other considerations the territory was 'essential to Australian security'. Hughes then demolished Wilson's final point, namely that 'the World dreaded annexations.' This did not apply to Australia since the world only dreaded annexation 'for imperialistic purposes'. He was certain that 'no one dreaded the annexation of New Guinea by Australia' on this account. Moreover his nationalist ideology rebelled against the amorphous notion of the 'World' which was at the heart of Wilson's liberal vision of a new order. It was not the 'World' which had won the war and would make the peace. This was the achievement of 'peoples in particular', most notably the British, French and Americans. They had not reached the commanding heights of international power and influence because the 'World' had put them there but 'because they had worked out their own salvation.' Here Wilson came face to face with the most intractable enemy of his peace, and he hardly bothered to hide his contempt for the man.

By 28 January the Dominions, the Japanese and the French had all appeared before the council and pressed their claims to the German colonies in their possession. Wilson took umbrage at this defiance. He complained that 'the discussion so far had been in essence, a negation in detail – one case at a time of the whole principle of mandatories.' It looked as though they were reaching 'a point where their roads diverged'. The world would not understand if they parcelled out the German colonies before the League of Nations was formed. Indeed the world would not accept such a decision. The very existence of the League of Nations was in the balance. If they failed here, then they would return to the old ways, and America would 'have to have a greatly increased navy and maintain a large standing army.' It was a scarcely veiled threat. Moreover, he continued, the people of the world would turn to more extreme solutions such as Bolshevism, and 'this great wave from the East … would gather fresh volume.' Wilson would make no concessions. He would not agree to make exceptions to the mandatory rule or to allot mandates before the League was constituted. He wished to leave the question of the disposal of the German colonies until after the League of Nations had been established.

---

[23] Sensing the inadequacy of his first address to the Council of Ten Hughes had asked Latham to give him a brief setting out the Australian case for annexing the German colonies. Adapting a long paper that he had written on the subject on 19 December, Latham handed Hughes a copy the following day. See letters, Latham to Ella Latham, 24 and 26 January 1918, and Paper on 'Australian Claims to the German Pacific islands', distributed to BED on 25 January, Latham Papers, NLA MS 1009/21/1424–26 and 1342.

Lloyd George tried to appease the annexationists by assuring them that the mandatory system was not too different from complete control; the League of Nations would interfere only when the rights of the native peoples were 'scandalously abused'. Likewise he pleaded with Wilson not to postpone the selection of mandatories until after the League was established. This was important not only for the Dominions but also for Britain. The world needed to be settled, and Britain at great expense was maintaining 170,000 troops from the Caucasus to East Africa, many in areas where Britain had no desire to become a permanent trustee power. But neither Hughes nor Wilson was won over by these arguments.[24] After the meeting Hughes informed Lloyd George 'quite plainly that [sic] mandatory principle would not be satisfactory to the people [sic] Australia; that it meant destruction [sic] White Australia and of our trade.'[25] What Lloyd George had hoped would be a simple matter to settle became the first great trial of strength between the world views and security strategies of the Australian Prime Minister and the American President.

The British Prime Minister realised that the talks were in danger of breaking down. In the following twelve hours, Smuts and Hankey – at the Prime Minister's behest and with the help of some officials from the Dominion delegations – sought to find a formula which would satisfy all parties. Smuts had found himself in a difficult position. On the one hand he shared Wilson's liberal vision of a better world and saw the League of Nations as the way forward; indeed Wilson's ideas about mandates derived from Smuts's booklet, *The League of Nations; A Practical Suggestion*. On the other, as Minister for Defence for South Africa, he agreed with Botha, Hughes and Massey that the Dominions should be exempted from this principle. Caught between these two opposing positions he was anxious to find a compromise.[26] Likewise, Hankey, as Lloyd George's trouble-shooter, wanted to find a way of healing the division between members of the BED and between the Empire and Wilson. Hankey had already addressed this problem in December when the Imperial War Cabinet had been preparing for Wilson's visit. In a paper, which all the Dominion leaders had approved, he had proposed that the British Empire should put all the captured German and Turkish territories, apart from South-West Africa and the South Pacific islands, under a League of Nations mandate; the latter were to be incorporated respectively into South Africa and Australia and New Zealand.[27] But this resolution of the problem would no longer serve, and Hankey and Smuts, after engaging in 'an infinity of delicate negotiations',[28] managed to put together a mandate policy which they hoped would meet the occasion.

Adapting a scheme which Smuts had put to the BED on 27 January, they devised a three tier mandate plan. Under the first, where peoples had reached a relatively advanced stage of develop-

---

[24] Minutes of the Council of Ten Meetings, 27 and 28 January 1919, *FRUS*, 'PPC, 1919', Vol.III, pp.735-71. Wilson adapted his anecdote about a man with real estate hunger from a story retailed to him by Senator Robert L. Owen. See letter, Owen to Wilson, 17 January 1919, Wilson Papers, LC mm 73046029 VIIIA. This letter is not included in Link's *Papers of Woodrow Wilson*.
[25] Cable, Hughes to Watt, 29 January 1919, NAA CP360/8 B1/3.
[26] W.K. Hancock, *Smuts: The Sanguine Years, 1870–1919* (Cambridge: Cambridge University Press, 1962), pp.496–504.
[27] Memorandum, Hankey to Lloyd George, 21 December 1918, Lloyd George Papers, House of Lords Record Office, F/23/3/31.
[28] Roskill, *Hankey*, Vol.2, p.53.

ment – as in the case of the peoples of the former Turkish Empire – the role of the mandatory would be to guide them to full independence. Under the second, where peoples had not reached that stage – such as those of Central Africa – the mandatory would have to assume complete responsibility for the administration of these territories, to protect them from abuses such as the slave trade and the arms and liquor traffic, to permit military training only for police purposes, to abstain from building military fortifications or naval bases, and to secure equal opportunity for trade to all other members of the League of Nations. The third class of mandates contained the essence of the compromise. Here it was provided, 'that there are territories, such as South-West Africa and the Pacific islands, which owing to the sparseness of their population, or their small size, or their remoteness from the centres of civilisation, or their geographical contiguity to the mandatory state, and other circumstances, can be best administered under the laws of the mandatory state as integral portions thereof, subject to the safeguards above mentioned', namely those applying to the second class mandates. Probably they were drawn to this solution as a result of Borden reminding them of Wilson's statement that under a mandate, as he envisaged it, 'South Africa would have practically the same control over South-West Africa as if the territory were annexed.'[29]

From Lloyd George's perspective this scheme had the best prospect of success. It accommodated Wilson by bringing all the conquered territories under a League mandate while at the same time defining the third class mandate in a way that enabled the Dominions, most particularly Australia, to extend their own laws in the most important respects to the territories. Hughes had made much of the fact that under a mandate Australia would not be able to exclude Japanese from the South Pacific islands and that, if this were so, 'the territory would become a Japanese or Japanese and German country within ten years.'[30] By treating these territories as 'integral portions' of Australia this objection would be overcome. And so early on the morning of 29 January, Lloyd George gave this clever compromise his blessing, and sent Smuts to ask House whether the President would be likely to approve it. After House intimated that he was in principle 'ready to accept it',[31] Lloyd George took it immediately to a BED meeting.

Hughes and Massey, however, had been kept in the dark. Lloyd George no doubt hoped to present them with a *fait accompli*. For Hughes this was a critical moment. He had been anxious for some time about the outcome of the Peace Conference negotiations. Wilson's wartime speeches opposing annexations, the incorporation of the Wilsonian principles into the armistice and Lloyd George's report to the Imperial War Cabinet of his discussions with Wilson had warned the Australian of what lay ahead. As Hughes saw it, President Wilson was 'the trouble'. Hughes had quite accurately discerned that Wilson's determination to secure international control over the German colonies was based as much on concerns for American national security as for a new liberal world order. That is, he recognised that it proceeded as much, if not more, from apprehensions about Japan as from a commitment to the League of Nations. Nevertheless he

---

[29] Minutes of BED Meeting (4), 27 January 1919, TNA: PRO CAB 29/28.
[30] *Ibid.*
[31] House diary, 29 January 1919, House Papers, Yale MS 466, Vol.15, p.26; Link, *Papers of Woodrow Wilson*, Vol.54, p.347.

thought that he could rely on the support of Britain and the other Dominions as well as France, Italy and Japan. Wilson alone was 'dangerous'. The American President had even cast doubt on whether Hughes, in seeking absolute control of the South Pacific islands, truly spoke for the Australian people.[32] When then Lloyd George put the plan hatched by Smuts and Hankey before the BED, Hughes was on his guard.

At the meeting Hughes wanted to know firstly, whether the third class mandate would cover all the islands that Australia had seized from the Germans and secondly, when the mandates would be formally allocated. Lloyd George indicated that he wished to keep the Japanese out of the arrangement. He thought it unwise to link the principle to allocation of mandates. From his first meeting with Wilson he had perceived that a major, even possibly the major, reason for Wilson's resistance to the Dominions' pleas for annexation was his fear that Japan would seek the same concession. And this impression had been confirmed by further discussions with Wilson in Paris.[33] The British Prime Minister was worried that if the third class mandate could be applied to the North Pacific islands Wilson would feel compelled to reject the compromise proposal. To this end, Lloyd George insisted that the mandate, designed for the Dominions, should be restricted to South-West Africa and the South Pacific, and in Australia's case to German New Guinea. If this were agreed to it would, since some islands would be left outside the third class mandate category, prevent the Japanese from drawing a direct analogy from the treatment of the South Pacific islands to the North Pacific islands. Lloyd George, realising how much this counted in Wilson's thinking, pressed the point very strongly.

Hughes, however, would have none of it. When Hughes protested that Australia would not be able to enforce its immigration policy unless it controlled all the islands, the British Prime Minister would go no further than to promise to consult with Wilson about the matter. This did not satisfy Hughes who said that he 'desired this policy to operate throughout the Bismarck Archipelago, and Australia wanted these islands, which were almost continuous, for purposes of defence.' On Lloyd George's initiative, the final paragraph in the mandate statement was amended to change 'Pacific Islands' in the original to 'certain of the South Pacific Islands', and it was agreed that, subject to a further discussions among the relevant Dominion leaders – presumably to obtain Hughes's consent – Lloyd George was to take the amended version to the Council of Ten.[34]

---

[32] Cable, Hughes to Watt, 26 January 1919, NAA CP360/8 B1/3. In order to refute Wilson Hughes asked Watt to issue a public statement endorsing Hughes's demand for the annexation of the islands and to organise public meetings for the same purpose. On 28 January Watt issued a press release which expressed the government's 'emphatic objections to any form of International Government of those islands'. Because of the influenza epidemic all public assemblies were banned and so he was unable to do anything to meet Hughes's other request. See cable, Watt to Hughes, 28 January 1919, *ibid.,* and also *SMH,* 28 January 1919.
[33] Minutes of BED Meeting (5), 28 January 1919, TNA: PRO CAB 29/28. Lloyd George, reporting a personal conversation with Wilson, told the meeting that 'President Wilson had also stated that if exceptions were made from the mandatory principle as proposed by the British Delegates, it would be difficult to refuse to make an exception in the case of Japan.'
[34] Minutes of BED Meeting (6), 29 January 1919, *ibid*. The record of this meeting is clearly incomplete and quite anodyne. The Secretary in compiling the minutes of these meetings as a general rule emptied the exchanges of much of the emotion and confrontation. This would seem to be particularly true here. Borden

An immediate decision had to be made, and so Hughes hastened to seek the advice of his cabinet in Melbourne. In two cables he summarised for Watt what had transpired at the 'Rather stormy' BED meeting and during the subsequent negotiations. In the first he explained that the third class mandate would only apply to the 'mainland of New Guinea', whereas in the second he stated that it would cover 'the South Pacific Islands', adding that this would enable Australia to extend its immigration, navigation and tariff laws to all the islands. It may be that in the interval he had had a further talk with Lloyd George and received the concession in return for his willingness to go along with the arrangement. Hughes added that Wilson would not agree to award mandates until after the League had been established.

Hughes found himself in a quandary. Lloyd George had made it clear that if Hughes persisted with his demand for direct control Britain would not back him and the 'British Navy would not support Australia in any attempt to secure it [annexation of the islands].' It was a pseudo ultimatum. The three affected Dominion prime ministers were 'bitterly disappointed', but since Britain had abandoned them they felt they had no choice but to fall into line. Hughes urged the cabinet not to agree unless Australia was to be named 'forthwith' as mandatory for the territory and unless the mandate gave Australia 'complete control over immigration, trade and tariff, over New Guinea and the principal adjacent islands'.[35] At the end of the dispute he had no choice but to yield. It was not Lloyd George's threat to deny Australia the protection of the Royal Navy which forced his hand; it was hard to believe that any power would attempt to eject Australia from the islands. Rather since Australia identified itself with the British race Hughes, when pressed, could not seriously contemplate a break with the British Empire.

The cabinet in Melbourne shared his 'bitter disappointment' over the treatment accorded Australia but were agreed that this bitterness should not be allowed to cause a rupture with Britain and the Empire. They considered that the British Government's actions in acceding to American wishes over the South Pacific islands created a situation 'fraught with the gravest possibilities to the people of this country'. If Australia were forced to accept a mandate then it should, as Hughes had demanded, have 'the control over immigration, tariff and trade matters', and for the cabinet 'immigration' was the most important of these powers. Without it 'Australia's racial policy will be challenged and injured, if not destroyed.' It would mean the 'eventual predominance of mixed and inferior races in the Islands'. They could not understand why America did not 'sympathise with a people isolated and adjacent to unnumbered colored millions, but resolutely facing its duty to keep this fertile continent and its intimately associated islands for

---

in his diary recorded that 'Mr. Hughes was very persistent, desiring to incorporate not only New Guinea but a large adjacent island and several other groups of islands stretching some 500 miles to the North and East of the Australian continent. After a somewhat heated discussion Mr. Hughes reluctantly accepted the proposal.' See Borden diary, 1 February 1919, General Memorandum No.6, Borden Papers, LAC.

It may be that Kerr had given Lloyd George the idea that the Americans might separate New Guinea from the Bismarck Archipelago and the Solomon Islands. George Louis Beer, a member of the American Inquiry, who was an expert on the colonial question, had made such a suggestion at a lunch with Kerr on 28 January. See Beer diary, 28 January 1919, Beer Papers, LC mm 79004954.

[35] Cables, Hughes to Watt, 29 and 30 January 1919, NAA CP360/8 B1/3. It is clear from internal evidence that the second cable message was also written on 29 January.

the selected white races.' Here Watt spelt out the way in which ideas of race were interwoven with those of geopolitics. Yet despite this concern for Australia's vital racial interest in the region, the cabinet nevertheless was clear that 'Australia could not endanger relationship with motherland and antagonise America without placing its whole future in jeopardy.'[36]

Only on this latter point was there any difference with Hughes. Hughes might have hoped for American support for Australia's Pacific interests, but in Wilson he found an American leader who not only showed no concern for Australia, but contrariwise was intent on pursuing a policy which, from Hughes's perspective, threatened the nation's security. Thus, believing that there was nothing to be lost, he had no qualms about antagonising Wilson. Indeed he gained personal pleasure from the exercise.

Hughes could not help but see this setback as a direct consequence of the Allies' ignoring his warnings at the time the armistice was being negotiated. Everything that he had then predicted was coming to pass. As he told Watt, 'The present position, in which Australian interests are in greatest danger of being sacrificed, arises entirely through the most unfortunate and unwise acceptance of Wilson's Fourteen Points by the Allies in November last.' He emerged from the battle with Lloyd George disgruntled and resentful. And no sooner had he acquiesced in the inevitable than he sought out a British journalist, Montagu Smith, to whom he confided his jaundiced view of what had happened.

On the morning of the next day – the very day on which Lloyd George was taking the British Empire's mandatory proposal to the Council of Ten – the Paris edition of Lord Northcliffe's *Daily Mail* carried an inspired story in which it was asserted that, as a result of the BED decision to support the mandatory principle, the Dominion representatives were 'greatly perturbed' and 'that the step threatens the existence of the British Empire.' Furthermore it stated the Australians believed 'rightly or wrongly, that the firm stand President Wilson is taking … is due at bottom to his fear that the Japanese occupation of them [North Pacific islands] would cause a great outcry in America.' It was a rather muddled treatment of the subject. It posited that, as Wilson had taken his rules for mandatories from British colonial principles, it meant that the result would be 'annexation in fact but not in theory'. On the one hand the implication seemed to be that Wilson was either a hypocrite or an egotistical fool in insisting on adhesion to the mandatory forms. But on the other it might have been thought that, if it were annexation in fact, the Dominions should have had no grounds for objection. The article nevertheless concluded by complaining that major questions had not been addressed; namely, who was to pay for the administration of the mandates, what conditions would govern tariffs and, most apposite for Australia 'in the case of the Far Eastern Lands, whether the mandatory Powers are to be allowed any right of excluding people or capital that they do not wish to enter there.'[37]

---

[36] Cable, Watt to Hughes, 31 January 1919, NAA, CP 360/8 B1/3.

[37] *Daily Mail* (Paris edition), 30 January 1919.
 Hughes never openly admitted that he had had any part in producing this article. Apart from the content and style the circumstantial evidence of the article's composition shows that Hughes was its effective author. On the 29 January, Eggleston recorded that Hughes after the BED meeting had lunched with the *Daily Mail* correspondent. (Eggleston diary, 29 January 1919, Eggleston Papers, NLA MS 423/6/80.) Kerr in complaining to Milner about this 'very mischievous article' noted that the British had learned that 'Hughes

It is difficult to know what Hughes believed he would achieve by these attacks on Lloyd George and Wilson. Hughes, if he had rationally considered the matter, should have realised that a man like Wilson, a man like himself in this respect, would only be made more implacable. If it were intended to stir up French and British public opinion the language was ill-chosen for the purpose. Hughes was merely venting his sense of outrage against those who had rejected what he knew were just and necessary peace terms and who thereby had allowed the true interests of Australia and the Empire to be sacrificed on the altar of personal vanity and mindless moralism.

While Hughes was engaged in this subversive activity, Wilson was conferring with House and the American Commission about the BED's proposed mandate terms and in the process revealing at this critical moment more fully the most pressing reason for his obstinacy. House, in sending Wilson a copy of the uncorrected draft, had scribbled on it that 'It seems fair to me.' Wilson was not convinced. He would, he told House, agree to it 'if the interpretation in practice were to come from Gen'l Smuts (and on the understanding that the conditions – slave trade &c – are illustrations).' But there were two big problems, 'the demands of men like Hughes and the *certain* [Wilson's emphasis] difficulties with Japan.' And of the two, the latter was more important: 'The latter looms large. A line of islands in her possession would be very dangerous to the U.S.' Fear of Japan was, as it had been when this issue was first aired in December, the crucial consideration. The American President, who had told Hughes that his preoccupation with Pacific security was misplaced and showed a lack of confidence in the League of Nations and collective security, was judging mandate matters on strategic grounds; and this even though America, unlike Australia, was a great power and well able to fend off any threat to its territories. That evening, at a meeting of the American commissioners where they discussed the BED proposal, Wilson made it clear that he 'was not ready to accept it as a whole or at once.'[38]

When the Council of Ten assembled the next morning – all the Dominion prime ministers again being present – to discuss the BED mandatory formula there was a certain tension in the air. After Lloyd George had briefly introduced the scheme, stressing the great concession the Dominions had reluctantly made in the interest of harmony, Hughes had spoken up and

---

had seen his article in proof and made corrections to it in his own hand.'(Letter, Kerr to Milner, 31 January 1919, Bodleian Library, MSS. Milner C700/193–200.) Further, in a letter of apology to House, Northcliffe wrote that he 'was distressed to hear of the bad break made by one of my reporters in regard to Mr. Hughes … Mr. Hughes succeeded in capturing one of my young reporters who had been in the army for three years and was unaware of my views of Mr. Hughes's antics.' (Letter, Northcliffe to House, 5 February 1919, Northcliffe Papers, BL Add 62180, Vol.XXVIII.)

Lord Riddell, Lloyd George's press manager, saw the *Daily Mail's* political correspondent shortly after the publication of the article and he told Riddell that he had interviewed Botha and Massey as well as Hughes about the article and shown them the proofs at which time they had suggested the sentence about the break up of the Empire. (Riddell, *Lord Riddell's Intimate Diary of the Peace Conference and After, 1918–1923* (New York: Reynal and Hitchcock, 1934), p.16). But this cannot be true of Botha who could not dissimulate and who denounced the article both inside and outside the Council of Ten. It seems unlikely also that Massey was party to the article's publication. In every way the mark of Hughes was upon it. It was common knowledge that it was his work.

[38] House diary, 29 January 1919, and note, House to Wilson, 29 January 1919 and letter, Wilson to House, 29 January 1919, House Papers, Yale MS 466, Vol.15, p.26; Link, *Papers of Woodrow Wilson*, Vol.54, p.347.

explained that since 'grave interests' were at stake he had acceded to Lloyd George's proposed terms for a South Pacific mandate. Even so, he added that he was obliged to withhold his formal assent until he had heard from his government.

Wilson replied 'with unaffected good humour' – how he must have gritted his teeth. Firstly he complained of the articles appearing in the English language press in Paris which stated that he did not know how his ideals would work and suggested that there were differences between himself and the Dominions. He threatened that if this were to continue he would feel obliged 'against his own wishes to make a full public expose of his views.' Turning to the matter in hand he stated that while the BED document which had been distributed, 'made a long stride towards the composition of their differences', he did not think that 'they could have a final decision immediately.' He then declared that until the League was established and the terms of the mandates settled it was impossible to know definitively how they would work, and nations could not be expected to accept mandates until they knew their precise conditions. He denied that he was 'a hopeless Idealist'. On the contrary he maintained that 'he never accepted an ideal until he could see its practical application.' It may be here that he had made the statement which was later, at his request, excised from the minutes; namely that 'he ... would like to be able to say that religion was a good working proposition, but he regretted that this was not the case', and that 'In the case of the League of Nations he did not want to make the mistake that had been made in regard to religion.'[39] This new would-be practical saviour had little to offer the Dominions, and, expressing himself rather awkwardly, said that they 'should build upon this agreement the solid foundations which would carry this superstructure.'

Lloyd George was dismayed. Wilson's response 'filled him with despair'. He had a sense of what Hughes's reaction would be. He again emphasised that it was 'only with the greatest difficulty' the Dominions had been induced to accept the compromise. The council could not delay every decision until the League of Nations was a going concern. He hoped therefore that it would 'provisionally adopt the resolutions he had submitted ... subject to such reconsideration as might be required when the complete scheme of the League of Nations was formulated.' Wilson, somewhat taken aback by Lloyd George's words, endorsed his solution.

But this was not good enough for Hughes. As Borden noted, 'Unfortunately he [Wilson] emphasised the weak features of the arrangement from the Australian viewpoint, with the result that he brought Mr. Hughes to his feet with practically a repudiation of the whole arrangement as far as Australia was concerned.' Hughes was in no mood to accept anything but an unambiguous adoption of the BED principles and the immediate allocation of the mandates. He was angry that Wilson should have dealt so slightingly with concessions which he had made under duress and against his better judgment. Having listened to the President, all that he could tell the Australian people about a mandate was – and here he sarcastically threw Wilson's own words back at him –

---

[39] Roskill, *Hankey*, Vol.2, p.54. Hankey, in a letter to his wife, wrote that 'It was almost tantamount to saying that he did not intend to make the mistake Jesus Christ had made! It drew some rather nicely veiled comments from our Dominions' people ...' See also Riddell, *Diary of the Peace Conference*, p.19, 'Wilson made an unfortunate speech at the Conference ... he himself thought it so unfortunate that he asked that it should be deleted from the *procès-verbal* which was done.'

that it would 'fit like a glove'. He thought that the Council of Ten, the *de facto* League of Nations, should act as the executive of the League and immediately distribute the mandates.

Borden, the peacemaker, recognising that personal animosities were putting at risk the prospect of an agreement, used the lunch hour to 'urge upon Mr. Lloyd George and upon President Wilson that the resolution should be passed with as little further discussion as possible.'[40] But his efforts proved fruitless. When the council resumed its sitting, Massey felt compelled to follow Hughes's lead and express his disappointment that Wilson had failed to make 'a clear and definite statement' about the BED mandate scheme. Wilson was maddened by this challenge, and, as House later put it, 'lost his temper'. There are a number of accounts, published after the event, of the exchanges which subsequently ensued. These vary in detail and colour. But probably Hankey's minutes of the meeting convey the essence, if not exactly the full flavour, of what was said. Wilson demanded to know whether Australia and New Zealand were presenting an ultimatum to the conference, whether the British proposal was the most that they were willing to concede, and whether, if they did not have their way, they proposed 'to do what they could to stop the whole agreement'. Hughes answered that the President had 'put it fairly well', reminding him at the same time that, as far as Australia was concerned, even consent to the BED proposal was subject to his government's approval.

Lloyd George was infuriated by this scene which threatened to destroy all he had worked so zealously to accomplish. And in a rather exasperated tone he suggested that 'after everyone had made his position clear and when nobody was under any illusions as to Mr. Hughes's position, or General Botha's position, or Mr Massey's or anybody else's' they should take the document he had placed before them 'as a provisional decision subject to revision'. He returned them to what he believed the morning debate had settled. When Wilson himself concluded that they should in their press statement say that 'they had arrived at a satisfactory provisional arrangement with regard to dealing with the German and Turkish territory outside Europe',[41] Lloyd George, it seemed, had won the day.

Neither Wilson nor Hughes, however, was happy with the outcome. At the end of the meeting, Wilson confided his concerns to David Hunter Miller, the American legal adviser, about how the British scheme would affect Japan's claims to the North Pacific islands.

> He [Wilson] then spoke of the limitation in the resolution to the islands in the South Pacific and asked me to consider this question in respect of the islands in the North Pacific which Japan held. He said that these island lie athwart the path from Hawaii to the Philippines and that they were nearer to Hawaii than the Pacific coast was, and that they were of little use for anything else and that we had no naval base except at Guam.

These were Wilson's first thoughts as he emerged from this critical meeting over mandates. What came off the top of his head was Japan. His immediate reaction was not misgivings about the plight of the native peoples under the proposed rules but rather anxiety that Japan might benefit strategically at America's expense. His statement of the security issue followed very closely the

---

[40] Borden diary, 1 February 1919, General Memorandum No.6, Borden Papers, LAC.
[41] Minutes of Council of Ten Meetings, 11am and 3.30pm, 30 January 1919, *FRUS* 'PPC, 1919', Vol.III, pp.785–816.

Naval Board's briefing paper. It was ironic that Wilson and Hughes should have had the same objective in mind in battling over the question of mandates.[42] Had their authoritarian personalities not been so identified with their conflicting theories of international relations they should, under ordinary diplomatic rules, have been working in close cooperation to limit Japan's expansion in the Pacific.

Hughes too remained dissatisfied, but not as dissatisfied as he appeared to be. What the provisional decision meant was a mystery: as he told Riddell, 'The whole thing is in so much confusion. They never put a resolution as there is no voting.'[43] Yet in informing Melbourne of what had happened he painted a rather optimistic picture. The BED mandate resolution that the Council of Ten had adopted had its advantages, even if only provisionally. The Council's decision meant that:

> Our position is in some respects better under the mandatory system, if we get it in the above form [that is, the third class form], than if we were in outright control because Japan under mandatory system cannot and must not fortify Marshall and Carolines or use them for submarine or naval bases.
>
> Cook and I think this of tremendous importance.

Hughes, the 'realist', only came belatedly – indeed after Wilson – to see that a mandate rather than annexation was a better basis for security against Japan than direct annexation. That is, Japan would only accept for the North Pacific islands the same conditions adopted for the South Pacific islands. Since Australia had no intention or ability to fortify the South Pacific islands, such a restriction forbidding the building of naval bases would not weaken its defences; whereas if the North Pacific islands were placed under a mandate Japan would not be able to use the islands for naval or military purposes. Similarly Hughes, as a result of his discussions with the Italians, French, Japanese and British, had no doubt that Australia would be awarded the mandate for the South Pacific islands and that it would be able to apply its immigration and trade laws to the mandated territory. Hughes recommended that the government be willing to accept a mandate on the understanding that Australia could extend its laws to New Guinea, New Britain, New Ireland and adjacent islands. At the same time he warned that the Australian Government should not

---

[42] David H. Miller, *My Dairy at the Conference of Paris with Documents*, 21 vols (New York: Appeal Printing Company, 1924), Vol.I, p.100.

It is noteworthy that though from at least 1917 Wilson voiced this distrust of Japan both to American and British confidants, including Lloyd George, he himself only on one occasion, at a high point in the mandate controversy put his 'selfish' national security concern in writing.

House, whom the European delegates commonly thought was more attuned to strategic considerations, did not seem to understand the Japanese question and thought that Wilson had taken too hard a line in dealing with the British Empire delegates. Commenting on Wilson's refusal to embrace the British compromise, House wrote that 'the British had come a long way, and if I had been in his place, I should have congratulated them over their willingness to meet us more than half way.' See House diary, 30 January 1919, House Papers, Yale MS 466, Vol.15, p.28.

[43] Riddell, *Diary of the Peace Conference*, p.17.

'hint anything publicly that would indicate that we are satisfied with mandatory principle or with anything less than (immediate) settlement of question.'[44]

Despite this positive assessment Hughes did not abandon his campaign against Wilson's mandates policy and thereby against Wilson himself. Through the French, British and American press he continued to rail against the delay in allocating mandates. On 2 February in *Le Matin* Hughes denied that a solution had been reached and repeated much the same arguments he advanced in the Council of Ten in favour of an immediate decision on the mandatory powers. Regardless of whether there was or there was not a provisional agreement he declared that *'moi, je sais, en tout cas, que je n'y ai pas souscrit, que je n'y souscrirai pas ...'* He refused to wait for the allocation of the mandate from some future League of Nations. For Australia the question of New Guinea was a matter of life or death, and he continued, comparing Australia's strategic vulnerability to that of France, *'Ce n'est à la France que j'ai besoin de dire que pour certains peuples situés dans certaines conditions de géographie, les problèmes de frontière ont une gravité exceptionelle.'* In making his demand he could not help but cast aspersions on those who would thwart Australia's wishes. Appealing for French sympathy he pointed out that Australia had not been tardy in coming to the defence of France and civilisation. Australia indeed had suffered heavier losses than America.[45] He implied that Australia had a better right than America to be heard at the peace table.

Simultaneously Hughes composed a memorandum, calling for an immediate distribution of mandates, and sent it to Clemenceau as president of the Peace Conference. Aware that before Wilson returned to America in the middle of February there was to be a Plenary Meeting of the conference to receive the report of the League of Nations Commission, Hughes wished to use the

---

[44] Cable, Hughes to Watt, 31 January 1919, NAA CP360/8 B1/3.

Watt immediately grasped Hughes's point that a mandate might serve Australian interests better than direct annexation. In his reply he said, 'I quite agree that special mandate may be preferable to free annexation in that it binds Japan concerning Naval bases etc.' See cable, Watt to Hughes, 3 February 1919, *ibid*.

Cook, perhaps under Latham's influence, also recognised the strategic advantage for Australia of applying the mandate system to the German Pacific islands. Under the heading 'Danger of Japanese ownership of Islands North of Equator', he wrote '1. Mandate neutralises their strategic value ... 2. Brings America definitely into Pacific to keep it clear of Eastern menace. 3. Our White Australia & Economic aspirations & ideals are preserved.' Notebook 1919, Vol.II, Cook Papers, NAA M3580.

The Japanese were under no illusion about the intent of the British Empire's third class mandate formula. Makino recommended that Tokyo approve the mandate resolution. He saw it as a device to save Wilson's face while ensuring the effective annexation of the Pacific islands. See Noriko Kawamura, 'Wilsonian Idealism and Japan's Claims at the Paris Peace Conference', *Pacific Historical Review*, LXVI (November 1997), 517.

[45] *Le Matin,* 2 February 1919. See also article by 'Victorian' on 'Mr Hughes's Hard Fight: The Battle for the Islands', in *Morning Post*, 11 February 1919, and Hughes's message sent to the Australian Commissioner in America, *New York Times*, 9 February 1919. In his campaign against Wilson Hughes had the full sympathy of the Governor-General who wrote in his diary, 'Hughes opposition to America justified. He alone speaks for the Empire ... Wilson, c'est l'ennemi – and more impudent than any cuckoo.' See Novar diary, Novar Papers NLA MS 696/36, 5 February 1919.

opportunity to have the conference award the mandates and define the conditions under which they would be held. The Council of Ten had failed him and so he was hoping to appeal to the full conference.

In the memorandum, Hughes required that the mandate spell out the conditions of Australia's control over the South Pacific islands. This was 'absolutely necessary for Australia's security'. The country's first priority was to maintain inviolable White Australia. The well-established racial and geographical arguments customarily advanced in defence of White Australia were revisited. The United States had shown 'the evils which follow from the introduction into a country of large populations of widely different race, type and habits of life – a population which cannot, without the most disastrous social and racial consequences, either be absorbed or remain absorbed.' It was important that 'at any cost and at any sacrifice Australia shall be kept free from these evils.' Its geographical position made this all the more urgent in that a country of five million white people faced the teeming millions of alien races to their north. Australia was 'deeply convinced of the strategic importance of the islands which lie like ramparts to the north and east.'

Thus Hughes urged Clemenceau to have the Peace Conference declare itself the 'provisional executive' of the League of Nations and without further delay settle the whole matter.[46] But he was disappointed. The whole session was taken up by President Wilson's speech introducing the Covenant, which included the BED resolution on mandates, and by supporting speeches from representatives of other major powers. Hughes could only obtain Clemenceau's assurance that there would be an opportunity at a later time for a general discussion of its terms.[47]

During March and April the issue continued to simmer. A BED meeting on 13 March discussed a memorandum from Milner setting out conditions which might be applied to the three classes of mandates, named A, B and C. For Hughes the proposal to allow the native people to choose to unite with their mandatory power was dangerous in that if the inhabitants of the Marshall and Caroline islands voted to become part of Japan, then Japan would be able to fortify the islands. When Lloyd George, still wishing to meet American sensitivities, expressed a strong desire to put the North Pacific islands under the B regime, Cecil, who had spoken to Makino about this, made it clear that the Japanese would insist on holding their mandates on the same terms granted to Australia and New Zealand in the South Pacific. Accepting that this was unavoidable, Hughes conceded that in order to keep the Japanese out of the South Pacific,

---

[46] Memoranda by Hughes, WCP 71, 'Australia and the Pacific Islands' and WCP 116, 'Memorandum Regarding the Pacific Islands', 6 and 8 February 1919, Latham Papers, NLA MS 1009/1300-06. See also cable, Hughes to Watt, 10 February 1919, NAA CP360/8 B1/3.

Hughes sent his memorandum to Clemenceau without consulting the BED.

The French Secretary to the Council of Ten informed Hankey of Hughes's action and gave him a copy of the document. Hankey was much alarmed by this unorthodox behaviour and spoke to Garran, pointing out that what Hughes was doing was 'precisely what the Dominions had, in the past, complained that we did, namely to discuss matters of policy affecting them without first consulting them.' Garran apparently saw Hughes and told Hankey that the Australian Prime Minister had promised that in future he would communicate direct with Hankey. See letter, Hankey to Lloyd George, 21 February 1919, Lloyd George Papers, House of Lords Record Office F/23/4/18.

[47] Record of Third Plenary Conference Meeting, 14 February 1919, *FRUS*, 'PPC, 1919', Vol.III, pp.205-30.

Australia would not oppose Japan shutting out Australian trade from the North Pacific islands.[48] He was willing to sacrifice the established rights of the Burns Philp trading company in these islands so as to acquire absolute control over the South Pacific. Commercial interests had to play second fiddle to racial purity and strategic security.

Having reconciled himself to the Japanese keeping the North Pacific islands, Hughes tried to enlist them in his campaign to achieve an early decision on the allocation of the mandates. From a 'very secret source' the British Ambassador in Paris heard that Hughes, in a meeting with Makino, had told him that Australia would raise 'no objection to Japan becoming mandatory for the islands North of the Equator, and considered that the appointment of mandatories for the Pacific Islands whether North or South of the Equator was a matter of urgency and he would undertake to cooperate with the Japanese on the point.'[49] Nevertheless this search for allies failed to advance the cause.

At the end of April, as the League Covenant and the Peace Treaty were being completed, preparatory to summoning the representatives of Germany, Hughes renewed his efforts to have the mandatories named and the conditions specified. At a BED on 28 April he complained that the Peace Treaty was shortly to be handed to the Germans and nothing had been done about the mandates. All the Dominion leaders shared his anxiety and Borden was deputed to convey their views to Lloyd George and through him to the Council of Four or Three.[50] Hughes, desperate for action, was not content to leave the matter there, and he approached House, the 'universal conciliator, smoother-over, connector!', seeking his help 'to arrange for the mandatory system to go into effect at once as far as the Pacific Islands are concerned.' Why Hughes turned to House is not easy to understand. House himself was rather bemused that the man who had been 'fighting us ever since the Congress assembled' should have sought his aid. Again for no evident reason, House promised to forward a summary of Hughes's view to the President and 'see what could be done.'[51]

A few days later Hughes sent House the requested memorandum. It put the Australian view as starkly as ever. The matter was one of 'vital urgency'. The islands were 'the defensive ramparts of Australia against naval attack'. They were 'bound up with the White Australia policy as to which public opinion in Australia is very sensitive and impatient.' In the case of the Class Three mandates there was no good reason for not proceeding to frame the mandate terms and appoint the mandatory power. If the peace was signed before this happened Australians would have 'grave misgivings that both the territorial integrity of the country and the White Australia policy, which is the cornerstone of the national edifice, were in serious danger.'[52] Whether Wilson would have

---

[48] Minutes of BED Meeting (13), 13 March 1919, TNA: PRO CAB 29/28. For Cecil's account of his discussions with Makino about mandates, see letter, Cecil to Lloyd George, 10 March 1919, Lloyd George Papers, House of Lords Record Office F/6/6/16.

[49] Letter, Curzon to Milner, 22 March 1919, Milner Papers, Bodleian Library, MSS. Milner C699/466.

[50] Minutes of BED Meetings (28 and 29), 23 and 28 April 1919, TNA: PRO CAB 29/28.

[51] House Diary, 2 May 1919, House Papers, Yale MS 466, Vol.16, p.164.

The description of House comes from the diary of Ray Stannard Baker, see Link, *Papers of Woodrow Wilson*, Vol.56, p.338.

[52] Miller, *My Diary at the Peace Conference*, Vol.I, pp.296–97 and Vol.IX, pp.287–92.

found these arguments persuasive is a moot point since before House could act the leaders of the Great Powers, prompted by Lloyd George, reached a decision.

On 5 May in response to the pressure from the BED, Lloyd George in the Council of Three said that he wished to settle the mandate issue before the Peace Treaty was handed to the Germans. Surprisingly, Wilson, though he reaffirmed his desire to avoid the appearance of a division of the spoils, was quite cooperative, stating that 'to all intents and purposes', harking back to the 30 January decision, it had been agreed that South-West Africa should go to South Africa, New Guinea and adjacent islands to Australia and Samoa to New Zealand. Perhaps having lived with the peacemaking for so long and being wearied by the many constant and complex disputes they had dealt with he had no desire to allow lesser issues to hold up the settlement.

At a BED meeting later that day Lloyd George assured the Dominion prime ministers that the Council of Three intended to agree on a schedule of mandatories for the German colonies and to publish it at the same time as the Peace Treaty. The charters for each class of mandate were, however, to be left for a League of Nations Commission to determine. On the very day that the Peace Treaty was handed to the Germans, the Council of Three approved the mandatories for the German Colonies. In the Pacific Japan was allotted all the islands north of the equator, New Zealand was given Samoa and Australia all the other islands south of the equator with the exception of Nauru.[53] Nauru, which the Australians had occupied since the early months of the war, was very rich in superphosphate, and Britain and New Zealand contested Australia's right to be the mandatory power. As a result, Nauru was made a mandate of the British Empire and it was left to the three governments to work out how it should be administered. The result of all his effort left Hughes still discontented. Until the terms of the mandate were fixed and Australia was handed the title deeds he would not be able to rest.[54]

Hughes's Pacific island policy and the methods he adopted in pursuing it had little or nothing to be said for them. They were counterproductive and only served gratuitously to antagonise the Japanese, the putative enemy, alienate the Americans, a putative friend, and to irritate the British and other Dominions, who were the assumed mainstay of Australian security. Nothing was to be achieved by trying to prevent Japan from keeping the German North Pacific islands. The Japanese occupied them and had made it clear that they had no intention of handing them over to Australia or any other power. Neither Britain nor the United States had given the slightest indica-

---

[53] Minutes of BED Meeting (30), 5 May 1919, TNA: PRO CAB 29/28; Minutes of Council of Three Meetings, 5, 6 and 7 May 1919, *FRUS* 'PPC 1919', Vol.V, pp.472-73, 492, 496-500.

[54] For the fullest account of Hughes's struggle to obtain the Nauru mandate for Australia see Peter Spartalis, *The Diplomatic Battles of Billy Hughes* (Sydney: Hale and Iremonger, 1983), pp.145-50.

Hughes was again irate at having been denied what he thought was Australia's just reward for its efforts in the war. In an angry cable to Watt, in which he reported the Council of Three's decision on the mandates, he declared, in a characteristically hyperbolic manner, that if Australia 'were to be robbed of Nauru that is for me the end.' As a protest he would refuse to sign the treaty and to accept the mandate for the other islands. Watt again was a calming voice. While sympathising with Hughes the cabinet believed that, after putting up the best fight he could, he should sign the treaty and rely on subsequent negotiations with Britain to achieve Australia's objective. See cables, Hughes to Watt, 7 May 1919 and Watt to Hughes, 9 May 1919, NAA CP360/8 B1/4.

tion that they were willing to use force to compel Japan to give up these wartime gains. The Americans did not like the fact that Japan was ensconced in these territories from which it might be able to attack Hawaii or the Pacific coast. But they were not prepared to go to war to eject Japan from the islands. The British Government for its part would not press Japan to give up the territories. Apart from other considerations it held that the Empire was bound by the Anglo-Japanese Treaty of February 1917 to support Japan's desire to keep these territories.

Likewise Hughes's insistence on Australia's right to annex the South Pacific islands would, if it had been successful, have had the contrary result of what was intended. His fear that, if Australia held these islands under a League mandate, Japanese migrants would swarm over them and so threaten White Australia, was groundless. As he recognised, after he had been more or less forced to accept the mandatory principle, the mandate was in all the circumstance the best option available to protect Australia against Japan. Since Japan was determined to have the same condition for settling the fate of the North Pacific islands that Australia accepted for the South Pacific islands, it was in Australia's interest to place the islands it occupied under a League mandate. By so doing it obliged the Japanese to agree to a mandate over the North Pacific islands and thereby to deny themselves the right to build naval bases which could menace Australia. This was the most that Australia could hope to achieve in limiting Japan's ability to use these islands for aggressive purposes.

Australia itself lost nothing that it would otherwise have had. It had no desire or capacity to build naval bases in the South Pacific islands. As Smuts and Botha understood, the third class mandates gave the Dominions all they needed in order to control immigration and commerce. While the formal allocation of the mandates was not accomplished until the end of the conference it was as certain from the outset that Australia would be awarded the mandate for New Guinea and associated islands as it was that Japan would receive a mandate for the Marshalls, Marianas and Carolines, and for the same reason – namely that they occupied them. Hughes's absolute and simple-minded idea of power and possession, which he believed to be the only sure basis for security and which informed his demand for annexation, was in effect a danger to Australia's national security.

Japan's racial equality principle and the challenge to White Australia

For the Japanese, racial equality was fundamental to their modern national identity. From the end of the nineteenth century they had become very sensitive to Western ideas of superiority. As a result, they had pursued a diplomacy aimed first at ridding themselves of the 'unequal treaties' that the Western powers had imposed upon them and then at persuading the Pacific rim 'Anglo-Saxon' powers to give up or modify their racially-based policies which discriminated against Japanese immigrants and Japanese residents.[55] During the war Japan, having been accorded the

---

[55] Carol Gluck, *Japan's Modern Myths: Ideology in the Late Meiji Period* (Princeton: Princeton University Press, 1985); Ian Nish, 'Japan Reverses the Unequal Treaties: The Anglo-Japanese Commercial Treaty of 1894', *Journal of Oriental Studies*, 13 (1975).

status of a great power by its Western allies, was encouraged to press its campaign against these humiliating distinctions. With the signing of the armistice and the coming of the Peace Conference, especially the proposal for a League of Nations, this objective moved to the centre of Japanese diplomacy. If Japan were to be truly equal to the other great powers it was important that the new international organisation should in one form or another acknowledge the equality of all peoples, regardless of race.[56]

For Australia, Japan was a migratory as well as a military threat. Japan was seen as a danger in racial as well as *Realpolitik* terms. It appeared not only as a challenge to national security but also as a symbol of Asian peoples' general designs against Australia. This concern for White Australia, which was evident in the debates over the future of the German possessions in the South Pacific, was even more clearly present in the Australian reaction to the Japanese desire to include a racial equality provision in the League Covenant. In Hughes's eyes the Japanese desire to incorporate such a principle in the charter of the new international body was of a piece with the pressures they had brought to bear on Australia to sign a Commercial Treaty. To his fevered imagination Japan intended to use this principle to break down Australia's 'Great White Walls' and so allow a *tsunami* of Asian migrants overwhelm the British race in the South Pacific. The Japanese action put at risk the white British identity which the Australians had adopted at the end of the nineteenth century and subsequently made the foundation principle of their Commonwealth.

As Hughes had noted, Japan's war had been essentially limited to the Pacific theatre. Japan never showed any interest in becoming involved militarily in Europe where the decisive battles were being fought. Indeed the Japanese had only a conditional commitment to the Allied cause. Some Japanese political leaders and newspapers, especially at times of military setbacks for the Allies, had voiced doubts about the desirability of the Anglo-Japanese alliance and had shown an interest in reaching a rapprochement with Germany. In the early months of 1918 when the German offensive on the Western Front seemed to be on the point of carrying all before it, the government of General Masatake Terauchi, which contained some ministers with German associations, had shown a willingness to reconsider their stand on the war.[57] After it became clear, however, that Germany was in full retreat, the Terauchi government was replaced by one more sympathetic to the Allies. James Murdoch, the Professor of Oriental Studies at Sydney University, who had at the end of the year been sent by Watt on a secret mission to investigate Japanese attitudes to the post-war world, reported that:

> The collapse of Germany has had its effects – German militarism is now being held up as a terrible example: and able editors are everywhere preaching to their public the advisability of taking warning & turning over a new leaf ... and on the whole the country has become reasonable. In short, things are much more hopeful than they have ever been since 1914.[58]

---

[56] See D.C.S. Sissons, 'The Immigration Question in Australian Diplomatic Relations with Japan, 1875–1919', paper presented to the Australian and New Zealand Association for the Advancement of Science, Brisbane, May 1971, and Naoko Shimazu, *Japan, Race and Equality; The Racial Equality Proposal* (London: Routledge, 1998), especially pp.164–66.

[57] Nish, *Alliance in Decline*, pp.240–41 and 245–46.

[58] Letter, James Murdoch to 'McRae' (E.L. Piesse), 22 December 1918, Piesse Papers NLA MS 882/5/5.

The new government of Kei Hara had the task of framing the instructions which its plenipotentiaries were to take to the Paris Peace Conference. Following discussions in the Foreign Relations Advisory Council it was agreed that Makino and Chinda should seek to retain all the German North Pacific territories and, if they could not secure the postponement of a League of Nations, they were 'to make efforts to secure suitable guarantees against the disadvantages to Japan which would arise ... out of racial prejudice.' Like Hughes the Japanese policy-makers were suspicious of Wilson's league proposal. They knew little of how it was supposed to operate. Like Hughes they feared that it might impinge upon national sovereignty. And they were worried that the League might become, as Hughes had wished, a means to entrench the global hegemony of the English-speaking powers.[59] But the Japanese understood that if the League were established they could not afford to stay aloof and become isolated, and so they insisted that their delegates should try to ensure that Japan's status as a great power was protected.

Once the Japanese delegates, Makino and Sutemi Chinda, had grasped that Wilson was intent on making the League Covenant an integral part of the peace they attempted to have a provision inserted in the covenant which would make racial equality a founding principle of the world body. It proved to be a very difficult task. Unlike the retention of their territorial gains where others made the running, the Japanese themselves had to take the lead in pursuing the racial equality objective both in meetings of the League of Nations Commission and at the Plenary Session of the Conference. As the representatives of the only non-Western great power, they felt uncomfortable in a gathering dominated by European problems, ideologies and languages. Nevertheless it was so important to their nation's self-esteem that they persevered against all the odds with their campaign.

Thus on 4 February, after the second meeting of the League of Nations Commission, Makino and Chinda consulted House about how best to proceed in order to incorporate 'some broad principle of racial equality' in the League Covenant. For the Japanese it was the Americans who were the key to the problem. The League of Nations was President Wilson's pet project, and considering the Pacific coast states' hostile attitude towards Japanese residents it was thought that if the Americans could be won over then the objective would be effectively achieved. House was seen as a sympathetic figure. In July 1918 he had given the Japanese Ambassador to the United States, Kikujiro Ishii, the impression that he understood Japanese feelings, and, true to this image, he reassured Makino and Chinda that he 'deprecated racial, religious or any other kinds of prejudice'. The Japanese did not wish to take the responsibility for placing a resolution before the League of Nations Commission, and were hoping that President Wilson would himself propose a suitable amendment to the covenant. House urged them to prepare two resolutions, one being what they most desired and the other being what they would accept. That is, he suggested that they should indicate their maximum and minimum positions.[60]

---

[59] Shimazu, *Japan, Race and Equality,* pp.46–49; Frederick R. Dickinson, *War and National Intervention: Japan in the Great War, 1914–1919* (Cambridge, Massachusetts: Harvard University Press, 1999), pp.224–25.
[60] House Diary, 4 February 1919, House Papers, Yale MS 466, Vol.15, p.23.

For House's account of the meeting with Ishii on 6 July 1918, see letter, House to Wilson, 6 July 1919, Link, *Papers of Woodrow Wilson*, Vol.48, pp.540–41.

During the following week the Japanese, American and British Empire delegates wrestled with the problem. Both House and Wilson disapproved of the mandatory character of the first Japanese proposed amendment which declared that:

> The equality of nations being a basic principle of the League of Nations, the High Contracting Parties agree that concerning the treatment of aliens in their territories, they will accord them equal treatment in every respect, making no distinction, either in law or fact, on account of their race or nationality.

For the Americans such a requirement would cause difficulties on the Pacific coast; Wilson had had firsthand experience of the problem in 1913 when he had found it impossible to persuade California to abandon its discriminatory legislation. The Japanese compromise proposal had more appeal. After 'will accord', it added the phrase 'as far as it lies in their legitimate powers'. Indeed Wilson agreed that if the Japanese were willing to substitute 'as soon and as far as practicable' for their qualifying phrase then 'it might do.' When Chinda was shown the American suggestion he thought it 'would be satisfactory'.[61]

The British Empire, however, proved immovable on the subject. The Dominion leaders were unhappy with the Japanese initiative; and probably Smuts, certainly Borden and most vehemently Hughes opposed the inclusion of the principle of equality in the covenant in any form. The Dominion leaders saw it as a threat to their race-based immigration and domestic policies. Balfour, who discussed the matter with House, seems to have shared the Dominions' view. He considered that, if it were agreed to, it would raise expectations which would not be fulfilled, and as a result the League would be burdened 'with perpetual controversy incapable of satisfactory solution'.[62] The British, conscious that the dispute over the German colonies had endangered imperial unity, were loath to allow another crisis to arise, and so felt obliged to leave it to the Dominions to set the policy for the Empire. Balfour and Cecil, when approached by the Japanese, were therefore unable to give them any encouragement.[63]

House was dismayed by British intransigence. It seemed possible that the Japanese might make the acceptance of the racial equality principle a condition for their adhering to the League. His troubles were multiplied when the Japanese after further consideration rejected President Wilson's compromise as being 'practically meaningless'.[64] House tried his hand at devising other formulae, but all to no good purpose. Either the Japanese turned them down because, as was intended, they had no legal effect or the Dominion leaders vetoed them because they still committed the League to the notion of human equality. House was frustrated and, throwing up his hands in despair, told the Japanese that every solution which he and they had proposed had

---

[61] House Diary, 5 February 1919, House Papers, Yale MS 466, Vol.15, p.26.
[62] Balfour's record of conversation with House, 10 February 1919, Balfour Papers, BL Add 49751.
[63] Cable, Japanese Peace Delegation to Japanese Foreign Minister, Yasuya Uchida, 15 February 1919, cited in Sissons, 'The Immigration Question in Australian Diplomatic Relations with Japan, 1875–1919', p.2. See also House Diary, 12 February 1919, Yale MS 466, Vol.15, p.41, which recorded that 'Viscount Chinda called again and said that he could get nothing definite from the British.'
[64] *Ibid.*, 6 February 1919, Vol.15, p.30.

been blocked by Hughes.[65] Apparently the Americans by 12 February had reached an agreement with the Japanese on the wording for an amendment which was 'as mild and inoffensive as possible', and which, according to House, all the members of the British Empire Delegation except Hughes were willing to go along with. Hughes was 'the stumbling block'.[66]

As Wilson hastened to complete the draft covenant before he returned to America, the Japanese, even though they knew they would be defeated, determined to put their amendment before the League of Nations Commission. For the standing of their government at home they had to show an aroused public opinion that they had done their best. Thus at the last meeting of the commission on 13 February before the final draft went to a plenary session of the conference, Makino moved an amendment to article 21 which dealt with freedom of religion. Defiantly, the amendment was couched in very strong terms, indeed the very terms which the Americans had earlier rejected.[67] That is, the amendment stated that:

> The equality of nations being a basic principle of the League of Nations, the High Contracting Parties agree to accord, as soon as possible, to all alien nationals of States members of the League, equal and just treatment in every respect, making no distinction in law or fact, on account of their race and nationality.

Cecil who was in the chair said that the subject 'had raised extremely serious problems within the British Empire' and he thought it would be wiser for the moment to postpone its examination. Other members agreed, and as had been expected the amendment was set aside.[68]

Hughes had been warned beforehand of what the Japanese intended. In sending Watt his appraisal of the League Covenant, he expressed alarm at Makino's proposal. Hughes told Watt that though Japan probably would not be successful it was 'insisting that open door to all nationalities shall be accepted.' Japan's action had alerted him to yet one more hazard that would have to be faced if the League Covenant were adopted. Australia would have 'no guarantee … that League will uphold us in our policy of excluding Asiatics, and if overcrowded countries represented on the League demand entrance Commonwealth and League gives decision against us, forces of League will be directed against us.'[69] Under the League, White Australia would always be in

---

[65] *Ibid.*, 9 February 1919, Vol.15, p.37.

[66] *Ibid.*, 13 February 1919, Vol.15, p.45.

It is possible that the amendment House referred to was of his own devising, and borrowing its opening line from the Declaration of Independence, it ran, 'Recognising that all men are created equal, the High Contracting Powers agree that the Executive council may consider any external grievances affecting the nationals of any of the High Contracting Powers and may make such recommendations in respect thereof as are deemed equitable.' See Miller, *My Diary*, 9 February 1919, Vol.V, p.215.

House was very pleased to think that he had convinced the Japanese that the British were the stumbling block. It had, as he congratulated himself, 'taken considerable finesse to lift the load from our shoulders and place it upon the British.' See House Diary, 13 February 1919, House Papers, Yale MS 466, Vol.15, p.46.

[67] *Ibid.*, 12 February 1919, Vol.15, p.41. The form of this amendment was first given to the Americans on 9 February 1919, See Miller, *My Diary*, 9 February 1919, Vol.V, p.195.

[68] Minutes of the Ninth Meeting of the League of Nations Commission, 13 February 1919, Link, *Wilson Papers*, Vol.55, pp.138–40.

[69] Cable, Hughes to Watt, 13 February 1919, NAA CP360/8 B1/3.

jeopardy. It was Hughes's fiercely held belief in his country's race-based identity that made him so unyielding.

The Japanese Government did not allow this reverse to deflect them from their course and directed their delegates to renew their efforts to have the principle accepted. Makino and Chinda, knowing that Hughes was the key to gaining British and American assent, met with him on 14 March and stressed that Japan only wanted recognition of the principle. Its practical application, notably on immigration, could be left for subsequent bilateral negotiations, meaning a gentleman's agreement along the lines of those already signed with the Americans and Canadians. According to the Japanese records Hughes stated that he was not personally opposed to the principle but had 'to give adequate consideration to public opinion in Australia and to Australia's position'. As a result, he would have to give the wording of any resolution 'careful thought'.[70] Hughes, in saying that he did 'not disagree with the abolition of racial discrimination', was not merely being diplomatic. That is, he could, like many other Australian political leaders, accept the equality of the races, especially the Japanese with the European. But, on the other hand, since he believed with the vast majority of Australians that different races could not mix without corrupting each other and endangering social cohesion, the acceptance of the equality of the races did not mean that Japanese should have same rights as Europeans to enter Australia. Likewise he had no objection to the Japanese excluding Europeans from their country. He did not, however, spell out his racial theory when speaking to the Japanese. He apparently left them with the impression that if the right wording could be found he might be able to accede to their wishes.

Makino and Chinda, having revised the wording of their amendment, sought another meeting with Hughes. But they could not pin him down. He appeared to be adopting once again a policy of studied avoidance. They therefore sent their proposal to Garran to be passed on to Hughes. The earlier version had been slightly modified by replacing 'agree to accord as soon as possible … equal and just treatment' with 'agree to endorse the principle of equal and just treatment to be accorded'. The major cause of Hughes's objection, namely the principle of equal treatment for individuals regardless of race, remained unchanged, and so he declined to accept it.[71] Indeed from the outset he had shown no interest either in giving the matter 'careful thought' or engaging with the Japanese in discussions about the wording.

In public statements to the press Hughes made his position clear. As reported in the *Sydney Morning Herald*, he said that 'it was impossible for the British Dominions to agree to the Japanese demand for equality of treatment towards all nationals.' It was Australia's hope 'to build up an all British population of 15,000,000 as early as possible.' This was his answer to Japan's campaign on behalf of racial equality. In an interview with the *New York Sun* he was even more blunt in closing the door against any concession to the Japanese.

> Australia cannot agree to the incorporation of the principle of equality of races in the League of Nations Covenant. Australia will not agree to the adoption of the principle of equality of

---

[70] Cable, Keishiro, Japanese Ambassador to France to Uchida, 15 March 1919, cited in Sissons, 'The Immigration Question in Australian Diplomatic Relations with Japan, 1875–1919', pp.2–3 and Shimazu, *Japan, Race and Equality,* pp.23–24.

[71] Sissons, 'The Immigration Question in Australian Diplomatic Relations with Japan, 1875–1919', pp.3–4.

races in any other form by the Peace Conference if it conflicts with our interests. We cannot deviate an inch from our expressed position in regard to the Japanese question.[72]

By this time a controversy had arisen in America over Japan's proposed amendment, and the ensuing outcry gave heart to Hughes even as it made House and Wilson much more cautious in dealing with the subject. On 14 March the Japanese Ambassador in Washington had called for American backing for the inclusion of the racial equality principle in the League Covenant. Though he had assured the Americans that Japan was content to continue the restrictions on labouring class emigrants to America and looked to future talks to resolve this problem, the very act of focusing attention on the subject stirred up a hornet's nest among political leaders from the West Coast states. Senator James Phelan, a Democrat from California, claimed experience of Japanese settlement had shown that they were unassimilable, that they used devious means to gain the best lands and that what was occurring on the Pacific slopes amounted to a Japanese invasion. Unless existing discriminatory policies were maintained the western states would be delivered, without a blow being struck, into the hands of those who, he said, had been described as the 'Huns of the East'. It was time to stand firm and cooperate with Britain and its Dominions, especially Australia and Canada, against this menace to America's domestic peace and Christian civilisation.

Phelan cabled the American Delegation in Paris, warning Wilson against allowing any declaration dealing with racial equality in the covenant and calling on him to exclude explicitly such domestic matters as immigration, naturalisation, the right to vote and marriage laws from the jurisdiction of the League. The West Coast states were united in opposing any provision which might require 'Oriental peoples' to be treated on a basis of equality with the white race. Phelan used language almost identical with that of Hughes. As for Hughes's Australia so for Phelan's America it was a 'vital question of self-preservation'. The senators from the western states publicly declared that, 'If Japan insists upon equality for her citizens in immigration that simply means that either Japan or the United States will not be a signatory to the League of Nations compact.' A number of them also sent cables to Paris endorsing Phelan's sentiments.[73] As a result of the emergence of the Japanese question, Phelan was also courting William E. Borah, a Republican Senator from Idaho who was totally opposed to America joining a world organisation.[74] Since Phelan was a member of the President's own party and had supported the creation of a League of Nations this furore over racial equality augured ill for Wilson in his efforts to secure the Senate's approval of the League Covenant.

---

[72] *SMH*, 22 March 1919 and *New York Sun*, 19 March 1919.

[73] *New York Times*, 16, 22 and 25 March 1919.

Ishii, in an interview published in the *New York Times*, 21 March 1919 tried to pour oil on troubled waters, but only served to inflame the situation further.

For examples of the messages to Wilson, see cable, Senator W.L. Jones to Ammission, Paris, 26 March 1919 and cable, Oliver Sharp, Governor of Colorado, 26 March 1919. Wilson Papers, LC mm 73046029 File VIII A. These cables are not included in Link, *Papers of Woodrow Wilson*.

[74] For the development of the Phelan-Borah relationship, see letters, Phelan to Borah, 24 March 1919 and Borah to Phelan, 24 March 1919, Borah Papers, LC mm 77013276, Box 552.

When therefore the Japanese put the new version of their amendment to House, he insisted that it should be put in the preamble, which would have the effect of depriving it of any binding force. Desperate, the Japanese acquiesced. They produced a phrase to be added to the list of the means by which the League's objective of promoting international peace and security would be accomplished, namely 'by the endorsement of the principle of equality of all nationals of states members of the League'. The references to 'race' and 'equal and just treatment' of all nationals were excised. In this form the Japanese initiative won the approval of both House and Wilson.[75]

What remained was to gain the cooperation of the Dominions. On 25 March Makino and Chinda met the Dominion leaders for this purpose. It was a difficult meeting. All the Prime Ministers found fault with the latest wording. They could not accept 'the equality of all nationals'. Even in the preamble a reference to racial equality, no matter how indirect, was seen to be a threat to their immigration, naturalisation, industrial and franchise policies. After much argument over phraseology, all parties with the exceptions of Hughes and Massey – the New Zealand Prime Minister felt obliged to follow the Australian lead – were prepared to accept a Canadian formulation which rejigged the Japanese wording to read, 'by the endorsement of the principle of the equality between nations and just treatment of their nationals'. Foreign nationals were to be entitled to 'just' but not 'equal' treatment.[76]

Hughes sensed that Makino and Chinda, in pressing for the insertion of a racial equality provision in the Covenant, were acting on strict instructions from Tokyo. Nevertheless he told Watt that though the Japanese delegates had 'modified their demands many times' he had 'stated plainly that Australia cannot agree'. Regardless of whether the British Government abandoned him or the Japanese refused to join the League, he was determined not to give way on the issue.[77] To bolster his position he looked to the West Coast of the United States. In yet another interview with an American journalist he said that he thought the people of that region shared Australia's view. The Japanese amendment, 'no matter how drafted', was unacceptable for it 'strikes at the root of a policy vital to the existence and ideals of Australia.'[78]

As the League of Nations Commission hastened to complete a final review of the covenant, the Japanese, assisted by the Canadians and the South Africans, attempted to find a way to deal with Hughes's objections. Borden and Smuts, both of whom thought Hughes's attitude unreasonable, knew that much was at stake. If the Japanese failed to obtain a satisfactory amendment they would probably not join the League and their anger would be directed against the British Empire.

---

[75] Cable, Matsui to Uchida, 25 March 1919, cited in Sissons, 'The Immigration Question in Australian Diplomatic Relations with Japan, 1875–1919', p.4.

House, mulling over the West Coast demands for protection of domestic matters from league interference, saw that Wilson was faced with a dilemma: 'a statement that the League of Nations is not to interfere in domestic affairs would please Senators from the Pacific Slope but displease Senators of pro-Irish tendencies for they would declare that it was done at the instance of the English to keep the Irish question out of the League of Nations.' See House Diary, 18 March 1919, House Papers, Yale MS 466, Vol.15, p.102.

[76] Borden Diary, 29 March 1919, General Memorandum 14, Borden Papers, LAC.

[77] Cable, Hughes to Watt, 27 March 1919, NAA A981 Japan 101, Pt.1.

[78] *New York Times*, 28 March 1919.

Hughes had become 'greatly concerned' that the White Australia policy was under siege. Shortly after the Dominion leaders' meeting with the Japanese he had learnt that the International Labour Commission, which the Plenary Conference had established in February to propose guidelines for industrial conditions, was proposing not only to bind all League of Nations members to a Labour Convention but also to insert into the League Covenant a clause requiring that member nations accord the same industrial and social conditions to foreign workers as to their own. As he explained to Watt this would mean that 'all Japanese Chinese and other Asiatics would have to (1) be admitted to all Unions and (2) enjoy same privileges under labour and factory legislation.' Since both this labour provision as well as the Japanese racial equality principle were to be incorporated in the League Covenant which was itself to be incorporated in the Peace Treaty, Hughes saw Australia 'being enmeshed in a web' from which it would be impossible to free itself. It would only be able to obtain mandates, a share of reparation and any other benefits accruing from the peace if it were willing to sacrifice the White Australia policy.

Smuts therefore found Hughes rather unresponsive to the suggestion that he reconsider the Borden formula. Pressed by Smuts, the Australian Prime Minister would only assent to it if the Japanese agreed to a declaration in the covenant excluding immigration and naturalisation from the jurisdiction of the League.[79] But the Japanese when informed of this turned it down. They feared that if this were adopted the forms of equality which they had already acquired through gentleman's agreements with the United States and Canada would become valueless. As a last resort they appealed to Lloyd George to use his good offices, but though he expressed sympathy he was not willing to challenge Hughes on a matter which might cause a breach in imperial unity.[80]

Hughes's intransigence carried the day. He had promised that if the Japanese were successful in having any resolution included in the League Covenant, 'no matter how mild and inoffensive', he would attack it in the meeting of the full conference which was to be called to approve the draft treaty and he would 'raise a storm of protest not only in the Dominions but also in the western part of the United States.' Both the Americans and the Dominions knew that these were no idle threats. Thus House told the Japanese that 'while we would agree to the pallid formula they desired, yet unless Hughes promised not to make trouble we would be against putting it in.' Smuts likewise made it clear to the Japanese that if Hughes persisted in his opposition the British Empire would have to vote against their proposal in the League of Nations Commission.[81]

Makino nevertheless felt obliged to put the watered-down preamble amendment at the final meeting of the commission on 11 April. Speaking with great dignity he saw the amendment as

---

[79] Borden Diary, 7 April 1919, General Memorandum 15, Borden Papers, LAC; *Borden Memoirs*, Vol.II, pp.925–28 and 931; cable, Hughes to Watt, 31 March 1919, NAA CP360/8 B1/3.

[80] Cables, Matsui to Uchida, April 1919, cited in Sissons, 'The Immigration Question in Australian Diplomatic Relations with Japan, 1875–1919', pp.4–5 and 7–8; Shimazu, *Japan, Race and Equality,* pp.25 and 27.

[81] House Diary, 29 March 1919, House Papers, Yale MS 466, Vol.15, pp.122–23.

House, in front of Smuts, told Makino and Chinda that the Japanese press should not blame America for the failure of the racial equality proposal, and the Japanese delegates promised 'to let their people know just where the trouble lay', namely with Hughes.

responding to the struggle of 'the oppressed nationalities' of Asia and Africa against Western imperialism. 'The wrongs of racial discrimination' were 'the subject of deep resentment on the part of a large portion of the human race.' And alluding to Japan's special concern, he added that the 'feeling of being slighted had long been a standing grievance with certain peoples.' Only Cecil offered a serious challenge to the Japanese motion.[82] Since he sympathised with the Japanese intent he found himself in an embarrassing position. As the representative of the British Empire he was caught in Hughes's net and had no choice but to take a stand against the Japanese proposal. Indeed he even used Hughes's argument that the Japanese words were either 'vague and ineffective or they were of practical significance.' If the former, then there was no point in urging their acceptance. If the latter, and repeating the point that he had made when the matter had first been raised in the February meeting of the commission, he declared that it 'opened the door to serious controversy and to interference in the domestic affairs of States.'

When Wilson, who was presiding, called for a vote, an overwhelming majority of the delegates supported the motion. Without calling for the negatives, Wilson, however, declared the motion lost since it had failed to gain unanimous support. This manoeuvre enabled the Americans to avoid having to show their hand. Wilson would have been content to see an addition to the preamble adopted. He was willing to make this modest concession to obtain Japanese consent for the inclusion of the Monroe Doctrine amendment in the covenant and to persuade them to give up Shantung. But since he knew, as House warned, that if the Japanese motion were passed 'Hughes would fight it and make an inflammatory speech in the Plenenary [sic] Session' and so stir up the Japanophobes in the West Coast states, the President let British opposition become an excuse for its defeat. In order to mollify the Japanese Wilson asserted that the decision should not be interpreted as a rejection of the principle embodied in the motion. Makino, however, was not mollified and stated that he would take up the matter again at the first opportunity.[83]

In Melbourne there were increasing doubts about the wisdom of Hughes's diplomacy. From the beginning of the conference Watt had been annoyed by Hughes's unilateral policy-making and his public statements which offended the Japanese, alienated the Americans and revealed divisions in the Empire delegation.[84] Hughes's handling of the racial equality question brought these reservations to the fore. While there was no dissent from the view that White Australia had to be kept inviolable, Watt and his chief advisers, E. L. Piesse and Professor James Murdoch,

---

[82] Cecil Diary, 11 April 1919, cited in Link, *Papers of Woodrow Wilson*, Vol.57, p.247.

Cecil complained that when the issue arose Smuts had fled and left him to speak for the Empire; 'I ... had to grapple with the Japanese as best I could, which was not very well.'

[83] Letter, Cecil to Lloyd George, 15 April 1919, Lloyd George Papers, House of Lords Record Office F/6/6/29; David Hunter Miller, *The Drafting of the Covenant*, 2 vols (New York: G.P. Putnam's Sons, 1928), Vol.I, pp.463–64 and Vol.II, pp.387–91; House Diary, 12 April 1919, Yale MS 466, Vol.15, p.151. According to House – and there is no reason to doubt his word – 'the President was for accepting' the Japanese motion and was only dissuaded from doing so by House.

[84] Cable, Watt to Hughes, 24 January 1919, NAA CP360/8 B1/3. Watt urged on Hughes the 'wisdom and necessity of communicating with Cabinet and securing its concurrence before any policy pledging Government is announced.'

feared that Hughes's egregious stand against any concession to the Japanese might prove to be counterproductive. Through reading Japanese newspapers Piesse had become aware of the public agitation over the issue of racial discrimination. Murdoch on returning from his government-sponsored intelligence mission to Japan confirmed this perception. He informed Piesse that 'this racial discrimination business is the most important issue in the country.' The agitation over the subject disturbed the whole nation. It had been 'engineered by the military party', and he believed that 'it may well become dangerous if not met properly.'[85]

Profoundly troubled by Hughes's confrontationist policy towards Japan, Piesse prepared a report in late March setting out both the gravity of the problem and the most desirable way of meeting it. He was alarmed that the pro-Western liberal tendency which Murdoch had noticed when he first arrived in Japan might give way to a new wave of jingoistic imperialism. In a memorandum to the Chief of the General Staff, Piesse contended that 'in the essential features of her polity, Japan has hitherto been a second Germany', that its foreign policy had been 'dictated by its military chiefs' and that these militarists and imperialists had sought to strengthen their position by making Japan the leader of a 'Pan-Asia' movement which was directed against Western discrimination and exploitation. These reactionary elements had seized upon popular antagonism to racial discrimination to further advance their cause. They had stirred up public resentment against the Western powers' failure to write a racial equality principle into the League Covenant.

The consequences of these developments boded ill for Australia. The anti-Western elements might prevent Japan from entering the League of Nations and, if that were to occur, 'the spectre of a race war between East and West ... looms up in the not very distant future.' In the light of this possibility, Piesse criticised the Australian Prime Minister for his uncooperative attitude in dealing with Japan. Hughes at Paris had emphasised 'the national distinctions between the Japanese and ourselves in a way that could not fail to be offensive to a high-spirited people.' In Japan the effect of Hughes's speeches had been 'most serious'. They had given ammunition to those ultra-nationalists who desired to keep Japan out of the League. As a result of Hughes's attitude it was probable that Australia would have to look to the United States to counter a Pan-Asian movement led by Japan, and American aid in such an eventuality was most uncertain.[86]

A few days later Piesse sent the Acting Prime Minister a set of proposals, prepared by Murdoch, which aimed to appease Japan by removing the most offensive aspects of Australia's

---

[85] Letter, Murdoch to Piesse, 14 March 1919, Piesse Papers, NLA MS 882/5/11.

[86] Memorandum, 'The Present Movement in Japan against Racial Discrimination', Piesse to Legge, 24 March 1919, NAA MP729/2 1877/5/152.

Captain A.W. Jose of Naval Intelligence took issue with Piesse's assessment of the Japanese threat to White Australia. He threw doubt on Piesse's reading of the Japanese press and thought his claim that Japan was seeking 'a general removal of racial discrimination' which would give it the leadership of East Asian peoples – which was not a fair summary of Piesse's position – was 'exaggerated'. He pointed out that the Chinese hostility towards Japan made it impossible for Japan to achieve such a role. In his judgment, Japan was more interested in the commercial exploitation of China than in 'the matter of racial prejudice'. Moreover he thought that the critical references to the Prime Minister were 'scarcely justified'. See Memorandum, Jose to First Naval Member, 8 May 1919, NAA MP1049/1 18/0491.

racially-based policies. Murdoch recommended that Australia should follow the Canadian and American examples and sign a treaty with Japan giving the Japanese the same rights of entry as Europeans while at the same time signing a 'Gentleman's Agreement' which, through Japan's control over the issue of passports, would ensure that only Japanese acceptable to Australia, such as merchants, students and tourists, took advantage of this formal right. He also suggested that the provision in the Australia's *Naturalisation Act* preventing Asians from becoming citizens should be deleted, and that Australia, if it could not reach a reciprocal arrangement on the matter, should repeal all legislation which excluded Asians from engaging in certain classes of employment or business.[87]

Watt was impressed by these reports. He had talked to James Murdoch after his return from Japan and had discussed these questions with Piesse against the background of Australia's post-war relations with the Pacific region. Watt was much affected by the dark picture which Piesse had painted and thought Murdoch's proposals provided 'a policy which is workable and looks acceptable',[88] and this despite the fact that the arguments which underpinned them were at odds with Hughes's views and critical of his stand at Paris. There is no question but that Watt, as a result of these discussions, continued for the remaining period of the Paris Peace Conference to be worried by Hughes's brash and uncompromising diplomacy at Paris.

The Melbourne *Herald*'s summary of an interview which Makino had given to Keith Murdoch seemed to confirm Piesse's assessment of the problem. Makino, no doubt in response to Hughes's press campaign, had summoned Murdoch to air Japan's grievance against the Australians. This 'moderate, kindly old man' had issued a 'grave warning that public opinion in Japan would hold Australia accountable for the failure to secure an amendment of the League of Nations Covenant providing for the recognition of racial equality'. Since the 'whole rising democratic feeling and pride of Japan' demanded the conference acknowledge that 'all men are born free and equal' and believed that Australia's lone opposition had defeated it, Japanese-Australian relations would be 'seriously compromised'. Makino had also said that Wilson had claimed Dominion opposition had made it impossible for the American delegation to assent to Japanese wishes. Wilson thus had laid the blame for Japan's humiliation at Australia's door. The following day the Melbourne *Argus* reported that the Japanese press in an outburst against the rejection of a racial equality declaration in the covenant were blaming Hughes for this snub and demanding that Japan should turn its back on the League and 'create her own Monroe doctrine in the Orient'.[89]

The Acting Prime Minister conveyed his misgivings to Hughes. Makino's warning that Japan held Australia responsible for the rejection of the racial equality principle was, as he wrote Hughes, 'clearly most unfortunate'. Watt continued that:

> Recent comments in Japanese papers, which I have been closely following for months, are couched in a tone which bodes no good to Australia. All information which I have indicates

---

[87] Copy of 'Discrimination against Asians – Notes for an Australian Policy', 27 March 1919, Piesse Papers NLA MS 882/2/118–31.
[88] Letters, Piesse to Watt, 27 March 1919 and Watt to Piesse, 31 March 1919, NAA A3934/1 SC12/6.
[89] Melbourne *Herald*, 10 and 14 April 1919 and *Argus*, 15 April 1919.

growing irritation in Japan against Australia's reaffirmation of its principles. This is obviously being fanned by Japanese Military Party, whose power has been rapidly declining. Nothing so calculated, however, to revive it as this atmosphere of irritation.

Watt was shaken up by the picture painted by Piesse, the two Murdochs and press reports. Thus he told Hughes that 'Generally situation surrounding relations between Japan and Australia appear to be assuming new and dangerous features', and he advised him that 'public activities or utterances calculated to specially inflame Japanese feeling against Australia ought to be moderated or eliminated.' In summing up, he requested Hughes to send cabinet his views 'on the whole question'.[90]

Replying to this implied criticism Hughes denied that there was any cause for alarm and blamed the Americans for all the trouble with the Japanese. While he shared Watt's view about the danger to Australian-Japanese relations, he claimed to have solved the problem by explaining his position to the Japanese press. In this interview with a representative of the *Asahi Shimbun* he derided, without naming them, the Americans who had opposed the Japanese racial equality amendment in the League of Nations Commission while simultaneously posing as the friends of Japan. They spoke 'with forked tongues'. Thus he not too subtly accused the Americans of deception and asserted that they were equally responsible for the defeat of the racial equality motion. He crudely flattered the Japanese, saying that they were 'a very keen and wise people' who would not be taken in by 'insidious rumours'. The Japanese standing at the Peace Conference showed that the world accepted them 'on a footing of equality with the other nations'. Giving White Australia a more acceptable gloss he said that the racial equality amendment could not be accepted because it 'would vitally affect Australia's industrial welfare.' He readily admitted that the Japanese were Australians' equals 'before the bar of the world', but insisted that it did not follow that one should invite everyone whom one considered one's equal into one's house.

Hughes, without attempting in any way to weigh the evidence, asserted that his words had convinced the Japanese. His interview had 'greatly pleased the Japanese here.' They preferred a 'straight-out opponent to those who promised support or led them to believe they would support.' Makino's eyes had been 'opened to that truth'. The implication was that Australia would not suffer from a Japanese backlash as a result of the manner of his defence of White Australia. He concluded with the simple reassurance, 'Do not worry.'[91] Watt's words in no wise affected Hughes's treatment of the Japanese. His flimsy self-serving argument failed to placate the Japanese while at the same time further alienating the Americans.[92]

As the treaty-making moved into its final phase, Hughes had to contend with proposals for including the racial equality principle in the Labour Charter as well as the Preamble to the League

---

[90] Cable, Watt to Hughes, 15 April 1919, NAA CP 360/8 B1/4.

[91] Cable, Hughes to Watt, sent 17 April and received 26 April 1919, NAA CP360/8 B1/4.

For Murdoch's summary of Hughes's statement to a representative of the *Asahi Shimbun*, see Melbourne *Herald*, 17 and 19 April 1919, and for the full report of the interview, see the *Japan Advertiser*, 25 April 1919.

[92] Cable, House to Frank Lyon Polk, State Department, Washington DC, 21 April 1919, containing House's response to Hughes's attack on the American delegation, cited in Link, *Papers of Woodrow Wilson*, Vol.57, pp.570–71.

Covenant, and he resisted to the last all attempts at conciliation. Hughes was unhappy with the Labour Charter which the Labour Commission wanted embodied in the covenant. He especially objected to Point Eight which required members of the League to accord equality of status and treatment to foreign workers. If this remained in the covenant Hughes averred Australia would not sign it.[93] Borden and Smuts, whose own countries' laws were as discriminatory as Australia's, took a similarly hard line on this provision.[94] The three Dominion leaders were also fearful that Japan might take advantage of the exceptions which allowed less industrialised countries to delay giving effect to the charter's conditions and so expose their economies to unfair competition.

In order to meet the Dominions' difficulties Balfour drafted a new version of the charter and this became the basis for that incorporated in the Covenant. The rephrased charter, instead of containing mandatory obligations, merely set down 'methods and principles which all industrial countries should endeavour to apply, so far as their special circumstances will permit'. More importantly it emasculated Point Eight so that the members of the League were only required to 'have due regard to the equitable treatment of all workers lawfully resident' in their countries. Hughes was quite satisfied with this solution and left Borden and Balfour to settle the matter behind closed doors.[95] In this case Hughes's hostility to the principle of racial equality did not receive public exposure.

Under pressure from Tokyo the Japanese renewed their efforts to have the racial equality clause added to the covenant's preamble. Having been defeated in the League of Nations Commission they were intent on putting their case to the Plenary Conference when they were asked to approve the final version of the Peace Treaty. Hughes, despite the warnings from Melbourne, stood his ground. He would only accept the Borden formula if the Japanese would agree to an amendment to the Covenant naming immigration and naturalisation as domestic matters outside the jurisdiction of the League – a proposal that the Japanese had already rejected. On the morning of 28 April the BED was informed that Makino intended to make a declaration setting out the events which had led to the failure to include the racial equality principle in the Peace Treaty. Hughes, fearing that the finger might be pointed at him, made it known that he might be obliged to respond. It was an awkward moment. Smuts, anticipating Hughes's likely response to this news, had advised the Japanese that if their declaration was 'provocative' the Dominions might have to reply.[96] That afternoon Makino made a measured speech in which he set out the Japanese case and reaffirmed their determination 'to continue in their insistence for the adoption of this principle by the League in the future.' The Japanese had again given notice that this was not the end of their campaign. Hughes, however, had won the day and was content to let the matter pass.[97]

---

[93] Minutes of BED (17), 3 April 1919, TNA: PRO CAB 29/28.
[94] *Ibid.* (18), 8 April 1919.
[95] *Ibid.* (24), 17 April 1919; James T. Shotwell (ed.), *The Origins of the International Labor Organisation*, 2 vols (New York: MacMillan, 1934), Vol.I, pp.199–220 and Vol.II, pp.368–78; Borden, *Memoirs,* Vol.II, pp.933–43.
[96] Minutes of BED Meeting (29), 28 April 1919, TNA: PRO CAB 29/28.
[97] *FRUS*, 'PPC, 1919', Vol.III, pp.289–91.

Despite Hughes's assurances, Watt was still worried that Japan would continue to vent its resentment against Australia. Further reports from Paris appearing in the Melbourne *Herald* fed this anxiety. Keith Murdoch reported that the Japanese delegates, in their endeavours to find a compromise, 'profess(ed) the utmost mortification … that Hughes had refused to talk to them.' Watt therefore took the opportunity on the occasion of an Empire Day speech to lecture his fellow Australians about the new attitude they should adopt towards their wartime ally. Speaking 'as a man in the full responsibilities of his office' he maintained that even though Japan before the war had been regarded as 'an utterly inferior race' and that 'this prejudice' still existed in certain parts of the country, Australians 'should cherish the friendship of Japan.' During the war Japan had 'stood by our side as the lonely sentinel in the Pacific, guarding our boys while they were going across the oceans … and even guarding Australia itself.' [98] The burden of his message was that Australia could not afford gratuitously to antagonise Japan.

Hughes's blocking of Japan's desire to include racial equality in some form in the League Covenant was, as Watt, Piesse and James Murdoch understood, unnecessarily provocative. His stand, instead of protecting White Australia, had endangered it.

There were no good grounds for Hughes's rejection of Borden's 'pallid formula' on racial equality. Japan had accepted it even though it did not provide specifically for racial equality. The words, vague as they were – that is they only suggested that member nations seek to treat nationals of other members justly – were only to appear in the preamble to the League Covenant. They were not to be part of the covenant itself and therefore, Japan, even if it sought to use the phrase to attack the White Australia policy, would not be able to base their argument on commitments made by members of the League. More substantially, it was inconceivable that the British and American Governments would allow Japan to use the League to interfere with the racially-discriminating policies of Australia or the other Dominions. For the British, should they do so, it would mean the end of the Empire; and for the Americans, Japan's actions would be seen by analogy to be directed at their western states.

Smuts and Borden, who were as aware as Hughes of the domestic political implications inherent in the subject, were convinced that this amendment to the preamble would not adversely affect their countries' racial policies. Borden in justifying the amendment to his government in Ottawa put the case quite well:

> As Japan is already recognised as one of the Great Powers and as each nation already acts upon the principle of what it conceives to be just treatment the proposed amendment does not seem to alter existing conditions. Immigration and Naturalisation are regarded under international law as matters of domestic concern and the new draft of Covenant contains a clause providing that League of Nations shall not interfere in matters of domestic concern. Further the position of Great Britain and the United States as the most important Powers on League of Nations Council and the fact that no action can be taken except by unanimous

---

[98] *Argus*, 24 May 1919 and *SMH*, 24 May 1919.

consent seems to remove absolutely any danger of attempted interference by the League with these domestic questions.[99]

Hughes's willingness to stand alone against the rest of the delegates at the conference was a reflection of his need to have absolute barriers against the dangers that beset Australia and the Empire. His answer to Makino's assurance that the Japanese proposal was a matter of principle which was not meant to have any practical effects had all the marks of this style. He argued that it must have practical effects or there would be no point in pressing the matter. The Japanese tenacious pursuit of the cause, even in its limited form, was itself evidence of a sinister intent. Hughes had no appreciation of the national sensitivities which lay behind the Japanese initiative. There was no subtlety in his response to the question. Heedless of the considerations that Borden had advanced to show that the final formula raised no difficulties for the Dominions' domestic policies, Hughes would only accept it if the Japanese would agree to an amendment of the covenant explicitly excluding immigration and naturalisation from the jurisdiction of the League. That the Japanese refused to concede this point was for him further evidence of their ulterior motives. Underlying these Japanese efforts was a dastardly plot aimed at overthrowing White Australia. Hughes was alone in placing this interpretation on Japanese efforts to secure recognition of the racial equality principle. The Canadians and Americans, as a result of their experience of Japan's administration of the 'Gentleman's Agreements', were satisfied that Japan had no desire to overturn their immigration policies.

The consequence of Hughes's stand was, as James Murdoch and Piesse observed, to provide ammunition for Japanese imperialists and militarists who wanted nothing to do with a Western-dominated League of Nations and instead hoped to lead a Pan-Asian movement to oust the Europeans and Americans from the region.[100] Furthermore, since Hughes was responsible for preventing the racial equality principle from being included in the covenant, much of Japanese hostility was directed against Australia. It was totally consistent with Hughes's overweening self-confidence that he should think a few words to a Japanese journalist in which he pointed the finger at America, could deflect Japanese anger from Melbourne to Washington. His assertions lacked the most superficial credibility. Wilson was quite willing to accept the Borden formula as an amendment to the preamble. Only Hughes's threat that he would make inflammatory speeches in the western states caused Wilson to withdraw his support.

In an interview which the Japanese Prime Minister had granted Adam McCay, a journalist whom the Melbourne *Herald* and *Sun* had sent to Japan in May, Takashi Hara used the understated language of Japanese diplomacy to deplore Hughes's role in the rejection of the racial equality principle:

> Japan was disappointed at the attitude adopted by the Australian representative on the subject of racial discrimination. We had expected that the resolution would be easily passed through the Conference, and I think that the opposition must have been due to a misunderstanding of

---

[99] Cable, Borden to Acting Prime Minister Sir Thomas White, 15 April 1919, Link, *Papers of Woodrow Wilson*, Vol.57, p.573.

[100] For the backlash in Japan against the Peace Conference's rejection of the racial equality principle and the focus on Hughes's role, see Shimazu, *Japan, Race and Equality*, pp.46–66.

Japan's desires … Japan was free from motives of territorial expansion and other objectives and merely desired the assertion of an inalienable principle.[101]

Hughes's attitude towards the racial equality principle, as towards the issue of the Pacific islands, was counterproductive. Both the positions he took and the manner in which he prosecuted them did nothing to help the very objectives which, he claimed, underpinned his policies. Contrariwise his attitude caused Japan to become more suspicious of the West and antagonistic towards Australia. It fuelled the fires of the forces most inimical to the League and caused the Japanese to see Australia as the chief obstacle standing between them and their aim of achieving equality with the West.

Nevertheless this ultramontane stand against any concession probably did not harm him politically at home. His underlying justification was at one with that of nearly all political leaders since the end of the nineteenth century in defining Australia and adopting the 'White Australia' immigration policy. The great majority of Australians, unlike Piesse and James Murdoch, were not aware of the precise form of the Japanese delegates' proposals and their willingness to accept a symbolic statement of the equality of nationals in the preface to the League Covenant. Rather they were easily swayed into seeing the issue in Hughes's terms and thus to view the Japanese actions as a threat to the racial principles underpinning their society. In backing Hughes the Melbourne *Argus* reaffirmed these principles. The cause of Australians' antipathy to non-white migration was 'deeper and more instinctive' than mere fear of labour competition and the lowering of standards of living for the working class. The leader writer proclaimed that:

> The East and the West are too far apart in tradition in ethos or ethical tone and way of feeling, in religion and social instinct, in all the elements which really go to make up what is called civilisation … The intimacy and the meeting, the mixing and the mingling of two differing civilisations means demoralisation; means social, ethical and religious decadence.[102]

Reparations and the repression of Germany

'Reparations' was probably the most contentious issue at the Peace Conference. From the moment that Lloyd George, on 22 January, proposed to the Council of Ten that a commission be set up to look into the question, the lines were drawn.

The British Prime Minister, wishing to push on with the work that the Inter-Allied Council had begun, moved that a commission on reparations and indemnity be established to examine what the enemy countries ought to pay; what they were capable of paying and the method and form that such payments ought to take; and the guarantees which would be required. Lloyd George, as a result of the Imperial War Cabinet's instructions, had conjoined 'indemnity' with 'reparation' as the objective which should define Germany's liability. Woodrow Wilson immediately challenged the word 'indemnity'. He was aware that Hughes had had 'indemnity' included alongside 'reparation' at the time the Inter-Allied Council was establishing its commission. This word symbolised all that was wrong with the old world 'power politics' which

---

[101] Melbourne *Herald*, 3 June 1919.
[102] *Argus*, 19 April 1919.

his Fourteen Points were intended to transcend and he was determined not to let the 'pestiferous varmint'[103] who was the standard bearer for all those opposed to America's new diplomacy have his way. Lloyd George agreed to omit the word, but in order to keep faith with his colleagues only on the condition that 'reparation' was 'taken in its widest terms'.[104]

Three days later the Second Plenary conference approved the appointment of the commission's members; there were to be no more than three from each of the five Great Powers and two representatives each from Belgium, Greece, Poland, Rumania and Serbia. Following the recommendations of the BED Committee Hughes and Cunliffe with Lord Sumner, an eminent British jurist who specialised in commercial law, were chosen to represent the British Empire. Louis-Lucien Klotz, the French Finance Minister, was elected chairman and Hughes, as the senior member of the British team, was made one of the two vice-chairmen. To organise their work they appointed three subcommittees, the first chaired by Sumner to investigate the sum that the enemy powers should pay, the second chaired by Cunliffe to inquire into Germany's capacity to pay and the third, chaired by Hughes, to consider the means by which Germany should be compelled to carry out its obligations. But as soon as the commission settled down to business it was evident that there was a great gulf between the views of the Americans and the British who were supported by the French, the Japanese and, at least initially, by nearly all the other representatives.

The United States position as expounded by their legal adviser, John Foster Dulles, was a narrow legal one. It had Wilson's full approval. In short the Americans argued that the Germans were only liable for costs prescribed in the armistice contract and for damages arising out of violations of international law. This meant according to Dulles that Germany was responsible for all Belgium's war costs, for restoring the occupied areas of France and Belgium and for compensating the civilian populations for all damage to property and person 'caused directly by German military operations'. In judging whether Germany was responsible to make reparations it was 'not enough that an act be immoral, that it be cruel, that it be unjust, unless at the same time it is illegal.'[105]

Hughes drew up and defended the British case before the commission. He adapted the arguments in the Imperial War Cabinet's report to the new forum. Taking the very grounds that the Americans had chosen, he declared that the tax burden which the Allies had to bear as a result of fighting the war was 'as much damage to the civilian populations as was the cost of property damage' and therefore legally a cost that should be sheeted home to the Germans. But he was not content to leave the matter there. Even more, justice – a vaunted principle of the Wilsonian peace – demanded that Germany, the aggressor, should pay the full cost of the war. Nothing less. 'Reparation' should not be construed as a legally technical word. Hughes cited Wilson's speeches for his purpose. In particular he stressed Wilson's assertion that 'the final settlement must be

---

[103] Stephen Bonsal, *Suitors and Suppliants: The Little Nations at Versailles* (Port Washington, New York: Prentice-Hall, 1946), p.229.

[104] Secretary's Notes of a Conversation held in M. Pichon's Room at the Quai d'Orsay, 22 January 1919, *FRUS*, 'PPC, 1919', Vol.III, p.682.

See also for the American version in which it is recorded that Lloyd George agreed to accept 'the one word "reparation" provided that this included "restitution"', *ibid.*, Vol.III, p.690.

[105] Burnett, Vol.I, pp.21–23 and Vol.II, pp.302–07 and 310.

based upon the essential justice of the particular case' so as to bring a 'peace that is permanent'. It was transparently unjust that the Allies should be left to shoulder the costs of the war, for in that case the aggressor would emerge from the war better off than those who had given their blood and treasure to defend its victims. It would be wrong 'to let the arch criminals go free'. It would 'make the coming League of Nations a subject for mockery and derision for those who plotted wars hereafter.' Whether one relied on law or justice the conclusion was the same, namely that the Allies were 'entitled to reparation for the full cost of the war'.[106] It is noticeable that while the American case had rested on legalism, Hughes had additionally appealed to broad principles of international justice and order. Both sides acted out of a moral expediency, ignoring the economic, political and moral complexities of the problem and selecting their arguments to serve their self-righteous ideologies.

It was quickly apparent that the American and British approaches to reparations were irreconcilable. In the commission and its subcommittees this conflict blocked progress. Hughes was determined that the Americans should not be able to deny the Allies the full cost of the war, and he confided to Philip Kerr that 'if he could not get the unanimous report he wanted, he would get a majority report!!'[107] On 19 February, Dulles, however, in an effort to avert a vote being taken on the principles which would govern the bill to be presented to the Germans, suggested that the authors of the armistice terms – that is the American, British, French and Italian leaders – should be asked for guidance about the meaning of reparations.[108]

Hughes's expectation that the British Empire would be engaged in a broad-ranging struggle with the Americans over the peace was being realised. He was highly indignant at the American stand. As he told Watt, the American attitude fully justified his earlier criticisms of the terms of the armistice. This foolish act had 'tied a millstone round our necks'. Just as he had predicted, he found that 'At every step in Peace negotiations these accursed Fourteen Points meet us and bar our way.' Since the American members of the commission were not likely to be converted – they were 'merely there to register Wilson's opinions' – he anticipated that there would be 'a tremendous outbreak in Britain when people learn that they have been sold.'[109] Hughes believed that he, not Wilson, was the true voice of the people, and he did his best to marshal that opinion for his purposes. He pressed Watt to have cabinet give their support and to obtain resolutions in favour of indemnities from the Australian public.[110] Likewise he took every opportunity to spread his message through interviews with the British, American and French press. The *New York World* reported Hughes as saying that he intended 'to get something out of our dear brother Germany' and that Australia would share in the indemnity. *Le Matin* was loud in its praise of Hughes's approach to the problem of reparations. Citing his harsh and unforgiving views of the matter, it

---

[106] *Ibid.*, Vol.II, pp.296, 298–301 and 320–22. See also, for the full text of Hughes's reply to the American case at the Reparation Commission meeting on 14 February 1919, Bernard M. Baruch, *The Making of the Reparation and Economic Sections of the Treaty* (New York: Harper and Brothers, 1920), pp.298–315.
[107] Minute, Kerr to Lloyd George, 16 February 1919, Lloyd George Papers, House of Lords Record Office F/89/2/18.
[108] Burnett, Vol.II, pp.337–38.
[109] Cable, Hughes to Watt, 10 February 1918, NAA CP360/8 B1/3.
[110] Cable, Watt to Hughes, 13 February 1919, *ibid.*

looked to him as the statesman, 'rude, clair, irréfragable', who could bring 'le bon sens' to the discussion of the subject. [111]

The response of the United States to the confrontation with the British was equally unyielding. On 19 February the American members of the commission sent a radiogram to Wilson, who was aboard the *George Washington* returning home for a brief visit. In it they set out the difficulties they were having with the British claims for the full cost of the war. They summarised Hughes's appeal to 'general principles of justice enunciated in other portions of your address[es] and which are likewise to be considered as forming part of the terms of peace.' They themselves were willing to be as liberal as possible in applying the American principles since 'our opponents make a strong popular argument difficult to answer without appearing to be bound by legal technicalities.' It was clear that the other nations' representatives were bound by political commitments which 'all our inquiries show the people of the Allied countries feel to be just and their due.' Nevertheless the Americans considered that the inclusion of war costs would 'open the way to a complete departure from the agreed terms of peace based on the Fourteen Points and subsequent addresses.'

Wilson in reply conceded nothing. The war cost could not be included. He who had so unwillingly accepted the Anglo-French reservations now declared that, 'The time to think about this was before the conditions of peace were communicated to the enemy.' The American delegation in rejecting the British proposal were, if necessary, to express their dissent publicly and, in doing so, should argue 'not on the intrinsic justice of it' but rather on what the enemy had been led to expect. Wilson in taking this narrow legal position was thereby admitting that his Fourteen Points, at least in this respect, were not based on the idea of justice which he had consistently declared underpinned the new world order. Hughes had hoisted him on his own petard. In threatening to go public Wilson was overlooking the commissioners' advice that the people of the Allied countries believed Germany should pay the full cost of the war. It was all too hard for the President, and his answer showed up once again the superficial nature of his liberal peace principles.[112]

Lloyd George too had learnt that the Reparation Commission had reached an impasse. Hughes, like his American counterparts, sought advice from the head of his delegation. He explained to Lloyd George that the Americans would not allow war costs under the heading of reparations and that as a result the countries which would gain most from the American formula, such as Belgium, were becoming cool towards the British position. They had come to see that, if Germany did not have the capacity to pay the full costs and the total figure was divided up on a percentage basis, their share of whatever compensation could be exacted would be severely reduced. To overcome this difficulty, Sumner and Cunliffe, to Hughes's dismay, had proposed that, without giving up the demand for war costs, certain claims might be given priority. The British Prime Minister saw clearly that if the Americans prevailed the British Empire would receive little since 'there may be nothing left with which to pay indemnity.' Thus his immediate

---

[111] *SMH*, 23 January 1919; *Le Matin*, 9 February 1919.
[112] Radiogram, Lansing, House, Baruch, Davis and McCormick to Wilson, 19 February 1919 and radiogram, Wilson to Lansing, 23 February 1919, Link, *Papers of Woodrow Wilson*, Vol.53, pp.219–20 and 231.

response was to steel Hughes's resolve, telling him that the British representatives on the commission should hold out for the cost of the war and insist on proportional, not priority, payments. Lloyd George's rationale, however, was not Hughes's.[113] The British leader did not seek this full-blooded indemnity in order to crush or punish Germany or even to restore the British Empire's global pre-eminence. Rather it was an expedient tactic intended to appease the British press and parliament and to ensure that the British Empire received the maximum possible share of what Germany ultimately might pay.

A few days later, Hankey aired his disquiet about the Reparation Commission in a letter to Lloyd George. Like House, Hankey had a keen nose for emerging problems and a well-honed talent for seeking practical solutions. As he reported it, the whole process was bogged down. In Sumner's subcommittee the British and the Americans were equally 'obdurate' in respectively advocating and rejecting war costs. Cunliffe's subcommittee was having similar problems in trying to estimate Germany's capacity to pay. Private sources had told him that Cunliffe favoured a sum of £25,000 million – which was, not surprisingly, equal to Hughes's Imperial War Cabinet committee's estimate of the cost of the war – while it seemed that the Americans and the Treasury thought £4000 million a more reasonable figure. Cunliffe's estimate, according to Hankey's informant, was not arrived at 'on any particularly scientific basis but one drawn rather by that peculiar instinct on which … high financial authorities in the City often work.' What impressed him above all was, however, that the British and American members of the commission 'do not work together at all, and are unsympathetic to one another.' He considered that Lloyd George would 'before long' have to take up this matter with Colonel House, who during Wilson's absence represented America on the Council of Ten, 'with a view to some agreement on broad lines'. Since it was unlikely that a 'scientific' determination could be reached either on the amount of damages or Germany's ability to pay he presumed that it would be necessary to resort to a 'rough and ready method' and so 'to close on a lump sum', part of which would be paid immediately and the rest over a period of years.[114]

Stirred into action by Hankey's warning, Lloyd George invited Hughes and the other two British Commissioners to come to London to discuss the situation with the British Cabinet.[115] Lloyd George was compelled to give his mind to the problem in all its ramifications. At the cabinet meeting he canvassed every side of the question. What he sought was to find the best way, within all the limiting conditions, to maximise the amount of reparations which the British Empire could obtain. He recognised that it was not practical to demand too great a sum from

---

[113] Letters, Hughes to Hankey, 15 February 1919 and Lloyd George to Kerr, 16 February 1919, Lloyd George Papers, House of Lords Record Office F/89/2/18.

Hughes's approach to Lloyd George was probably instigated by a letter from Sumner in which he said that he and Cunliffe were of the opinion that failure to give way on priority claims for 'specific and material damage' would 'do us considerable harm', and that while Hughes might say that he had instructions to refuse such concessions, Sumner and Cunliffe had no similar instructions. See letter, Sumner to Hughes, 15 February 1919, Hughes Papers, NLA MS 1538/24/35.

[114] Letter, Hankey to Lloyd George, 21 February 1919, Lloyd George Papers, House of Lords Record Office F/23/4/19.

[115] Letter, Lloyd George to Hughes, 24 February 1919, *ibid.*, F/28/3/5.

Germany. If the Americans would not accept the figure which the British put on the table the Germans would be encouraged to resist, and it was impractical to think of renewing the war to enforce an unreal claim on the enemy. With Hughes's earlier advice in mind, about a post-war struggle with America for mercantile supremacy, Lloyd George was determined that Britain, in addition to being recompensed for £800 million worth of damage, should recoup, if possible, the £1000 million owed to the United States and the $900 million in securities and bullion which they had forfeited to America in payment for war goods. He did not seem to have much confidence that the debts owed to Britain by its European allies would be repaid.

The problem of the war debt and its potential effect on Britain's economic recovery hung over the meeting. Lloyd George's preferred way forward was to establish what Germany could reasonably pay, to commit the Americans to that sum and to find means by which it could be extracted from Germany without undue delay. He was very sceptical about binding Germany to pay tribute to the Allies for longer than ten years. Likewise he did not want to grant Belgium and France a priority of payment, for if this were allowed he feared that Britain might in the end receive nothing. Thus he thought they should endeavour to reach a private agreement with the French which would, in allocating shares of the spoil, take into account the destruction caused by the invasion of their territory.

While Sumner and Cunliffe did to some degree appreciate Lloyd George's analysis of the problem, Hughes refused to give any ground. For him the British Empire's only path to salvation lay in being able to claim the cost of the war. If the Supreme War Council leaders accepted that in signing the armistice they had given up their claims to full compensation for war losses, 'Britain and the Empire would get little or nothing.' It was clear that he wanted Lloyd George to force the issue with Wilson and, with the aid of the French, try to persuade the Americans to yield the point. If no other way was open, the British victory over the Americans should be a triumph of the will. Though most of Lloyd George's colleagues seemed to see merit in his arguments they were reluctant to overturn the Imperial War Cabinet instructions to the British delegation, and so Hughes won the day. [116]

It was, however, a hollow victory. Hughes's doctrine of will power was not a sustainable one. By early March, Hankey and Kerr seemed to have concluded that the question of reparations should be taken out of the hands of the commission, that the British should no longer press for war costs and that the British Prime Minister and House should negotiate a lump sum. To this end Kerr set out in a Minute for Lloyd George the implications of reparations policy for Britain's future prosperity. In particular he urged that before a fixed figure was accepted the British should know what share of reparations they would be entitled to and what the Americans proposed to do about Allied debts.

The connection between reparations and inter-allied debt had been in the background during all the discussions of reparations and indemnity. For the British the war debt owed to America was a crucial consideration. As Kerr observed:

> The Americans are expecting us to pay them an indemnity of a thousand to fifteen hundred million [pounds] in the shape of the repayment of loans which they made to us during the

---

[116] Minutes of British War Cabinet Meeting (536), 25 February 1919, TNA: PRO CAB23/9.

first three years of the war. They have not said one word as yet about reducing the figure of that indemnity on the ground that it is bound to cripple us in the work of reconstruction … On the other hand they say to us that we are not entitled to ask Germany to indemnify us for what she practically came and took from us through her aggression, on the ground that it would be crippling to the German people. I see no reason why, if we are to be expected to pay interest and sinking fund to America for the next fifty years, Germany should not be required to pay us interest and sinking fund on her debt for the next fifty or sixty years … I should like therefore before finally determining what we are going to ask of Germany to put it to the Americans that if there is to be a diminution of indemnity in the one case there must be a diminution in the other. They cannot possibly expect us to let off our German debtor – to say nothing of our French, Italian and Russian debtors – unless we are equally liberated on the other side.

For this purpose he also recommended that Lloyd George should without further ado 'take the matter up with House'.[117]

Almost from the moment the armistice had been signed British officials had been informally sounding out their American counterparts about sharing the costs of the war or cancelling all war debts – that is those owed by France, Italy and Russia and the lesser allies to Britain – and those owed by Britain and France to the United States. In return the British had intimated that they would not demand war costs from Germany but would settle for a more reasonable sum. Wilson, however, was unalterably opposed to these proposals. He had instructed American officials that the issue of Allied debts was not to be brought into the negotiations over reparations. At the time the Reparation Commission was being set up he told Vance McCormick, one of the American Commissioners, that 'the Allies want to pool the total expense of the war and have us pay our proportionate share.' This was 'not to be considered'. The President was 'considerably exercised over this proposal', and he directed McCormick to inform the other American advisers and experts that 'we were to confine ourselves only to our own [and] Allied financial or other problems in which the enemy countries are involved, thereby keeping clear of embarrassing discussions which have nothing to do with Germany.'[118]

---

[117] Minute, Kerr to Lloyd George, 2 March 1919, Lloyd George Papers, House of Lords Record Office F/89/2/37.

[118] Diary of Vance Criswell McCormick, 21 January 1919, Link, *Papers of Woodrow Wilson,* Vol.54, p.196. See also cable, American Secretary of the Treasury, Carter Glass to Wilson, 19 December 1918 and cable, Wilson to Carter Glass, 23 December 1918 in which Wilson assures Glass that 'There can be no proper basis for a discussion of our foreign loans in connection with the Peace Conference', *ibid.*, Vol.53, pp.441–42 and 472–73.

Though the Americans were unshakeable in their refusal to allow war debts to be included in the discussion of the amount of reparations, the British hoped right to the end that the two might in some way be connected. As late as 23 April Lloyd George sent Wilson a proposal drawn up by Keynes which had that intent, but as with all earlier schemes the Americans rejected it. Keynes estimated that if all inter-allied war debts were cancelled then, at least on paper, the Americans would forego £1688 million net owed to them, the British would lose £651 million net and all the other Allies would lose relatively little or nothing at all. See Dan P. Silverman, *Reconstructing Europe after the Great War* (Cambridge, Mass: Harvard University

Returning to America at the end of February he explained to his cabinet that the British and French had pressed to have 'the cost of the war borne equally by all engaged', and that this was out of the question for to do so 'Would mean that this country would renounce all British, French & Italian debts & then some.' He had cleverly 'fenced to keep this direct proposition from coming to a head.' For a President whose boast it was that America had, unlike the European belligerents, entered the war to serve mankind and to create a peace based on just principles this pride in rejecting proposals that might not only assist the recovery of those nations who had borne the major burden of the struggle but also help resolve the vexed question of reparations and revive the international economic system might seem surprising. Certainly there were strong domestic reasons for his stand. Any concessions over debts would have faced overwhelming difficulties in Congress and put America's acceptance of the League of Nations at risk. On the other hand, nowhere did Wilson express regret for being so constrained. Indeed nowhere did he ever explain his attitude in these terms. He never even hinted that for the greater good of achieving the League of Nations he was forced to rule out a financial arrangement which in its essence was just and would best serve the peace of the world.

Lloyd George may have taken Kerr's concerns to House when he met him on 7 March, but whether he did or not it is clear that the British leader never seriously tried to push the argument. He recognised that the Americans in negotiating reparations would agree neither to bring Allied war loans into the discussion nor to accept the costs of the war as the basis of Germany's liability. From this time he saw that the British Empire's primary interest was to obtain as large a portion as possible of whatever Germany in the end would be required to pay.

At a BED meeting on 13 March when Hughes raised the subject of the 'deadlock' on the Reparation Commission and asked for guidance on the principles to be applied in establishing the amount Germany should have to pay, Lloyd George revealed the new direction that he was taking in talking to House and Clemenceau. As he had earlier intimated, Lloyd George's approach was governed not by abstract principles but practical outcomes. His fundamental concern was that if Belgian and French claims were to have priority 'he would not give the British claim much hope.' This was the first question that had to be settled. In talks with Clemenceau it had been suggested that France should receive 50 percent, Britain 33 percent and Belgium 17 percent of the sum for which Germany was liable. In order to increase the British share he had been advocating that the capitalised cost of pensions should be included in the total amount of reparations. House had agreed to his distribution formula and had indicated that, provided war costs as such were not included, America would 'stand aside' in the argument over what categories of damages went into the final bill. Lloyd George was against the amount of reparations being so great 'as to induce the Germans to throw up their hands and invite the Allies to take over the administration of their country.'

Hughes was aghast. It seemed that all he had striven for, all his previous victories in the Imperial War Cabinet were to go for nought. Undoubtedly he had sought the BED's view in order to strengthen his hand in dealing with the waverers on the British team and in the commission

---

Press, 1982), p.33 and Elizabeth Johnson (ed.), *Collected Writings of John Maynard Keynes*, Vol.XVI, 'Activities 1914–1919: The Treasury and Versailles', p.421.

itself. Lloyd George's change of course had left him isolated. He might protest that 'in waving our right to demand from Germany the cost of the war, we should place ourselves under a great disadvantage financially, economically and politically', but not one other voice was raised in support of his view.[119] The writing was on the wall. Another betrayal was at hand. Another cause was lost.

From this time Hughes was bypassed. The commission's subcommittees continued to meet and eventually produced inconclusive or nugatory reports. After the American President's return to Paris on 14 March the settlement of the reparations question slowly emerged out of negotiations between Lloyd George, Wilson and Clemenceau, and occasionally Orlando, and their expert advisers. Lloyd George used Sumner and Cunliffe as well as Keynes, Smuts and others, but, as in the case of the armistice, Hughes was purposely left out of the picture. The other two members of the British Reparation Commission team were to some extent malleable, and Lloyd George needed them in order to shore up his position at Westminster. By contrast, Hughes, the leader of the British Empire representatives, could not be easily managed. He had an independent status as Australian Prime Minister and a member of the BED. Moreover, given his truculent manner and propensity for stirring up trouble through the press, he would under any circumstances be a thorn in the side. Lloyd George had had many unhappy experiences dealing with Hughes.

By early April the British, Americans and French, after three weeks of intense and often confused debate, had made considerable progress. Lloyd George had abandoned the claim for the cost of the war, had offered to settle for a total reparations bill of £11,000 million and had, through the good offices of Smuts, persuaded Wilson, against the advice of his experts, to accept German liability for pensions for disabled soldiers, soldiers' widows and children. This latter addition to the categories for which Germany would be held responsible increased the British Empire's share of the total claim for compensation and therefore of whatever Germany ultimately paid to the Allies. This, from Lloyd George's point of view, was the most important aspect of the settlement. The abandoning of the cost of the war, however, carried great political risks. In response to rumours reaching London, the British press and parliament – especially the Coalition government's own supporters – were becoming agitated over the question. On 9 April, 233 unionist MPs published a letter in the *Times* calling on the leaders of the victor nations to demand from Germany nothing less than the full cost of the war.[120]

To bolster his position Lloyd George then asked the BED to approve the general direction he had been taking. At a BED meeting on 11 April Lloyd George gave a sketchy outline of his policy – and it was sketchy, if the minutes of the meeting are an accurate account of what was said. In introducing the subject he made three points. The enemy states would be required to accept that their aggression made them responsible for all loss and damage which the Allies had suffered. Since, however, their resources were not sufficient to cover the total reparations for which they were responsible, they would only have to make compensation for all damage to civilians and their property, including pensions and separation allowances. He added that he had had

---

[119] Minutes of BED Meeting (13), 13 March 1919, TNA: PRO CAB 29/28.
[120] *Times* (London), 9 April 1919. See also Lloyd George, *Truth about the Peace Treaties*, Vol.I, pp.558–64.

'considerable difficulty' in inducing the Americans to accept the 'wide' list of categories of damage. Lloyd George asserted that if this basis for a settlement were rejected they would be thrown back to where they were before the Council of Four had taken it up. They would be confronted once again with a stalemate and Wilson might well go home. In the course of the debate he stressed that if they asked for the unobtainable they would have to keep 1,500,000 men under arms for an indefinite period, and he pointedly asked whether the Dominions would be willing to provide their quota.

Hughes alone, of all the Dominion prime ministers and British ministers present, refused to give his consent to this solution to the reparations question. In contrast to the March meeting he had to face the opposition of all the other members. Over a very long meeting as he set out his case he had to fight off objections from every direction. He had learnt nothing and forgotten nothing and returned to his well-worn themes. The Fourteen Points were to blame for the difficulties in which they found themselves. They had 'truckled to the United states of America too long.' He was not at all appeased by the news that the enemy states would have to accept a theoretical responsibility for all the Allies' losses. The Germans should be presented with the Bill for the full cost of the war and be required to prove that they could not pay. No-one knew what the Germans could pay. No-one could foretell what Germany's wealth might amount to in ten or thirty years. Hughes was troubled that the British Empire, as a result of not pushing for the cost of the war, would be entitled to a lesser share of the pot than would otherwise be the case. At no point and in no way did he argue on the basis of Australia's own claims. Rather what moved him were the consequences for the future of the British Empire of accepting this lesser sum. Aware of the discontent in the Unionist ranks he feared for the repercussions in Britain and what that might mean for the future of the Empire and the world; 'Great Britain was not only the heart of the Empire, but it was the sheet anchor of the civilised world at the present time.'

Sumner and Cunliffe, having been invited by Lloyd George to the meeting, showed their new colours. They served their master well. Sumner was convinced that the interpretation of reparations under the proposed scheme was extremely liberal. Cunliffe had had another epiphany and discovered belatedly that what Germany could pay was £12,000 million rather than the £25,000 to £30,000 million he had previously estimated to be the case. In response to queries both agreed that the reparations bill would probably add up to about £11,000 million and that the British Empire's share would be twenty percent or £2200 million. Borden once again told Hughes that America could not be ignored, that the British Empire had to work with its Allies to produce a peace. He thought that unless they approved what Lloyd George proposed they might 'get nothing at all', an argument which Massey found compelling. General Botha, the South African Prime Minister, never expected such a good result as that which Lloyd George had set before them.

For domestic reasons, however, the British Prime Minister needed unanimity. He would not proceed without the assent of all. He could not afford to allow Hughes to become a rallying point for his critics in Britain. Indeed it was because of this that the meeting dragged on for so long. Hughes had to be won over. After four hours he was still recalcitrant, and Bonar Law, who had taken the chair when Lloyd George had to depart, suggested that Hankey should draft a letter for Hughes's consideration. The letter, by placing the responsibility for the abandonment of the cost of the war on Lloyd George and on his assurance that what he proposed was the best deal available, was intended to enable Hughes to consent to the scheme. But Hughes would not sign.[121] It did not meet his objections. Perhaps also the fact that Lloyd George had taken the issue out of his hands still rankled.

Instead Hughes composed his own letter in which he complained that the cost of the war was excluded and that Germany was not to pay much more than £10,000 million. Because of this he thought that he should not be asked to agree to the scheme. He could not see why Lloyd George needed his compliance since the Imperial Cabinet acted like all cabinets on a majority vote. This latter point was Hughes's sophistry at its worst. It was patently clear that the Imperial Cabinet by its very nature did not and could not act in any other way than by unanimity. At the end he, however, allowed that if no better terms could be had he would follow the lead of the British and the other Dominion prime ministers and sign the Peace Treaty.[122] It was a difficult letter for him to write. This concession was wrung from him. Yet despite his deep-seated reservations about what was proposed he understood that he could not stand apart. Irrespective of other considerations, he knew that he would be held responsible in Australia for any failure to act with the rest of the Empire. Even so he could not refrain from once again sniping at the Americans whom he blamed for his defeat.

---

[121] Minutes of BED Meeting (19A), 11 April 1919, TNA: PRO CAB 29/28.

It is worth considering whether he was encouraged to resist by his knowledge of the demand in the Coalition parties and press that Germany should be humbled and made to pay to the last penny. Certainly, four days before the BED meeting he had met with Christabel Pankhurst, the ultra-nationalist suffragette, who was in Paris lobbying Hughes to hold fast to his resolve to have a peace of annexation and indemnity. See a scribbled note on letter, Sumner to Hughes, 7 April 1919, Hughes Papers, NLA MS 1538/24/88.

Three days later after seeing Hughes she was back in London warning Lloyd George in a public address that he had to choose between 'the great patriotic majority which placed him in power, and the gang of Asquithian pacifists, pro-German money grabbers who put their pockets before their country, and Bolshevists and cranks of all sorts who compose the unpatriotic minority.' See Mitchell, *Queen Christabel*, p.277.

[122] For Hankey's draft letter, see appendix to Minutes of BED Meeting (19A), 11 April 1919, TNA: PRO CAB 29/28.

For Hughes's draft letter, which Hankey returned to him as unacceptable, see letter, Hughes to Lloyd George, 11 April 1919, Hughes Papers, NLA MS 1538/24/92. For Hankey's rejection of the draft, see letter, Hankey to Hughes, 11 April 1919, *ibid.*, 1538/24/95.

For Hughes's letter, see letter, Hughes to Lloyd George, 11 April 1919, Lloyd George Papers, House of Lords Record Office F/28/3/26. Lloyd George sent Hughes a testy reply implying that he was trying to escape the political consequences of the necessary reparation settlement. But this was not true. Hughes had never been afraid of shouldering consequences, no matter how burdensome, for what he regarded as a vital cause. There was no reason for him to think that by following the lead of the British and other Dominion prime ministers he would suffer any backlash at home either from within the National Party or from the Labor opposition. It was with great reluctance that he had fallen into line, and finally allowed political considerations to overrule his ideological commitment. That is, he could not afford not to sign the Peace Treaty and so be separated from the rest of the British Empire in resolving the war issues; too much hung on joining with the rest of the Empire in the peace settlement.

For Lloyd George's letter, see letter, Lloyd George to Hughes, 14 April 1919, Lloyd George Papers, House of Lords Record Office F/28/3/27.

> Some nations coming into the war later sought to deflect the path of peace, but he hoped we would make peace in the same spirit as that in which we made the war. Those who fought from the beginning had the right to make peace. He did not want an emasculated peace ... for which over a million Frenchmen and 60,000 Australians had died. If he was a Frenchman he would make no peace that did not prevent the danger of a recurrence of war.[123]

In reporting back to Melbourne Hughes gave a self-serving account of the dispute, and his cabinet colleagues expressed complete sympathy with his dilemma. Watt in reply expressed their grave disappointment. If Australia's war debt were not to be covered by reparations then for at least two generations the people of the Commonwealth would have 'to face taxation which will blight Australia's prosperity.' If only those European countries which had suffered direct damage from invasion were to receive reparations payments then the settlement would be 'inequitable between European Allies and the more distant peoples of the Dominions'. Should this not be recognised in the terms of the Peace Treaty they 'regretfully' felt that it would 'reflect itself on the sentiment of Empire which all through the great war had animated the Commonwealth and its people.' They understood Hughes's difficulty in responding to Lloyd George, but thought that Hughes's solution was right and unavoidable since the alternative could not be entertained. And they repeated here what they had already said at the high point of the dispute over the future of the South Pacific islands; 'Rejection might have meant a breach of relations between Britain and America and a dislocation of whole Peace settlement ... or, if Britain determined to accede to Wilson's position, virtual secession from Empire partnership.'[124] Both for sentimental and security reasons the Australian Cabinet could not contemplate the alternative to acquiescence. Watt's explication of this point might well be seen as an implied criticism of Hughes's behaviour throughout the armistice negotiations and the Peace Conference.

Hughes had no say in fashioning the reparation clauses of the Peace Treaty that were presented to the German representatives on 7 May. In the month following the BED meeting, British and American quarrels over the reparation terms, especially the question of a lump sum figure, continued. After an exhaustive and inconclusive exchange of views the leaders of the great powers took the easy way out of the impasse and agreed that all contentious matters should be handed over to a permanent Reparation Commission which would, after the treaty had been signed, determine the total bill, the amount of annual instalments and the apportionment to the various claimants. The commission was by May 1921 to compute, on the basis of the categories of damages set out in the treaty, the amount of Germany's reparation liability. These categories covered, as Lloyd George had told the BED, damages to civilians and their property, including pensions to military victims of the war and their dependants. These provisions were embodied in Articles 231–244 and the Annexes to the Peace Treaty.[125]

Shortly before the Allies presented the Germans with their peace terms Hughes, apparently ignorant of the Council of Four's decision, informed Watt that reparations had been 'fixed at

---

[123] *SMH*, 15 April 1919.
[124] Cables, Hughes to Watt, 13 and 15 April 1919, and cable, Watt to Hughes, 17 April 1919, NAA CP360/8 B1/4.
[125] Burnett, Vol.I, pp.51–60, 72–77, 99–106 and Vol.II, pp.215–42.

about 11,000 million pounds' and that the British Empire's share was to be about twenty percent and Australia's share four percent of that, all of which was to be paid 'over twenty or fifty or a million years, more or less'.[126] Australia was to receive, if it were lucky, £88 million to cover its war costs, newly estimated to be £345 million. His disillusionment was still evident, if somewhat subdued. It was expressed now not in the angry language of defiance but in the sarcastic aspersions of defeat.

Since Hughes thought that Germany had been dealt with 'far too leniently' he had no sympathy for the German protests against the reparation bill. When Garran sent a message to Hughes in London saying that the German delegation was denying responsibility for the war and therefore the Allies' claims for compensation for losses suffered in the war Hughes would brook no argument. Though Klotz, the President of the Reparation Commission, had proposed a point by point rebuttal, Hughes agreed with Garran that this would merely invite further exchanges of notes. The Allies should simply respond with 'a curt statement of the position'. It would be best to reply 'that Germany's responsibility is undoubted and that the question has been considered in all its aspects: and that the decision arrived at is final.' Garran was to let Lloyd George know his views. If, however, it was decided to go ahead with Klotz's draft, Hughes was willing that Garran should initial the document on Australia's behalf, which he did since the Allied leaders preferred Klotz's more reasoned reply.[127]

The final review of the Treaty

The German Delegation's Notes of 13 and 24 May and their detailed 'Observations on the Conditions of Peace' on 29 May caused many of the British leaders to have second thoughts about the justice and wisdom of the terms that were being offered to the defeated enemy. The treaty was the result of a complex compromise between the major allies who in this process had failed to give proper consideration to how the Germans might regard its provisions or how, should the Germans not sign, these terms might be enforced. So widespread was the unease sparked by the Germans' reaction that Lloyd George felt compelled to consult the BED in lengthy meetings on 31 May and 1 June. From different viewpoints the British and Dominion ministers pressed for revisions. For Smuts the draft treaty was unjust in that it ignored or was contrary to the Fourteen Points as they had been accepted in the armistice. Furthermore he believed that the reparations scheme was unworkable. By seizing Germany's industrial infrastructure, denuding it of capital and denying it access to raw materials the Allies 'must kill the goose which is to lay the golden eggs.' Moreover the treaty should fix a precise sum for reparations. Germany should not be asked to give a blank cheque to the Allies. The German people should know from the outset what the bill was to be. It should not be left to the Reparation Commission to decide the question at some

---

[126] Cable, Hughes to Watt, 4 May 1919, NAA CP360/8 B1/4.
[127] Cables, Garran to Hughes, 15 May 1919 and Hughes to Garran, 16 May 1919, Hughes Papers, NLA MS1538/24/232 and 251.
   For the German Note and the Allies' reply, see Burnett, Vol.II, pp.6 and 24–25.

future date. He suggested £5000 million as a possible figure.[128] Milner, Chamberlain and Churchill, as Minister for War, all shared Smuts's concern about having to maintain an army of occupation if the Germans refused to sign or if they failed to carry out its provisions.

True to himself Hughes, on the other hand, was loath to make any concession. He had been against giving up the claim to the cost of the war and was unwilling to retreat another step. He joined with his former colleagues on the Conference's Reparation Commission, Sumner and Cunliffe, in resisting any back down. Having read the German replies and Smuts's paper Hughes could still not see that the Germans had 'a leg to stand on'. As for Wilson's Fourteen Points, if the draft treaty violated them then he would expect the American President who was an author of the treaty to be the first to denounce it; 'He assumed that President Wilson would be the last man to admit any inconsistency between his points and the Draft Treaty which he proposed.' There was no evidence, apart from their own statements, that the Germans would refuse to sign the treaty as it stood, and since they belonged to 'a nation of liars' there was no reason to take their word seriously. On reparations he concluded that it would be 'most unwise to agree to any alteration'. The only change he would countenance would be a revision of Germany's eastern boundaries. He had become convinced that the treaty had erred in being too generous to the Poles. Being a believer in nationalism as the only true basis for identity and sovereignty, he considered it 'monstrous to put Germans under Polish rule'. Thus he favoured a plebiscite to determine the future of Silesia.

Lloyd George asked the BED to authorise him at the Council of Four to press for four amendments to the draft which hopefully would make the Germans more willing to sign and implement the conditions of the Peace Treaty. On its Eastern frontier Germany was to retain all territory which had a predominantly German population. Provided that it was performing its obligations under the treaty Germany might be admitted to the League of Nations at an early date. The Allied military forces would remain in Germany for as short a time as possible. The most subtle and significant of all was the 'concession' on reparations. Here Lloyd George offered two possibilities. Both were intended to place the responsibility for coming up with a precise and acceptable figure for compensation on the Germans themselves. In the first case, Germany would agree immediately to undertake the task of restoration in Belgium and Northern France and offer a fixed sum for other liabilities and, if this were satisfactory to the Allies, the nominated amount would be incorporated in the treaty. In the second, Germany would be given three months after signing the treaty to make an offer of a fixed amount for reparations, but, if it did not do so or if the Allies did not accept the offer, Germany would remain bound by the existing reparation clauses. Yet though it would appear that the Germans were under both schemes being given an opportunity to fix their obligations, their offers were subject to the Allies' agreement that what was offered was fair and reasonable. The proposal had the virtue of seeming to meet the critics in the Allies' ranks. Both those who sought a high and those who wanted a low figure could believe that it would serve their purpose, while at the same time making it more likely that the Germans would pay up, and so set at rest the awkward question of military occupation and enforcement.

---

[128] Letter, Smuts to Lloyd George, 22 May 1919, Lloyd George Papers, House of Lords Record Office F/45/9/35.

Lloyd George played up both these advantages, and was so successful that he gained the unanimous support of his colleagues. Hughes, in giving his consent, insisted that it was for these Lloyd George revisions only and not for those that the more thoroughgoing critics of the treaty had put forward.[129] Lloyd George had convinced Hughes that these amendments, if adopted, would still allow the Allies to obtain the maximum reparation – the categories of damages for which Germany was held responsible remained unchanged – while at the same time securing more willing German cooperation.

From this time Lloyd George was left to negotiate the Allies' response to the Germans along these lines. At the Council of Four, the French quickly dismissed the first alternative and the Americans returned to their original position. They wanted without further ado to fix a sum of £5000 million, a figure that the Germans themselves had offered. Learning of this, the three British members of the Conference Reparation Commission – Hughes, Cunliffe and Sumner – wrote to Lloyd George urging him to reject any fixed sum. The commission's subcommittees had been unable to decide what the total bill would add up to or how much Germany would be able to pay. It was unfair to all the victims of Germany's aggression to accept less than they were entitled to and Germany could fund. It had to be remembered also that while waiting for Germany to meet its obligations Britain would be 'paying many millions per annum for interest to the United States, to say nothing of our vast losses on the American securities which we sold.' It was their view, and especially Hughes's view, that 'Substantial concession on our part would encourage the Germans to make further demands.' Lloyd George thus joined once again with the French to oppose the American solution. The outcome was that the Germans were offered the second alternative which put off the decision about the full cost of reparations until after the treaty was signed.[130]

Hughes's demand for an indemnity to cover the cost of the war, like his demand for the annexation of the German Pacific islands, left him at the end as a voice crying in the wilderness. Even when the case was irretrievably lost he held firm. He still hoped that a very large sum would be extracted from Germany, and, regardless of whether that eventuated, he believed the enemy ought to acknowledge the full price of its war guilt. There was an awful consistency in his pursuit of what he believed to be the necessary reparation terms. He argued his case with passion. He appealed to interest and sentiment, to justice and revenge, to reason and emotion. There was a logic to his oft repeated assertions that it was unjust for Germany to emerge from the war financially stronger than the British Empire; that unless Germany paid the full bill the British race would lose its economic leadership to the United States, and so its role as the world's great civilising power and peacemaker; that Germany as the aggressor ought to be forced to pay for its crime against humanity; and that the German people should be so humbled and crippled that they could never again attempt to impose their military despotism on the world.

---

[129] Minutes of BED Meetings (33–35), 30 May and 1 June 1919, TNA: PRO CAB 29/28.
[130] Minutes of Council of Four Meetings, 2, 3, 7, 10 and 11 June 1919, *FRUS*, 'PPC, 1919', Vol.VI, pp.139–42, 155–57, 240, 265–80, 290–300 and 305–10; President Wilson's Discussion with the American Delegation, 3 June 1919, Link, *Papers of Woodrow Wilson*, Vol.60, pp.45–71; letter, Hughes, Sumner and Cunliffe to Lloyd George, 9 June 1919, Lloyd George Papers, House of Lords Record Office F/28/3/40.

But that logic was the logic derived from an adamantine nationalism. Unlike Keynes, a Cambridge 'Apostle' and member of the Bloomsbury Group who put personal friendships before abstract identities such as nationalism,[131] Hughes subordinated all other considerations to the security of the British race. Since all wars were struggles for the nation's survival or supremacy, the victor's task was to crush the enemy. Any generosity shown to the enemy would be seen as weakness. Any concession to the defeated must be a loss to the victor. Seeing the enemy only in nationalist terms, Hughes did not believe that the collapse of the German Empire and the creation of a democratic republic should make a difference to the way in which the Allies approached the peace. No matter what form of government the Germans adopted they would always remain Germans, and so a potential rival to the British peoples and their ideas of liberty and civilisation.

While Hughes, when he saw he was losing the battle for war costs, might resort to expedient arguments in defence of his position, namely that insisting on war costs would increase the British Empire's and so Australia's share of whatever reparations Germany eventually paid, there would seem to be no doubt that his demand for indemnity was primarily motivated by a righteous and vengeful nationalism. If Lloyd George was a chameleon, Hughes was Hughes was Hughes. Throughout the negotiations over reparations he maintained the position that he had taken from 1917, a position which he neatly summarised just as the Paris Peace Conference was about to begin its business:

> The Kaiser may have led Germany, but she followed not only willingly, but eagerly. Upon the shoulders of all classes and all sections lies the guilt. They were drunk with bestial passion, with the hope of world conquest – Junker, merchant, and workman alike, all hoped to share in the loot. Upon the German nation, then, rests the responsibility for the war, and she must pay the penalty for her crime.[132]

All the other members of the BED, no matter how much some might have shared his desire for war costs, understood the fundamental flaws in Hughes's approach to peacemaking. Hughes could not imagine that the Germans, having been brought to their knees, might refuse to accept his draconian terms, and he therefore gave little consideration to the difficulties of compelling them to submit. He never properly assessed the political and economic price of maintaining a permanent occupation force. Certainly he was not willing that Australian troops should be part of such a force.[133] He also gave little thought to the means by which Germans should pay the huge compensation bill or to the consequences of the transfer of gold and goods for the health of the Allies' post-war industry, finances and employment.

---

[131] Robert Skidelsky, *John Maynard Keynes* (London: Penguin, 1983), Vol.I, 'Hopes Betrayed, 1883–1920', especially pp.354–75.

See also John Maynard Keynes, *The Economic Consequences of the Peace* (London: Macmillan, 1920). Writing in criticism of those like Hughes who demanded that Germany should pay the full cost of the war Keynes stated that 'nations are not authorised by religion or natural morals to visit on the children of their enemies the misdoings of their parents or of rulers.'

[132] *Times* (London), 10 January 1919.

[133] Cable, Hughes to Watt, 9 February 1919, NAA CP360/8 B1/3; 'am writing British Government, to notify them that scheme of demobilisation will not permit of retention of Australian troops as an army of occupation.'

Hughes's mantra that the German nation should be presented with the whole bill and then, if they were unable to meet it, be required to show that this was so, represented not a practical process but a vengeful crusade. The overthrow of the imperial dynasty and the establishment of the Weimar Republic had no effect on his view of the indemnity that Germany should pay. Not even the possibility that such harsh terms might bring the Bolsheviks to power deterred him from demanding his pound of flesh. His constant plea that it was the Fourteen Points in the armistice which had cruelled his pitch was a nonsense. Though without the Fourteen Points it is true that the rhetorical context in which the debate over reparations took place would have been different, the problems with which the Allies had to contend would have been much the same, and most likely the outcome itself would not have been dissimilar. Hughes's claims for the full costs of the war did not serve British Empire or Australian interests.

'Not a good peace'

In every aspect of the peacemaking, from the wartime planning until the signing of the Treaty of Versailles on the 28 June, Hughes had followed the simple-minded 'realist' philosophy of international relations that he had held from the first time he had given thought to these matters. It was a philosophy which, while it claimed to be based on a realistic appreciation of the role of power in international affairs, was also infused with the romantic ideal of nationalism. British Australians had experienced a very acute form of the socio-psychological crisis brought on by modernisation, and had responded overwhelmingly to the appeal of nationalism as a means of dealing with the sense of social dislocation and disorientation. Being newcomers dwelling uneasily on the edge of an alien Asia they gave their Britishness a white racial intensity. As Watt put it, in writing to Hughes towards the end of the conference; 'League or no League, we must always remember that more than half the people of the world look with hungry eyes across narrow seas at our great empty land. We must guard this British outpost.'[134]

Hughes, from the beginning of the war, had been the great champion of British race nationalism. He had proclaimed the righteousness of the British cause and expounded a British race vision of what the Empire and Australia must achieve from the conflict. Among the leaders of the British Empire he had stood alone in his unwavering and unqualified demand for a peace of annexation and indemnity. Despite President Wilson's contrary ideas of the peace, despite the Allies' acceptance of the Fourteen Points as the basis for the armistice and despite Lloyd George's equivocation and the Imperial Cabinet's indecision, Hughes at the opening of the Peace Conference still believed that it would be possible to achieve his major goals. As Hughes considered Wilson to be 'a man firm in nothing that really matters' and that if given a League of Nations he would 'give us all the rest', he approached the negotiations over the settlement with some optimism.[135] By tackling his opponents head on he would bludgeon them into submission. To fight and struggle, even against the greatest odds, this was the persona that he had shaped for himself out of history.

---

[134] Cable, Watt to Hughes, 1 May 1919, NAA CP360/8 B1/4.
[135] Letter, Hughes to Munro Ferguson, 17 January 1919, Novar Papers, NLA MS 696/2762.

Yet as the diplomacy of peacemaking proceeded Hughes was cast into the depths of despair. As the conference had proceeded, all his objectives were being thwarted. He had failed to dislodge the Japanese from the German North Pacific islands. He had had to abandon the annexation of the South Pacific islands, and even though a League of Nations mandate promised to give the substance of what he had sought the conditions governing the mandates had still not been officially determined. Furthermore the Japanese, though defeated in the League of Nations Commission, had given notice that they would continue to press for the adoption of the racial equality principle. Lloyd George had usurped Hughes's role on the reparations question, and it seemed that Germany would escape having to pay the cost of the war and that the British Empire would recover only a small proportion of its total expenditure. Unlike most of his colleagues on the BED, he had little or no faith in the League of Nations as a possible instrument for achieving his kind of new world order. As all these issues slipped away from him he lamented to Watt that 'Things are not going well … I feel and am rotten', and then again later, 'My position here is absolutely unbearable. Australian vital interests – are at this moment being decided by four [the Council of Four]. All sorts of influences are at work and my task of protecting Australia is no easy one.'[136]

After the Council of Three and Four had decided the terms of peace nothing was left to him but to bewail the fate of Australia and the Empire. It was a bitter lament. And he railed against the two powers that had won out at the expense of the British peoples.

In the first place Germany had not been crushed or cowed. When on 7 May the German plenipotentiaries had received the Allies' peace terms in the Hall of Mirrors at the Palace of Versailles, they had assumed a defiant manner. For Hughes this was visible proof of everything he had believed about the German people. He was so indignant at the behaviour of Count Ulrich Brockdorff-Rantzau, the head of the delegation who had continued to sit while giving his response, that he went to Lloyd George and asked whether Clemenceau, who was presiding, was 'going to allow this fellow to go on like this'.[137] In giving the Governor-General a vivid account of these proceedings, Hughes said of Brockdorff-Rantzau that:

> He looks what he is: a typical Prussian Junker: arrogant, intolerant unrepentant. The War had taught him nothing.
>
> He poses as the mouthpiece of Socialdemokratie: talks about workers of the world: about Justice About: Peace: about Right, about Democracy!
>
> He talks for purposes of propaganda: he produces a *very* bad impression on the Allied delegates. They all saw in him the very incarnation of all against which the world had been fighting for over 4½ years.

In the second place America had emerged from the peacemaking triumphant, financially and commercially. It had become a global threat to the British Empire. As he told Munro Ferguson, it was:

---

[136] Cables, Hughes to Watt, 15 and 22 April 1919, NAA CP360/8 B1/4.
[137] A.J.P. Taylor (ed.), *Lloyd George: A Diary by Frances Stevenson* (London: Hutchinson, 1971), p.183.

a good peace for America. *She* who did not come into the war to make anything has made thousand of millions out of it. *She* gets the best ships: *She* has a good chance of beating us for the world mercantile supremacy. *She* prevented us getting the cost of the war.

Hughes had misjudged Wilson. The American President, he whom Hughes mocked as 'The Heaven-born' or 'THE GREAT, ONE', had not been content with his League of Nations. Hughes had to admit that 'Wilsons [sic] 14 points has been the millstone round our necks all through this conference.' Consequently the United States had frustrated Hughes's program for a new world order and emerged from the war a potential rival to Pax Britannica.

It was his considered view that the Treaty of Versailles was '*not* a good peace for Aus: nor indeed for Britain.'[138] In stressing the '*not*' he underscored his sense of betrayal and failure. Though Australia had been allotted the mandate for German New Guinea and the associated island groups which it had occupied early in the war, though the Japanese had been prevented from including any kind of race equality principle in the League Covenant – an achievement that gave Hughes a great deal of satisfaction[139] – the peace was in Hughes's view neither in principle nor practice one of 'annexation and indemnity'. Australia's security in the Pacific was still in jeopardy. Japan was to keep the North Pacific islands. Australia was denied the right to have unqualified title to the South Pacific islands. The French too whom he had approached about ceding their interest in the New Hebrides were also uncooperative.[140] Even his subsequent efforts to persuade the French – now considered a natural ally against Japan – to enter into economic and defence agreements to protect their common interest in the South Pacific proved abortive.[141] Furthermore, while the decision about the amount of reparations Germany should pay and the principles for its distribution was left to a Reparation Commission he was convinced that Germany would not be required to pay the cost of the war. It seemed certain that the British Empire would see very little of whatever sum Germany did ultimately pay. Germany's arrogance had not been curbed. It retained the ability to rise again to challenge the British race. Among the British Empire leaders Hughes was the only one to have such a pessimistic view of the results of the Paris Conference.

Back in Australia Piesse, reviewing the final form of the peace, shared Hughes's pessimism about its effects on Australia, but for diametrically opposed reasons. As he wrote to Latham:

> The whole business seems to have gone badly for us, from our apparent lack of cordiality towards the United States to the barren victory over racial discrimination. How much better it would have been to accept the Japanese amendment in one of its least noxious forms and rely on the opportunities of the Covenant of the League gives us to protect ourselves from any

---

[138] Letter, Hughes to Munro Ferguson, 17 May 1919, Novar Papers, NLA MS 696/552.
[139] Cable, Hughes to Watt, 4 May 1919, NAA CP360/8 B1/4. 'Japan gets Marshalls and Carolines and Kiao-chou. This is very good for her; she went down badly on racial equality. That is one for us.'
[140] Cable, Hughes to Watt, 26 June 1919, NAA CP360/8 B1/4.
[141] London *Observer*, 18 July 1920, in NAA A981 Control of New Hebrides 24. It was reported that at this meeting with Simon in July 1919, 'The idea was even examined whether, in case a Federal Council should be set up in Sydney for the whole of British Australasia, the French Colonies in the Pacific should not be represented on the Council, and thus become part of an Anglo-French Federation of the Pacific.'

> unfavourable interpretation. As it is we have been perhaps the chief factor in consolidating the whole Japanese nation behind the imperialists ...

In particular, he was puzzled and dismayed by the Council of Four's decision to allow Japan to keep the German territories on the Chinese mainland – which some commentators thought to be a *quid pro quo* for Japan's failure to obtain its racial equality amendment. Given the resurgence of Japanese imperialism – for which he held Hughes primarily responsible – it needed 'little imagination to see how serious that may be with Japan's now assured opportunities for expanding her power through China's resources.' Thus he concluded, 'I withdraw all my optimism about our future relations with Japan. We shall need all our wits to look after ourselves now.'[142]

As Piesse argued, if Australia had lost out at the Peace Conference it was Hughes himself who had compromised the nation's position, and this was true not only in relation to Japan but also reparations. Hughes prided himself on understanding human nature. In his letters and speeches, his anecdotes and humorous sallies he satirised moral pretensions and appeals for a better world where peace and justice would prevail. He played on human foibles and failings. People were irredeemably self-interested and their greatest interest, the interest with which their ideals were connected, was the preservation of their nation or race. Blind to the consequences of the policies that he had decided were essential for the safety of Australia and the Empire he fought what was for the most part a lonely battle against the Japanese and the Americans, and frequently also against his British and Dominion colleagues. He in the process had antagonised the British, disappointed the other Dominion leaders, alienated the Americans and deeply offended the Japanese. And all to no good end.

L. F. Fitzhardinge, in his well-documented official biography, is at pains to defend or excuse Hughes at the Paris Peace Conference. On the annexation of New Guinea and the associated island groups he does not show any understanding of the strategic argument for putting all the former German islands under mandates, claiming that 'neutralisation on both sides of the equator could only have worked if it was guaranteed either by an effective League of Nations or an actively interested United States', neither of which was possible. Fitzhardinge does not appreciate that even while the mandate in itself would not prevent Japan from exploiting the islands militarily, it could only do so at some diplomatic cost. Of the alternatives available mandates for the Pacific islands was the best option for Hughes's own purpose and Hughes himself, after he had been more or less compelled to accept a mandate, realised that it served his purpose better than annexation. Summing up, Fitzhardinge contends that, 'The events of the Second World War proved Hughes's point'; that is the need for annexation. Even if Hughes was so prescient it is difficult to see how

---

[142] Copy of letter, Piesse to Latham, 7 May 1919, Piesse Papers, NLA MS 882/5/25.

These brief comments on the peace settlement and 'The Far Eastern question' were a summary of a paper Piesse had written the previous day. In this paper he had developed his arguments about the significance of Japan's domination of China for Australia, the strengthening of Japan's claims to be accepted as the leader of a pan-Asian movement and Hughes's role in focusing Japanese resentment on Australia and stirring up public support for Japan's anti-Western militarist party. See 'The Far East Question – Notes on its Solution at the Peace Conference', 6 May 1919, NAA A2219, Vol.5.

annexation would have been preferable to League mandates for the purpose of protecting Australia against this future possibility.

On the racial equality issue Fitzhardinge states that it was 'hard to judge' its significance. But he then proceeds to set out Hughes's defence, namely that 'If the Japanese did not intend to include immigration [under the various versions of a race equality insertion in the Covenant], let them say so explicitly, otherwise the inference must be that they did.' Likewise Fitzhardinge, trying to meet the criticisms of Piesse, Murdoch and Watt, claims 'it seems highly improbable' that the rejection of the racial equality principle was 'an important factor in discrediting the struggling liberal party in Japan, and so paved the way for militarism and Pearl Harbour.' The argument here, which is now beyond dispute, is not that the rejection led to Pearl Harbour; and Hughes should have foreseen this. It is rather that Hughes unnecessarily gave ammunition to the militarist party in Japan at that time. By doing so he directed Japanese resentment against Australia and by this acted against his country's best interest.

A similar explaining away is offered for Hughes's stand on reparations. Hughes was denied what he sought which, according to Fitzhardinge, was deterrence against future aggression and some compensation for Australia's war expenditure. But Hughes's aims were much more wide-ranging and vindictive than this. He wished to punish and crush the German nation which he saw as an enduring threat to the supremacy of the British Empire. In response to Hughes's detractors, Fitzhardinge says that he never claimed to be an 'economic expert' and 'if he had not taken the position he did, others, French or English, would have done so.' A wise statesman or even a practical politician, recognising the limitations of his knowledge, would have treated professional advisers with more respect, but Hughes being who he was would listen to no-one. Moreover, as with the racial equality question, it is difficult to see why the claim that there were others at Paris who supported Hughes's policy and who were happy to leave it to him to take the lead, mitigates Hughes's responsibility for the policy or makes his advocacy of it more defensible.[143]

At the end of the conference, after the signing of the Treaty of Versailles, Hughes made a series of speeches in Britain and Australia explaining the meaning of the Treaty of Versailles for the future of Australia, the Empire and the world. This public appraisal of the significance of the war and the peace culminated in his address to the Commonwealth Parliament on 10 September when he moved the ratification of the treaty. On this latter occasion, he gave a masterly overview of what, from his world view, had been won and what had been lost. Perhaps with the memory of his colleagues' criticisms still fresh in his mind, he once again revisited the dispute that he had engaged in with Lloyd George over taking the Fourteen Points as the basis for the armistice. It was the Fourteen Points which had denied the British Empire and the Allies the fruits of a 'victorious peace'. It was the Fourteen Points which had denied Australia the right to possess freehold the South Pacific islands and threatened to limit its control over tariff policy and to demand indemnities from the enemy. In his view, 'this peace, whatever may be said, it is not a harsh Peace to Germany, and it is not a just peace to us.'

As a result of this experience Australia, along with the other Dominions, had realised that they needed to be represented in their own right at the Peace Conference. Britain had 'very many

---

[143] Fitzhardinge, *The Little Digger*, pp.416–17.

interests to consider besides ours, and some of those interests do not always coincide with ours.' In the conference itself there were 'men of all colours and from every part of the world.' In this cauldron of 'diverse and clashing interests' there were nations with ideals very different from those of Australia. In particular, White Australia was 'not understood, by those with whom we consorted.' Among 'the clashing of warring interests each nation desired what it considered necessary for its own salvation, though it might trench on the liberties, rights, or material welfare of others.' As Hughes reported it, the whole exercise had been a conflict of national interests in which each delegation pressed its own advantage as far as circumstances permitted, and Australia had been left out in the cold.

In giving his account of the Peace Conference Hughes said nothing directly either about the changing relation of the Dominions to the Mother Country or about the Imperial War Cabinet or the British Empire Delegation. He announced that Australia, as a result of being separately represented at Paris, 'became a nation, and entered into the family of nations on a footing of equality.'[144] His experience of the Imperial War Cabinet, especially at the critical moment when the armistice was negotiated, and of the BED where he had been at loggerheads with Lloyd George over both mandates and reparations and alone in resisting the Japanese-sponsored racial equality principle, had caused him to embrace Australia's national elevation. Likewise, he was happy to back Borden and Smuts in their demands that the Dominions and India should sign the Peace Treaty separately under the general heading of the 'British Empire' and that they should, following the precedent set at the Paris Peace Conference, become founding members of the League of Nations and the International Labour Organisation with a status identical to that of other small powers.[145]

Even so, Hughes had no desire to turn his back on the Empire. Despite the disappointments and betrayals he could not renounce his vision of a world-wide British race united inside a confederated British Empire. As he had done in 1916, so in 1919, while preparing to return home, he made a series of speeches reaffirming Australia's identification with the Empire. They echoed what he had campaigned for during his stay in Britain, namely commonly agreed imperial foreign, defence and trade policies. Australia wanted 'to see the idea of Empire expressed in something more than lip service.' It wanted 'a declaration of policy which will make for the permanency of the Empire.'[146] These speeches were not ritualistic gestures. They were inspired by more than a need for the protection of the Royal Navy and British markets for primary exports. As important – and this can be not be easily separated from the other motives – was the image of Australia as a British people.

The two sides to Hughes's view of the Empire were not easily reconciled. He himself recognised the problem, a problem which was to bedevil Australia's approach to the world for two further generations. To the question, 'How were we to reconcile that which on the face of it

---

[144] *CPD*, 1918–19 session, LXXXIX, 12164–79, 10 September 1919.
[145] Borden Memorandum on Dominions as Parties and Signatories to Peace Treaties, 12 March 1919, *Documents on Canadian External Relations* (Ottawa: Queen's Printer, 1969), Vol.2, 'The Paris Peace Conference of 1919'.
[146] *SMH*, 27 June 1919; *Times* (London), 26 June 1919.

seemed irreconcilable – the sovereignty, the political and economic independence of each of the parts – with the concept of an Empire presenting a united front to the world?', he gave a considered answer which tried to connect his deeply-felt sense of identity with his hard-earned experience:

> Events might seem to point to each part of the Empire slowly but certainly turning to the development of its heritage and achievement of its destiny along different roads. But the ties of race and common interests were not lightly torn asunder. The Empire was a great, a mighty factor, standing for everything that was best and highest in the world's civilisation and progress. Precisely how we were to create such machinery as would enable the voice of every part of the Empire, not only to be heard but also to make itself felt in determining what may be termed an imperial policy, remained to be seen.
>
> One thing appeared certain, neither the self-governing Dominions nor Britain would agree to surrender one jot or tittle of their political independence. The idea of an Imperial parliament was a vision which could never take substantial shape for it was in its very nature incompatible with the status of sovereignty which now more than ever, the self-governing Dominions prized. But we must hope that somehow means would be found whereby the great confederation of free nations calling itself the British Empire would work, live, and develop together in the highest interests of civilisation and the welfare of mankind.

Hughes looked to improvements in communications through fleets of fast steamships and airships and a chain of wireless stations to help solve this problem. Through these means he hoped that the great geopolitical divide would be bridged and 'the bonds of Empire ... so firmly cemented that neither corroding time nor the rude buffets of adversity would batter them.'[147] It was not a satisfactory resolution of his dilemma – there was, of course, no satisfactory solution – but it showed very clearly that, despite the difficulties he had encountered in dealing with the British Government and the conflicts over difference of interests, he could not abandon the idea of the unity of the Empire in facing the world.

Hughes proudly boasted that his greatest achievement at the Peace Conference was to safeguard White Australia, 'the foundation of all that Australia stands for'. But this White Australia was a White British Australia. Australia had the distinction of 'being the only community in the Empire, if not, indeed in the world, where there is so little admixture of race.' Australians were 'all of the same race and speak the same tongue in the same way.' They were 'more British than the people of Great Britain'. Australians believed 'in our race and in ourselves, and in our capacity to achieve our great destiny which is to hold this vast continent in trust for those of our race who

---

[147] *Times* (London), 2 July 1919.

Cook, a more naïve believer in the British race patriot faith, saw in the Imperial War Cabinet and the BED signs of an inevitable movement towards integrating the Empire. He was more certain than Hughes that a way would be found to achieve this desirable objective. See Cook's 1919 Notebooks, Vol.I, NAA M3580; 'The Imperial War Cabinet is tentative Imperial Federation. We have like Topsy grow'd into it. What form the future structure will be – whether Imperial Parliament or Imperial Council. Fact already there – Sooner or later structure will fit fact as body clothes mind and soul .... We slip inadvertently into some of our most cherished institutions. First facts jostle each other – then find appropriate resting place in some organic & orderly relation.'

come after us, and who stand with us in the battle of freedom.'[148] And, in doing so, they would share the fate of the British race. In summing this up he declared, at a farewell dinner given by Andrew Fisher, that 'the only virtue he had was that in his veins flowed the blood of our race.'[149]

That the League Covenant was incorporated in the Treaty of Versailles did not alter Hughes's scepticism about the organisation. In asking parliament to approve the Treaty of Versailles he struck a seemingly more positive note than he had customarily adopted in discussing the League. Since Australia was a founding member of the organisation it was incumbent on him to say something favourable about it:

> I can only say that the League of Nations may be regarded as the foundation of the new temple of civilisation. It is for the world to erect on that foundation an edifice worthy of the ideals for which the Allies have fought, and of the sacrifices by which those ideals were maintained.

But this was not assured:

> if the world should take another road; if it should seek as men have sought from the very beginning, to settle their quarrels by the sword, the League of Nations will prove to be but a house of cards ...

This commendation of the League was useful for the purpose at hand. He no more expected the League to usher in a new era of peace than he had the pre-war Hague international courts. It might light the way 'to a better road' but it 'did not make it or carry us along on it.' He did not believe that human nature had changed or could change. He wore with élan the accusation levelled at him 'of being a very virulent anti-German'. Germany still had 'the will, the lust for vengeance, the desire to kill'. Its defeat might have made the Empire safe for a generation but the desire remained and Germany might well rise again.[150] His expectation of the League and its possibilities was to be found in his conditional endorsement. He judged the League against Wilson's extravagant promise. That is, it had to be an effective policeman of world order or it was nothing. There were no shades of grey. For Hughes unless the League could act instantly to protect its members and had the appropriate naval and military force at its disposal then it would be a failure.

In his speeches in London and to various audiences on his return to Australia he reiterated this point. In his farewell addresses to the Empire Parliamentary Association and British Empire League he put these reservations about the League in their starkest form. If the League was to be effective then it would be 'incompatible with the Empire as we know it today, since the Empire relies on a dominant navy, and the League also must have its own army and navy capable of carrying out its decisions against any Powers or combinations of Powers.' If Britain and the Dominions had to choose between relying on the League or on the British navy then 'there can only be one decision.' The Empire 'would not abandon the substance for the shadow.' Even if the

---

[148] *CPD*, 1918–19 session, LXXXIX, 12174–75, 10 September 1919.

[149] *Times* (London), 8 July 1919.

In his speech, which was reported very briefly, Cook 'believed that the Britishers in the Empire today were in Australia, The Australians were 98 percent British and they liked to call themselves Britishers first of all.'

[150] *CPD*, 1918–19 session, LXXXIX, 12170–72, 10 September 1919.

League did have a composite navy made up of contributions from its great power members, Australia would draw no comfort from having to depend upon 'a polyglot, heterogeneous force … which probably will include our deadly enemy.'[151] As Germany was not a member there was only one possible 'deadly enemy' to which Hughes could be referring.

With this in mind, Hughes exploited the United States unilateralism that is its demand for the inclusion of the American Monroe Doctrine in the League Covenant. He resuscitated Australia's demand for a Monroe Doctrine for the South Pacific. During his ratification speech Hughes averred that Australia was entitled to have an equally free hand in the Pacific.

> I say – and this surely is a matter far outside of party politics – that, so far as the Pacific is concerned, at least within the area and sphere of our influence, it, too is covered by a doctrine that it is for us to settle, and for nobody else …
>
> While the Monroe Doctrine exempts the whole of the two Americas from the jurisdiction of the League of Nations, we will not allow anything relating to our sphere in the Pacific to be regarded as a proper subject for submission to that tribunal.[152]

Hughes allowed that the war in which Australia had been engaged was a titanic struggle, a conflict which engaged ideals as well as interests. It was 'not merely a struggle of opposing nations but a war between clashing ideals, between military Autocracy and Democracy, between those who passionately loved liberty and those who sought to lay upon free peoples of the world a despotic yoke.' To this extent Hughes shared Wilson's own picture of the European conflict. But it was the British peoples who were the natural guardians of liberty and democracy. These ideals were part of their particular racial inheritance. Therefore the British Empire was entitled to exercise the global police authority. Or if a greater force were required then Hughes still held to the position he had taken when the Imperial War Cabinet had first considered peace terms: 'The best assurance for the world's peace is not the Versailles treaty, but an Alliance of Britain, America and France.'[153]

The debate in the Commonwealth Parliament over the Treaty of Versailles did not engage Hughes's world view. A general election was in the offing and the vexed issues arising from the conflicts over conscription influenced many of the speeches. The most relevant comments were directed to the interconnected issues of White Australia, the danger of Japan and the Pacific island settlement. Even Hughes's most bitter Labor enemies, such as the pacificist Frank Brennan, complimented the Prime Minister on the fight he had put up in defending White Australia at the Paris Peace Conference. The most vitriolic attack on Hughes came from J. H. Catts who accused him of agreeing during the war to let the Japanese keep the North Pacific islands.[154] No voices were raised in opposition to the ratification of the Treaty or the associated American, British and

---

[151] *SMH*, 23 and 26 June 1919; *Times* (London), 26 June 1919.
[152] *CPD*, 1918–19 session, LXXXIX, 12172, 10 September 1919.
[153] *SMH*, 23 and 27 June and 2 July 1919.
[154] *CPD*, 1918–19 session, LXXXIX, 12573, 18 September 1919 and 12425, 17 September 1919. For other comments on Japan, the Pacific islands and Japan see *ibid.*, 12333, 17 September 1919 (Millen), 12535, 18 September 1919 (Fleming), 12544–45, 18 September 1919 (Finlayson), 12554–55, 18 September 1919 (Dr Maloney) and 12561–63, 18 September 1919 (Archibald).

French Treaty under which the British Empire and the United States promised to come to the aid of France should it be attacked again by Germany. With varying degrees of optimism the Australian Parliament endorsed the brave new world created by the Treaty of Versailles. For Hughes, however, the promise of a peace under the auspices of Wilson's League of Nations was still an illusion. Japan still remained a menacing presence and he looked where he had always looked for reassurance, to Australia's own national defence and close cooperation with Britain and the Empire.

The Lessons of War, the Decline of Empire and 'Détente' in the Pacific

Australia's world crisis did not end with the war in Europe, the signing of the Treaty of Versailles or the creation of the League of Nations. Though the 'hot war' against Germany was over, the 'cold war' against Japan remained and in the eyes of the Australian national security community it looked even more menacing.

The British peoples might have emerged triumphant from the Great War but they had suffered great losses of men and treasure and the new world which was emerging out of the ashes of the old had within it the seeds of fresh challenges. While Hughes considered that a revived Germany might at some distant time seek revenge, he was more immediately concerned that revolutionary Bolshevism might subvert the loyalty of the working class, the Sinn Fein-led rebellion in Ireland weaken the Empire and the United States replace Britain as the dominant financial and commercial power. Above all, he and his government feared that Japan, with its position in the region greatly enhanced, might embark on an aggressive course aimed at White Australia.

Though Australian policy makers established a 'Foreign Office' for the Pacific to meet what they conceived to be their vulnerable situation and drew up comprehensive plans for military, naval and air defence, they quickly found their resources inadequate for the task. So they looked for protection, as they had before the European war, through the establishment of a British Imperial naval force in the region. The 1921 Imperial Conference could not reach an agreement on either a common defence or foreign policy. Hughes was faced with disappointment. The British would not contribute to a Pacific fleet and the Canadians and South Africans indicated that they would not share in the cost of an Empire-wide defence program. Once again the cultural bonds of Greater Britain were not sufficient to overcome the diverse strategic interests of its constituent nation states.

It was the intervention of the United States that resolved Australia's Pacific dilemma. America seeking to return to an isolationist policy convened a conference of the major powers at the end of 1921 for the purpose of easing tensions in the Pacific and ending expensive naval armament competition. At the Washington Conference, all the powers accepted limits for capital ships and naval bases and promised to respect the existing territorial sovereignty of China and the Pacific islands. The Australians were impressed by the ensuing treaties and even more by the co-operative spirit which Japan showed in negotiating and carrying out their terms. As a result the great majority of the nation's leaders were at last convinced that Japan was 'peaceful', and with some reservations viewed these treaties as marking the end of their 'cold war' in the Pacific and thus the close of an era in the history of Australian defence and foreign policy.

15

A Pacific 'Foreign Office', the Japanese Threat and Defence Planning

Creating a Pacific 'Foreign Office'

Since the Russo-Japanese war the Australians had been obsessed by the idea of a Japanese threat. Britain, distracted by the German challenge to its naval supremacy in the North Sea and determined to preserve the balance of power in Europe, had shown almost no understanding of their Pacific concerns. Australians had come to believe that Britain might leave them to fend for themselves, and so, in Alfred Deakin's words, Australia was 'being forced into a foreign policy of its own.'[1]

The Great War had reinforced this sense of danger. The war had given Japan an even freer hand in the Western Pacific. It had taken advantage of the European conflict to seize all German territory in the North Pacific. It had attempted to make China into a client state. It had spread its commercial influence throughout the whole region. And it had pressed Australia to sign a treaty to give Japan most-favoured-nation tariff status and so water down the White Australia policy. This expansion of Japanese power accelerated Australia's decision to set up its own formal structures for collecting and analysing information about Pacific affairs. By early 1919 the Australian Government's conviction that the Britain saw the world through different geopolitical spectacles led them to establish a Pacific Branch of the Prime Minister's Department and to give it the key functions of a foreign office or perhaps, more precisely, the functions of what is today known as the Office of National Assessment.

In early 1915, immediately after the Japanese had expressed their intention of keeping the German North Pacific islands, the Australian Government, as we have seen, had begun to look for more authoritative and up-to-date information on Japan's attitude to Australia and the Pacific. It had asked the British Government to instruct its ambassador in Tokyo to send such material to Melbourne. So vital had the Japan question become that, without telling the British, the Fisher Government had also asked the New South Wales Government to have its Trade Commissioner in Kobe report independently on the same issues. For the remaining years of the war the Australian authorities received regular and often disturbing reports from both sources.

These surveys of and commentaries on Japanese opinion influenced greatly the Australian Government's policy towards the Pacific problem. The Navy Department's extensive analysis of 'The Japanese Danger' drew upon this material to bolster its arguments.[2] Likewise in April 1916 the Acting Prime Minister had been prompted by a report from the New South Wales Trade

---

[1] *CPD*, 1910 session, CIX, pp.6859–60, 25 November 1910.
[2] Section II of the Naval Board's Report, 'The Japanese Danger', enclosed in letter, Naval Secretary, G.L. Macandie to Secretary, Prime Minister's Department, 21 December 1915, NAA MP1049/1 14/0285.

Commissioner to have the Defence Department appoint James Murdoch to a lectureship in Japanese at Sydney University and Duntroon Military College and to advise the government more generally on Japan. This initiative was a direct response to Suttor's claim that, 'The esoteric working of the Japanese brain is always more or less clouded in mystery ... and it is really only by a knowledge of the language of the country that one can get an insight into the secret working of the Japanese mind and form an estimate of the future aspirations of the people.'[3]

Of all members of the national security community it was Major E. L. Piesse, the Director of Military Intelligence, who was most concerned to base Australia's appreciations of Japan's intentions on the best available evidence. Piesse brought an exceptional background to his role. He held degrees in Science and Law from the University of Tasmania and had read mathematics at King's College, Cambridge. His father had been present at the foundation of the Commonwealth and was elected as a senator to the first federal parliament. Before the war Piesse, a lieutenant in the Intelligence Corps, had accepted the full picture of the 'Australian Crisis'.

After being appointed Director of Military Intelligence in March 1916, Piesse gave increasing attention to the Japanese question. Investigating German espionage was subordinated to this potentially greater and more immediate peril. He well understood that Japan's status as an ally could not be depended on. Indeed he was keenly aware of all the issues which had alarmed both the Fisher and Hughes governments. He read the reports of the British Ambassador and the New South Wales Trade Commissioner with great care and began to keep notes on 'the expansion of Japanese influence in other countries' and 'Japanese plans and ambitions for further expansion.' Perhaps impressed by Suttor's observation about language, Piesse started also in 1917 to teach himself Japanese so that he could read the Japanese newspapers and other relevant literature for himself. James Murdoch, a congenial colleague and friend, assisted Piesse in his studies and shared with him the fruits of a long experience of Japan.[4]

The following year, at the behest of Major-General J. G. Legge, Chief of the General Staff, Piesse prepared an assessment of all the information which he had been collecting on Japan. It showed that Japan, during the war, had grown in wealth and power, had sought to dominate China, and had expressed an interest in southward expansion and sponsored 'Pan-Asianism' as a means of seizing the leadership of the region from the West. Yet though Piesse had drawn on a wide range of sources – including despatches from British officials in East Asia, the 'War Diary of the General Staff in the Straits Settlements', and Japanese, American and European newspapers – he was not satisfied with his conclusion. As a good scholar he realised that the value of the evidence for Japanese ambitions found in these documents depended on their authority and interpretation. Thus he had at Legge's suggestion consulted Murdoch and also sought the opinion of G. E. Morrison, an Australian-born former China correspondent for the London *Times* who had become a trusted adviser to the Chinese Republican Government and was visiting his

---

[3] Letter, Holman to Pearce, 7 March 1916, enclosing copies of letters, Suttor to Holman, 24 and 31 January 1916, NAA MP729/5 393/1/272. See also Chapter 7, pp.5–7.

[4] For this section which deals with the evolution of Piesse's ideas about Japan as a threat and his influence on the creation of the Pacific Branch of the Prime Minister's Department, see Neville Meaney, *Fears and Phobias: E.L. Piesse and the Problem of Japan, 1909–39* (Canberra: National Library of Australia, 1996), pp.3–32.

homeland at the beginning of 1918.[5] The two 'experts' did not settle the matter since they offered different evaluations of Japanese intentions. While Morrison argued that Japan was intent on conquering China and might then use that nation's resources to undertake even greater imperial adventures, Murdoch more reassuringly stated that there was 'a growing school that abhors the expansion of Japan through the domination of other countries.' Piesse himself had to admit that 'the sources of information available to me contain only rarely any sign of Japanese interest in Australia.'[6]

Acting Prime Minister Watt was so impressed with the report that he proposed sending it to the British Foreign Office. When, however, Piesse, demurred, saying that it was based on inadequate knowledge Watt instructed him to compile 'a summary of all information in all Departments about Japan' in order to obtain a more authoritative overview of the question.'[7] After seeking out and collating a great deal of material under such headings as the 'Anglo-Japanese alliance', 'Japanese espionage in Australia' and 'Japanese-nanyo (southward) expansion' Piesse in October produced a paper, 'The Far Eastern Question: Recent Developments and their Significance for Australia', which painted a troubled picture of Australia's position in the Pacific. According to this new evaluation of Australia's post-war strategic situation the United States would probably block Japan's economic and political expansion into the Asian continent and that if this came to pass 'the Southern school of Imperialists will come forward with their familiar arguments of the danger of continental entanglements for an island power and will urge that Japan's true destiny lies in the South.' He thought it likely in such circumstances that 'the relations of Australia and Japan will come into question – to the extent at all events of the restrictions of the White Australia policy and of further opportunities for Japanese trade?' On the other side of the ledger he was willing to allow that it was 'possible' President Wilson's League of Nations might through the principle of collective security 'relieve us from the immediate need of preparations for defence against Japan.'

But these opinions were based on imperfect knowledge. What was most important and urgent, given the imminent end to hostilities in Europe and the remaking of the international geopolitical map, was to 'have more certain and adequate means of information from the East.' The despatches from the British Embassy and the New South Wales Trade Commissioner were

---

[5] For an authoritative study on Morrison, especially his continuing concern since the Russo-Japanese War about Japanese expansion in the region, see Eiko Woodhouse, *The Chinese Hsinhai Revolution: G.E. Morrison and Anglo-Japanese Relations, 1897–1920* (London: Routledge Curzon, 2004), pp.17–24 and 182–84.

[6] Report, 'Japanese Expansion and Ambitions', attached to letter, Piesse to Legge, 14 May 1918, DMI Secret 180/1, NAA MP1587/1 184J. For the origins of Morrison's antagonism to Japan, see Eiko Woodhouse, *The Chinese Hsinhai Revolution*, pp.17–24 and 173–89.

The Governor-General gave a more alarmist report of Murdoch's view about Japan's ambitions. He recorded Murdoch as saying that Japan's demands on China showed that 'Germany is Japan's model'. Novar Diary, 11 May 1918, Novar Papers, NLA MS 696/36.

[7] Letter, Piesse to Latham, 2 May 1918, Piesse Papers, NLA MS 882/5/1 and foreword to 'Index and Summary of Information about the Relations of Australia and Japan and about some Far Eastern and Pacific Questions (No.I)', 30 September 1918, NAA A2219, Vol.IA.

deficient. As far as the former were concerned it was 'not sufficient to rely on what we got from British representatives.' The British did not understand the Australian perspective on the Pacific.

> There seems to be a blight over British policy in the East – most British representatives are not in sympathy with our interests – and there are other reasons which, if I am not mistaken, have been stated to ministers by one in whose judgment they have complete confidence, why we should supplement by our own arrangements the information we now get from British sources.

As for the latter, Piesse was quite scathing about the kind of Australians that the government had used for gathering intelligence about the region. What was required was 'quiet inquiry by a person who knows the East, and who has a competent knowledge of world politics'. After this expert had submitted his findings an Australian commissioner might be appointed to carry out 'the more formal and ornamental tasks of diplomacy'. Clearly Piesse had in mind for the role of the quiet Australian his friend James Murdoch in whom the ministers already had 'complete confidence'. Likewise Piesse may also have seen himself as the future commissioner or head of a quasi foreign office. He urged that it would be worthwhile investing £2000 or £3000 in this intelligence-gathering program for the next two or three years. Given the 'vast expenditure we have planned for defence and ... the magnitude of the interests at stake if White Australia be challenged', he pointed out that this sum would be 'a trifling premium for an assurance of full and exact information'.

This report reached the Defence Minister and the Acting Prime Minister at an opportune moment. The Germans were suing for peace and the Australian Government was turning its mind to post-war policy. Since the war had burdened the country with a huge national debt, a heavy repatriation bill and pension commitments that would place strains on the federal budget for many years to come, the government was anxious to curb expenditure, including, if possible, defence expenditure. Indeed with this in mind cabinet had decided to appoint a board to look into public expenditure 'with a view of effecting economies.' Thus it was important for every reason to secure the best advice possible about the likely threats facing Australia, most notably from Japan. Accordingly on 11 November, Pearce asked Piesse 'to put on paper, in a personal note', his ideas about 'the organisation of a foreign service for the Commonwealth.'

Piesse set himself to the task and two days later sent the result to Pearce. This informal submission raised doubts about Japan as a future danger to Australia and therefore about the level of defence appropriations necessary for post-war national security. After reviewing the records about Japan in all the Departments he considered that Australia's 'policy of defence against Japan is inadequately supported by evidence.' He concluded from his research that 'hitherto her eyes have not been turned to us', and he added that Japanese public opinion was 'coming to have more influence' and that there was a 'growing opposition to any aggressive policy that might lead to war.' He allowed that heavy defence expenditure might be 'prudent' in the absence of more complete understanding of Japan's intentions. If, however, the government were willing to establish a 'foreign affairs section' which could provide it with 'full and reliable information' on Japan's attitude to White Australia, the renewal of the Anglo-Japanese alliance and, more generally, 'the need for defence against Eastern nations', it might discover that it could avoid the 'vast expenditure' on defence which its naval and military advisers were recommending.[8] In effect Piesse was pressing for the creation of an Australian foreign office.

By October 1918 Piesse had won the trust and respect of both Watt and Pearce. They consulted him on Japan and Pacific affairs. He was already acting in a *de facto* capacity as their official adviser on foreign policy. Surveying Japan's reported peace aims he advised the government that Japan had imperialist ambitions in China, Siberia and the Pacific. Since Britain had agreed to back Japan's claims to the German North Pacific islands, Australia could only look to the United States which also had differences with Japan 'to deliver us from danger', that is to prevent Japan from annexing the islands. This, however, could only be achieved if Australia refrained from claiming the South Pacific islands. He saw no problem in Australia conceding this and allowing the islands it occupied to come under international control. Foreshadowing the criticism he was later to make of Hughes's demand for annexation he pointedly asked, 'If the choice be between international control of the islands north and south of the equator, and Japanese control of those to the north and our control of those to the south would not the former be preferable for our defence?'[9] Japan's intentions had become an urgent question and at his suggestion Watt agreed to finance a trip by Murdoch to Japan so that he could discreetly sound out his contacts in high places, both in the Japanese and Western communities, about Japan's attitude to the post-war world.[10] Under the guise of buying books and recruiting lecturers for an expanded Japanese language program Murdoch was instructed to undertake an intelligence gathering exercise.

During his five month visit to Japan, Murdoch sent Piesse four letters giving frank impressions of the Japanese approach to the post-war world. These letters were directed to a 'Mr

---

[8] 'The Far Eastern Question and Australia', sent by Chief of the General Staff, Major-General Legge to Defence Minister Pearce, 22 October 1918, NAA MP1587/1 184 J. Copies also in NAA A981 FAR9 and NAA A2219/XR1, Vol.1, Pt.1. The latter contains much of the written material which Piesse drew upon for the report. See also letters, Piesse to Christina Piesse, 11 and 12 November 1918, Piesse Papers, NLA MS 882 Additional papers.

For the cabinet decision to establish a Commission to inquire into ways and means of securing economy in public expenditure, see NAA A460 A5/12/-.

Piesse stated that in forming his opinions on the Far East he had consulted two experts, 'one was European and the other an Asiatic' and 'both of them have exceptional qualifications for forming judgments on the contemporary affairs of the Far East.' The European was undoubtedly Murdoch. The second, however, is a mystery. It might well be that he is referring in this case to a Japanese resident of Melbourne, Inagaki, who was tutoring him in Japanese. But it was more likely a Chinese resident, 'Mr Ouei' with whom Piesse discussed 'the latest news from China'. See letters, Piesse to Christina Piesse, 17 and 19 November 1918, Piesse Papers, NLA MS 882 Additional papers.

[9] The Navy Department which during the war gave great attention to the 'Japanese Danger' had suggested to the government on a number of occasions that 'a suitable representative of Australia' who was fluent in Japanese and well-informed about Far Eastern affairs should be sent to Japan for the purpose of producing a report based on first-hand knowledge of the nation's intentions. See Naval Intelligence Report of Captain W. Thring on 'Japan', 21 May 1918, NAA MP 1587/1 184J.

[10] Report on 'Japan's Reported "Basic Peace Clauses"', 26 November 1918, DMI S180/22, NAA A2219, Vol.6.

McRae' – using Mrs Piesse's maiden name – at the Piesse family address. Murdoch adopted this method of correspondence because, he said, 'the Japanese were watching all correspondence very carefully' and he feared that any letter addressed to Major Piesse at Victoria Barracks might attract their attention.[11] Murdoch's initial views were quite reassuring. The Allies' defeat of Germany had had a salutary effect on both the official and public mind. There was no question but that 'the Empire will be much more amenable to "sweet reasonableness" than it has been for the last decade or so.' After conferring with British Embassy officials, the American Ambassador and former students and friends, and meeting the Japanese Vice-Minister for Foreign Affairs, Shidehara Kijuro, Murdoch came away convinced that:

> The collapse of Germany has at last had its effect; – German militarism is now being held up as a terrible example; and able editors are everywhere preaching to their public the advisability of taking warning and turning over a new leaf. Japanese policy in China is now altering greatly for the better; and on the whole, the country has become reasonable, very reasonable. In short, things are much more hopeful than they have ever been since 1914.[12]

Yet even as these good tidings were reaching Melbourne both Piesse and Murdoch were disturbed by a sudden reversal in the Japanese attitude towards the Western powers. The Japanese people had reacted sharply when they learnt that their erstwhile allies were opposing the inclusion of a racial equality provision in the League Covenant. There were mass demonstrations in the streets of major cities and public denunciations of Western arrogance in the press. Piesse in scouring the Japanese and Australian newspapers had been alerted to this dangerous development and Murdoch on his return reinforced these apprehensions, telling Piesse that 'this racial discrimination business is the most important issue' in the country and that it 'may well become dangerous if not met properly'. As we have seen in the previous chapter, Piesse, in late March, prepared a briefing paper for the Acting Prime Minister in which he explained the gravity of the problem and criticised Hughes's handling of the racial equality issue at Paris. Shortly after this he sent Watt a set of proposals from Murdoch for revising the White Australia policy and domestic discriminatory legislation so as to remove the formal grounds for Japan's complaint. Watt found the well-informed and well-argued views of Piesse and Murdoch quite persuasive and considered Murdoch's proposals to be a policy which was both 'workable and looks acceptable'.[13] Alarmed by

---

[11] Letter, Murdoch to Piesse, 14 March 1919, Piesse Papers, NLA MS 882/5/10.

It would appear that the Japanese were not unaware of the Defence Department's purpose in having Murdoch appointed to a lectureship in Japanese at Sydney University. Piesse in recounting a conversation which he had had with the Japanese Consul-General told Watt that while Shimizu was pleased to hear of the advances in the teaching of Japanese in New South Wales and Victoria he 'was perhaps rather less cordial in his appreciation of the enlightenment of Australian opinion which the study of Japanese, and the activities of the Professors [sic] of Oriental Studies in Sydney might bring about.' Memorandum, Piesse to Pearce, 7 December 1919, NAA A981 Japan101, Pt.1.

[12] Letters, Murdoch to 'McRae', 6 and 22 December 1918 and Murdoch to Piesse, 25 January 1919, Piesse Papers, NLA MS 882/5/3, 5 and 9.

[13] Piesse to Legge, 24 March 1919, Memorandum on 'The Present Movement in Japan against Racial Discrimination', NAA MP729/2 1877/5/152 and NAA A2219, Vol.6; copy of paper, 'Discrimination against

Piesse's picture of a militarised Japan leading a Pan-Asian movement against the West, he cautioned Hughes against speaking out against the Japanese efforts to insert a racial equality provision in the Covenant.[14]

From Piesse's point of view the Paris Peace Conference was a disaster for Australia. Hughes's vetoing of the racial equality principle not only stirred up anti-Western feeling in Japan and made Australia the chief target of Japanese resentment but also forced Wilson and Lloyd George, as a gesture of appeasement, to leave Japan in possession of the German territories in China. When Piesse read of this concession he, perhaps influenced by Murdoch, saw in it a new source of possible peril, and on 6 May he produced another memorandum on 'The Far Eastern Question' which set out his misgivings. In his estimation Japan's imperialists had emerged triumphant and 'the way now seems open for her to put into force any plans she may have for completing her economic and political domination of China.' He predicted that since Japan had achieved so much so easily its 'power would probably develop very rapidly' and its new position might enable it 'to challenge any power that stands in her way.' Australia's strategic position could 'therefore turn out to be far worse than it was at the outbreak of the war.' In these circumstances he believed that Australia's leaders should 'give their minds' to maintaining cordial relations with the United States, avoiding misunderstandings with India and China, revising the White Australia policy to remove its offensive appearance and encouraging those Japanese liberals who opposed an imperialist course.[15] He was putting before the government an outline of an Australian foreign policy for the Pacific, an alternative policy to that which Hughes had pursued at Paris.

Watt, who had only reluctantly assumed the post of Acting Prime Minister, had had little experience with foreign policy. Unlike Hughes, however, he understood the need for the government to act on good advice. He accepted Piesse's argument that Britain did not see the world from the same perspective and therefore Australia needed to have its own foreign service. Both he and Pearce had found Piesse's discussion of the strategic problems facing Australia very enlightening. Given the great financial problems that the government had to contend with in the post-war era, they were particularly attracted by Piesse's insistence on obtaining the best intelligence about Japan's attitude and intentions before committing themselves to greatly increased defence expenditures. For these reasons both ministers consulted him directly and from the end of 1918 were giving serious consideration to establishing some form of a foreign office which could continue to supply them with well-based and well-thought-out strategic appreciations.[16] Following the receipt of Piesse's March report in which he had once again stressed that 'the need for more and better information is obvious and urgent – more information from the United States, more information from China, more information from Japan', Watt appointed a cabinet committee to look into the matter. On 8 May cabinet agreed to the creation of a Pacific

---

Asiatics – Notes for an Australian Policy', 27 March 1919 and letters, Piesse to Watt, 27 March 1919 and Watt to Piesse, 31 March, NAA A3934/1 SC12/6.

[14] Cable, Watt to Hughes, 15 April 1919, NAA CP360/8 B1/4.

[15] Memorandum on 'The Far Eastern Question – Notes on its Solution at the Peace Conference, 6 May 1919, NAA A2219, Vol.5. See also, letter, Piesse to Latham, 7 May 1919, Piesse Papers, NLA MS 882/5/25.

[16] Letter, Captain W. Thring to Latham, 12 November 1918, Latham Papers, NLA MS 1009/1/981–82.

Branch of the Prime Minister's Department, and Watt, in no way deterred by Piesse's trenchant criticisms of Hughes, offered him the position of Director.[17]

Piesse was the obvious choice and he accepted with alacrity. From the time he had conceived the idea he had set his mind on obtaining the position. Since November he had applied himself to his Japanese studies with renewed energy and had begun a course of reading in diplomatic history and international relations.[18] Watt's respect for Piesse was such that he invited the Director of Military Intelligence to the meeting of the cabinet committee which decided the terms and conditions of the Director's appointment and gave Piesse a free hand in drawing up a statement defining the functions of the Pacific Branch. This statement embodied aims which Piesse had distilled from his wartime experience. Australia's defence and diplomacy had to be underpinned by a better and more accurate understanding of international affairs, especially Pacific affairs. Thus the 'principal duty' of the office was 'to study the affairs of the countries of the Far East and of the Pacific (including the United States of America) in so far as they may in the immediate or distant future affect the foreign relations or domestic affairs of the Commonwealth and to study the policy of the Commonwealth on questions arising from relations with these parts of the world.'

The Pacific Branch would not only advise the government about changes in the international environment but also 'study' and so critically evaluate and guide Commonwealth policy. It was to be an 'intelligence' not an administrative arm of government. It was to concern itself 'with general tendencies and broad questions of policy.' Possibly as a conciliatory gesture to the intelligence sections of other interested departments, Piesse allowed that 'while the general tendencies of the political and economic imperialism would be studied', the Branch would leave the more specialised aspects of Japan's policy to the Departments of Navy, Defence and Trade. Furthermore Piesse saw the Branch also helping to educate Australians about Asia and the Pacific. It was 'to take every opportunity to assist in the instruction of public opinion.'[19] By this means he hoped in particular to combat the ignorance which permitted crude ideas of race to dominate attitudes towards Japan, and so to make it easier for the government to modify the White Australia policy.

One of the first questions which came before him in this new role was the Japanese proposal to raise the status of their consulate-general to that of a legation and thereby establish formal diplomatic relations with Australia. Hughes himself on both his first and second wartime trips overseas had suggested to the cabinet that steps should be taken to arrange for diplomatic representation in the United States and Japan. Australia's Pacific security required that it should have direct access to these major regional powers, one the putative enemy and the other a desired protector. Each time difficulties had arisen to prevent the fulfilment of the objective. It raised

---

[17] Indeed Hughes was not consulted about the setting up of the Pacific Branch or about the appointment. Cabinet decision, 1 April 1919, NAA A3934/1 SC12/6; copy of letter, M.L. Shepherd, Secretary of Prime Minister's Department, to L.E. Groom, Minister for Works and Railways, 12 April 1919, *ibid.*; Cabinet decision, 8 May 1919, *ibid.*; copy of letter, Watt to Pearce, 16 May 1919, *ibid.*

[18] Letters, Piesse to Christina Piesse, 14 and 19 November 1918, Piesse Papers, NLA MS 882, Additional papers.

[19] Letter, Piesse to Watt, 16 April 1919, NAA A3934/1 SC12/6; copies of letters, Watt to Piesse, 16 May 1919 and Shepherd to Piesse, 28 May 1919, *ibid.*; Cabinet decision, 20 June 1919, *ibid.*

constitutional issues about the diplomatic unity of the Empire. His cabinet colleagues had reservations and Hughes did not have time or energy to pursue the matter. In the case of America the government, as a result of the stand taken by the Governor-General, had had to be content with the appointment of a trade commissioner. As for Japan the matter had been left on the shelf. In April 1919, however, at the height of the bitter dispute over the racial equality principle in the League Covenant, Baron Makino seems to have warmed to the idea. Since Hughes was the chief obstacle in the way of Japan achieving its goal Makino had told Keith Murdoch that Japan hoped 'for a clearer understanding between Japan and Australia by the exchange of visits, the improvement in representation, and perhaps an increase in the status of the consulates.'

On 1 July when Consul-General Shimizu was saying his farewells just before returning to Tokyo he indicated to Piesse that a suggestion, referring back to Makino's remarks, had been made that the consulate might become a legation. In reporting this to the Acting Prime Minister Piesse surmised that the Japanese might wish to influence Australian public opinion or, even more troubling, to settle 'directly the questions that now exist between us'. To his mind Australia would be well advised not to encourage this initiative. Australia would be in a stronger position if it kept the British intermediary as a barrier against Japanese claims and arguments.[20] The Japanese did not press the matter and so the opening of formal diplomatic relations was postponed for a generation, until almost the eve of the outbreak of the Pacific War. This early interest in opening formal diplomatic relations came not from a desire for national status but from a concern about national security.

The government believed that Piesse's first task in his new role should be to undertake an extensive fact-finding tour of East Asia. During this tour, which from September 1919 to March 1920 took him to Portuguese Timor, the Dutch East Indies, Singapore, French Indo-China and China, and culminated in a five-week stay in Japan, he inquired into Japanese influence on and penetration of the region. For example at the British Consulate at Batavia he read 'a large number of files on the internal political situation and the activities of Japanese in the Indies', and at Singapore he found the most interesting files in the offices of the Colonial Government to be 'those relating to the attempt made during the war to limit the acquisition by Japanese of land in the Malay Peninsula'.

On returning home he wrote reports on all the colonies and countries that he had visited but, of them all, the most significant and substantial was that on Japan.[21] In Japan Piesse sounded out a wide range of people and made arrangements, including the posting of Pacific Branch officers to the British Embassy, to ensure that he would be kept fully informed about Japanese affairs. Piesse was surprised to find that British officials at all levels and from all departments seemed 'keenly interested in the Australian point of view towards the Far East' and that 'they had a spontaneous and intensive interest in the relations of Australia and the Far East.' It was ever the case that 'in the discussion of such questions as the future of the Anglo-Japanese alliance … British officials placed

---

[20] Melbourne *Herald*, 10 April 1919; letter, Piesse to Secretary, Prime Minister's Department, 14 July 1919, NAA A981 Japan 101, Pt.1.

[21] 'Report on Tour of Duty of Director of the Pacific Branch, September 1919–March 1920', Piesse to Shepherd, 18 March 1920, Piesse Papers, NLA MS 882/5/1–65.

Australia's interests in the forefront'. How he had come to this conclusion remains a mystery. Nevertheless this revelation, he allowed, had 'an important bearing on the question of Australian representation in the East'; that is, since the British, at least in East Asia, were, contrary to his earlier judgment, giving proper attention to Australian interests the Commonwealth Government would have no good reason to seek separate representation in the region.[22]

But of all those he consulted during his tour the most important was the Japanese Vice-Minister for Foreign Affairs, Masanao Hanihara. At the meeting with Hanihara – organised by Shimizu – Piesse raised all the issues which since 1905 had created fear and suspicion in Australia and which had 'led to the present attitude of Australia towards Japan which unfortunately was not quite cordial.' Speaking with undiplomatic candour he said that Australia had been concerned not only with immigration and espionage questions but also had 'watched the development of Japan since the Russo-Japanese war at the expense of her neighbours.' Australians were troubled by the influence of imperialists on Japanese policy, especially those who advocated a Nan'yo or South Seas expansion. The Vice-Minister answered all points. He told Piesse that the Australians had provided no specific evidence to support their charge of spying and that Japan's proposed amendment to the League Covenant was directed not at removing restrictions on immigration but at 'the elimination of racial discrimination ... which, for no other reason but of the colour of skin deprived men of equal opportunity in life and often subjects them to an unbearable humiliation.' Further he denied that Japan had an imperialist policy. It sought only to achieve 'the security of the Empire through legitimate means'. This response helped to convince Piesse that Japan was not a danger to Australia.[23]

As a result of his investigations, Piesse played down the Japanese threat to Australia. In a paper entitled 'Japanese Expansion as it Affects Australia', he reported that nearly all the British and Americans whom he had met in Japan, including some 'whose opinion should be of the highest value', were agreed that expansion for expansion's sake had only a relatively small influence on Japan's foreign policy. They believed that Japan's territorial expansion could be explained more convincingly by a 'need of satisfying economic wants and security against overseas attacks'. They further held that Japan did not support emigration of its nationals, but in order to feed a growing population it, like many European countries, had been compelled to seek control of economic resources necessary for its survival. Japan's increased defence appropriations

---

[22] Piesse's unqualified praise for the assistance and understanding of the British officials in Tokyo sits a little oddly with the fact that he was denied full access to the Embassy archives. In a letter to the British Foreign Secretary, the British Charge d'Affaires in Tokyo said that Piesse had requested 'the fullest possible information on all aspects of Japan's foreign policy' for which purpose he wished to consult the Embassy archives and make notes on relevant matters. The Charge d'Affaires had, however, refused to 'permit a gentleman with whom I was unacquainted ... to have unrestricted access to the archives of His Majesty's Embassy.' See copy of letter, B. Alston, British Charge d'Affaires, to Lord Curzon, British Foreign Secretary, 23 January 1920, NAA A3934/1 SC12/6.

[23] 'Note of statements made by Major E.L. Piesse in a conversation with Mr. Hanihara, Vice-Minister for Foreign Affairs and Mr. S. Shimizu, Consul-General for Japan at Sydney', at *Gaimusho* (Japanese Foreign Office), 25 December 1919, and Hanihara's note in reply received at Manila, 20 February 1920, Piesse Papers, NLA MS 882/5/43–52 and 58–65.

in December 1919 were a response to the United States naval build-up. The Japanese were only preparing for 'a war of defence in their home waters'. Piesse's informants could find nothing in Japan's behaviour which 'threatened distant countries such as America and Australia'. Indeed, as far as Piesse could discover, it appeared that Japan was not interested in Australia. British and American diplomats and their naval and military attaches 'never heard Australia mentioned by the Japanese with whom they mixed.' Japan's occupation of the German North Pacific islands was 'clearly a precaution against the United States'. The publicists who had agitated for a southward policy were 'not representative of general opinion'. The authorities he had consulted found it 'quite incredible' to think that 'Japan could have any plans of aggression in the immediate future against Australia.'[24]

Only one conclusion could be drawn from this account of Piesse's discussion with Western authorities in Japan. While he did not directly endorse their judgments nevertheless their views pervaded his reports. He discounted all the argument that had been advanced to justify Australia's fear of Japan. He did not cite one opinion or observation which might have modified this positive assessment of Japan's foreign policy. Unlike his customary careful use of evidence he offered no critical analysis of the expert opinions. Perhaps his informants were so unanimous that there seemed nothing more to be said. Perhaps since this was his first overseas trip as head of the Australian foreign office he was a little overawed by the authority of the British and American professionals. Or perhaps he was happy to let the material speak for itself since it confirmed ideas to which he was already moving. Whatever the explanation the tour marked a turning point in Piesse's view of the Japanese threat.

It is not known whether Hughes read Piesse's reports. Certainly, if he did, he was not influenced by them. The Prime Minister continued throughout 1920 and 1921 to see Japan as a menace to Australia and to seek a defence policy aimed at countering a hostile Japan. Moreover Hughes had no sympathy for Piesse's proposals for amending the White Australia policy and so quieting Japan's sense of grievance. Piesse challenged the orthodoxies of White Australia most fully in a series of papers prepared for Senator E. D. Millen before the latter left at the end of 1920 to represent Australia at the first meeting of the League of Nations. It was expected that the Japanese would, as they had foreshadowed at Paris, once again raise the issue of racial equality. Piesse's visit to Japan had confirmed him in his view that Australia's opposition to including a racial equality statement in the League Covenant was unnecessary and had only served to give ammunition to extreme militarist and imperialist elements, and he took this opportunity to set out his convictions most fully.

In his first paper, 'Racial Prejudice and Racial Discrimination: Miscellaneous Notes', he set out the result of his reading on the subject of biological determinism and racial discrimination. He cited a number of authorities who upheld 'the equality in innate capacity of the various peoples of the world', and claimed that 'racial differences [were] due to environment more than to biological heredity.' These authorities also showed 'how racial dislike arises' and how 'the white feeling of racial superiority is recent.' He was manifestly using these authorities to express his own

---

[24] Report, 'Japanese Expansion as it Affects Australia', Piesse to Secretary, Prime Minister's Department, 22 March 1920, *ibid.,* NLA MS 882/5/66–74.

thoughts on the matter and to lay a theoretical foundation for specific changes to White Australia's theory and practice.

In a second paper he listed all the state and federal laws discriminating against non-Europeans who were British subjects, naturalised Australian or otherwise resident in Australia and he urged the government to consider 'the effect of our policy on the attitude towards us of Japan and of the Asiatic countries which Japan may in the future be able to influence.' He suggested that it would be 'wise for us, so far as we can, to shape our policy so that we shall not incur the enmity of Asiatic countries.' With this in mind he recommended that on issues such as naturalisation and the right to vote there was in the case of the Japanese 'probably little reason for applying discrimination based merely on the ground of race.' Moreover he added that this would 'probably be true for the Chinese, and even in India there are many people who are our equals.'

On the more vexed question of immigration Piesse applied the same argument. Australia should stress that its discriminatory policy was economic and not racial. He repeated his earlier contention that Australia should appease Japan by entering into an agreement placing its nationals on the same basis as Europeans and leaving it to the Japanese to prevent unwanted immigration through their control over the issue of passports. He pointed out that this arrangement had proved satisfactory in both Canada and the United States.

Senator Millen, perusing these papers on board ship on his way to Europe, was astounded by their contents which seemed to undermine the one agreed principle of Australia's national life. He thus wired Hughes to inquire whether cabinet had read and approved these papers. Millen thought that 'they recommend such a whittling away of existing restrictions as would result in complete abandonment of the White Australia Policy.' Hughes, when he read them, was equally appalled. He could not contain himself and scribbled critical remarks against the most offensive passages. He was particularly incensed by the assertion that 'the utterances of Australian public men have attracted much more adverse criticism in Japan than have those of American public men' – which was patently aimed at the Prime Minister – and pencilled over it, 'Where is there any proof of this? I know of none & don't accept it.' No doubt it reminded him of Watt's rebuke during the Paris Peace Conference and perhaps he could discern here the source of Watt's opinions. Even more tellingly Hughes crossed out Piesse's key proposition, namely that there was 'probably little reason now for applying discrimination based on race' to the Japanese as compared to 'less advanced European nations', and wrote 'rot' against it. It offended his biological determinism. Piesse's arguments were anathema to Hughes and he told Millen that he disagreed 'entirely' with the briefing papers and that they should be ignored.[25]

Piesse persisted with his critical assessments of government leaders' alarmist speeches which implicitly pointed to Japan as a threat to White Australia and was dismissive of further claims of Japanese espionage in Australia. In the first case he reported that Hughes's speech on Australian defence policy on 9 September and Millen's on his departure to represent Australia at the first meeting of the General Assembly of the League of Nations had gained wide currency in the

---

[25] 'Papers Prepared in the Pacific Branch in Connection with the First Assembly of the League of Nations, Geneva, November 1920', NAA A3934/1 SC42; cables, Millen to Hughes, 17 October 1920 and Hughes to Millen, 23 October 1920, *ibid.*

Japanese press and that as a result, 'To the Japanese public we again, as we did during the Peace Conference, thus seem to have a foremost place among her enemies.'[26]

Such criticism did not endear Piesse to Hughes and it seems clear that he came to distrust Piesse and took steps to limit his influence. Perhaps the fact that Piesse had been appointed by Watt, who in June had resigned from the ministry and become a thorn in Hughes's side, also helped to fuel the Prime Minister's suspicions of the Director of the Pacific Branch. From this time there is no evidence that Hughes gave any attention to Piesse's reports. In early 1921 he instructed the Governor-General that British Foreign Office papers were to be reserved exclusively for the Prime Minister's use, thus cutting Piesse off from access to one of the most important sources of the material he needed to carry out his official duties.[27] Hughes did not take the Director of the Pacific Branch with him to the 1921 Imperial Conference. Piesse resented Hughes's actions in sidelining him and came to despair about this first experiment in setting up an Australian foreign office. Hughes, at the same time as isolating Piesse, had revived the office of the Minister for External Affairs and added that portfolio to his own. It was not intended to acknowledge the need for a foreign office, that is for expert advisers, but rather to emphasise that he would not only decide Australia's foreign policy but also act as his own adviser on all issues.

Planning for post-war defence

The Watt Government's establishment of the Pacific Branch of the Prime Minister's Department and its concern about Japan's future intentions were directly related to its post-war defence policy. During the war Australia's anxieties about Japan had intensified. From 1916 the Australian Government had begun to make plans to meet the Japanese challenge which they believed might well emerge at the end of the war. The naval and military intelligence officers were preoccupied with the Japanese question. To this end, the Naval Board and the Military Board had warned the government about the dangers inherent in allowing Japan to gain permanent rights over Germany's Pacific possessions. Likewise they had supported a proposal to restructure the Council of Defence to enable it to provide the country with a more comprehensive and effective machinery for preparing the country to resist foreign threats. This reformed organisation would integrate all the nation's resources – the armed forces, the industrial, technological and scientific infrastructure, the transport and communication systems and intelligence gathering. Pearce, in

---

[26] Memorandum on 'Japanese Comment on Australia's Attitude to the White Australia Policy', Piesse to the Secretary. Prime Minister's Department, 15 November 1920, *ibid.*, and NAA A2219, Vol.17.

Millen in being farewelled for his trip to the League of Nations meeting at Geneva echoed Hughes, stating that 'The White Australia principle is an as essential to Australia as the Monroe Doctrine is for America and the Freedom of the Seas to Great Britain ... We must fill Australia with white men, otherwise we run the great risk of other nations endeavouring to fill Australia for us ... If the policy is to be successfully maintained the population of Australia must be very considerably increased by men of our own kith and kin, and more especially British soldiers who fought side by side with our own boys.' *SMH*, 24 September 1920.

[27] Letter, Piesse to George H. Blakeslee, Professor of History and International Relations, Clark University, Worcester, Massachusetts, 14 October 1920, Piesse Papers, NLA MS 882/1/93–96.

recommending this new scheme to Hughes, endorsed the idea of appointing a full-time secretary for the council who would 'keep in mind continually the possibility of war with foreign powers.'[28] What Pearce had in mind in this latter respect was achieved partially through the appointment of Piesse as the Director of the Pacific Branch of the Prime Minister's Department.

This new Council of Defence was a response to the European conflict in that it was a reflection of the need to organise the country for total war. While in principle aimed at preparing for war from whatever quarter the challenge might arise it was inspired fundamentally to meet a perceived threat from Japan. The idea emerged from the Munitions Committee which the government, following Britain's example, had established in 1915 to systematise the production of all the requirements of a modern army. Captain W. H. C. S. Thring, the Director of War Staff in the Naval Office and the naval representative on the committee, argued for a central war planning authority which would coordinate all the relevant elements of the economy, the technical professions and the defence forces. While the scheme had arisen out of the problems associated with supplying the AIF with uniforms, rifles and ammunition and manufacturing high explosive shell and other military equipment, the intention from the beginning was to make Australia 'self-contained' for defence purposes. That is, the new body was to carry forward the defence policy that Prime Minister Andrew Fisher had laid down in his pre-war administrations and again in his statements of Australian defence policy after assuming office in September 1914.[29]

This initiative also fitted well with the Navy Department's briefing papers about the Japanese danger that Thring had written and the Naval Board approved at the end of 1915. From the first draft in 1916 to the inauguration of the Council of Defence two years later Fisher's policy remained the rationale for creating this national security council. The Thring report was headed 'Organisation for promoting the security and welfare of the Commonwealth of Australia'. In the midst of war it asserted that this new body would 'coordinate the work of the Departments of the Commonwealth in order to make the best uses of all resources for the defence of the Empire.' Even so, the announced purpose of this reformed Council of Defence was 'that some definite line of policy may be laid down for the adequate defence of Australia' and 'to make the Commonwealth self-supporting as may be'. Pearce, in calling together a preliminary meeting of the Council of Defence in March 1918, justified the innovation by asserting that 'some closer connexions should exist between the Commonwealth Government and the Council of Defence in order that definite lines of policy may be laid down for the defence of Australia.' Looking towards the post-war era he added that, 'It is important to make the Commonwealth self-supporting in respect to war materiel as far as may be.'[30]

---

[28] Letter, Pearce to Hughes, 10 August 1917, Hughes Papers, NLA MS 1538/117/3.

[29] *Search for Security*, p.178; *Argus*, 5 August 1914; *CPD*, 1914–17 session, LXXXVII, 1338-48, 3 December 1914 and 4095-96, 17 June 1915.

[30] Report, 'Organisation for promoting the security and welfare of the Commonwealth of Australia', Federal Munitions Committee to Pearce, 4 April 1916, NAA MP729/2 1851/2/47; Memorandum upon the Establishment of a Council of Defence, 15 March 1918, NAA A9787/2 2.

In 1918 and 1919 the council, apart from its abortive efforts to set up a loyalist Australian Protective League, concentrated mainly on forming its eight standing subcommittees and attempting to lay down the basis for a post-war air-force. The council itself was a complex structure; the subcommittees covered 'strategy and combined operations', 'manufactures and trade', 'intelligence', 'inventions', 'war economics', 'transport', 'censorship' and legal matters. It was nothing if not comprehensive in its planning. Much attention was given to defining the scope of each of these subcommittees and choosing the personnel who would serve on them. The council itself, made up as it was of the Prime Minister, the Minister for Defence, the Minister for the Navy, the Treasurer and two representatives each from the navy and the army, was designed to be a decision making body which would determine national security policy and give energy and direction to the whole establishment. Yet, despite this grand administrative blueprint, in the nine meetings between 23 March 1918 and 15 April 1919 (the last meeting for that year), the council achieved very little. In this period it operated under several grave handicaps. Firstly, its senior members – Hughes, Cook and latterly Pearce – were in Europe, and so it lacked authority; secondly, the shape of the post-war world, including the role of the proposed League of Nations, was unclear; and thirdly the accumulating war debt forced the government to look for savings in every area of expenditure. The financial problems weighed heavily on Watt's shoulders. At the April 1919 meeting, the first and most important item of business concerned defence expenditure and a motion was carried asking the responsible ministers 'to effect all savings possible',[31] a task which they had to admit could not be addressed until the council was able in the aftermath of the Peace Conference to perceive clearly the country's strategic position.

The only substantive issue which the council dealt with in this interim period was the creation of an air force. The European war had demonstrated that air power was a weapon with great potential. Early in 1918 Chief of the General Staff Major-General Legge, who in the decade before the war had been the Australian staff officer most convinced of the high possibility of a Japanese threat and had in 1917 urged that more attention should be paid to home defence, was worried that Australia might have to repel an invasion. He urged the government to look to its land defences, including the building of a military arsenal, the construction of strategic railways, and especially the acquisition of a powerful air force; 'The urgency of preparation is a vital question for Australia.'

Legge argued that Australia's naval strength for many years would be 'weaker … than any country that can attack us' and in making this statement he had in mind Japan. He seemed to have no expectations of receiving help from the British navy. Adequate and thorough measures for land defence were of 'pressing importance' and therefore Australia should build an air force which could contribute greatly to 'breaking the strength of an attack or increasing the value of an inferior defending force.' For this purpose he recommended that it should set up an Australian air

---

See also Minutes, Council of Defence meeting 15 April 1919, *ibid.*, when the Council authorised its subcommittee on 'Resources and Manufactures' to draw up a conspectus 'showing the requirements for Defence purposes … on the basis of Australia being self-contained.'

The *Defence Act* Regulations which gave legal status to the new Council of Defence were not gazetted until 9 October 1918 but were backdated to 23 April 1918.

[31] Minutes, Council of Defence Meeting, 15 April 1919, NAA A9798/2 2.

service and begin the manufacture of 200 aeroplanes and 12 balloons.[32] The Military Board and Navy Department endorsed Legge's plan. The Military Board claimed that it was 'absolutely essential in the interest of the safety of Australia' and the Chief of the Naval Staff wanted four Australian air bases established to the north of Australia 'as far advanced in the direction of the enemy as possible'.[33]

Pearce and Watt were convinced by Legge's argument and after cabinet approved the plan in principle it went to the Council of Defence for advice about the size, nature and control of the air service.[34] The council had to decide whether the land and sea forces should continue to maintain their own air arms or whether it should establish an air force as a separate entity. In August 1918 the cabinet promised £3 million spread over three years for the construction in Australia of 200 planes and the payment of salaries and maintenance. This scheme was almost immediately caught up in the problems which arose from the armistice. Given the uncertain post-war circumstances and the need to cut costs, the council agreed to set up only a temporary organisation designed to meet the needs of the naval and military services and to limit its budget for 1919–20 to £500,000. Since the British offered to make a gift of the Australian Flying Corps' 100 machines there was no longer any urgency about manufacturing aircraft in Australia and this idea was put on hold. The Air Services Committee, set up to supervise the temporary air arm, cut their cloth to suit the government's purse. They recommended that the air service should have two stations or bases, one at Corio Bay in Victoria and the other in the vicinity of Sydney and that they should house only two half squadrons of 30 planes each; the British were to be informed that at this stage Australia could only usefully accept 60 planes. Watt was pleased with the outcome, commenting that the scheme was 'not beyond Australia's capacity to handle'.[35] And it was this scheme, a severely modified version of the original plan, which was adopted.

The government faced similar constraints in giving thought more generally to its post-war defence policy. During the war it had endeavoured to maintain the compulsory military training for home defence that had been in operation since 1910. But the war-driven pressures on financial and human resources made this task very onerous. With but a brief break in late 1915 the training of boys and young men for the citizen army or Australian military force had, however, continued in a considerably modified form and Pearce had attempted in 1917 and 1918 to strengthen home forces by seeking voluntary enlistments.[36] As a result, the formal strength of Australia's home

---

[32] Legge, 'Military Memorandum on the Air Service in Australian Defence, 29 April 1918, NAA MP729/2.
[33] Military Board, 'Recommendation' on 'Australian Flying Corps in the Australian Military Forces', 9 December 1918 and Captain W.H. Thring, Director of Naval War Staff, 'Naval Aviation, Naval Requirements', July 1918, NAA MP729/2.
[34] Minute by Watt on Legge's 'Military Memorandum on the Air Service in Australian Defence', 29 April 1918 and 30 April 1918, NAA MP729/2.
[35] Minutes, Council of Defence Meetings, 6 June, 28 August and 4 November 1918 and 20 January and 14 February 1919, NAA A9798/2 2; *Argus*, 21 April 1919.
[36] Scott, *Australian During the War*, pp.196–97; *SMH*, 7 February 1917 and cable, Pearce to Hughes, 1 May 1918, NAA CP360/8 B1/1.

defence establishment, that is excluding all junior and senior military cadets, rose from 45,645 in 1914 to 122,186 in 1918.[37]

As the Peace Conference drew to its close the government, having to make provision for defence expenditure in framing a budget for 1919–20, appointed an expert committee, composed of Generals Legge, White and McCay and the government's financial watchdog George Swinburne, to advise on the post-war requirements. The committee agreed that the pre-war system of universal military training should continue and be made more effective. Despite the complete defeat of Germany and the lack of any evidence that the British or the Americans intended to continue with universal training after the Peace Treaty was signed the Australians remained committed to this pre-war preparedness program. Even the creation of the League of Nations was not seen as a reason for Australia giving up its concerns about Japan. Though under pressure to secure economies the government's advisers would not give up what was the most expensive single item in the defence budget.

The committee recommended that each quota of 18 year olds should, over a four year training period, be in camp in the first year for thirteen continuous weeks and for shorter periods in the subsequent years. By the mid-1920s the citizen force would comprise six infantry divisions and two mounted divisions which, with the returned AIF in the reserve, would give Australia a total military force of 180,000 men – the minimum number required 'to protect Australia … during any temporary loss of Imperial sea command in the Indian and Pacific oceans.' The committee also proposed that the government should in the same period establish an arsenal which would make 'the country self-contained' in the manufacture of rifles, ammunition, artillery and aircraft.[38]

For Watt the cost of this scheme was formidable when set against the heavy burden of the war debt. Defence expenditure for the financial year 1918–19 exceeded all previous levels. When all AIF repatriation and pension costs and interest on war loans were added together it amounted to over £77.56 million or 20 times the last pre-war defence budget.[39] He was torn between the need to make drastic economies and the concern to ensure that Australia was not exposed to external dangers. Thus he was happy to accept the committee's recommendations that the compulsory system should be suspended for the 1918–19 financial year to allow for the training of the officers and the return of Hughes, Cook and Pearce who would 'be fully acquainted with the latest arrangements with regard to the Peace Conference and the League of Nations'.[40]

The only military issue touching home defence that the government had to decide before the Peace Conference was a British proposal for Dominion contributions to a post-war imperial army. Encouraged by the very substantial expeditionary forces which the Dominions had raised in

---

[37] *Official Year Book of the Commonwealth of Australia, 1919–1920 (No.14 – 1921)* (Melbourne: Commonwealth Bureau of Census and Statistics, 1921), p.919.

[38] Letter, E.J. Russell, Acting Minister of Defence, to Watt, 30 June 1919, containing the 'Report on certain matters of defence policy', NAA MP367/1 629/1/741.

[39] *Official Year Book … 1921*, p.927.

[40] 'Notes of a Conference Held at Prime Minister's Office between Members of the Committee Considering Questions of Defence and the Acting Prime Minister and the Acting Minister of Defence and Assistant Minister of State for Defence', 9 July 1919, NAA MP367/1 629/1/741.

support of the Mother Country the War Office, reviving the idea it had put to Australia at the end of the Boer War, drew up a plan for an imperial army which would be available to serve not only for the occupation of Germany but perhaps also for the defence of the Empire more generally. Initially when Pearce was approached by General Birdwood, he had agreed to appoint General Brudenell White to a committee to discuss the plan, though he made it clear that Australia would not be bound by any decision that the committee might reach. But Hughes, who had been forewarned as a result of a discussion of the topic in the Imperial War Cabinet, cabled Watt that Australia should have nothing whatever to do with the scheme and should not even send a representative to sit on the committee. At the Imperial War Cabinet meeting Hughes had joined Borden in opposing the scheme. Hughes, as a result of the unilateral action of Lloyd George over the armistice, had become convinced that there was no Imperial Government, that the Imperial War Cabinet under Lloyd George's leadership was an empty vessel. Moreover he was convinced that the Australian people would want their troops to be brought home as soon as possible. He told Watt that 'this idea must be killed at its inception.' On reconsideration the cabinet agreed and Birdwood was informed that Australia would not participate in the committee.[41]

The navy raised even more formidable problems. In 1912, in response to Britain's abandonment of plans for an imperial Pacific fleet, Prime Minister Fisher had adopted Admiral Henderson's report which had recommended the acquisition of a self-sufficient Australian navy comprised of eight armoured cruisers, ten light cruisers, eighteen destroyers, twelve submarines, three depot ships and a fleet repair ship. In addition Australia would construct three major naval bases and associated shore facilities. The Fisher Government believed that, in the absence of an imperial Pacific fleet, this naval force should at the least be able to deter Japan from attempting any hostile move against Australia. The carrying out of the naval scheme was to be spread over twenty-two years and was estimated to cost £23.29 million. During the first of the four stages of its development – that is from 1911 to 1918 – Henderson had laid it down that in addition to completing the fleet unit agreed to at the 1909 Imperial Defence Conference, the government should build the naval bases from which it could operate. It should also build three more submarines by 1916, and three more destroyers in 1917 and another three in 1918.[42]

During the first years of the war the government, despite the expense, had tried to keep to the Henderson program. In 1913 it had begun building the light cruiser *Brisbane* and two destroyers, and in 1915 another destroyer. The following year the naval shipyard at Cockatoo Island in Sydney harbour laid down a further light cruiser, the *Adelaide*.[43] Likewise in 1914 and 1915 the Naval Board had commenced work on the Henderson base at Cockburn Sound near Fremantle and the Flinders base in Port Phillip Bay. By 1917, however, the mounting cost of the bases and the naval vessels was imposing a heavy burden on the over-stretched war economy and it forced

---

[41] Memorandum, Secretary of Defence to Secretary of Prime Minister's Department, 30 December 1918, NAA A3934 SC15/62; cable, Hughes to Watt, 18 December 1918, NAA CP360/8 B1/2; cable, Watt to Hughes, 16 January 1919, *ibid.*; Minutes of Imperial War Cabinet Meeting (42), 12 December 1918, TNA: PRO CAB 23/42.

[42] Meaney, *Search for Security,* pp.228–29.

[43] C.E.W. Bean, *Official History of Australia in the War of 1914–18,* Vol.IX, 'The Royal Australian Navy' by A.W. Jose, Appendix 4.

the responsible ministers to consider whether they should proceed further with the construction of ships and bases.

The matter was brought to a head when the Naval Board, in accordance with the Henderson timetable, recommended that the government commit itself to completing the first stage in the development of the bases. By mid-1917 almost £1.5 million had been spent on the Henderson base at Cockburn Sound and the Naval Board accepted a somewhat abridged version of the original scheme which would cost £5.5 million over ten years. The government was alarmed at the total cost of naval expenditure. It had risen from about £2 million in 1913–14 to just over £6 million in 1916–17; £2.5 million of the latter was charged to local as opposed to war costs, with almost £900,000 being spent on building naval vessels and naval bases. Therefore the government wanted to know whether the experience of the war might have provided grounds for revising the Henderson scheme.[44] Though Creswell, the First Member of the Naval Board, could offer no reason for believing that this was likely to be so, the ministers insisted that the Admiralty should be asked for their advice. The Admiralty, occupied with more urgent war tasks, procrastinated and Australia had to wait eight months for a reply. When a cable arrived in May 1918 it offered very little guidance and the guidance it did give still involved continuing some investment in the naval bases.[45]

Watt, by then Treasurer and Acting Prime Minister, was greatly exercised by the problem. He was an inveterate worrier as well as a stickler for proper procedures. Having served as Victorian Treasurer for five years he took a much greater interest in managing the economy and controlling government expenditure than his federal predecessors or Hughes. Though the accumulated war debt and its implication for post-war budgets weighed heavily upon him he could not ignore the possible strategic risks which might be entailed in abandoning the Henderson program. Thus he still felt it necessary to seek reassurance that any cutbacks or delays would not be at the cost of

---

[44] Minute Paper by W.R. Creswell, First Naval Member, 14 March 1917 and Minute by Joseph Cook, Minister for the Navy, 29 August 1917, NAA MP1185/5 17/021; Minutes of Meeting of the Naval Board, 16 and 19 March 1917, NAA A2585/1; *Official Year Book … 1921*, pp.926–27.

[45] Minute, Naval Board Secretary to Cook, 30 September1917, NAA MP1185/5 17/021.
The Naval Board in replying to Cook stated that if existing government policy was to remain premised upon the Henderson assumptions of Australian self-reliance for naval defence rather than on an Imperial naval force for the defence of all British possessions in the Pacific, then 'only very minor modifications of the Henderson scheme are necessary as the result of the war.' Indeed, if the latter, which was the Board's estimate of the more likely possibility, this alternative policy would require 'amplification' of the Henderson scheme of bases in order to accommodate the larger fleet. Since no decision had been reached on post-war policy the Board had limited base development to the more limited scheme which, as they had previously explained, would cost £5.5 million over ten years.
Letters, W.A. Watt, Minister for Works and Railways who had oversight of the base-building, to Cook, 5 and 22 September 1917 and cable, Naval Office, Melbourne to Rear-Admiral Haworth Booth, Australian Representative at the Admiralty, London, 28 September 1917, *ibid*. Both ministers were unhappy with this answer and agreed that the Admiralty should be asked to advise whether the war experience and new naval technology might require a 'fundamental revision' of the Henderson scheme both in respect to bases and the fleet unit. A cable containing the request was sent on 28 September 1917.

national security and for this reason supported Piesse's efforts to obtain a more accurate assessment of the Japanese danger.

From well after the signing of the armistice, the Australian Government was still seeking more precise advice from the Admiralty. By that time, however, Australia's specific concerns were caught up in the larger question of post-war plans for imperial naval defence and the proposal for a senior British Admiral to visit the Dominions to report on their naval requirements. Thus Cook suggested that all naval base works could be 'safely suspended' to await the recommendations of the British naval expert. [46]

The Jellicoe mission

Before the war the Pacific Dominions had openly criticised the British Government for reneging on its promise to contribute to the creation of an imperial Pacific fleet. At the 1917 Imperial Conference the New Zealand representatives, in the absence of the Australians, took the lead in complaining about the British failure to honour this commitment to Pacific naval defence, and as a result the Empire's leaders had asked the Admiralty:

> To work out … what they consider the most effective scheme of naval defence of the Empire for the consideration of the several Governments … with such recommendations as the Admiralty consider necessary … for the Empire's security.[47]

In response the Admiralty in May 1918 presented a memorandum dealing with the future structure of the Empire's naval forces for the consideration of the Imperial War Cabinet. It maintained that the experience of the war had reaffirmed the wisdom of the 'one Empire, one ocean, one navy' doctrine and concluded that 'the whole naval forces of the Empire' should be 'under the control of an Imperial Naval Authority in peace and war'. The Admiralty recognised that in the light of the changes in Dominion status achieved during the war years this Imperial Authority would have to include representatives of the Dominions, and it suggested that until these changes took a clear constitutional form the Dominions' navy ministers should attend meetings of the Authority at least once a year and that in their absence the First Lord of the Admiralty would stand in for them.[48]

The Admiralty's answer to New Zealand's question did not satisfy the Dominions. Borden and Hughes insisted that it would not do. Hughes's reservations, deriving as they did from the

---

[46] Cable, Long to Munro Ferguson, 27 May 1918 and despatch, Long to Munro Ferguson, 23 May 1918 (arriving 5 August 1918) containing Admiralty's reply and cables, Watt to Cook, 24 August 1918, Watt to Cook, 22 November 1918 and Cook to Watt, 27 November 1918, NAA CP360/8 B1/2 and MP1185/5 17/021.

After receiving Cook's message cabinet agreed to complete the Flinders base at a cost of £150,000 and to cease all work on the Henderson base until they received the advice of the visiting British naval expert. See copy of letter, Watt to A. Poynton, Acting Minister for the Navy, 28 November 1918 and extract from cable, Watt to Australian High Commission, London, 30 November 1918, NAA A981 Defence 350, Pt.1.

[47] Minutes of the 1917 Imperial War Conference, TNA: PRO CO 532/97/585–618 and 864–66.

[48] Admiralty Memorandum for the War Cabinet, 'Naval defence of the British Empire', 17 May 1918, TNA: PRO ADM116/1815.

pre-war experience, took issue with the one ocean premise. They were encapsulated in a paper which Latham had written for the Australian ministers in which Latham took to task the Admiralty's 'The Seas Are One' doctrine and laid it down that though the Admiralty's principle 'was no doubt correct until the advent of Japan as a Sea Power', Australia since that time had rejected it as a proper basis for determining the Empire's naval strategy. On the contrary, Latham contended that 'the Oceans of the world [were] divided into two parts' – the Atlantic Ocean and the Mediterranean Sea on the one side, and the Pacific and Indian Oceans on the other. Since 'the centres of sea power in Europe and Japan [were] as distant from one another as they can well be … a predominant sea power in Europe [was] no longer able to make good a well-organised success by Japan in the other hemisphere.' What followed for imperial naval policy was that:

> For the defence of Australasia it [was] necessary that a naval force should be stationed in the Pacific or Indian Ocean which would be powerful enough to prevent Japan from establishing or maintaining herself in strength in Australasia …

Replying to the Admiralty, the Dominion prime ministers declared that what was proposed was not practicable. It was their view that, provided the character and armament of naval vessels and the training and organisation of each navy remained the same, the ability of the Dominion navies to act with the British navy in time of war would be preserved. While they were not willing to place their naval forces under a London-centred authority over which they had no effective control, they allowed that as their navies grew in size it might be possible to establish 'a supreme naval authority upon which each of the Dominions would be adequately represented'. It would be a defence counterpart to the Imperial Cabinet. In the meantime the Dominions would welcome visits from a well qualified representative of the Admiralty who could advise them on the future structure of their navies. [49]

As the war drew to its close the Admiralty felt able to oblige the Dominions. The Australians were the most importunate and Cook on 16 November requested the Admiralty to send Lord Jellicoe, who had commanded the Grand Fleet at the Battle of Jutland, to review 'the whole naval position in the light of the circumstances of the war, and more particularly, with respect to the building scheme suggested by Henderson.'[50] The Admiralty agreed and commissioned Jellicoe to tour all the self-governing Dominions and India and report on their naval requirements. Though the British naval authorities had not resiled from their centralising principle they were nevertheless willing that Jellicoe's remit should be limited to advising the Dominions how best to organise their naval forces to meet local needs and to secure 'the greatest possible homogeneity and cooperation between all the Naval Forces of the Empire'. If, however, the Dominions should express a desire 'to take a more effective share in the Naval Defence of the Empire' he was given authority to draw up a scheme for their consideration.[51]

---

[49] 'The Seas Are One', NAA MP 1587/1 184J; copy of letter, Borden to Sir Eric Geddes, First Lord of the Admiralty, 15 August 1918, NAA A981 Defence 350, Pt.1.
[50] Letter, Cook to Geddes, 16 November 1918, TNA: PRO ADM 116/1831 and 1/8548.
[51] Copy of letter, Secretary to the Admiralty to Lord Jellicoe, 23 December 1918 enclosing 'Instructions for Lord Jellicoe', TNA: PRO ADM 116/1815.

The Naval Board saw Jellicoe's visit as a decisive event in preparing Australia to meet the post-war problems of defence in the Pacific. At its instance Watt asked Jellicoe to report also on 'Naval strategical problems affecting Australian waters and the Pacific'. In an attached document the Australian problem was spelt out; it asked about 'Probable routes of attack on Australia with special reference to occupation by a foreign power of Islands north of the Equator', 'Probable composition of Imperial Fleet in Pacific' and 'Suggested organised cooperation in Pacific Defence by Canada, New Zealand, India and Malay States'.[52] Since 1905 the Australian Government had come to believe that the best answer to Australian security lay in the creation of a Pacific imperial fleet. The Allies' victory had revived hope that the British Empire might at last have such a fleet.

Admiral Jellicoe set out on this mission in January. He was a protégé of Lord Fisher who had, as First Sea Lord of the Admiralty, been the author of the 1909 Imperial Defence Conference proposal for a Pacific Fleet. Jellicoe was fully informed about both that plan and the Henderson scheme. He took his task seriously and recognised that Australia, as its pre-war actions had shown, was the lynchpin for the development of imperial naval defence in the Pacific. South Africa was too distant from the centre of the problem; indeed imperial cooperation was so divisive an issue that he was forced to cancel his visit to that country. Canada under the protection of the United States Monroe Doctrine was lukewarm about naval defence. New Zealand was too small to be more than a follower of Australia or the Admiralty. And India under British rule could not act freely and its native representatives were not sympathetic to spending money on imperial defence. Thus Jellicoe gave more attention to Australia than to any other Dominion and produced a four volume report which was more comprehensive and detailed than those which followed his visits to India, New Zealand and Canada.

On reaching Australia in May, Jellicoe saw that his recommendations must be based on an assessment of threats to Australian and other British interests in the Pacific. Indeed Watt's questions could not be answered without identifying likely enemies or denying that there was an enemy. The Admiralty had not provided Jellicoe with any guidance on the strategic question and so he was left to determine the matter for himself. In the fourth volume of his report, a secret volume – the other three were made public – he set out an elaborate case for taking Japan as the potential menace against which the British Empire had to plan its naval defence.

Setting aside the United States as a possible enemy, he contended that Japan was 'the only nation in the Far Eastern Waters which would be in a position to inflict any permanent injury on the British Empire'. Like the Australian leaders, he had no faith in the Anglo-Japanese alliance. He pointed out that during the war 'the relations between Great Britain and Japan were characterised by mutual distrust.' When the course of the war was going badly for the Allies, Japan's press became very critical of the alliance and expressed 'ill-feeling' towards Britain. He noted that when London had asked for military and naval assistance Tokyo always refused the former and exacted a price for help of the latter kind. What is more there were substantial sources of friction in the relationship, such as Japan's commercial penetration of India, its attempts to exert control over China and Australia's exclusionary immigration policy. For these reasons he concluded it was 'almost inevitable that the interest of Japan and of the British Empire will eventually clash.'

---

[52] Letter, Watt to Jellicoe, with attachment, 1 May 1919, NAA A981/4 DEF Pts I and II.

Though for diplomatic reasons this strategic threat assessment was put in a secret volume, the chapter in the first volume which dealt with 'Naval Requirements in the Far East' did little, apart from refraining to name Japan, to hide the identity of the enemy against whom the Empire's naval policy was to be directed.

To meet this contingency he accepted, at least to some extent, the Australian argument that distance from the British Isles meant the Empire should have a fleet in the Indian and Pacific Oceans as well as in European waters. That is, he accepted in principle the 1909 Imperial Defence Conference proposal for an imperial fleet in the Pacific to which the Dominions would make contributions. For the purpose he maintained that, in the light of Japan's wartime naval building program, the British Empire would need 'a fleet of capital ship … stationed in the Pacific … composed of not less than eight battleships and eight battle cruisers' with all the ancillary light cruisers, destroyers, submarines, minesweepers, oilers and so forth, in total 130 vessels. Jellicoe was prescribing a 'Grand Fleet' for the Pacific for, as he wrote, 'nothing less than equality in modern capital ships can be relied upon to give security in the future against war with Japan'. In making his recommendations he accepted that Australians of all political persuasion were insistent that their ships would comprise a distinct squadron.

On the question of control, the former First Sea Lord had difficulties in adapting his acceptance of the Empire's geopolitical division to the Admiralty's doctrine of 'one sea, one fleet, one Empire', and its fundamental principle of global concentration and centralised command. In essence he remained orthodox. Thus he asserted that in war the Empire's fleet would still have 'to come under the single control of the British Admiralty' and that if the main theatre of war was in European or Atlantic waters, 'some portion of the ['Far Eastern'] fleet might be required in those waters.' Nevertheless because of the 20,000 kilometres separating Australasia from the United Kingdom the Admiralty should delegate command of the Far Eastern Fleet to a high-ranking flag officer stationed in Singapore. In time of war all Dominion squadrons as well as British squadrons in the Pacific and Indian oceans would come under his control. This solution, though a concession to the Australian Naval Board's views, did not go as far as Latham and others had proposed in giving assured protection to the British Dominions in the Pacific and allowing the Australian and other Dominion governments a say in the deployment of an imperial fleet. The new 'Grand Fleet' was intended to contain Japan in the Pacific in the same way that the original Grand Fleet had been devised to contain Germany in the North Sea. But there was a significant difference between the two circumstances. Since the Admiralty had control over the Pacific fleet it could, as it had in 1905, move the capital ships to the North Sea even if this left the British Dominions exposed to an attack.

There was some confusion in Jellicoe's proposals for the defence of Australia. On the one hand he argued that his East Asian fleet would be as strong as that of the Japanese in capital ships, and superior to the Japanese in seamanship, and therefore adequate to deter or prevent the Japanese from attacking the British Empire or British interests in the Pacific. Yet on the other he had in assuming Japan's 'final aim' to be 'the invasion of Australia' stated that Australia should prepare local defences to meet the possibility since Britain might not be able to despatch 'any naval forces to reinforce the Far Eastern Fleet'. This local naval defence was to include bases, submarines, aircraft, early warning intelligence system in the northern islands and self-sufficiency through manufacturing guns and munitions and maintaining reserves of fuel.[53] The cost of Australia's squadron for the Pacific Fleet alone was estimated to be almost £4 million in the 1920–21 financial year rising to £6 million by the end of the decade. This did not include the possible cost of the additional destroyers and submarines, needed for harbour defence. If not obtained as gifts from Britain then their cost as well as the cost of naval works for bases, amounting to more than £750,000, would have to be added to the Jellicoe estimates.[54]

Jellicoe's mission was a great event in the history of Australian naval policy. His report was the departure point for all Australian policy-makers' discussions of naval defence from the end of the war until the Washington Conference. Its analysis of the Empire's Pacific problem confirmed Australia's worst fears about Japan and its intentions. Jellicoe's recommendations seemed to offer Australians what they had long sought as the most secure shield against an Asian threat, namely an imperial fleet permanently stationed in the Pacific. Jellicoe was somewhat disappointed that he had to leave Australia before Hughes and Cook returned from Europe but it is doubtful that his failure to meet them made any difference to their response.

Nevertheless the Australian ministers had to face up to two major problems. Would the British Government play its crucial part in the scheme and how, even if it did, could Australia pay for its share of the Pacific fleet? Watt, even though keenly aware of Australia's post-war straitened circumstances and anxious to cut back government expenditure, was won over by Jellicoe's argument. Answering the claims of the Royal Commission on Government Economy that, following victory in the war and the establishment of the League of Nations, all peacetime defence expenditure should be suspended, he cited the Jellicoe report in arguing that such savage cuts would expose Australia to grave risks. The report was 'a warning as to the future and an admonition to be prepared'. This, he said, should be 'the doctrine presented to the Australian people at this time.'[55]

---

[53] 'Report of Admiral of the Fleet Viscount Jellicoe of Scapa on Naval Mission to the Commonwealth of Australia May-August 1919', Vol.IV, NAA A65/2 and A981 Defence 350, Pt.1, pp.221–34; *ibid.*, C of A, *Parliamentary Papers*, 1917–18–19 session, IV, No.177, Vol.I, pp.5–7, 10–11, 13–25.

Jellicoe's fear of Japan does seem to be genuine; he produced evidence of Japan's wartime behaviour and imperial ambitions and also argued the case to the Admiralty. In the covering letter to his report he told the Admiralty that he could not advise on naval forces in the Dominions without taking into account the whole Pacific problem. He had left the United States out of his calculations 'partly because naval strategy against the United States would demand concentration in home waters, and partly because of the strong feeling of friendship at present existing between the two nations.' Japan was another matter. It had to be taken into account 'as a possible enemy' and consequently the Empire's defence in the Pacific had to match Japan's growing navy. Letter, Jellicoe to Secretary of the Admiralty, 21 August 1919, TNA: PRO, ADM 116/1831. See also copy of covering letter for his final report on his mission, Jellicoe to Secretary of the Admiralty, 3 February 1920, Jellicoe Papers, BL Add 49045/217–24 in which he justified more elaborately his view of Japan as the Empire's potential enemy in the Pacific.

[54] C of A, *Parliamentary Papers*, 1917–18–19 session, IV, No.177, Vol.I, p.25, Table IX.

[55] *CPD*, 1919 session, LXXXIX, 13892 and 13898–900, 23 October 1919.

Australia's post-war defence policy

When Hughes landed in Fremantle in late August, he was, as had been the case on his return from Europe in 1916, greeted by cheering crowds. As he proceeded to the eastern states this enthusiastic welcome was repeated. He came among them as the victor who had represented Australia at the Peace Conference. He had been celebrated in the press as the hero who had fought for Australian interests and made White Australia's name known among the nations.

But international peace had not brought domestic harmony. Unlike 1916 there were no trade unionists to lift him up and carry him in triumph to the forum; this time it was the repatriated soldiers who so honoured the 'little digger'. The bitter social divisions which the conscription 'loyalty' campaigns had engendered intensified during Hughes's absence. A militant labour movement, some of whose leaders were inspired by the Bolshevik revolution, had initiated widespread strikes. There was even a breakdown of discipline and social order among the returning armed forces. Soldiers rioted in the streets and sailors 'mutinied' on the RAN's flagship, *Australia* and the light cruisers *Melbourne* and *Sydney*.

The Governor-General, once again showing himself to be out of sympathy with the democratic mores of the colonials, was so incensed by this lack of deference to authority that he denounced Australia as a 'most extraordinary barbarous society'.[56] The British naval officers who had responsibility for dealing with the series of 'mutinies' which occurred on board the Australian naval vessels on their return to Australia in 1919 held much the same view. When questions were asked in parliament about the severity of the sentences the commander of the fleet, Commodore J. S. Dumaresq, protested against any remission claiming that the actions of the ratings on HMAS *Australia* in disobeying an order to get steam up when the vessel was about to leave Fremantle amounted to mutiny and that if they had faced this charge they would have incurred either a very long-term of imprisonment or the death penalty.[57] The officers on a Court of Inquiry investigating similar acts of insubordination on HMAS *Sydney*, all but one being British, explained the Australian sailors' actions as being primarily the result of 'a species of innate vanity peculiar to the class to which they belong, which includes the state of mind which is known vulgarly by the expression "Jack's as good as his master"'. This state of mind proceeded from fundamental defects in Australian society, especially 'the shocking example set them on shore by the Masses [sic] in the manner of strikes' and 'out and out Shinn Feinism [sic]' as well as 'the curious adulation of the "Independent spirit"'.[58]

---

[56] Novar Diary, 23 August 1919, Novar Papers, NLA MS 696/36.

[57] Memorandum, Dumaresq to Naval Board, 30 July 1919, NAA A3934 SC15/25.

Five sailors were tried on the charge of 'joining in a mutiny not accompanied by violence'. The action of the sailors was comparable to a strike. The five were 'prominent among a group who tried to persuade others not to carry out the orders of the Captain, and to prevent the ship going to sea'. When the court martial hearing took place on 16 June, they were all found guilty and sentenced from one to two years imprisonment. See copy of letter, Secretary of the Admiralty to Under-Secretary of the Colonial Office, 10 September 1919, NAA A3934 SC15/46.

[58] Report of Court of Enquiry into grievances of the lower deck of HMAS *Sydney*, 8 November 1919, *ibid*.

Hughes, with the public at large, had some sympathy for the sailors who had just returned to their own country after four years away on war service. The punishment was considered to be excessive, and so two weeks before the federal election he announced, after gaining the consent of the Admiralty but without consulting the Naval Board, that because of their good record and youth the *Australia* 'mutineers' were to have the rest of their sentence remitted and to be released just before Christmas. In response both Dumaresq and Grant sent their resignations to the Minister for the Navy. They were only persuaded by Hughes to withdraw their notice when the official reason for freeing the sailors was changed to a general amnesty to mark the coming of peace.[59]

Yet while Hughes might have some sympathy for sailors who, after four years away from their homes, were in peacetime showing some unwillingness to submit to the absolute discipline of the Royal Navy, he made it clear that he would take on all the enemies of Australia whether at home or abroad. For him the true Australians were those who had contributed to the war effort, especially the soldiers and sailors who had risked their lives in defence of the freedom of their country and race. It was 'those who saved the country who had every right, human and divine, to say what shall be Australia's destiny.' He would be their Prime Minister and fight the Bolsheviks who had infiltrated the labour movement and the others who had shirked their responsibilities. He believed 'in constitutional modes and the rule of the majority' but warned that if these 'parasites of labour' pursued their revolutionary course and attempted to impose their will on the country he would 'smite them hip and thigh'.[60]

As for the peace settlement and the League of Nations he continued to express a sceptical view of what it promised and to throw doubt on its ability to protect Australia from the threat from the north. He had insisted on speaking out at the Paris Peace Conference because British leaders did not understand that Australia was 'an outpost' of the Empire 'situated at the extreme fringe of the world, surrounded by a thousand million men whose ideals and ideas differ essentially and materially from ours in almost every particular.'[61] The American Senate's refusal to give its consent to the United States joining the League increased Hughes's reservations about the League and what it might achieve. It gave him the opportunity to reiterate more easily what had from the first been his view of Wilson's panacea of collective security. 'Happily', he said, '… we are a member of a League of Nations which has been tried and tested in war – I mean the British Empire and on that Empire we must continue, as in times past, to depend for an effective instrument for the preservation of the world's peace.'[62]

---

[59] *Daily Telegraph*, 22 November 1919; letter Grant to Cook, 14 December 1919 and cable, Dumaresq to Naval Board, 10 December 1919, NAA A3934 SC15/25; *Argus*, 20 December 1919.
[60] *Argus*, 27 August 1919.
[61] *SMH*, 15 September 1919.
[62] *SMH*, 22 November 1919.
  Hughes, alluding to American senate objections to the Dominions having independent representation in the League of Nations, maintained that 'should a dispute be likely to lead to a rupture between Australia and Japan … Australia could not present her own case to the League.' What, he asked, did Australia have 'to gain from a League of Nations when not only her own voice is to be silenced but also those of her sister

Profound suspicion of Japan underpinned Hughes's post-war attitude to Australian defence. Japan was the particular embodiment of the Asian menace which he had since the Russo-Japanese war invoked to justify his demands for preparation against invasion. He lived daily with the threat of invasion, never knowing the day or the hour when the alien enemy would be upon them. Perhaps his unrelenting antagonism towards Japan at Paris over the racial equality issue had made him even more excitedly anxious about this prospect. Indeed at the beginning of October, moved by these fears, he was seized by a fit of panic. A week or so previously Rear-Admiral Sir Percy Grant, a British officer who had succeeded Creswell as First Member of the Naval Board, submitted a memorandum to cabinet which set out a picture of a clear and present danger. In this paper Grant, who from 1915 to 1917 had been Commander-in-Chief of the China squadron and responsible for liaising with the Japanese – an experience which had caused him to have grave misgivings about their aims – carried Jellicoe's strategic analysis to greater lengths. He considered 'the grand ideal' of White Australia, which both Hughes and Cook had declared to be the defining principle of Australia's public life, to be in great peril. While the European powers were exhausted by the war, Japan had emerged unscathed and as a result 'the near future would be a psychological moment to press her claims with all the strength of a great fleet which lies behind those claims.' He thought 'it would be wrong to place any faith in America coming to our assistance.' There was 'a very black cloud … gathering in the North which I feel certain … will burst sooner or later if we are not prepared to meet it.' After stating that Jellicoe's recommendations were the minimum naval force necessary for Australian security. Grant drew cabinet's attention to the 'grave position in which the country is today owing to the fact that there is practically no coal reserve, no ammunition reserve and a very inadequate oil reserve for the fleet.'[63]

When therefore Grant's tale of doom was followed by a report that the Japanese fleet was manoeuvring in the North Pacific, Hughes took alarm and cabled Lloyd George expressing his government's 'great uneasiness' about what this might mean and asking Lloyd George to send 'immediately' a squadron of battleships into the Pacific. When the First Lord of the Admiralty replied, denying that there was 'any emergency' and stating that the Japanese naval exercises did not justify the despatch of a naval force to the Pacific, Hughes responded at once, elaborating his argument and pleading with the British Government to reconsider its decision. He believed that Australia was in imminent danger of attack.

> It is a long way from Tokio to Whitehall, but we are within a stone [sic] throw. I desire again to emphasise that our fleet is practically without fuel, and in any case quite unequal to meet Japanese with any hope of success; that there are no British squadrons in eastern waters fit to do so; that we profoundly distrust Japan; that experience of Port Arthur shows she strikes first and declares war afterwards; present belligerent mood evident in attitude to Shantung; and as you doubtless know, her strong animosity has been roused by our opposition to her desire for an equal treatment of their [nationals?] and their entry into Australia.

Dominions in the only matter out of which war in the future is like directly to menace her.' Cable, Munro Ferguson to Milner, 14 November 1919, TNA: PRO CO 418/178/139.
[63] Rear-Admiral E.P. Grant, Memo on Naval Estimates 1919–1920 to Minister for consideration of cabinet, 22 September 1919, NAA A3934 SC15/46.

Hughes added that he had been informed that Admiral Jellicoe 'strongly endorses our request'. But the British were unmoved and reaffirmed their earlier decision.[64]

Cook shared his leader's view of the post-war world. Though, in accord with his liberal Methodist background, he sometimes expressed a sentimental view of the League of Nations and its possibilities for world peace, nevertheless his main message did not differ in essence from that of Hughes. As he told a Methodist Conference, 'If the League of Nations does not function outside and above the separate nations, and function with power, then you had better get ready for the last great throw of your civilisation, for it is very near'. Even as peace was being made in Paris, new clashes of interests were appearing to breed hostility among the nations, even between the Allies. Australians should 'trust in the League of Nations, but keep our powder dry'. Likewise he joined with Hughes in seeing in the British navy a superior basis for maintaining world peace as 'the seas were never as free as when they were patrolled by the British navy … and held in trust for the benefit of the world'. Carrying his romantic view of nationalism further – 'the spirit of the nation … or the soul of a nation' was to be found in a common language – he looked towards the peoples of the British Empire and America being drawn closer together for in that 'lay the one hope of salvation for the world'.

Cook was also concerned about the rise to power of Japan and shared the gloomy forebodings of Hughes and Grant. Shortly after Hughes had asked the British Government to send a naval force to the Pacific to deter Japan from proceeding with what they conceived to be a likely attack on Australia, Cook – using imagery borrowed from Grant – spoke of 'the many dark and ugly clouds lowering in the sky'. He noted that Japan had since the armistice been engaged in building up its navy. By the end of 1923:

> she would have eight of the largest and latest dreadnoughts in the world in addition to a fleet of battle cruisers of a very powerful type. Her militarists were clamouring for another eight dreadnoughts. The Japanese navy was carrying out manoeuvres on a grand scale in the presence of her Emperor to the southeast of the main islands. She proposed to build 25,000.000 [pounds] worth of aircraft in the next four years. She was building 10,000 ton oil tankers and constructing huge oil reserves for her fleet.

He concluded that in dealing with 'the overmastering question of national defence' they must be 'sane and wide and wise'. Australia had 'to still stand on the watchtower and see that her ramparts were strong and well-fortified'.[65]

---

[64] Cable, Hughes to Lloyd George, 7 October 1919 and draft of cable, Lloyd George to Hughes 10 October 1919, Lloyd George papers, House of Lords Record Office F28/3/42 and F133/2/75 (a) and (b); minutes of Finance Committee of British War Cabinet, 17 October 1919, TNA: PRO CAB 27/91 and Conclusions of War Cabinet Meeting (633), 22 October 1919, TNA: PRO CAB 23/12.

[65] *SMH,* 20 and 24 September, 20 October and 4 November 1919 and 10 February 1920.

Cook was also alarmed by the news that Japan's new battle cruisers made provision for aircraft. He had noted that Haig, Marshal Ferdinand Foch (the French Commander-in-Chief of Allied Forces), and Major-General Erich Ludendorff (the German Commander-in-Chief of the German army on the Western Front in 1918), had all said that 'in the next war there will be a great air battle before either armies of fleets can move effectively.' Cook Notebooks 1919. Vol.II, Cook Papers, NAA M3580.

Despite the urgency of the issue Hughes and Cook accepted that before giving serious thought to a defence policy, they would first have to go to the people and seek renewal of their mandate to govern. Defence had become a contentious issue. Following the conscription referenda and the remaking of the Labor Party there was no longer a consensus on the question. At their 1919 federal conference, Labor made not only conscription for overseas deployment but also compulsory military training for home defence, tests of loyalty to the party. Moreover Hughes and his ministers had to contend with war weariness and a general demand for the reduction of government spending, especially on defence. In the election campaign though he did not resile from his fundamental position that defence policy had to be 'dictated by common prudence and our geographical position' he made some formal concessions to his critics. Even as he asserted that the White Australia policy was 'not calculated to endear us to some of our neighbours' and the 'only way ... to hold this country was by the way we held it during the war' he promised that the Nationals would not indulge themselves 'with grandiose schemes of defence' and would cut expenditure 'to the bone'.[66]

The results of the election in December were not encouraging. The exuberant welcome in the streets and great halls of the capital cities could not be converted into votes. Labor gained seats; a new rural-oriented group also took seats from the Nationals; and inside his own party there were those who openly showed dissatisfaction with his leadership. Hughes did not command a secure majority in the new parliament and often had to depend on the support of at least some members of what came to be called the Country Party to stay in office. It was not a good platform from which to carry out a strong defence policy.

Defence was the most pressing issue awaiting their attention. The Royal Commission on Economies, which was composed of businessmen, had thrown out a challenge to those who wished to continue the pre-war defence program.[67] But before any decisions could be arrived at on compulsory military training or the Jellicoe report, ministers had to agree on Australia's position in the post-war world. And so they turned to their official advisers.

On 22 January the Minister for Defence, having summoned a conference of senior military officers to advise on future defence policy, opened proceedings by setting out the changes wrought by the war and he instructed the officers to bear these in mind in producing their report. Firstly they were to keep before them Australia's financial difficulties and 'the undesirability of hampering overmuch the economic development of the country'. Secondly, they were not to

---

[66] *SMH*, 7 November 1919.

[67] First Progress Report of the Royal Commission appointed to consider and report on the Public Expenditure of the Commonwealth of Australia with a view to Effecting Economies, *Parliamentary Papers*, 1917–18–19 session, No.176.

While this report formally advocated the cessation of compulsory training only until government made its mind up about post-war defence policy nevertheless it considered that 'evidence is not lacking that there is a desire in some quarters to maintain the military spirit, and permanently saddle the country with an expenditure for Defence which would be exceedingly onerous.' Furthermore it argued that since Australia would be able to call on returned soldiers who were 'thoroughly and efficiently trained in the most modern methods of war' if required and the League of Nations might well 'operate to minimise the risk of war' it seemed unnecessary to incur heavy expenditure for defence preparedness. (*ibid.*, p.6).

forget Australia's new and, by implication, greater defence responsibilities that would follow from their acquisition of mandates over the German islands in the South Pacific. Finally and most importantly he drew their attention to the creation of the League of Nations and, alluding to the Jellicoe report, 'the probable increase of British Naval Power in the Pacific'. In noting these latter new possibilities he was in effect asking his generals to review their post-Russo-Japanese war history which had governed Australia's defence policy from 1905 and to see whether there was another history in the making which might free Australia from the spectre of a Japanese invasion and thereby the heavy burden of the compulsory military training scheme.

The conference contained a great deal of experience, being composed of generals H. G. Chauvel, J. J. T. Hobbs, J. G. Legge, J. W. McCay, John Monash and Brudenell White, all of whom had served with the AIF and played, to a greater or lesser degree, a leading role in the pre-war military scheme. These officers took their task very seriously. They met almost continuously for a fortnight and produced a report which accomplished for the army what the Jellicoe report had done for the navy. Their recommendations covered resources, citizen forces, system of organisation, permanent forces, munitions, fixed defences, rifle clubs and reserves, and the Council of Defence. It was by far the most comprehensive and ambitious survey of Australia's military defence needs since Federation.

Like the Jellicoe report, which they had read, the officers began with an assessment of Australia's strategic position in the post-war world, and, like Jellicoe, the military officers argued that Japan represented a serious danger to Australia, and they framed their recommendations accordingly.

They took as the philosophical underpinning for their understanding of war and international relations a quotation from Spencer Wilkinson, a British authority on geopolitics and subsequently Chichele Professor of History at Oxford University; 'The absolute case of inevitable war is when each of two states regards as ... indispensable to its own welfare action diametrically opposed to that similarly regarded as necessary by the other.' That is, when differences between states could not be settled by diplomacy through compromise or concession then the resort to arms naturally ensued. Whether the League of Nations could overcome this principle which had in the past governed international relations and so prevent future wars and protect the weak from the strong, time alone would show. Citing Theodore Roosevelt, the generals were willing that the League should be assisted and promoted, 'but in addition to, and not in substitution for the provision of a nation of its own defence by its own strength.' In their view this approach to the post-Versailles world was peculiarly apt for Australia.

Looking at the consequences of the war for Australia's geopolitical position they noted that with the defeat of Germany and the devastation of Europe there was no nation from that continent able to mount a challenge to the Empire's naval supremacy. America and Japan were the only great powers to emerge with their military and naval power enhanced. Setting aside the possibility of a war with America, they declared that Japan remained 'in the immediate future the only potential and probable enemy'. Indeed they held that Australia would be a great prize. Its sparsely settled land with its rich resources would provide Japan with an outlet for its surplus population and supply it with the means for developing its industries. The White Australia policy would be 'easily capable of being made a casus belli.' They showed that Japan was rapidly increasing its armed forces. It had a naval building program which would, by 1924, add eight battleships and eight battle cruisers, all of the most advanced Dreadnought models, to its fleet. Similarly Japan was maintaining in peacetime an army of 25 divisions which could be expanded to 42 divisions in time of war and enable the country to put an army of 600,000 men in the field. Its mercantile navy had also grown apace and would be able to transport an army of 100,000 men in one convoy to attack Australia.

The role of the British Empire in such a contingency was a central consideration. The Japanese would have to reckon with the prospect of the Empire coming to Australia's aid. But while Australians might properly assume that the whole of the British Empire would come to their aid against an aggressor, the conference thought that Australia's policy-makers should 'not … lose sight of' the question of whether 'the people of the British Isles, of India, of Canada and South Africa, for example, [would] be prepared to exert their whole strength in maintaining against Japan every tenet of Australian policy'. And clearly the conference had the White Australia policy in mind when raising this troubling matter.

Moreover Australia could not rely on Britain to prevent a Japanese invasion. Since the British Empire had such limited naval forces and bases in the Pacific, Japan would initially be able to move unchecked against Australia and land troops wherever it wished on Australian soil. If Japan seized Singapore and Fremantle it would be in an advantageous position to engage any British fleet subsequently despatched to the region. The military officers agreed that the best security against a Japanese threat lay in the creation of a British imperial fleet for the Pacific along the lines prescribed by Jellicoe and they urged that Australia should devote 'its first effort … to contributing in full [its] share of an adequate Far Eastern Fleet.' Yet, as the officers also observed, perhaps looking back at the pre-war German challenge to British naval supremacy, this too had its limitations, for Britain could at its discretion remove its ships from the Pacific to meet an 'international situation elsewhere'. Because the British ships would represent the greater part of the Pacific fleet it would in such circumstances lose its effectiveness as a shield against Japan.

The conference therefore concluded that it would be possible for Japan to inflict great damage on Australia before the Empire's full resources could come to the rescue, and to meet this possibility Australia had to maintain an army 'capable of preventing an enemy from attaining a decision on shore.' The members believed that 'the accumulated mass of evidence points irresistibly to the gravity of the situation, to the compelling necessity of recognising it, and to the unavoidable need of organising to insure against its dangers.' Given that Australia's population was so small and the logistics of defending its coasts so difficult, it was *essential that the military force, like the naval force, be the maximum obtainable.*

For this purpose the report recommended a dual response to the Japanese threat – a five year plan to raise through an improved and intensified compulsory training program a citizen army of 180,000 men; and a short term measure to deal with the period which would elapse before the permanent scheme came fully into operation. The military officers thought it not impossible to imagine that in this interim period, Japan would see a window of opportunity and so begin 'challenging Australian political tenets, and leaving us only the choice between war and the surrender of some of our rights of self-determination'. The officers therefore urged that the demobilised AIF should at once be organised into an emergency force.

Finally the report called for a revision of the *Defence Act* to remove the prohibition against the use of compulsion for overseas defence. It was argued that the best defence was often offence and that it was better to fight in the enemy's territory than one's own. Moreover if Australians could be compelled to serve wherever they were needed no time would be wasted in raising and training a volunteer force.

Though the officers' disappointment with the outcome of the 1916 and 1917 conscription referenda may well have been lurking behind this proposal the examples they cited related only to assistance to the League of Nations and regional defence. These were vaguely expressed but their meaning seems clear; 'As an Eastern outpost of Western Civilisation', Australia might be asked on behalf of the League 'to take up duties which cannot at present be defined'. The League, presumably under the influence of the West, might develop so as 'to be able to exercise effective control, particularly in those directions from which Australia has most to fear.' In such circumstances Australia would be 'called upon to find her share of "the world police"'. They also allowed that acquisition of Germany's colonies in the South Pacific might require Australia to send troops to defend them. In every respect the imperative driving the report and its recommendations was fear of Japan.

The report's list of requirements for the defence of Australia reflected the gravity of the perceived danger. Many of the specific recommendations repeated the 30 June 1919 military committee's findings, which was not surprising since the conference contained the military members of the earlier body. Following the earlier committee, the conference urged the revision of the established compulsory military system. They wanted to replace the annual eight day camps which occurred over eight years with a more intense and concentrated four-year training program. This new training program would begin in the first year with preferably a thirteen-week camp, to be followed in successive years by four-, three- and one-week camps. The officers had found that this longer period of continuous training had been necessary to turn AIF volunteers into effective soldiers. The report also set out the need for accumulating arms and armaments to add to those which the AIF had brought back from Europe and the Middle East: in particular the government should acquire 218 pieces of field and heavy artillery and set up an arsenal to make Australia as self-contained as possible in armaments and munitions. Finally it called for the strengthening of coastal defences, the establishment of an air force and the expansion of the railway system to make it more strategically useful. The cost under ordinary votes and appropriations for this 'fortress Australia' defence program was estimated to be £4.2 million in the first year and on average £3.8 million for the subsequent four years which was more than double the 1913–14 military expenditure. These sums, however, did not include capital items, such as artillery, ammunition and arsenal, the total cost of which over five years was reckoned to be more than £5.75 million.[68]

---

[68] Letter, Lieutenant-General H.G. Chauvel to Pearce, 6 February 1920, with attached 'Report of the Conference of Senior Military Officers Constituted by the Minister for Defence on 22/1/20 to Advise the Government upon the Military Defence of Australia', NAA MP729/2 1855/1/42.

See also letter, Pearce to Hughes, 9 February 1920 with attached copy of the Report of the Senior Military Officers Conference, Hughes Papers, NLA MS 1538/10/4.

At a meeting of the Council of Defence on 9 February at which Hughes presided, the reports of the naval and military committees and the Air Board were considered – the first of these reports being in line with the Jellicoe scheme and the last with the earlier Council of Defence decision. There was a long discussion about the recommendations and the cost involved in giving effect to them. Watt, as Treasurer, entered a protest at the total bill, which amounted – without including the capitalised costs – to £12.5 million or three times the last peacetime defence budget. As a result, the council decided that the army and navy officials should meet and produce a joint report which would make some concessions to the need for economy.

The next day the service representatives did as they were bid. They first set out an agreed strategic appreciation which was an amalgam of that already set down in their original reports. Japan was 'the only potential and possible aggressor'. Because of Australia's limited resources its defence was an 'Imperial problem'. For this reason 'the centre of the Empire should study this problem', and preferably in Australia. Jellicoe's proposal for a Pacific fleet was the best solution and it should be proceeded with immediately. Even if this were done, it was asserted that Australia might still be attacked and therefore the strength of the military forces 'should be the maximum obtainable'. Both these arms of the defence forces also required 'adequate air defence' and the Air Board's recommendations were 'a minimum requirement'. If the government approved the proposals of its advisers Japan would understand that Australia was resolved 'to uphold Australian policy' and these defence preparations might deter Japan from setting out on an aggressive adventure.

They nevertheless were willing to make some concessions to the demands for economy. Since 'The critical period' was 'the immediate future' they stood by what they still considered to be the minimum sum to meet this contingency. The navy and army agreed to reduce their budget recommendations – the navy to £3.62 million and the army to £3.5 million – but only on condition that some items would be treated as capital costs outside the regular defence budget. With provision of £1 million for the nucleus of an air force, the total defence budget was cut back by almost a third. Even so the revised estimate, after allowing for cost inflation, was still approaching double that of the last peacetime budget.[69]

Hughes agreed completely with his defence advisers that Japan was Australia's potential enemy and represented a clear and present danger. It was this very belief that had a few months earlier informed his desperate appeal for the immediate despatch of a British battle-cruiser squadron to the Pacific. He also regarded White Australia as an ideal that had to be fought for against all odds. A British White Australia was at the core of his nation's identity and he would brook no compromise on the question. Despite his public denials he had returned from Europe very conscious that the Japanese resented deeply his opposition to including a racial equality principle in the League Covenant and he suspected that they might seek their revenge. In an Australia Day address, he had declared that 'the next war ... was most likely in the Pacific' and

---

[69] Letter, Pearce to Hughes, 11 February 1920, attaching a copy of the report of the joint meeting of the Naval and Military Members of Council of Defence on the Naval, Air & Military scheme, Hughes Papers, NLA MS 1538/19/4.

that Australia was 'hemmed about by nations which lusted after her.' His message was that 'we must … be ready.'[70]

In the period between his appeal for the despatch of a British naval squadron and the April 1920 Council of Defence meeting Hughes's apprehensions were further excited by reports coming from many quarters about Japan's naval and military build-up, its expansion into Southeast Asia and the South Pacific islands, the general assertiveness and secretiveness of the crews of visiting ships and even of Japanese clandestine landings in northern Australia.[71] Newspapers highlighted the details of Japanese increased spending on their naval and military forces.[72] Despatches from the British Embassy in Tokyo warned of 'the penetration of Japanese' into all parts of that region called the 'South Seas'. They mentioned Japanese colonies being established in the Philippines, Japanese settling in 'points of strategic importance', business men seeking commercial concessions and influence in Malaya and the Dutch East Indies and individuals suspected of espionage.[73] At the same time Australians interested in exploring for oil in Portuguese Timor, which was of great importance to the Naval Board, reported that Japan was trying to pre-empt them and gain control over this new source of energy so essential for naval supremacy.[74] A message from Piesse that he had seen despatches from the British Consul-General in Batavia which 'might be of interest to the

---

[70] *SMH*, 26 January 1920 and *Argus*, 28 January 1920.

Professor Murdoch's inaugural lecture, which was delivered in early December and subsequently published, may well have helped in a balanced way to give some academic support to Hughes's overall view of Japan. Murdoch had opined that in the twentieth century 'the centre of interest in the great drama of History bids fair to be transferred to the Pacific' and that Japan would be likely to play a large part in that drama. It 'Already as an industrial and manufacturing nation had to be seriously reckoned with; even now her mercantile marine is the chief carrier on the Pacific.' Moreover 'as a great naval power' it ranked third 'among the States of the World and she is sedulously expanding and perfecting her armaments.' It seemed that Japan's rulers 'seem to trust rather in keeping their powder dry than in the League of Nations.' James Murdoch, *An Inaugural Lecture Delivered in the Union Hall on December 3, 1919* (Sydney: Angus and Robertson, 1919), p.29.

[71] For a summary of these latter reports, see *Herald* (Melbourne), 4 October 1920.

[72] *Age*, 8 November 1919, 29 December 1919 and 9 February 1920; *Argus*, 28 February 1920; *SMH*, 24 March 1920.

[73] Letter, Milner, Colonial Secretary, to Munro Ferguson, 5 November 1919, enclosing for ministers, despatch. Beilby Alston, British Embassy, Tokyo, to Lord Curzon, 15 August 1919, NAA A981/4 JAP38, Pt.2.

See also letter, Atlee Hunt to Shepherd, 3 January 1920 in which Hunt related that a business friend of his who travelled on business in the southern Pacific was worried the Japanese traders were establishing themselves in Fiji and Tonga and were intent on 'extending their operations to other Groups in the South Pacific.' He also pointed out that the British officials in the Pacific placed no obstacles in the way of the Japanese, even allowing them to settle in the islands they administered. Hughes thought that Hunt should ask his friend to continue 'to keep the Comlth [sic] posted as to movements in the Islands.' *Ibid*.

[74] Extract from Minutes of Meeting of Naval Board, Secretary of the Board to Cook, 3 November 1919, Hughes Papers, NLA MS 1538/19/4 and NAA MP1049/1 16/085. Cook in forwarding this document to Hughes commented that 'the Japanese are after this concession & I think you should communicate with the Imperial Govt with a view to their getting the whole thing over from the Portuguese. It is I believe a most valuable field & the whole matter is a strategic one of the greatest concern to us.'

Commonwealth', caused the Australian Government to ask London to inform them of 'any movements threatening the Dutch administration of the islands' and likewise of any 'political' material about Portuguese Timor. All these signs taken together formed a sinister pattern.[75]

This picture of the Japanese preparing for dominance in the region – and even war if it found itself thwarted – was given further plausibility from reports of Japanese visitors' hostile attitude to Australians and their excessive interest in Australia. In October the Sub-district Naval Officer at Newcastle informed his superiors that he had received numerous representations from a range of people, including some engaged in mercantile shipping, that during the previous months Japanese crews had ceased to be models of 'deferential politeness' and had instead evinced 'an aggressive self-assertion, at times positively offensive'. The captain of the *Kenkon Maru* in an argument with a stevedore over coal was supposed to have 'violently condemned the White Australia policy, and threatened that his countrymen would come here in spite of prohibition, when ready.' The Australian officer stated that the Japanese on shore 'would have appeared to have exceeded previous efforts to acquire local knowledge' through frequent motor drives through the country side and making 'constant use' of cameras, especially at the steel works, coaling operations and other sensitive industrial and strategic points in the port. He concluded by making the observation that it was 'generally agreed that the present manner of the Japanese is strongly reminiscent of the German attitude before the war.'

This report spoke to all the fears that the Naval Board had been expressing in their strategic appreciations. Though further investigation, especially through seeking the views of naval, military and customs officers in other ports, showed little support for this supposed new hostile attitude, Admiral Grant remained convinced that the officer's suspicions were well-founded, reflected the Japanese post-war attitude towards Australia and illustrated their involvement in espionage or at least intelligence gathering. Grant himself had come across two Japanese in Sydney whom in his eyes were engaged in clandestine activities. While staying in a hotel he noted that these Japanese 'gentlemen' who occupied two rooms across from his own received guests in their rooms up to 1am or later. During this time it seemed from his own attempts to discover the identity of the visitors that the Japanese had 'set a watch' in the corridor. Seeing these two Japanese at the theatre Grant and his companion observed them closely and noticed not only that they were 'well acquainted with the English language' but also that one of them had 'the distinct "cut" of a Japanese naval officer'. On consulting the hotel records he discovered also that the Japanese had been 'visiting Newcastle & other places'. This experience brought home to him that Japanese intelligence gathering was indeed a 'very serious' matter. As a result, he directed that all the information which the Navy Department held on the Japanese in Australia, including the report from the naval officer in Newcastle, should be sent to Cook for forwarding to the Prime Minister.[76]

---

[75] Letter, Munro Ferguson to Milner, 24 December 1919, TNA: PRO CO 418/178/575–76.
[76] Report, Commander P. Fearnley to District Naval Officer, Sydney, 9 October 1919; letter, Boarding Inspector, Sydney, to the Collector of Customs, Sydney, 13 October 1919; letter, District Naval Officer, Sydney to Secretary, Navy Department, 25 November 1919; minute, Captain A.W. Jose, Naval Intelligence Section to Grant, 1 December 1919 containing a scribbled commentary by Grant on his spy hunting in Sydney, 2 December 1919; memorandum, Acting Controller-General of Customs to Secretary, Department

With all this in the immediate background Hughes was shocked to learn that the Japanese Ministry of War was sending two officers on a month long trip professedly 'to see as much as possible of Australia and New Zealand and to consolidate friendship with Japan.' He cabled the British to express his surprise that military officers should be sent on a friendship mission and declared that his government was 'very much embarrassed by the visit'.[77]

Indeed Hughes's response to nearly every foreign policy question was determined at bottom by the fear of Japan. The League of Nations' failure to transfer promptly the formal control of the German imperial possessions to the respective mandatory powers was one such issue. After returning home Hughes continued to press for a quick transfer of the mandate for the German South Pacific islands to Australia. He blamed the Japanese, who wished to obtain free access to trade in the League's mandates, for delaying this process and saw in their actions a desire to take advantage of the unsettled state of affairs to advance their influence in the Pacific. In complaining to London he contended that:

> Every day the Japanese are ousting our traders, are intriguing with the Germans for mining, land, freight, trading and other rights. Agents Japanese ships now threaten to send ship to Rabaul with cargo from Japan and to lift cargo for Sydney in defiance of our refusal to grant permit: naturally we cannot allow that: what will follow no-one can say …
>
> Unless we act without delay, the great bulk of the trade of these very rich islands will go to Japan. She will secure shipping, trade, land and other rights and generally exercise such influence and so strengthen her claim for rights of her nationals to settle in islands as will be most difficult to answer before League of Nations. As Australia cannot in any circumstances agree to this, the policy of the Empire is obvious. The mandate must be settled forthwith.[78]

---

of the Navy, 7 January 1920 containing reports from all major ports on Japanese; letter, Captain C. Wood, Military Intelligence Section, Brisbane, to Director of Military Intelligence, Melbourne, 9 December 1919; letter, Captain Longfield Lloyd, Military Intelligence Section, Sydney, to Director of Military Intelligence, Melbourne, 10 December 1919; memorandum, Grant to Secretary, Department of the Navy, 22 December 1919, with instructions that the Fearnley report and other documents be sent to the Minister for the Navy to be forwarded to the Prime Minister. NAA MP1049/1 20/193.

It is noteworthy that when Fearnley later tried to use a mistranslation of a *SMH* leading article of 13 November 1920 which appeared in the *Japanese Advertiser* to suggest a Japanese Government conspiracy aimed at Australia, Piesse used his greater knowledge of Japan and the Japanese newspapers to show that Fearnley misconstrued the incident and that there was no basis for his conspiracy theory. Memorandum, Piesse to Director of Naval Intelligence, 3 February 1921, NAA MP1049/1 20/093.

[77] Letter, Shepherd, Secretary, Prime Minister's Department to Governor-General's Official Secretary, 24 January 1920, containing instructions to send cable, NAA A981 Japan 101, Pt.1.

In the event the trip was cancelled, apparently because the Japanese Consul-General in Sydney let the Japanese Foreign Office know that it was not 'the opportune moment' for such a visit. See copy of letter, Beilby Alston, British Embassy, Tokyo, to British Foreign Secretary, Lord Curzon, 14 February 1920, *ibid*.

By contrast the Australian Government was willing to welcome visits by American war vessels 'at all times'. It was thought that such visits would 'further Australian and American interests in the Pacific'. Letter, Munro Ferguson to Milner, 17 December 1919, TNA: PRO CO 418/170/142.

[78] Cable, Hughes to Milner, 2 February 1920, NAA CP360/9 B1. See also cables, Munro Ferguson to Milner, 26 September 1919 and 15 November 1919, TNA: PRO CO 418/178/151.

Likewise when the British sought the Dominion leaders' help in overcoming the American Senate's objections to the League of Nations Covenant, Hughes made Japan the core reason for refusing. One of the key American stumbling blocks was that the British Empire had six votes to the United States' one in the General Assembly and that when the United States was involved in a dispute with the United Kingdom or one of the Dominions, while both parties would be unable to take part in the debate and vote, the British party would still have five voices and votes from the outset to support its case. The British Government, anxious to have the United States as a member of the League, wanted the Dominions to accept a reservation to the Covenant which would mandate that when one of the British Empire countries was in dispute with a member of the League, all British members would be barred from taking part in the debate or voting on the matter. Despite the pressure brought to bear on him Hughes would not give way. In explaining himself he said that 'should a dispute be likely to lead to a rupture between Australia and Japan over, say, immigration equal(ity) treatment for all nationals', Australia would not be able to put its case to the League, nor would its fellow Dominions. Australia, he continued, might well ask 'what she had to gain from a League of Nations when, not only her own voice is to be silenced but also those of her sister Dominions in the only matter out of which war in the future is likely directly to menace her.'[79]

How to account for this overpowering sense of a looming Japanese threat – a threat indeed which not only Hughes but also his defence ministers and nearly all his official advisers (Piesse was the only exception)[80] agreed carried with it the possibility in the immediate future of an invasion of Australia?

Their strategic appreciations, whether formal or informal, contained a set of overlapping arguments.

The policy makers were agreed that Japan's behaviour during the war showed it was bent on an imperial course. Japan had given little assistance to the Allies and had demanded a price for what little aid, nearly all in the Pacific, it had supplied. It had used the opportunity afforded by the European conflict to seize the German territories in the North Pacific, to attempt to reduce China to the status of a protectorate and had sent military forces to occupy Siberia. The Australians moreover did not believe that the Anglo-Japanese alliance would protect them from Japanese aggression.

Similarly they saw in Japan's post-war defence and trade policies further evidence of its intention to dominate the Western Pacific. At the end of hostilities Japan had emerged as the third greatest naval power in the world and was embarking on a massive naval building program which when added to its large conscripted army gave it the means to achieve its ambitions. It was engaged in a commercial offensive which was penetrating the markets of East Asia and the South Pacific, and there were claims that it was involved in extensive espionage. Australia would be an outlet for its surplus population and a valuable source of raw materials for its rapidly expanding industries. Moreover Australia's discriminatory immigration policy had raised the ire of the

---

[79] Cable, Munro Ferguson to Milner, 14 November 1919, TNA: PRO CO418/178/139.
[80] See report, Piesse to Secretary, Prime Minister's Department, 22 March 1920, Piesse Papers, NLA MS 882/5/66–74. If Hughes read the report it was clear that he was not at all influenced by its content.

Japanese and Hughes's opposition to the inclusion of a racial equality provision in the Covenant had given them a convenient *casus belli*.

Australia's military and naval advisers doubted whether the Royal Navy would be able to deter Japan. They even questioned whether, if the Japanese did attack British territories in the Pacific, Britain would be able to send a force which would match that of the Japanese. Even if a British fleet did come it might very well arrive too late to prevent an invasion. The military officers even speculated whether, if the Japanese moved against Australia in defence of the rights of their people to equal treatment, the British might hesitate to come to Australia's rescue for fear of a backlash from their Asian and African colonies.

This seemingly prudential justification for Australia's post-war defence policy, however, failed to take into account some important considerations, especially as Piesse had noted, Japan's preoccupation with Northeast Asia and the growing tensions in Japanese-American relations. In 1919 and 1920 Japan's defence policy was predominantly concerned with meeting these challenges. While Japan's army was committed to fighting the Bolsheviks in Siberia, putting down a rebellion in Korea and preparing to retaliate against Chinese who opposed Japan's occupation of Shantung and its railway concessions in Manchuria, the navy was looking with apprehension at the United States creation of a Pacific Fleet, and its plans to strengthen its naval base at Honolulu and build a new major base at Guam.

It was Japan's distrust and resentment of America which underpinned the Hara government's naval construction program.[81] The Americans from the onset of the European war had been troubled by Japan's attempt to make China into a client state and to undermine the Open Door policy, and this anxiety about Japan's desire to carve out for itself an exclusive sphere of influence in northeast Asia continued into the early years of the peace.[82] They had also been alarmed by Japan's seizure of Germany's North Pacific island possessions. At the Peace Conference, as the Australians well knew, President Wilson had insisted on mandates for the former German Pacific territories in order to prevent Japan fortifying these islands, and even though these islands were placed under mandates the Americans were still concerned that they might be used as bases from which to launch attacks on United States territory. Japanese-American antagonism was further fuelled by the revival of anti-Japanese movements in California and other West Coast states which were aimed at halting Japanese migration and preventing Japanese *nisei* from owning land or exercising other rights of citizenship.[83]

These causes of ill-will when taken together caused the Americans to look with disfavour on the Anglo-Japanese alliance. Josephus Daniels, the Secretary of the Navy, sent President Wilson an extract from a report from Admiral Albert Gleaves, Commander-in-Chief of the Asiatic fleet, summing this up:

---

[81] Roger Dingman, *Power in the Pacific; The Origins of Naval Arms Limitation, 1919–1922* (Chicago: Chicago University Press 1976), pp.128–35; Nish, *Alliance in Decline*, pp.282–83.

[82] Ron Watson Curry, *Woodrow Wilson and Far Eastern Policy, 1913–1921* (New York: Bookman Associates, 1957), chapters 4–10.

[83] Roger Daniels, *the Politics of Prejudice: The Anti-Japanese Movement in California and the Struggle for Japanese Relations* (New York: Atheneum, 1968), chapters VI and VII.

> The Japanese have firmly established themselves in Siberia and intend to remain not only in Eastern Siberia, but also in Shantung and Manchuria and to dominate the government of China. That such a course will lead to war between the United States and Japan from economic causes, appears to be certain, unless concerted action by Great Britain, France and United States forces Japan to with-draw. From such information as I have been able to obtain, it seems unlikely that such concerted action can be obtained. The Alliance between Japan and Great Britain is still in effect and the general impression is that it will be renewed in some form upon its expiration next year.[84]

The Americans made no secret of their suspicions about Japan. As the *Sydney Morning Herald* reported it, Josephus Daniels, the Secretary of the Navy, in calling for the construction of a new major naval base at Guam and a 'great submarine, aviation and destroyer base at Honolulu', declared that 'our friends today may be our enemies of tomorrow'.[85]

Even though the press reported international developments which gave cause for Australian anxiety, such as Japan's 'extraordinary armaments preparations' and Canada's decision 'to abandon all pretensions at naval defence', they also covered these other and even more relevant factors that dominated the geopolitics of the north Pacific.[86] There was no good strategic reason to explain why Australian policy makers should have failed to take into account the significance of Japan's military involvement in northeast Asia and its troubled relationship with the United States. How could Japan find a military force for an invasion of Australia when its armies were committed to containing the Russian Communists and suppressing Korean and Chinese nationalist movements? How could Japan risk sending a major fleet to attack British territories in Southeast Asia and to convoy an invading force to Australia when it was faced with deteriorating relations with America?

Australia's defence officials may have had self-interested institutional motives for exaggerating the external threat but there is no direct evidence to support this view. While the strategic and logistical arguments which they advanced to justify the Japanese threat were not balanced they were complex and in their own terms compelling. It would seem that their blindness to countervailing conditions derived from their racial assumptions about the nature of international politics. Both the naval and military reports made much of the 'White Australia ideal' and the need to defend it against its enemies. Even if the British naval officers were playing up the race question for their own ends – for which there is hardly any evidence – there is no question but that the Australian military officers were swayed by racial assumptions about social identity and world politics which made a Japanese move against Australia inevitable. These racially influenced conclusions about Japan and its aggressive intentions chimed in neatly with the views of Hughes and his defence ministers.

---

[84] Message, Daniels to Wilson, 10 June 1920, Wilson Papers, LC mm 73046029 File II. This document does not appear in Link, *Papers of Woodrow Wilson*, Vol.65.
[85] *SMH*, 11 March 1920.
For a good account of the Navy Department's identification of Japan as the probable enemy against which they should prepare their defences, see Braisted, *United States Navy in the Pacific*, pp.468–90.
[86] *SMH*, 24 March 1920. See also 'Japanese Question in Canada and United States 1920–1924', NAA A3934 SC23/3.

Totally possessed by this spectre of Japan hovering over the future of Australia and the Pacific, Hughes summoned the members of the Council of Defence to a meeting in the Cabinet Room on 12 April to consider the recommendations of the joint navy-army committee. Though the cost of the proposed defence policy was still much greater than the last peacetime budget and would add significantly to the government's financial and political difficulties Hughes, Cook and Pearce did not hesitate to approve it. Watt, the Treasurer, having left a few days earlier for London to negotiate a settlement for the outstanding war debt owed to the British Government and to raise a loan to help cover the federal deficit, was not present and therefore the cost of this policy was not given the attention it might otherwise have received. Indeed Hughes might well have postponed calling the meeting until he knew that Watt was on the high seas.

As a result of the adoption of this policy, the existing naval force was to be kept in fighting condition ready to join a British fleet that would, it was hoped, be despatched in time of crisis to the Pacific. There was, at least at the council meeting, no debate about the need to continue with compulsory military training, including a thirteen-week camp in the first year for all eighteen year old young men; as before the war Australia, with New Zealand[87], was alone among the English-speaking countries in having such a program. Watt was to be asked to approach the British Government for surplus artillery and shells either as a gift or at low cost. The plan for an air force, including the setting up of an aeroplane industry, which had been developed in the previous year was also approved. It was thought, as the minutes put it, that taking it altogether 'this minimum expenditure would give Australia a "sporting chance" of holding out till British command of the Pacific can be established.'[88]

How the British were to take command of the Pacific remained unclear. Hughes already knew that the Canadians had decided against contributing to a Pacific fleet and that the British were compelled to make deep cuts in defence expenditure in order to pay off the domestic and foreign debts accumulated during the war. Furthermore he knew that the British authorities wanted to put off dealing with the Jellicoe report until the next Imperial Conference.[89] The best that he

---

[87] W.D. McIntyre, *New Zealand prepares for War: Defence Policy, 1919–1939* (Canterbury: Canterbury University Press, 1988), pp.47–48.

[88] Minutes of a Special Meeting (11) of the Council of Defence, 12 April 1920, NAA A9787/2.

Shortly after this meeting Hughes, who had contacted the British firm Vickers Ltd while in England about setting up an aircraft industry in Australia, pressed the company for a concrete proposal. 'What is wanted', he cabled the head of the company, was 'definite offer from you to build aeroplanes and engines for the Government … A concrete proposal will, I feel sure, lead to business. We are going in for a large air programme.' Vickers replied that, excluding the cost of the site, it would cost £750,000 to erect and equip a factory and provide the working capital for the production of the planes; and that if the government would guarantee orders worth £800,000 annually for five years it might be possible to raise a loan in Britain to fund the venture. Hughes, increasingly overwhelmed by financial problems, abandoned the project. Cables, Hughes to Sir Vincent Caillard, London, 11 May 1920 and Caillard to Hughes, 25 May 1920, NAA CP360/9 B1.

[89] Cable, L.S. Amery to Munro Ferguson, 23 February 1920, enclosing letter, W.F. Nicholson, Secretary to the Admiralty to Under-Secretary of State, Colonial Office, 30 January 1920, NAA A981 Defence 350, Pt.1 and TNA: PRO CO532/153/103–04; *SMH*, 24 March 1920.

could do was to approach the British Government to ask whether the Admiralty in conformity with the Jellicoe recommendations proposed to station three battle cruisers of the Lion class in 'far Eastern waters' in the near future. But once again he was disappointed. The Admiralty denied having such a plan and reminded Hughes that the issue of naval defence in the Pacific was to be determined at the next Imperial Conference.[90] Even if the Admiralty had had such a plan these three battle-cruisers would not, as the Jellicoe report disclosed, be a match for Japan's navy. Britain did not possess any battleships to equal in fighting power the eight latest Japanese battleships, and even though it had battle-cruisers which were at least equal to the best of the Japanese, only the Lion class were able to be despatched to the Pacific since there were no naval bases with docking facilities able to accommodate the other British battle-cruisers.

Hughes was in a quandary, and his anxieties were increased by the press and political agitation for drastic cuts in government expenditure, especially defence. When cabinet met in May to discuss the budget for 1920–21, Hughes was aware that his government might be defeated unless cuts were made. He accepted very reluctantly the need to pare back the naval and military commitments which had been adopted by the Council of Defence – the navy by almost 18 percent, the army by 14 percent and the air force by 25 percent. It marked a significant retreat from the policy that the Council of Defence had insisted would give the country no more than a 'sporting chance' of survival. To attempt to counteract any encouragement these cutbacks might give Japan, Hughes planned to have the Prince of Wales during his coming visit to Australia review the Commonwealth's naval force at Rabaul, on the outer edge of the country's new northern frontiers. When the Governor-General said that the Prince's itinerary was exhausting him and that the Rabaul trip should be omitted, Hughes at first would not have it; to do so 'would be an act of weakness in the face of Japan'. Hughes was only convinced to forego this demonstration of Australia's defence capacity when it was pointed out to him that 'it would be pure camouflage' since as soon as the RAN returned its major warships were to be placed in mothballs. One of the Prince's entourage declared that he should not be associated with such 'a piece of empty gesticulation'.[91]

Admiral Grant shared Hughes concerns about British naval power in the Pacific: indeed he may have prompted Hughes to ask the British whether they intended to send battle cruisers to the region. Even before he was aware of the government's decision to cut the defence budget further, Grant had had reservations about the April Defence Council's decision to split the available funds more or less equally between the army and the navy. Though he had for expedient reasons gone along with this principle in the February consultation and the April Defence Council meeting he was much troubled by its strategic implications. And so on the very day that the Council of

---

[90] Cables, Munro Ferguson to Milner, 21 April 1920, and Milner to Munro Ferguson, 14 May 1920, TNA: PRO CO532/153/183–84 and NAA CP78/22 1920/337.

[91] Novar diary, 1 June 1920, Novar Papers NLA MS 696/36; letters, Edward Grigg, Military Secretary to the Prince of Wales during the Prince's visit to Australia, to Kerr, 29 June and 5 July 1920, Lothian Papers, NAS GD40/1714/8/4 and 40/1714/16/1.

In his diary Munro Ferguson wrote that Hughes was 'resolved to provide for Defence Fleet 'n all'. He recognised that 'without bases the Home Fleet could not help & that relations with Japan give cause for being on the alert.' Novar Diary, 23 June 1920, Novar Papers NLA MS 696/36.

Defence had approved the services' recommendations he had sent Cook, at the minister's request, a personal 'APPRECIATION OF THE PRESENT POSITION OF AUSTRALIA WITH REGARD TO DEFENCE' which called for a redistribution of defence funding, to favour the navy at the expense of the army. He argued that no Australian military force would be able to withstand a Japanese invasion of Australia and that only the Jellicoe scheme could secure the country against Japan. The expensive universal military training scheme was a waste of money, for '*if the British Fleet were beaten this Army could not hold out against the teeming millions which the Japanese would bring to Australia.*' Only a limited military force was needed for the defence of bases and capital cities against enemy raids. He thus urged that the compulsory training scheme should be abandoned and the navy given the lion's share of the defence funds so that Australia could make its contribution to the proposed British Pacific armada. To achieve this he estimated that the navy, including its air arm, should receive three-quarters and the army, including its air arm, a quarter of the moneys available for defence purposes.[92]

When he subsequently learnt that his political masters were requiring additional cuts, Grant moved quickly in order to protect the navy. With the unanimous approval of the Naval Board he sent formally a more elaborate version of his 'Appreciation' for submission to the cabinet in which he again set out the navy's view of Australia's strategic position and the need above all to give preference to the navy in distributing defence funds. In a covering note he reaffirmed that it was 'unsound and unwise merely to split the money available for defence purpose equally between the army and the navy'. Rather it should be allocated in accordance with 'the relative importance of the army and navy in the defence scheme for the Country' as determined by the government's foreign policy.

Reiterating the fundamental argument of all the post-war strategic assessments, the document posited that Japan, like pre-war Germany, possessed a powerful military caste that was independent of parliament and people and responsible for the nation's formidable armaments program. This massive arms build-up could not be justified in defence terms: neither the United States nor Britain 'cherished any designs to attack Japan'. The only possible explanation for Japan's behaviour was its determination 'to be on an equal footing with all other Great Countries'. Given its demands at the Paris Peace Conference for recognition of racial equality, Japan as soon as it considered it was strong enough would demand that Australia accord equal treatment to the Japanese people. Australia would then have only two choices. It would either have built, in harmony with the Jellicoe scheme, a sufficiently powerful naval force able to deter the Japanese or it would have to give up the White Australia policy.

Citing Jellicoe's claim that 'a strong far Eastern Naval Unit, properly based, would remove almost entirely the probability of aggression' it repeated the earlier claim that an Australian army could never prevent a Japanese invasion and that only a naval defence could secure Australia. With this as its premise it then concluded that no local defence whether 'small crafts' such as destroyers and submarines or the largest army that could be raised would ensure Australia against

---

[92] 'AN APPRECIATION OF THE PRESENT POSITION OF AUSTRALIA WITH REGARD TO DEFENCE', 21 April 1920, attached to letter, Grant to W. Laird Smith, Assistant Minister for the Navy, 18 June 1920, NAA MP1049/1 20/0215.

a Japanese invasion. Thus military defence should be limited to protection against raids and the greater proportion of defence funds – and again it suggested three-quarters – should be allocated to the navy so that it could make its proper contribution to the Empire's Pacific fleet. To decide how best to contribute in the coming year to the Jellicoe scheme it suggested that the Admiralty should be asked to advise whether the Australian naval policy should give priority to maintaining the Australian naval unit as a seagoing force or to building up the bases, docks, magazines and fuel reserves.[93]

Grant had accompanied Jellicoe during his visit to Australia and saw in the Jellicoe report the only safe answer for the Dominion's security. He could see no other solution for Australia's Japanese problem. He could not imagine that the British Government would reject Jellicoe's recommendations or, at the least, would not provide a significant naval force for the Pacific, should Japan make a threatening move. However, he dismissed too easily the deterrent effect of a substantial trained and equipped army supported by a land-based air force. His assumptions reflected his faith that the British Government, as the guardian of the Empire's integrity, would never fail in its duty to Greater Britain. Thus Australia's only role was to maintain a naval unit that would be ready to take its part in the defence of British interests in the Pacific. No doubt in taking such a strong stand he was also influenced by his awareness that unless the navy received a substantially greater share of the defence he would be presiding over not a powerful unit of an imperial fleet but a depleted and demoralised local force, comprising only destroyers and submarines.

The government's immediate response to the Naval Board's warning about the strategic consequences of the proposed cut in the defence budget was to send a cable to London inquiring about British naval policy and asking for advice on how best to spend the limited moneys apportioned to the navy. Grant himself had urged this as the first most logical step. Assuming that British policy for the Pacific would be the Jellicoe scheme or its equivalent he had, after stating that the funds allocated for the navy would be 'inadequate for the Australian part of the of Jellicoe scheme', suggested asking for the Admiralty's view on how this inadequate amount could 'best be expended in order to help the general imperial scheme for the security of the Pacific.'

Hughes's message to London, however, was quite different. He, unlike Grant, understood that it would be wrong to assume that Britain would adopt the Jellicoe report or commit itself to any other substantial plan for the defence of the Empire in the Pacific. He remembered the Admiralty message of the previous February which had said that the matter had to be left over until the next Imperial Conference. He understood that as a result of the Great War the British, like the Australians, were 'circumscribed by financial considerations'. The result was that Australia found itself 'groping in the dark'. It did not know 'whether Britain approves the whole or any part of Lord Jellicoe's scheme' nor did it have any information as to intentions of the other Dominions. Even if the question of naval defence was not to be determined until the forthcoming Imperial Conference, Australia, in spending what was available for the 1920–21 appropriations – and the limits adopted by the government were 'insurmountable' – ought not to use them in a way

---

[93] Covering letter Naval Board to Minister, 1 July 1920 attached to 'An appreciation of the Present Position of Australia with Regard to Defence', Hughes Papers, NLA MS 1538/19/4 and NAA MP1049/1 20/0215.

inconsistent with the policy which would be agreed to at that time. It ended with a plaintive plea, 'Will you therefore let us know views of British Government on Imperial Defence policy for the Pacific?'

Six weeks later the British in replying did not give Hughes an answer to the fundamental question. They noted that both Canada and New Zealand had not taken any serious steps to carry out Jellicoe's recommendations because of financial strictures, and were awaiting the deliberations at the Imperial Conference before making a decision about naval policy. For Australia in the meanwhile they suggested that its battle cruiser *Australia* should be placed on reserve and used only for training, and the rest of the squadron be kept in commission. It also thought that Port Stephens just north of Newcastle, whose bay was twice the size of Sydney's, should be developed as a base for capital ships and a start made towards acquiring and storing large reserves of fuel oil.[94]

Given the government's decision to limit the Navy Department's vote to £3.25 million, the Admiralty's advice was of little practical use. Grant and his Naval Board continued to harass Cook and through him, Hughes. They pressed for a response to their 'Strategic Appreciation', but never received one. For Hughes and Cook the issues raised in the Board's appreciation – the dismissal of the army's potential role in Australia's defence, the need to accept that a British imperial fleet was the only answer to Australia's defence dilemma, the proposed redistribution of defence funds in favour of the navy – were too difficult to be responded to in any logical or safe political manner. They totally agreed with Grant about the threat from the north but, regardless of this, financial constraints and political expediency compelled them reluctantly to take a large slice from the defence budget. Likewise, when Grant, unabashed by the minister's insistence that the navy reconcile itself to what was unavoidable, asked for the naval vote to be increased to over £4 million, Cook ignored him and demanded that naval estimates be furnished to the Treasury on the basis set down by the government. Grant, frustrated and indignant, had no choice but to act as directed. Yet even as the Naval Board complied, it informed the minister that it could 'not recommend the drastic cutting down of the Navy ... as this cutting down will to a large extent destroy the efficiency of the fleet.'[95]

At the end of these prolonged and confused exchanges Grant lost out. Hughes, Pearce and W. Laird Smith, who had replaced Cook as Minister for the Navy, accepted that they were taking a risk. They sought more information about Japan's activities. They sent James Murdoch on a second intelligence gathering mission to Japan and he took with him two military officers who were to study the Japanese language over two years and prepare themselves to become experts on

---

[94] Cables, Munro Ferguson to Milner, 3 July 1920 and Milner to Munro Ferguson, 13 August 1920, NAA A981/4 DEF Pts 1 and 2, and A981 Defence 350, Pt.1.
[95] Minute, Naval Board to Treasurer through Minister for the Navy, 9 July 1920, Hughes Papers, NLA MS 1538/136/7: Minute, Naval Board to Laird Smith, 19 August 1920, NAA MP1049/1 20/0215: Minute, Naval Board to Laird Smith, 25 August 1920, *ibid*.

Japanese armed forces.[96] Likewise they pressed London to resume sending them copies of the reports of the British consuls-general at Manila and Batavia and requesting that a British naval vessel visit Truk in the Carolines archipelago to find out whether the Japanese were, in defiance of the mandate terms, fortifying the island.[97] But these initiatives did not help with the immediate problem. At bottom since the British Government would not give them any assurances about Pacific naval defence, their surrender to financial stringency was a gamble. They looked to the coming Imperial Conference to somehow find the means of securing Australia against the ever-present threat of Japan.

After a year of wrestling with the issue, the government finally announced its defence policy. Hughes took the lead and in a masterly speech in parliament on 9 September, perhaps the most comprehensive of all his speeches on defence and foreign policy in his eight years as Prime Minister, he gave voice to all the concerns which he, his ministers and defence advisers shared about Australia's position in the post-war world. The speech was very carefully composed so as to avoid offending Japan directly and to meet all the domestic objections to the government's policy.

Hughes began by putting Australia's position in the context of the pre-war Australian crisis. He maintained that had it not been for the Great War he and his government 'should have considered the present state of affairs as the most menacing that has confronted us in the last fifty years.' What he meant by this was that the serious threat to Australia's security in the Pacific, which had first been discerned at the time of Japan's victory in the Russo-Japanese war, had now reached a critical point.

Hughes asserted that though peace treaties had been signed with all the enemy powers, the world was still a dangerous place. New wars raged in Eastern Europe, the Germans remained unrepentant and Sinn Feiners and Bolsheviks spread propaganda that disturbed the safety of the Empire and the peace of the world. Tactfully he omitted Japan and its aggressive actions in East Asia from the list of menaces and left it to his listeners to fill in this space on the geopolitical map. This 'cursory survey of the world' plus 'the teachings of history, and the experience of the ages' showed that it was 'only by sufficient preparations for effective national defence' that 'the political integrity and the freedom of nations can be maintained.' The existing state of affairs was 'not a world in which any prudent nation can afford to allow its war insurance policy to lapse, and to trust to luck for protection against invasion and attack.'

How then was Australia to be shielded from the slings and arrows of this dangerous world? What did Australia's membership in the League of Nations or its partnership in the British Empire mean?

While, as was his custom in making public speeches on international relations he admitted as a sop to naïve optimists that the League of Nations represented 'a noble ideal', he immediately followed this by a declaration that in the world in which they found themselves, it provided no

---

[96] Memorandum, Secretary, Prime Minister's Department to Official Secretary, Governor-General, 28 August 1920, NAA A981 JAP 28.

In January 1921, the Naval Board proposed sending a naval officer for two years for the same purpose. See Minutes of Naval Board, 6 January 1921, NAA A2585 1921.

[97] Cable, Munro Ferguson to Milner, 28 July 1920 and cable, Milner to Munro Ferguson, NAA CP290/15 1920/782, Bundle 3.

guarantee of national security. Its effectiveness depended on 'the growth of the peace spirit', and it would be foolish not to recognise that 'at the present the will to war exists as keenly in the mind of man as it ever did.' In the case of the Russian Bolsheviks' invasion of Poland the League had shown itself to be powerless to protect one of its members against aggression. If the League's leading members with their headquarters in Europe could not help Poland, then Australia could not expect any help from that organisation, especially given its distance from Europe.

Moreover he pointed out yet again that there were interests so vital to national existence that league members, including the leading supporters of the League, would not allow them to be submitted to the arbitration of that body. The Americans had insisted on exempting their 'Monroe Doctrine' and the British their right to 'the freedom of the seas' from the League's oversight, and the Australian people regarded the White Australia policy in the same light. Hughes admitted that this latter policy was 'calculated to be one of the most fruitful means of provoking international complications' but he averred that 'on this principle there could be no concessions whatever.' For Australia the assertion of this principle would be futile unless it was supported by 'the utmost resources of the nation'.

Turning to the British Empire he rejected President Wilson's demand that there should be 'no leagues within the League'. This principle was 'not only undesirable but impossible to apply to our Empire.' The British Empire was 'a federation of free nations ... having the same ideals' and 'springing from the same mother'. Thus, as history had shown, it was a much more reliable league for protecting its members and policing the peace of the world. Australia, however, should not rely on the British navy and the British taxpayer for its security. The Great War had drained the Mother Country of its resources and so Australia had to play its part and make its contribution to the common defence of the British world.

Hughes's argument for the development of a strong defence was posited on georacial as well as geopolitical grounds. Australia was a continent as remote as possible from Europe and remoteness meant vulnerability. As a result, it was 'the advance guard of the white population of the whole world ... ringed about by half the population of the world.' Australia had to guard a coastline of approximately 17,000 kilometres – the same distance separating Melbourne from London. In addition it had acquired control of substantial island territories and had a vast international and coast trade to protect. The centre of political gravity had moved from Europe to the Pacific. Summing up, he concluded that if Australians were to maintain this continent 'as their own' they had to be prepared to defend it.

Having outlined Australia's strategic problem he then announced in general terms the government's plans for the army, navy and air force for the financial year 1920–21. These would be stopgap measures to be reassessed after Britain and the Dominions had met and arrived at an imperial defence policy. For the army, as the military officers had advised, compulsory military training was to be retained, the training period in the first year to be extended – Hughes left it to Pearce to explain that this was to be a continuous camp of ten weeks – and the returned members of the AIF invited to cooperate 'to engrave the traditions and exploits of that splendid body on the Citizen Forces'.

On the navy he made some gestures to Grant's point of view. If the enemy came to Australia's shores 'we shall do our best, but it is better that they should not come here at all' and therefore

Australia's main lines of defence should be on the sea and in the air. Battleships were still the deciding factor on the high seas and since Australia, because of its relatively small population, could not hope to create a high seas fleet it was hoped that what Hughes called the 'Imperial Defence Conference' – perhaps looking back to the Imperial Defence Conference of 1909 – would 'evolve a real imperial policy' to which Australia would contribute its fair share. And then he passed over the question of how the proposed £3.25 million allocated for the navy would be spent. The issue was too messy. What the Naval Board had proposed offered only some thin coastal defence by destroyers and submarines. Naval policy would survive or sink on what was to be decided at the forthcoming conference. In the meantime the government, because of the need for economy, was adopting a policy 'very near to danger point'.

On air defence Hughes waxed lyrical. Always attracted by new technological marvels which would break through economic, political and military barriers he found 'something exhilarating about the conquest of the last element by mankind'. Keith and Ross Smith's pioneering flight from England to Australia in 1919 had made a great impression on him. It was an augury of the future: 'with one machine [a Vickers-Vimy bomber] we have bridged the enormous gap between Britain and Australia.' The conquest of the air was particularly relevant to Australia: it would 'be of incomparable service in defending us against an enemy'. The government was going to encourage manufacturers to make engines and aeroplanes in Australia. It was providing £500,000 in the estimates for establishing an air force and £100,000 to aid in setting up commercial aviation in the country.[98]

Hughes had confessed that they were taking risks. Given the nature of the perceived threat the £8 million which they had squeezed out of the Treasury for defence was much less than was advisable.

Both the navy and the army had had to accept much less than what they had thought necessary to meet the perceived danger from Japan. While Grant had failed to convince the cabinet to dispense with compulsory military service, the army had been compelled to cut back the first year training camp from thirteen to ten weeks and for 1920–21 it would operate only 'to a limited degree'. On the navy side, the gap between what was desired and what was possible was even greater. Grant in a secret memorandum for Cook wrote that the government's naval policy meant that Australia had abandoned its 'high seas fleet policy'. The government seemingly had given up the idea of contributing a battle cruiser-led squadron for a Pacific imperial fleet. The failure to make provisions for bases, docks and fuel and ammunition reserves was even more disastrous in that the Royal Navy would not be able to come to Australia's aid unless it brought its own floating docks, oilers, colliers and ammunition carriers. The six submarines and six destroy-

---

[98] *CPD*, 1920 session, XCIII, 4386–94, 9 September 1920.
See also his speech on 'the Hour Dark with Menace' to a National Party rally in Bendigo on 15 August when he expanded on this picture of the world, including India, Asia Minor and China, where trouble was brewing, and argued that while 'the family of nations of the British Empire' were 'bound together to protect the individual and collective interests the dominions could no longer look to Britain bowed down as she was by a mountain of debt' and had to assume responsibility for their own defence. Australia, 'This richest prize. that now exists in the world, must be defended by our own hands.' See *SMH*, 15 August 1920. He might make this assertion but he was powerless to do anything to give it meaning.

ers could only give a very limited local defence to Sydney and Melbourne, and with the one light cruiser in commission provide some protection for coastal trade.[99]

What the government had agreed to fund for defence for 1920–21 was greatly at odds with the strategic views of the ministers and their advisers. There can be no doubt but that Hughes, Pearce, Laird Smith and Cook believed Australia faced a grave threat from Japan. Nevertheless they had been compelled by a war weary public, resistance from some of their own supporters and their dire financial circumstances, to put aside what they thought was prudent. Even though it seemed irrational, they felt obliged to take a gamble on the coming year and place their hopes in the forthcoming Imperial Conference.

Bolshevism and Sinn Fein

Paralleling this deep concern about Japan was a great uneasiness about the success of the Bolshevik Revolution and the outbreak of the Anglo-Irish War. For the government and its supporters, these events were considered to imperil not only the safety of the British Empire but also the existence of Australia as a British dominion. These external movements stirred the internal enemies who had led the struggle against conscription to even greater expressions of disaffection and this in turn brought the issue of loyalty into sharper relief. Even as the government was wrestling with the need to defend Australia against Japan, it was embroiled in a fiery campaign at home against those who espoused revolutionary socialism or supported Sinn Fein's struggle to free Ireland from British rule. For Hughes, the first meant 'the overturning of responsible government and order as we have known them', and the second 'the disintegration of the British Empire'. This was a formidable combination and what was of central importance to Hughes was that 'Nationalism could not make headway against this phalanx.' These alien movements which challenged Australia's physical security and cultural identity had 'at all costs' to be defeated.[100]

Since the Bolsheviks' seizure of power in Russia the more radical and romantic elements in the labour movement had become more militant. The IWW and its sympathisers were confirmed in their belief in direct action by workers on the factory floor; the industrial unionists were moved to seek One Big Union, preparatory to a general strike; and socialist ideologues became convinced that only by converting the proletariat to the pure doctrine of Marxism-Leninism could revolution be accomplished.

In Brisbane and Sydney, Russian émigrés – many of them refugees from the 1905 uprising in St Petersburg – embraced the Bolshevik revolution and gave disaffected Australians a direct focus for their revolutionary fervour. They revelled in acts of defiance such as flying the Red Flag at demonstrations and urging the overthrow of capitalism. Peter Simonov, whom the Soviet Govern-

---

[99] Letter, Secretary of the Navy to Captain Thring, RAN Liaison Officer to the Admiralty, 10 September 1920 containing Grant's 'MEMORANDUM TO THE MINISTER FOR THE NAVY SHEWING THE EFFECTS ON THE ROYAL AUSTRALIAN NAVY OF THE REDUCTION OF THE NAVAL ESTIMATES ...', 9 September 1920, NAA MP1049/1 1920/0215; cable, Munro Ferguson to Milner, 24 September 1920, NAA A981 Defence 350, Pt.1.
[100] *SMH*, 20 August 1920.

ment had appointed consul, acted as their chief spokesman and was reported to have told unionists that 'the politician is a hindrance … the only salvation is "go slow", sabotage and industrial organisation.'[101] Jock Garden, the secretary of the New South Wales Labour Council, regarded the coming to power of the Bolsheviks as the beginning of a new era for the emancipation of the working class, and on the occasion of the second anniversary of the revolution he declared that 'we recognise the good work that has been done in Russia, and we know that their victory is our victory, their defeat is our defeat. If they fail in Russia we will fail here … Do not wait for the people to be educated: if you do you will be waiting for ever. You are educated enough to know that you are being robbed. Let us take action and do less talking.'[102]

But this very vocal and active minority achieved little. There was no planning for a revolution or accumulation of arms or other weapons for the overthrow of the capitalism system. There was in this period only one very modest and amateur armed confrontation of state authority, and it would seem to have been motivated not by sympathy for the Bolshevik cause but by anger against the sentences imposed on the ratings convicted of 'mutiny' on the *Australia.* In the early evening of 20 July 1919 a sailor from the *Melbourne*, accompanied by another person in 'military clothes', pointed a pistol at the guard at the entrance to military and naval headquarters at Victoria Barracks, Melbourne and demanded that he hand over his rifle. After a brief altercation the guard had grabbed the pistol and seized the sailor and, on seeing about 100 supporters 'congregating on St Kilda road', had called for further assistance from the mounted police who very quickly and without any injury to either side caused the crowd to disperse.[103]

The New South Wales militants' venture into conventional politics was also a failure. In 1919, wearied of the Labor Party's timidity, radical unionists led by Garden and others formed a breakaway Industrial Socialist Labor Party; but in the ensuing state election it had returned only one member – Percy 'Jack' Brookfield from Broken Hill – and it disappeared almost as quickly as it had arisen. Unionists, like Labor voters, were primarily interested not in grand dreams of a future utopia but in improved conditions for their workaday lives. Nevertheless in this period the antagonism between employers and employees generated by the war reached a high point. Strikes were widespread across all the major industries and some lasted for many months. Indeed 1919–

---

[101] Raymond Evans, *The Red Flag Riots: A Study of Intolerance* (St Lucia, University of Queensland Press, 1988), p.81.

The Australian Government in harmony with British practice refused to recognise Simonov's official status. They were especially antagonistic to him because he was a member of the IWW. See Australian cabinet decision, 8 October 1918, NAA A981 Soviet Union 42, Pt.1 and Long to Munro Ferguson, 1 March 1918, TNA: PRO FO 371/3298/498.

[102] *Sun* (Sydney), 7 November 1919.

Many of these admirers of the Bolshevik revolution were not so much bent on violent revolution as on helping the underprivileged. Garden, who had been a Church of Christ minister, even as a Communist, could not cut himself off from his Christian upbringing and in 1922 on his way back from the Soviet Union where he had been elected to the executive of the Comintern, he took part in a Christian revival movement in Scotland. See Bede Nairn, 'John Smith Garden', *ADB* (1891–1939), Vol.8, p.615.

[103] Letter, Commandant, 3rd Military District to Secretary, Department of Defence, 21 July 1919, Hughes Papers, NLA MS 1538/16/137.

20 marked a high point in the number of working days lost as a result of industrial disputes: 6.3 million in 1919 and 1.9 million in 1920. At Broken Hill, the miners' and associated craft unions' strike over wages, hours of work and health problems lasted from May 1919 to November 1920.[104]

This militant spirit had some influence on the Labor Party. It was influential in having the party adopt resolutions opposing Australian, British or Allied intervention in Russia, and in causing the party to press for the pardoning of the twelve Sydney IWW members who had in 1917 been found guilty of arson and the Brisbane radicals who had been imprisoned in 1919 for publicly displaying Red Flags. The Labor premiers in both New South Wales and Queensland took steps to secure these men's release. More generally the party at its 1919 conference had adopted two resolutions which reflected these pressures: the first, affecting its objectives, sought the 'peaceful' overthrow of capitalism; and another, affecting their defence policy, opposed not only conscription for overseas service but also compulsory military training for the protection of Australia.[105]

This latter resolution had immediate consequences for the parliamentary debates over the government's 1920 defence policy and budgets. Labor members of parliament attacked compulsory military training, especially in its new extended camp form. Reflecting their resentment of the army's increased control over civil affairs during the war, most notably through censorship and intelligence, they denounced the measure as a new militarism, a potential instrument of the National Party and its capitalist backers for suppressing the labour movement. A number who had in the pre-war era supported the Fisher Government's introduction of compulsory military training now either denied that Japan constituted a threat or that, if it did, the natural fighting abilities of Australians as exemplified by the ANZACS would be quite sufficient to beat off an Asian enemy. In the debate over the Hughes government's *Defence Appropriations Bill*, David Charles McGrath, a moderate member of the party who had served in the AIF, speaking in the House of Representatives asserted that there would be 'open revolt and mutiny' if the government should attempt to force eighteen-year-old young men into a military camp for seventy days. He claimed, moreover, that the government's whole scheme was unnecessary since he did not think that there was 'any fear of war for the next twenty years'.[106] Yet while the Labor federal members might speak about the defence budget as if there were no serious Pacific threat, the Labor premiers of New South Wales and Queensland were not so complacent and spoke in Hughes-like language of the next big war as being one 'for the mastery of the Pacific' in which, within ten years, a Sino-Japanese conflict might well embroil 'every nation whose shores abutted on the Pacific'.[107]

The Sinn Fein cause was very different from that of Bolshevism. It was a grass-roots movement expressing sympathy for the Irish struggle for national independence. While Bolshevism

---

[104] Ian Turner, *Industrial Labour and Politics*, chapters 8 and 9, especially pp.194–95, 197–99 and 223–26; Brian Kennedy, *Silver, Sin and Sixpenny Ale: A Social History of Broken Hill, 1883–1921* (Carlton, Vic: Melbourne University Press, 1978), pp.138–39 and 158–74.

[105] Ian Turner, *Industrial Labour and Politics*, pp.213–17; Murphy, *T.J. Ryan*, pp.439–40.

[106] *CPD*, 1920 session, XCIV, 6521, 16 November 1920.

[107] *Sunday Chronicle*, 18 July 1920 and *Argus*, 17 August 1920.

had revolutionary implications for Australia and the world, the Sinn Fein insurgency only directly affected Ireland and the British Empire. Likewise whereas the Bolshevik revolution was taking place in a country about which Australians, apart from a small group of Russian exiles, knew little there were many Australians of Irish Catholic descent who still had family and friends in the 'Old Country' and thus had a fellow feeling for those fighting for their independence.

By the time of Hughes's return from the Peace Conference, Sinn Fein's demand for independence had taken a more substantial form. No sooner had the Great War ended than the Anglo-Irish war began. At the December 1918 British parliamentary election, the Irish people had returned 73 Sinn Fein members – the great majority coming from the Catholic dominated southern counties – who constituted 70 percent of the total Irish representation in the House of Commons. The Sinn Fein members refused to go to London and instead, in January 1919, sat as an Irish Parliament called Dail Eireann in Dublin. There they unilaterally declared for independence, chose Eamon de Valera as the first President of the Republic and established the Irish Republican army for the purpose of imposing their authority over the island. By the end of that year a guerrilla insurgency aimed at British institutions and officials had broken out, and like all such wars in which military discipline was weak and civilians could not be easily distinguished from combatants it was marked by many atrocities.

These developments helped to intensify the Australian Irish Catholics' hostility towards the British attempts to suppress the insurrection. Mass meetings reaffirmed even more uncompromisingly their support for Sinn Fein and Irish independence. A number of the hierarchy denounced British brutality and, led by Mannix, called for Ireland to be set free. In November 1919 Mannix, following an American precedent, organised an Irish Race Congress in Melbourne which attracted some 2000 delegates among whom were clergy and laity from as far away as New Zealand and Western Australia. In Mannix's opening speech he lambasted the Allied statesmen at the Paris Peace Conference who had claimed to go to war to support small nations and the right to self-determination and yet failed to give justice to Ireland. The greatest cheers were given for his story of an Irish child in an English school who when asked when Ireland was conquered replied, 'It began in 1170 and it is not finished yet.'[108] Many leading members of the Labor Party of Irish descent were present, including Queensland's Premier Ryan who presided over the convention, and they joined in passing resolutions endorsing Ireland's right to self-government and giving support for De Valera and by implication also for Sinn Fein's Dail Eireann and so the establishment of a republic outside the British Empire.[109]

Mannix contrived his speeches in an archly satirical manner, as was his wont in Australia, so as on the one hand to express loyalty to the Empire, even if a qualified one; and on the other to identify with the Easter Rising martyrs and the Sinn Fein and their demand for an Irish republic. On St Patrick's Day 1919 just after the Sinn Fein had set up its own parliament in Dublin and chosen De Valera as its president, he made a speech of this kind. In addressing 'a great gathering in the Melbourne Town Hall' which was bedecked with the white, green and gold colours of the Sinn Fein flag, he mused on how differently Ireland would have been treated at the Peace

---

[108] Ebsworth, *Archbishop Mannix*, p.216.
[109] Murphy, *T.J. Ryan*, pp.468–69.

Conference if Germany had been Ireland's oppressor; 'unfortunately for Ireland the enemy during these years had not been Germany, but England.' If President Wilson and America failed them then Ireland would have no choice but to 'rely on God and the stout hearts and hands of her sons.'[110]

In the middle of 1920, just at the time the war in Ireland was entering its 'most brutal and ruthless' stage,[111] Mannix on his *ad limina* trip to the Vatican to report on his stewardship discarded these nuances. Crossing America, he met De Valera and addressed Irish American gatherings in a most forthright and often inflammatory manner. In Chicago he stressed Australian-American friendship, especially in facing 'the Asiatic menace which is always lurking near' and he assured his audience that 'Australia looks to the United States for support and friendship in time of crisis', hinting that Britain could not be relied upon to protect White Australia. In New York he claimed that he and not Hughes spoke for Australia and averred that Americans should understand that 'England was your enemy. England is your enemy today. England will be your enemy for all time.'[112] These outbursts reported back in Australia and coming on top of numerous expression of sympathy for Sinn Fein and an Irish republic created an almost hysterical response among the loyalists, who from the time of the conscription debate had believed that their British heritage was menaced by an enemy from within.

In response New South Wales loyalists sponsored a monster meeting in the Sydney Town Hall where they gave vent to their outrage and founded a King and Empire Alliance.[113] The aim of this new body was 'To build up and maintain a strong national pride of race and Empire' and 'to strongly oppose all attempts to introduce and encourage disloyal doctrines'. Those responsible for summoning the meeting hoped that they would be able to found a national movement through linking up their organisations with similar bodies which already existed in Queensland and the other states.

Mannix's American statements were the flashpoints for the occasion. The American Consul at Sydney was present and spoke, disavowing Mannix's sentiments. He stated that there was 'no American citizen ... who does not regret, aye, and who does not resent – some of the statements being cabled from the United States in the last few days.' He indeed identified himself with the purpose of the meeting 'because the people of the United States and of the British Empire are bound in bonds of blood and a community of common interests.' His words were greeted with great applause and the assembled throng stood up and sang 'The Star Spangled Banner'.

While one Australian speaker made a passing reference to 'disturbances being fomented throughout our industrial, social and political life' the chief target was Mannix along with the

---

[110] *Age*, 18 March 1919.

[111] Michael Hopkinson, *The Irish War of Independence* (Montreal and Kingston: McGill-Queen's University Press, 2002), p.79.

[112] *SMH*, 5 July 1920; Ebsworth, *Archbishop Mannix*, p.229.

[113] This title was borrowed from Queensland which had established a similar organisation in April 1919 following the Red Flag riots. The Queensland King and Empire Alliance, however, was directed primarily against Russian émigrés and their Australian associates who agitated for Bolshevik and Socialist causes and it pressed for the deportation of 'disloyal aliens, especially Russians'. See Evans, *Loyalty and Disloyalty*, p.171.

challenge to British rule in Ireland. As another put it, 'Some – a few – were Bolsheviks but the others, the worst were of British stock [Irish Catholics], were disloyal. It was to combat men of that type that they proposed to combine.' To the loyalists these renegades were traitors who had betrayed the essence of Australian life, their British cultural identity and political allegiance. Set against Mannix's history of the British Empire as one of English oppression and exploitation, the speakers told the story an Empire of liberty, of Britain as it spread its Dominion across the globe bestowing on benighted peoples law, justice and enlightenment. Looking back at the Empire's role in the recent war, at Britain's action in coming to the aid of Belgium, 'Those … of British stock … could only feel pride in this Empire of ours.' Wherever the British flag flew, men had rushed to join the colours: 'A flame of loyalty had gone out to the uttermost ends of the earth' and Australians, had played their part, and it was 'that sacred flame of loyalty that we propose to keep alive at its best.'

Even as they seethed with animus towards Mannix and his followers, the speakers insisted that their organisation was open to all Australians regardless of class or religion. They asserted, as they had to do (since they claimed to be defending national ideals), that the movement did not belong to an elite but to all citizens equally. Australia in the new world had created something approximating a pantisocracy. It was their boast that 'there was not another country in the world where the wealth was more equally divided.' They could proudly affirm that in Australia, 'a boilermaker could rise to a premier [a reference to John Storey, the Labor Premier of New South Wales], an umbrella mender to a prime minister [a reference to Hughes] and a Scottish coalminer to be Commonwealth high commissioner [a reference to Fisher]', and the mention of each of these examples of democratic equality was greeted with applause. In asserting that their cause was not opposed to any religion, they also pointed out that many Irish Catholics had joined the AIF and laid down their lives for the Empire. Similarly they cited leading Catholic laymen who had been deeply offended by those members of the hierarchy who sang the praises of Sinn Fein and denounced the British Government for putting down the Irish insurgency.

Yet these speakers closed their eyes to what had been evident since the conscription crisis; namely that those who had assumed the mantle of loyalism came overwhelmingly from the rulers and respectability. Among the list of sponsors of the movement there were knights of the realm, AIF generals and other officers, company directors, leading lawyers, university professors and National Party state and federal members but no representatives of the labour movement, whether from the state Labor Government or the trade unions. Indeed the Chief Secretary in the Labor Government dismissed the loyalist meeting as the work of self-advertising individuals who wanted to prove that their 'virtue' was superior to that of others.

Though a number of Protestant ministers graced the platform at the inaugural meeting, no Catholic clergyman was present and the two Catholic laymen – one a judge and the other a company director, who were cited as exemplifying the non-sectarian nature of the organisation – were there as representatives of class not religion. Some members of the Catholic hierarchy had joined Mannix in openly condemning the British suppression of the Sinn Fein and associated themselves with those demanding independence for Ireland. By contrast a special meeting of 180 Anglican clergy from the Sydney diocese, called at the instance of the Clerical Prayer Union, gave its blessing to the loyalist movement. They passed resolutions condemning the Catholic Church 'as being a menace to our liberties and largely disloyal to the Throne and Empire'. Thankful for 'the benefits the British race and Empire have long enjoyed' they welcomed the formation of the King and Empire Alliance and the Protestant Federation as means by which disaffected elements could be combated.

How then could the proponents of this loyalist alliance claim to be the mouthpiece of the whole people irrespective of class or religion?

The short answer is that the Great War, the first great war of peoples, had made loyalty to nation or 'race' the highest social value and in Australia many of those who had embraced the idea of British identity most fervently would tolerate no qualifications or reservations to that allegiance. For the self-proclaimed 'loyalists' religious, class and ethnic differences had to be subordinated to the British idea of identity and for those who had reservations this made difficulties. They did not have another national myth which could vie with Britishness and were forced onto the defensive. The New South Wales Labor Chief Secretary in putting down the King and Empire League had not declared that these 'loyalists' were traitors to Australia. Rather he said that they were grandstanding and wanted to show that they were more 'virtuous', meaning that they had superior claims to being the guardians of Australia's Britishness. But for the loyalists Britishness had a much more complete psychic importance. Nationalism was for them what nationalism in its purest form claimed for itself, the only social idea which would make people whole. Their intense belief in Britishness as all-saving was essential for making sense of the world and their place in it. They saw themselves as the true inheritors of the British race patriotism which had swept the country at the outbreak of the war. In their eyes unwillingness to sacrifice everything for the race smacked of treason. The very liberty for which the Empire stood had arisen out of the special genius of the British race and was merged with British identity itself. Therefore any disparagement of the British Empire was an attack on the ideals of being British, including their parliamentary system of government. This British heritage was responsible for allowing Australians to enjoy religious toleration and to enable the representatives of the labour movement to form governments and pass legislation sympathetic to the working classes. This liberty, however, could not be loyally used to undermine or attack the Mother Country, especially when the very existence of the British race was at stake.

That Mannix should have aligned himself so wholeheartedly with the enemies of the Empire at the very time that the Prince of Wales was visiting Australia, made his disloyal statements that much more insufferable. The Prince, a lineal symbol of the British race and its heritage, had had a right royal reception in every city and town. After observing the huge, reverential and enthusiastic crowd who greeted the Prince on his arrival in Melbourne Herbert Brookes, the great champion of the loyalist cause, was thrilled to the core of his being. After the setbacks of the conscription referenda his belief in the Australian people's Britishness and their love for the Empire seemed vindicated. Writing to the Rev. T. E. Ruth he rhapsodised on the experience; 'It was an inspiration. It was joy unspeakable. It was balm to souls like ours, that have been troubled with the Enemies of Empire in our midst.'[114] Even some of those who, like John Fihelly, the Acting Premier of Queensland, had been regarded as among the worst of the Sinn Fein persuasion, showed

---

[114] Letter, Brookes to Ruth, 26 May 1920, Brookes Papers, NLA MS 1924/1/6219.

themselves to be as enamoured of the Prince and to greet him as warmly and loyally as their critics. Fihelly at the welcoming state banquet in Brisbane stated that, 'The Prince had endeared himself to all who came in contact with him … The traditions of our race and of his race will live and be inspired by him.' And he maintained that though Queensland was 'only an outpost of the Empire, it was a very loyal one.'[115] Indeed so infatuated had Fihelly become by this brief brush with royalty that when the Prince was leaving the state the putative Sinn Fein republican hired an aeroplane and followed the royal train to the New South Wales border in order to say his farewells.

Mannix's embrace of the Irish rebels' cause fractured this picture of social harmony. His assertions of English enmity towards the United States spurred the loyalists into action. Shortly after the founding of the King and Empire Alliance, the Prime Minister, one of their heroes, added his voice to those condemning the wayward prelate. Mannix was the leader of the 'disloyalists and extremists' in the country. He pulled the strings from behind the screen and made 'the marionettes' in the Labor Party dance to his tune. 'Envenomed with age-long hatred of England', he and his followers were 'prepared to destroy us if they can only aim a blow at England.' Mannix's mischief-making in America was offensive and unforgivable. Australia needed the United States' help in the Pacific and Hughes announced that to counter the claims of Mannix and his ilk the cabinet had decided to appoint 'a High Commissioner' to the United States who could speak 'with authority' about the Australian people's view of these matters.[116] Australia was sending 'a diplomatic representative to Washington' who would 'work with but not necessarily through the British Ambassador'. He assured the correspondent for the *Chicago Tribune* that Australia rejoiced in the launching of each new United States battleship as, 'It was another brick in the citadel of safety.'[117]

---

[115] *SMH*, 30 July 1920.

As the Prince was about to leave Australia Fihelly sent a cable assuring him of the Queensland people's 'greatest delight in your presence among them', and of their continuing regard for him 'as a new link uniting the British peoples'. And he asked the Prince to inform his father that the 'lofty ideals which inspire our race are a living active force in Australia.' Copy of cable, Fihelly to Prince of Wales, 18 August 1920, Lothian Papers, NAS GD40/17/1418/6.

Munro Ferguson had been so concerned about Fihelly and the Labour government in Queensland and their supposed disloyalty that he had wondered whether Queensland should be on the Prince's itinerary. 'Fihellyism' had from the first conscription campaign become a byword for disloyalty. Fihelly, while acting minister for justice in the Ryan government, had, in response to Britain's ruthless treatment of the Easter Rising rebels, told an Irish Association meeting that many young Australians believed that 'every Irish Australian recruit means another soldier to assist the British Government to harass the people of Ireland.' Comparing the British denunciation of the German arbitrary shooting of Captain Fryatt and Nurse Edith Cavell with the summary execution of the Irish rebels, he had declared that England was 'the home of cant, humbug and hypocrisy' and he had urged his audience, 'If they thought of contributing to local patriotic funds' to 'divert the money to relieve the distress in Ireland.' See *Catholic Advocate* (Brisbane), 7 September 1916.

[116] *SMH*, 26 July 1920.

[117] *Argus*, 4 September 1920.

It would seem clear that Hughes had also discussed the Mannix question at length with the Prince of Wales who in a letter of farewell echoed the Prime Minister's sentiments and encouraged him to take a hard line in dealing with this enemy of the Empire:

> let me again congratulate you on all your utterances against that – dangerous Mannix. As you know I have no politics but I don't look on the Irish R.C. question as a politics at all so feel I am not doing wrong in expressing my views … I need hardly tell you that I intend this to be a strictly private letter!! I think it was a great mistake that he is allowed to land in the U.K. & I only trust you will be very firm & and not let him return to Australia.'[118]

But what could the loyalists do to counter the influence of Mannix and punish the enemies of the Empire? What could be done to silence the renegades? How could they be punished?

Mannix being out of reach they seized the opportunity afforded by an impassioned outburst from Hugh Mahon, a Labor member of the federal parliament, to make him their sacrificial lamb. Mahon was born in Ireland and in his early years had been involved with Charles Stewart Parnell's National Land League. After being imprisoned for his political activities he had migrated to Australia and, like Hughes and many others, had come to see Home Rule in the Empire as the proper solution for the Irish problem. He had initially supported the British cause in the European war – two of his sons enlisted in the AIF – but after Britain's harsh treatment of the Easter rising rebels he threw in his lot with the anti-conscriptionists.

In the autumn of 1920, as the British met guerrilla attacks with increasingly savage reprisals, Mahon became enraged by the actions of Lloyd George and his ministry. His feelings were given a precise focus by the fate of the Lord Mayor of Cork, Terence McSwiney – a Republican sympathiser, who after being imprisoned had gone on a hunger strike and after 70 days of refusing food had died. This brought Mahon's ire to the boiling point. Having been denied the right to debate the matter in the House of Representatives, he launched into a tirade against the British Government on 7 November, while chairing a meeting of the Irish Ireland League in Melbourne. In the presence of other Labor leaders, including Tudor, the Protestant leader of the opposition, he heaped praise on Mannix and the Sinn Fein republicans and declared that the British rule in Ireland was 'a bloody and accursed despotism'. His speech was a scarifying indictment of the British Government's behaviour. After Mahon and Tudor had left, the meeting 'pledged its support to any movement for an Australian republic'.[119] It is noteworthy that such a movement did not eventuate. The resolution was merely a gesture registering the strength of feeling about the British repression of the Sinn Fein-led Irish independence struggle.

This outburst enraged Melbourne loyalists and, egged on by the *Argus,* they demanded action. These champions of conscription, who had been shamed by the failure of Australia to do its duty by the Empire, saw in Mahon the personal embodiment of the demonic forces responsible for that humiliating chapter in the history of the country and all the subsequent expressions of sympathy and support for the enemies of the Empire. The President of the British Empire League called upon the government 'to prosecute or deport those latter-day rebels.' The Council of the Australian Women's National League wanted Mahon expelled from parliament and the

---

[118] Letter, 'Edward (P)' to Hughes, 20 August 1920, Hughes Papers, NLA MS 1538/16/312–13.
[119] *Argus*, 8 November 1920.

Commonwealth constitution amended to ensure that anyone convicted of such disloyal utterances as those for which Mahon was responsible would never be allowed to occupy a seat in parliament. The Council of Public Education was likewise moved to advise the Victorian Minister for Education that all teachers be required to sign a declaration that they would 'not directly or indirectly seek to influence their pupils or students in any way prejudicial to the interests of the Crown and Empire.'

The Protestant churches were united in condemnation of Mahon. The Secretary of the United Protestants Clubs urged the government to 'clear Australia's fair name, and also its presence of that "patriot" and his confederates.' The Vicar-General of the Anglican Melbourne Diocese, in his presidential address to the Synod, warned of a 'new peril from within' which was 'more malignant, more bitter in its hatred of the Empire, and especially of the English, than any that had hitherto been known.' Its 'evil designs' encompassed 'civil-war in Australia and a world-wide war between English-speaking people.' It envisaged 'the surrender of the protection of Australia by the British fleet, and exposure of Australia to what was called "the yellow peril"'. The Synod, all standing in silence, carried a motion urging the government 'to use all possible means to check the campaign of slander which is being carried on against Britain and which has for its aim the disintegration of the Empire and the overthrow of the social order.' And the Methodists, the Presbyterians and the Baptists were not behindhand in adding their voices to this great wave of Protestant indignation.

On Armistice Day the British Empire League of Victoria held a 'Great Citizens' Meeting' in the Melbourne Town Hall in order to enable loyalists, in a more general way, to denounce Mahon and affirm their loyalty to the British Empire. The meeting was supported by the Commonwealth and Victorian governments, the National Federation, the Melbourne City Council and representatives from Protestant churches, the Union of Soldiers' Wives and Mothers, the Soldiers' Fathers' Association, the Australian Women's League, the Masonic Order of Victoria and the Automobile Club. Mahon's condemnation of the British Government's treatment of the Sinn Fein and the Irish meeting's support for a republic had touched sensitive nerves. It challenged Australia's British identity as this section of the British people defined it. The emotional meeting passed resolutions affirming loyalty to Crown and Empire and assuring the Commonwealth Government of their full backing in any action it might take 'for the rigorous suppression of disloyalty and the maintenance of the integrity of the Empire'. Though the Labor Party was not represented and the only clergy present were Protestant there were again here the necessary denials that the meeting was about class or religion. The words of Mahon and the talk of a republic were viewed as an insult to those who had sacrificed their lives for the Empire in the Great War. It was asked, rhetorically, whether they could forget their forebears and 'the struggles to maintain the supremacy of the British race'. To this idealised myth of the British race as the source of Australian identity Senator Pearce added the idealised myth of the British navy as the great protector of White Australia in the Pacific:

> The British throne typified the freest form of political governing institution ... and the Empire represented the bulwark of civilisation in the world today ... Every Australian who loved Australia had to declare his loyalty to the Empire, if only for the sake of self-preservation. If they looked at the position in the Pacific they would realise that but for the might of the British navy we could not live for a day ... Those in Australia who would strike a

> blow at the unity of the Empire were not only enemies and traitors to the Empire, but enemies and traitors to Australia ... They would not only bring crashing to the ground the greatest bulwark against Bolshevism, but they would bring down the shield that enabled Australia to work out its destiny in peace, and which enabled us to implant on our banners the principle of a white Australia. [120]

Hughes and his ministers fully shared the sentiments of this jingoistic festival and intended to make an example of Mahon. Afraid that the courts would not convict him on the available evidence they took it upon themselves to accuse him of 'seditious and disloyal utterances' and used their majority to expel him from the parliament. There was no well-attested evidence that Mahon had used the phrases which were alleged against him. There was no argument advanced to show that his attack on the British Government amounted to sedition or that he advocated armed rebellion against British or Australian authorities. This partisan use of a political majority to remove a member from parliament had no precedent in the Commonwealth. But the expulsion of Mahon gratified the self-styled loyalists who for so long had sought action against those whom they deemed enemies of the Empire. And they felt further vindicated when in the subsequent by-election Mahon was defeated by a Nationalist candidate.

Throughout the first half of the following year the loyalist organisations remained very active and reflecting what the Prime Minister had hinted at in public and the prince had urged in private they pressed the government to refuse to allow Mannix to land on Australian soil or, at the least, to demand that he sign a pledge of loyalty to the Crown and Empire before being allowed to do so.[121] By the time of his return to Australia in early August 1921, however, Lloyd George had signed a truce with De Valera and was engaged in negotiating a peace with the Sinn Feiners, and as a result the heat was going out of the Anglo-Irish confrontation and the Australian Government accepted that it would be impolitic to hinder the prelate's homecoming.[122] When in December Britain granted southern Ireland autonomy as a Dominion inside the British Empire, most Irish Catholic Australians were satisfied with this resolution of the problem. Thus following the establishment of the Irish Free State, mass protests against the British Government ceased but the bitterness stirred up by the issue remained an open sore on the body politic for at least another generation.

Hughes and the national security community had no illusions about the post-war world. Victory over the European enemy, the imposition of a humiliating peace on Germany and its allies and the establishment of a League of Nations did not give Australian leaders confidence about their future in the Pacific. The limitations of the League were evident. America, its sponsor, had refused to become a member. Wars and threats of war had not disappeared. The spectre of a Bolshevik proletarian uprising overhung the British world and national uprisings against London's authority, most notably that in Ireland, seemed a further sign of division and decline. While Hughes and his advisers hoped for the restoration of the Pax Britannica, Britain's post-war naval policy and its response to the Jellicoe report remained unsettled.

---

[120] *Argus*, 10–12 November 1920.
[121] 'Representations re Mannix', from 91 'loyal' organisations, NAA 1606/1 SC F42/1.
[122] *SMH*, 29 July 1921.

For Australia, in particular, the 'cold war' with Japan had reached a critical point. Japan, ostensibly an ally of Britain, had taken advantage of the European war to extend its influence into the Pacific and onto the mainland of Northeast Asia. It was spreading its commercial tentacles into Southeast Asia, building a great modern navy with the capacity to defeat British forces in the region and thus positioning itself to mount an invasion of White Australia. All the anxieties generated by the Russo-Japanese war and intensified by the European war remained in place and underpinned Australians' strategic discourse and defence planning. With the exception of Piesse, policy makers in Melbourne, their judgment distorted by a race-based world view, were unable to adjust their pre-war threat analysis to the changed geopolitical circumstances. Thus they believed that, initiated by the Japanese, the next great war would shortly break out in the Pacific. Perceiving the international arena in this way, the Australians were at a loss to know what could be done to avert the dreaded prospect of the downward thrust of Japan towards their frontiers.

16
The Crisis of Empire and a Pacific Settlement

Preparing for the imperial gathering

With the menace of Japan looming large, Hughes felt frustrated by his inability to provide for Australia's security. Seemingly insuperable economic, political and imperial obstacles stood in the way. Both the Mother Country and the Dominions were suffering from the huge economic and psychological costs of the war. Furthermore Britain was committed to quelling rebellion in Ireland, putting down nascent nationalist movements in India and Egypt, imposing order on the dissolved Ottoman Empire and taking the leading part in trying to keep the peace in Europe. Despite being aware of these inhibiting factors, Hughes still believed that Britain and the Dominions, acting together on foreign and defence policy, could restore the global position of the Empire and, more immediately, produce a Pacific fleet to hold Japan at bay. He could envisage no other answer to Australia's perceived defence dilemma. As a result, on 7 October he cabled Lloyd George to seek a meeting with the Dominion prime ministers in London.

This meeting had been in his mind for some time but by October it had become 'absolutely essential'. In his typically breathless style he told the British Prime Minister that the Empire should not allow itself to drift along; 'The necessity for a clear understanding-policy-call it what you will – on certain matters vitally affecting the Empire is urgent and vital.' These matters included, in addition to foreign relations, 'Empire shipping, trade resources, wireless and defence – quotas for naval defence in particular': Jellicoe's Pacific fleet was of prime importance. More generally he was alarmed by the existing state of Britain and the Empire. The British peoples were:

> confronted by a host of enemies. Britain herself must fight for her trade and financial as well as national supremacy. We must circumvent our enemies. Empire problems are many and complex: they clamour for settlement and I feel quite sure that as time goes on a solution will be less easy.

He acknowledged that the path to a common foreign policy for the Empire was fraught with difficulty. The Canadians had demanded and the British had agreed that Ottawa should be able to appoint its own minister plenipotentiary to Washington. The British Government was returning to its old habits of making decisions without consulting the Dominions, even on such subjects as Egypt and India where Australia and New Zealand had a salient interest. Though the Imperial parliament idea was 'chimerical', Hughes still believed, as he had in 1916 when first facing up to these questions of interest and identity, that 'a working understanding would be possible and machinery could be devised to make this practicable.' He did not, however, venture to say what a working understanding might mean or how it would be arrived at or what kind of machinery might produce the desired result. He knew, as he admitted, that there were 'formidable' problems to overcome.¹

Hughes's cable arrived at Whitehall at an opportune moment. Milner, the *eminence grise* behind the formation of the Round Table and the creation of the Imperial War Cabinet, had on becoming Colonial Secretary made it clear that he saw in the Imperial Cabinet the answer to maintaining the unity of the British race. By 1920 however, he and his acolyte, Leo Amery, were beginning to despair. Lloyd George's proposal – that the Dominion prime ministers should appoint special representatives to London who could act for them on the Imperial Cabinet during the absence of the Dominion leaders – had not worked. Amery, writing to Milner, complained that the scheme was in danger of dying from desuetude. Some of the Dominions, including Australia, had not appointed representatives and Lloyd George had reverted to the old pattern and taken decisions without consulting the Dominions.

> … in all matters of real importance we are back in the old rut.
>
> We were conceivably on the verge of a war with Germany over the demands for a floating dock … but in the whole discussion which had led up to our ultimatum, the Dominions were no more consulted than they were in July 1914.²

Milner still preached the Round Table gospel of imperial unity in facing the world. In a speech to the House of Lords he celebrated the achievement of the Imperial War Cabinet. The British Government accepted that there was no kind of authority in practice that the parliament and people of the United Kingdom claimed over the parliaments and peoples of the Dominions. The Dominions were accepted as partners equal in status, even if Britain by common consent held the position of head of the family. Nevertheless it was 'supremely important for the Empire and the world that the self-governing Dominions and the United Kingdom should continue to pursue a common policy on all the great questions of international affairs.' Looking back to the wartime experiment with the Imperial War Cabinet he said that they should establish 'an instrument of government able not only to discuss Imperial affairs but able to take action as representing the Empire.'³

---

¹ Cable, Hughes to Lloyd George, undated, Lloyd George papers, House of Lords Record Office F/39/2/22 and copy, dated 7 October 1920, in NAA CP 360/9 B1.

² Letter, Amery to Milner, 8 January 1920, Milner Papers, Bodleian Library MSS. Milner C703/25–26.

When Hughes had protested that he had only learnt from the press that the British Government had at the San Remo Conference proposed reducing Germany's reparations bill, Lloyd George had replied in a message prepared by Milner that:

> As to consultation with the Dominions … I would remind you that the British Government invited the Dominions to send a representative Minister to London for the precise purpose of obtaining information about Imperial and Foreign affairs … and I promised to have regular meetings of the Imperial Cabinet for the purpose. The Australian Government has not made use of this machinery which is the only practical machinery for maintaining inter-imperial consultations about international questions.

See copies of cables, Hughes to Lloyd George, 29 April 1920 and Lloyd George to Hughes, 12 May 1920, Hughes Papers, NLA MS1538 Series 16 Sub-series (ii) and copy of cable Lloyd George to Hughes, 12 May 1920, Lloyd George Papers, House of Lords Record Office F/28/3/45.

³ *Argus*, 21 June 1920.

On reading Hughes's cable Milner was given fresh hope. What Hughes was proposing seemed to him to be the way forward and so without delay he wrote to Lloyd George urging action. Hughes's suggestion was 'on the right lines'. Britain and the Dominions had become tangled in the confusing titles which were being used to describe their desire to work together, namely '"Imperial Cabinet", "Imperial Conference" and "Constitutional Conference" etc. etc. etc.' Knowing how potentially divisive and destructive any attempt to define the new empire might be he was certain that what was wanted was 'to keep up the touch so profitably established during the War between the Governments'. They should not attempt to create a new imperial constitution 'but to *discuss and settle* on the basis of our existing institutions' the various '*practical and urgent* problems, which affect the Dominions as well as the Mother Country, and to ensure harmony and cooperation between them.' And so he advised Lloyd George that what was required was to call a meeting of 'the "Imperial Cabinet" or something like it'. Within five days of the receipt of Hughes's message, cabinet had agreed to sound out the other Dominions and on 13 October Lloyd George sent a cable, drafted by the Colonial Secretary, inviting them to a meeting of the 'Imperial Cabinet' not later than June. Milner's wording expressed very clearly his view of the nature of this first post-war gathering of the leaders of the far-flung British world and his hopes for what they might achieve. The 'Imperial Cabinet' should be conducted 'on the lines of the Imperial War Cabinet meetings in 1917-1918' and the Prime Ministers should 'try to devise some practical working method for arriving at a common imperial policy in foreign affairs.'[4]

In order to allay any misgivings that the Canadians might have about his use of the term 'Imperial Cabinet' Milner wrote a personal letter to Arthur Meighen, Borden's successor as Prime Minister, admitting that this title was 'something of a misnomer'. He understood the problems associated with the title and assured the Canadian leader that it was not meant to suggest 'an Executive Body having supreme authority over the whole Empire'. It did 'not ... attempt to dictate to the several Governments represented on it each one of which retained its independence and remained responsible to its own Parliament.' On the other hand, what had been established during the war was 'more than a debating society. It did in practice decide by discussion resulting in general agreement on many questions affecting the conduct of the war ... From this point of view it was not inaptly described as an Imperial Cabinet.' In order to give expression to 'the essential oneness of the Empire' and the need to enable the five or six governments to pursue a 'common international policy' an early meeting of the 'Imperial Cabinet or whatever we want to call it' was required. As it might have been expected it was the British world community not Dominion autonomy which was stressed. Somehow race patriots, like Milner and Hughes, believed that the cement of 'blood' and culture could overcome the diversity of interests and enable Britain and the Dominions to agree on a common defence and foreign policy. As part of his reassurance Milner

---

[4] Letter, Milner to Lloyd George, 8 October 1920, and letter, A.C.C. Parkinson, Lord Milner's Private Secretary to J.T. Davies, Lloyd George's Private Secretary, 13 October 1920, Lloyd George Papers, House of Lords Record Office F/39/2/22; cables, Colonial Secretary to Governors-General of Canada, New Zealand and South Africa, containing message from Lloyd George for their Prime Ministers, 13 October 1920, *ibid.*, F/39/2/23.

For Lloyd George's invitation to Hughes, see cable, Lloyd George to Hughes, 1 November 1920, NAA A981 IMP106.

told Meighen that the 'Imperial Cabinet' should be understood as more akin to an alliance like the 'War Council of the Allies', but he believed that in practice the bonds of sentiment would mean that members would not betray each other, never abandon the alliance, and never fail to make sacrifices for the good of the whole. Meighen responded – as Hughes and indeed even Borden might have – that he was 'in complete sympathy with your purpose'. The Dominion leaders readily accepted the invitation and raised no objections to Milner's description of the meeting and its objective.[5] Perhaps the Dominion leaders' seeming acceptance of Milner's idea of a common imperial policy was based on a view that such a policy would necessarily serve their respective interests and needs.

This common imperial policy had to be based on shared knowledge and decided through consultation. Hughes, during 1920, had complained repeatedly about the British Government's failure to keep Australia informed about British negotiations with France over the New Hebrides, Japanese activities in the Pacific, and the Admiralty's naval policy. Indeed shortly after receiving the invitation to the 'Imperial Cabinet', Hughes had read in the press that Milner himself, having headed a commission to look into the nationalist disturbances in Egypt, had recommended giving the country its virtual independence. Here was yet another example, an egregious example, of British unilateralism. This action drew yet another protest. Hughes dashed off a garbled cable asserting that the grant of independence meant nothing less than handing over the Suez Canal, 'the gateway to India, and East, including Australia' to an enemy. Australia and the other Dominions depended 'upon complete control by Britain or the Empire of all waterways'. Hughes asked that the British Government postpone making a decision until the Prime Ministers' meeting when the Empire's foreign policy would be discussed.[6]

To the Colonial Office's initial agenda for the conference, which included a 'common imperial policy in foreign affairs', naval policy, the Anglo-Japanese alliance, and the long-promised review of the Empire's constitution, Hughes added 'communications'. Though other topics were subsequently added, these remained the core business for the meeting. What the Australian leader wanted above all was a commonly determined imperial defence and foreign policy, especially one

---

[5] Copy of letter, Milner to Meighen, 4 October 1920, and letter, Meighen to Milner, 22 October 1920, Milner Papers, Bodleian Library MSS. Milner C700/300–16.
[6] Cable, Hughes to Lloyd George, 18 November 1920, Lloyd George Papers, House of Lords Record Office F/28/3/47.

For an excellent account of Milner's mission, see John Darwin, *Britain Egypt and the Middle East: Imperial Policy in the Aftermath of War, 1918–1922* (London: The Macmillan Press, 1981), especially chapter 4. Darwin shows that Milner's aim was identical with that of Hughes, namely that Britain should retain 'a strong foothold in Egypt as being a vital link in the chain of empire', but his analysis of the nationalist problem was much more intelligent and his recommendation as to the proper British policy much wiser. Hughes had no desire to become embroiled in the troubles of the Mother Country which did not immediately affect Australia. Thus when Munro Ferguson in September 1920 sounded out Hughes about supplying troops to assist the British, who were hard pressed in trying to put down a serious uprising in the mandated territory of Mesopotamia, Hughes turned him down. For the crisis in Mesopotamia, see Darwin, *Britain, Egypt and the Middle East*, pp.198–203 and for Hughes's answer to Munro Ferguson, see Novar Diary, 22 September 1920, Novar Papers NLA MS 696/36.

which would provide a sure shield against Japan in the Pacific. He recognised that holding Prime Ministers' meetings more regularly, even annually, would not be adequate to ensure that the Dominions had a continuous say in the Empire's policy-making. Thus he looked for improved communications between London and Melbourne as the best method for achieving this primary goal.

On naval defence there was little more that could be done to prepare the Australian case. Hughes and his chief naval adviser, Admiral Grant, were of one mind and saw in the Jellicoe plan the only sure means of deterring the Japanese. The Naval Board formally advised the government to adopt the Jellicoe plan and stated that 'as the other Dominions would derive benefit from that Policy, their cooperation should be invited in carrying out Lord Jellicoe's Scheme.'[7]

While the Naval Board was preparing its advice to the government, the Admiralty was seeking to arrange a meeting of the commodores of the East Asia, China and Australian squadrons in March 1921 to discuss war plans and other forms of cooperation for the British naval forces in the Western Pacific. After some rather strained negotiations during which the Australians sought unsuccessfully to have the meeting held in Sydney, the Admiralty grew cold about the idea – probably fearing that if the Australian commodore were included he might raise the troublesome matter of a Pacific fleet. Nevertheless when Grant learnt that the Admiralty had changed its mind and was proceeding with a meeting of the commanders of the other two squadrons, he persuaded Hughes to seek an invitation on the grounds that it would be of 'the greatest importance to the Prime Minister in dealing with the Naval Pacific problem at the June Conference.' The Admiralty could not easily refuse, and the First Naval Member, seconded for the purpose to the position of commander of the Australian naval forces, attended the meeting at Penang.[8]

The Penang conference worked under the direction of an Admiralty 'War Memorandum' which regarded war between Japan and the British Empire as the only contingency worth considering and ruled out for the foreseeable future the possibility of stationing a fleet permanently in the Pacific. The briefing paper stated that 'for the present and near future, financial and also in all probability political limitations prevent maintenance by the British Empire in the "Pacific" of a Fleet in any way comparable with the Japanese Fleet.' It anticipated that the Admiralty would only keep small squadrons in the Pacific and that if the Japanese should act aggressively a British fleet would be despatched to the Pacific to meet the threat. In a later paper on 'Empire Naval Policy and Cooperation, Part 1' dated 3 December they estimated that that would mean 'in all except the most adverse circumstances' the fleet would arrive within six weeks to two months of the outbreak of hostilities.

The squadron commanders had been asked to make recommendations to deal with the so-called 'Defensive Period'. To this end they agreed that a Higher Command of the Pacific should be set up at Singapore – a base which should be made 'impregnable' – and when the warning

---

[7] Extract from Minutes of Naval Board, 4 October 1920, NAA MP1049/1 20/0304.
[8] Copy of cable, Baron Forster of Lepe (hereinafter Forster), Governor-General, to Milner, 16 November 1920; cable Milner to Forster, 21 December 1920; copy of cable, Forster to Milner, 15 January 1921; cable, Milner to Forster, 31 January 1921, NAA A981/4 DEF Parts 1 and 2.

message was received all squadrons, including the Australian, should automatically come under the control of the Higher Command at Singapore. In addition to planning for protection of trade, improved organisation of wireless communications and maintenance of reserves stocks of oil, coal and other supplies, they also urged that the squadron forces should be increased and the minimum naval force include two battle cruisers as well as more light cruisers and a seaplane carrier.[9]

When the Prime Minister and the Minister for the Navy read this report it must have startled them somewhat. Though there had been earlier intimations of the Admiralty's plans for the Pacific this was the first definite news of the British Government's decision not to adopt the Jellicoe scheme. The Naval Board, however, remained convinced of the need for the scheme and assumed that Grant, who was to be Hughes's naval adviser at the London Conference, would persist in pushing this answer to the problem of the Pacific.[10]

On foreign policy, the pressing question was whether or not the Empire should support the renewal of the Anglo-Japanese alliance. The British Government had, in the light of the post-war circumstances, to consider the effect that continuation or abrogation would have on relations with Japan, the United States, China and the general power balance in the Pacific. In July 1920, after the two parties had informed the League of Nations that they intended to revise the treaty to make it conform to the covenant, this became a more urgent question. The British regarded this step as giving the required one year notice for the termination of the treaty and as a result, unless action was taken before that time it would end.[11] They also recognised that they would have to consult the Dominions, as had happened in 1911 when the alliance was revised and extended. Thus it became the most important issue for the coming conference.

By early 1920 Hughes had become aware from a number of sources, including the British and Australian press, that the British were giving thought to the future of the alliance. Piesse after returning from Japan had himself drawn the Prime Minister's attention to the question and had written a paper on 'Australia and the future of the Anglo-Japanese alliance' based on his discussions in Tokyo. Alerted to the problem Hughes asked the British to inform him of 'any negotiations or conversations' about a possible 'modification, termination or extension' of the Anglo-Japanese alliance. The Australian Government wanted the opportunity to have a say on the matter, 'not only as it may affect questions now pending between Australia and Japan, but also as it may affect the general situation in the Far East, and in particular its bearing upon the racial equality amendment of the Covenant.'[12] Hughes claimed a right to have a voice in the decision both because of the implications for Australia's general strategic position in the Pacific and of its ongoing issues with Japan – namely Japan's objections to the New Guinea mandate conditions and its threat to raise the racial equality issue at the first meeting of the League of Nations. The British Government might feel free to act unilaterally on European and Middle Eastern problems but

---

[9] Letter, Grant to Laird Smith, 11 April 1921 containing 'Report … of Conference at Penang, 7 March 1921, NAA MP1049/1 21/0641.
[10] Minutes of the Naval Board, 20 April 1921, NAA A2585.
[11] Nish, *Alliance in Decline*, pp.295–98.
[12] Cable, Munro Ferguson to Milner, 21 April 1920, NAA A981 Japan 96. Hughes himself had scrawled this last phrase on the draft.

they knew that the Dominions, especially Australia and Canada, would take umbrage if not fully consulted on the Japanese alliance. Thus Milner replied that no conversations or negotiations had taken place and that he was sending a Foreign Office memorandum on the question and looking forward to hearing Hughes's view.[13]

The British Foreign Office memorandum and Piesse's paper were quite thorough and tended to support the continuance of the alliance. The British thought that renewal would give 'a sort of insurance for the Empire in the Far East'; would safeguard the Empire against the possibility of Japan entering into an alliance with Russia and Germany; and would enable London 'to retain a certain hold over Japan's policy in China.' The major difficulty would be its impact on the Empire's relations with the United States. It was admitted that America was, in 1920, Japan's potential enemy – as Russia had been in 1902 when the alliance had been originally negotiated. But, in contrast to the British attitude to Russia at the time of the making of the alliance, the Empire's relationship with the United States was 'of prime importance … both from the point of view of material and racial affinity' and thus it was imperative to ensure that America was not antagonised. The best outcome would be a tripartite understanding in East Asia – which might later be extended to France. Until that 'ideal' could be realised they should 'content themselves with the next best arrangement – alliance with Japan: intimate friendship and cooperation with the United States of America and France.'[14]

Piesse's analysis, which was written without knowledge of the British Foreign Office's view, was more hard-headed and looked directly at how the continuation of the alliance would affect Australia's interests. For him neither Australia nor the British Empire needed the alliance against a third power enemy. If the British Empire did need the alliance against a potential enemy, it was Japan itself against whom it should be directed. That is, it should be entered into in order to exercise a restraining influence upon Japan. Unlike the Foreign Office he did not think that it would give British possessions in East Asia 'some sort of insurance'. In tune with the pre-war views of Fisher and Cook he took 'the cynical view that Japan, like most other countries, will find ways if not of breaking obligations at all events of avoiding them, if her vital interests seem to require it.' Likewise since he had become convinced that Japan's naval and military build-up was motivated by fear of the United States he did not see that the retention of the alliance would make any difference to Australia's security. For those in Australia – and he was clearly excluding himself – who believed that the Japanese might turn their armed forces against the Dominions he did not see how continuing the alliance would reduce the threat. Thus he concluded that 'On any such big issue as our national safety then, I doubt if a renewal of the Alliance is of much value.'

Nevertheless he did think that there might be some possible benefits from maintaining the alliance. He was convinced from his reading of the Japanese press and discussions with diplomats and others in Tokyo that Japan was 'extremely anxious that the Alliance remain in force' and if the British Empire and Japan were 'to remain close friends, minor questions will be easier to adjust,

---

[13] Cable, Milner to Munro Ferguson, 3 May 1920, *ibid*.

[14] 'Foreign Office Memorandum on the Effect of the Anglo-Japanese Alliance upon Foreign Relationships', 28 February 1920, in despatch, Milner to Munro Ferguson, 10 May 1920 (arriving in Melbourne 24 June 1920), *ibid*.

and we may expect that Japan may be induced to refrain from any active policy contrary to our interests.' He thought that Australia might be able to exploit Japan's desire to keep the alliance to extract concessions. In return for the British Empire's assent, Australia might be able to secure from Japan 'a recognition of our policy in the former German islands, an undertaking that the question of immigration will not be raised, a recognition of our policy of refusing to enter into a commercial treaty, and adjustments of any other questions that may exist.' If the alliance were to be renewed he did not envisage that America would be a difficulty. The Japanese had in principle conceded at the time of the 1911 renegotiation of the treaty that it could not be invoked against the United States, and there was no sign that Tokyo wanted to abandon that position.[15]

During 1920 Hughes and his ministers were concerned not so much with the alliance itself, but with Japan's demand for the inclusion of the open door trade principle in the C class mandate terms and with rumours that it would raise the issue of racial equality at the first meeting of the League of Nations Assembly in December. Almost immediately after the signing of the Versailles treaty, the Japanese – affronted by Australia's refusal to allow their ships the right to pick up cargo at Rabaul and their merchants to expand their activities in New Guinea – had blocked the Supreme Council's attempts to confirm the allocation of the mandates. This obstructive behaviour, combined with press suggestions that Japan would seek again to have the League incorporate the racial equality principle in its Covenant, infuriated Hughes. For Hughes Japan's stand on these questions was further evidence of its aggressive intentions towards Australia.[16] These questions were to come to a head at the meeting of the League and therefore as Hughes told Milner, 'Pending meeting of Assembly of League in November, statement of views of Commonwealth Government [on the alliance was] postponed.'[17] Perhaps Hughes had in mind Piesse's idea that Australia might be able to exploit the Japanese desire for the renewal of the alliance to obtain concessions on the racial equality and mandate questions.

As the inaugural meeting of the League of Nations drew closer, the anxieties about Japan and its objectives grew. Despite pressure from the press and some of his parliamentary colleagues,[18] Hughes had to abandon the idea of going to Geneva himself to defend Australian interests. Since the Prime Ministers' conference could not be held around the same time and he could not make two trips to Europe within a six-month period, he delegated the task to Senator E. D. Millen, the

---

[15] 'Australia and the Future of the Anglo-Japanese Alliance', 22 March 1920, NAA A2219, Vol.8. It is not known whether Hughes or Cook perused these documents.

[16] See copies of cables, Hughes to Milner, 2 February and 29 April 1920, NAA A3934 SC12/5 Part 1 and letter, Hughes to Munro Ferguson, 21 May 1920 containing cable for transmission to Milner, *ibid.*, A3934 SC12/15 Part 1.

During 1920 Hughes and Cook rarely expressed a view on the question of renewal of the alliance. The only two statements of their attitude appearing in the press came from interviews. The *Chicago Tribune* reported Hughes to have said that 'a modified Anglo-Japanese agreement instead of harmfully affecting Australia would rather protect us', and the *Argus* reported Cook as saying that 'he hoped with all his heart that the Anglo-Japanese alliance would continue based on a thoroughly good understanding between the two countries.' See *Argus*, 4 September and 11 August 1920.

[17] Cable, Munro Ferguson to Milner, 7 August 1920, NAA A981 Japan 96.

[18] *SMH*, 12 August 1920 and *CPD*, 1920 session, XCIII, pp.408–09, 22 September 1920.

Minister for Repatriation. Millen, a former Defence Minister and vehement supporter of White Australia, set out his uncompromising position on the eve of his departure. Speaking of the issues that might be brought up at the meeting of the League of Nations he declared that there was:

> none more vital to Australia than the policy of a White Australia. The White Australia principle is as vital and as essential as the Monroe Doctrine is to the United States or the Freedom of the Seas to Great Britain. (Applause). I will endeavour to maintain the stand taken by Mr Hughes at Versailles. We must fill Australia with white men.[19]

Millen was true to his word. Arriving in London he was emphatic about his mission, telling the *Daily Telegraph* that the 'White Australia policy was more than a doctrine. It was a religion.'[20] Hughes reinforced Millen's mission, protesting to the Colonial Secretary that he could not understand why the conditions for the C class mandates were still being discussed. They had been settled at Paris and incorporated in the Peace Treaty. He told Milner that what the Japanese Government was doing in attempting to amend these terms was 'to introduce thin edge of wedge of racial equality and the conditions obtaining for class "B" Mandates in regard to trade' and that the Commonwealth Government would 'resolutely resist both these proposals.'[21] In all the official and unofficial discussions that took place with the British and the Japanese, Millen gave no quarter; and in the end the Japanese capitulated and agreed to accept the provisions of the C class mandates as they had been determined at Paris. The Japanese on 13 December stated that while not acquiescing in discriminatory treatment of their nationals they would, 'From spirit of conciliation and consultation and reluctance to see question of settlement longer delayed', sign the mandate in its present form. The Japanese also declared that they would not submit a concrete proposal on racial equality to this first session of the League's General Assembly.[22] Given their circumstances the Japanese had no alternative but to retreat before the intransigence of the Australians. Having as their prime objective the renewal of the alliance – especially at a time of

---

[19] *SMH*, 24 September 1920.

[20] *Daily Telegraph* (London), 5 November 1920.

[21] Copy of cable, Hughes to Milner, 12 November 1920, NAA A3934 SC12/20.

See also cable, Hughes to Millen, 12 November 1920, *ibid.*, 'The safest plan is to stand fast and agree to no modifications.'

[22] Cables, Millen to Hughes, 4, 10, 13 and 17 December 1920, NAA A3934 SC12/5 Part 2 and A3932 SC18.

At a meeting of the British Government with representatives of the British Dominions and India on 5 November 1920, Millen not only refused to make any concession to the Japanese over the mandate question but also affirmed Hughes's view, against the South Africans and others who wished to invite Germany to join the League of Nations without delay, that Germany should be required to apply for membership and before being admitted should 'give evidence that she was making a real effort to carry out her obligations and had generally shown her *bona fides.*' See minutes of Conference, TNA: PRO CAB 29/28.

On 30 November Viscount Ishii stated that though Japan had failed at the Paris Peace Conference to have a racial equality provision included in the League Covenant it would continue to seek its adoption. Since, however, the league was still in the process of establishing itself, the Japanese considered it not appropriate to 'insist upon an immediate revision'. He said that they would 'patiently bide the time until the opportune moment would present itself.' The League Council agreed on the form of the C class mandates on 17 December and they were issued by the Assembly on 17 January 1921. See Millen's report to the Senate. *CPD*, 1920–1 session, XCIV, pp.7349–56, 13 April 1921.

strained relations with the United States – they knew that Britain would not agree to an extension without the Dominions' consent. They could not risk an Australian veto and as a result they could not afford to press their case further.[23]

With these matters satisfactorily resolved Hughes turned his attention to the Imperial Conference, especially to the matter of the renewal of the Anglo-Japanese alliance. On 7 April in a major parliamentary speech he set out his understanding of the chief problems to be discussed at the meeting. He assured the house that he was opposed to changing the time-tested constitution of the British Commonwealth and would, in particular oppose the setting up of an Imperial Federation or any similar body which would limit Australia's autonomy and self-government; 'the ties of race, of kindred, of common tradition, of language – all these taken together go to weave that which neither the storms of adversity nor the passage of time has been able to destroy.' Similarly he promised that he would bring back any cooperative scheme for naval defence to the parliament for its ratification and would only consent to a renewal of the Anglo-Japanese alliance in a form that had America's approval and did not compromise any of Australia's interests, such as White Australia.

Hughes found the reasons for supporting the renewal of the Anglo-Japanese alliance to be compelling. The next war would arise out of Pacific problems. As a result of the European conflict, British resources had been stretched to the limit and in the post-war struggle for economy its leaders had admitted that they could no longer maintain a navy 'at a strength necessary for the complete protection of the Empire and that the Dominions must do their share.' Australia, above all the other Dominions, was placed in jeopardy by this development. The Australian navy was 'ludicrously inadequate to defend' the country against the Japanese who were 'an ambitious and an intensely passionate, patriotic people' and who 'imagined that they have causes for quarrel, or, rather complaint, with ourselves because of our policy of a White Australia.' Hughes, having grasped that the Jellicoe scheme for an imperial Pacific fleet was not likely to be realised, implied that Australia could not afford to offend Japan unnecessarily. It was 'a thing more precious than rubies that we should have an alliance with the greatest Power in the East.' In his hyperbolic manner he declared that the alliance 'means everything to us.'

Australia's dilemma was that Japanese-American relations were strained and the two countries were involved in a naval-building armaments race. Australia, equally with Britain and the other Dominions, could not contemplate being drawn into a war against the United States. It was well known that America was suspicious of the alliance and did not look kindly on its renewal. Hughes acknowledged that the alliance was 'anathema to the Americans', and since he regarded 'an alliance, an understanding, call it what you will, between the two great branches of the English-speaking peoples' as the hope of the world the form of the renewal of the alliance had to 'be acceptable to Britain, America, Japan, and ourselves.' He refuted those who seemed to think

---

[23] The AAP representative at Geneva stated that Japan had abandoned its proposed amendment to the C class mandates and its intention to raise the racial equality question at the League Assembly; firstly because it wanted to secure a renewal of the Anglo-Japanese alliance on the most favourable terms, and secondly because it did not wish to have the status of Shantung brought up and thereby its policy towards China. See *SMH*, 14 December 1920.

America could never be reconciled to the continuance of the treaty. The Empire had to retain the friendship of Japan while not making an enemy of America.

From this speech there emerged three issues that pointed to the problems which Hughes would encounter at the Prime Ministers' conference. Firstly, he had not explained how the Americans could be brought to accept the alliance nor what Australia's position would be if the Americans remained hostile to its renewal. Secondly, he had, with Canada in mind, declared that since Australia was, of all the Dominions, the most exposed to invasion it should have the dominant say on the question. Thirdly, and most remarkably, he showed an unaccustomed sensitivity to Japan in enthusiastically endorsing the Anglo-Japanese alliance. It would seem that having won his battle over mandates and racial equality he was happy to court Japanese goodwill and to reveal his hand on the renewal question.

He called on all members who were to follow him in the debate to exercise discretion, signalling that they should avoid saying anything that would antagonise the Japanese. Hughes was, for the first time in his public career, seriously intent on placating the Japanese and he praised them for their loyalty during the European war and their assistance in convoying Australian troops across the Indian Ocean.[24] He assured them that the White Australia policy was not meant to give offence. The immigration law was not meant to suggest that Australians considered Japanese as inferiors. He declared that Australians admired their bravery and 'their splendid patriotism', and added that 'we stand among those who are loudest in admiration of their magnificent achievements.' He said Australians did not complain about the many restrictions which Japan had imposed on foreigners in order to protect its own way of life.[25] Hughes's embrace of the alliance and his advocacy of its renewal was music to Japanese ears, and Japanese public figures were effusive in expressing their appreciation. The Japanese Ambassador in London applauded Hughes's speech, saying that it would have 'good results and be welcomed in Japan.' The Acting Japanese Consul-General said that he was glad to learn from the Prime Minister that the Commonwealth was 'desirous of maintaining the most friendly relations with Japan'. And he

---

[24] It is difficult to believe that Hughes considered the Japanese to have acted as good allies in the European war. In February 1921 Piesse at Hughes's behest, sent the Prime Minister a paper from the Naval Board on 'Japanese Naval Assistance during the War'. It concluded that Japanese assistance consisted merely of a single cruiser helping to escort the first contingent of the AIF across the Indian Ocean, the maintenance of a Japanese cruiser squadron on the Australian coast for ten months in 1917, the escorting of several merchant ships from Fremantle to Colombo at intervals in 1917 and 1918 and the maintenance of a single cruiser on the Australian coast during 1918. See memorandum, Piesse to Secretary, Prime Minister's Department, 2 February 1921. NAA A981 Japan 53.

[25] *CPD*, 1920–21 session, XCIV, pp.7262-69, 7 April 1921.

Hughes, no doubt drawing on Piesse's research paper on 'Disabilities of Foreigners in Japan', listed the numerous restrictions of movement, immigration and naturalisation that Japan imposed on foreigners. See E.L. Piesse's 'Papers Prepared in the Pacific Branch in connection with The First Assembly of the League of Nations, Geneva, November 1910, Paper, No. V, Disabilities of Foreigners in Japan.' NAA A3932 SC42. Piesse, however, noted that though Japan discriminated against foreigners its laws, unlike Australia's, were applied to all foreigners regardless of race, and so the citing of these restrictions on foreigners would not meet the gravamen of the Japanese complaint. See *ibid.*, 'Paper No.1, Discrimination against persons of Non-European Race in Australia', p.14.

added rather archly that these sentiments would be 'gratifying news to the Japanese in Japan some of whom may be disposed to believe that the radical and sensational statements sometimes promulgated in Australia express the unanimous belief of the Commonwealth.'[26]

In Australia there was still much apprehension about what the future might hold. Hughes had set his discussion of the Anglo-Japanese alliance against the background of a troubled world. Germany was challenging the terms of the Versailles treaty. Eastern Europe was being ravaged by war, the Middle East was in disarray and in the Pacific Japanese-American tensions were fuelling a naval arms race. The United States election of an isolationist Republican president was a blow to the League of Nations. It was especially a blow to many Australians who looked to the United States, even if rather vaguely and uncertainly, as a fellow Anglo-Saxon country that might protect them against Japan. Tudor, the leader of the Labor opposition, who thought more faith should be placed in the League of Nations, nevertheless agreed with Hughes that the world had not entered into an era of lasting peace. He too considered that the next war would be fought in the Pacific and that White Australia, which was 'irrevocable', could lead Australia into war. He believed that Australia's salvation lay with the United States.[27] The *Sydney Morning Herald* was also preoccupied with the naval situation in the Pacific and the possibility of war, and on hearing rumours of a possible visit of an American naval squadron to Australia proclaimed that it would 'receive an even greater welcome' than that given to the Great White Fleet in 1908.[28]

Taking as axiomatic that war was 'still the one dominating factor of national life' and that it might 'come upon us from the most unexpected quarter and upon the most trivial pretext', Hughes was in despair and did not place much confidence in American aid. If Great Britain were 'to economise, and commences with her Navy, how' he asked, 'will it go with us? What shall we do?' Racial and cultural affinities might suggest the possibility of an alliance or understanding between the United States and the British Empire as the natural and desirable answer. But since America had voted for a return to isolation, that was not a practical proposition. It was in these circumstances that the Anglo-Japanese alliance became 'a thing more precious than rubies'.[29] His philosophy of international relations taught him that treaties were only as reliable as the interests which underpinned them. Piesse, and probably James Murdoch also,[30] had told him, if he needed

---

[26] *SMH*, 11 April 1921; *Argus*, 9 April 1920.
[27] *CPD*, 1920–21 session, XCIV, pp.7389–93, 13 April 1921.
[28] *SMH*, 9 and 18 March 1921.
[29] *CPD*, 1920–21 session, XCIV, p.7266, 7 April 1921.

The alliance was not 'a thing more precious than rubies' because of the certain protection it gave Australia. Hughes throughout these early months of 1921 continued to take a personal interest in the many reports of Japanese spying in Australian ports that crossed his desk. See NAA A981 JAP 55, 'Japanese Espionage-General' (1920–34).

[30] Murdoch was on another intelligence gathering mission to Japan from September 1920 to January 1921. He had had an interview with Hughes before he left Australia and on his return had requested another meeting to give his views about the renewal of the Anglo-Japanese alliance. See letter, Murdoch to Hughes, 3 March 1921, Hughes Papers, NLA MS 1538/25/413. The Professor of Oriental Studies might well have seen Hughes and, amongst other matters, asked the Commonwealth Government to provide £250 annually for

telling, that Britain and Japan no longer shared common enemies and interests. As Piesse had put it, the British and Australian interest in renewal flowed from the need to contain Japan. Continuing the alliance would enable Britain to exercise greater restraint on Japanese ambitions in the East Asia and Pacific region than would be possible if it were terminated. For these reasons – reasons quite similar to those Fisher had invoked in approving the treaty in 1911– Hughes supported the renewal of the Anglo-Japanese alliance.

The crisis of Empire

From the signing of the Versailles treaty the British Government had been struggling to find and to define its role in the post-war world. In Ireland they were fighting to suppress a rebellion. In India, Egypt and the Arab mandated territories they faced nationalist-based insurgencies. In Europe they had, by default, been compelled to take the lead in trying to settle the manifold problems which were the legacy of the war. In the Pacific rising tensions between the two new great naval powers, the United States and Japan, brought to the fore the question of *Pax Britannica* and its future.

Keenly aware of these constraints, the British leaders looked to Greater Britain to come to their aid. They believed that just as the Dominions had helped Britain in war so they might be persuaded to assist in restoring the Empire's fortunes in peace.[31] This first post-war meeting with the Dominion leaders was intended to realise these expectations.

The Imperial War Cabinet was the precedent to which they looked in order to establish the institutional machinery which could achieve this objective. The Colonial Office in putting together a memorandum on 'A Common Imperial Policy in Foreign affairs' for the guidance of the imperial meeting traced out the evolution of the Dominions' status as independent nations and their role in the making of imperial policy through the Imperial War Cabinet. The authors mistakenly assumed that the same impulse which had underpinned this wartime experiment would continue to justify it in the peace. The memorandum asserted that:

> The practical community of interests between the different members of the British Commonwealth has not been lessened in any degree either by the actual outcome of the war, or by recent developments [The Dominions' separate membership of the League of Nations and Canada's right to have its own diplomatic representation in Washington]. In their future policy towards the United States or Japan, towards the problems of the Pacific or the Middle

---

three years to subsidise the teaching of Chinese at Sydney University. See Cabinet Notes, 17 March 1921, *ibid.*, 1538/16/953.

[31] Lloyd George, shortly after sending out the invitations to the conference, had at a meeting of the Committee of Imperial Defence where Britain's post-war policy in the Pacific was being canvassed declared that if the Dominions could be persuaded to cooperate with the Mother Country the Empire would be able to stand up against the United States and remain supreme as a world power. See Minutes of Meeting of CID (134), 14 December 1920, TNA: PRO CAB2/3.

East, they can afford to be disunited even less than they could afford to be disunited in their policy towards Germany.[32]

The British saw the imperial gathering as an epoch-making event and prepared well for the occasion. All the relevant departments and instrumentalities – the Committee of Imperial Defence, the Overseas Defence Committee, the Foreign Office, the Admiralty, the War Office, the Air Ministry, the Treasury, the Colonial Office, the India Office and the Home Office – provided detailed briefs for their respective topics on the agenda. Lloyd George led the way and, even while dealing with serious coal strikes, peace negotiations with the Sinn Fein, and complex European issues, presided over the thirty-four formal meetings and nearly all the informal meetings of the conference. On 20 June, the British Prime Minister, in greeting the delegates, set out the Empire's problem in dramatic terms:

> The Conference falls at a time of great stress in this country and of serious problems in many parts of the world. It was inevitable that the nations which had put forth such colossal efforts and sustained such unparalleled losses of life, limb and treasure during the war, should feel all the consequences of overstrain and exhaustion.

Looking back to the war, he reminded them of 'what our unity has meant'. Making a gesture to the multiracial and multicultural empire, he praised Australia and New Zealand as the Dominions of sole British heritage; Canada and South Africa as those of mixed British and French, and British and Dutch cultures; and India as the representative of the 'blending of East and West'. It was the duty of all to take counsel together for the progress and welfare of all, and 'to keep our strength both moral and material, a united power for justice, liberty and peace.' In seeking their counsel he told them, somewhat disingenuously, that while 'There was a time when Downing Street controlled the Empire: today the Empire was in charge of Downing Street.'[33]

But this British vision of mutually agreed policies which would enable the Empire to face the world as a united body had grave problems. The very naming of the institution through which this ideal would be realised was contentious and the debate about the naming went to the heart of the matter. Like Hughes and Milner, Hankey who had responsibility for the formal planning of the gathering, keeping the minutes of its meetings, and issuing its public statements, recognised that the term 'cabinet' while conveying the idea of government for the whole Empire was misleading since it implied responsibility to one parliament and thus limitations to Dominion autonomy. On the other hand, he was reluctant to use 'Conference' which suggested that the meeting of the Empire's leaders was merely for an exchange of views and not for arriving at an agreed imperial policy. Thus in the end he evaded the issue by using for all official purposes the rather literal, if long-winded, formula, 'Meeting of the Representatives of the United Kingdom, the Dominions and India'. Most delegates, including Lloyd George, did not, however, have such

---

[32] 'Memorandum prepared in the Colonial Office on a common Imperial policy in Foreign Affairs', March 1921 (E6), TNA: PRO CAB 32/6.
[33] 'Stenographic Notes of a Meeting of Representatives of the United Kingdom, the Dominions and India' (Hereinafter 'Conference Notes of Meeting'), 20 June 1921 (E1), TNA: PRO CAB 32/2.

sensitivity to language and used 'cabinet' and 'conference' interchangeably, believing somehow that the two different views of Empire embodied in those terms could be reconciled.[34]

The Australian Prime Minister shared the British hope that this conference would be a path-breaking event. Like Deakin, Fisher and Cook before him Hughes, impelled by a sense of vulnerability to Japan, wanted to find a way by which the British Empire could act in the world as a united body and so enable Australia to have its Pacific interests integrated into an idea of Greater Britain. He was impatient with the semantic issue that so troubled Hankey. The name given to the meeting of the leaders of the Empire was immaterial and he used both terms indiscriminately in his speeches. As he frequently put it, he wanted the substance not the shadow. Throughout the long Conference, which lasted for almost seven weeks, he joined with Massey of New Zealand in pressing the case for a united imperial policy, especially on foreign and defence policy. He fully accepted the British view that if the Dominions were going to help shape the Empire's foreign policy then they should be willing to contribute to the cost of its defence. This was the inescapable price for seeking imperial protection. Responding to Lloyd George, Hughes stated that if the Conference were 'not to be a last magnificent flare of a dying illumination' then the Dominion leaders must be accepted on a basis of equality in the 'Council of the Empire' and the great problems which they were to deal with, namely 'Foreign Policy in general, Anglo-Japanese Treaty in particular, and Naval Defence', must be 'not only considered but settled'.[35]

The Conference proper opened with the Foreign Minister's survey of the state of the world and the challenges facing the post-war British Empire. Lord Curzon's outlook was even more sombre than that of Lloyd George. The whole of planet earth was 'still in a state of disturbance'. Sitting in the Foreign Office contemplating the international scene he imagined it as being like 'one of those lava-lakes with which some of you are familiar in the islands of the Pacific, where you observe a great liquid expanse – an uneasy movement trembling the surface, a seething and a bubbling going on; from time to time a violent explosion occurs; here the banks slip into the mud and are engulfed, while there you see new landmarks emerge.'

Introducing the Anglo-Japanese alliance as the most pressing issue before the conference, Curzon, aware of Britain's weakness in Asia and the Pacific came down on the side of renewal of the treaty. Curzon, knowing that the Dominion leaders were divided over the question, put the cases for and against but at the end recommended that the treaty be extended either for a year or a longer period to allow time for consultation with America and China and thereby hopefully the achievement of a wider regional settlement. He felt that the Japanese would resent being rejected, and might in retaliation seek other friends, such as the Germans and the Russians. Even more tellingly Britain would lose its ability to restrain Japan. The alliance had enabled Britain 'to exercise a very powerful and controlling influence on the sometimes dangerous ambitions of Japan.'[36] Expressing the same point more bluntly at a meeting of the Committee of Imperial Defence, he had said that:

---

[34] For convenience from this point the term 'Conference' is used when referring to the meeting of the Empire leaders' Meeting.
[35] Conference Notes of Meeting, 21 June 1921 (E2), TNA: PRO CAB 32/2.
[36] Ibid., 22 June 1921 (E4), TNA: PRO CAB 32/2.

there would be a concrete danger if the alliance was not renewed. The Japanese were insidious and unscrupulous in their methods, and if they were not controlled and kept in order by their Alliance with this country they would be at liberty to pursue their aggressive policy in China and elsewhere unchecked, even to the extent of waging war on the United States of America.[37]

Speaking for the Committee of Imperial Defence, Balfour addressed the question from a more strictly strategic perspective. While he understood that an alliance was not 'a permanent safeguard', he nevertheless considered that since Britain was 'in a relatively unprepared condition' in East Asia and the Pacific, because of the drain on its resources, it was necessary not to offend the Japanese and to hold to the alliance. The British fleet would be stationed in the North Sea and the Atlantic in peacetime and, as a result, if Japan should threaten British interests it would be necessary to despatch the navy to the Pacific. But the ships of the line would require a base for concentrating, refitting and refuelling. Until such a base was built at Singapore the navy was 'at a relative disadvantage undoubtedly in the Pacific, and that is why we should remain on the most friendly terms with Japan and why we should continue a policy … of joint action with Japan in the Far East.'[38] In the meantime, British interests were exposed and would be at the mercy of Japan.

Once broached, this issue brought to centre stage the differences between Australia and Canada not only over the renewal of the Japanese alliance but also over the nature of the Empire itself. Whereas Hughes had urged the need for a united foreign policy, determined and settled jointly by the leaders of the Empire, Meighen stressed the right of a Dominion 'to have its consent obtained before being bound, and in cases where the interest of a Dominion is paramount to have its voice accepted.' In this latter respect, Meighen had Canada's relations with America in mind. In the months leading up to the conference, the Canadian government, primarily out of concern for American opinion, had made it clear to the British Government that they were opposed to the Anglo-Japanese alliance and its renewal, and Meighen carrying this position into the conference declared that he 'would regret to see the Treaty continued in any form at all.' He declared that Canada had a 'right to be specially heard' on the subject since it was impossible for him to believe that 'any agreement for an exclusive confidential relationship … with Japan, will not injure our relationship with the United States … no matter what the terms.' What was implied was that such a treaty must have adverse consequences for Anglo-American relations, and that Canada would feel the full effects of this ill-will. He looked forward to Britain initiating negotiations with America and Japan for a conference on Pacific security which hopefully would supersede the Anglo-Japanese pact and hasten on naval disarmament. He considered that the renewing of the treaty would not encourage American participation in this process.

Hughes was infuriated by Meighen's claims and went on the attack, caricaturing and critiquing the latter's argument. Meighen had set out 'not the case for the Empire, but … the case for the United States of America.' The Canadian Prime Minister had not given thought to the Empire 'as a whole' and the need to have a policy satisfactory to all members. Hughes denied that Canada's interest in the renewal question was greater than Australia's. Canada might share a

---

[37] Minutes of the CID Meeting (134), 14 December 1920, TNA: PRO CAB 2/3.
[38] Conference Notes of Meeting, 28 June 1921 (E8), TNA: PRO CAB 32/2.

continental-wide border with America, but this did not give the Dominion a right to a greater say in determining the future of the Japanese alliance. Canada would not suffer if the alliance continued, but Australia would be left at the mercy of Japan if the Empire did not renew it.

Here Hughes yet once more gave vent to his racial geopolitics, and laying out a map of the region – probably the same one he had unfolded before the Council of Ten at the Paris Peace Conference when seeking to annex the German South Pacific islands – he explained the 'menace' of Japan:

> Now these circumstances are operating in Japan today. She has a rapidly increasing population crowded together in a scattered group of small islands. She must burst the bonds that cramp her natural growth. This is the explanation for the great army and of the ever-increasing strength of her navy. This is the reason she is spending more than half her income on naval and military armaments. But she cannot continue indefinitely … this tremendous drain upon her resources. Her ambitious projects must be realised in the near future or the hour in which realisation is possible will pass. What, then, is likely to happen? Will anybody who looks at that map say that, living as we do, remote from Europe, from the Western World, occupying a rich and almost empty continent, dependent absolutely on sea power, not only for our prosperity … but dependent for our very existence on sea power, say that it would be wise for us to alienate by a rude and abrupt refusal to renew this Treaty, our nearest neighbour, a great and powerful nation, whose circumstances compel her to seek new territory for her overcrowded population, and who has behind her effective means of making us feel the full force of her resentment?

Hughes charged that the Canadian Prime Minister did not appreciate Australia's vulnerable position and that what he had sought was 'fraught with menace to this Empire.' The British had no significant naval force in the Pacific and lacking oil depots and secure bases they would not be able to send the fleet to the Pacific. As a result, the Empire was 'not today in a position to challenge or invite a conflict with a great Power.' Because of Meighen's fortunate 'geographical and political circumstances … he has at his door a powerful neighbour which for its own sake, if not for his, will defend him.' Canada was comfortably nestled within the arms of America's Monroe Doctrine. Australia would happily accept a similar assurance as an alternative to the Japanese alliance. Repeating what he had said to the parliament before leaving for London, Hughes declared that, 'We desire to be – we are resolved to be – friends with America.' There was no question but that 'if Australia was asked whether she would prefer America or Japan as an Ally her choice would be America.' Since, however, it was not given that choice, what it was offered as against the substance was merely the shadow. And so, in direct contradiction of Meighen, he concluded, 'I am for the renewal of this Treaty, and I am against delay.'[39]

Both Prime Ministers, acting on behalf of their Dominion's perceived interests, had taken an absolute stand. Their arguments, however, did not justify this intransigence. Meighen's key point, that continuing the alliance would alienate America and cause difficulties for a conference on naval disarmament and Pacific security, made much out of very little. In the 1911 renegotiating of the treaty Britain had insisted and Japan had accepted that the alliance could not be invoked against the United States. Renewing it at this time may have made the American administration a

---

[39] *Ibid.*, 29 June 1921, (E9) and (E10), TNA: PRO CAB 32/2.

little more suspicious about British motives but that it would have had a decisive influence of any kind on American behaviour seems quite far-fetched. Certainly Meighen adduced no evidence to support this latter contention. Likewise while it is certain that Japan would have been offended by a British refusal to maintain the alliance, Hughes's prediction of the dire consequences which would immediately follow for Australia, as well as his expectation of the degree of restraint which the alliance would place on Japan, were greatly exaggerated. What stood out in this exchange was that the Canadian and Australian leaders were not willing to make any concessions of their respective Dominion's perceived interests in order to achieve a united imperial foreign policy, and this even when their positions seemed so far out of kilter with the nature of the problems they identified.

Lloyd George was disturbed by this confrontation. It did not auger well for his desire to achieve a common naval defence and foreign policy. The two Dominion leaders had seemed to rule out any compromise and roiled the conference. Hastily summoning a British Cabinet meeting on the morning of 30 June the British Prime Minister sought to find a way through this impasse. Ever resourceful in resolving political disputes, he 'wondered whether it would not be possible to get out of the difficulty' by not treating the notification to the League of Nations as a notice for termination of the alliance, and he immediately instructed Birkenhead, the Lord Chancellor, to review all the legal material which had convinced the Foreign Office to reach their opinion and to bring the fruits of this review to the late afternoon meeting of the Conference.[40] The reversal of the existing interpretation had two possible advantages: it would be welcomed by the Japanese who had adopted this position from the beginning and would place Meighen on the defensive in that if he persisted in seeking to end the alliance he would have to plead a case for ending the alliance rather than simply opposing its renewal.

When the Lord Chancellor duly did as he was bid and announced to the Conference that 'no denunciation had taken place' and therefore the alliance remained in force until one of the parties gave notice of termination, the battle between Meighen and Hughes was joined again. They adapted their arguments to this new development. Meighen wanted the alliance only to be allowed to continue for a year and nothing done that would impede American cooperation and the success of a possible Pacific conference. Hughes demanded that the alliance should be left to continue without any time limit and the agenda for the Pacific conference be agreed to beforehand in order to ensure that Japan was not offended or sidelined. Both Hughes and Massey, the New Zealand Prime Minister who shared Hughes's concerns, were troubled that they might not be able to attend this Pacific conference which would decide matters vital to their interests.

Curzon drew up a compromise plan of action to which the Dominion leaders grudgingly assented. Japan was to be informed that the British were now of the view that the joint letter to the League did not represent a notice of intention to terminate the alliance. The Japanese, American and Chinese missions in London would be approached to see whether their governments would take part in a conference on the Pacific question. They would also be told that the British would not end the alliance until the Pacific powers had 'by common agreement' drawn up a new treaty which could replace the existing one. If the Pacific conference failed in this task then the existing

---

[40] Minutes of the British Cabinet Meeting (56), 30 June 1921, TNA: PRO CAB 28/26.

Japanese alliance, adapted to meet the requirements of the League of Nations, would remain in force.[41] Hughes was worked up about the matter. Fearing that the Anglo-Japanese alliance might be sacrificed to the desire for a Pacific settlement, he sent an undated note – probably after this meeting of the Conference – to Lloyd George. In the note he pressed him 'not [to] agree to any course involving a postponement of a public announcement of our intention to renew the Treaty – in the form compatible with the Covenant: and excluding America from its operations until after this Pacific Power conference is held.' It was vital that Lloyd George 'made clear that we *propose to renew the Treaty*' as 'anything less is full of danger to us.'[42]

Following this meeting a great deal of confusion arose. On 8 July (the very day that the American Ambassador in London, George Harvey, sent Curzon's message to Washington inviting President Harding to summon a conference to deal with Pacific security), the Foreign Secretary received a message from Charles Evans Hughes, the American Secretary of State, asking whether the British Government would be willing to take part in a Washington conference on the limitation of armaments. The new American Government had found considerable resistance among the press, the public and the Congress to its very large *Naval Appropriation Bill* which was intended to pay for the completion of the 1916 battleship and battle-cruiser program and the building of a formidable naval base at Guam. The Congress, in putting off a decision on the Bill, had passed a resolution calling on the President to call a conference of the three major naval powers to seek reductions in defence expenditure. Since the British proposal fitted neatly into this movement for disarmament the Americans quickly adopted it and announced that they had invited the relevant powers to a conference which would deal with both issues.[43]

The Australian and New Zealand leaders were troubled by the American initiative.[44] Because of their parliamentary commitments they had to begin their journey home by late August, or at the latest early September, and so would be unable to attend the Washington conference which was scheduled for the late northern autumn. Lloyd George and Curzon, misled by the American Ambassador,[45] believed that the United States might consent to the holding of the Pacific and East Asia Conference or at least a preliminary conference on the subject in London in August and thus allow the Dominion prime ministers to take part in its deliberations. During a weekend at the British Prime Minister's country residence, Chequers, Hughes and Massey had taken the opportunity of Harvey's presence to impress upon him their need to be present at the Pacific and East Asia Conference and, according to Hughes, the American envoy had agreed with them.

---

[41] Conference Notes of Meeting, 1 July 1921 (E12), TNA: PRO CAB 32/2.
[42] Letter, Hughes to Lloyd George, undated, Lloyd George Papers, House of Lords Record Office F/28/3/51.
[43] Cable, United States Secretary of State, Charles Evans Hughes to United States Ambassador in Great Britain, George Harvey, 8 July 1921 and cable, Harvey to C.E. Hughes, 8 July 1921, *FRUS, 1921*, Vol.I, pp.18–21; *Times* (London), 11 July 1921; William Reynolds Braisted, *The United States Navy in the Pacific, 1909–22* (Austin and London: University of Texas Press, 1971), pp.492–502.
[44] Letter, Hughes to Lloyd George, 18 July 1921, Lloyd George Papers, House of Lords Record Office F28/3/50.
[45] For this sorry story of gross incompetence, see cable, Sir A. Geddes, British Ambassador to Washington, to Curzon, 30 July 1921, *Documents on British Foreign Policy, 1919–1939* (London: Her Majesty's Stationery Office, 1966), First Series, Vol.XIV, 'Far Eastern Affairs, April 1920–February 1922, pp.357–58.

Hughes nevertheless remained concerned that the Americans would not cooperate and he and Massey would not have a say in the making of any Pacific security arrangement. Reporting to Cook, the Acting Prime Minister, he wrote:

> ... it would be nothing short of a calamity if Australia were not represented at conference which is to settle the outstanding Pacific problems. Question of Disarmament is another matter, and Britain could speak for us if we could not attend, but as Pacific problems raise two questions both vital to us – White Australia and the safety of Australia – on which Britain cannot speak for us, since she must consider India and other Asiatic subjects, Australia must be directly represented.[46]

Hughes's empire was not, like that of Lloyd George and Curzon, one of 'blended' races and diverse cultures but rather one composed of the British race and those European settlers who could assimilate to British culture. India's membership of the High Council of the Empire, even though its representatives were appointed by the British Raj, was an anomaly not easily reconciled to this vision of Greater Britain. Its inclusion in these conferences was symbolically a further obstacle blocking the path to the united empire of Hughes's imaginings. Britain's commitment to this multi-racial, multi-cultural notion of empire limited its ability to appreciate Australia's Pacific predicament and to embrace fully Australia' attitudes to defence and foreign policy.

Curzon, acting on behalf of Britain and the Dominions, sent the Americans a number of proposals about the form, venue and agenda for this preliminary conference. But owing to the incompetence of Harvey it took until the end of July to elicit from the Americans a clear response, and that was an unequivocal rejection of the whole idea. All that the Secretary of State would concede to Hughes and Massey was that they might, if they wished, by travelling home through Washington take the opportunity to confer with the American Government. This was no consolation and neither leader took advantage of the offer. The American decision was a blow, and a blow for which the Conference had no answer. Indignant at the way they had been used the Conference members washed their hands of the matter and instructed the Foreign Minister to reply that they would 'leave the responsibility for all the arrangements for the Conference to the United States Government.'[47] For Hughes it meant giving up all that he had striven for. The imperial gathering had been unable to solve the problem itself. What he had feared had come to pass. The question of the future of the Anglo-Japanese alliance and with it Australia's security in the Pacific was to be left to the Washington conference.

Discussions on naval defence were conducted in tandem with those on foreign policy.

Lord Lee, the First Lord of the Admiralty, in opening the subject showed in great detail the limits of British naval strength and spelled out what was required of the Dominions and India if the British navy were to maintain even a one power standard, that is for the post-war era a navy equal to that of the United States. Britain, in setting its standard for naval supremacy, had moved from requiring, at the end of the nineteenth century, a navy equal to the next two largest navies, to

---

[46] Conference Notes of Meeting [minutes], 11 July 1921 (E21), TNA: PRO CAB 32/2; cable, Hughes to Cook, 15 July 1921, NAA A4311 395/4.

[47] Cable, C.E. Hughes to Harvey, 28 July 1921 and 2 August 1921, *FRUS,* pp.47–48 and 50–51; Conference Notes of Meeting, 1 August 1921 (E32-B), TNA: PRO CAB 32/4.

requiring a sixty percent superiority over the German navy in the years before the war. Despite the destruction of the German fleet, Lee had to admit that 'our historic position as the greatest Sea Power; still more our undisputed command of the sea are both challenged.' Britain 'under the stress of financial circumstances had to retreat from both those advanced positions.' The Admiralty even had 'grave doubts' whether a one-power standard could be maintained 'unless the whole Empire combines, in some measure and to the best of its ability to assist … in sharing the burden and responsibilities.'

Lord Beatty, the First Sea Lord, then explained that the Admiralty viewed the British navy as an 'Imperial weapon'. It was intended to be 'just as much for the defence of any other portion of the Empire as of the defence of the British Isles.' This being so it was 'just as much the Navy of Australia, of Canada, of South Africa and India as it is of the British Isles.' He then proceeded to explain the strategic policy which had been developed to give effect to this purpose in the post-war world. Firstly, because of financial stringency the Admiralty could not afford 'to station strong fleets within striking distance of the fleets of potential enemies' – meaning Japan. Secondly, the main fleet was to be kept in a 'central position' – meaning 'Home Waters' and the Mediterranean Sea and despatched 'in the event of war with Japan … to reach the Far East in the shortest possible time.' Thirdly, in order to make this work the fleet would need to have a strongly fortified first-class base at Singapore equipped with fuel and repair facilities. Thus he concluded that 'With Singapore firmly held' there was 'no danger of a Japanese attack in force on Australia or New Zealand.'

Hughes was taken aback by this picture of Britain's proposed defensive strategy for East Asia and the Pacific and he subjected Beatty to a searching inquisition. When Beatty told him that it would take six weeks for the main fleet to reach Singapore, Hughes wanted to know what would happen if 'you fail – your six weeks become eight weeks!' Even though the Jellicoe scheme had been scrapped, Hughes thought that 'the margin of time there ought to be filled up by something more than the present China squadron.' Beatty did 'not think that Japan would be so unwise as to exhaust her resources by attempting to attack Australia at such a distance.' For Hughes this was at odds with all that he had long believed and that Jellicoe and Grant had advised, and he mumbled in shock, 'It is a new view to me. It seems a little staggering.' Clearly the British did not share the view that he had expressed in his November 1919 alarmist cable to Lloyd George, namely that Japan was merely a 'stone throw' away from Australia. Indeed the shock was so great that he was, unusual for him, dumbstruck for a time. When he had recovered a little he pointed to yet another disturbing aspect of the Admiralty's outline of future policy, namely Lee's statement that unless they began a substantial building program the British Empire would, by 1925, slip to the position of third naval power. Reminding Lee that he had said the Americans were building sixteen capital ships and the Japanese eight, he asked how many Britain was building. On being told they were not building any but had approved four, he commented, 'Is that not rather beating the air?' Despite this rather disheartening news he had no choice but to accept what the Admiralty was offering and make the best of it.[48]

---

[48] Conference Notes of Meeting, 4 July 1921 (E14), TNA: PRO CAB 32/2.

After the Dominion and India representatives had private discussions with Admiralty officials about how the Dominions could best assist the Mother Country in providing naval defence in the Pacific, Lee took the Admiralty's recommendations to the Conference. The Admiralty's paper proposed that imperial defence should have priority over local defence; and Australia, New Zealand and India should contribute 'a considerable portion' of the cost of developing Singapore as a base for the fleet, and Canada should give equal importance to the Pacific coast in establishing oil fuel reserves.[49] Lee asked for even more assistance and, perhaps anticipating the difficulties which were to come, made it clear what the consequences would be if the Dominions and India failed to pay their fair share of imperial naval defence.

> Therefore we come down to this, that if the requirements which the Admiralty and the Government here have ascertained to be the minimum that are compatible with the general security of the Empire, if the money for those cannot be found between the different portions of the Empire, and if the whole burden is left, as it is now on the shoulders of the mother-country, it will be quite impossible to provide those forces to the extent even of the minimum that is considered absolutely essential.[50]

Once more Hughes and Meighen were at loggerheads. Meighen argued that Canada was in a different position from Australia and New Zealand in that it was not dependent upon the Empire's naval defence and therefore should not be required to contribute to the cost of the Singapore base policy Hughes, however contended that if the Empire were to have a common foreign policy determined by the Dominions along with the Mother Country then it followed that all parts of the Empire 'must bear the share of naval defence of the Empire upon some fixed, definite and equitable system.' He said that he 'could not admit for one moment the principle that there could be, as it were, a separate responsibility for naval defence imposed upon any one Dominion by reason of its geographical circumstances.' He then pointed out the great difference in the financial burden borne by Britain and the different Dominions in providing for defence; Britain paid per capita £1-18s-8½d, Australia 15s-4½d, New Zealand 4s-4½d, South Africa 3s-5½d, and Canada 1s-6d. Hughes summed up by asserting that 'there is no equitable distribution of the burden, and such a state of things ought not to continue, or, at any rate, ought not to continue with the sanction of this Conference.'

Smuts attempted to find a way through this difficulty. He, like Meighen, feared that his parliamentary colleagues would not raise taxes to help maintain the British navy and suggested instead that they all contribute to the naval defence of the Empire by making it a first charge on the reparations expected from Germany. Meighen, however, would have none of it. That scheme would still amount to the Dominions paying a contribution to the British navy and he did not think that the Canadian Parliament would accept it. Hughes then declared that unless all the other Dominions were willing to play their part then he did not think he would be able to persuade the Australian Parliament to approve the plan. Meeting succeeded meeting. Hankey tried to find words which would still leave at least some vague notion of shared responsibility for

---

[49] 'Empire Naval Policy: Brief Summary of the Recommendations of the Admiralty', 11 July 1921 (E32), TNA: PRO CAB32/6.
[50] Conference Notes of Meeting, 19 July 1921 (E26), TNA: PRO CAB 32/2.

imperial naval defence in a resolution. But all in vain. Much to the annoyance of Lloyd George the Dominion leaders could only agree to a resolution on imperial naval defence which essentially left matters where they were at the beginning of their discussion. The resolution accepted that the imperial navy should as a minimum be equal to any other power. It recognised the necessity for cooperation on naval defence and agreed that the method of cooperation would be determined by each individual parliament, and that nothing further would be done about the matter until after the coming disarmament conference.[51]

For Hughes the discussions on defence were even more disappointing than those dealing with the Anglo-Japanese alliance. The experience of the Conference was making him wonder whether his vision of the Empire could ever be realised. Sometime in late July, probably about the time that the defence talks were beginning to founder, Hughes wrote a hurriedly scribbled letter to Hankey intended for Lloyd George, in which he expressed his disillusionment with the Conference and its failure to obtain clear decisions.

> I am getting most seriously alarmed at the prospects of this Mountain of a Conference being delivered of a very small Mouse & one half dead at that. I have had no opportunity to speak to the Prime Minister but as I see it the position is this.
>
> Aus & N.Z. cannot continue to send their P.M.s away for 6 months merely that they may be entertained by Society & hear the views of British Ministers & of each other. All this is good: but if we are to come often enough to do any good: – I mean to have a *real* voice in Imperial affairs such as will satisfy them and the people of the Dominions that they really are *partners* and not pawns – then we must do something: decide something in a definite way & in a way which will appeal to the Dominions Britain and the World & prove to all doubters and sneerers at Empire, that our foreign policy is decided by reps of the whole Empire and not merely by Britain: that Naval Defence is the business of the whole Empire and not merely that of Britain. And so on. If we do nothing: if we postpone the qu[estion] of the Treaty: do nothing very definite on Naval Defence: Imperial Communications then one thing is certain these Conferences will fall into disrepute: Aus will not attend or send someone other than her P.M. And we shall begin to drift apart. Perhaps you will think me a pessimist. But I am not. And I am most certainly if any man is a whole-hearted champion of Empire. But I get a little tired of so much talk and nothing definite done.[52]

For Hughes the failure of the Conference to reach positive decisions on specific issues was in large part owing to the different views held by the Dominions about their role in the Empire and therefore the proper function of imperial conclaves. When the Conference turned its attention to the questions of how the experiment of Dominion participation in the making of imperial foreign policy could be institutionalised and whether the post-war changes in the relations between the Dominions and the Mother should be given some constitutional form, these differences surfaced, and Hughes renewed his battle with Meighen over the issue. Hughes, who believed the pillars that held the Empire together were 'complete autonomy of the various parts and unity of the whole'

---

[51] *Ibid.*, 19 July 1921 (E26) and 5 August 1921 (E24), TNA: PRO CAB 32/2; Notes of a Meeting of Prime Ministers of the Empire, 19 July 1921 (E26-A), 20 July 1921 (E26-B), 22 July 1921 (E26-C), 27 July 1921 (E31-A) and 29 July 1921 (E32-A), TNA: PRO CAB 32/4.
[52] Letter, Hughes to Hankey, undated, Lloyd George Papers, House of Lords Record Office F/25/2/5.

considered that Meighen's principles for governing imperial policy-making stressed too much the rights of the Dominions and so endangered the integrity of the whole. In particular he took further his objection to Meighen's claim that in determining the Empire's foreign policy 'in spheres in which any Dominion is peculiarly concerned, the view of that Dominion must be given weight commensurate with the importance of that decision to that Dominion.' Since Meighen then applied the principle to Canada's relations with the United States, this principle, if accepted, would, in Hughes's estimation, mean that Canada would control the making of the Empire's policy towards America. American policy would be decided before the Conference. If all the Dominions insisted on exercising their autonomous rights to the extent implied in the Canadian principle then the 'effect will not be immediate, but as I see it, inevitable that we shall drift apart.' It was 'only by wise restraint, by refraining from exercising our undoubted rights as self-governing communities, that an Empire such as ours … can endure'.

'Wise restraint' was similarly required in formalising the Empire's constitutional arrangements. Following on from the 1917 Imperial Conference decision that at the end of the war there should be a constitutional conference to clarify and codify the changes in the relations of the Dominions to the Mother Country, the Colonial Office had proposed that this first post-war Conference should consider the time and agenda for such a meeting. The Prime Ministers had varied views of the new relationship. Smuts and Meighen tended to stress equality and autonomy while Hughes and Massey stressed the need for equality in unity. Symbolising this Meighen wanted future meetings to be called imperial conferences while Massey insisted that they should be known as 'Imperial Cabinets'. Hughes was indifferent to these battles over terminology and condemned the efforts to produce draft statements of the existing constitutional relationship. For him these latter would be 'in effect declarations of rights'. Such statements were only needed when rights were threatened. Otherwise they were dangers to unity. The British Empire's constitution having grown up organically from precedent to precedent was 'illogical'. Its success, what made it work so well, was not declarations of rights but 'the circumstances of origin and race', the 'common stock from which the white inhabitants of the British Empire sprang.' Thus he was opposed to any attempt to lay down an agenda for a constitutional conference or even the holding of such a conference. In the end the Dominion leaders all accepted that any mention of a constitutional conference was too fraught with possibilities of divisions and disputes both among themselves and their home constituencies. They decided that practical developments had made the 1917 resolution redundant and that 'substantial improvements in communication' were required in order to achieve continuous consultation. The phrase 'imperial foreign policy' was not mentioned in their published conclusions.[53]

Calls for better communications spoke to Hughes's concept of how a common imperial policy could be made to work. He had nominated the topic for the Conference agenda for that very reason. In order that this idea could work the Dominions needed continuous access to information and opportunities to consult with London before decisions were made. He had learnt of Milner's proposal to give Egypt some form of self-government from the press and this had

---

[53] Conference Notes of Meeting, 11 July 1921 (E22) and 23 July 1921 (E23), TNA: PRO CAB 32/2; Notes of a Meeting of the Prime Ministers of the British Empire, 27 July 1921 (31-B), TNA: PRO CAB 32/4.

brought home to him the difficulties inherent in imperial policy-making. Milner had acted unilaterally. Control of the Suez Canal was essential for Australia's strategic security. For Hughes this Egyptian affair 'demonstrated in convincing fashion' the need 'for the establishment of some machinery by which the foreign policy of the Empire might be guided by the representatives of Great Britain, the self-governing Dominions, and India …' The idea of granting self-government to the Egyptians, he claimed, derived from 'a glittering phrase' in Wilson's Fourteen Points, which was 'responsible for this and much more'. The Egyptians were 'a corrupt people … As a self-governing country in the sense we mean it … is impossible.' Since Egypt controlled 'the Gateway to the East' it was of 'vital importance' to the Empire and Australia. It 'affected the national safety of Australia.' Hughes was 'disturbed greatly by what was done.'

Introducing the subject of imperial communications the Australian stated that the purpose of the present Conference was 'to discuss the principles upon which the foreign policy of the Empire is to be governed and to devise means that will give an opportunity for the Dominions overseas to apply those principles to definite questions as they arise which were formerly decided by Great Britain.' But as things stood distance prevented the Dominions from being able to take part continuously in the discussions that shaped imperial policy. In Hughes's view, 'The key to the whole position is communications. There is no other.' In 1918 it had been suggested that the Dominions station resident ministers in London who could act for their governments between conferences. Hughes, however, did not think this an adequate answer for the problem. Such representatives would soon lose touch with their home base. Moreover only Prime Ministers could speak for their governments. Hughes's scheme for improved communications 'would enable the various parts of the Empire to be brought into such close, intimate and daily touch with each other as to enable them, by the common possession of facts upon which opinion is to be formed, to exercise a real voice in determining the destiny of the Empire.' Firstly he wanted to make it possible to hold more frequent meetings of the Imperial Conference and to this end suggested the establishment of an air ship service from England to Australia. He also joined with Massey to see whether the British could provide a light cruiser or fast yacht to take the antipodean leaders to London. This would take only four weeks and would cut the commercial steamer time by two weeks each way. In addition he proposed a system of telegraphic and telephonic wireless which would allow the Prime Ministers to communicate with each other more quickly and directly and in a more interactive way than the seabed cables. These more efficient means of communication would have the added advantage of helping to cultivate an 'Empire spirit' in Britain and the Dominions. Only Hughes and Massey were enthusiastic about these proposals. Meighen was indifferent and the British were worried about cost and practicality. At the end there was no agreement. Hughes's grand scheme to give substance to the new vision of Empire did not get off the ground.[54]

---

[54] Conference Notes of Meeting, 5 July 1921 (E16) and 11 July 1921 (E22), TNA: PRO CAB 32/2; Stenographic Notes of a Meeting of Representatives of the United Kingdom, the Dominions and India, 13 July 1921 (E-SC2) and 14 July 1921 (E-SC3), TNA: PRO CAB 32/3; Notes of an Informal Conversation, 12 July 1921 (E-24A), TNA: PRO CAB 32/4;; Secretary's Notes of a Meeting of Representatives of United Kingdom, the Dominions and India, 1 August 1921 (E-32B), TNA: PRO CAB 32/4.

This Conference marked a critical moment in the history of the British Empire. Lloyd George's hopes for enhancing Britain's world status by bringing the Dominions into the imperial policy-making process and so committing them to a united defence and foreign policy had failed. Geopolitical and geocultural differences made collaboration in facing the world as a united empire impossible. The clash of Hughes and Meighen over the nature of the Empire and foreign and defence policy, in particular in the debates over the renewal of the Anglo-Japanese alliance and contributions for the British navy, made this clear. As a result, what Hughes feared would happen did happen. The centre did not hold. The individual self-governing nation states drifted apart from the Mother Country and each other. The term 'Imperial Cabinet' disappeared from the lexicon of these gatherings. No future Prime Ministers' conference attempted to lay down a common policy for the whole Empire.

For Hughes, the Conference was a failure. Though he advocated the cause of a common imperial policy more vehemently than Lloyd George he was motivated more by his perception of Australia's interests than by ideas of race and culture. After the establishment of the Imperial War Cabinet he had publicly attacked Lloyd George over the terms of the armistice and as a member of the British Empire Delegation at the Paris Peace Conference he had threatened that Australia would go its own way if defied over the disposition of the German South Pacific islands or the Japanese proposal for a racial equality provision in the League Covenant. When Massey, the most ardent supporter of 'Imperial Cabinets' and British imperial unity, proposed that Britain and the Dominions should give up their individual representation on the General Assembly of the League of Nations and take their seats as part of a British Empire delegation Hughes was as quick as Meighen to dismiss the idea. At the conference, Hughes in arguing with Meighen not only stressed how Australia, unlike Canada, was exposed to danger in the Pacific from a land-hungry Japan but also explained why for these reasons it was important for Australia to maintain unity with Britain and the Empire.

> Quite apart from those other things which bind us together: race, language, ideals, free institutions of government and trade, the sea power of Britain – the Motherland of the Dominions-is a sufficient reason why the Dominions although in name and fact, nations, should exercise their rights of self-government in a way what you [Lloyd George] said the other day, 'a living force' ... Or to put it in other words, but for the British navy, they would not now be self-governing Dominions-nor in all human probability be in existence as British or even free communities at all.[55]

Since Australia of all the Dominions spent by far the most per capita on defence, Hughes wanted Canada to make an equivalent contribution to the Empire's defence and so help the British to provide a naval force for the Pacific, a force which was fundamental to Australia's security but which served no fundamental Canadian interest. Meighen, knowing that Canada, unlike Australia, had no enemy to guard against would not accept any responsibility for a common defence.

At the Conference Hughes had been rebuffed on all that counted. It was true that the constitutional conference had been abandoned – even the declaration of principles that Meighen

---

[55] Conference Notes of Meeting, 11 July 1921 (E22), TNA: PRO CAB 32/2.

and Smuts had initially wanted was not pursued – but nothing substantial had been done to improve communications between the Dominions and Britain so that continuous consultation would become practicable. The specific topics which were central to Australia's security, the Anglo-Japanese alliance and British naval defence in the Pacific, had been postponed to await the outcome of the Washington conference. The British had made it clear that whatever might happen at Washington there would be neither a Jellicoe Pacific fleet nor an increased naval force of any kind for the Pacific. While the imperial meeting had agreed that should the negotiations in Washington not produce a satisfactory result the Japanese alliance would continue, there was no agreement about what 'satisfactory' might mean. Likewise if the disarmament talks led nowhere, the Conference had not considered what the British Empire would need to do to maintain its claim to equality with the strongest naval power. Hughes's only consolation was that the Admiralty were determined, regardless of what happened at Washington, to proceed with their plans for a major naval base at Singapore.

The Washington conference

In reporting to parliament on 30 September, Hughes put the best face he could muster on the Conference's proceedings. He had prepared his account of its doings very carefully and provided an overview which gave prominence to his own role. Marking 'a new era in Empire government' the Conference was 'most successful'. It had 'not completely solved the great problem insuring united action in foreign affairs, side by side with complete autonomy of the component parts', but had made substantial progress. Nevertheless his tale could not avoid revealing that the great questions which had come before the delegates, namely the future of the Anglo-Japanese Treaty and imperial naval defence, had not been resolved but rather deferred until after the Washington conference on disarmament and the Pacific. These questions were at the core of Australia's Pacific problem, which was 'for all practical purposes the problem of Japan'. He, along with all the other Empire's representatives, had favoured a tri-partite preliminary conference dealing with the Pacific and the Anglo-Japanese alliance to be held in London or North America so that the Australian and New Zealand delegates could express their views; but the Americans had rejected the idea and maintained that the two problems should only be dealt with at the Washington conference in November. As a result – and implicitly the American Government was blamed – Australia would 'not be directly represented at a Conference … at which questions vital to its welfare will be raised and possibly decided.'[56]

After the collapse of the preliminary conference plan and just before leaving England, Hughes had joined with Massey to give the British the right to represent them at the Washington conference.[57] After being away from home for five months, Hughes could not risk leaving his minority government for another lengthy northern hemisphere conference. Furthermore just as he was never willing to appoint a resident minister to London to act for Australia between imperial conferences so he did not want another member of his government to go to Washington to speak for Australia. Yet this was not the end of the matter. Meighen had left London weeks

---

[56] *CPD*, 1920–21 session, XCVII, pp.11629, 11640 and 11644, 5 October 1921.
[57] *Ibid.*, p.11711, 6 October 1921.

before Hughes and was not amenable to surrendering Canada's right to attend the Washington gathering, and, as soon as rumours about the nomination of delegates reached him, he cabled Lloyd George to inquire about Dominion representation. The British Prime Minister, given his commitment to the equality of the nation states within the Empire, could not refuse Canadian representation on the British Empire Delegation, and having conceded it to Meighen he then had to give the same opportunity to the other Prime Ministers. And so a few days after Hughes had given the account of his stewardship to the parliament he received a cable from Lloyd George making a similar offer to Australia.[58]

The invitation was embarrassing. He had been attacked in the press and parliament for giving up the right for Australia to send an envoy to Washington, and under constant fire in the House he in a fit of pique blurted out that it was the Americans who were to blame. They had 'slammed the door in our faces.'[59] He thus muddled the American rejection of the preliminary conference with the Washington conference and confused the issue. In the circumstances he was left with no option but to accept Lloyd George's invitation and appoint an Australian to the British Empire delegation. Hughes selected George Pearce, the long-serving Minister for Defence, for the post.

The confusion accompanying the question of Dominion participation in the Washington conference raised once again the divisive issue of national status. Smuts on receiving his invitation for South Africa to be represented in the British Empire delegation had taken umbrage at what he considered to be a derogation from the independent status which the Dominions had achieved at the Paris Peace Conference, He cabled the Prime Ministers of Canada, New Zealand and Australia urging them to press for a direct invitation from the host nation, the United States, so that they would be present at Washington in their own right. If they did not act on this it would set a retrogressive precedent. If the Dominions took a stand and the United States acquiesced then 'the battle for International recognition our equal status' would be 'finally won'. Smut's missive arrived after the delegates had been chosen and in Pearce's case had taken ship for North America and so all three replied politely saying that it was too late to review their decision.[60] Their representatives, however, were appointed to the British Empire Delegation by the king on the advice of their respective governments and, in accordance with the precedent set in the Treaty of Versailles, they were instructed to sign any treaties coming out of the Washington conference separately under the names of their respective Dominions.

For Hughes, Smuts's cable was another sign of South Africa's desire to break up the Empire, and he warned Lloyd George against making any concession to the Afrikaner. To do so would be to 'make impossible that unity of Empire which is the rock on which it rests.' He explained that:

> General Smuts' concept of Empire and mine do not coincide. Our origin and circumstances explain this sufficiently. If the circumstances of every Dominion and of every leader were

---

[58] Cable, Lloyd George to Hughes, 3 October 1921, NAA A4311 395/4.
For the Meighen-Lloyd George correspondence on Canadian representation at the Washington conference, see Canada, *Sessional Papers*, 1922, No.47A.
[59] *CPD*, 1920–21 session, XCVII, p.11716, 6 October 1921.
[60] Cable, Hughes to Smuts, 22 October 1921, NAA A4311/395/4.
For Meighen's response see cable, Meighen to Smuts, 23 October 1921, Canada, *Sessional Papers*, 1921, No.47A.

those of New Zealand and Australia and for example myself and Massey it would be immaterial how far it went in the direction which I have referred to but they are not. And that being the case I hope you will go very slowly, and give ground only when there is clear indication that this is essential in the interests of the Empire, and not merely the wish of one Dominion. You may take it that among the Dominions there is not a majority in favour of the view of General Smuts.[61]

The 'origin' was their British descent and their 'circumstances' the Japanese danger in the Pacific. These reinforcing factors of culture and interest made Australia and New Zealand hold fast to the Empire. South Africa had entered the British Commonwealth after a bloody and bitter war and lacking both cultural affinity and external threat, was of all the Dominions the most assertive about its national independence. Since nothing at this late hour could enable South Africa to achieve its desired independent status Smuts decided that his Dominion would not be represented at the Washington conference.[62]

At the Washington conference the major topics those which had dominated the Imperial Conference, that is the future of the Anglo-Japanese alliance and naval building rivalry. The two British representatives were A. J. Balfour, who headed the British Empire Delegation, and Lord Lee, the First Lord of the Admiralty. Both men had played central roles in the work of the imperial gathering and had come to Washington well-informed about the Dominions' views of these topics. The Americans who saw Japan as their naval rival and potential enemy in the Pacific looked forward to working closely with the British Empire. The General Board of the Navy, as it had done before Wilson had left for the Paris Peace Conference, prepared a briefing paper for their government on how to treat the British and the Japanese. Its report which was sent to Secretary of State Hughes stated that 'Great Britain aims at a dominant commercial position … She is now looking to her great Dominions to assist in maintaining her position and the Dominions in consequence are demanding a voice in the decisions of the Empire.' Japan was a more sinister and dangerous opponent. It aimed at dominance of East Asia, 'by peaceful means if possible, by conquest if necessary'. Since the United States was 'bound to Great Britain by laws, customs, a common ancestry and literature, and similar ideals' it should seek to cooperate with the English-speaking peoples to solve the outstanding Pacific problems. By contrast 'the Japanese people had been educated to regard themselves as a superior combatant race', and therefore there was little to be gained by seeking their goodwill.[63] In general, the Secretary of State would seem to have followed this advice. He worked very well and easily with Balfour but not in such an overt or exclusive manner so as to alienate the Japanese.

Pearce had a much milder temperament and a more stolid personality than his Prime Minister. Hankey, who was once again secretary to the BED, carried on a practice that he had

---

[61] Cable, Hughes to Lloyd George, 25 October 1921, Lloyd George Papers, House of Lords Record Office F/10/1/24 and TNA: PRO CO 532/175.

[62] Cable, Smuts to Hughes, 27 October 1921, conveying the text of Smuts's cable to Lloyd George declining the invitation to have representation on the BED, NAA A4311/395/4.

[63] Report of the United States General Board of the Navy, 12 September 1921, enclosed with letter, Edwin Denby, Secretary of the Navy to Charles Evans Hughes, 30 September 1921, C.E. Hughes Papers, LC mm 78026708, Box 169.

adopted from the wartime meetings of the Imperial Cabinet and offered Lloyd George at the outset of the conference a thumbnail sketch of the Dominion representatives. Of Senator Pearce he wrote, with perhaps Hughes's past performances in mind, that he was 'not likely to contribute very much wisdom, but not I think likely to be obstructive as we shall be very solicitous of Australia's point of view, which we know so well.'[64] In the event, the British gave Pearce no reason to quarrel with them and so he was on almost every aspect of the negotiations content to follow their lead. But even so he did watch over Australian interests and kept his Prime Minister fully informed of proceedings.

The two major treaties which came out of the conference went far towards resolving the problems which had beset the Empire's leaders at their meeting in London. The Four Power Treaty which was to replace the Anglo-Japanese alliance committed the United States, the British Empire, Japan and France 'as between themselves to respect their rights in relation to their insular possessions and Dominions in the Pacific region', and these powers agreed that in case of any disputes arising among themselves or from a threat from another power they would consult together. To counter American critics who might argue that a tripartite pact was an extension of the Anglo-Japanese alliance, Secretary of State Hughes insisted that France should be invited to be a party to the arrangement.

For Australia this agreement went far towards meeting what Hughes had sought at London. Even though, unlike the Anglo-Japanese treaty, there was no provision for automatic support for members, should they face a threat of aggression, nevertheless this was not an element of the alliance that Australia felt important. What the British Empire had lost and Hughes had felt to be of more value than rubies was its privileged influence on Japanese policy. On the other hand the termination of the alliance did have the advantage of removing the obstacle to American cooperation on naval disarmament in the Pacific. The only distinctively Australia issue which Pearce had to consider was the Japanese request, after the signing of the treaty, that its home islands should be exempted from the protection of the pact. The Japanese felt that since the home territories of the other signatories were not covered by the terms of the treaty it reflected on their status as a great power to be included. For Australia the question then was whether if Japan's main territories were to be excluded, should Australia follow suit and have its main territories also excluded.

Piesse, who had accompanied Pearce to Washington as an adviser on Pacific affairs, argued in a paper prepared for the minister that Australia had nothing to lose by accepting the Japanese proposal and remaining itself covered by the treaty. By its terms, that is the recognition of the existing status quo, Japan had tacitly recognised the White Australia policy,[65] and abandoned the reservation it had attached to Australia's mandate for German New Guinea. Furthermore through

---

[64] Letter, Hankey to Lloyd George, 11 November 1921, Lloyd George Papers, House of Lords Record Office F/62/1.

[65] See cable, Pearce to Hughes, 13 December 1921, NAA A981 Disarmament 1 Part 2 in which Pearce informed Hughes that the rights which the signatories to the Four Power Pact had agreed to respect were in effect 'all rights … whether relating to matters within domestic jurisdiction of any signatories or not, but that agreement to submit controversies to consideration and adjustment by all signatories refers only to questions not within domestic jurisdiction.'

the treaty Australians had engaged the interest of America 'in our future progress as a white country' and 'obtained an assurance of peace for the next ten years at least'. If in the light of this Australians were able to convince themselves that Japan had no aggressive intent towards them then this might 'well justify us in abandoning much of our preparation for defence'. The Japanese sought the amendment merely out of a sense that their inclusion affected their status as one of the great powers. Australia's only objection to this could be that if Japan withdrew its main islands from the coverage of the treaty then Australia might be seen to lose prestige. But 'such ideas as honour and prestige ... deserve to be examined with extreme suspicion, and ... accepted only if they can be confirmed by more concrete reasons.' The benefits were so great that Australia should be willing to go along with Japan's wishes in this matter if this were required to ensure the ratification of the treaty.[66] Pearce was convinced. Two days later he reported to Hughes that 'Some opposition ... here to including mainland Japan in terms of Pacific Treaty' and that when asked by Balfour about Australia's attitude he had replied, 'whilst it might be held somewhat derogatory to status Australia, advantages on the other hand of making sure ratification by [United States] Senate in my judgment outweighed this.'[67]

Disarmament proved to be a more difficult problem. It was impossible to obtain any agreement for the reduction of military forces. Even on the naval question, which was the more immediate cause for the conference, negotiations had to be limited to capital ships, aircraft carriers and fortifications of naval bases in the Pacific. Unlike the Four Power Pact, which emerged out of discussions among the three major Pacific powers, the basis for the Treaty on the Limitation of Naval Armaments was solely an American initiative. On Armistice Day, Charles Evans Hughes gave his inaugural address as president of the Conference. Having decided that reductions in naval armaments must be the main American objective, he laid out a set of principles for this purpose. He called for a ten year 'Naval Holiday' on building capital ships and the reduction of existing battleships and battle-cruisers for the three major naval powers. He proposed a total tonnage of roughly 550,000 tons each for the United States and the British Empire and 315,000 tons for Japan. He also wanted to extend the 'Naval Holiday' and the reductions – in lesser ratios – to the capital ships of France and Italy and he hoped that all the powers would agree to stop building aircraft carriers and other naval vessels and make proportional reductions as well in these categories. These principles provided the basis for the treaty.

Pearce only took issue in the British Empire Delegation on two matters. On the first, which concerned imperial naval policy he sided with the Admiralty against Borden and the British ministers. After their initial study of the American plan for naval limitations the Admiralty was willing to accept the reductions in the size of their fleet but they baulked at stopping all further building of capital ships. The British battleships and the battle cruisers were as a group older than

---

[66] Piesse, 'The Quadruple Pacific Treaty, its application to Japan proper from the Australian point of view', 27 December 1921, Piesse Papers, NLA MS 882/7/2 170–72.

[67] Cable, Pearce to Hughes, 29 December 1921, NAA A981 Disarmament1 Part 2.

For copies of the Four Power Pact and the subsequent amending Agreement requested by the Japanese, see *FRUS*, 1922, Vol.I, pp.33–36 and pp.46–47.

those of United States and Japan and therefore the Empire's fleet would always be at a strategic disadvantage. In order to maintain the effective fighting ratio they needed to be able to replace their older warships continuously throughout the decade. In addition they argued that as a result of a shut down of their naval building they would lose both the industrial infrastructure and the labour skills necessary for constructing new capital ships. Since British naval vessels – as opposed to the American and Japanese – were built by private enterprise, the government would face a considerable time lag and great cost in trying to bring their fleet up to date at the end of the ten year moratorium. Lloyd George and the Committee of Imperial Defence were not persuaded, and informed the Delegation in Washington that 'the advantages of a ten year's absolute naval holiday in capital ships are so great for the cause of peace and disarmament that we are prepared to face the technical objections and inconveniences inseparable from it.'[68]

Pearce was so perturbed by the Admiralty's arguments that he cabled his Prime Minister explaining that the British Empire Delegation was divided, Canada supporting the British Government's view and he and the New Zealand representative the Admiralty. He asked for the cabinet's view and Hughes promptly replied that the cabinet agreed with Pearce in backing the Admirals' judgment.[69] At the meeting of the Delegation on 9 December, Pearce reinforced the arguments of Admiral Sir Ernle Chatfield. The 'Naval Holiday' would tip the balance of naval power in the Pacific in favour of Japan. In such a development, he and his government saw a state of affairs that they 'could only view with alarm.'[70] Despite this, the British Government once again overruled the Admirals and the replacement option was not pursued further. [71]

The other matter affected Australia more nearly. The Japanese, in return for consenting to a capital ship tonnage sixty percent less than that of the American and British, wanted a freezing of the status quo on naval bases and fortifications in the Pacific islands belonging to the three powers. The Japanese initially wanted to include Australian and New Zealand island territories in the agreement but Pearce, remembering Jellicoe's recommendation that Australia should consider building a northern island base, had protested against this. Pressed by Balfour, the Japanese relented and Australia was left free to establish a naval base and to fortify harbours in Papua.[72]

In Australia the work of the Washington conference was greeted with great enthusiasm. Pearce was given a warm welcome on his return and all the treaties when they came before parliament in the winter of 1922 were approved without a division. Hughes in commending them to the House of Representatives did issue a word of warning. He admitted that the conference had 'achieved great things' and heaped praise upon the Four Power pact which had replaced the Anglo-Japanese alliance – 'Nothing has been done at any Conference or by any Treaty, which means so much to us in Australia as that done in Washington in the Quadruple Treaty.' Yet he drew attention to the fact that, unlike the Japanese alliance, this treaty did not oblige the parties to

---

[68] Cable, Curzon to Balfour, 1 December 1921, *Documents on British Foreign Policy, 1919–1939*, Vol.I, p.527.
[69] Cable, Pearce to Hughes, 5 December 1921 and Hughes to Pearce, 9 December 1921, NAA A981, Disarmament I, Pt.2.
[70] Minutes of British Empire Delegation meeting, 9 December 1921, TNA: PRO CAB 29/28.
[71] Cable, Curzon to Balfour, 9 December 1921, *Documents on British Foreign Policy, 1919–1939*, Vol.I, p.544.
[72] Cable, Balfour to Curzon, 24 January 1921, *ibid.*, p.620; Cable, Pearce to Hughes, 25 January 1921, NAA A981, Disarmament I, Pt.2.

this arrangement to give military aid should any one of them be attacked. The agreement only offered a 'guarantee of peace in the Pacific, as far as any effort of man can guarantee it while human nature remains unregenerate.' In the meantime it was his view that Australia was 'as dependent as ever on the Navy of the Empire.'[73]

Pearce, by contrast, had no such reservations. He considered that the treaties had laid down a firm basis for a Pacific settlement. In moving for their ratification in the Senate he not only pointed out the contribution which the treaties themselves made to removing the possibility for war but also stressed the importance of the 'friendly understanding, full and complete' between the British Empire and the United States in producing this successful outcome.

He was even more impressed by the Japanese attitude at the conference.[74] He repeated what had become a commonplace of Australian rhetoric in speaking of international affairs, namely that while Australians were racially Europeans they were geographically 'Asiatics' and their 'immediate interests are more nearly concerned with what is happening in China and Japan than with what is happening in Belgium and Holland.' Moreover he acknowledged that he had gone to the conference 'as one who suspected Japan and her intentions in regard to the Pacific.' Yet as the conference had proceeded he had noticed that the Japanese delegates were determined to avoid the fate that had overtaken Germany and its 'moral isolation from the rest of the world'. The Japanese had entered fully into the spirit of the meeting and had not only agreed to the four and five power treaties but also a nine power treaty under which the parties committed themselves to respect China's territorial integrity and the right of equal access to trade and investment in that country. At the same time the Japanese had volunteered to withdraw their forces from Shantung and Siberia and had already begun to carry out these promises. Pearce had become convinced that 'Japan is peaceful.' Expanding on this novel assertion, an assertion which overturned almost two decades of dread of the Japan menace, he stated that:

> It is a great source of satisfaction for us in Australia to know that this powerful neighbour should desire to turn away from military aggression and the policy of force and to tread the path of peace ... While ... I suspected Japan I believe now that Japan is earnest and sincere, and that the course which her statesmen took at Washington, and which her Prime Minister has announced she intends to pursue, is actually the policy which she proposes to follow.[75]

---

[73] *CPD*, Vol.XCIX, 1922 session, pp.789 and 793, 26 July 1922.

For an account of the negotiations over maintaining the *status quo* in the island territories of the three Pacific powers, see Braisted, pp.609–14.

[74] Under the leadership of the Minister for the Navy, Admiral Tomosaburo Kato, the Japanese government had decided that since they could never compete with the United States in a naval building race, national security could be best achieved by supporting limitations on capital ships and naval bases. See Schencking, pp.217–222.

[75] *CPD*, Vol.XCIX, 1922 session, pp.822–23, 29 June 1922.

Pearce in May sent Hughes a secret report on the Washington conference which set out his new view of Japan. In particular he stressed that Japan, by agreeing not to build new naval bases or fortifications on its insular possessions, had given up the possibility of being able to launch an attack against Australia, and he said that 'To my mind, this action on the part of Japan is significant, as indicating that she does not harbour any designs on Australia.' See 'Report to the Prime Minister', May 1922, NAA A2219, Vol.23, 'External

In the debates over the ratifying of the treaties, while some members of parliament still voiced concerns about Japan's long-term ambitions, it was Pearce's optimism that prevailed. With the new expectations of peace in the Pacific the rationale for Australia's defence policy had lost its validity and the demand for cuts to defence expenditure could not be resisted. Even before the Washington conference had concluded, Pearce's successor as Minister for Defence, Walter Massy-Greene, was bending before the war weary mood of the public and the parliament. Writing to Pearce he confided that 'whether or not the results achieved go as far as popular opinion ... thinks ... it does connote in the popular mind a very definite advance towards disarmament which in the present temper of public opinion the Government cannot fail to recognise in some substantial way.' If the government was to survive, it 'cannot neglect the general feeling in regard to defence matters, which can be described by no other term than drastic.'[76] The government's 1922–23 defence budget estimates were accordingly reduced by £1,177,453 to £4,212,788 – that is by just more than a fifth of that of the preceding year. After allowing for inflation these defence estimates were approximately forty percent less than defence expenditure in 1913–14. All the ambitious defence schemes of 1920 were abandoned. Australia was no longer planning to make a contribution to an imperial Pacific fleet. Following the terms of the naval limitations agreement the dreadnought *Australia* was in due course scuttled off Sydney Heads and, in addition, three out of the six light cruisers, four out of the seven destroyers and all the submarines were mothballed. The military training scheme was no longer universal. Only a quarter of the eligible eighteen-year-olds were to be called up and they were to have only four days in camp and four single days training during the year. In an explanatory statement the Defence Minister cited the Washington conference as a justification for this radical policy. Its achievements were 'the fortunate consummation of the bright hopes inspired by the summoning of the Conference by President Harding' and these hopes had enabled 'the nations of the world a means of relief from the burden of armaments at a time when the financial and economic situation is most difficult and complex.'[77]

By the time that Hughes's government was forced from office in early 1923 Australia's 'cold war' against Japan in the Pacific had come to an end.

Relations'. To what degree Piesse influenced Pearce in arriving at these revolutionary views of Japan and its intentions is unknown. Likewise it is not known whether or to what degree Piesse was responsible for this report.

[76] Letter, Massy-Greene to Pearce 31 December 1921, Pearce Papers, AWM 3DRL2222.

[77] 'Department of Defence Estimates of Expenditure 1922–23. Explanatory Statement Prepared by Direction of the Minister for Defence', *CPP*, 1922 session, Vol.II, pp.1265–80.

Conclusion

Australia's world crisis 1914–23 was composed of two main elements, a 'hot war' in Europe and a 'cold war' in the Pacific. It was against this background of nation-state violence and putative threats of nation-state violence in these two distinct spheres that Australia's leaders responded to the global tensions and turmoil which marked these years. Australia's policy-makers in dealing with both 'wars' were contending with substantive and complex issues of national survival and national security.

The 'hot war' in Europe was an outcome of an era of rising mass nationalism. Australians in this era had defined themselves as a British people and saw their own welfare, both cultural and strategical, linked inextricably to that of Britain and the British Empire. Thus in August 1914, when Britain went to war to prevent Germany from dominating Europe and challenging the global supremacy of the Royal Navy, Australians were almost unanimous in agreeing to go to the aid of the Mother Country. By the end of the war almost four out of ten of all eligible men had voluntarily enlisted in the AIF, an extraordinary social phenomenon expressing the Australian identification with the Empire and the British race. But the European 'hot' war against Germany was Britain's war. Because of this it was the British Government, for the purpose of this war, that determined the Empire's military and naval strategy and its wartime diplomacy.

The 'cold war' against Japan was very different. It was peculiarly Australia's war. From its origins – that is from Japan's triumph in the Russo-Japanese war – Australia had viewed Britain's Asian ally as a potential enemy. Japan had emerged from that conflict as the dominant power in the West Pacific. Learning from its European mentors it had set out on an imperial course, seizing Taiwan, annexing Korea, acquiring spheres of influence in Manchuria and seeking to gain a supreme influence in northern China. It resented the White Australia policy and took offence at the racial discrimination suffered by its nationals. The British had little sympathy for Australia's distrust of Japan. Even if they had shared Australia's anxieties, the British, hard-pressed at home in trying to outmatch the German navy in the North Sea, were in no position to assist Australia. As a result, Australian policy-makers, their fears heightened by racial ideas of international politics, pursued their own defence and foreign policies, raising their own military forces, acquiring their own navy and seeking the cooperation of the other British Pacific Dominions and even the United States.

Japan's entry into the European war on Britain's side did not in any way assuage these concerns. It served rather to intensify Australia's 'cold war' apprehensions about Japan. During the European conflict and in the early post-war years, Australian leaders were constantly scanning the geopolitical horizons for signs of Japan's hostile intentions. Japan's limitation of its role in the war to the Pacific, its seizure of Germany's colonies in China and the North Pacific, its attempts to turn China into a client state, its outspoken pro-German press and politicians, its persistent efforts to persuade Australia to sign a non-discriminatory commercial treaty and to allow its traders to extend their commercial interests in the South Pacific, all these actions were taken as signs of Japan's intention to take full advantage of the distractions of the Western powers in order to impose its will on the region.

Throughout the war Australia's leaders in their dealings with Britain, America and Japan tried to ensure that the Japanese threat would be kept at bay. Recognising Australia's helplessness, the government put the problem of Japan at the centre of their policy-making. They obtained secret sources of intelligence about Japanese intentions and established a lectureship at the University of Sydney to train the officer cadets at Duntroon Military College in the Japanese language. Likewise the naval and military authorities continued to prepare briefing papers about the Japanese threat and to carry out as far as possible both the local naval and military pre-war plans for local defence. During the referendum campaigns over conscription for the European war, both those for and against conscription argued their cases at a strategic level around the problem of Japan. Should they put at risk their immediate safety and send all their men and materiel to Europe in the hope that this would help achieve a quick victory and so allow the triumphant Empire to make available the British fleet to deter Japan from intimidating or invading Australia? Or should they not take such a gamble and try to preserve as much of their resources as possible for home defence against the Asian foe? The debate over the issue of conscription brought out most clearly the tensions inherent in the dual commitment to a 'hot' and a 'cold' war and in the associated ideas of British loyalty and Pacific security.

In looking towards the peace, Australian policy-makers were as concerned about containing Japan as about crushing Germany. Victory in Europe offered little comfort. Japan had become a world power. It had extended its empire in East Asia and moved its southern frontier to face Australia across the equator. It was maintaining a very substantial conscript army and building a fleet composed of the most advanced warships and aircraft carriers. At the Paris Peace Conference, Prime Minister Hughes had courted Japan's ill-will by frustrating its desire to include a racial equality provision in the League Covenant and had thereby focused Japan's hostility on Australia. Britain was economically and psychologically exhausted and unable to maintain a two ocean navy, and it was unclear what assistance Britain would be able to offer in the case of a Japanese move against Australia. Hughes's hopes of uniting Greater Britain behind a common imperial policy which would give security to the Pacific Dominions were dashed at the 1921 Imperial Conference. Even so he could never abandon the notion that Australia's goal must be to unite all the British peoples behind one imperial policy which would provide equal security to all parts of the Empire. That was the only imaginable solution for its 'cold war' predicament.

The European war had placed Australian society, like those of the other belligerents, under great stress. As the war had proceeded, with the parties locked in an ever more violent and bloody embrace and with neither side able to deliver a final blow, the increasing demands for sacrifice, the ever lengthening lists of casualties, the accumulation of power in the hands of the warfare state and the restraints on the labour movement and the freedom of the press stretched social bonds almost to breaking point. Simultaneously the Sinn Fein rebellion in Ireland and the Bolshevik revolution in Russia gave a symbolic legitimacy to the most disaffected. These internal divisions had important repercussions for defence and foreign policy in both the war and its immediate aftermath. They destroyed the pre-war national consensus and spawned conflicts over ideas of loyalty which made rational debate impossible.

The great problems that faced the country at this time called for able and wise leadership. Australian leaders understood these issues through the lens of their respective world views, and fashioned their specific defence and foreign policies accordingly. As heads of government, Andrew Fisher (for the first year of the European war) and William Morris Hughes (for the remaining years of the world crisis) bore the chief responsibility for Australia's response to these problems. They were agreed about the disastrous consequences for Australia that would follow from a British defeat in Europe. The emergence of Germany as the master of Europe would have global implications. Depending on the extent of the victory it might mean a considerable expansion of German influence and authority into the Pacific. At the least it would leave Japan, perhaps in alliance with Germany, free to extend its empire into the South Pacific and possibly to impose the equivalent of its Chinese 'twenty-one' demands on Australia. Both Fisher and Hughes accepted that Japan's preponderant power in the western Pacific posed a threat. The two leaders, however, differed markedly not only about how best to meet the crisis – that is how far Australia should go in assisting the Mother Country as against pursuing its pre-war policies for the defence of Australia – but also about the nature of the peace that the Empire should strive to achieve at the end of the war.

As war approached, Fisher had given voice to the sentimental catchcry of aiding Britain 'to the last man and last shilling'; but after war was declared he had reaffirmed what had become Australia's pre-war doctrine – namely to provide first for Australia's own defence and then offer aid to Britain, and it was to this latter policy that he gave the greater weight. Thus once elected as Prime Minister he aimed to ensure that Australia's own defence plans were not abandoned and that Australia was not left vulnerable to Japan. His earlier experience of both the 'Dreadnought' affair and the failure of the 1909 Empire Pacific fleet agreement had made a deep impression on him. While willing to accept all those who volunteered to join the AIF he did not at first encourage recruitment campaigns. He gave priority to national development and insisted on maintaining compulsory military training for home defence, the building of light cruisers and naval bases, and the completion of the transcontinental strategic railway. After the Japanese moved into the German North Pacific islands he had asked the British Government to summon the promised Imperial Conference to discuss Pacific naval defence. It was his view that while Australians were fighting for the Empire in Europe or the Middle East, the British should not be allowed to ignore the needs of Australian defence in the Pacific. There should be limits conditioned by Australia's 'cold war' against Japan on the extent of the aid that Australia gave Britain.

Hughes, by contrast, had from the beginning seen the war above all as a global struggle of the British race for survival and, as a result, he was adamant that this required a total commitment to the Empire's cause. While fearful of Japan he was convinced that the only way for Australia to keep the White Australia flag flying – the racial symbol he put before the Australian public time and time again when seeking support for his policies – was to defeat Germany as quickly as possible and so restore British global supremacy. From its own resources, Australia could never hope to keep the Japanese at bay. The only effective barrier to Japanese land hunger and racial hostility was the British navy and its ability to deploy in the Pacific Ocean. Not only British race loyalty but also Australia's strategic interests dictated his single-minded approach to the war. For the period of the war, Australia had to run the risk of leaving itself vulnerable to Japan in order that the British Empire could regain its global pre-eminence – the only acceptable outcome of the war. It was these considerations which underpinned the two leaders' defence and foreign policies during Australia's world crisis. Strategically both analyses carried great risks but, given the difficult choices the Australian Prime Ministers had to face, they were both plausible bases for policy-making.

When in 1915 the Allies failed to achieve their promised quick victory and suffered serious reverses in Europe and the Middle East these difference came to the fore and were centred on the issue of conscription. Fisher, as an inheritor of the Enlightenment tradition of human progress, was a liberal romantic who held a belief in the essential goodness of all peoples, a belief tempered by a certain Scottish common sense. He had supported the war not only out of loyalty to Britain and concern for Australian security but also from a belief that Britain and the Empire were fighting against German militarist autocracy which when defeated would enable the German people to join with other civilised nations to bring into being a new cooperative era of world peace and justice. Following many British Labour and Liberal leaders who shared this tradition, Fisher met the new demands of the war by supporting increased enlistments for the AIF while at the same time resisting pressure to introduce conscription for overseas service.

The path he had chosen for himself was a difficult one. It was not that he was opposed to conscription in principle. He had himself supported compulsory military training for the defence of Australia. In promising to aid Britain 'to the last man and the last shilling' he had hoped to limit Australia's contribution to the European war and to leave to the future the question of when the last man should be sent and the last shilling raised. The emergence of a Universal Service League calling for the conscription of the whole manpower of the country for the war effort forced the issue. And it was followed by the formation of an Anti-Conscription League that feared compulsion would bring further attacks on industrial unions and the further militarisation of society. Fisher was in a quandary. Both sides appealed to the Prime Minister, and he knew that this Pandora's box once opened would be impossible to close and would leave the Labor Party and the community irrevocably divided. It was impractical to think that Australia could adopt conscription before Britain itself had done so and his political acumen told him that to opt for conscription or to rule it out altogether would cause a domestic schism which would be disastrous for Australia and the Empire. All his instincts were against conscription and so he fudged the issue and let it be known that he would not agree to consider the question unless it was first put to the people. This was not cowardice but the only way he could keep, at least for the time being, the party and the country together.

Hughes brought a very different vision of the world and leadership to the office of Prime Minister. Hughes was drawn to the romance of nationalism. In his philosophy it was through belonging to the 'British race' that Australians were made psychologically, culturally and morally whole. While humanity remained unregenerate one did not expect human progress. The international arena had always been a jungle in which nations and races were driven to compete with one another for supremacy. In the European war the Germans had thrown down the gauntlet to the British peoples. In this collision the Empire had no choice but to subordinate everything to achieving total victory. The enemy had to be crushed so that it could never rise again, and this enemy was not only the German militarists but the whole German people. He prided himself on his clear-eyed 'realism' and ridiculed those who took a more optimistic view of international cooperation as 'babblers of peace and the brotherhood of man'. Hughes had such self-confidence in his understanding of international politics and what needed to be done to save Australia and the Empire, that he had no tolerance for those who dared to dissent. For him there could not be, at least on war issues, a loyal opposition. There was not a reflective bone in his body. He was rarely troubled by doubt but when the world did not bend before his imperious will, he often had to accept disappointment.

For all the great problems of defence and foreign policy facing Australia in the world there were simple and absolute answers. On becoming Prime Minister he had declared that his administration would be devoted solely to the winning of the war, since on its outcome depended the ultimate safety of Australia and the Empire. After Britain in 1916 had introduced military conscription, he demanded of his party and people that they follow suit, and was confident that through achieving a great majority in a referendum on the subject he would silence his opponents. He flatly rejected those who would appease Germany and called for a liberal peace of 'no annexation and no indemnity'. Defiantly taking up this slogan, he turned it on its head and demanded a peace of 'annexation and indemnity'. In the spirit of Cato the Elder's call for the destruction of Carthage at the end of the second Punic War, Hughes believed *Germania delenda est*. The German Empire had to be reduced to its national borders, to be stripped of all its colonies, deprived of its High Fleet, allowed but a token army, denied access to the economic resources of the Allies, compelled to pay the full cost of the war and to be treated as a pariah nation.

At the Paris Peace Conference Hughes fought for Australia's unfettered control over the German islands it had seized in the South Pacific, and had even raised the issue of Japan's control of the North Pacific islands. Likewise he was adamant that the Japanese should not be allowed to include in the League Covenant any words which might in any possible way imply racial equality and therefore endanger White Australia. Having made himself Japan's enemy at the Paris Peace Conference, Hughes became alarmed about that country's intentions. The world crisis had moved more decisively to the Pacific. On returning home he even imagined that a Japanese invasion fleet was headed south and would, as it had done in attacking Russia in 1904, strike without warning. In the post-war years, under his leadership, the national security community planned a substantial defence program to meet the expected onslaught, and at the 1921 Imperial conference Hughes hoped, as it turned out unsuccessfully, to persuade Britain and the other Dominions to join Australia in creating a Pacific fleet and to keep the Anglo-Japanese Alliance as a restraint, even if only a limited one, on Japan's expansionist ambitions. After the Washington conference had succeeded in bringing the Pacific powers, including Japan, to agree to limits on their navies and naval building and to respect the Pacific islands and China's territorial integrity, Hughes, even as he praised these treaties, could scarcely bring himself to believe that they had solved Australia's Pacific problem and remained sceptical. While human nature was unregenerate he assured his fellow Australians that the world was still the dangerous place that it had always been and as a result they would still have to depend ultimately on the British navy.

From the beginning to the end of his term as Prime Minister Hughes's uncompromising realist approach to both the 'hot' and 'cold' wars was often counter-productive and self-defeating, and it was not that he lacked voices from many quarters warning him about the adverse consequences which would follow from his polices.

He denounced his opponents in the conscription referenda as either pro-German traitors in the pay of Berlin; Sinn Fein republicans bent on the break-up of the British Empire; or IWW anarchists intent on destroying civilisation. By so doing, he divided society into the 'loyal' and the 'disloyal' and thereby put the bonds of civil society under great stress. As a result, after the defeat of the referendum many 'loyalists' considered the voluntary system dishonourable, and many of those defamed as 'disloyalists' saw it as collaboration with their traducers. Both sides increasingly refused to take part in recruiting campaigns and so the numbers of volunteers coming forward shrank. Hughes's attempt to bully Australians into accepting conscription in order to increase Australia's military contribution to winning the war ended in producing the opposite of what was intended. The Treasurer in Hughes's first cabinet, W. G. Higgs, amongst others, warned the Prime Minister that if he took up the cause of conscription he would break up the Labor Party and cause dissension in society.

Hughes's attempt to demand from Germany the full cost of the war, while not in the end successful, did set the terms of the debate over reparations at the Paris Peace Conference. Both Lloyd George and J. M. Keynes pointed out the unreality of Hughes's draconian claim. They recognised the impossibility of Germany being able to pay the Allied war costs and the dire consequences for the European and world economies if Germany was burdened with such a debt. They showed that Germany's gold holdings and other transferable assets could not meet the sum demanded and argued that if it was stripped of its industrial machinery it would be deprived of the very means it would need to produce the goods necessary for paying off the debt. Moreover if the Germans were to pay through earning money by exporting abroad, this would affect the Allies' own industries adversely and widespread unemployment would be unavoidable. But Hughes would not listen and answered that if it were shown that they could not pay then the matter could be renegotiated. He insisted that in the Peace Treaty, Germany's guilt should be expressed economically as well as morally. It did not cross his mind that the German people would associate their new Weimar democratic republic with Allied vindictiveness and national humiliation and therefore give this experiment with Western ideas of civil liberty and parliamentary government an unhappy beginning and weak roots.

At the Paris Peace Conference, Hughes persisted in demanding the right to annex the German South Pacific islands. In replying to President Wilson's wish to place all the former German colonies under League of Nations' mandates he argued in the presence of the Japanese delegates that these islands were Australia's ramparts guaranteeing its protection against future enemies. A member of the Australian delegation, Frederic Eggleston, had recognised that the most effective way of using the islands as a barrier against Japan would be to place them under League Mandates because Japan would then have to place the North Pacific islands it held similarly under Mandates. Japan would then be prevented from building naval bases and thus from bringing Japanese naval power that much closer to Australia's own frontiers. Australia had no desire to build naval bases in the South Pacific islands and so such a settlement was clearly the most desirable in order to protect Australian national security. Though he had ignored his advisers Hughes, indeed, when forced to accept a mandate, did himself after the event justify his action in these terms. The Americans had from the beginning understood this reason for imposing mandates on the South Pacific territories. They were anxious to ensure that Australia did not provide Japan with an excuse not to accept a mandate. Not trusting Japan, it was important to the Americans as it was to the Australians that Japan should not be able to fortify the North Pacific islands.

At the conference, Hughes also blocked Japanese attempts to include a statement of racial equality or anything approximating it in the League Covenant. He even rejected it when the Japanese agreed to reduce and simplify what they sought, namely 'the principle of equality between nations and just treatment of their nationals', omitting all reference to 'race', and to include it as merely one more objective in the Preamble to the Covenant. Smuts of South Africa and Borden of Canada along with the other members of the British Empire Delegation were willing to accept this revised Japanese proposal. Only Massey of New Zealand, fearing a political backlash at home, stood with Hughes. Hughes made it clear that if the British supported this Japanese formula at the League of Nations Commission he would make a public row over the matter and refuse to sign the Peace Treaty. Likewise he threatened the Americans that he would rouse the West Coast states against the administration if President Wilson, the chairman of the commission, allowed it to pass. Hughes's blackmail was successful and though a majority of the states represented on the commission voted for the motion, the British opposed it and Wilson declared it lost.

Hughes had been fighting a phantom created out of his own psychological insecurity and racial imagining. The wording of the Japanese proposal was very vague and said nothing about racial equality or the right to equal treatment of peoples of different races. Moreover as part of the preamble it did not bind League members. Even if the Japanese had been able to persuade a majority of the members of the League that the proposed preamble's wording meant that members should not discriminate in their immigration policies on the basis of race, it would be impossible to believe that the British and American Governments would have allowed this interpretation to be enforced. Smuts's South Africa was based even more thoroughly on racial discrimination than Hughes's Australia. Borden had a problem with racial discrimination in British Columbia. Neither of these Dominion leaders, however, could take seriously the hysterical scenarios which Hughes contemplated. Hughes's was a hollow victory. This blow to the Japanese attempt to secure a formal recognition of their equality with the Western nations stirred up nationalist feelings. Those imperialist and militarist forces which had lost influence at the end of the war had a revival and became a focus for popular feeling. In the Japanese press the responsibility for this rebuff was sheeted home first and foremost to Hughes. Australia was seen as the major obstacle blocking Japan's aspiration to acquire equal respect in the West. Australia's two leading Japanese experts –James Murdoch (who had just returned from an intelligence gathering visit to Japan), and E. L. Piesse (who had been reading the Japanese newspapers and other material on Japan) – understood fully the stupidity of Hughes's language and behaviour. They warned Watt, the Acting Prime Minister, of the adverse consequences for Australian interests and, convinced by their arguments, he had urged Hughes to take a more measured and moderate stand in dealing with the Japanese. Hughes paid no heed to this advice and went his own way.

At the 1921 Imperial Conference, Hughes's most important general aim was to establish the basis for a united imperial defence and foreign policy, and this, even if somewhat impracticable, was not an unreasonable objective. The strain of the war had weakened Britain's material and military resources and with this, its ability to provide for the security of the Empire in the Pacific. By following the precedent set by the Imperial War Cabinet Hughes's plan was that all the self-governing Dominions would take part in the making of the Empire's policy and thus assume a joint responsibility for the consequences of those collective decisions, including the decisions to go to war. Yet in dealing with the two most immediate issues facing the Empire, namely the renewal of the Japanese alliance and imperial naval defence in the Pacific, Hughes's intransigence only served to harden differences between the Dominions. In arguing for the renewal of the alliance he made it appear that Australia's very survival depended upon it.

One might make allowances for hyperbole in parliamentary speeches, such as Hughes's address to the House of Representatives when he described the Anglo-Japanese alliance as 'more precious than rubies'; but to give the alliance such a high value when confronted by Canadian opposition at the Imperial Conference only served, quite unnecessarily, to undermine any sense of collegial cooperation which was fundamental to achieving his aim of a united imperial foreign policy. As he knew himself he desired renewal, not because Australia shared common interests with Japan, but rather hopefully to enable the Empire to exercise some restraint over Japanese policy in the Western Pacific. He wanted to use the Japanese alliance against the Japanese, and while it was clearly better from Australia's point of view to keep the alliance rather than abolish it, its relative value as a protection against Japan was quite small. When naval defence was discussed he took an equally absolute position, asserting that a right to discuss imperial foreign policy carried with it the responsibility to contribute to the common defence, especially the British navy. On both topics he made no allowances for the different cultural politics and geopolitical circumstances of his Canadian and South African colleagues. He would not, in the face of their difficulties, consider attempting to find some agreed, even if limited, means of assisting with the common defence. Since the Dominions would not offer to pay proportionate contributions, he washed his hands of the whole idea. His handling of these issues did nothing to advance his wider goal. But failure did not in any way cause him to waver from his ambition to create a Greater Britain and to achieve a common imperial policy which would give effect to it. And in continuing, against all experience to urge this, he was expressing not only a vague hope that such a policy would somehow give security to Australia in the Pacific but also that it would fulfil the Australians' sense of their British identity.

This Australian commitment to a British world was so deeply felt across the community that after the trauma of the conscription controversy some 'loyalists' gave irrational, even bizarre, interpretations of the idea. Walter Marks, the National Party member for Wentworth, in entering the debate on defence just before the opening of the Washington conference, announced to the House that the Bible had shown that Armageddon – which would be accompanied by Christ's second coming and the beginning of the millennium for the Kingdom of Christ on earth – was to take place in 1934 in Palestine and that the British peoples had been divinely chosen to lead the forces of righteousness to bring this about. The Bible had revealed that:

> The British nation from the start ... – I hardly know how to express it – ... has been ordained by the Almighty to take this part [that is to take the main role in the great battle on behalf of the legions of the righteous] on Christ's final return to earth; nothing can ever undermine the British Empire to our utter destruction because it is marked out, and our name is marked on His final coming to play a great part. Without us He cannot return in 1934. We play a great part in these "latter days", "the time of the end."

There was no reason to fear a Japanese invasion since, 'as far as we can ascertain' the Japanese 'will, at the millennium, go into Palestine with Christ'. All the signs for the imminent coming of this final battle and Christ's return to earth were now appearing, and

> the main one is this, which is rather remarkable – is that the Turkish Empire must disappear before 1922. There is one year to go; and what is the position today? The Turks – the oppressors of the Christians – have nearly disappeared.[1]

Ensuing events, however, could not have been more unkind to Marks and his prophesies about the Turks and the British. The Turks did not disappear. Within a year they were challenging the British Empire at the Dardanelles. As peace was spreading across the Pacific, tensions were rising in the Middle East. Led by Mustafa Kemal, the hero of the resistance to the Allied invasion of Gallipoli, a Turkish national movement had sprung up in defiance of the victor's terms that the Allies had imposed on the Ottoman Empire. The Treaty of Sèvres had not only divested the Sultan of his Arab lands but also reduced Turkey itself to a rump centred on Ankara. Constantinople and the Straits were to be internationalised. The Greeks were given the Aegean islands, Smyrna, its hinterland, and the Gallipoli peninsula. The Allies were to supervise the Empire's army and finances and to have spheres of influence in Turkey itself. The Allies had established themselves in Constantinople but were unwilling to enforce their harsh peace and left it to the Greek army to put down the insurgency. By early September 1922, in contrast to what the peace terms had laid down, the Turks had occupied Smyrna, pushed the Greeks into the sea and advanced against a small detachment of British forces at Chanak, a small town on the Asian side of the Dardanelles. The peace settlement was in tatters. The British Government while willing to renegotiate the Sèvres treaty wanted to do it from a position of strength so at the least to preserve the internationalisation of the Straits, and they called on their European allies, great and small, to send forces to hold Chanak and Constantinople. In their panic they also decided to appeal to the Dominions to associate themselves with these preparations and to agree to furnish military aid.[2]

---

[1] *CPD*, 1921–22 session. XCVII, pp.12406–09, 3 November 1921.

Marks, who had been educated at Sydney Grammar School and was a partner in a Sydney law firm, had been influenced to adopt these ideas by Charles P. Wauchope, a Christodelphian, who had published two works on these eschatological themes, *The Troubled Nations* (Adelaide: G. Hassell and Son, 1916) and *Four Lectures on Armageddon* (Adelaide: Commercial Printing House, 1921). A month later Marks was appointed Parliamentary Under-Secretary for External Affairs and he held this post until the fall of the Hughes government in February 1923.

[2] Cable, Churchill to Forster, 16 September 1922, NAA CP78/32.

Once the British announced through the press that they were making these approaches to the Dominions, Hughes, having given hostages to British loyalty, had no choice but to respond positively. To uphold Britain's prestige in its confrontation with the Turks he issued a public statement that Australia would back the British Government 'in whatever action it … deemed necessary to insure the freedom of the Straits and the sanctity of the Gallipoli peninsula', and 'would be prepared, if circumstances required, to send a contingent of Australian troops'. Matthew Charlton, who had succeeded Tudor as leader of the opposition, dissented and gave what was now the orthodox position of the Labor Party on defence and foreign policy. It was his view that no troops should be committed before the people had been consulted. He had supported the sending of the AIF to assist Britain in the Great War but he thought the League of Nations should find a peaceful settlement to this problem; 'Australian should not be dragged into troubles affecting other countries.'[3] Labor just did not want to know about these happenings in distant foreign parts. They played into the hands of their opponents. The Labor leaders wished to be able to ignore these problems of the outside world which had the potential for causing domestic difficulties both inside the party and in the electorate.

Armageddon did not come. After lengthy negotiations a new Peace Treaty was signed at Lausanne in July 1923 which gave the Turks control over their homeland in Asia and Europe. Hughes therefore did not have to worry about raising troops for another overseas adventure. His central concern arising out of the incident was the implication of Britain's actions for a united imperial foreign policy. He was aghast at how the whole matter had been handled and two days after his public declaration of support sent a furious, almost 2000-word cable to Lloyd George to give vent to his anger at Britain's unilateral action. The request for Australia's aid had come 'as a bolt from the blue'. He had been neither informed about the events leading up to the British ultimatum nor consulted about the decision which clearly carried with it the risk of war with the Turks.

In his reply to Lloyd George, Hughes protested about the British conduct of the whole matter. By issuing a press release before the cable had reached Melbourne, the British had forced Australia's hand; 'A Dominion ought not to be stampeded into action by premature press statements.' More generally he complained about the British ignoring all the processes of consultation which had been intended to give substance to the idea of a united imperial foreign policy. This was the point that he emphasised 'most strongly':

> The Dominions ought to be consulted before any action is taken or irrevocable decision made by Britain, then and then only can our voices be heard and our counsels heeded. The Empire is one and indivisible or it is nothing. If the Empire is only another name for Britain and the Dominions are to be told that things are done after they have been done, that Britain has decided upon war, and asking whether they wish to be associated with her and to stand by her side, when in fact they have no other alternative, then the relations between the Dominions and Britain being what they are it is perfectly clear that all talk about the Dominions having a real share in deciding foreign and imperial policy is empty air.

---

[3] *SMH*, 18 September 1922; *Statement Made By Prime Minister re Turkish Situation*, NAA CP78/32.

If the British Government were to continue to follow the course which had marked the Chanak affair he warned that 'such action would gravely imperil the unity of the Empire.'[4] When at the end of October he was informed that the Dominions were not to be represented at the Lausanne Conference, and that the British Empire was to be represented by Lord Curzon and the British High Commissioner at Constantinople he repeated his criticism of the British.[5] In this further arbitrary decision, Hughes saw confirmation of his earlier view that, much as he disliked admitting it, the British Government seemed indifferent to the whole idea of a united imperial foreign policy and was intending 'to go on the same bad old way.'

In his reply he pointed out that Australia's loyalty had not received any recognition. Though not consulted about the events leading to the crisis it had been willing 'to stand by Britain – to be represented if need be not by a mere contingent of troops but by a great army'. And yet it was not to be invited to the conference that was to settle the issues which had fuelled this dangerous confrontation. That the Dominions would be left free to sign any treaty emerging from the conference was for Hughes no consolation. He admitted that this solution might be satisfactory for Canada and South Africa but they held a very different idea of the Empire from Australia. They did not accept that when Britain was at war they were committed to giving aid to the Mother Country, and this had been seen when they failed to offer troops for Chanak. Australia, unlike these two Dominions, accepted that if the British assumed responsibilities under a revised treaty then it was automatically caught up in any consequences that might follow. If, however, the British continued to take advantage of Australian loyalty it would have disastrous effects on the unity of the Empire. The British 'habit of asking Australia to agree to things when they are done and cannot be undone, and when in practice there is only one course open to us – and that is to support Britain – is one which if persisted in, will wreck the Empire. You have already seen Canada and South Africa standing aloof on the plea that they had not been consulted.' He then once more, in a kind of plaintively hectoring tone, offered his solution to the problem of Greater Britain: 'What is wanted, I have said many times in the Imperial Cabinet, and what we are entitled to, is a real share in moulding Foreign and imperial policy. The Empire must speak with one voice in foreign affairs.'[6]

Setting out Australia's view of its role in the world Hughes never wavered in public from this mantra. In opening the National Party's election campaign in late October 1922, he set out the full doctrine of his Greater Britain.

---

[4] Copy of cable, Forster to Churchill, 20 September 1922, NAA CP78/32.
At a later point in the revising of the draft copy of this cable it would appear that Hughes agreed to insert the latter phrase in place of a more comprehensive statement accusing the British, despite constant promises to the contrary, of behaving towards the Dominions in just the same way that they had prior to the outbreak of the Great War. The initial draft had stated that 'despite all the declarations by British Ministers in the Imperial Conference in the British parliament on the platform and in the press this latest act of the British Cabinet is exactly on all fours with the position in 1914 but divested of all the circumstances that led up to the Great War which could not have been foreseen but made it inevitable.'
[5] Cables, Lord Devonshire, Colonial Secretary, to Forster, 27 and 28 October 1922, NAA CP78/32.
[6] Cable, Forster to Devonshire, 2 November 1922, NAA CP78/32.

> The National Party stands for the maintenance of the Empire: that is the rock on which the house is built, the cross to which it clings. We believe our very existence as a free Commonwealth depends upon the unity and greatness of the Empire. As the power of the Empire lies in its unity, it is obvious that in its relations with foreign countries it must have one policy and speak with one voice. In determining the foreign policy of the Empire, the Commonwealth claims, and has been freely conceded, the right to sit around the council table, and to be consulted in moulding that policy.

While proudly recalling Australia's offer to support the Mother Country in the Chanak crisis he excused the British Government's failure to consult in its own terms; namely that 'the situation, which could not have been foreseen, demanded instant action', and so preserved the appearance of imperial unity and harmony.[7]

Why, it must be asked, given the long and sorry history of this idea, did Hughes persist in pursuing this mirage of imperial unity, of one imperial defence and foreign policy being fashioned out of the joint consultations of Britain with the Dominions? And why was he so passionate and tenacious in pursuing this ideal?

His experience with these new forms of imperial cooperation from the Imperial War Cabinet through the British Empire Delegation at the Paris Peace Conference to the 1921 Imperial Conference and Chanak had not been a happy one. He had become aware of the ethno-cultural and geopolitical differences between Australia and the New Zealand on the one hand, and South Africa and Canada on the other, and how 'the different origin and circumstances' of the latter Dominions caused them to resist the adoption of a united imperial policy. He had attributed the failure of the 1921 Imperial Conference to produce a common imperial policy to just these differences. But Hughes was disappointed not only with South Africa and Canada. Britain itself on a number of issues where Australian interests were at stake had acted unilaterally, such as the armistice at the end of the European war, the proposal for giving national autonomy to Egypt and most recently the Chanak crisis. The British had their own idea of Empire which did not in many respects sit harmoniously with Hughes's. Their Empire was not simply white and British but rather a 'blended' one made up of peoples of many races and cultures. The Dominions, being self-governing, had a special place in the hierarchical structure but Britain saw itself as the centre of the Empire, held the ultimate power and authority and conducted foreign relations through its diplomatic machinery.

A further problem for Hughes's united imperial foreign policy was that his scheme had no means, apart from ordinary diplomacy, for resolving differences either between Britain and the Dominions or between the Dominions themselves. Australia had its own view of the world, most particularly of the Pacific, and had its own distinctive defence and foreign policy interests. On a number of occasions Hughes, in pursuing these interests, had clashed with Britain and the other Dominions and stretched the idea of Dominion autonomy to its limits and beyond. After Lloyd George's failure to consult him about the armistice, Hughes had expressed his disillusionment with the Imperial War Cabinet by joining Borden in demanding separate Dominion representation at the Paris Peace Conference and separate Dominion membership of the League

---

[7] *SMH*, 25 October 1922.

of Nations. At the Peace Conference he had found himself at loggerheads with Lloyd George over the question of mandates for the South Pacific islands and was willing to act independently of the British Empire Delegation, should he not get his own way. On the Japanese proposal to include recognition of the principle of racial equality in the League Covenant he, out of all the members of the British Empire Delegation, stood alone in opposing it, and was only able to keep the appearance of imperial unity by blackmailing Britain and the other Dominions into accepting his view. At the 1921 Imperial Conference he confronted the Canadian Prime Minister over the renewal of the Anglo-Japanese alliance and imperial naval defence, refused any compromise and so contributed to the failure of the conference to achieve a united imperial policy.

Why, in the face of all this harsh experience, would Hughes not follow the South Africans and the Canadians and be content with Imperial Conferences which merely discussed common interests and problems? Why could he not, like the leaders of these other Dominions, accept that Australia should accept the status of a small, intimate ally of a great power, even if a great power with which Australia shared a common history and heritage?

The answer was threefold. Firstly, Australians could only realise their national mythology of Britishness if they were able to unite with all their fellow Britons across the globe and so face the world as one. Secondly, Australians saw in the consolidated strength of Britain and the Empire the most potentially reliable source of protection against an alien Asia. Thirdly, Hughes and his National Party had partisan reasons for supporting a united imperial policy. Hughes and his supporters needed to show that their loyalty to Britain in the war had been justified. By showing that Britain had invited Australia to participate in the making of the Empire's defence and foreign policy and thereby assured Australia of protection they could vindicate themselves and deny ammunition to those they had dubbed the disloyal.

Australia's world crisis had been marked by uncertainty and tension, anxiety and discord. In its short history modern Australia had never had to face up to such a threat to its survival. Until the very last months of the war in Europe the fate of the British Empire and its Allies hung in the balance. With Japan taking advantage of the war to extend its power in East Asia and the West Pacific, Australians' pre-war fears about its ambitions gained a new intensity and they could not but worry about how far Japan could be relied upon to keep its alliance commitments. These considerations were central to the nation's war and post-war policy. They contributed to the domestic conflict over conscription, induced the establishment of professional intelligence gathering about Japan and the Pacific, informed post-war defence schemes, led to overtures to the Americans and determined the nation's concerns at the peacemaking. At the Paris Peace Conference the Australian Prime Minister was intent on destroying Germany as a great power, restoring the British Empire's global supremacy, acquiring an island barrier against Japan and defending White Australia. Convinced that the Pacific was the new centre for world politics and most likely arena for a new war, the Australian government, seeing Asia through racial spectacles, continued to be apprehensive about Japan and to plan for a very substantial defence force to meet this supposed threat. It looked to British imperial defence cooperation in the Pacific and the renewal of the Anglo-Japanese alliance to solve this problem. But in the end, peace and security came about under the auspices of the United States, whose Washington conference brought a halt to the competition for naval building and a promise from all the major Pacific powers to respect each other's existing island territories in the region.

This marked the end of an era. The major war leaders, who had had responsibility for guiding their countries through the world crisis, were, like the world crisis itself, disappearing from the stage. President Wilson had left the White House in March 1921, a broken and bitter man. In the wake of the Chanak disaster, Lloyd George's Conservative colleagues, in October 1922, withdrew their support for the wartime coalition and he was forced from office. Following hard on his heels, Hughes, after losing what was already an unstable majority in a general election, was forced by the Country Party and his enemies in the National Party to resign in February of the next year. S. M. Bruce, who had served as a captain in the British army in the war, on succeeding Hughes as Prime Minister accepted the general conclusion that the Washington Conference had caused the spectre of Japan to recede into the background and thus reduced the need for large defence expenditure. Australia would rely for its defence on the British navy – whatever that might mean – and perhaps contribute to the building of the Singapore base. Bruce persisted in pursuing Hughes's culturally derived chimera of a united imperial defence and foreign policy. But from every direction this vision was being challenged. In 1924 a British Labour Government unilaterally decided to cease work on the Singapore base, and at the 1923 and 1926 Imperial Conferences the Canadian, South African and Irish Free State pressures for formal statements of complete Dominion independence made Bruce fear for the survival of the British Empire as 'one great nation'.[8]

One particular legacy from this era had very harmful consequences for Australia's ability to meet another and greater world crisis which appeared on the international scene in the 1930s. The social and political divisions created by the fight over conscription had domesticated the issue of Empire loyalty and with it the issues of defence and foreign policy. This legacy made it very difficult for either side to treat these issues on their own terms. They had become a function of internal politics. On the one hand, the conscriptionists, who had organised themselves behind the National Party had enlisted British loyalty on their side of politics and thus they needed to show, regardless of the facts of the matter, that Britain had earned Australians' loyalty by giving Australia a say in imperial policy-making and credible assurances of naval protection. On the other hand, the anti-conscriptionists who had rallied to the reformed Labor Party had been made suspicious of the conservatives' close ties to the British Governments and so demanded that Australia should not go to war until the question had been put to the people. Their antagonism to the Nationals also caused them to oppose military conscription not only for overseas wars but also for the defence of Australia itself.

And so Hughes and his successors, unlike Deakin, Cook and Millen and other conservatives in the pre-war period, could not afford to be openly critical of Britain or British policies or throw doubt on the viability of the Singapore base or on British promises to send a fleet to defend Australia. Likewise the new Labor leaders, in contrast to Fisher and Pearce in the earlier era, could not allow that there might be advantages for Australian security in imperial cooperation and compulsory military training for the defence of Australia. Thus in the 1930s as war clouds spread

---

[8] *CPD*, 1926 session, CXIV, 4772, 3 August 1926.

across Europe and the Pacific and Australia had to face up to the strong possibility that the Empire might have to face a war on two fronts and in circumstances which were even more dangerous than those that existed at the outbreak of World War I, the nation and its leaders still held fast to these partisan slogans and prejudices. This failure of leadership in the earlier crisis contributed greatly to Australia's inability to prepare properly for this greater global conflagration.

As an afterword it might well be pointed out that when World War II did arrive this irrationality quickly evaporated. When the two sides of politics faced up to this new world crisis they found that they had much in common. In April 1939 R. G. Menzies, one of the more militant supporters of conscription and loyalty in World War I, as his first act as prime minister broke with the diplomatic unity of the Empire. He recognised that Australia would have to take 'the responsibilities and risks' in the Pacific and announced his intention to appoint Australia's own representatives to Washington, Tokyo and Chungking. Similarly after the outbreak of the war he refused to heed British pleas to send an Australian military contingent to Europe until he was convinced that Japan would not immediately join the Axis powers and be drawn into the conflict.[9] John Curtin, who had been a leading figure in the anti-conscription movement in World War I, when he became Prime Minister supported conscription not only for home defence but also for the 'Southwest Pacific Area'. After the Japanese attack on Pearl Harbour he declared in a radio broadcast that 'we Australians ... shall keep this territory and keep it as a citadel for the British-speaking race.'[10] Looking to the peace he revived Fisher's and Hughes's vision of empire and shortly before setting out for the 1944 British Commonwealth Prime Ministers' meeting told the ALP conference that the British peoples were on the cusp of a 'Fourth Empire' in which 'the trend' was 'to augment an association of independent sovereign peoples by a common policy that concerns the Empire as a whole' and that it was his intention to urge this reform upon his fellow Prime Ministers at the coming meeting in London.[11]

---

[9] *SMH*, 27 April 1939; cable, Menzies to S.M. Bruce, Australian High Commissioner to London, 11 September 1939, R.G. Neale (ed.), *Documents on Australian Foreign Policy, 1937–1949* (Canberra: Australian Government Publishing Services, 1976), II, '1939', 232.

[10] *SMH*, 9 December 1941; *CPD*, Vol.173, pp.264–65, 3 February 1943;

[11] Cited in James Curran, '"An Organic Part of the Whole Structure": John Curtin's Empire', *Journal of Imperial and Commonwealth History*, 37 (March 2009) 51–75.

Bibliography

Primary Sources

Official Records (unpublished)

Australia
National Australian Archives (Canberra)

A1	A981 Japan 38 Pt 2
A63/48	A981 Japan 53
A1108	A981 Japan 55
A1606/1	A981 Japan 96
A1632	A981 Japan 101 Pt 1
A2032	A981 Japan 181
A2219	A981 MARS2 Pt 3
A2939	A981 Soviet Union 42 Pt 1
A2585	A981/4 DEF Pts 1 and 2
A3688	A11803
A3932	A11804
A3934	CP78/22
A4311	CP78/23
A9787	CP78/32
A9791	CP103/3
A981 Control of New Hebrides 24	CP290/15
A981 Defence 350 Pt 1	CP351/1
A981 Disarmament I Pts 1 and 2.	CP360/8
A981 FAR9	CP360/9
A981 IMP104	CP447/1
A981 IMP106	CP447/2
A981 Japan 28	CP717
A981 Japan 36	M3580 (Sir Joseph Cook Papers)
A981 Japan 38 Pt 1 General	

National Australian Archives (Melbourne)

B197	MP 729/2	MP 1587/1–5
B543	MP 729/5	
MP 133/2	MP 729/6	
MP 367/1	MP 826/1	
MP 493/3	MP 1049/1	
MP 729/1	MP 1185/5–6	

Canada
Library and Archives Canada
Sir Robert Borden fonds

United Kingdom
The National Archives of the United Kingdom: Public Record Office (TNA)

ADM 116	CAB 32/2
ADM 137	CAB 32/3
CAB 21/187	CAB 32/4
CAB 23/1	CAB 32/6
CAB 23/8	CAB 38
CAB 23/9	CAB 41/37/26
CAB 23/12	CO 209
CAB 23/14	CO 418
CAB 23/17	CO 532
CAB 23/40	CO 616
CAB 23/42	FO 371
CAB 23/43	WO 32
CAB 23/44A	WO 158
CAB 27/43	WO 163
CAB 27/91	Balfour, A. J. Papers FO 800/199–217
CAB 28/26	Geddes, Sir Eric Papers ADM116/1809
CAB 29/9	Grey, Sir Edward Papers FO 800/35–113
CAB 29/28	Lord Reading Papers FO 800/222–226
CAB 29/100	

National Archives of Scotland (NAS)
Kerr, Philip; Lord Lothian GD 40

United States of America
National Archives and Records Administration (NARA)
RG 59

Official papers (published)

Commonwealth of Australia
Parliamentary Debates, 1914–23
Parliamentary Papers
——, 1914–17 session, X, Vol. V, 'Naval and Military Assistance afforded to H.M.' Government by H.M.'s Overseas Dominions-Correspondence Regarding the'.

——, 1917–18–19 session, CLXXVII, Vol. IV, 'Report of Admiral of the Fleet Viscount Jellicoe of Scapa on Naval Mission to the Commonwealth of Australia (May-August 1919)', Vols.I-IV.
——, 1917–18–19 session, Vol. IV, 'Report of Proceedings of the Conference Convened by His Excellency the Governor-General at Federal Government House, Melbourne, April, 1918.'
——, 1922 session, Vol II, 'Department of Defence Estimates of Expenditure, 1922–23. Explanatory Statement by Direction of the Minister.'

Canada
Department of External Affairs (Canada), *Documents on Canadian External Relations* (Ottawa: Queen's Printer, 1967).

Japan
Nippon Gaiko Bunsho (Ministry of Foreign Affairs, 1967).

United Kingdom
British Documents on Foreign Affairs, general editors, Kenneth Bourne and D. Cameron Watt, Part II, Series 1, 'From the First to the Second World Wars', edited by M. Dockrill, 'The Paris Peace Conference', Vols 1–15 (University Publications of America, 1989–91).
Cd. 7979, Correspondence respecting Military Operations against German Possessions in the Western Pacific, November 1914.'
Parliamentary Debates (Commons).

United States of America
Link, Arthur S. (editor and translator). The Deliberations of the Council of Four (March 24–June 28 1919), Notes of the Official Interpreter, Paul-Joseph Mantoux (Princeton: Princeton University Press, 1992).
Foreign Relations of the United States, Papers Relating to.

Personal papers (unpublished)

Australia
Australian War Memorial
    Birdwood, Field Marshal William Riddell. MS 92/3DRL.
    Pearce, G. F. 3DRL.
Mitchell Library
    Holmes, General William and Colonel R. J. Travers. MSS 15
National Library of Australia
    Brookes, Herbert. MS 1924.
    Cook, James Newton Haxton Hume (Hume-Cook). MS 601.
    Cook, Joseph. MS 762 and 2212.
    Eggleston, Frederic. MS 423.
    Ferguson, Ronald Craufurd Munro (Novar). MS 696.
    Fisher, Andrew. MS 2919.

Garran, R. R. MS 2001.
Groom, Littleton MS 236.
Hughes, W. M. Ms 1538.
Hunt, Arthur Atlee. MS 52.
Latham, John T. MS 1009.
Murdoch, Keith Arthur. MS 2823.
Pearce, G. F. MS 213.
Piesse, E. L. MS 882.
White, C. B. B. MS 5172.

University of Melbourne Archives
Barrett, James
Deane, Percival

United Kingdom

Bodleian Library, Oxford
Asquith, Herbert Henry. MSS. Asquith 1–152.
Harcourt, Lewis. MSS. Harcourt 1–751.
Milner, Lord. MSS. Milner C699–703.
Round Table Papers. MSS. Eng. hist. C797–98.

British Library
Balfour, Arthur James. Add 49751.
Hutton, Edward Thomas Henry. Add 50085–89.
Jellicoe, Lord. Add 49045.
Murray, Archibald James. Add 52461.
Northcliffe, Lord. Add 62153–397.

Churchill College, Cambridge
Churchill, Winston S.
Hankey, Maurice

House of Lords Record Office
Davidson, John Colin Campbell
Law, A. Bonar
Lloyd George, David

Imperial War Museum
Birdwood, William Riddell

Liddell Hart Centre for Military Archives
Lt.-General Sir Launcelot Kiggell
Field-Marshall Sir William Robertson

Wiltshire Record Office
Long, Walter Hume. MS947.

United States of America

Library of Congress (LC)
Beer, George Louis. mm 79004954.

Borah, William Edgar. mm 77013276.
Hughes, Charles Evans. mm 78026708.
Lansing, Robert. mm 78029454.
Wilson, Woodrow. mm 73046029.

Yale University Library (Manuscripts and Archives)
House, Edward Mandell. MS 466.

Private papers (published)

Official Report of sixth Commonwealth Conference of the ALP, held in Adelaide, 31 May–7 June 1915 (Sydney: Worker Trade Union Printery, 1915).

Report of the seventh Commonwealth Conference of the Australian Labor Party opened at Perth, June 17, 1918 (Perth: The Party, 1918).

Australian Council of Trade Unions. Australian trade unionism and conscription: being report of proceedings of Australian Trade Union Congress, together with the manifesto of the National Executive (Melbourne: Labor Call Print, 1916).

Hancock, W. K. (ed.). *Selection from the Smuts Papers* (Cambridge: Cambridge University Press, 1966), Vol. IV.

Johnson, Elizabeth (ed.). *The Collected Writings of John Maynard Keynes*, Vol. XVI, 'Activities 1914–19: The Treasury and Versailles' (London: Macmillan St Martin's Press, 1971).

Link, Arthur S. (ed.). *The Papers of Woodrow Wilson*, Vols 45–60 (Princeton: Princeton University Press, 1984–89).

Lo, Hui-min (ed.). *The Correspondence of G. E. Morrison*, 2 vols (Cambridge: Cambridge University Press, 1976–78).

Murdoch, James. An Inaugural Lecture Delivered in the Union Hall on December 3, 1919 (Sydney: Angus and Robertson, 1919).

Weller, Patrick (ed.). *Caucus minutes, 1901–1949: minutes of the meetings of the Federal Parliamentary Labor Party*, 3 vols, (Carlton, Vic: Melbourne University Press, 1975), Vol. I.

Newspapers

Australian

Advertiser (Adelaide)
Advocate
Age
Argus
Australian Worker
Brisbane Courier
Brunswick Star
Bulletin
Church of England Messenger
Daily Standard (Brisbane)
Daily Telegraph (Sydney)
Herald (Melbourne)
Labor Call
Mercury (Hobart)
Register (Adelaide)
Sun (Sydney)
Sunday Chronicle
Tribune
West Australian
Worker (Sydney)

Other

Le Matin
Daily Mail (Paris edition)
Evening Standard (London)
Japan Advertiser
Japan Chronicle

Morning Post
New York Sun
New York Times
Osaka Asahi Shimbun
Times (London)

Autobiographies, memoirs and diaries

Amery, L. S. *My Political Life*, 2 vols (London: Hutchinson, 1953).

—— *The Leo Amery Diaries*, 2 vols, John Barnes and David Nicholson (eds) (London: Hutchinson, 1980), Vol.I.

Baruch, Bernard. The Making of the Reparation and Economic Sections of the Treaty (New York: Harper and Brothers, 1920).

Bonsal, Stephen. *Suitors and Suppliants: The Little Nations at Versailles* (Port Washington, New York: Kennikat Press, 1946).

—— *Unfinished Business* (Garden City, New York: Doubleday, Doran and Company, 1944).

Borden, Henry (ed.). *Robert Laird Borden: His Memoirs*, 2 vols (London: Macmillan, 1938), Vol.II.

Burnett, Philip Mason. *Reparations at the Paris Peace Conference: From the Standpoint of the American Delegation.* 2 Vols (New York: Columbia University Press, 1940).

Catts, Dorothy M. *James Howard Catts, M.H.R.* (Sydney: Ure Smith, 1953).

Garran, Robert Randolph. *Prosper the Commonwealth* (Sydney: Angus and Robertson 1958).

Grey of Fallodon, Viscount. *Twenty Five Years, 1892–1916*, 2 vols (London: Hodder and Stoughton, 1925), Vol. II.

Hankey, Maurice. *The Supreme Command, 1914–1918*, 2 vols (London: Allen and Unwin, 1961).

Houston, David F. *Eight Years with Wilson's Cabinet*, 2 vols, (Garden City, New York: Doubleday, 1926), Vol. I.

Hughes, W. M. *Policies and Potentates* (Sydney: Angus and Robertson, 1950).

—— *The Case for Labor* (Sydney and Melbourne: The Worker Trustees, 1910).

—— *'The Day'-and after: War Speeches*, arranged by Keith A. Murdoch, with an introduction by the Rt Hon David Lloyd George (London: Cassell, 1916).

Lloyd George, David. *The Truth about the Peace Treaties*, 2 vols (London: Gollancz, 1938), Vol. I.

—— *War memoirs of David Lloyd George*, 6 vols (Boston: Little, Brown, and Company, 1933–36), Vol. IV.

Miller, David Hunter. *My Diary at the Conference of Paris with Documents*, 21 vols (New York: Appeal Printing Company, 1924).

Riddell, George Allardyce. *Lord Riddell's War Diary, 1914–1918* (London: Ivor Nicholson and Watson, 1933).

—— *Lord Riddell's Intimate Diary of the Peace Conference and After, 1918–1923* (New York: Reynal and Hitchcock, 1934).

Shotwell, James T. *At the Paris Peace Conference* (New York: Macmillan, 1937).

Smuts, J. C. *The League of Nations: A Practical Suggestion* (London: Hodder and Stoughton, 1918).

Secondary Sources

Bibliographies

Porter, Andrew (ed.). *Bibliography of Imperial, Colonial, and Commonwealth History Since 1600* (Oxford: Oxford University Press, 2002).

Books

Adams, R. J. Q. and Philip P. Poirier. *The Conscription Controversy in Great Britain 1900–18* (Basingstoke: Macmillan, 1987).
Baker, Paul. *King and Country Call: New Zealanders, Conscription and the Great War* (Auckland: Auckland University Press, 1988).
Bean, C. E. W. *Official History of Australia in the War of 1914–1918,* 12 vols (Sydney: Angus and Robertson, 1921–42).
Bean, C. E. W. *Two Men I Knew. William Bridges and Brudenell White, Founders of the AIF* (Sydney: Angus and Robertson, 1957).
Bell, Duncan. *The Idea of Greater Britain: Empire and the Future of World* Order, 1860–1900 (Princeton: Princeton University Press, 2007).
Boemeke, Manfred K. and others (eds). *The Treaty of Versailles; A Reassessment after 75 Years* (Cambridge: Cambridge University Press, 1998).
Bonsal, Stephen. *Suitors and Suppliants: The Little Nations at Versailles* (Port Washington, New York: Prentice-Hall, 1946).
Braisted, William Reynolds. *The United States Navy in the Pacific, 1909–1922* (Austin, Texas: University of Texas Press, 1971).
Brock, M. 'Britain Enters the War', in R. J. W. Evans and H. Pogge von Strandmann (eds), *The Coming of the First World War* (Oxford: Clarendon Press, 1988), pp.159–61.
Bunselmeyer, Robert E. *The Cost of the War 1914–1919: British Economic War Aims and the Origins of Reparations* (Hamden, Conn.: Archon Books, 1975).
Burgmann, Verity. *Revolutionary Industrial Unionism: The Industrial Workers of the World in Australia* (Melbourne: Cambridge University Press, 1995).
Butler, J. R. M. *Lord Lothian, Philip Kerr, 1882–1940* (London: Macmillan, 1960).
Burk, Kathleen. *Britain, America and the Sinews of War, 1914–1918* (Boston: Allen and Unwin, 1985).
Corbett, Julian. *History of the Great War: Naval Operations, Vol. I, 'To the Battle of the Falklands, December 1914'* (London: Longmans, Green, 1920).
Cunneen, Chris. *King's Men: Australia's Governors-General from Hopetoun to Isaacs* (Sydney: George Allen & Unwin, 1983).
Curry, Ron Watson. *Woodrow Wilson and Far Eastern Policy, 1913–1921* (New York: Bookman Associates, 1957).
Currie, George and J. Graham. *The Origins of the CSIRO: Science and the Commonwealth Government, 1901–1926* (Melbourne: CSIRO, 1966).

Daniels, Roger. *The Politics of Prejudice: The Anti-Japanese Movement in California and the Struggle for Japanese Exclusion* (New York: Atheneum, 1968).

Darwin, John. *Britain, Egypt and the Middle East: Imperial Policy in the Aftermath of the War* (London: The Macmillan Press, 1981).

Day, David. *Andrew Fisher: Prime Minister of Australia* (Sydney: Harper Collins, 2008).

Dickinson, Frederick R. *War and National Reinvention: Japan in the Great War, 1914-1919* (Cambridge, Mass.: Harvard University Press, 1999).

Dingman, Roger. *Power in the Pacific: The Origins of Naval Arms Limitation, 1914-1922* (Chicago: Chicago University Press, 1976).

Dockrill, M. L. and J. D. Gould. *Peace without Promise: Britain and the Peace Conference, 1919-1923* (Hamden, Conn.: Anchor Books, 1981).

Ebsworth, Walter A. *Archbishop Mannix* (Armadale, Victoria: H. H. Stephenson, 1977).

Egerton, George W. *Great Britain and the Creation of the League of Nations* (London: Solar Press, 1977).

Evans, Raymond. *Loyalty and Disloyalty: Social Conflict on the Queensland Homefront, 1914-18* (Sydney: Allen and Unwin, 1987).

—— *The Red Flag Riots: A Study of Intolerance* (St Lucia: University of Queensland Press, 1988).

Fic, Victor M. *The Collapse of American Policy in Russia and Siberia, 1918: Wilson's Decision Not to Intervene* (New York: Columbia University Press, 1995).

Fischer, Gerhard. *Enemy Aliens: Internment and the Homefront Experience in Australia 1914-1920* (St Lucia: University of Queensland Press, 1989).

Fitzhardinge, L. F. *William Morris Hughes: A Political Biography*, 2 vols (Sydney: Angus and Robertson, 1963-79).

Fowler, W. B. *British-American Relations: The Role of Sir William Wiseman* (Princeton: Princeton University Press, 1969).

French, David. *British Strategy and War Aims, 1914-1916* (London: Allen and Unwin, 1986).

—— *The Strategy of the Lloyd George Coalition, 1916-1918* (Oxford: Clarendon Press, 1995).

Fry, Michael G. *Illusions of Security: North Atlantic Diplomacy, 1918-22* (Toronto: Toronto University Press, 1972).

Gelfand, Laurence E. *The Inquiry: Preparations for Peace, 1917-1919* (New Haven: Yale University Press, 1963).

Gilchrist, Michael. *Daniel Mannix: Priest and Patriot* (Blackburn, Vic: Dove Communications, c.1982).

Gluck, Carol. *Japan's Modern Myths: Ideology in the Late Meiji Period* (Princeton: Princeton University Press, 1985).

Gollin, A. M. *Proconsul in Politics: a study of Lord Milner in opposition and in power* (London: Blond, 1964).

Guinn, Paul. *British Strategy and Politics, 1914 to 1918* (Oxford: Clarendon Press, 1965).

Hancock, W. K. *Smuts: The Sanguine Years, 1870-1919* (Cambridge: Cambridge University Press, 1962).

Hervey, Jeffrey. *The Spirit of 1914: Militarism, Myth and Mobilisation in Germany* (Cambridge: Cambridge University Press, 2000).

Hopkinson, Michael. *The Irish War of Independence* (Montreal and Kingston: McGill-Queen's University Press, 2002).
Jauncey, L. C. *The Story of Conscription in Australia* (Melbourne: Macmillan, 1968).
Kendle, John. *The Round Table Movement and Imperial Union* (Toronto: University of Toronto Press, 1975).
Kennan, George F. *Soviet-American Relations, 1917–1920, Vol. II, 'The Decision to Intervene'* (Princeton: Princeton University Press, 1958).
Kennedy, Brian. *Silver, Sin and Sixpenny Ale: A Social History of Broken Hill, 1883–1921* (Melbourne: Melbourne University Press, 1978).
Kennedy, P. M. *The Rise of the Anglo-German Antagonism* (London: Allen and Unwin, 1980).
Keynes, John Maynard. *The Economic Consequences of the Peace* (London: Macmillan, 1920).
Kriegel, Annie. *Le Pain et les Roses: Jalons pour une Histoire des Socialismes* (Paris: Presses universitaires de France, 1968).
Lavin, Deborah. *From Empire to International Commonwealth: A Biography of Lionel Curtis* (Oxford: Oxford University Press, 1995).
Lentin, A. *Lloyd George, Woodrow Wilson and the Guilt of Germany* (Leicester: Leicester University Press, 1984).
Link, Arthur S. *Wilson: Confusions and Crises, 1915–1916* (Princeton, New Jersey: Princeton University Press 1964).
Lloyd, M. E. (ed.). *Sidelights on two referendums, 1916–1917* (Sydney: William Brooks, 1952).
Louis, Roger. *British Strategy in the Far East, 1919–1939* (Oxford: Oxford University Press, 1971).
Lowe, Peter. *Great Britain and Japan, 1911–1915: A Study of British Far Eastern Policy* (London: Macmillan, 1969).
MacMillan, Margaret. *Peacemakers: The Paris Peace Conference and its Attempt to End War* (London: John Murray, 2002).
Martin, Laurence W. *Peace Without Victory: Woodrow Wilson and the British Liberals* (New Haven: Yale University Press, 1958).
McIntyre, W. D. *The Rise and Fall of the Singapore Naval Base, 1919–1942* (Hamden, Connecticut: Archon Books, 1979).
—— *New Zealand Prepares for War: Defence Policy, 1919–1939* (Christchurch, New Zealand: University of Canterbury Press, 1988).
McKernan, Michael. *Australian Churches at War: Attitudes and Activities of the Major Churches 1914–1918* (Sydney and Canberra: Australian War Memorial, 1980).
—— *The Australian People and the Great War* (Sydney: Collins, 1980).
Meaney, Neville. *Fears and Phobias: E. L. Piesse and the Problem of Japan 1909–39* (Canberra: National Library of Australia, 1996).
—— ' "In History's Page": Identity and Myth', in Deryck Schreuder and Stuart Ward (eds) *Australia's Empire* (Oxford: Oxford University Press, 2008).
—— *The Search for Security in the Pacific, 1901–1914. A History of Australian Defence and Foreign Policy Vol 1, 1901–1923.* (Sydney: Sydney University Press, 1976).

Meister, Walter and John A. Moses. 'The Brisbane German Club 1883–1983', in Johannes H. Voigt, John Fletcher and John A. Moses (eds), *New Beginnings: The Germans in New South Wales and Queensland* (Stuttgart: Institute for Foreign Cultural Relations, 1983).

Miller, David Hunter. *The Drafting of the Covenant*, 2 Vols (New York: Putnam's Sons, 1928).

Miller, J. D. *Norman Angell and the Futility of War* (London: Macmillan, 1986).

Milner, Susan. *The Dilemmas of Internationalism: French Syndicalism and the International Labour Movement, 1900–1914* (New York: Berg, 1990).

Mitchell, David. *Queen Christabel: A Biography of Christabel Pankhurst* (London: Macdonald and Jane's, 1977).

Mordike, John. *An Army for a Nation* (North Sydney: Allen and Unwin, 1992).

Morris, A. J. Anthony. *Radicalism Against War, 1906–1914: The Advocacy of Peace and Retrenchment* (London: Longman, 1972).

Murphy, D. J. *T. J. Ryan: A Political Biography* (St Lucia: University of Queensland Press, 1975).

Nairn, Bede and Geoffrey Serle (eds). *Australian Dictionary of Biography, 1891–1939* (Melbourne: Melbourne University Press, 1981).

Nedpath, James. *The Singapore Naval Base and the Defence of Britain's Eastern Empire, 1919–1941* (Oxford: Clarendon Press, 1981).

Nish, Ian. *Alliance in Decline: A Study in Anglo-Japanese Relations, 1908–23* (London: The Athlone Press, 1972).

O'Brien, Phillips Payson. *The Anglo-Japanese alliance, 1920–1922* (London: Routledge Curson, 2004).

Orde, Anne. *British Policy and European Reconstruction after the First World War* (Cambridge: Cambridge University Press.1990).

Peattie, Mark R. *Nan'yo: The Rise and Fall of the Japanese in Micronesia, 1885–1945* (Honolulu: University of Hawaii Press, 1988).

Pedersen, P. A. *Monash as Military Commander* (Carlton South, Vic: Melbourne University Press, 1985).

Perkins, Bradford. *The Great Rapprochement: England and the United States, 1895–1914* (New York: Atheneum, 1968).

Rickard, John. *H. B. Higgins: the rebel as judge* (Sydney: Allen and Unwin, 1984).

Robb, George. *British Culture and the First World War* (Houndmills, Basingstoke, 2002).

Roe, Michael. *Australia, Britain and Migration 1915–1940* (Cambridge: Cambridge University Press, 1995).

Robbins, Keith. *The Abolition of War: The 'Peace Movement' in Britain, 1914–1919* (Cardiff: University of Wales Press, 1976).

—— *Great Britain: Identities, Institutions and the Idea of Britishness* (London: Longman, 1998).

Robson, LL. *The First AIF: A Study of its Recruitment, 1914–1918* (Carlton, Vic: Melbourne University Press, 1970).

Roskill, Stephen. *Hankey, Man of Secrets*, 3 vols (London: Collins, 1970).

Scally, Robert J. *The Origins of the Lloyd George Coalition* (Princeton: Princeton University Press, 1975).

Schneer, J. *Ben Tillett: portrait of a labour leader* (London: Croom Helm, 1982).

Scott, Ernest. *Australia During the War* (Sydney: Angus and Robertson, 1936).
Serle, Geoffrey. *John Monash: A Biography* (Carlton, Vic: Melbourne University Press, 1982).
Searle, G. R. *The Quest for National Efficiency: A Study in British Politics and Political Thought, 1899–1914* (Oxford: Blackwell, 1971).
Shimazu, Naoko. *Japan, Race Equality: The Racial Equality Proposal* (London: Routledge, 1998).
Shotwell, James T. (ed.) *The Origins of the International Labor Organisation*, 2 vols (New York: Columbia University Press, 1934).
Silverman, Dan P. *Reconstructing Europe after the Great War* (Cambridge, Mass.: Harvard University Press, 1982).
Skidelsky, Robert. *John Maynard Keynes*, Vol. 1, 'Hopes Betrayed, 1883–1920' (London Macmillan, 1983).
Spartalis, Peter. *The Diplomatic Battles of Billy Hughes* (Sydney: Hale and Iremonger, 1983).
Steiner, Zara S. *Britain and the Origins of the First World War* (London: Macmillan, 1977).
—— *The Foreign Office and Foreign Policy, 1898–1914* (London: Cambridge University Press, 1969).
Strachan, Hew. *The First World War*, Vol. I, 'To Arms' (Oxford: Oxford University Press, 2001).
Stromberg, Roland N. *Redemption by War: The Intellectuals and 1914* (Lawrence: Regents Press of Kansas, 1982).
Thompson, Andrew S. *Imperial Britain: The Empire in British Politics, 1880–1932* (Harlow, Essex: Pearson Education Ltd, 2000).
Thompson, Roger. *Australian Imperialism in the Pacific: The Expansion Era* (Melbourne: Melbourne University Press, 1980).
Turner, Ian. *Industrial Labor and Politics: The Labor Movement in Eastern Australia* (Canberra: Australian National University Press, 1965).
—— *Sydney's Burning* (Melbourne: Heinemann, 1967).
Turner, John. *British Politics and the Great War: Coalition and Conflict, 1915–1918* (New Haven and London: Yale University Press, 1992).
Unterberger, Betty. *America's Siberian Expedition 1918–1920: A Study of National Policy* (New York: Greenwood Press, 1955).
Woodhouse, Eiko. *The Chinese Hsinhai Revolution: G. E. Morrison and Anglo-Japanese Relations, 1897–1920* (London: Routledge Curzon, 2004).
Wrigley, Chris. *David Lloyd George and the British Labour Movement: Peace and War* (New York: Barnes and Noble Books, 1976).
—— *Lloyd George and the Challenge of Labour: The Post-War Coalition, 1918–22* (New York: St Martin's Press, 1991).

Articles

Attard, Bernard. 'Andrew Fisher, the High Commissioner and the Collapse of Labor, *Labour History*, 68 (May 1995), 15–31.
—— 'Politics, Finance and Anglo-Australian Relations: Australian Borrowing in London, 1914–1920', *Australian Journal of Politics and History*, XXXV (August 1989), 142–168.

Curran, James. ' "An Organic Part of the Whole Structure": John Curtin's Empire', *Journal of Imperial and Commonwealth History,* 37 (March 2009), 51-75.

Fry, M. G. 'The North Atlantic Triangle and the Abrogation of the Anglo-Japanese alliance', *Journal of Modern History*, 39 (March 1967), 46-64.

Gilbert, Alan. 'Protestants, Catholics and Loyalty: An Aspect of the Controversies', *Politics*, 6 (May 1971), 15-24.

Gilbert, A. D. 'Religion, Loyalty and Conscription', *Politics*, 6 (May 1971).

Gilbert, Alan. 'The Conscription Referenda, 1916-1917: The Impact of the Irish Crisis', *Historical Studies*, 14 (October 1969).

Hamilton, Celia. 'Catholic Interests and the Labor Party: Organised Catholic Action In Victoria and New South Wales, 1910-1916', *Historical Studies*, 9 (November 1959), 62-73.

Hyslop, Robert. 'Mutiny on H.M.A.S. Australia, *Public Administration*, XXIX (September 1976), 284-96.

Kirby, David. 'International Socialism and the Question of Peace: The Stockholm Conference of 1917', *Historical Journal* 25 (1982), 709-16.

Iklé, F. W. 'Japan-German Negotiations during World War I', *American Historical Review*, LXXI (1965), 62-76.

Kawamura, Noriko. 'Wilsonian Idealism and Japanese claims at the Paris Peace Conference', *Pacific Historical Review*, LXVI (November 1997), 503-26.

Kwan, Elizabeth. 'Making "Good Australians"', *Journal of Australian Studies*, 29 (1991).

Matthews, H. C. G., 'R. I. McKibbin and J. A. Kay.' The Franchise Factor in the rise of the Labour Party', *English Historical Review*, XCI (October 1976).

May, Ernest R. 'American Policy and Japan's Entrance into World War I', *Mississippi Valley Historical Review*, XV, (1953), 279-90.

Meaney, Neville. 'Australia's Secret Service in World War I: Security, Loyalty and the Abuse of Power', *Quadrant*, XXIII (July 1979), 19-23.

—— 'Britishness and Australian Identity: The Problem of Nationalism in Australian History and Historiography', *Australian Historical Studies,* 32 (April 2001), 76-90.

—— 'Woodrow Wilson as Machiavelli's "Prince of Peace"', Proceedings of the First Biennial Conference of the Australian and New Zealand American Studies Association (Melbourne, 1964).

—— 'The British Empire in the American Rejection of the Treaty of Versailles', *Australian Journal of Politics and History*, X (November 1963), 213-34.

Nish, Ian. 'Admiral Jerram and the German Pacific Fleet', *Mariner's Mirror*, LVI (1970), 411-421.

—— 'Japan Reverses the Unequal Treaties: The Anglo-Japanese Commercial Treaty of 1894', *Journal of Oriental Studies*, 13 (1975).

Poynter, John. 'The Yo-Yo variations: Initiative and Dependence in Australia's External Relations, 1918-1923', *Historical Studies* XIV (April 1970), 231-49.

Prince, E. J. G. 'Towards National Railway Planning by the Commonwealth Government: Defence Considerations and the Constitutional Referenda of 1911 and 1913', *Australian Journal of Politics and* History, XXII (April 1976).

Stubbs, J. O. 'Lord Milner and Patriotic Labour, 1914–1918', *English Historical Review*, 87 (1972), 717–54.

Trachtenberg, Marc. '"A New Economic Order": Etienne Clementel and French Economic Diplomacy during the First World War', *French Historical Studies*, X (Fall 1977), 318–22.

Unterberger, Betty Miller. 'Wilson and the Bolsheviks; The "Acid Test" of Soviet-American Relations', *Diplomatic History*, 11 (Spring 1987).

Vinson, J. Chal. 'The Drafting of the Four-Power Treaty of Washington Conference', *Journal of Modern History*, 25 (March 1953), 40–47.

Walton, David. 'Feeling for the Jugular: Japanese Espionage at Newcastle 1919–1926', *Journal of Politics and History*, 32 (1986), 1, 20–38.

White, Richard. 'Motives for Joining Up: Self-Sacrifice, Self-Interest and Social Class, 1914–18', *Journal of the Australian War Memorial*, 9 (October 1986), 3–16.

Wilson, K. M. 'The British Cabinet's Decision for War, 2 August 1914', *British Journal of International Studies*, 1 (1975), 148–57.

Theses and Papers

Gow, Neil. 'The Formulation of Australia's Defence Policy, 1918–1925'. (MA thesis, University of Western Australia, 1972).

Kwan, E. H. 'Making "Good Australians": The Work of Three South Australian Educators'. (MA thesis, Department of History, University of Adelaide, 1981).

Metherell, T. A. 'The Conscription Referenda, October 1916 and December 1917: An Inward-Turned National War'. (PhD thesis, Department of History, University of Sydney, 1971).

Rushton, P. J. 'The Industrial Workers of the World in Sydney, 1913–1917; A Study of Revolutionary Ideology'. (MA thesis, Department of History, University of Sydney, 1969)

Sissons, D. C. S. 'Australia's first Professor of Japanese, James Murdoch (1856–1921)', David Sissons Papers, NLA MS 8230/58.

—— 'Attitudes to Japan and defence, 1890–1923', 3 vols. (MA thesis, University of Melbourne, 1956).

—— 'The Immigration Question in Australian Diplomatic Relations with Japan, 1875–1919', Paper presented to the Australian and New Zealand Association for the Advancement of Science' (Brisbane, 28 May 1971).

Verney, Guy. 'The Army High Command and Australian Defence Policy, 1901–1918'. (PhD thesis, University of Sydney, 1985).

Index

Admiralty, x, 1, 4, 29–31, 33, 37, 64–69, 71, 78–80, 128–130, 145, 153, 154, 157, 249–250, 267, 332, 334, 425–429, 432, 433, 447, 449, 450, 469–471, 479, 485–487, 492–497
Age, 58, 63, 214
Allen, Colonel James, 83
Amery, L. S., 49, 135, 187, 274, 275, 302, 346, 467
Anderson, Colonel Robert M.M., 9, 77, 170
Anderson, Sir John, 90
Angaur, 64, 72, 73
Angell, Norman, 10
Anglo-Japanese alliance, x, 56, 58–61, 100, 104, 106, 108, 126, 127, 144, 152, 160, 177, 364, 409, 410, 415, 428, 443, 444, 469, 471, 475–477, 480, 481, 484–485, 488, 491–497, 507, 512
Anglo-Japanese Commercial Treaty, 102, 103, 105, 126, 131, 145, 146, 153, 154
Argentina, 143
Argus, 214
Asquith, Henry Herbert, 3, 5, 135, 139, 140, 183
Australia, 65, 66, 72, 129, 431, 432, 450, 455, 499
Australia,
  attitude to Japan, x, 36, 42, 57, 77, 89, 147, 152, 253, 254, 262, 317, 321, 364, 373, 375, 403, 407, 416, 419, 442, 443, 446, 500
  attitude to resident aliens, 21, 35, 44, 138, 142, 214, 267, 418
  ideas of national security, 37, 38, 116, 235, 466
  military response and troop raising, 7, 28–32, 37–40, 42, 43, 46, 52, 117, 118, 173
  nationalism and identity, ix, x, 21, 151, 190, 200, 204, 211, 217, 267, 500, 512
  naval and defence policy, 82, 83, 109, 110, 127, 267, 360, 405, 419–424, 430, 433, 435, 437, 438, 449, 451, 512
  Pacific concerns, see also Australia Crisis, xi, xii, 62, 64, 70, 85, 88, 93–96, 133, 248, 251, 276, 317, 347, 348, 352, 362, 397, 407, 409, 415
  post-war economic considerations, 265, 277, 336
  relations with Great Britain, 3, 11, 59, 264, 275, 313, 490
  relations with United States, 258, 260, 262, 263, 280
Australian Crisis, 3, 11, 42, 56, 82, 90, 109, 127–129, 176, 318, 408
Australian Defence Scheme, 29, 31
Australian Enemy Contracts Annulment Act, 142
Australian Government
  Cook (1913), 6, 28, 107
  Fisher (1914), xii, 28, 31, 37, 41, 46, 52, 102, 107, 110, 117–118, 133, 407, 424, 456
  Hughes (1915), 118, 152, 154, 317
  Hughes (1916), 184, 419
  Hughes (1917), 251, 253, 456
Australian Imperial Force, xi, xii, 1, 13, 32, 33, 37, 39, 43, 44, 56, 78, 110, 117–119, 123, 161, 167, 169–174, 181, 182, 195, 196, 199, 204, 211, 215, 218, 220, 224,

239, 244, 269, 420, 423, 436–438, 452, 456, 459, 462, 500, 502, 503, 509

Australian Labor Party, 23
  Caucus, 6, 40, 47, 48, 165, 167, 169–171, 184, 194
  conferences, 15, 45, 46, 117
  division over conscription, 54, 55
Australian Natives Association, 158, 180
Australian Protective League, 230–232, 236, 239, 421
Austria and Austria Hungary, 3, 4, 57, 270
Bakhap, T. J. K., 57
Balfour, A. J., 210, 227, 270–272, 276, 285, 287, 302, 313, 316, 319, 325, 335, 343, 366, 376, 481, 494, 496, 497
Balkans, 119, 140, 183
Bamford, F. W., 48
Barton, Sir Edmund, 13, 180
Bavin, T. R., 50, 51, 54
Beatty, Lord, 486
Belgium, 4, 5, 282, 291, 304–306, 327, 336, 380, 392, 498
Bernhardi, Friedrich von, 7, 136, 137
Birdwood, General William R., 167, 173, 224, 424
Bismarck Archipelago, 65, 70, 101, 352
Boer War, 11, 23, 25, 29, 31, 424
Bolshevism, 212, 218, 232, 241–245, 270, 273, 333, 340–342, 349, 395, 405, 431, 432, 444, 451–456, 459, 464, 501, 527
Boote, Henry, 19, 155, 178
Borah, William E., 369
Borden, Sir Robert, 125, 126, 133, 137, 269, 274, 275, 303–307, 315, 325, 338, 342, 347, 351, 356, 357, 361, 366, 370, 371, 376–378, 388, 400, 424, 426, 468, 496, 506, 511
Botha, Louis, 150, 350, 357, 363, 388
Bougainville, 72, 99
Braddon, Henry Yule, 201, 263
Brennan, Frank, 35, 36, 403

Bridges, Brigadier-General William Throsby, 31, 32, 167
Brisbane, 116, 130, 196, 424
British Empire Delegation, 308, 341, 346, 350–358, 360–362, 367, 376, 380, 386, 387, 390, 391–394, 396, 400, 491, 493, 494, 496, 497, 506, 511, 512
British Empire League, 263, 265, 277, 402, 462, 463
Brockdorff-Rantzau, Count Ulrich, 396
Brookes, Herbert, see also Australian Protective League, 231–236, 460
Bruce, S.M., 513
Bulgaria, 115, 270, 287
Bulletin, 57
Burns, Colonel James, 70, 71, 85–87, 91
Buxton, Lord, 150
Canada, 30, 40, 82, 96, 103, 126, 128, 130, 133, 145, 147, 259, 303–308, 445, 476, 481, 482, 486–489, 493
Carolinas, 66, 69, 70, 72, 75, 85, 88, 89, 91, 94, 153, 320, 321, 360
Carr, Archbishop T. J., 24, 209
Carr, T. J., 24, 209
Catts, J.H., 102, 160–162, 176, 177, 222, 245, 246, 403
Cecil, Lord Robert, 277, 322, 343, 345, 360, 366, 367, 372
Ceylon, 80, 93, 129
Chile, 80
China, 1, 38, 58–60, 72, 80, 87, 100, 103, 398, 413, 480, 498
Chinda, Sutemi, 365, 366, 368, 370
Chisuka, Admiral, 108
Churchill, Winston S., 4, 67, 68, 69, 98, 149, 334, 338, 342, 392
Clemenceau, Georges, 284, 285, 288, 292, 327, 340, 345, 346, 347, 359, 360, 386, 387, 396
Clémentel, Étienne, 139, 141
Cobb, Frank, 288
Cockatoo Island, 196, 424

Cockburn Sound, 424, 425
Colonial Conference, 91
Colonial Office, 62, 67–71, 79, 90, 92, 93, 105, 111, 124, 125, 134, 145, 154, 157, 171, 184, 212, 273, 274, 278, 324, 469, 478, 479, 489
Colonial Secretary, 10, 30, 39, 61, 69, 81, 88–91, 95, 96, 98, 101, 105, 120, 125, 183, 185, 239, 249–250, 254, 257, 266, 267, 274, 286, 288, 323, 328, 346, 467, 468, 474
Committee of Imperial Defence, x, 29, 479–481, 497
Compulsory military training, x, 16, 41, 42, 48, 49, 110, 161, 176, 199, 245, 422, 435, 436, 446, 452, 456, 502, 503, 513
Conscription, 8, 13, 14, 43, 47–49, 53, 110, 158, 160, 164, 165, 168, 171, 181, 212
  British conscription measures, 119, 122, 158, 159
  opposition to, 169, 176, 177, 178, 180, 220
  overseas vs home defence, 168
  referenda and after effects, 8, 9, 13, 17, 171–176, 179, 180, 182, 193, 194, 213, 216, 219, 222, 223, 228, 505
Cook, Joseph, xii, 6, 7, 8, 26, 27, 35, 56, 58, 94, 95, 159, 187, 256, 296, 320, 323, 340, 342, 344, 427, 430, 434, 450, 485
Council of Ten, see also Paris Peace Conference, 306, 307, 340–342, 345–348, 352, 354–360, 379, 383, 482
Counter Espionage Bureau, 197, 228
Creswell, Rear-Admiral W.R., 85, 127, 322, 425, 433
Crimes Act, 34
Cunliffe, Lord, 328, 333, 380, 382, 383, 384, 387, 388, 392, 393
Curtis, Lionel, 179, 302
Curzon, Lord, 304, 338, 480, 483–485, 510
Daily Telegraph, 45, 57, 58, 474
Daniels, Josephus, 335, 444, 445

Dawson, Geoffrey, 135
Deakin, Alfred, 12, 41, 178, 258, 274, 407, 480, 513
Deane, Percy, 174, 179, 180, 195, 313, 343, 344
Defence Act, 31, 51, 53, 168, 172, 173, 181, 191, 438
Derby, Lord, 119–122, 123, 284, 285
Dreadnought crisis, 12, 14, 26, 437, 502
Dresden, 80
Dudley, Lord, 34
Duffy, John Gavan, 23, 189
Easton, 71
Eggleston, Frederic W., 127, 343, 344, 505
Egypt, 466, 469, 478, 489, 490, 511
Ellice and Gilbert islands, 70, 87
Elmslie, G, 23
Emden, 80
Entente cordiale, 18, 36, 56, 59
Expansion of England, 135
External Affairs Department, 69, 71, 84–86, 105, 109, 131
Falkland Islands, 38, 65
Federation (Australia), 338
Ferguson, Sir Ronald Munro, 5, 9, 14, 29, 34, 39, 41, 42, 55, 79, 80, 81, 90, 91, 92, 93, 94, 96, 99–102, 105, 121, 125, 131, 211, 212, 216, 229, 237, 238, 239, 249, 254, 258, 263, 273, 278, 396
Fihelly, John, 460
Fiji, 70
Finlayson, W. F., 25
Fischer, Gerhard, 213
Fisher, Andrew, 6, 9–12, 14, 26–28, 36, 55, 79, 81, 84, 85, 88, 90–94, 96, 97, 99, 102, 106–111, 118, 120–124, 134, 146, 167, 245, 300, 402, 420, 424, 480, 502, 503, 513
Fitchett, Rev W. H, 24
Foreign Office (British), x, 4, 67, 93, 144, 226, 409, 419, 472
Foster, Hubert, 156, 251, 322

Free Trade Party, 6
Fremantle, 37, 164, 179, 424, 431, 437
Gallipoli, 13, 44, 45, 51, 110, 280, 508, 509
Gardiner, Albert, 122
Garran, Robert Randolph, 35, 301, 302, 342, 343, 344, 368, 391
George V, King, 4, 10, 46, 163, 190
George Washington, 334, 382
Givens, Thomas, 122, 178
Gladstone, W.E., 5
Glynn, Sir P. McMahon, 35, 59, 69, 235
Gneisenau, 65, 66, 68, 72, 80
Grant, Admiral Sir Percy, 432, 433, 434, 441, 447–450, 452, 453, 470, 471, 486
Great Britain
  role in the Pacific, see also Pacific fleet, xiii, 79, 80, 87, 109, 426, 429, 434, 437, 447, 470, 482, 486
  Sinn Fein and relations with Ireland, 4, 24, 168, 185, 207, 209, 215, 243, 454, 456, 458, 461, 462, 478
Greater Britain, xi, 150, 301, 309, 339, 405, 449, 478, 480, 485, 501, 507, 510
Greece, 115, 380
Greene, Sir Conyngham, 73, 99, 126, 127, 144, 499
Grey, Sir Edward, 4, 5, 59–61, 63, 64, 66, 68, 73, 74, 75, 98, 145–149, 165
Groom, Littleton E., 30
Guam, 357, 444, 445, 484
Haldane, R.B., 4
Hankey, Sir Maurice, 272, 275, 283, 286, 288, 293, 304, 305, 326, 350, 352, 357, 383, 384, 388, 479, 480, 487, 488, 494
Hara government, 365, 378, 444
Harcourt, Sir Lewis, 39, 40, 41, 62, 64, 68, 69, 73, 79–81, 90–93, 95–97, 99–101, 103, 125, 145
Hawaii, 357, 363, 444, 445
Henderson Scheme, 31, 37, 128, 129, 425, 428
Hewins, W. A. S., 139, 328, 329

Higgins, Henry Bournes, 11
Higgs, W. G., 48, 165, 505
High Commissioners, Australia, 13, 55, 111, 134, 461, 510
Holman, W. A., 45
Holmes, Colonel William, 65, 69, 72, 84
Honolulu, 444, 445
House, Colonel E. M., 148, 272, 282, 288, 289, 290, 292, 295, 296, 303, 331, 351, 355, 357, 361, 362, 365, 366, 369–371, 383, 385, 386
Hughes, William Morris, 6, 15–19, 26, 27, 36, 45, 116, 133–139, 141, 148–150, 163, 164, 185, 187–189, 195, 246, 248, 256, 258–264, 270–273, 276–279, 282, 291–299, 309, 311, 313, 319, 327, 332, 334, 341–344, 349–359, 361, 362, 366–378, 386, 388, 390–392, 395–401, 417–419, 431, 432, 447, 449, 451–453, 462, 464, 466, 474, 475, 480–482, 485, 488, 490–493, 501–509, 511
Hunt, Arthur Atlee, 69, 71, 85–90, 105–107, 130, 131
Hutton, Lieutenant-General E. G. H., 32
Immigration Restriction Act (1901), 103
Imperial Conference (1911), 3, 30, 59, 97
Imperial Conference (1917 - War), 263, 266, 426
Imperial Conference (1921), 8, 405, 419, 454, 475, 501, 507, 511, 512
Imperial Defence Conference (1909), 78, 128, 424, 428, 429, 453
Imperial Federation, Imperial Council and Imperial Parliament, 137, 149, 150, 179, 188, 189, 246, 475
Imperial General Staff, 31, 42, 165, 171
India, 128, 129, 152, 177, 306, 340, 343, 400, 413, 418, 427, 428, 437, 466, 469, 478, 479, 485, 486, 487, 490
Inter-Allied Conference, see also Paris Peace Conference, 294, 303, 304, 329, 331, 333, 334, 379

International relations, global, 15, 16, 17, 20, 45, 241, 245, 314, 315, 338, 358, 468, 511
Irvine, Sir William, 6, 8, 9, 12, 13, 18, 27, 29, 30, 48, 94, 121, 160, 186, 194, 217, 237
Ishii, Kikujiro, 153, 258, 261, 365
Italy, 3, 17, 113, 144, 212, 218, 249, 287, 315, 317, 340, 352, 385, 496
Jambo, 85
Japan
  attitude to White Australia, 7, 126
  expansion in the Pacific, 13, 59, 66, 67, 73, 74, 84, 90, 91, 100, 103, 108, 110, 126, 162, 261, 318, 409, 413, 441, 512
  relations with Germany, 145
  relations with United States, 365, 475, 497
Jaurès, Jean, 10, 11
Jellicoe mission, 426–430, 433–439, 446, 448–450, 464, 466, 470–471, 475, 486, 492, 497
Jensen, J. A., 179
Kato, Takaaki, 61, 72, 73, 75, 92, 103
Kelly, Michael, 23
Kelly, W. H., 29
Kerensky, Alexander, 271
Kerr, Philip, 301, 314, 381, 384, 386
Keynes, John Maynard, see also reparations, 328, 329, 332, 333, 387, 394, 505
Kitchener, Lord, 36, 42, 43, 98
Knibbs, G. H., 191
Korea, 152, 444, 500
Laird Smith, W. H., 178, 450, 454
Lansdowne, Lord, 247
Lansing, Robert, 258, 259, 260, 261
Largie, Hugh de, 48
Latham, John, 50–54, 262, 301, 302, 318–322, 342–344, 348, 349, 397, 427, 429
Law, Andrew Bonar, see also Colonial Secretary, 105, 124, 125, 130–132, 135, 140–145, 149–151, 184, 265, 287, 292, 293, 304, 319, 325, 332, 343, 388
League Covenant, 347, 361, 364–367, 369, 371, 373, 376–379, 397, 402, 403, 412, 415–417, 439, 491, 501, 504, 506, 512
League of Nations, xiii, 10, 19, 266, 268, 275, 277, 281, 287–291, 295, 305, 311, 313–317, 325, 326, 333–338, 341–351, 355–360, 362, 364–378, 381, 386, 392, 395–400, 402–405, 409, 417, 418, 421, 423, 430–438, 442, 443, 451, 464, 471, 473, 477, 478, 483, 484, 491, 505, 506, 509, 512
Lee, Lord, 485–487, 494
Legge, Colonel J.G., 31, 39, 41, 42, 43, 65, 84, 100, 219, 231, 232, 255, 322, 408, 421, 422, 423, 436
Lippmann, Walter, 288
Lloyd George, David, 135, 148, 171, 174, 183, 184, 186–189, 247, 248, 266–270, 273, 275, 278, 283, 285–290, 292–294, 299–301, 314, 316, 326, 328, 329, 332, 335, 338, 343, 350, 353, 362, 387, 393, 464, 479, 491, 505
Long, Walter, 184–187, 229, 274–278, 328
Lusitania, 44
Mahony, W. G., 189
Makino, Baron, 348, 360, 361, 365, 367, 368, 370–378, 415
Maloney, Dr William R. N., 35, 176, 178
Mannix, Archbishop Daniel, 180, 182, 207–216, 218, 221–228, 231, 233, 239, 243, 457, 458, 459, 460, 461, 462, 464
Marianas, 66, 67, 70, 88–91, 320, 335, 363
Marshall Islands, 66, 69, 70, 72, 75, 85, 86, 88, 89, 91, 94, 95, 98, 153, 160, 171, 251, 253, 320, 321, 335, 358, 360, 363
Massey, William, 81, 83, 96, 125, 126, 133, 137, 275, 350, 351, 357, 370, 388, 480, 483, 484, 485, 489, 490–494, 506
Masson, Professor Orme, 52
McCay, General J. W., 378, 423, 436

Meighen, Arthur, 468
Melbourne, 431, 455
Menzies, Robert Gordon, 214, 261, 514
Military Board, 31, 42, 84, 419, 422
Military Service Referendum Bill, 175
Millen, E. D., 25, 29, 30, 31, 48, 106, 203, 216, 417, 418, 473, 474, 513
Milner, Lord, 49, 50, 135, 184, 186, 287, 333, 342, 346, 392, 467, 468, 469, 490
Monash, Colonel John, 33, 436
Monroe Doctrine (for the South Pacific), 128, 133, 255, 258, 260, 261, 318, 372, 374, 403, 428, 452, 474, 482
Murdoch, James, 156, 161, 364, 372, 374, 377–379, 408, 410–412, 450, 477, 506
Murdoch, Keith, 169, 186, 187, 195, 224, 260, 264, 273, 278, 344, 374, 415
National Review, 327
National Service League, 49, 50
Nauru, 62, 64, 72, 131, 153, 250, 362
Naval Board, 31, 37, 65, 69, 73, 85, 88, 92, 109, 126, 128–133, 152, 187, 358, 419, 420, 424, 425, 428, 429, 432, 433, 440, 441, 448–450, 453, 470, 471
Netherlands, 71, 305, 498
Netherlands, 59
Netherlands East Indies, 71, 127, 144, 145, 157, 249, 415, 440
New Caledonia, 70, 91, 92, 93, 99, 101, 109, 318
New Guinea, 62, 64, 66, 70, 73, 88, 93, 101, 252, 254, 259, 326, 337, 348, 349, 352, 353, 358, 359, 362, 363, 397, 398, 471, 473, 495
New Hebrides, 70, 91, 92, 93, 94, 99, 101, 109, 133, 318, 397, 469
Newfoundland, 97, 306
Nicolson, Sir Arthur, 144, 165
Nietzsche, Friedrich, 7
Northcliffe, Lord, 135, 149, 257, 258, 344, 354
Northern Territory, 34

Okuma, Count Shigenobu, 126, 131, 320, 321
Overseas Defence Committee, 479
Pacific Fleet, 130, 428, 429, 437, 444
Pacific Islands. See also under individual islands, 63, 86, 89, 125, 252, 270, 352, 353, 361
Papua, 251, 497
Paris Economic Conference, 1916, 148, 264, 265, 303
Paris Peace Conference (1919), xiii, 8, 15, 19, 246, 301, 303, 311, 313, 340, 365, 374, 394, 398, 400, 403, 413, 418, 432, 448, 457, 482, 491, 493, 494, 501, 504, 505, 511, 512
Parkes, Sir Henry, 315
Patey, George, 66
Pax Britannica, xi, 137, 256, 257, 327, 397, 464, 478
Peace, 268, 313
   Fourteen Points plan, 248, 276, 280, 281, 283, 285, 287–299, 302, 311, 313–316, 325, 327, 336, 340, 347, 354, 380–382, 388, 391, 392, 395, 399, 490
   Peace terms and negotiations, 34, 75, 79, 98, 109, 148, 184, 186, 187, 241, 244, 246–248, 251, 256–259, 276, 280, 282–298, 302, 307, 308, 311, 313, 314–316, 321, 325, 327, 334, 338, 340, 355, 381, 382, 391, 396, 403, 508
Peacock, Sir Alexander, 22, 26
Pearce, George, 40, 41, 42, 43, 69, 72, 73, 77, 82, 83, 85, 88, 92, 96, 100, 108, 118–120, 123–124, 132, 133, 138, 140, 145, 146, 148, 152–155, 157–161, 165, 173, 179, 191, 196, 197, 199, 200, 213, 216, 230–236, 251–253, 255, 261, 298, 410, 411, 413, 419–424, 446, 450, 452, 454, 463, 493–499, 513
Pearl Harbour, 399, 514
Pelew Islands, 61, 69, 75, 85, 88, 89

Pethebridge, Colonel S. A., 71, 73
Phelan, James, 369
Philippines, 157, 319, 357, 440
Piesse, E. L., xii, 232–235, 262, 320, 323, 372–379, 397–399, 408–420, 426, 440, 443, 444, 465, 471–473, 477, 495, 506
Pioneer, 71
Poland, 341, 380, 452
Port Phillip Bay, 424
Portugal, 305
Prime Minister's Department Pacific Branch, 407, 414, 415, 419
Privy Council, 266
Rae, Arthur, 26, 204
Ramaciotti, Brigadier-General G., 196, 197
Redmond, John, 24, 189
Reparations, 283, 288, 291, 292, 314, 326–329, 331–333, 379, 380, 387, 388, 390
Riddell, George Allardyce, 358
Roosevelt, Theodore, 263, 436
Round Table movement, 49, 50, 52, 125, 127, 129, 131, 179, 183, 184, 191, 194, 201, 274, 301, 302, 307, 343, 467
Royal Colonial Institute, 149
Royal Military College (Duntroon), 84, 156, 408, 501
Royal Navy, 3, 12, 19, 30, 116, 129, 266, 289, 334, 337, 353, 400, 432, 444, 453, 500
Runciman, W. R., 140, 141
Russo-Japanese War, 56, 109, 160, 162, 176, 407, 416, 433, 436, 451, 465, 500
Ryan, T. J., 52, 107, 212, 220, 221, 223, 229, 230, 237–240, 457
Samoa, 64, 65, 70, 362
Sarajevo, 3
Scharnhorst, 65, 66, 68, 72, 80
Serbia, 4, 115, 304, 306, 307, 380
Shimizu, Seizaburo, 86, 104–107, 130–132, 154, 252, 254, 415, 416
Siam, 306

Siberia, 271, 272, 292, 322, 335, 411, 443–445, 498
Sino-Japanese War, 58, 456
Smuts, Jan, 150, 274, 293, 304, 306, 316, 335, 345, 350–352, 355, 363, 366, 370, 371, 376–377, 387, 391, 392, 400, 487, 489, 492–494, 506
Social Darwinism, 115, 121, 135, 136
Solomon Islands, 70, 72, 93, 99, 101, 251, 254
South Africa, 83, 96, 128, 150, 268, 269, 275, 276, 289, 307, 314, 315, 325, 326, 335, 343, 348, 350, 351, 362, 370, 388, 405, 428, 437, 479, 486, 487, 493, 494, 506, 507, 510–513
South Australia, 22, 52, 174, 182, 190, 198, 223, 243
Steward, Major George, 197, 224, 225, 229, 234, 235
Strong, Archibald T., 110, 231, 232
Suez Canal, 469, 490
Sumner, Lord, 380
Suttor, J. B., 90, 127, 152, 153, 155, 157, 249, 318, 408
Sweden, 305
Sydney, 431
Sydney Morning Herald, ix, 58, 63, 126, 161, 177, 193, 368, 445, 477
Tasmania, xii, 57, 91, 408
Terauchi government, 364
The Herald (Melbourne), 278, 344, 374, 377, 378
The Times, 50, 111, 135, 320
Tonga, 70, 129
Trading with the Enemy Act, 34, 55, 116
Tudor, Frank, 202, 237, 238, 240, 244, 462, 477, 509
Turkey, 17, 44, 66, 270, 287, 508
Turnverein, 21, 36
Una (Komet), 71
Uncle Sam, 263

United States
  Californian discrimination against Japanese residents, 366, 369, 444
  fleets, 263, 477
Universal Service League, 14, 48, 50, 51, 52, 53, 55, 110, 117–119, 158, 159, 166, 167, 168, 183, 194, 200, 201, 217, 503
Unlawful Associations Act, 198, 200, 204
Valera, Eamon De, 457, 458, 464
Vaughan, Crawford, 52
Victoria Barracks, 412, 455
Wallin, F., 85
War Book (British), 29
War Census Bill, 46, 53–55, 110, 117, 167, 191
War Committee, 46, 49, 120, 159, 160
War Council (Britain), 98, 469
War Council (Supreme), 287, 290, 291, 297, 327, 340, 384
War Office, x, xii, 32, 40, 171, 251, 424, 479
War Precautions Act, 7, 8, 34, 35, 44, 116, 168, 205, 211, 236, 267
Ward, Sir Joseph, 83, 267
Washington Conference, xiii, 484, 485, 492, 493, 494, 497, 499, 504, 507, 512
Watson, David, 33
Watson, John Christian, xii, 50, 51, 52, 97
Watt, William Alexander, 231, 232, 234, 235, 261–263, 280, 283, 285, 287, 291, 295–299, 308, 318–322, 325, 331, 339, 341, 353, 354, 364, 367, 370–372, 374, 375, 377, 381, 390, 391, 395, 396, 399, 409, 411–414, 418, 419, 421–425, 428, 430, 439, 446, 506
Webster, William, 54
West Australian, 22
Western Australia, 25, 174, 175, 199, 200, 457
Western Front, 1, 37, 43, 115, 140, 160, 170, 172, 174, 176, 183, 195, 218, 228, 237, 256, 268, 269, 270, 364

'White Australia', xiii, 77, 107, 113, 147, 153, 165, 175, 176, 177, 178, 180, 221–223, 343, 350, 360, 363, 364, 367, 372, 375, 377, 378, 400, 401–405, 410, 418, 431, 433, 439, 445, 458, 463, 465, 474, 477, 504
White Australia policy, x, 10, 16, 18, 93, 106, 109, 127, 146, 148, 155, 160, 201, 221, 248, 254, 315, 317, 337, 347, 361, 371, 377, 407, 409, 412–414, 417, 418, 435–437, 441, 448, 452, 474, 476, 495, 500
White, Major C. B. B., 29, 31
Wilson, Thomas Woodrow, 134, 148, 162, 241, 243, 245, 246, 248, 256, 257, 258, 270–272, 276, 277, 280, 281, 283, 287–292, 302, 305, 306, 311, 314–316, 326, 327, 329, 334, 337, 342, 351, 354, 357, 360, 365, 366, 379, 392, 395, 409, 444, 452, 458, 505, 506, 513
Wise, G. H., 178
World War I, ix, x, xii, xiii, 1, 10, 48, 115, 116, 166, 205, 264, 311, 405, 407, 449, 451, 452, 457, 460, 463, 509, 514
World War II, 514
Wright, J. C., 23
Yap, 61, 64, 66, 67, 68, 69, 70, 71, 72, 73, 74, 98, 130
'Yellow Peril', 10, 58, 178, 267

www.ingramcontent.com/pod-product-compliance
Lightning Source LLC
Chambersburg PA
CBHW060302010526
44108CB00042B/2602